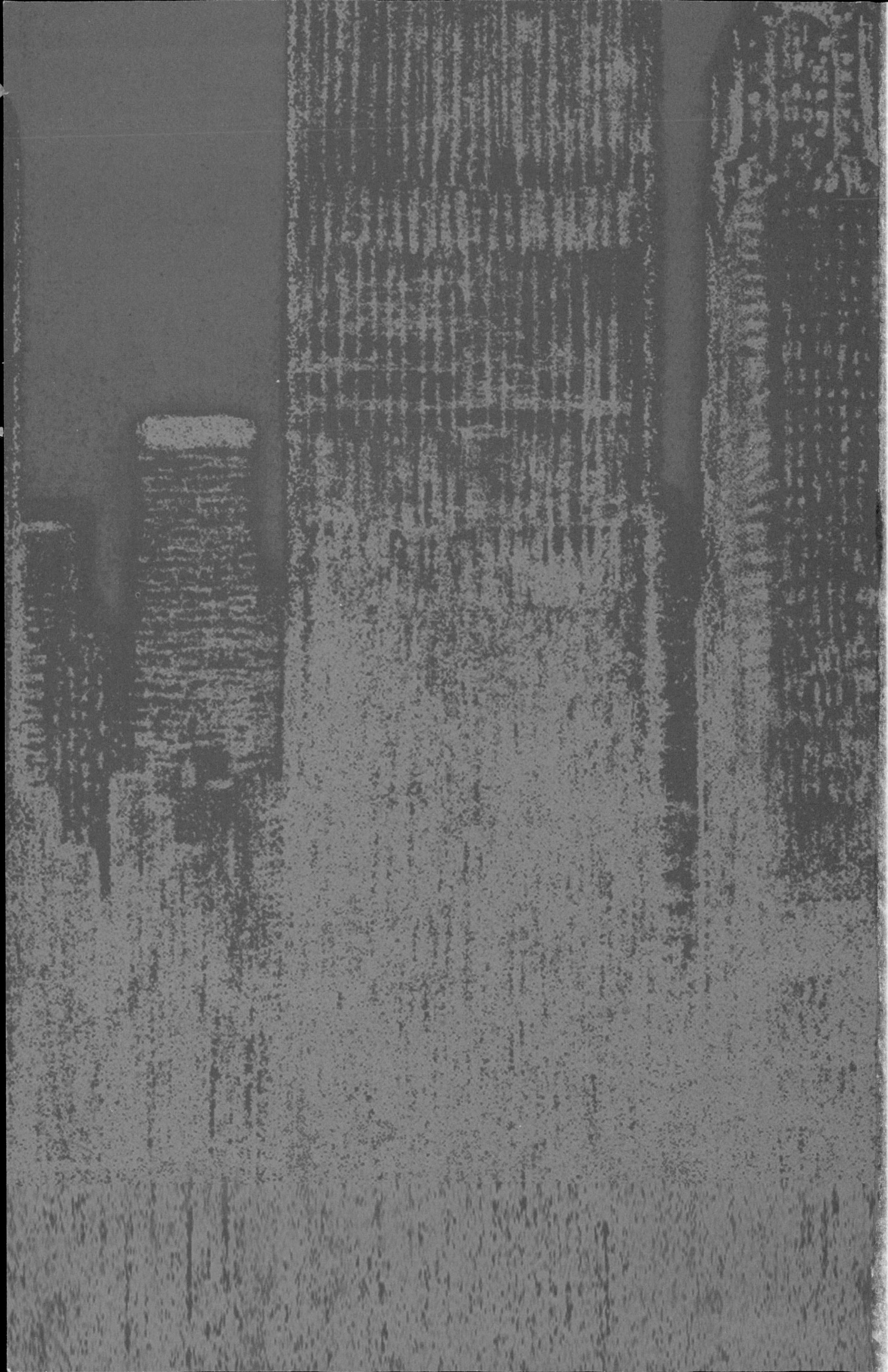

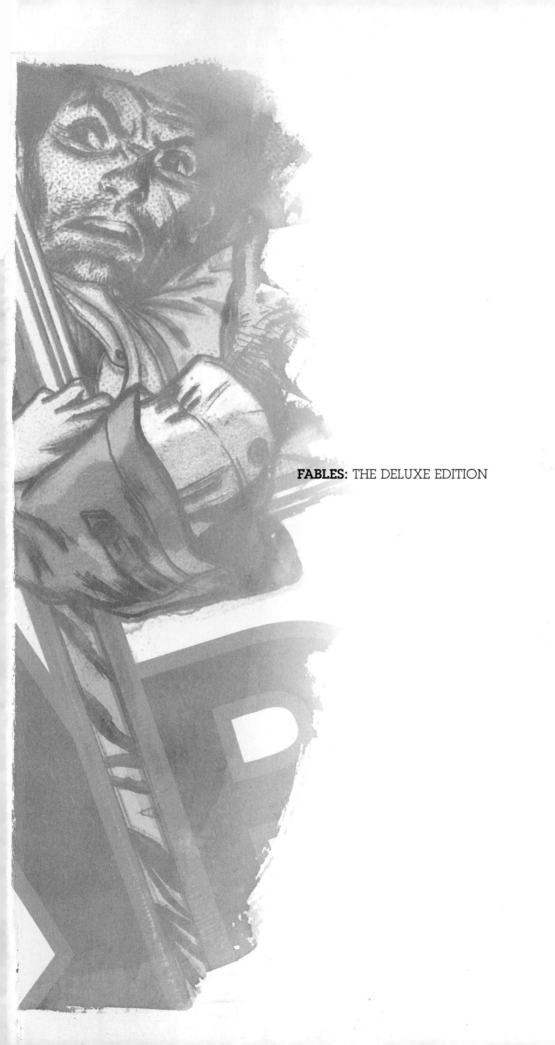

FABLES: THE DELUXE EDITION

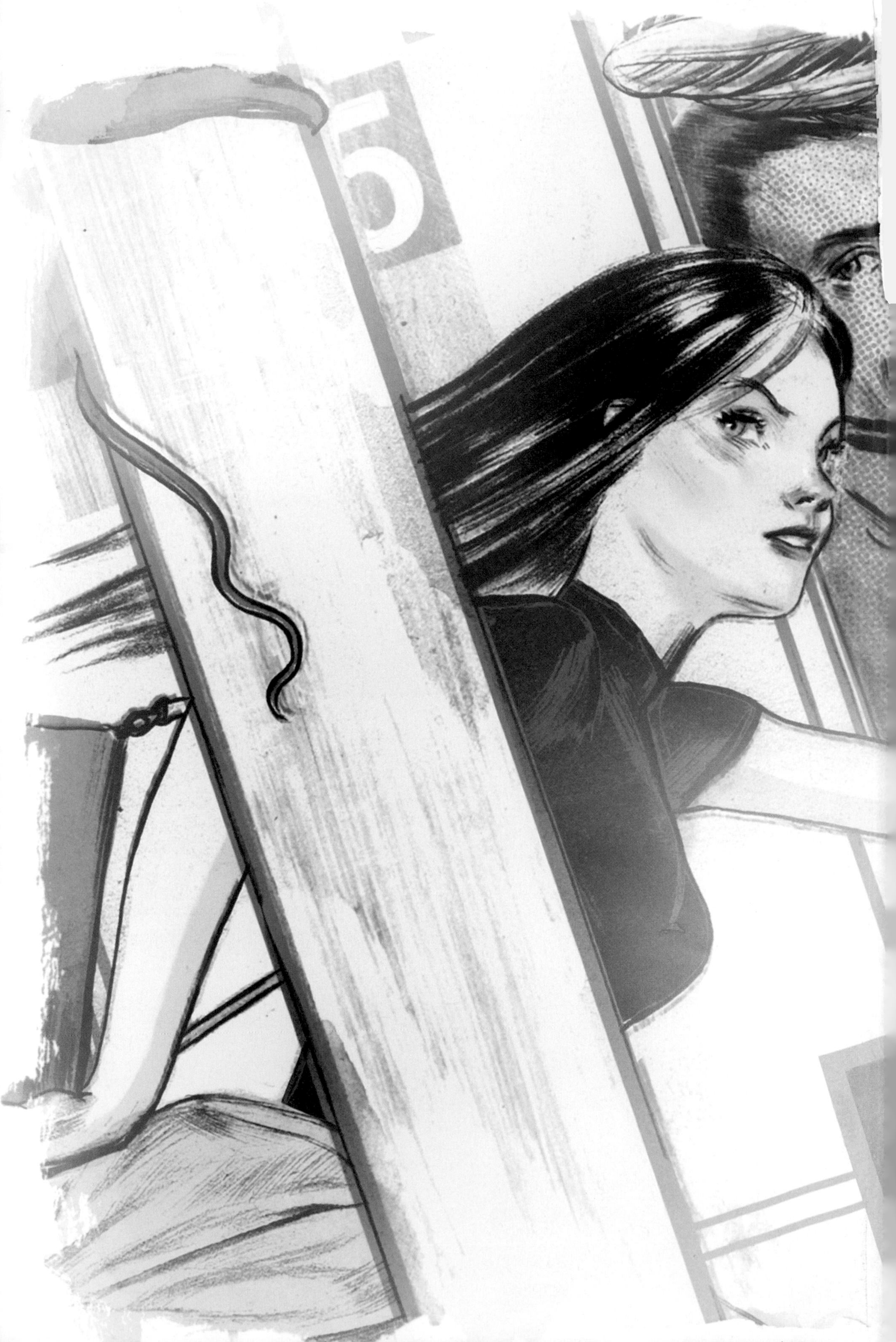

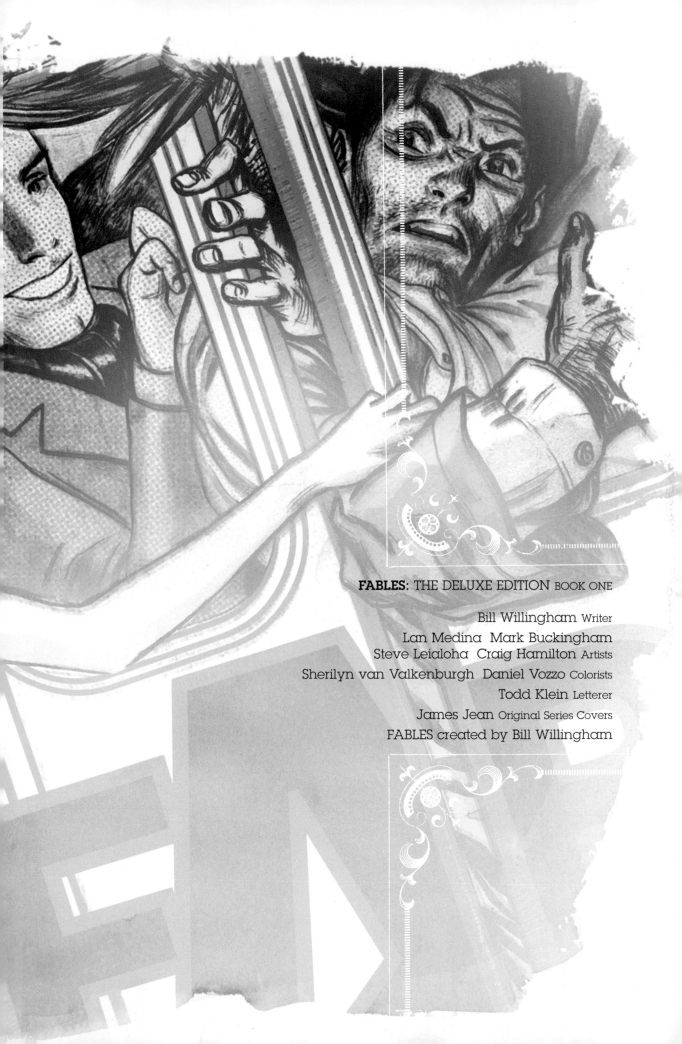

FABLES: THE DELUXE EDITION BOOK ONE

Bill Willingham Writer
Lan Medina Mark Buckingham
Steve Leialoha Craig Hamilton Artists
Sherilyn van Valkenburgh Daniel Vozzo Colorists
Todd Klein Letterer
James Jean Original Series Covers
FABLES created by Bill Willingham

To Lan Medina and Mark Buckingham.

Men of vision, fellow authors. You
carried the heaviest packs on this joint
expedition. You have my gratitude,
respect, and always my admiration.
— Bill Willingham

This book is dedicated to all those dearest
to me. My parents Valerie & John, my
sister Claire, her partner Jason and their
wonderful children Rudy and Matilda.
My dear friends Neil, Matt and Shane.
My wife and true love Irma. Thank you
for your constant love and support.
Thank you to Bill and Shelly for wanting
me to be part of FABLES from the start,
as well as everyone in the team, for
making this book so special.
— Mark Buckingham

Karen Berger SVP – Executive Editor
Shelly Bond Editor – Original Series
Mariah Huehner Assistant Editor – Original Series
Georg Brewer VP – Design & DC Direct Creative
Bob Harras Group Editor – Collected Editions
Scott Nybakken Editor
Robbin Brosterman Design Director – Books
Louis Prandi Art Director

DC COMICS
Paul Levitz President & Publisher
Richard Bruning SVP – Creative Director
Patrick Caldon EVP – Finance & Operations
Amy Genkins SVP – Business & Legal Affairs
Jim Lee Editorial Director – WildStorm
Gregory Noveck SVP – Creative Affairs
Steve Rotterdam SVP – Sales & Marketing
Cheryl Rubin SVP – Brand Management

Cover illustration by James Jean.
Logo design by Brainchild Studios/NYC

FABLES: THE DELUXE EDITION BOOK ONE
Published by DC Comics. Cover, introduction and
compilation Copyright © 2009 DC Comics.
All Rights Reserved.

Originally published in single magazine
form as FABLES 1-10. Copyright © 2002, 2003
Bill Willingham and DC Comics. All Rights Reserved.
All characters, their distinctive likenesses and related
elements featured in this publication are trademarks
of Bill Willingham. VERTIGO is a trademark of
DC Comics. The stories, characters and incidents
featured in this publication are entirely fictional.
DC Comics does not read or accept unsolicited
submissions of ideas, stories or artwork.

DC Comics
1700 Broadway,
New York, NY 10019
A Warner Bros. Entertainment Company.
Printed in the USA. First Printing.
ISBN:978-1-4012-2427-1

Table of Contents

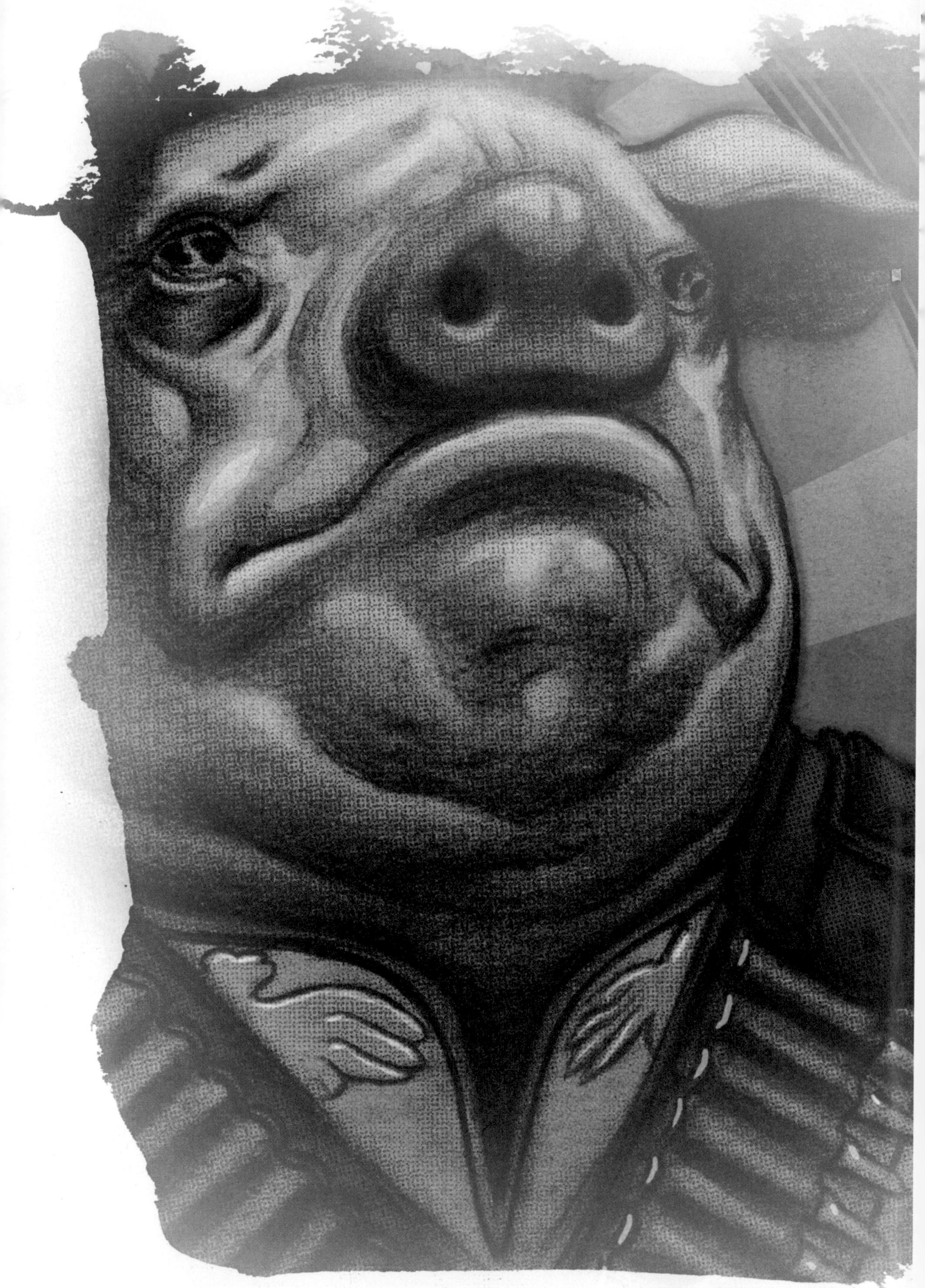

Down in the Deep Grand Green

Thank you for picking up this deluxe edition of the FABLES comic book series. This volume collects the first ten monthly issues of FABLES in their entirety, with a few extra tidbits thrown in. As I understand it, about once each year another deluxe FABLES volume will follow this one, until (one hopes) the entire sweeping FABLES saga is eventually collected. And because our "sweeping FABLES saga" is still ongoing, at the rate of one new issue each month, that finish line may be some time coming. And that's a good thing. I'm not in a hurry to see these stories come to an end. I hope you feel the same.

No doubt some of you are veteran FABLES readers, who've decided to revisit the past stories in this format. To you I don't have all that much to add to what we've already shared together, time and again, over the eight years (and counting) of FABLES' publication — except of course for the one thing that can't be repeated often enough: Thank you for reading. Thank you, not only for reading these tales once, but coming back to them again. C.S. Lewis used to say, "What good is a book you only want to read once?" I'm grateful that FABLES seems to be a series that merits those second and third readings. Thank you also for so often passing your copies and collections on to your friends, husbands, wives, fathers, mothers, and the occasional stranger. Your missionary efforts haven't gone unnoticed. And thank you, gentlewomen and gentlemen, for helping me make my living by telling these tall tales. Devoid of any respectable skills, unable to contribute to society in a meaningful way, and possessed of questionable character, I happily take my humble place among the other scurrilous liars, scoundrels and hoodwinkers of history.

But now, having spoken to you familiar and welcome old companions of previous adventures, I wonder if you'd excuse me a moment while I say a word or two to our new readers — to those who're about to read these first ten FABLES issues for the first time.

At the time I've had to pause in my normal routine to write this introduction, I have just completed the following line of dialogue for the 88th issue of the monthly FABLES series: "I'm here because all fairy tales take place in the woods, King Cole, even those that don't." Never mind who said those words, or why they were spoken to Old King Cole — yes, that fellow of the merry old soul. It doesn't matter. What does matter here is that this turns out to be an apt line with which to begin your introduction to the FABLES series.

Welcome to the woods, where all fairy tales take place — even those that don't.

Fables are fairy tales, folktales, whispered legends and ribald ballads, sung too loud and off-key, but with vigor and purpose. They're mysteries about things unknown, and perhaps unknowable, but desired, or feared, or both. The woods are and always have been a place of the deepest mysteries, the heart of the unknown. FABLES takes place in the woods.

Sure, you'll find out in the very first panel of the very first page that I've just told a whopper. Hey, I admitted to being the worst sort of liar not four paragraphs ago. I've lied, boldly and bald faced, because anyone can see with a glance that these stories take place in New York City, where our hapless characters are living in secret as refugees. Ah, but the woods are here, dear reader. Since we traffic in fairy tales, we have magic among our bag of tricks. And using such powers we've taken those enchanted glades with us, those ancient and venerable stands of oak and ash, yew and hawthorn, bright linden and cursed juniper. We've taken them and tarted them up in urban drag — the gaudy dress of stone, steel, plaster and glass. From the very first page, FABLES begins in a building called The Woodland, and its hallways are the dark and twisted trails of the deep forest. Its rooms, even the very big ones (and you'll quickly see that there are impossibly big ones), are close and brooding, with dense green canopies overhead that filter, edit, and rephrase what natural light gets through, until it is very unnatural indeed. The Woodland is a place where you only get to know what we tell you, and you should never trust a fraction of it. It's a place beyond the fields that you know, where the forgotten old monsters still lurk, and wait, and husband their years, until they can venture out again, stalking new young prey, that probably should have listened to the dotty old timers and heeded their dire warnings. It's a place where you can spread all the breadcrumbs behind you that you like; you're still going to get lost.

Lost, but not alone. You're about to meet some old friends that you haven't seen in a while. You already know their first stories — their adventurous tales from long ago. Now you get to find out what they've been up to lately. Some you can trust. Others you should never turn your back on. But isn't that always the way of things?

Welcome to the woods.

And now it's time for our stories to begin.

— Bill Willingham

25 June 2009

Written in the Woods

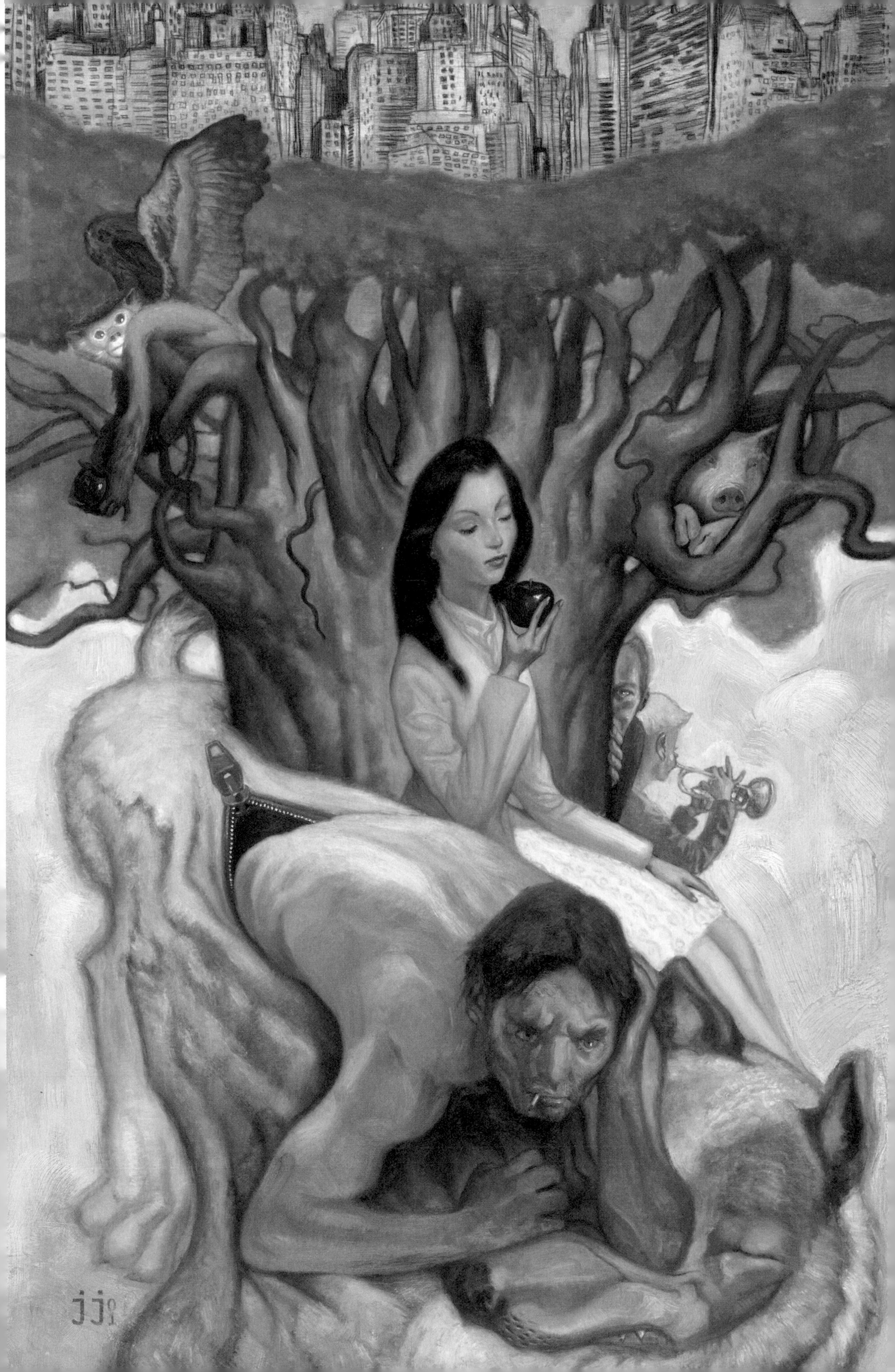

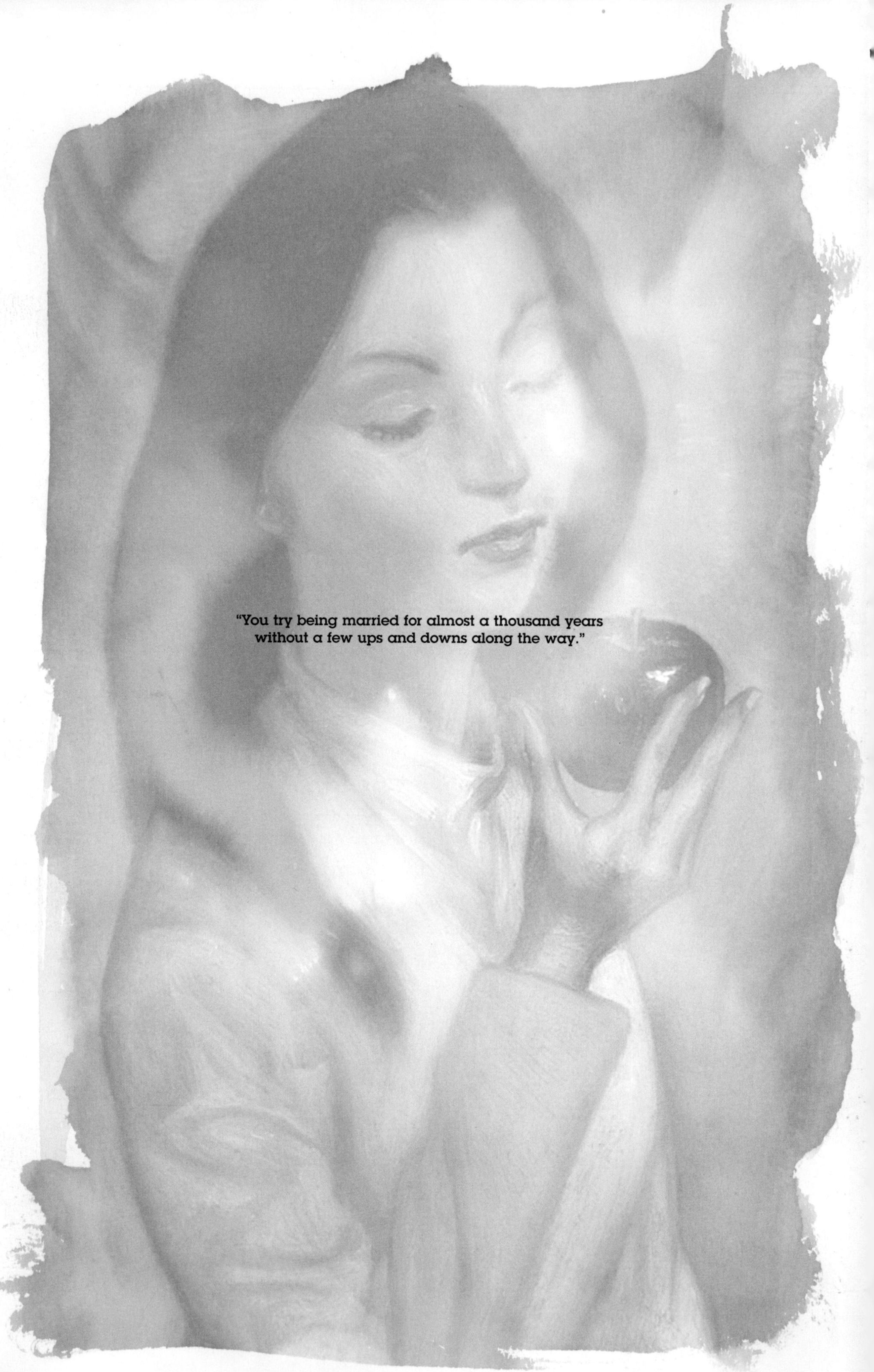
"You try being married for almost a thousand years
without a few ups and downs along the way."

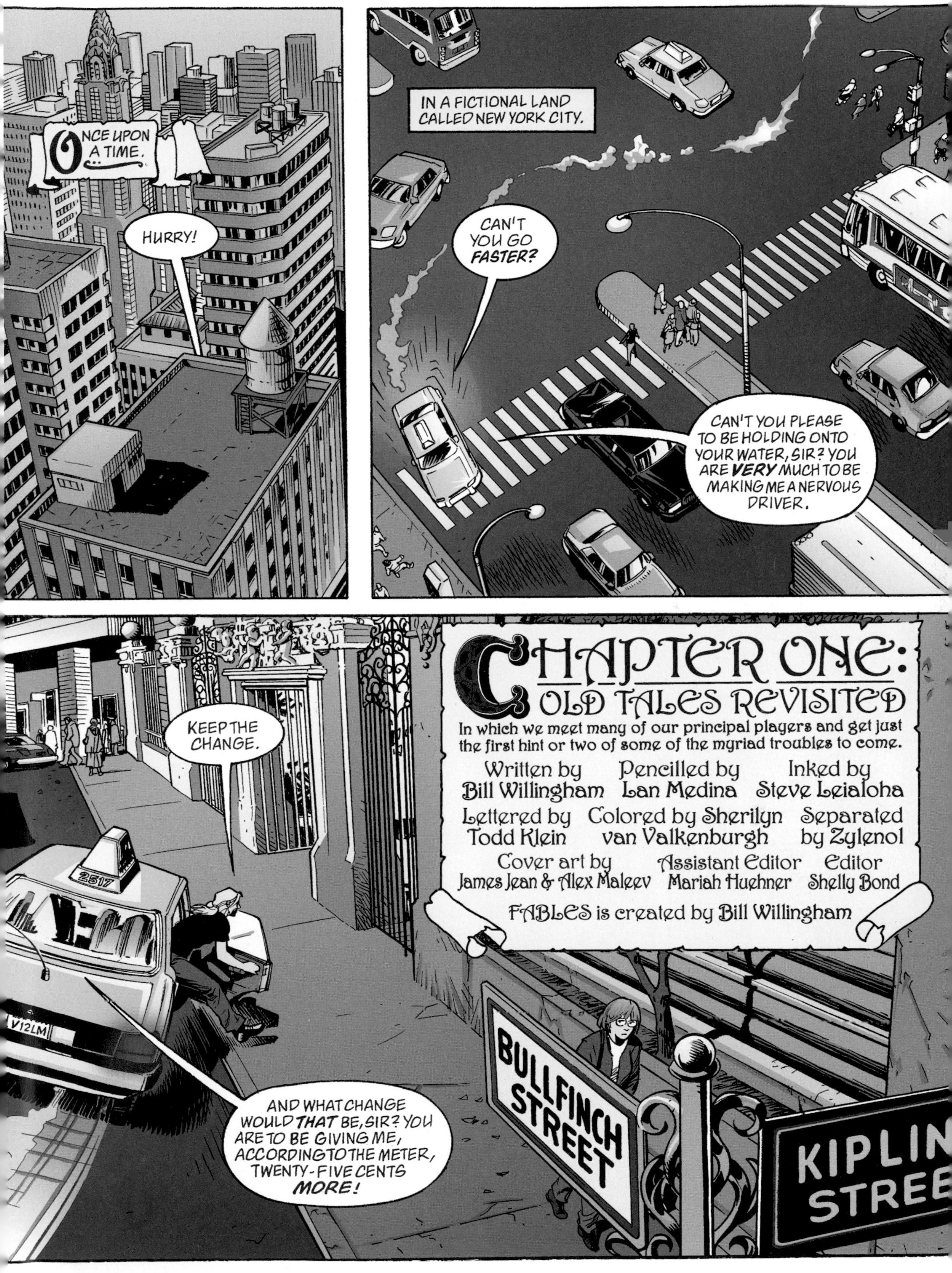

ONCE UPON A TIME...
HURRY!
IN A FICTIONAL LAND CALLED NEW YORK CITY.
CAN'T YOU GO FASTER?
CAN'T YOU PLEASE TO BE HOLDING ONTO YOUR WATER, SIR? YOU ARE VERY MUCH TO BE MAKING ME A NERVOUS DRIVER.
CHAPTER ONE:
OLD TALES REVISITED
In which we meet many of our principal players and get just the first hint or two of some of the myriad troubles to come.
Written by Bill Willingham
Pencilled by Lan Medina
Inked by Steve Leialoha
Lettered by Todd Klein
Colored by Sherilyn van Valkenburgh
Separated by Zylenol
Cover art by James Jean & Alex Maleev
Assistant Editor Mariah Huehner
Editor Shelly Bond
FABLES is created by Bill Willingham
KEEP THE CHANGE.
AND WHAT CHANGE WOULD THAT BE, SIR? YOU ARE TO BE GIVING ME, ACCORDING TO THE METER, TWENTY-FIVE CENTS MORE!
BULLFINCH STREET
KIPLIN STREE
2517

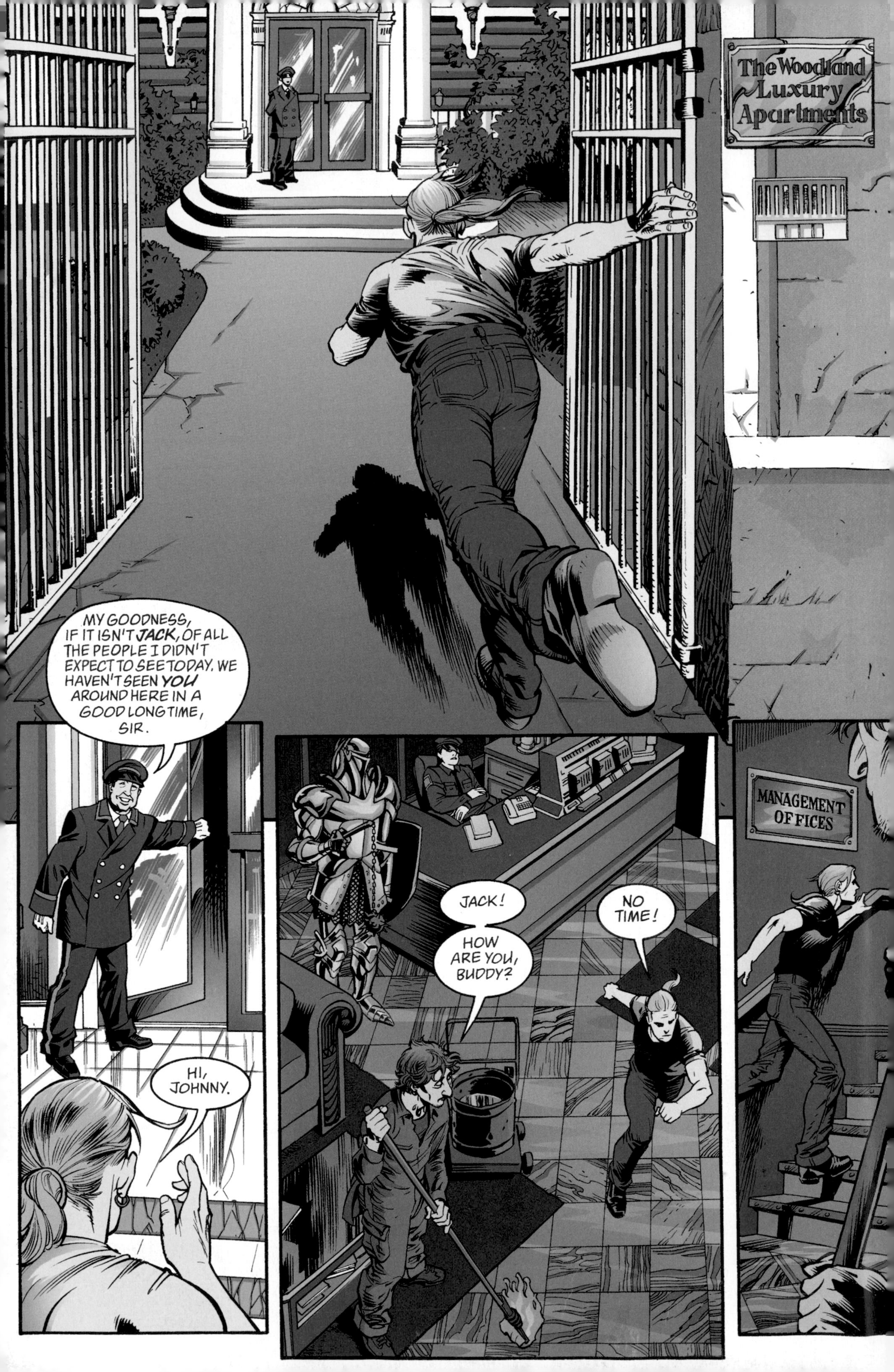
The Woodland Luxury Apartments
MY GOODNESS, IF IT ISN'T JACK, OF ALL THE PEOPLE I DIDN'T EXPECT TO SEE TODAY. WE HAVEN'T SEEN YOU AROUND HERE IN A GOOD LONG TIME, SIR.
HI, JOHNNY.
JACK!
HOW ARE YOU, BUDDY?
NO TIME!
MANAGEMENT OFFICES

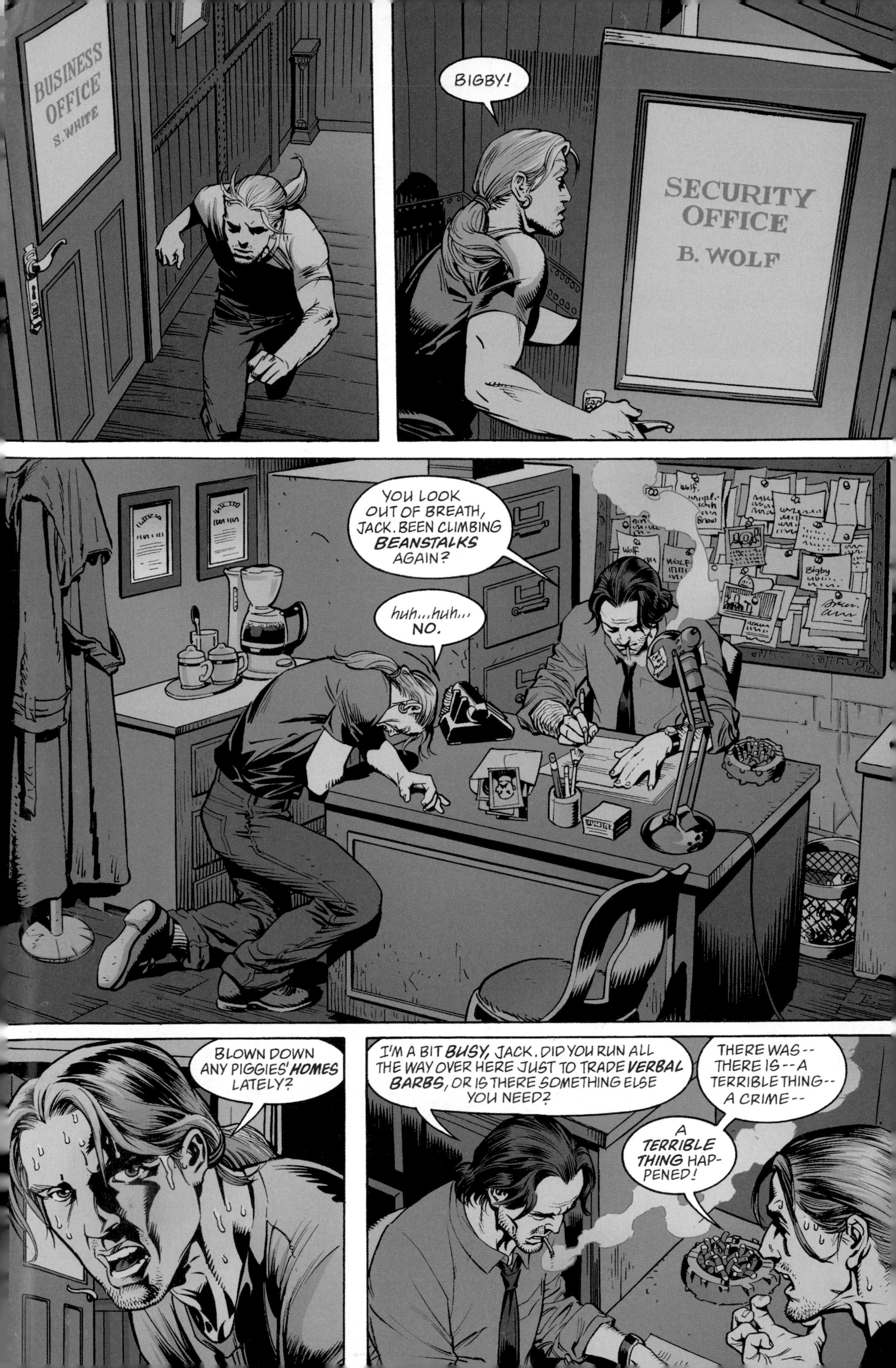
BUSINESS OFFICE S. WHITE
BIGBY!
SECURITY OFFICE B. WOLF
YOU LOOK OUT OF BREATH, JACK. BEEN CLIMBING BEANSTALKS AGAIN?
huh...huh... NO.
BLOWN DOWN ANY PIGGIES' HOMES LATELY?
I'M A BIT BUSY, JACK. DID YOU RUN ALL THE WAY OVER HERE JUST TO TRADE VERBAL BARBS, OR IS THERE SOMETHING ELSE YOU NEED?
THERE WAS-- THERE IS-- A TERRIBLE THING-- A CRIME--
A TERRIBLE THING HAP-PENED!

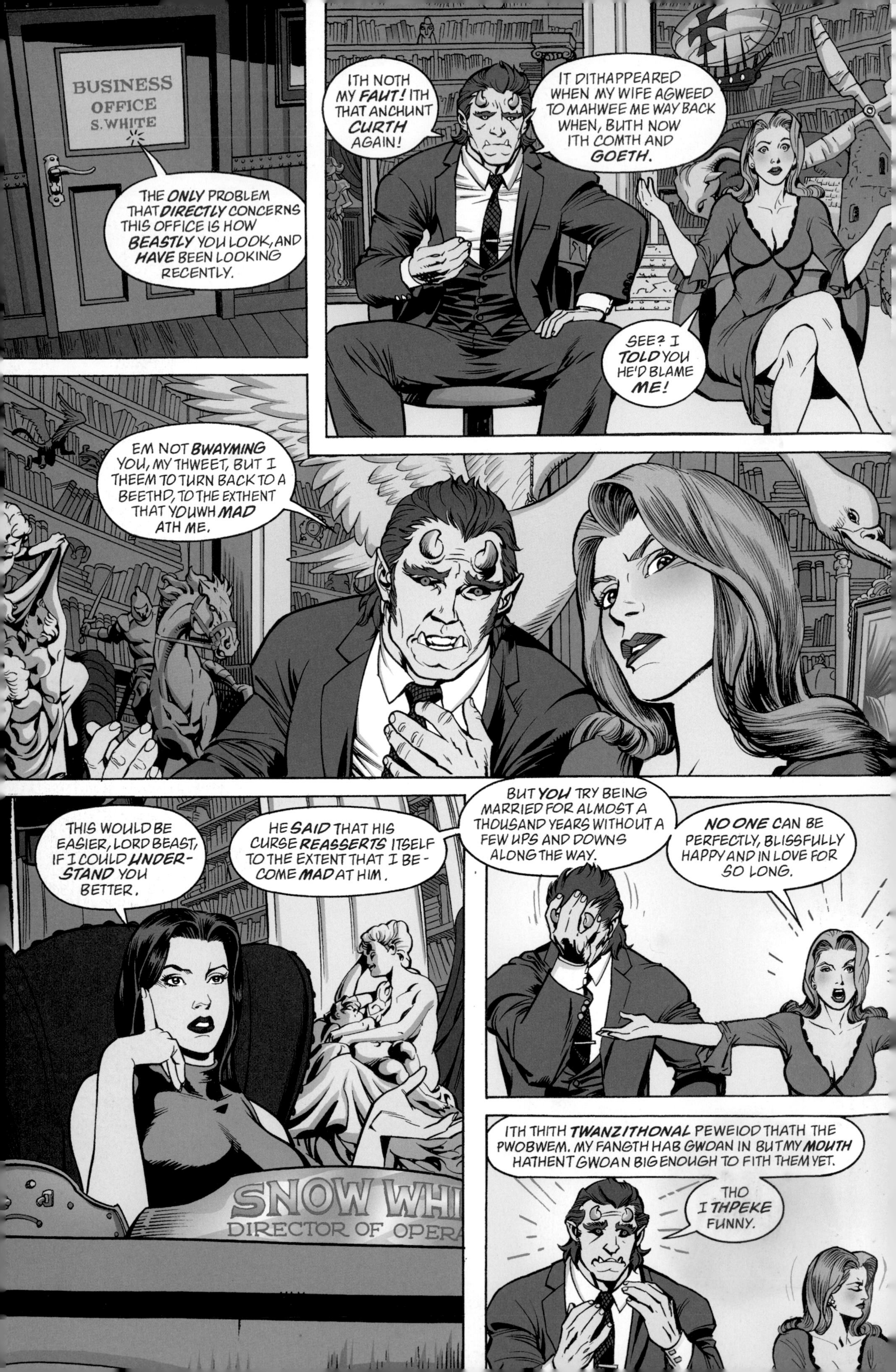
BUSINESS OFFICE S. WHITE
THE ONLY PROBLEM THAT DIRECTLY CONCERNS THIS OFFICE IS HOW BEASTLY YOU LOOK, AND HAVE BEEN LOOKING RECENTLY.
ITH NOTH MY FAUT! ITH THAT ANCHUNT CURTH AGAIN!
IT DITHAPPEARED WHEN MY WIFE AGWEED TO MAHWEE ME WAY BACK WHEN, BUTH NOW ITH COMTH AND GOETH.
SEE? I TOLD YOU HE'D BLAME ME!
EM NOT BWAYMING YOU, MY THWEET, BUT I THEEM TO TURN BACK TO A BEETHD, TO THE EXTENT THAT YOUWH MAD ATH ME.
THIS WOULD BE EASIER, LORD BEAST, IF I COULD UNDER-STAND YOU BETTER.
HE SAID THAT HIS CURSE REASSERTS ITSELF TO THE EXTENT THAT I BE-COME MAD AT HIM.
BUT YOU TRY BEING MARRIED FOR ALMOST A THOUSAND YEARS WITHOUT A FEW UPS AND DOWNS ALONG THE WAY.
NO ONE CAN BE PERFECTLY, BLISSFULLY HAPPY AND IN LOVE FOR SO LONG.
SNOW WHI
DIRECTOR OF OPERA
ITH THITH TWANZITHONAL PEWEIOD THATH THE PWOBWEM. MY FANGTH HAB GWOAN IN BUT MY MOUTH HATHENT GWOAN BIG ENOUGH TO FITH THEM YET.
THO I THPEKE FUNNY.

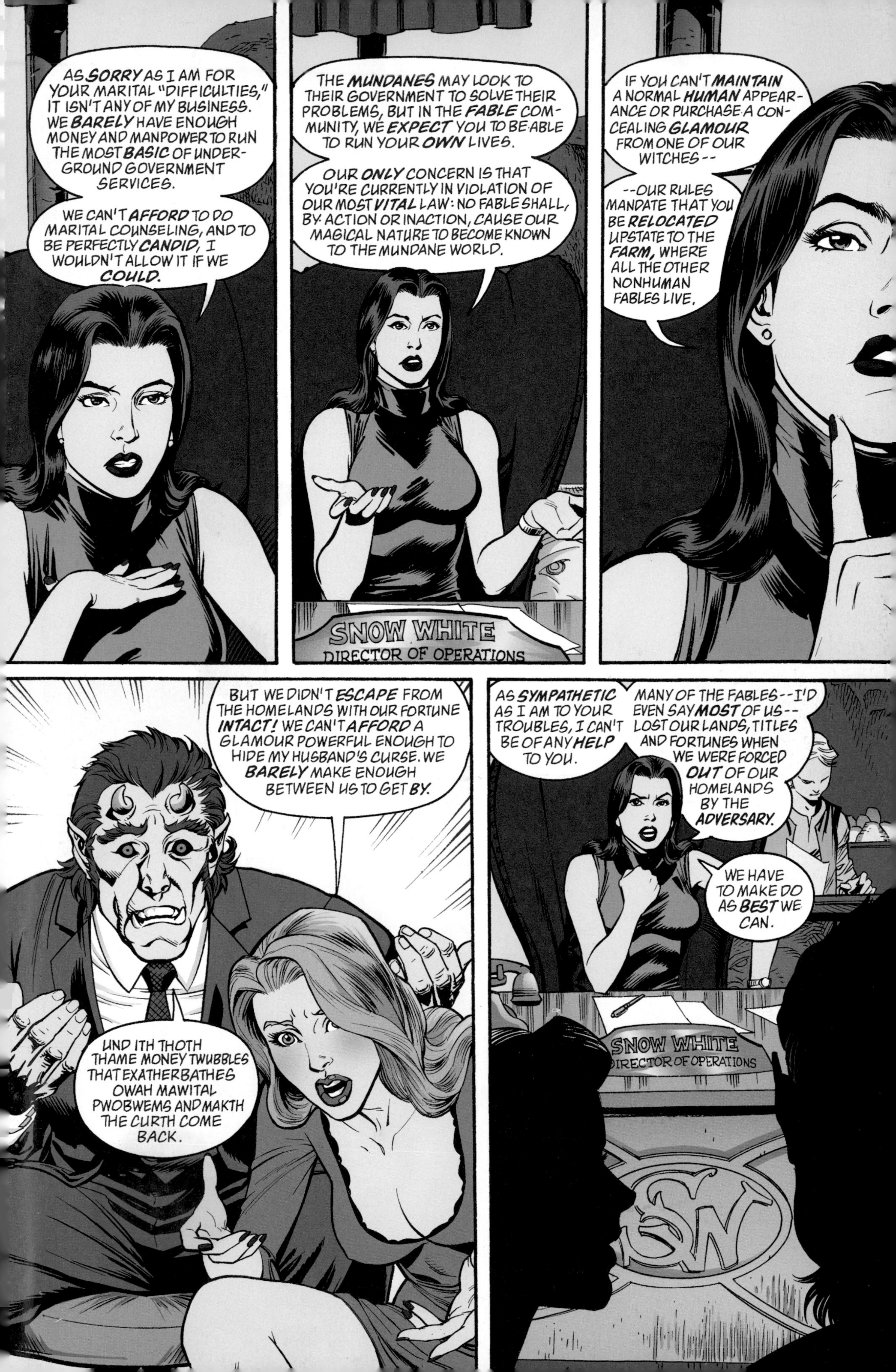
AS SORRY AS I AM FOR YOUR MARITAL "DIFFICULTIES," IT ISN'T ANY OF MY BUSINESS. WE BARELY HAVE ENOUGH MONEY AND MANPOWER TO RUN THE MOST BASIC OF UNDERGROUND GOVERNMENT SERVICES.
WE CAN'T AFFORD TO DO MARITAL COUNSELING, AND TO BE PERFECTLY CANDID, I WOULDN'T ALLOW IT IF WE COULD.
THE MUNDANES MAY LOOK TO THEIR GOVERNMENT TO SOLVE THEIR PROBLEMS, BUT IN THE FABLE COMMUNITY, WE EXPECT YOU TO BE ABLE TO RUN YOUR OWN LIVES.
OUR ONLY CONCERN IS THAT YOU'RE CURRENTLY IN VIOLATION OF OUR MOST VITAL LAW: NO FABLE SHALL, BY ACTION OR INACTION, CAUSE OUR MAGICAL NATURE TO BECOME KNOWN TO THE MUNDANE WORLD.
SNOW WHITE
DIRECTOR OF OPERATIONS
IF YOU CAN'T MAINTAIN A NORMAL HUMAN APPEARANCE OR PURCHASE A CONCEALING GLAMOUR FROM ONE OF OUR WITCHES --
--OUR RULES MANDATE THAT YOU BE RELOCATED UPSTATE TO THE FARM, WHERE ALL THE OTHER NONHUMAN FABLES LIVE.
BUT WE DIDN'T ESCAPE FROM THE HOMELANDS WITH OUR FORTUNE INTACT! WE CAN'T AFFORD A GLAMOUR POWERFUL ENOUGH TO HIDE MY HUSBAND'S CURSE. WE BARELY MAKE ENOUGH BETWEEN US TO GET BY.
UND ITH THOTH THAME MONEY TWUBBLES THAT EXATHERBATHES OWAH MAWITAL PWOBWEMS AND MAKTH THE CURTH COME BACK.
AS SYMPATHETIC AS I AM TO YOUR TROUBLES, I CAN'T BE OF ANY HELP TO YOU.
MANY OF THE FABLES -- I'D EVEN SAY MOST OF US -- LOST OUR LANDS, TITLES AND FORTUNES WHEN WE WERE FORCED OUT OF OUR HOMELANDS BY THE ADVERSARY.
WE HAVE TO MAKE DO AS BEST WE CAN.
SNOW WHITE
DIRECTOR OF OPERATIONS

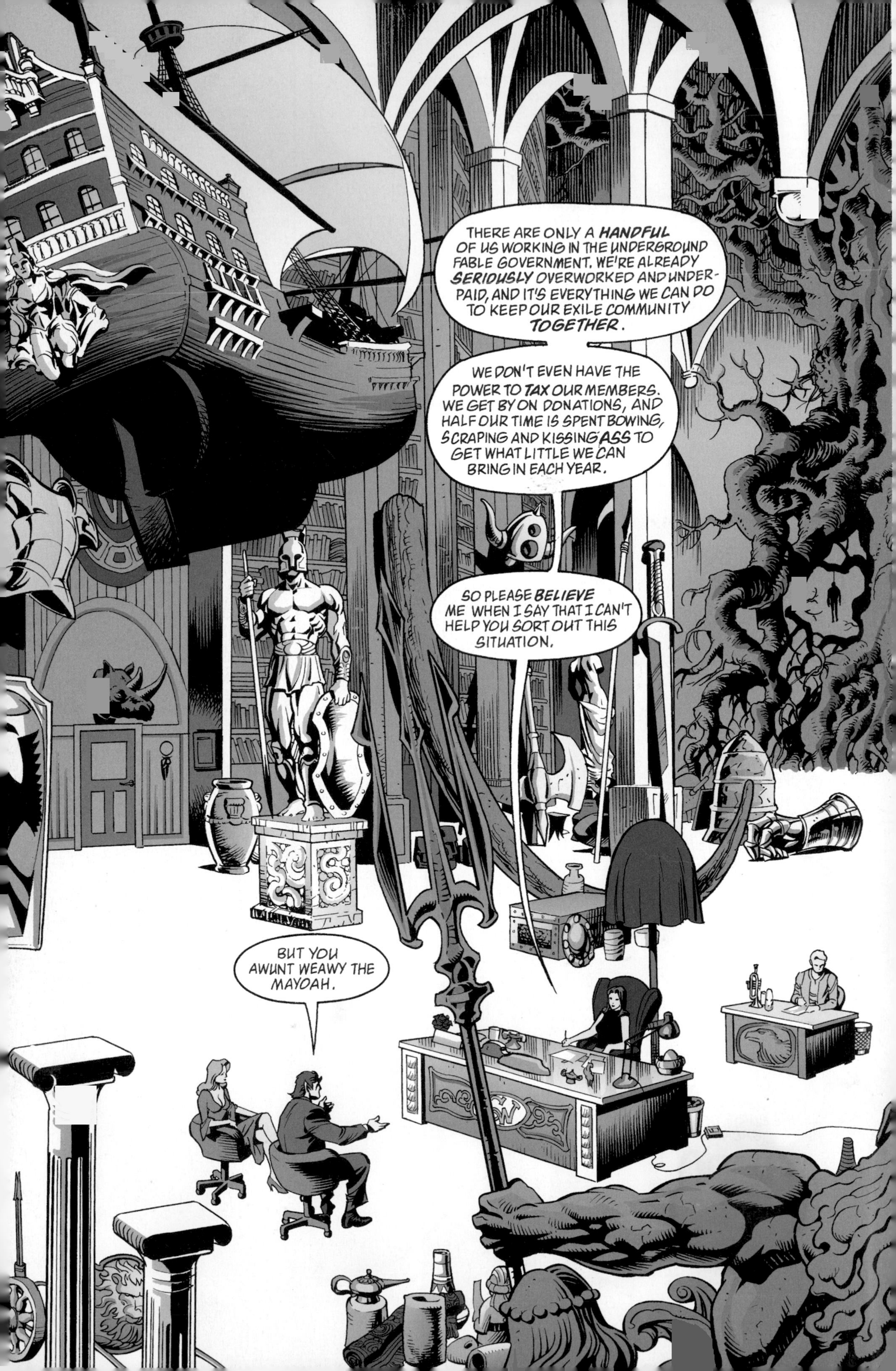
THERE ARE ONLY A HANDFUL OF US WORKING IN THE UNDERGROUND FABLE GOVERNMENT. WE'RE ALREADY SERIOUSLY OVERWORKED AND UNDER-PAID, AND IT'S EVERYTHING WE CAN DO TO KEEP OUR EXILE COMMUNITY TOGETHER.
WE DON'T EVEN HAVE THE POWER TO TAX OUR MEMBERS. WE GET BY ON DONATIONS, AND HALF OUR TIME IS SPENT BOWING, SCRAPING AND KISSING ASS TO GET WHAT LITTLE WE CAN BRING IN EACH YEAR.
SO PLEASE BELIEVE ME WHEN I SAY THAT I CAN'T HELP YOU SORT OUT THIS SITUATION.
BUT YOU AWUNT WEAWY THE MAYOAH.

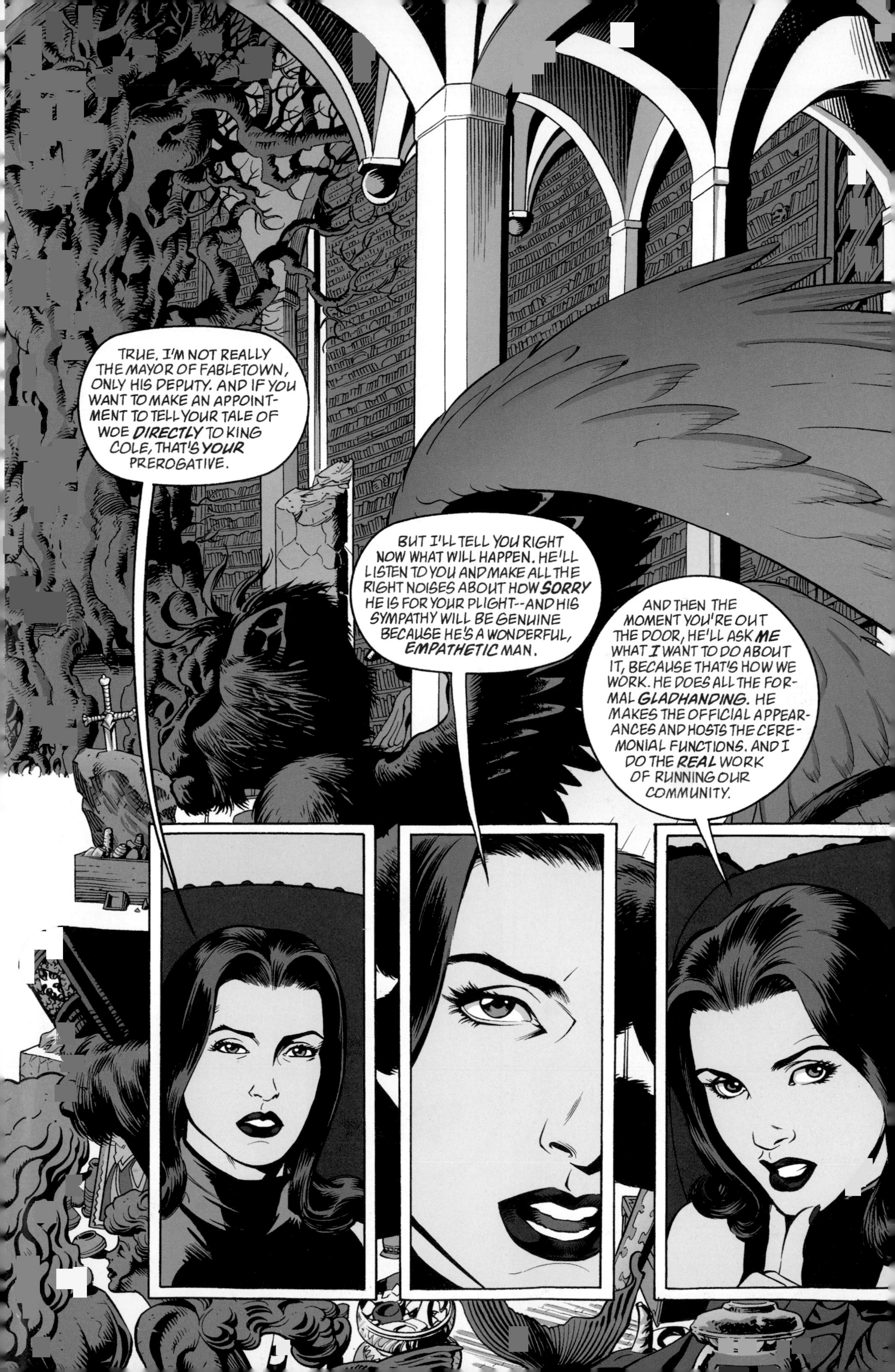
TRUE. I'M NOT REALLY THE MAYOR OF FABLETOWN, ONLY HIS DEPUTY. AND IF YOU WANT TO MAKE AN APPOINTMENT TO TELL YOUR TALE OF WOE DIRECTLY TO KING COLE, THAT'S YOUR PREROGATIVE.
BUT I'LL TELL YOU RIGHT NOW WHAT WILL HAPPEN. HE'LL LISTEN TO YOU AND MAKE ALL THE RIGHT NOISES ABOUT HOW SORRY HE IS FOR YOUR PLIGHT--AND HIS SYMPATHY WILL BE GENUINE BECAUSE HE'S A WONDERFUL, EMPATHETIC MAN.
AND THEN THE MOMENT YOU'RE OUT THE DOOR, HE'LL ASK ME WHAT I WANT TO DO ABOUT IT, BECAUSE THAT'S HOW WE WORK. HE DOES ALL THE FORMAL GLADHANDING. HE MAKES THE OFFICIAL APPEARANCES AND HOSTS THE CEREMONIAL FUNCTIONS. AND I DO THE REAL WORK OF RUNNING OUR COMMUNITY.

FOR BETTER OR **WORSE**, YOU'VE JUST HAD YOUR **APPEAL** TO CITY HALL.

YOU DIVORCED **YOUR** PRINCE **CENTURIES** AGO. YOU HAVE **NO IDEA** HOW HARD IT IS TO KEEP A MARRIAGE GOING SO LONG.

NOWAH, DEAH. THEWES NO WEASON TO GET **PERSONOAH**.

SNOW WHITE
DIRECTOR OF OPERATIONS

DON'T GET **PERSONAL?** AFTER SHE OPENLY **CRITICIZED** OUR MARRIED LIFE?

I DID **NO SUCH THING**.

AND JUST WHO IS **SHE** TO CRITICIZE **ANYONE'S** PERSONAL LIFE, AFTER WHAT **I** HEARD ABOUT HER TAWDRY LITTLE ADVENTURE WITH THOSE SEVEN DWARVES?

OKAY, FOLKS, BUSINESS IS PILING **UP** AND WE NEED TO MOVE THINGS ALONG TO MISS WHITE'S **NEXT** APPOINTMENT.

SNOW WHITE
Director of Operations

BUT--?

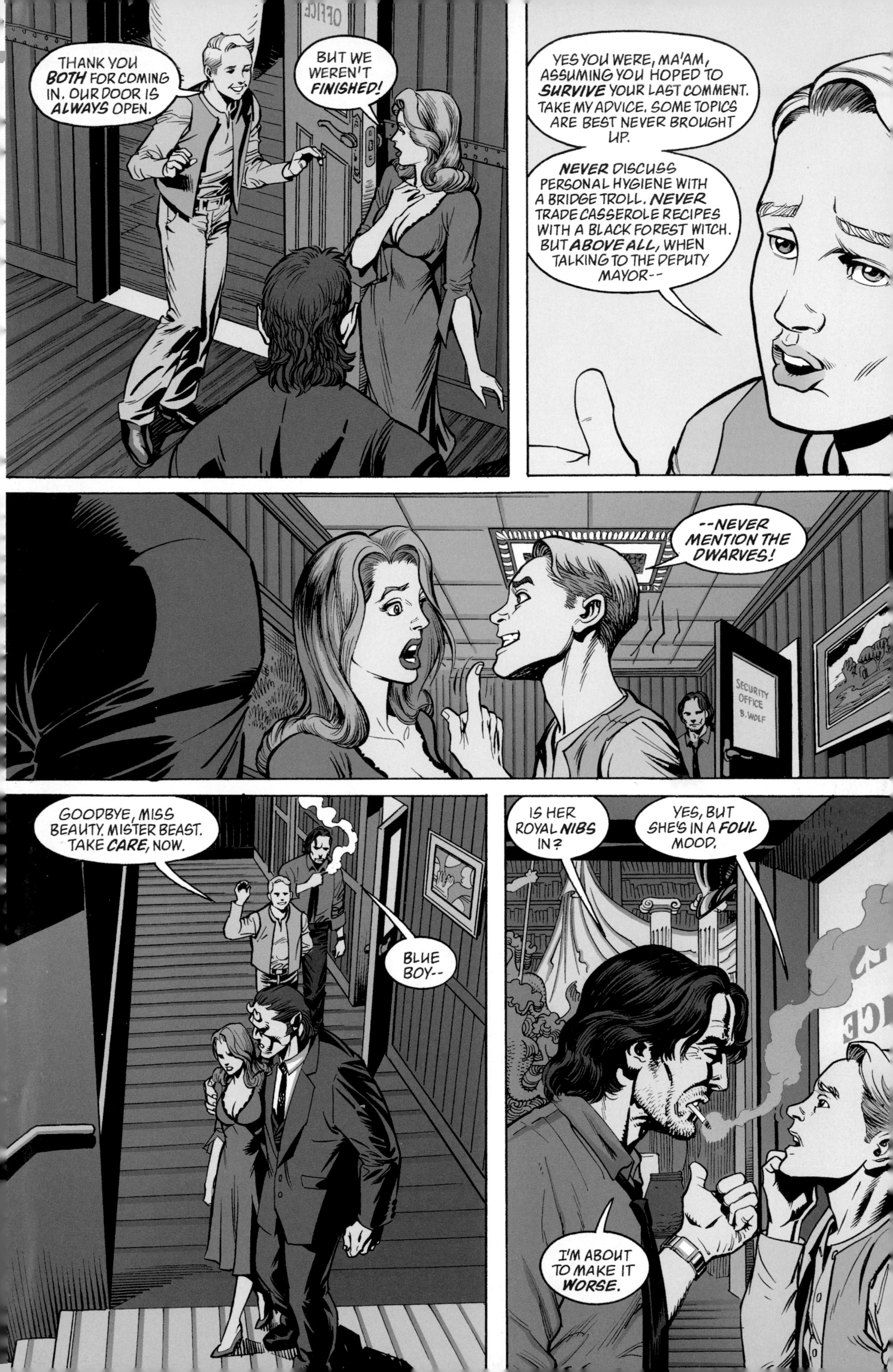

THANK YOU BOTH FOR COMING IN. OUR DOOR IS ALWAYS OPEN.
BUT WE WEREN'T FINISHED!
OFFICE
YES YOU WERE, MA'AM, ASSUMING YOU HOPED TO SURVIVE YOUR LAST COMMENT. TAKE MY ADVICE. SOME TOPICS ARE BEST NEVER BROUGHT UP.
NEVER DISCUSS PERSONAL HYGIENE WITH A BRIDGE TROLL. NEVER TRADE CASSEROLE RECIPES WITH A BLACK FOREST WITCH. BUT ABOVE ALL, WHEN TALKING TO THE DEPUTY MAYOR--
--NEVER MENTION THE DWARVES!
SECURITY OFFICE B. WOLF
GOODBYE, MISS BEAUTY. MISTER BEAST. TAKE CARE, NOW.
BLUE BOY--
IS HER ROYAL NIBS IN?
YES, BUT SHE'S IN A FOUL MOOD.
I'M ABOUT TO MAKE IT WORSE.

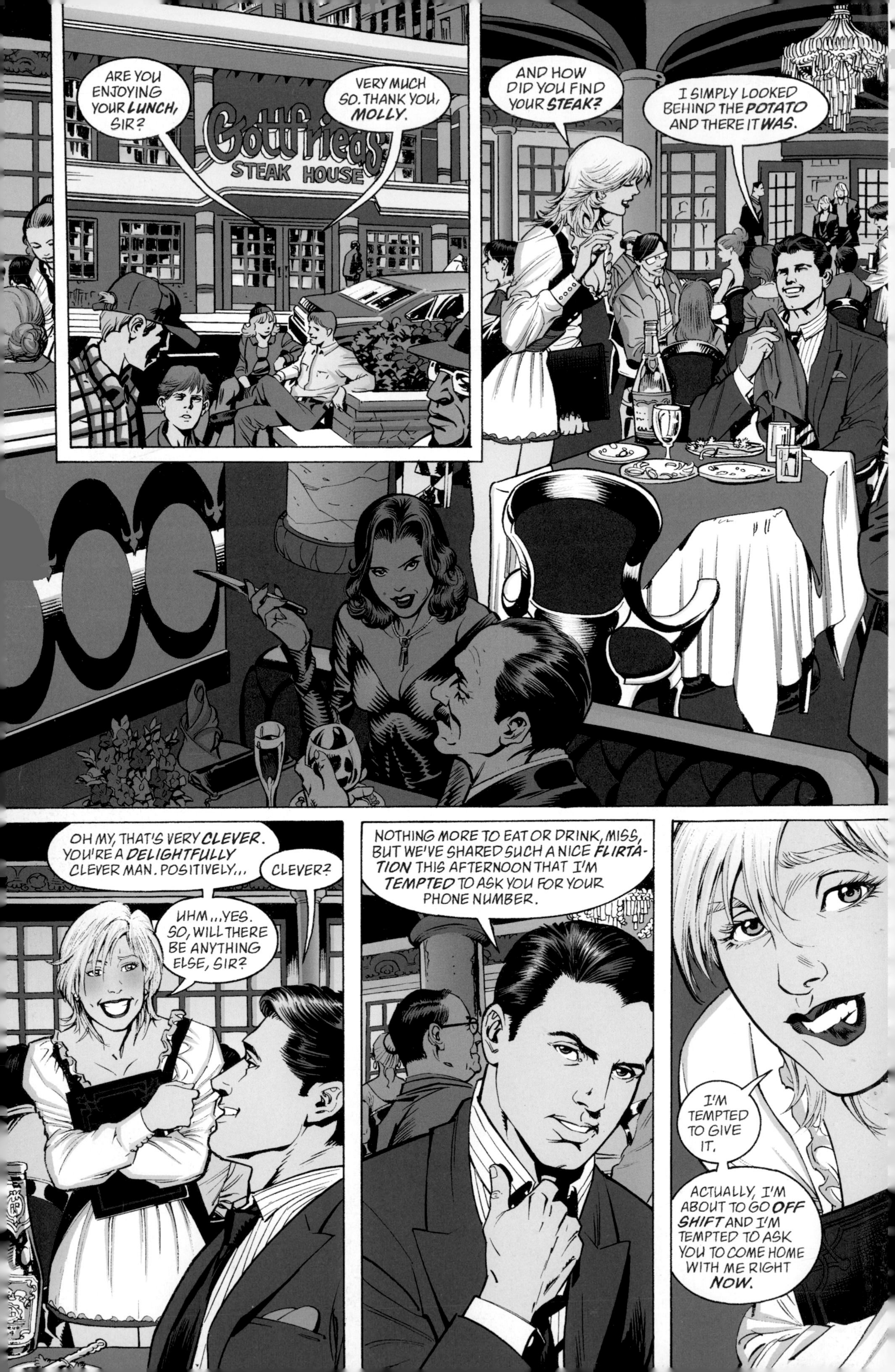

ARE YOU ENJOYING YOUR LUNCH, SIR?
VERY MUCH SO. THANK YOU, MOLLY.
Gottfried's STEAK HOUSE
AND HOW DID YOU FIND YOUR STEAK?
I SIMPLY LOOKED BEHIND THE POTATO AND THERE IT WAS.
OH MY, THAT'S VERY CLEVER. YOU'RE A DELIGHTFULLY CLEVER MAN. POSITIVELY...
CLEVER?
UHM ...YES. SO, WILL THERE BE ANYTHING ELSE, SIR?
NOTHING MORE TO EAT OR DRINK, MISS, BUT WE'VE SHARED SUCH A NICE FLIRTATION THIS AFTERNOON THAT I'M TEMPTED TO ASK YOU FOR YOUR PHONE NUMBER.
I'M TEMPTED TO GIVE IT.
ACTUALLY, I'M ABOUT TO GO OFF SHIFT AND I'M TEMPTED TO ASK YOU TO COME HOME WITH ME RIGHT NOW.

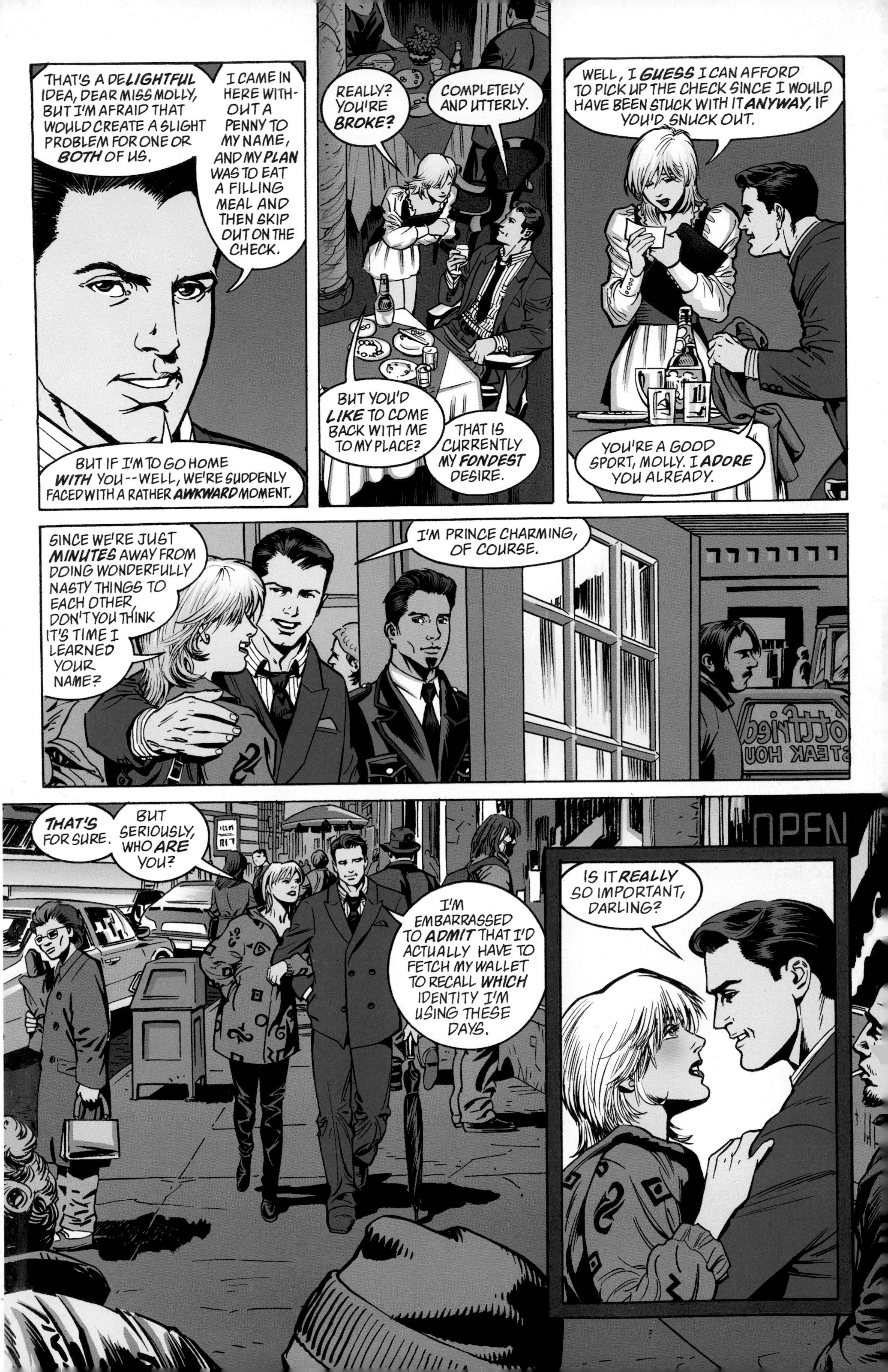

THAT'S A DELIGHTFUL IDEA, DEAR MISS MOLLY, BUT I'M AFRAID THAT WOULD CREATE A SLIGHT PROBLEM FOR ONE OR BOTH OF US.
I CAME IN HERE WITHOUT A PENNY TO MY NAME, AND MY PLAN WAS TO EAT A FILLING MEAL AND THEN SKIP OUT ON THE CHECK.
BUT IF I'M TO GO HOME WITH YOU--WELL, WE'RE SUDDENLY FACED WITH A RATHER AWKWARD MOMENT.
REALLY? YOU'RE BROKE?
COMPLETELY AND UTTERLY.
BUT YOU'D LIKE TO COME BACK WITH ME TO MY PLACE?
THAT IS CURRENTLY MY FONDEST DESIRE.
WELL, I GUESS I CAN AFFORD TO PICK UP THE CHECK SINCE I WOULD HAVE BEEN STUCK WITH IT ANYWAY, IF YOU'D SNUCK OUT.
YOU'RE A GOOD SPORT, MOLLY. I ADORE YOU ALREADY.
SINCE WE'RE JUST MINUTES AWAY FROM DOING WONDERFULLY NASTY THINGS TO EACH OTHER, DON'T YOU THINK IT'S TIME I LEARNED YOUR NAME?
I'M PRINCE CHARMING, OF COURSE.
THAT'S FOR SURE.
BUT SERIOUSLY, WHO ARE YOU?
I'M EMBARRASSED TO ADMIT THAT I'D ACTUALLY HAVE TO FETCH MY WALLET TO RECALL WHICH IDENTITY I'M USING THESE DAYS.
IS IT REALLY SO IMPORTANT, DARLING?
OPEN

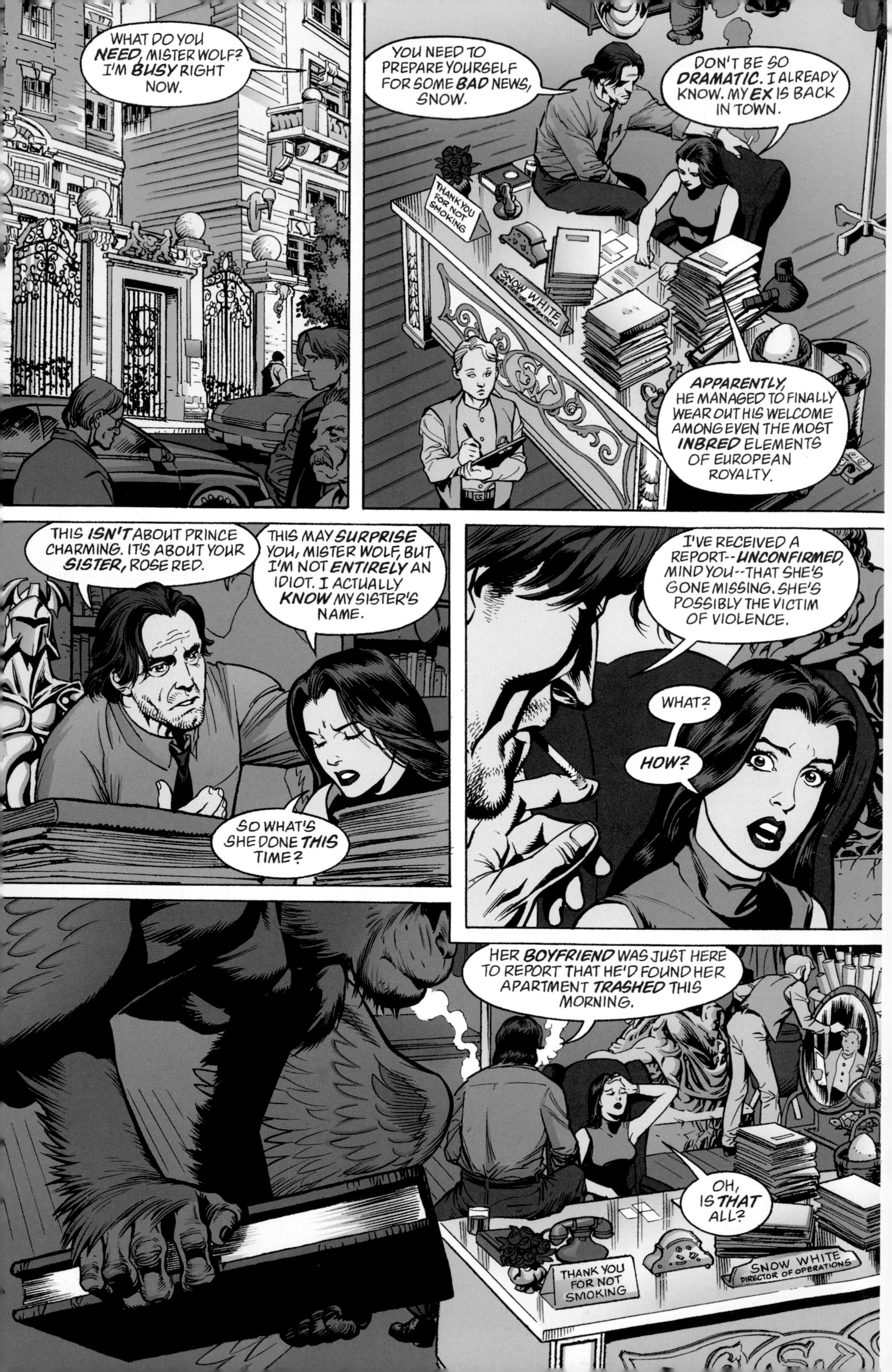

WHAT DO YOU NEED, MISTER WOLF? I'M BUSY RIGHT NOW.
YOU NEED TO PREPARE YOURSELF FOR SOME BAD NEWS, SNOW.
DON'T BE SO DRAMATIC. I ALREADY KNOW. MY EX IS BACK IN TOWN.
THANK YOU FOR NOT SMOKING
SNOW WHITE
APPARENTLY, HE MANAGED TO FINALLY WEAR OUT HIS WELCOME AMONG EVEN THE MOST INBRED ELEMENTS OF EUROPEAN ROYALTY.
THIS ISN'T ABOUT PRINCE CHARMING. IT'S ABOUT YOUR SISTER, ROSE RED.
THIS MAY SURPRISE YOU, MISTER WOLF, BUT I'M NOT ENTIRELY AN IDIOT. I ACTUALLY KNOW MY SISTER'S NAME.
SO WHAT'S SHE DONE THIS TIME?
I'VE RECEIVED A REPORT--UNCONFIRMED, MIND YOU--THAT SHE'S GONE MISSING. SHE'S POSSIBLY THE VICTIM OF VIOLENCE.
WHAT?
HOW?
HER BOYFRIEND WAS JUST HERE TO REPORT THAT HE'D FOUND HER APARTMENT TRASHED THIS MORNING.
OH, IS THAT ALL?
THANK YOU FOR NOT SMOKING
SNOW WHITE DIRECTOR OF OPERATIONS

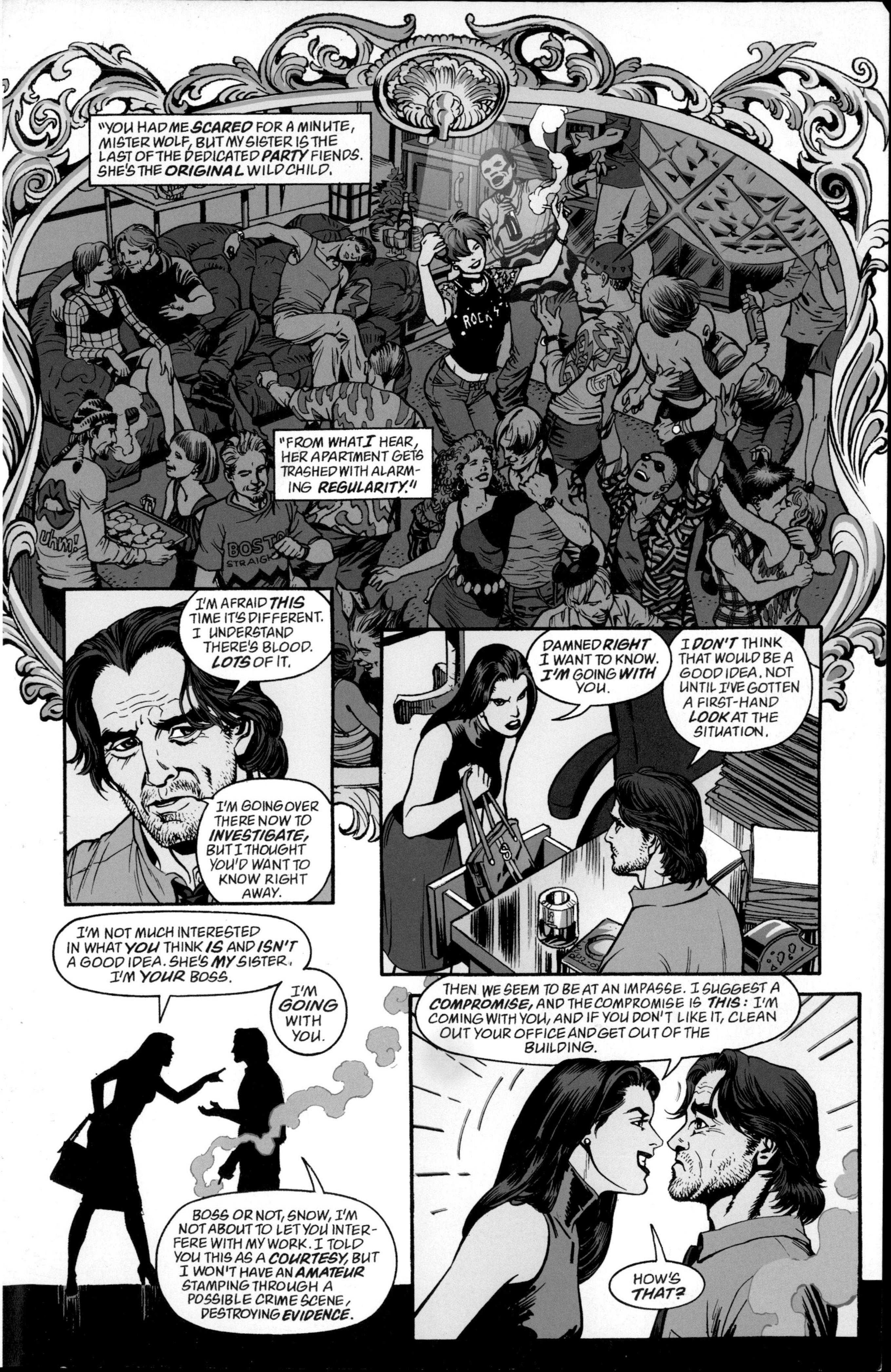
"YOU HAD ME SCARED FOR A MINUTE, MISTER WOLF, BUT MY SISTER IS THE LAST OF THE DEDICATED PARTY FIENDS. SHE'S THE ORIGINAL WILD CHILD.
"FROM WHAT I HEAR, HER APARTMENT GETS TRASHED WITH ALARMING REGULARITY."
I'M AFRAID THIS TIME IT'S DIFFERENT. I UNDERSTAND THERE'S BLOOD. LOTS OF IT.
I'M GOING OVER THERE NOW TO INVESTIGATE, BUT I THOUGHT YOU'D WANT TO KNOW RIGHT AWAY.
DAMNED RIGHT I WANT TO KNOW. I'M GOING WITH YOU.
I DON'T THINK THAT WOULD BE A GOOD IDEA. NOT UNTIL I'VE GOTTEN A FIRST-HAND LOOK AT THE SITUATION.
I'M NOT MUCH INTERESTED IN WHAT YOU THINK IS AND ISN'T A GOOD IDEA. SHE'S MY SISTER. I'M YOUR BOSS.
I'M GOING WITH YOU.
BOSS OR NOT, SNOW, I'M NOT ABOUT TO LET YOU INTERFERE WITH MY WORK. I TOLD YOU THIS AS A COURTESY, BUT I WON'T HAVE AN AMATEUR STAMPING THROUGH A POSSIBLE CRIME SCENE, DESTROYING EVIDENCE.
THEN WE SEEM TO BE AT AN IMPASSE. I SUGGEST A COMPROMISE, AND THE COMPROMISE IS THIS: I'M COMING WITH YOU, AND IF YOU DON'T LIKE IT, CLEAN OUT YOUR OFFICE AND GET OUT OF THE BUILDING.
HOW'S THAT?

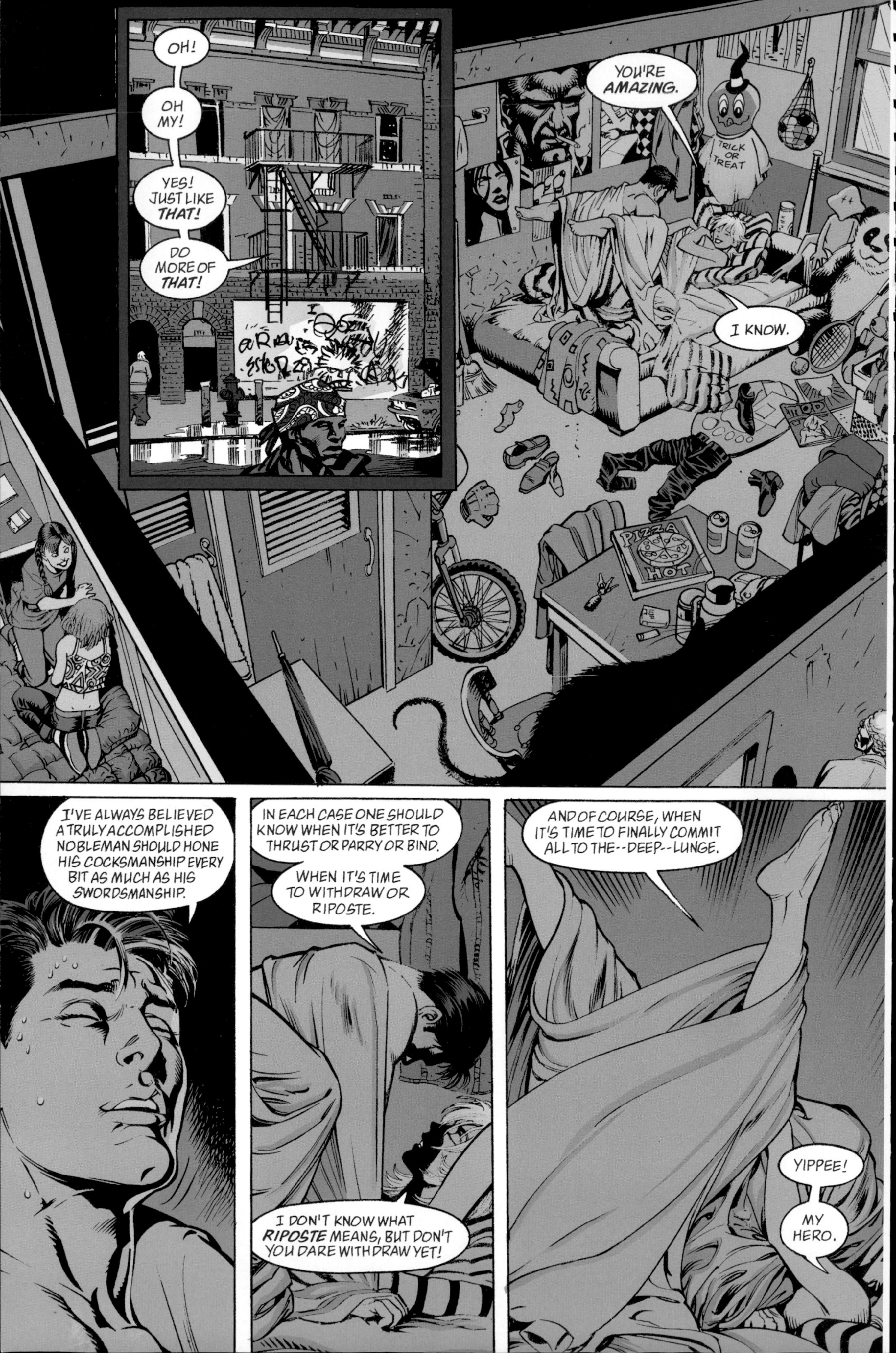

OH!
OH MY!
YES! JUST LIKE THAT!
DO MORE OF THAT!
YOU'RE AMAZING.
TRICK OR TREAT
I KNOW.
PIZZA HOT
I'VE ALWAYS BELIEVED A TRULY ACCOMPLISHED NOBLEMAN SHOULD HONE HIS COCKSMANSHIP EVERY BIT AS MUCH AS HIS SWORDSMANSHIP.
IN EACH CASE ONE SHOULD KNOW WHEN IT'S BETTER TO THRUST OR PARRY OR BIND.
WHEN IT'S TIME TO WITHDRAW OR RIPOSTE.
I DON'T KNOW WHAT RIPOSTE MEANS, BUT DON'T YOU DARE WITHDRAW YET!
AND OF COURSE, WHEN IT'S TIME TO FINALLY COMMIT ALL TO THE--DEEP--LUNGE.
YIPPEE!
MY HERO.

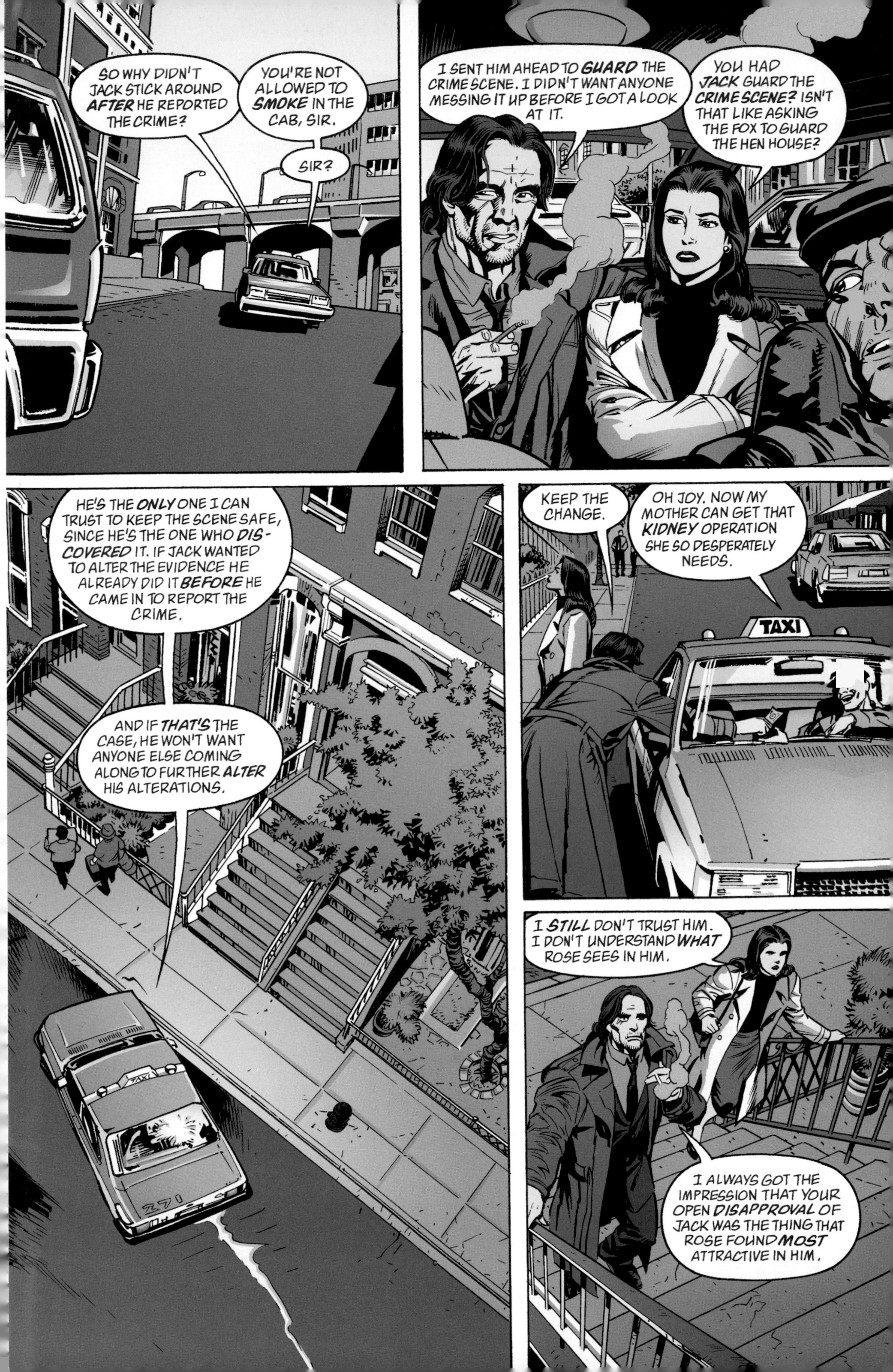
SO WHY DIDN'T JACK STICK AROUND AFTER HE REPORTED THE CRIME?
YOU'RE NOT ALLOWED TO SMOKE IN THE CAB, SIR.
SIR?
I SENT HIM AHEAD TO GUARD THE CRIME SCENE. I DIDN'T WANT ANYONE MESSING IT UP BEFORE I GOT A LOOK AT IT.
YOU HAD JACK GUARD THE CRIME SCENE? ISN'T THAT LIKE ASKING THE FOX TO GUARD THE HEN HOUSE?
HE'S THE ONLY ONE I CAN TRUST TO KEEP THE SCENE SAFE, SINCE HE'S THE ONE WHO DIS-COVERED IT. IF JACK WANTED TO ALTER THE EVIDENCE HE ALREADY DID IT BEFORE HE CAME IN TO REPORT THE CRIME.
AND IF THAT'S THE CASE, HE WON'T WANT ANYONE ELSE COMING ALONG TO FURTHER ALTER HIS ALTERATIONS.
KEEP THE CHANGE.
OH JOY. NOW MY MOTHER CAN GET THAT KIDNEY OPERATION SHE SO DESPERATELY NEEDS.
TAXI
I STILL DON'T TRUST HIM. I DON'T UNDERSTAND WHAT ROSE SEES IN HIM.
I ALWAYS GOT THE IMPRESSION THAT YOUR OPEN DISAPPROVAL OF JACK WAS THE THING THAT ROSE FOUND MOST ATTRACTIVE IN HIM.

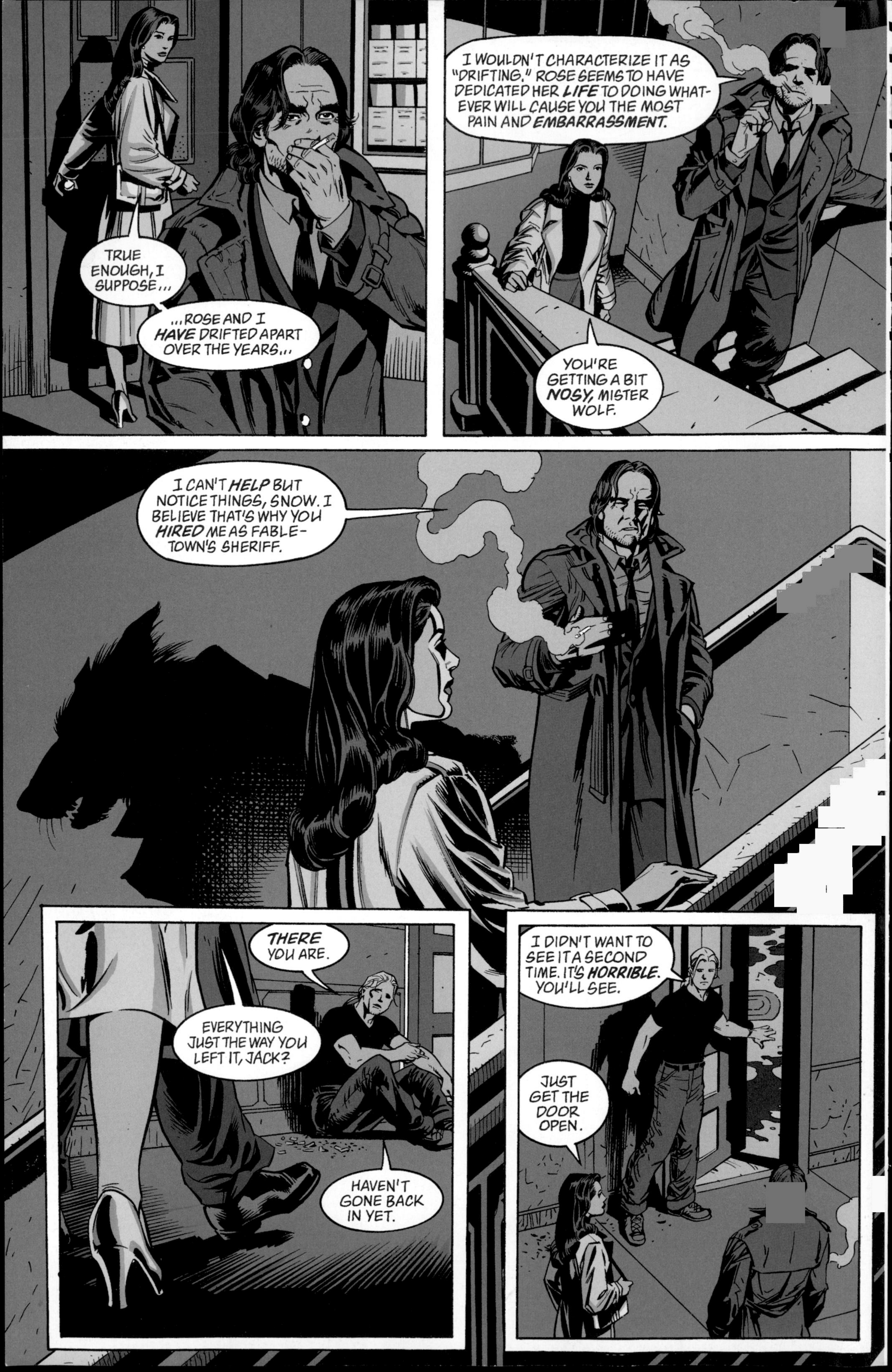
TRUE ENOUGH, I SUPPOSE...
...ROSE AND I HAVE DRIFTED APART OVER THE YEARS...
I WOULDN'T CHARACTERIZE IT AS "DRIFTING." ROSE SEEMS TO HAVE DEDICATED HER LIFE TO DOING WHATEVER WILL CAUSE YOU THE MOST PAIN AND EMBARRASSMENT.
YOU'RE GETTING A BIT NOSY, MISTER WOLF.
I CAN'T HELP BUT NOTICE THINGS, SNOW. I BELIEVE THAT'S WHY YOU HIRED ME AS FABLE-TOWN'S SHERIFF.
THERE YOU ARE.
EVERYTHING JUST THE WAY YOU LEFT IT, JACK?
HAVEN'T GONE BACK IN YET.
I DIDN'T WANT TO SEE IT A SECOND TIME. IT'S HORRIBLE. YOU'LL SEE.
JUST GET THE DOOR OPEN.

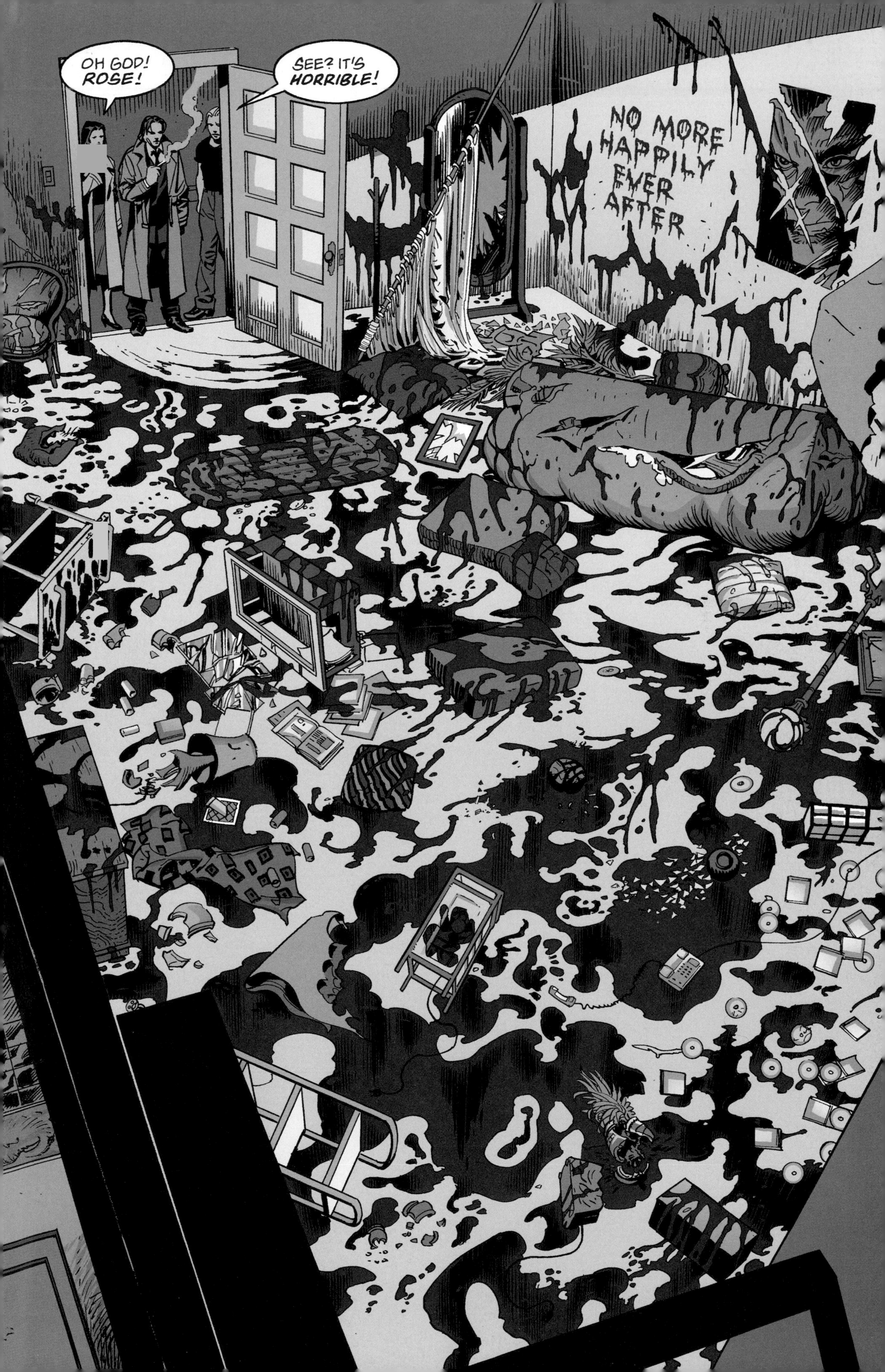
OH GOD! ROSE!
SEE? IT'S HORRIBLE!
NO MORE HAPPILY EVER AFTER

HOLD THIS. I'M GOING TO NEED MY SENSES *CLEAR*.

BOTH OF YOU STAY *HERE*.

DO NOT COME IN FOR ANY REASON.

IF SOMEONE COMES, CLOSE THE DOOR AND STAY OUT IN THE HALL.

THIS STAYS *STRICTLY* AMONG THE FABLE COMMUNITY. *NO ONE* LETS THE MUNDY COPS IN ON IT.

NO MORE HAPPILY EVER AFTER

WHAT ARE YOU *DOING?* WHY ARE YOU LOOKING AT THE *FLOOR?* YOU *SHOULD* BE LOOKING FOR *ROSE!* CHECK IN THE *BEDROOM* TO SEE IF SHE'S IN THERE!

I ALREADY CHECKED. SHE'S NOT HERE.

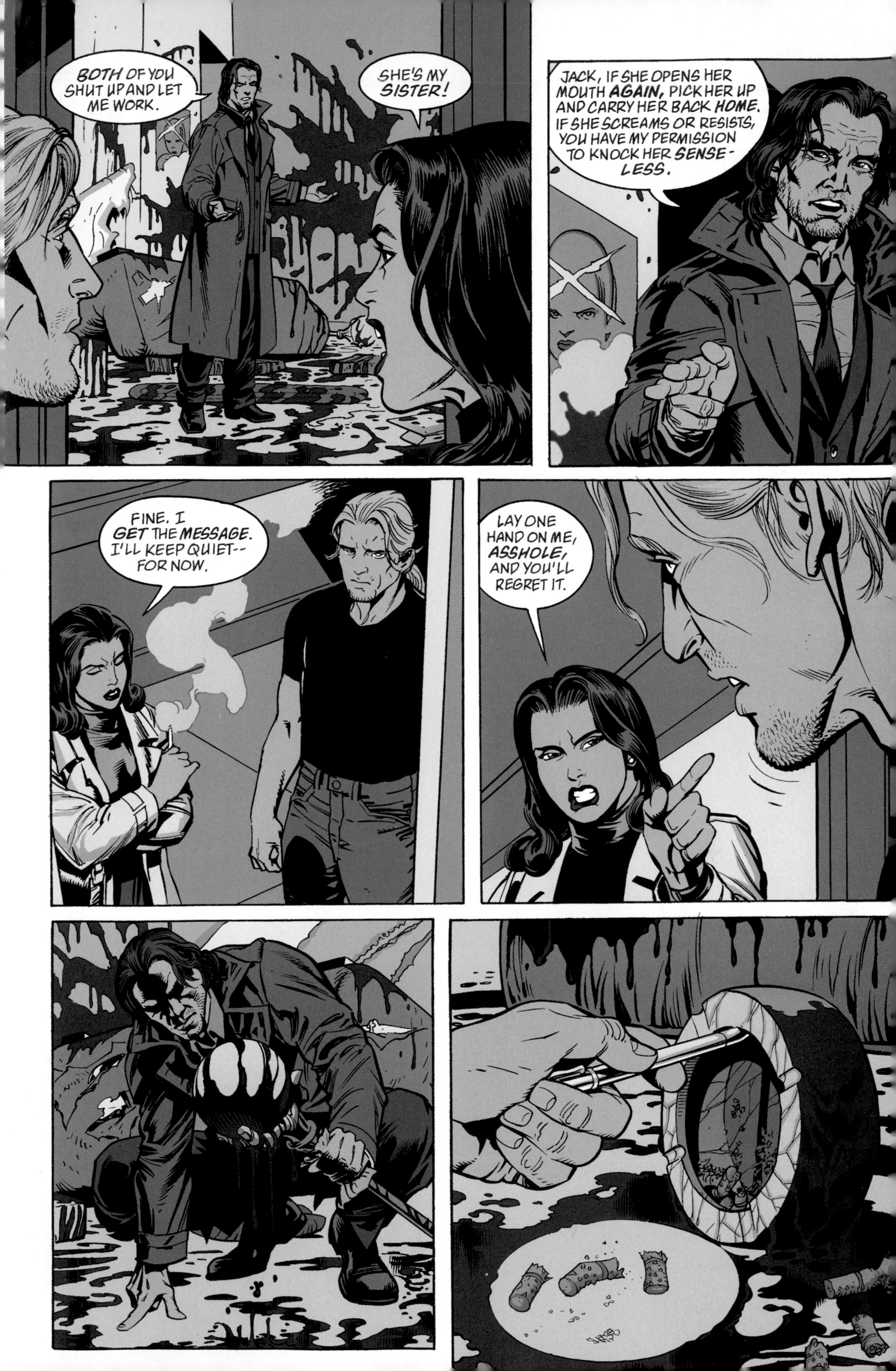
BOTH OF YOU SHUT UP AND LET ME WORK.
SHE'S MY SISTER!
JACK, IF SHE OPENS HER MOUTH AGAIN, PICK HER UP AND CARRY HER BACK HOME. IF SHE SCREAMS OR RESISTS, YOU HAVE MY PERMISSION TO KNOCK HER SENSE-LESS.
FINE. I GET THE MESSAGE. I'LL KEEP QUIET-- FOR NOW.
LAY ONE HAND ON ME, ASSHOLE, AND YOU'LL REGRET IT.

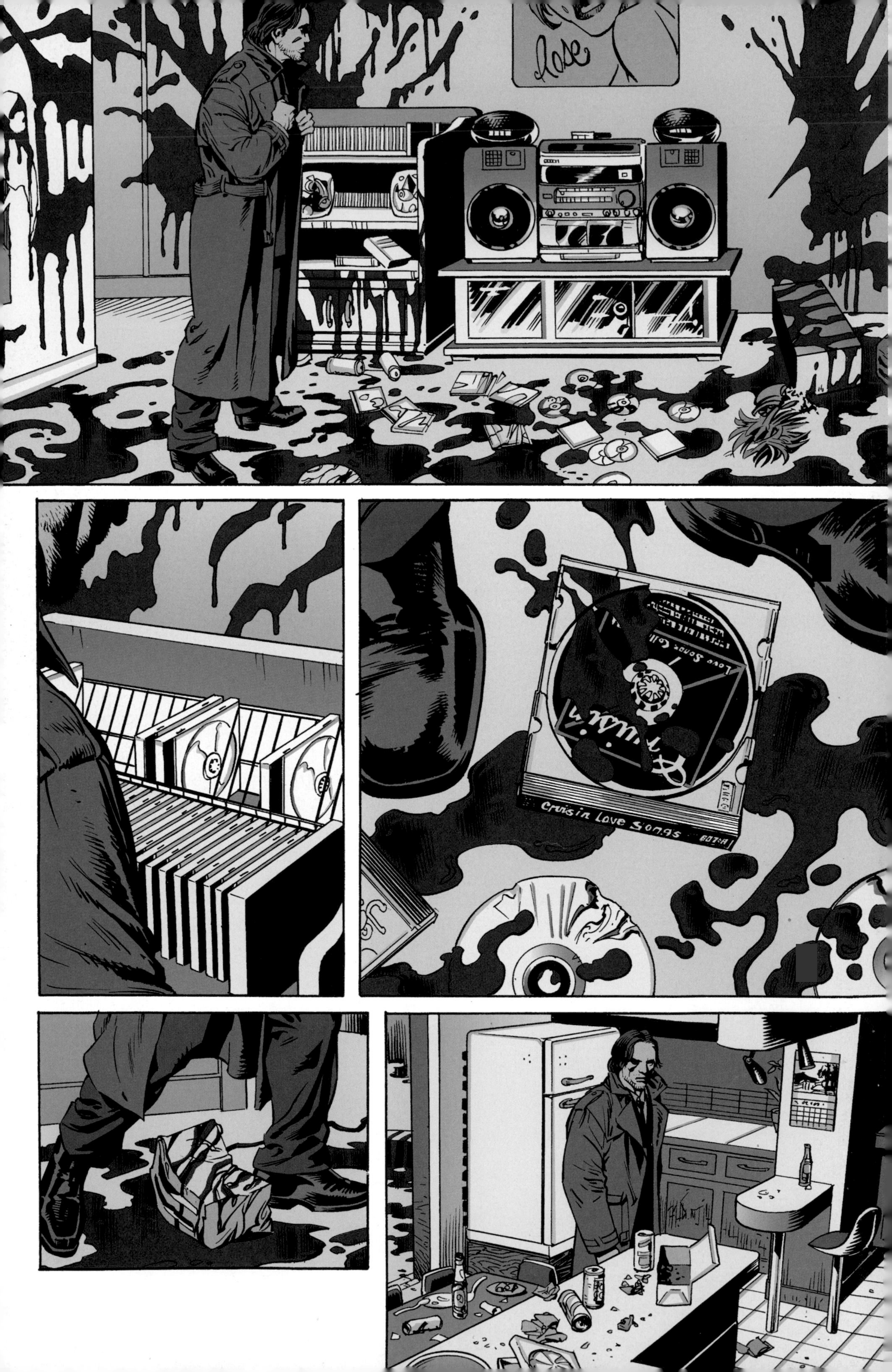
Rose
Cruisin Love Songs

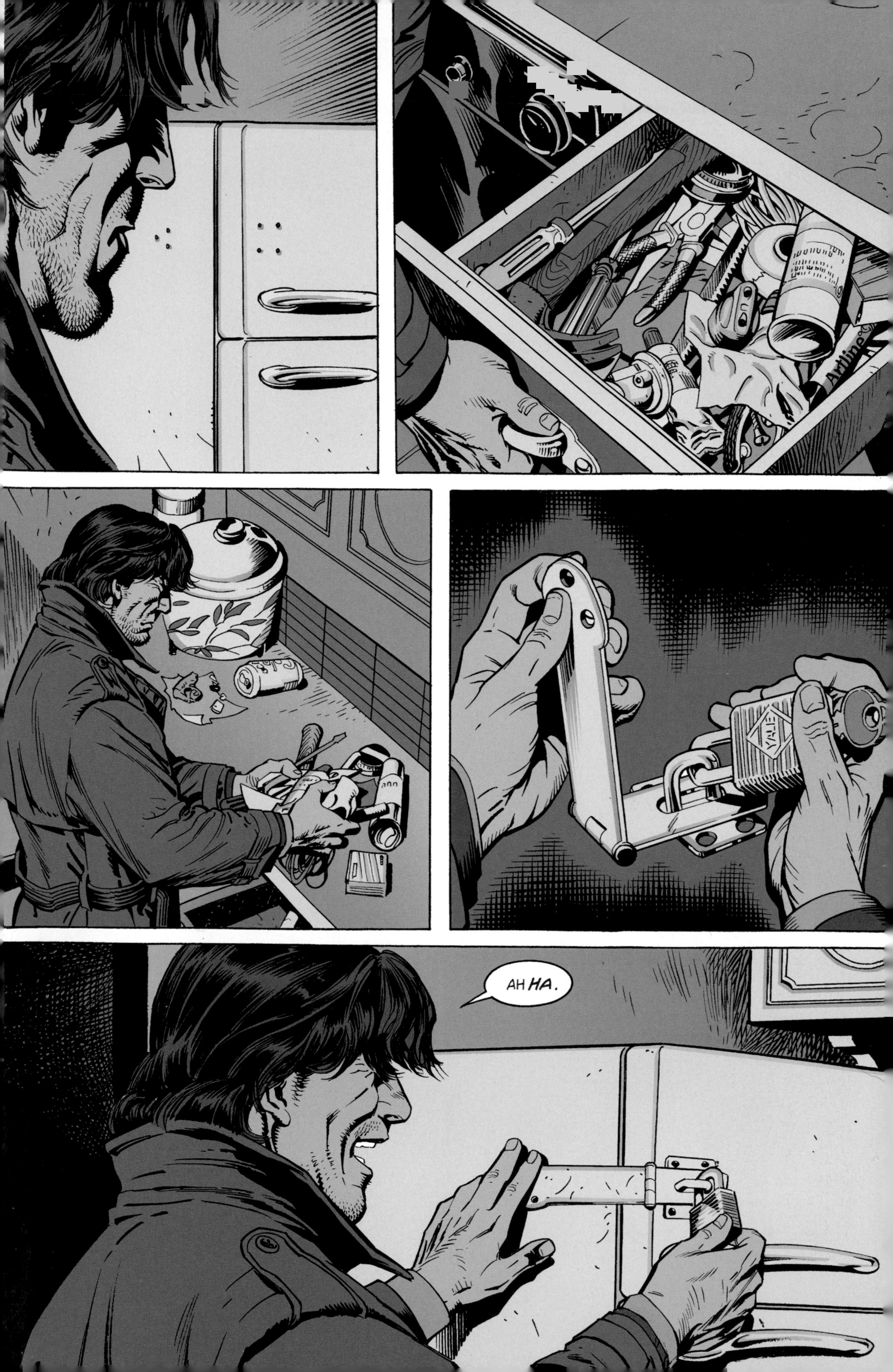
Artline
YALE
AH HA.

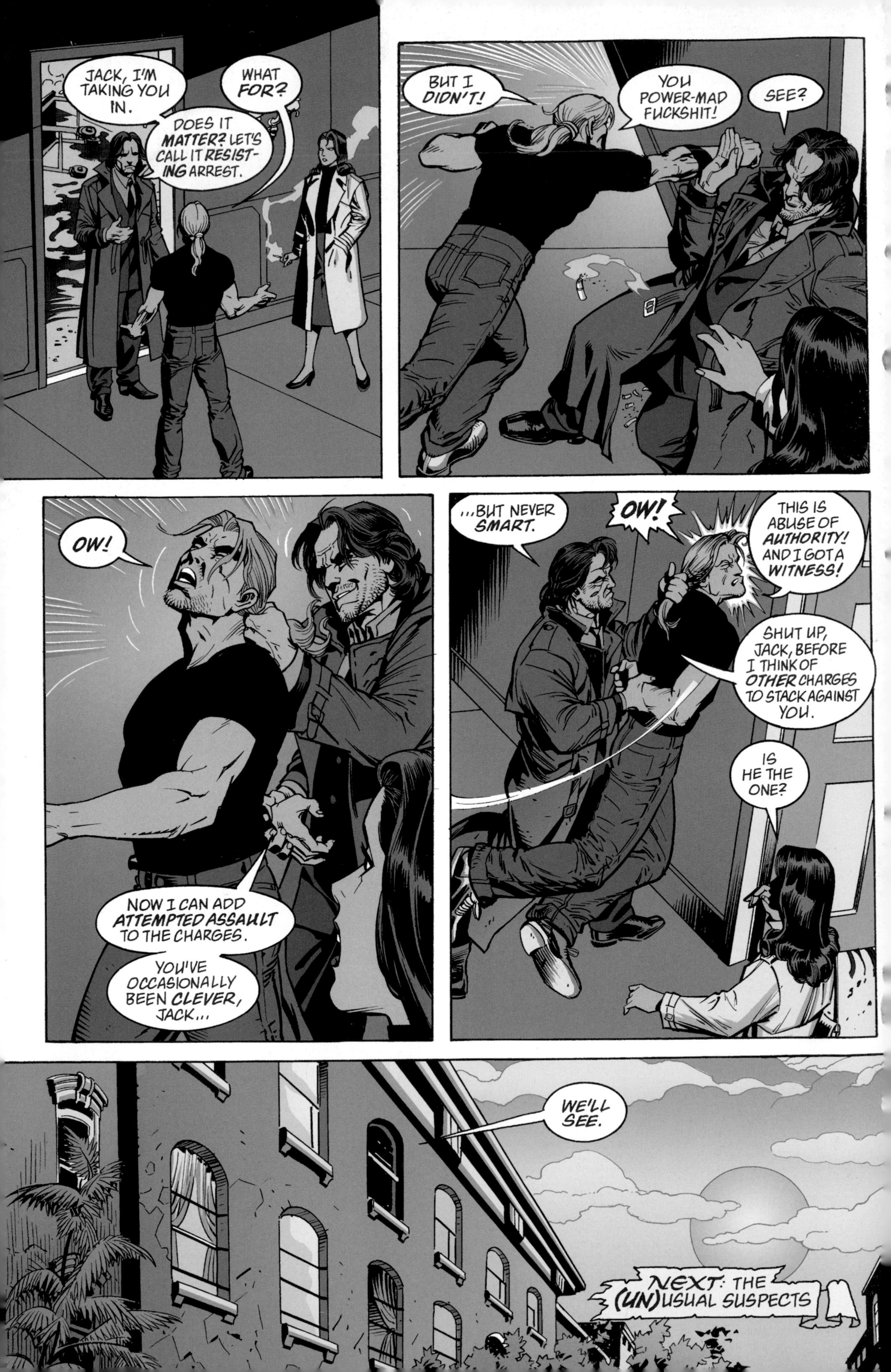

JACK, I'M TAKING YOU IN.
WHAT FOR?
DOES IT MATTER? LET'S CALL IT RESISTING ARREST.
BUT I DIDN'T!
YOU POWER-MAD FUCKSHIT!
SEE?
OW!
NOW I CAN ADD ATTEMPTED ASSAULT TO THE CHARGES.
YOU'VE OCCASIONALLY BEEN CLEVER, JACK...
...BUT NEVER SMART.
OW!
THIS IS ABUSE OF AUTHORITY! AND I GOT A WITNESS!
SHUT UP, JACK, BEFORE I THINK OF OTHER CHARGES TO STACK AGAINST YOU.
IS HE THE ONE?
WE'LL SEE.
NEXT: THE (UN)USUAL SUSPECTS

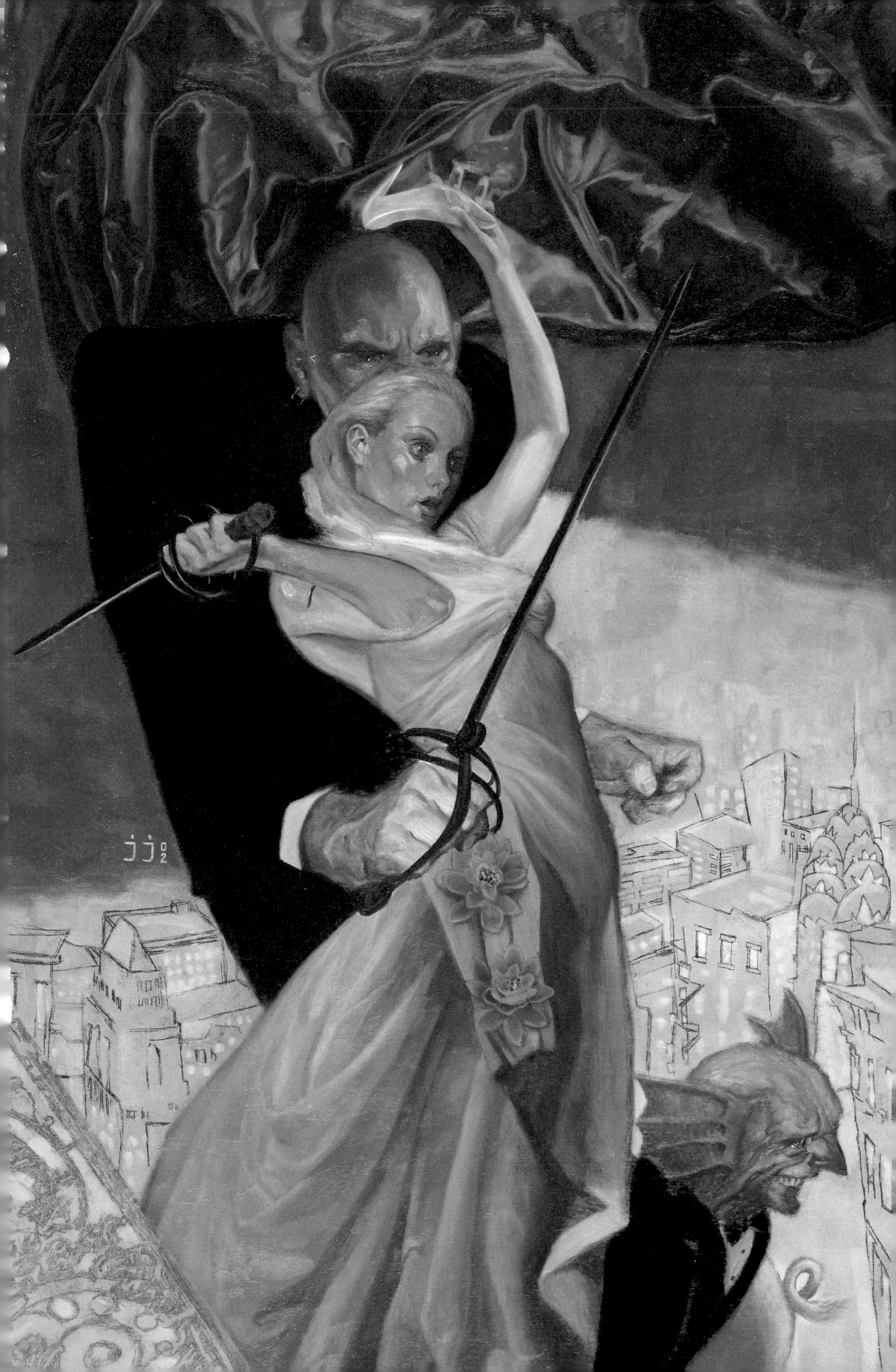

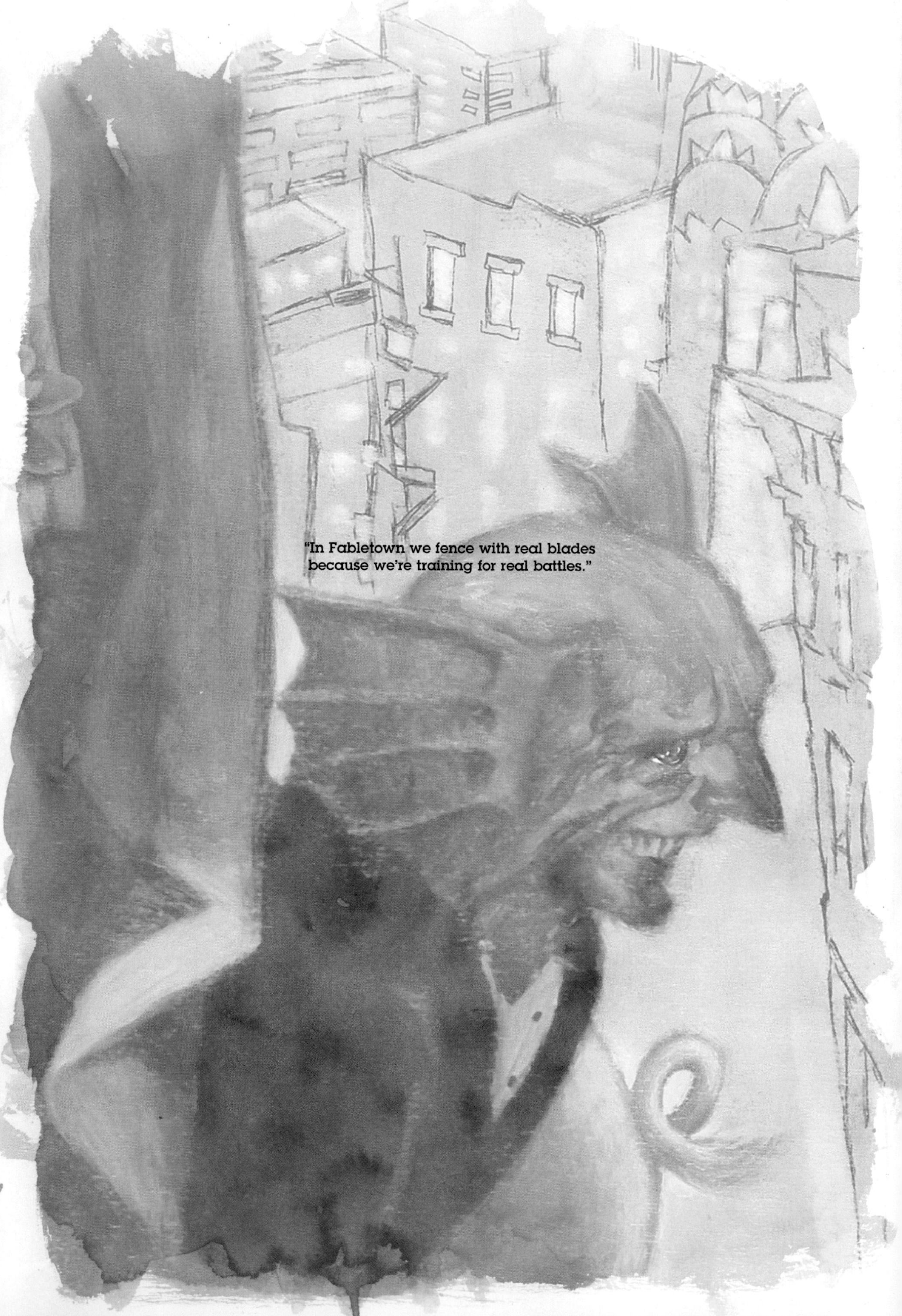
"In Fabletown we fence with real blades
because we're training for real battles."

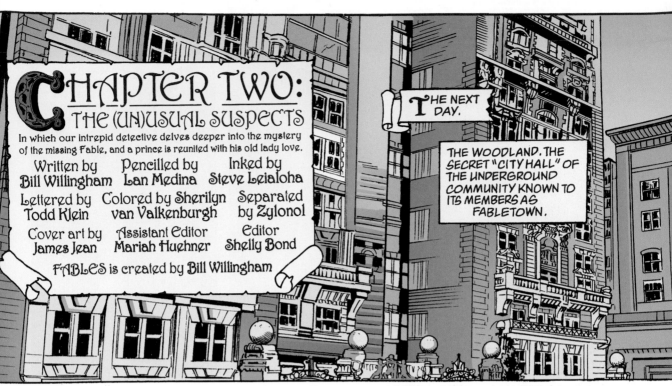

CHAPTER TWO: THE (UN)USUAL SUSPECTS

In which our intrepid detective delves deeper into the mystery of the missing Fable, and a prince is reunited with his old lady love.

Written by
Bill Willingham

Pencilled by
Lan Medina

Inked by
Steve Leialoha

Lettered by
Todd Klein

Colored by Sherilyn
van Valkenburgh

Separated
by Zylonol

Cover art by
James Jean

Assistant Editor
Mariah Huehner

Editor
Shelly Bond

FABLES is created by Bill Willingham

THE NEXT DAY.

THE WOODLAND. THE SECRET "CITY HALL" OF THE UNDERGROUND COMMUNITY KNOWN TO ITS MEMBERS AS FABLETOWN.

FROG WENT A-COURTIN'--

--HE DID RIGHT--

--UH-HUH.

GOOD MORNING, MISS WHITE.

GRAND DAY, ISN'T IT?

LOVELY.

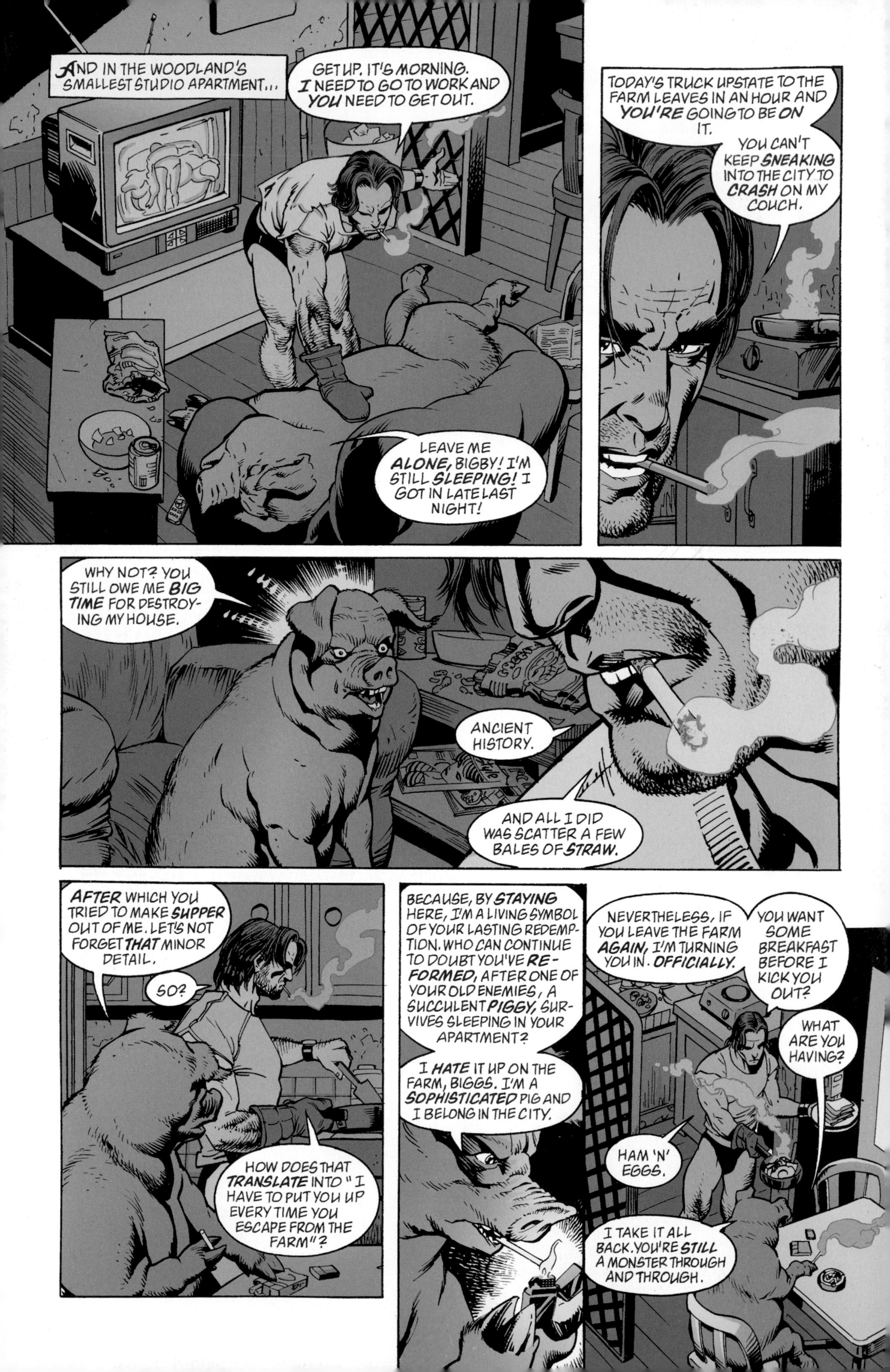
AND IN THE WOODLAND'S SMALLEST STUDIO APARTMENT...
GET UP. IT'S MORNING. I NEED TO GO TO WORK AND YOU NEED TO GET OUT.
LEAVE ME ALONE, BIGBY! I'M STILL SLEEPING! I GOT IN LATE LAST NIGHT!
TODAY'S TRUCK UPSTATE TO THE FARM LEAVES IN AN HOUR AND YOU'RE GOING TO BE ON IT.
YOU CAN'T KEEP SNEAKING INTO THE CITY TO CRASH ON MY COUCH.
WHY NOT? YOU STILL OWE ME BIG TIME FOR DESTROYING MY HOUSE.
ANCIENT HISTORY.
AND ALL I DID WAS SCATTER A FEW BALES OF STRAW.
AFTER WHICH YOU TRIED TO MAKE SUPPER OUT OF ME. LET'S NOT FORGET THAT MINOR DETAIL.
SO?
HOW DOES THAT TRANSLATE INTO "I HAVE TO PUT YOU UP EVERY TIME YOU ESCAPE FROM THE FARM"?
BECAUSE, BY STAYING HERE, I'M A LIVING SYMBOL OF YOUR LASTING REDEMPTION. WHO CAN CONTINUE TO DOUBT YOU'VE REFORMED, AFTER ONE OF YOUR OLD ENEMIES, A SUCCULENT PIGGY, SURVIVES SLEEPING IN YOUR APARTMENT?
I HATE IT UP ON THE FARM, BIGGS. I'M A SOPHISTICATED PIG AND I BELONG IN THE CITY.
NEVERTHELESS, IF YOU LEAVE THE FARM AGAIN, I'M TURNING YOU IN. OFFICIALLY.
YOU WANT SOME BREAKFAST BEFORE I KICK YOU OUT?
WHAT ARE YOU HAVING?
HAM 'N' EGGS.
I TAKE IT ALL BACK. YOU'RE STILL A MONSTER THROUGH AND THROUGH.

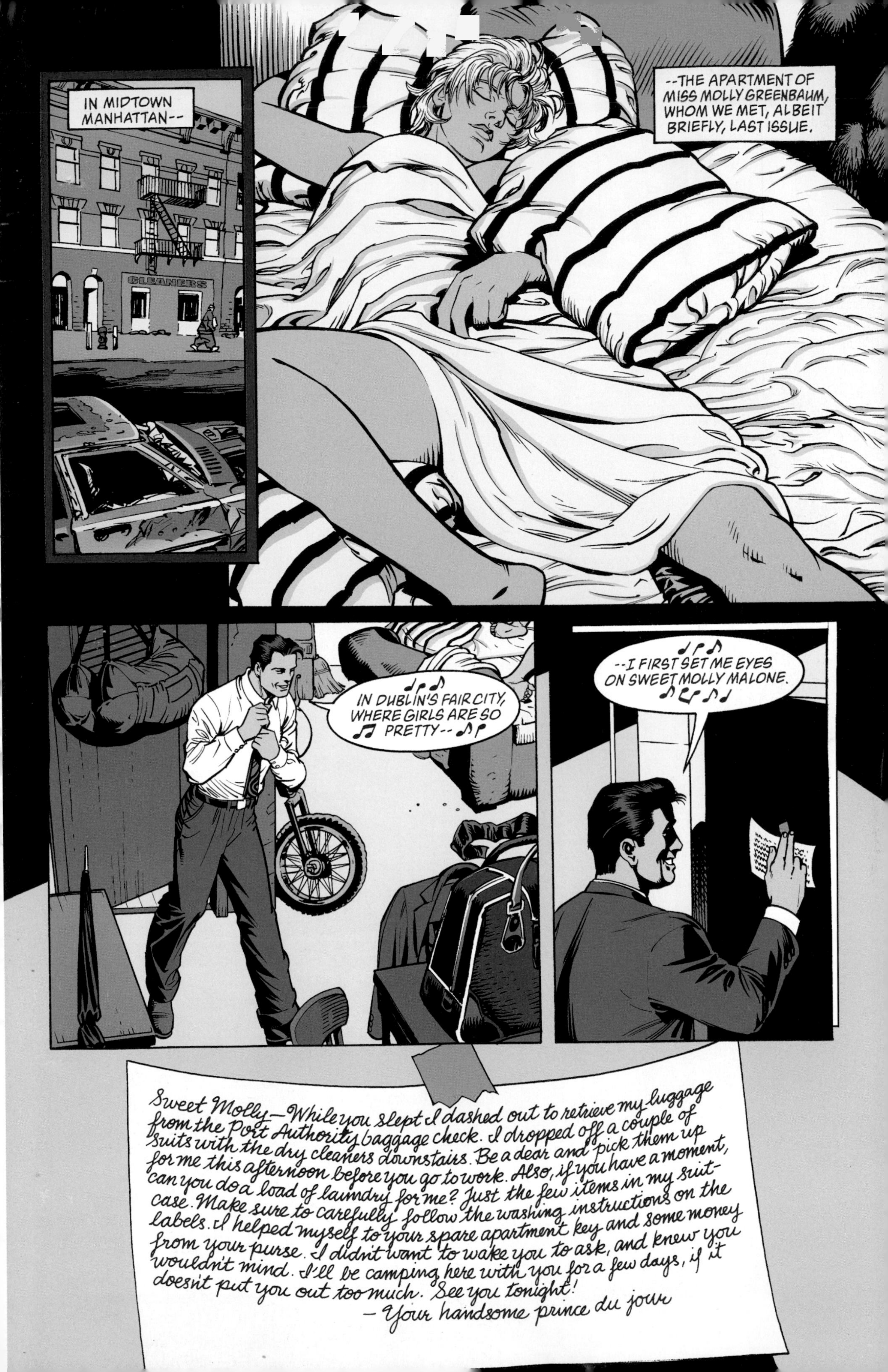
IN MIDTOWN MANHATTAN--
CLEANERS
--THE APARTMENT OF MISS MOLLY GREENBAUM, WHOM WE MET, ALBEIT BRIEFLY, LAST ISSUE.
IN DUBLIN'S FAIR CITY, WHERE GIRLS ARE SO PRETTY--
--I FIRST SET ME EYES ON SWEET MOLLY MALONE.
Sweet Molly— While you slept I dashed out to retrieve my luggage
from the Port Authority baggage check. I dropped off a couple of
suits with the dry cleaners downstairs. Be a dear and pick them up
for me this afternoon before you go to work. Also, if you have a moment,
can you do a load of laundry for me? Just the few items in my suit-
case. Make sure to carefully follow the washing instructions on the
labels. I helped myself to your spare apartment key and some money
from your purse. I didnt want to wake you to ask, and knew you
wouldn't mind. I'll be camping here with you for a few days, if it
doesn't put you out too much. See you tonight!
— Your handsome prince du jour

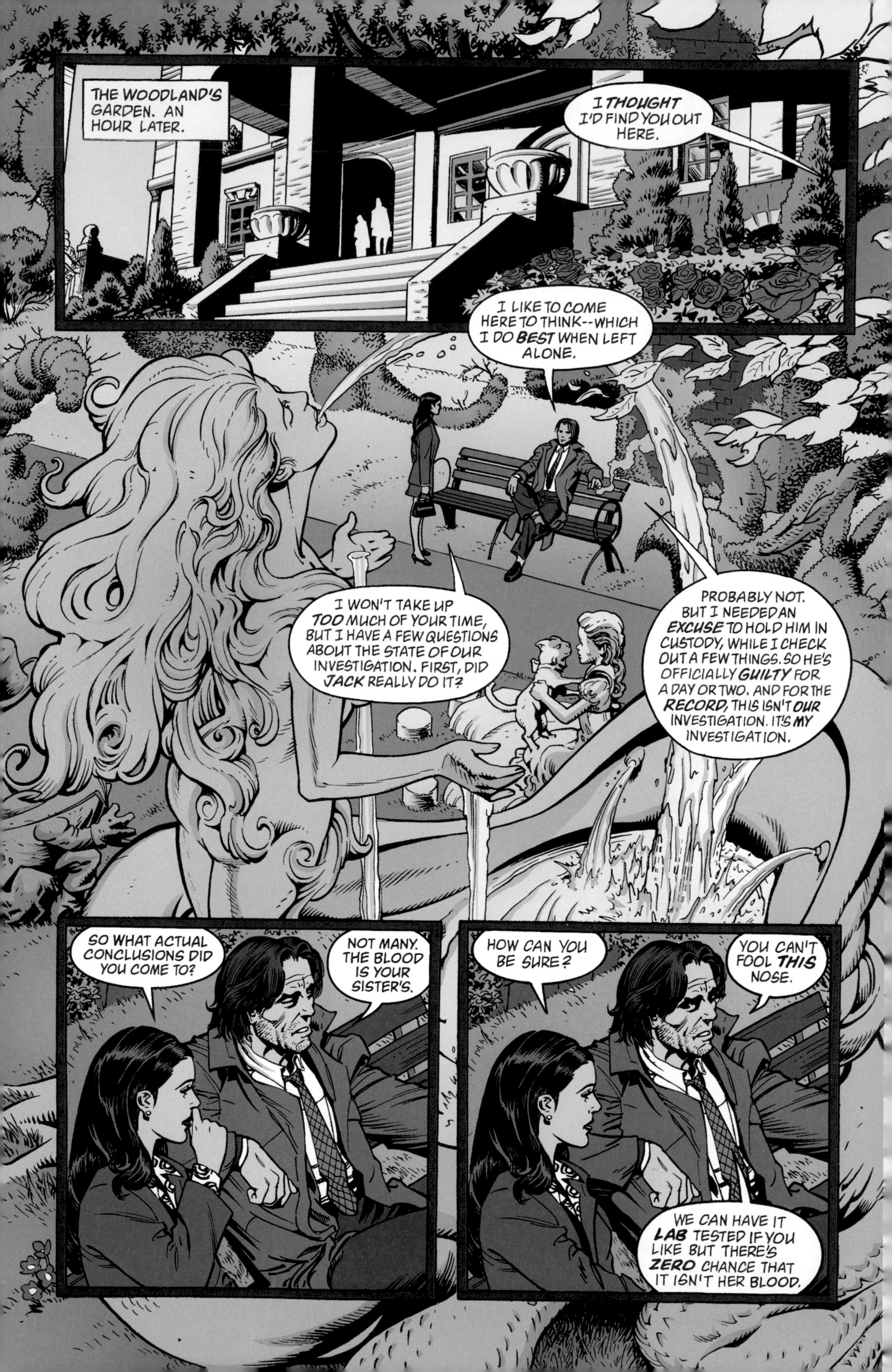
THE WOODLAND'S GARDEN. AN HOUR LATER.
I THOUGHT I'D FIND YOU OUT HERE.
I LIKE TO COME HERE TO THINK--WHICH I DO BEST WHEN LEFT ALONE.
I WON'T TAKE UP TOO MUCH OF YOUR TIME, BUT I HAVE A FEW QUESTIONS ABOUT THE STATE OF OUR INVESTIGATION. FIRST, DID JACK REALLY DO IT?
PROBABLY NOT. BUT I NEEDED AN EXCUSE TO HOLD HIM IN CUSTODY, WHILE I CHECK OUT A FEW THINGS. SO HE'S OFFICIALLY GUILTY FOR A DAY OR TWO. AND FOR THE RECORD, THIS ISN'T OUR INVESTIGATION. IT'S MY INVESTIGATION.
SO WHAT ACTUAL CONCLUSIONS DID YOU COME TO?
NOT MANY. THE BLOOD IS YOUR SISTER'S.
HOW CAN YOU BE SURE?
YOU CAN'T FOOL THIS NOSE.
WE CAN HAVE IT LAB TESTED IF YOU LIKE BUT THERE'S ZERO CHANCE THAT IT ISN'T HER BLOOD.

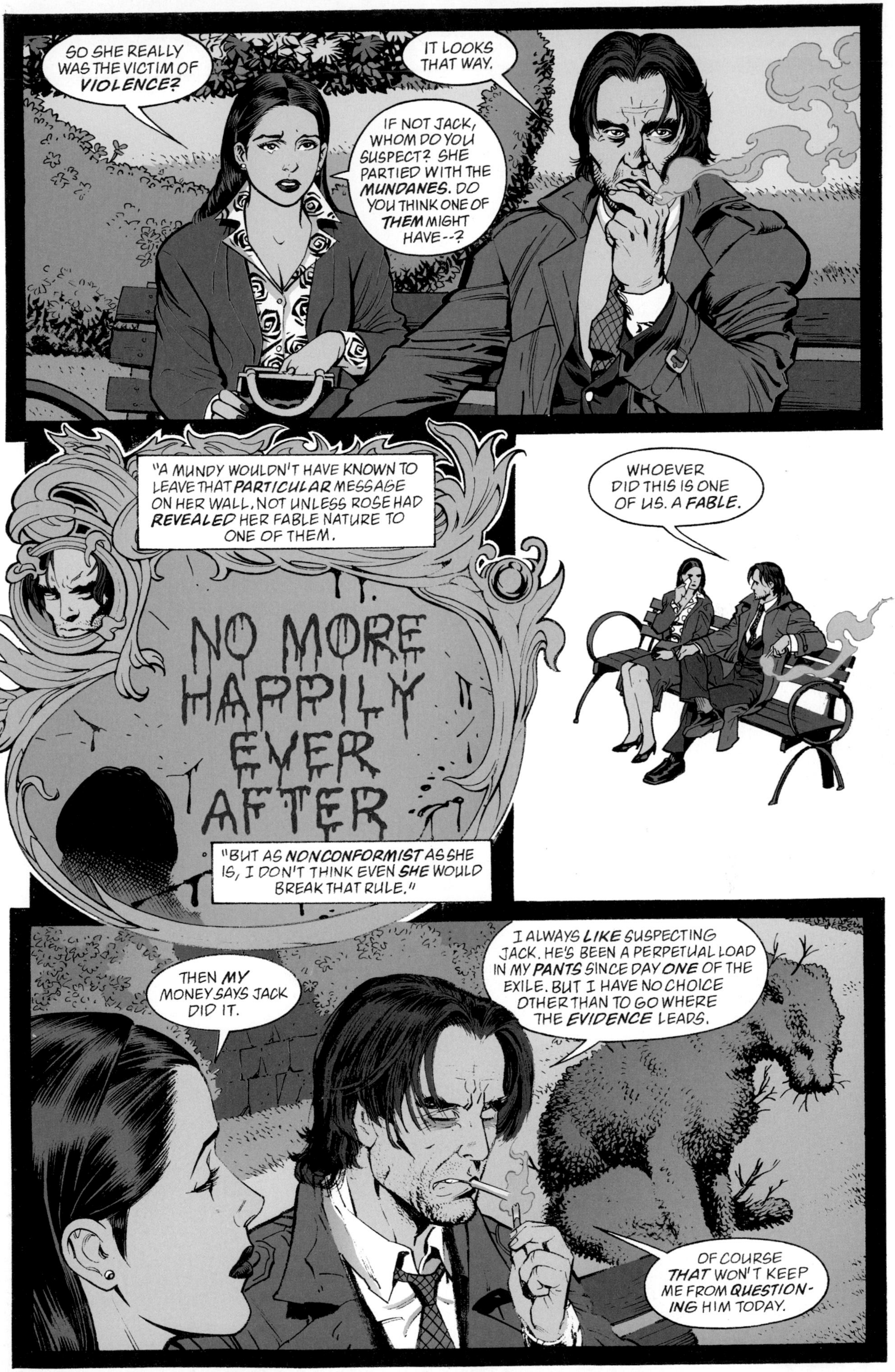

SO SHE REALLY WAS THE VICTIM OF VIOLENCE?
IT LOOKS THAT WAY.
IF NOT JACK, WHOM DO YOU SUSPECT? SHE PARTIED WITH THE MUNDANES. DO YOU THINK ONE OF THEM MIGHT HAVE--?
"A MUNDY WOULDN'T HAVE KNOWN TO LEAVE THAT PARTICULAR MESSAGE ON HER WALL. NOT UNLESS ROSE HAD REVEALED HER FABLE NATURE TO ONE OF THEM.
NO MORE HAPPILY EVER AFTER
"BUT AS NONCONFORMIST AS SHE IS, I DON'T THINK EVEN SHE WOULD BREAK THAT RULE."
WHOEVER DID THIS IS ONE OF US. A FABLE.
THEN MY MONEY SAYS JACK DID IT.
I ALWAYS LIKE SUSPECTING JACK. HE'S BEEN A PERPETUAL LOAD IN MY PANTS SINCE DAY ONE OF THE EXILE. BUT I HAVE NO CHOICE OTHER THAN TO GO WHERE THE EVIDENCE LEADS.
OF COURSE THAT WON'T KEEP ME FROM QUESTIONING HIM TODAY.

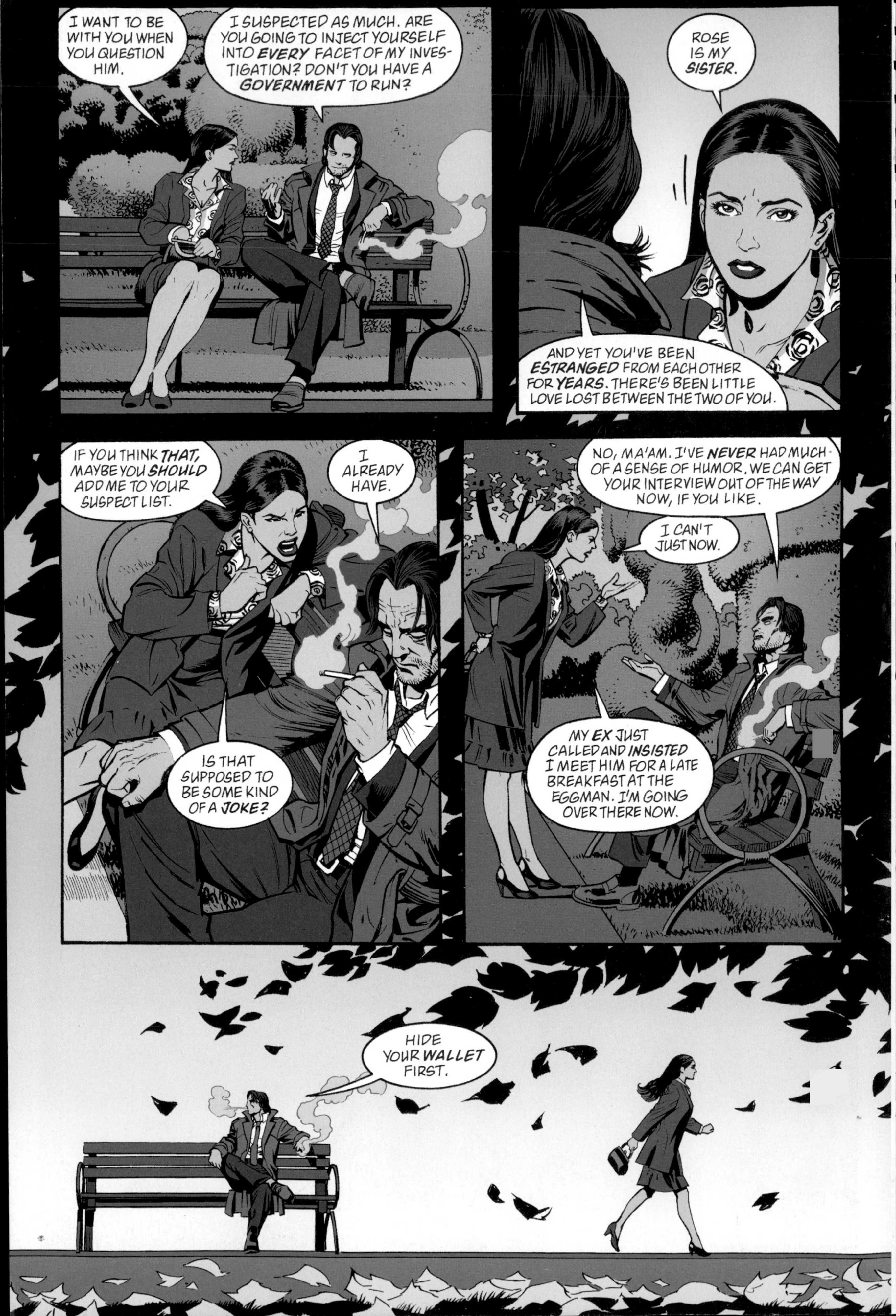
I WANT TO BE WITH YOU WHEN YOU QUESTION HIM.
I SUSPECTED AS MUCH. ARE YOU GOING TO INJECT YOURSELF INTO EVERY FACET OF MY INVESTIGATION? DON'T YOU HAVE A GOVERNMENT TO RUN?
ROSE IS MY SISTER.
AND YET YOU'VE BEEN ESTRANGED FROM EACH OTHER FOR YEARS. THERE'S BEEN LITTLE LOVE LOST BETWEEN THE TWO OF YOU.
IF YOU THINK THAT, MAYBE YOU SHOULD ADD ME TO YOUR SUSPECT LIST.
I ALREADY HAVE.
IS THAT SUPPOSED TO BE SOME KIND OF A JOKE?
NO, MA'AM. I'VE NEVER HAD MUCH OF A SENSE OF HUMOR. WE CAN GET YOUR INTERVIEW OUT OF THE WAY NOW, IF YOU LIKE.
I CAN'T JUST NOW.
MY EX JUST CALLED AND INSISTED I MEET HIM FOR A LATE BREAKFAST AT THE EGGMAN. I'M GOING OVER THERE NOW.
HIDE YOUR WALLET FIRST.

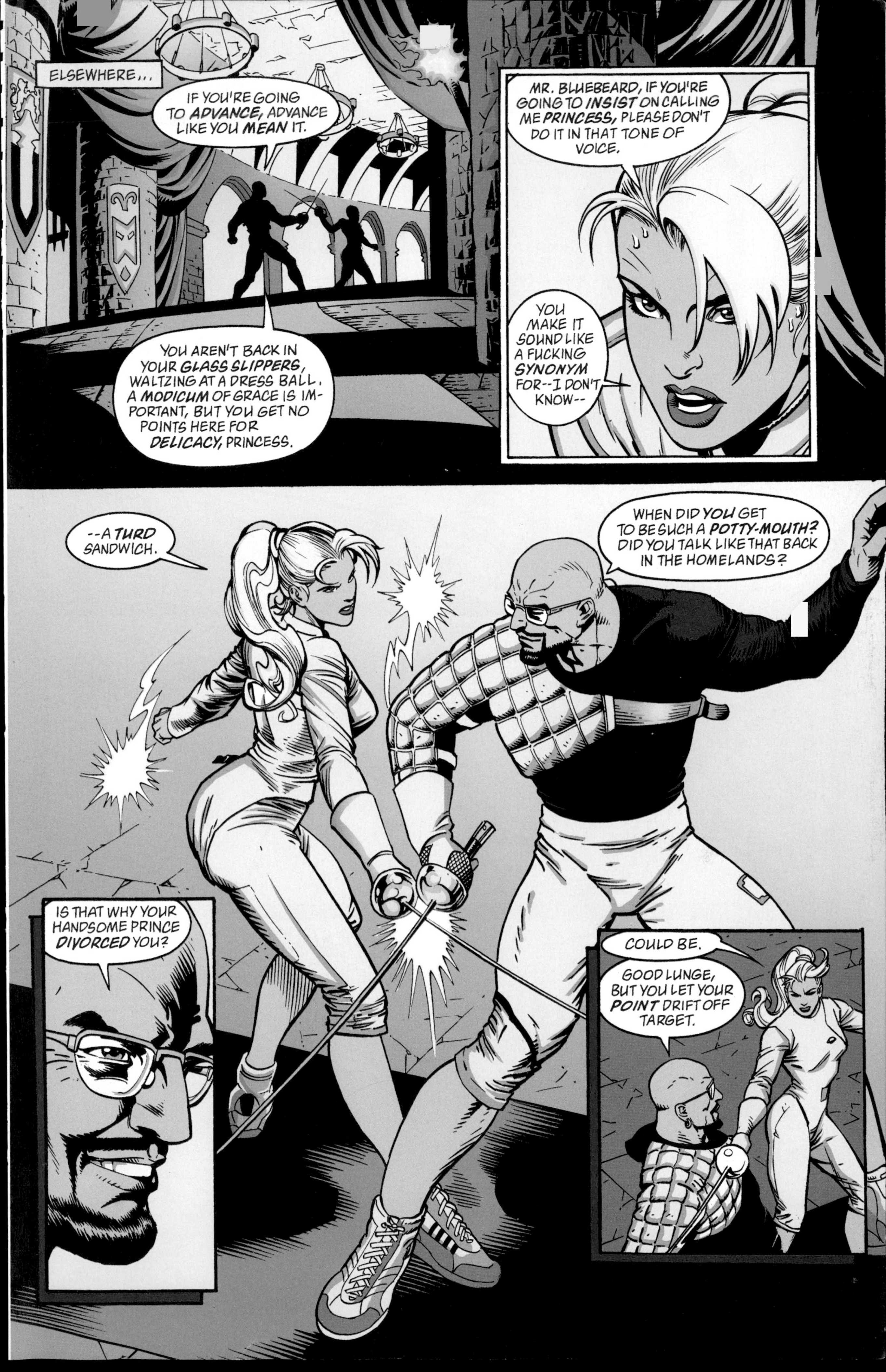
ELSEWHERE...
IF YOU'RE GOING TO ADVANCE, ADVANCE LIKE YOU MEAN IT.
YOU AREN'T BACK IN YOUR GLASS SLIPPERS, WALTZING AT A DRESS BALL. A MODICUM OF GRACE IS IMPORTANT, BUT YOU GET NO POINTS HERE FOR DELICACY, PRINCESS.
MR. BLUEBEARD, IF YOU'RE GOING TO INSIST ON CALLING ME PRINCESS, PLEASE DON'T DO IT IN THAT TONE OF VOICE.
YOU MAKE IT SOUND LIKE A FUCKING SYNONYM FOR--I DON'T KNOW--
--A TURD SANDWICH.
WHEN DID YOU GET TO BE SUCH A POTTY-MOUTH? DID YOU TALK LIKE THAT BACK IN THE HOMELANDS?
IS THAT WHY YOUR HANDSOME PRINCE DIVORCED YOU?
COULD BE.
GOOD LUNGE, BUT YOU LET YOUR POINT DRIFT OFF TARGET.

Panel 1:

I DIDN'T WANT TO RISK *SKEWERING* YOU.

THEN YOU'RE WASTING *MY* TIME AND *YOURS.* IN FABLETOWN, WE FENCE WITH REAL *BLADES* BECAUSE WE'RE TRAINING FOR REAL *BATTLES.*

YOUR *HUSBAND* FANCIED HIMSELF A DEFT HAND WITH A BLADE. IT'S A WONDER HE DIDN'T PASS ALONG ANY *USEFUL* SKILLS BEFORE HE SET YOU ASIDE. ON-GUARD POSITION, PRINCESS. *MY* TURN TO ATTACK NOW.

Panel 2:

ARE YOU PURPOSELY TRYING TO BE SO *BOOR-ISH?* IS THIS SOME CRYPTIC ASPECT OF YOUR *TEACHING* STYLE?

Panel 3:

COULD BE. DID YOU KNOW PRINCE CHARMING'S BACK IN TOWN?

OLD NEWS. *EVERYONE* KNOWS HE'S SCAMMING FREE EGGS OFF WIFE NUMBER ONE, EVEN AS WE SPEAK.

THE *REAL* NEWS IS WHAT HAPPENED TO ROSE RED. DID YOU *HEAR* ABOUT IT?

Panel 4:

NO. WHAT--?

SHE'S *DEAD*-- CARVED UP LIKE A CHRISTMAS TURKEY. AND *RUMOR* HAS IT THAT CREEPY *BOYFRIEND* OF HERS DID THE DIRTY DEED.

Panel 5:

JACK?

YEAH, I *THINK* THAT'S HIM. I HEARD HE WAS DANCING *NAKED* IN BITS OF HER SKIN WHEN THEY CAUGHT HIM--

OW! WHAT THE *FUCK*--!

Panel 6:

I'M *BLEEDING,* YOU SHIT! WHY'D YOU *DO* THAT?

BECAUSE THIS IS *SERIOUS* BUSI-NESS AND YOU WEREN'T PAYING ATTENTION. *THINK* ABOUT THAT BEFORE YOUR NEXT LESSON.

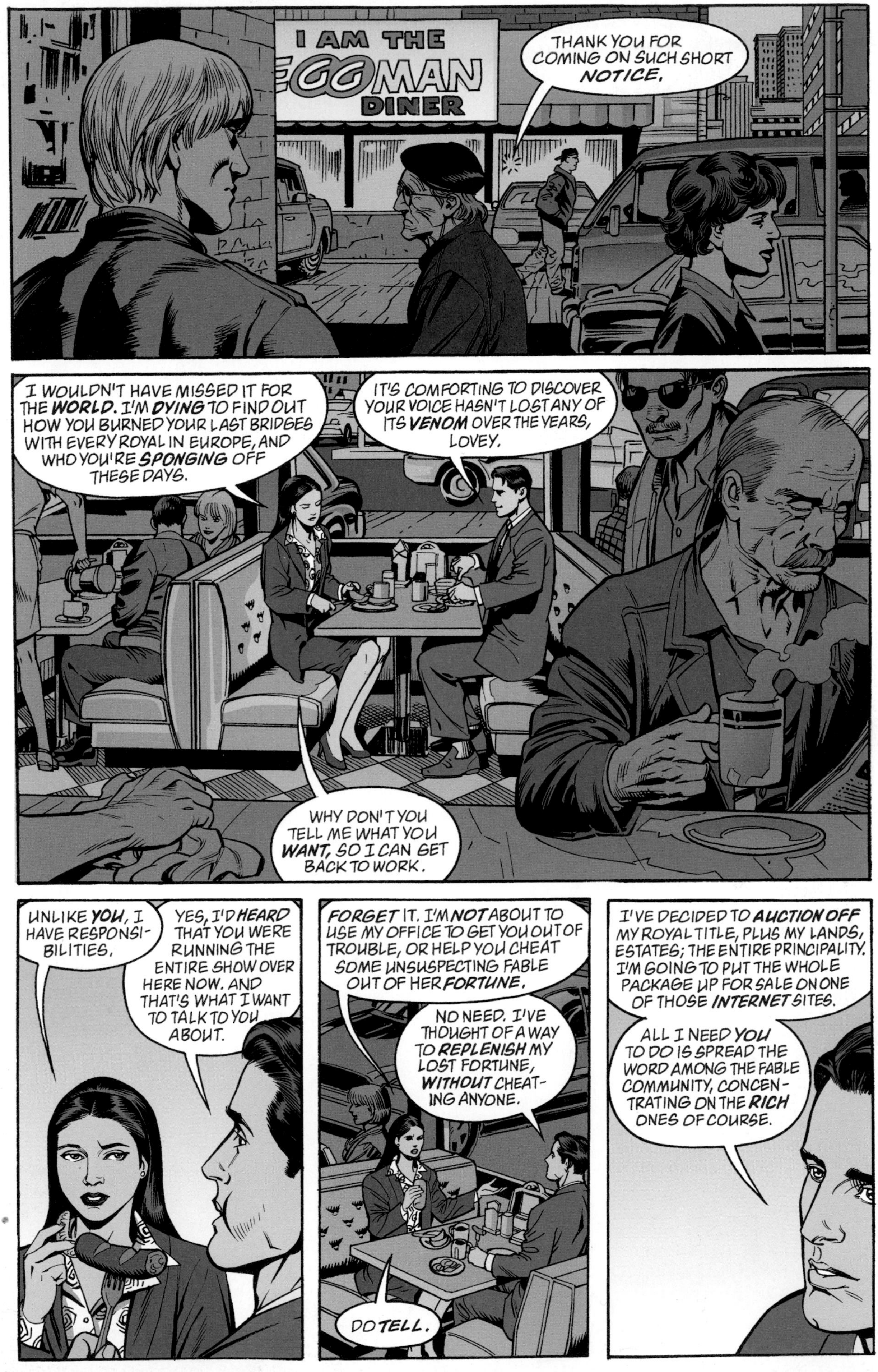
I AM THE EGGMAN DINER
THANK YOU FOR COMING ON SUCH SHORT NOTICE.
I WOULDN'T HAVE MISSED IT FOR THE WORLD. I'M DYING TO FIND OUT HOW YOU BURNED YOUR LAST BRIDGES WITH EVERY ROYAL IN EUROPE, AND WHO YOU'RE SPONGING OFF THESE DAYS.
IT'S COMFORTING TO DISCOVER YOUR VOICE HASN'T LOST ANY OF ITS VENOM OVER THE YEARS, LOVEY.
WHY DON'T YOU TELL ME WHAT YOU WANT, SO I CAN GET BACK TO WORK.
UNLIKE YOU, I HAVE RESPONSI-BILITIES.
YES, I'D HEARD THAT YOU WERE RUNNING THE ENTIRE SHOW OVER HERE NOW. AND THAT'S WHAT I WANT TO TALK TO YOU ABOUT.
FORGET IT. I'M NOT ABOUT TO USE MY OFFICE TO GET YOU OUT OF TROUBLE, OR HELP YOU CHEAT SOME UNSUSPECTING FABLE OUT OF HER FORTUNE.
NO NEED. I'VE THOUGHT OF A WAY TO REPLENISH MY LOST FORTUNE, WITHOUT CHEAT-ING ANYONE.
DO TELL.
I'VE DECIDED TO AUCTION OFF MY ROYAL TITLE, PLUS MY LANDS, ESTATES; THE ENTIRE PRINCIPALITY. I'M GOING TO PUT THE WHOLE PACKAGE UP FOR SALE ON ONE OF THOSE INTERNET SITES.
ALL I NEED YOU TO DO IS SPREAD THE WORD AMONG THE FABLE COMMUNITY, CONCEN-TRATING ON THE RICH ONES OF COURSE.

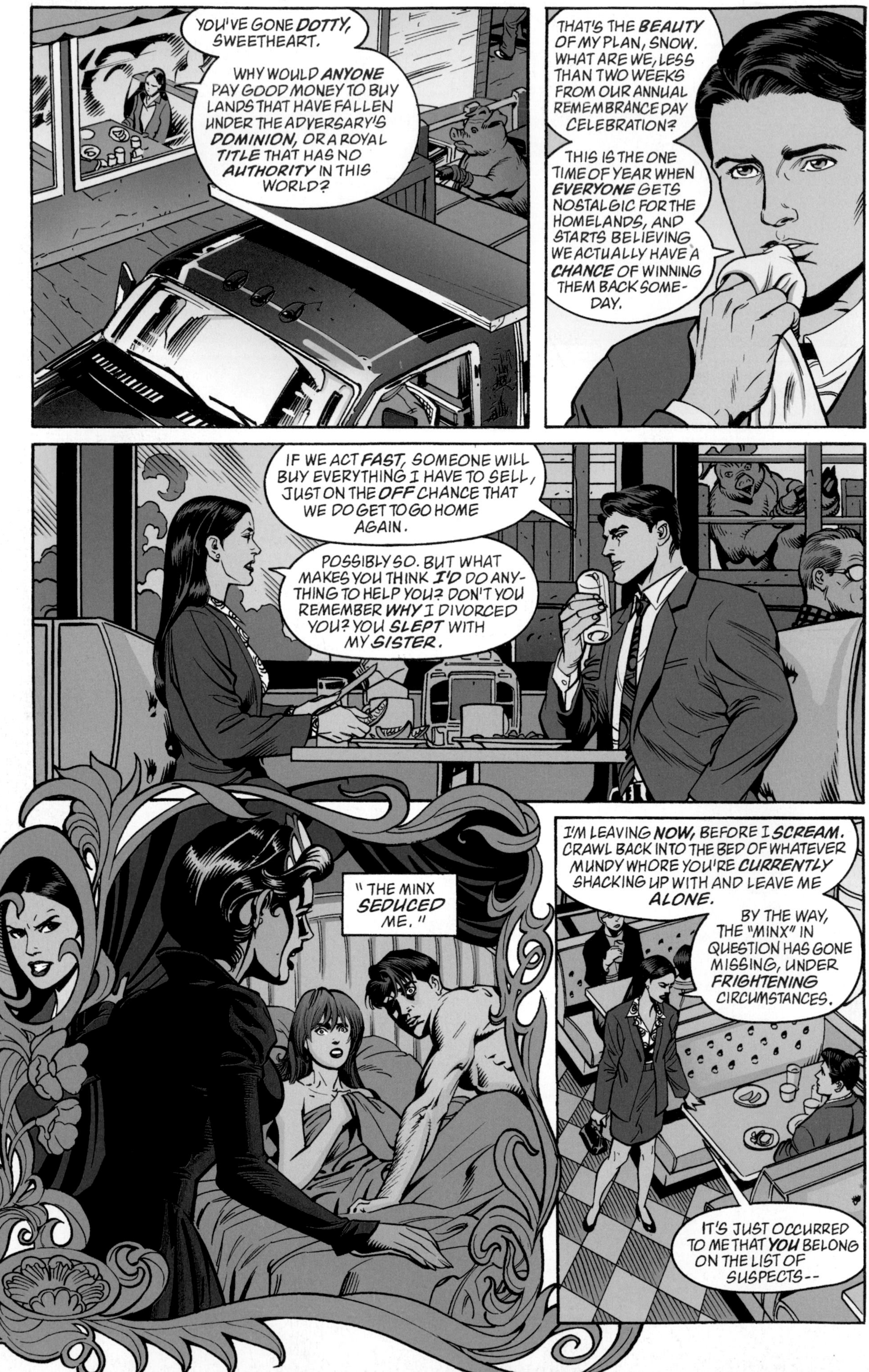

YOU'VE GONE DOTTY, SWEETHEART.
WHY WOULD ANYONE PAY GOOD MONEY TO BUY LANDS THAT HAVE FALLEN UNDER THE ADVERSARY'S DOMINION, OR A ROYAL TITLE THAT HAS NO AUTHORITY IN THIS WORLD?
THAT'S THE BEAUTY OF MY PLAN, SNOW. WHAT ARE WE, LESS THAN TWO WEEKS FROM OUR ANNUAL REMEMBRANCE DAY CELEBRATION?
THIS IS THE ONE TIME OF YEAR WHEN EVERYONE GETS NOSTALGIC FOR THE HOMELANDS, AND STARTS BELIEVING WE ACTUALLY HAVE A CHANCE OF WINNING THEM BACK SOME-DAY.
IF WE ACT FAST, SOMEONE WILL BUY EVERYTHING I HAVE TO SELL, JUST ON THE OFF CHANCE THAT WE DO GET TO GO HOME AGAIN.
POSSIBLY SO. BUT WHAT MAKES YOU THINK I'D DO ANY-THING TO HELP YOU? DON'T YOU REMEMBER WHY I DIVORCED YOU? YOU SLEPT WITH MY SISTER.
"THE MINX SEDUCED ME."
I'M LEAVING NOW, BEFORE I SCREAM. CRAWL BACK INTO THE BED OF WHATEVER MUNDY WHORE YOU'RE CURRENTLY SHACKING UP WITH AND LEAVE ME ALONE.
BY THE WAY, THE "MINX" IN QUESTION HAS GONE MISSING, UNDER FRIGHTENING CIRCUMSTANCES.
IT'S JUST OCCURRED TO ME THAT YOU BELONG ON THE LIST OF SUSPECTS--

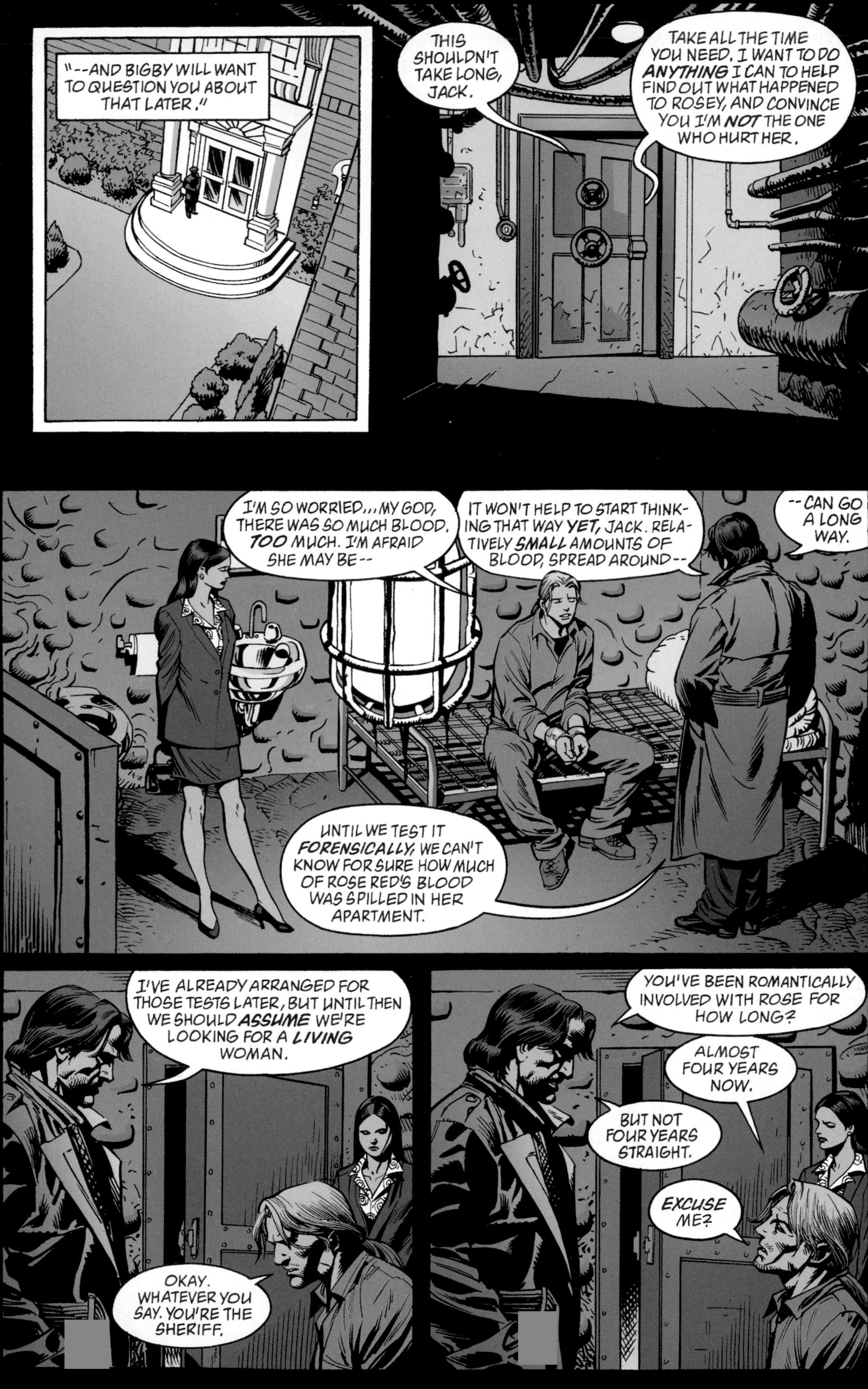
"--AND BIGBY WILL WANT TO QUESTION YOU ABOUT THAT LATER."
THIS SHOULDN'T TAKE LONG, JACK.
TAKE ALL THE TIME YOU NEED. I WANT TO DO ANYTHING I CAN TO HELP FIND OUT WHAT HAPPENED TO ROSEY, AND CONVINCE YOU I'M NOT THE ONE WHO HURT HER.
I'M SO WORRIED... MY GOD, THERE WAS SO MUCH BLOOD. TOO MUCH. I'M AFRAID SHE MAY BE--
IT WON'T HELP TO START THINKING THAT WAY YET, JACK. RELATIVELY SMALL AMOUNTS OF BLOOD, SPREAD AROUND--
--CAN GO A LONG WAY.
UNTIL WE TEST IT FORENSICALLY, WE CAN'T KNOW FOR SURE HOW MUCH OF ROSE RED'S BLOOD WAS SPILLED IN HER APARTMENT.
I'VE ALREADY ARRANGED FOR THOSE TESTS LATER, BUT UNTIL THEN WE SHOULD ASSUME WE'RE LOOKING FOR A LIVING WOMAN.
OKAY. WHATEVER YOU SAY. YOU'RE THE SHERIFF.
YOU'VE BEEN ROMANTICALLY INVOLVED WITH ROSE FOR HOW LONG?
ALMOST FOUR YEARS NOW.
BUT NOT FOUR YEARS STRAIGHT.
EXCUSE ME?

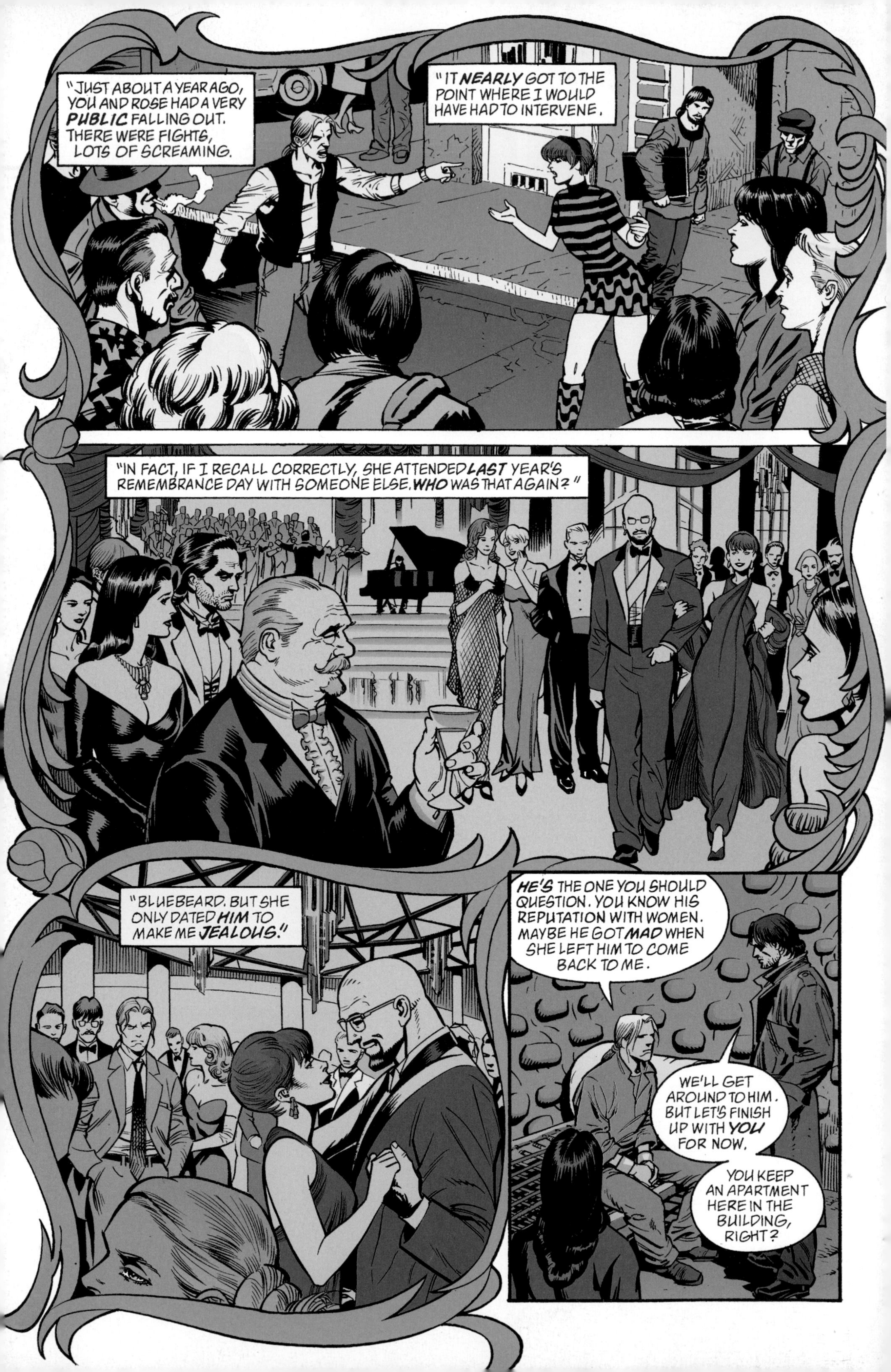
"JUST ABOUT A YEAR AGO, YOU AND ROSE HAD A VERY PUBLIC FALLING OUT. THERE WERE FIGHTS, LOTS OF SCREAMING.
"IT NEARLY GOT TO THE POINT WHERE I WOULD HAVE HAD TO INTERVENE.
"IN FACT, IF I RECALL CORRECTLY, SHE ATTENDED LAST YEAR'S REMEMBRANCE DAY WITH SOMEONE ELSE. WHO WAS THAT AGAIN?"
"BLUEBEARD. BUT SHE ONLY DATED HIM TO MAKE ME JEALOUS."
HE'S THE ONE YOU SHOULD QUESTION. YOU KNOW HIS REPUTATION WITH WOMEN. MAYBE HE GOT MAD WHEN SHE LEFT HIM TO COME BACK TO ME.
WE'LL GET AROUND TO HIM. BUT LET'S FINISH UP WITH YOU FOR NOW.
YOU KEEP AN APARTMENT HERE IN THE BUILDING, RIGHT?

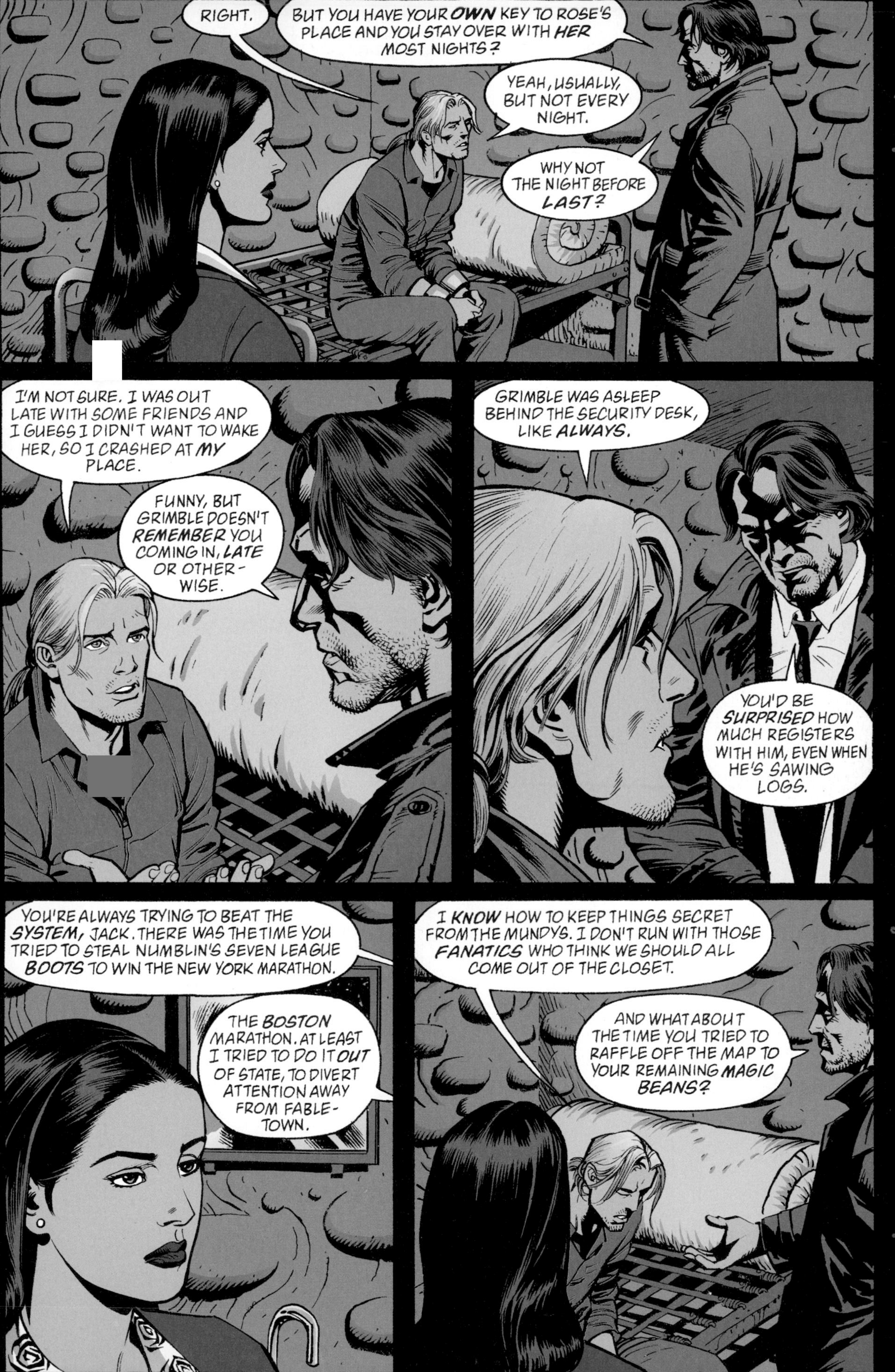
RIGHT.
BUT YOU HAVE YOUR OWN KEY TO ROSE'S PLACE AND YOU STAY OVER WITH HER MOST NIGHTS?
YEAH, USUALLY, BUT NOT EVERY NIGHT.
WHY NOT THE NIGHT BEFORE LAST?
I'M NOT SURE. I WAS OUT LATE WITH SOME FRIENDS AND I GUESS I DIDN'T WANT TO WAKE HER, SO I CRASHED AT MY PLACE.
FUNNY, BUT GRIMBLE DOESN'T REMEMBER YOU COMING IN, LATE OR OTHER-WISE.
GRIMBLE WAS ASLEEP BEHIND THE SECURITY DESK, LIKE ALWAYS.
YOU'D BE SURPRISED HOW MUCH REGISTERS WITH HIM, EVEN WHEN HE'S SAWING LOGS.
YOU'RE ALWAYS TRYING TO BEAT THE SYSTEM, JACK. THERE WAS THE TIME YOU TRIED TO STEAL NUMBLIN'S SEVEN LEAGUE BOOTS TO WIN THE NEW YORK MARATHON.
THE BOSTON MARATHON. AT LEAST I TRIED TO DO IT OUT OF STATE, TO DIVERT ATTENTION AWAY FROM FABLE-TOWN.
I KNOW HOW TO KEEP THINGS SECRET FROM THE MUNDYS. I DON'T RUN WITH THOSE FANATICS WHO THINK WE SHOULD ALL COME OUT OF THE CLOSET.
AND WHAT ABOUT THE TIME YOU TRIED TO RAFFLE OFF THE MAP TO YOUR REMAINING MAGIC BEANS?

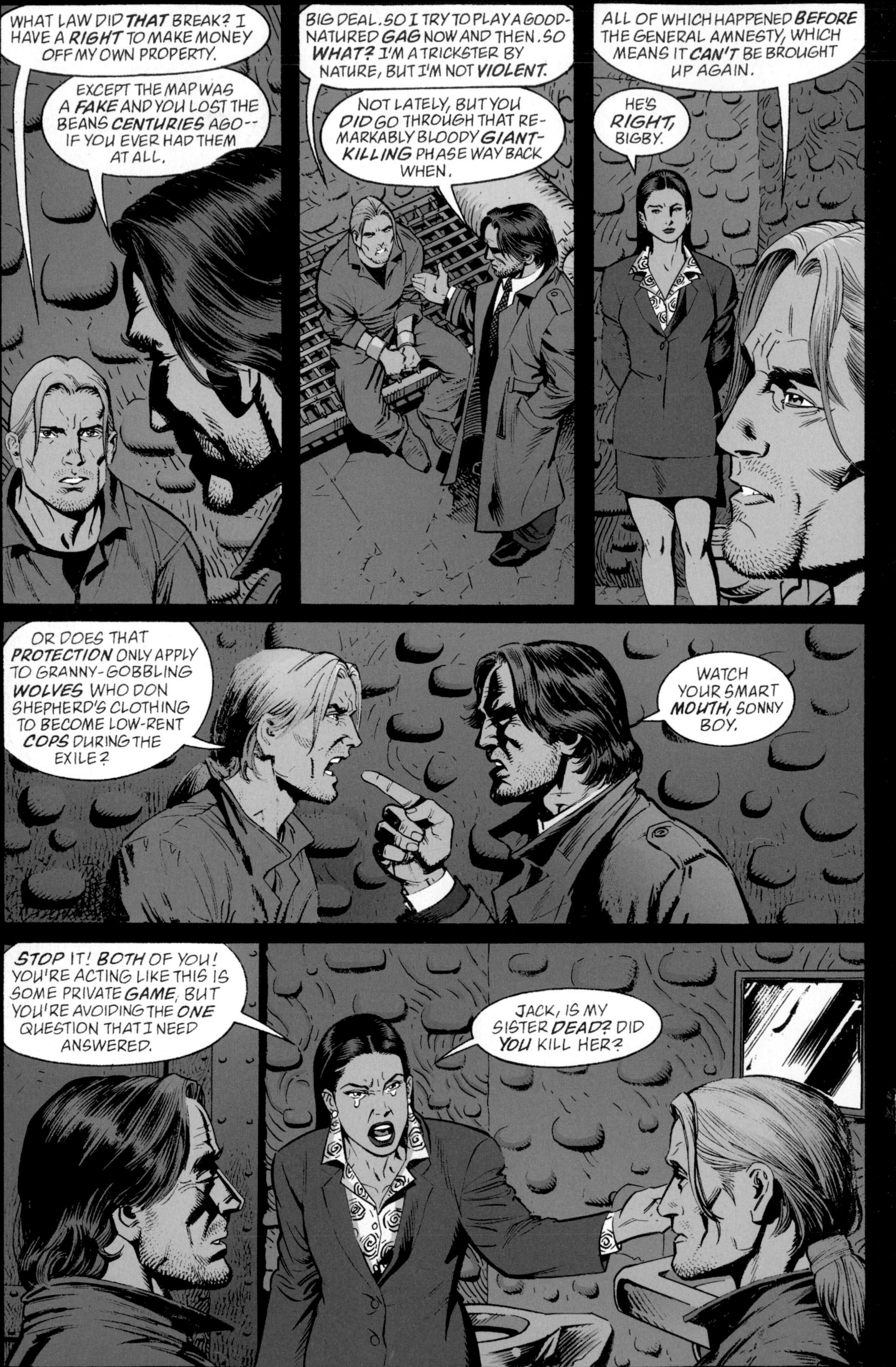
WHAT LAW DID THAT BREAK? I HAVE A RIGHT TO MAKE MONEY OFF MY OWN PROPERTY.
EXCEPT THE MAP WAS A FAKE AND YOU LOST THE BEANS CENTURIES AGO-- IF YOU EVER HAD THEM AT ALL.
BIG DEAL. SO I TRY TO PLAY A GOOD-NATURED GAG NOW AND THEN. SO WHAT? I'M A TRICKSTER BY NATURE, BUT I'M NOT VIOLENT.
NOT LATELY, BUT YOU DID GO THROUGH THAT REMARKABLY BLOODY GIANT-KILLING PHASE WAY BACK WHEN.
ALL OF WHICH HAPPENED BEFORE THE GENERAL AMNESTY, WHICH MEANS IT CAN'T BE BROUGHT UP AGAIN.
HE'S RIGHT, BIGBY.
OR DOES THAT PROTECTION ONLY APPLY TO GRANNY-GOBBLING WOLVES WHO DON SHEPHERD'S CLOTHING TO BECOME LOW-RENT COPS DURING THE EXILE?
WATCH YOUR SMART MOUTH, SONNY BOY.
STOP IT! BOTH OF YOU! YOU'RE ACTING LIKE THIS IS SOME PRIVATE GAME, BUT YOU'RE AVOIDING THE ONE QUESTION THAT I NEED ANSWERED.
JACK, IS MY SISTER DEAD? DID YOU KILL HER?

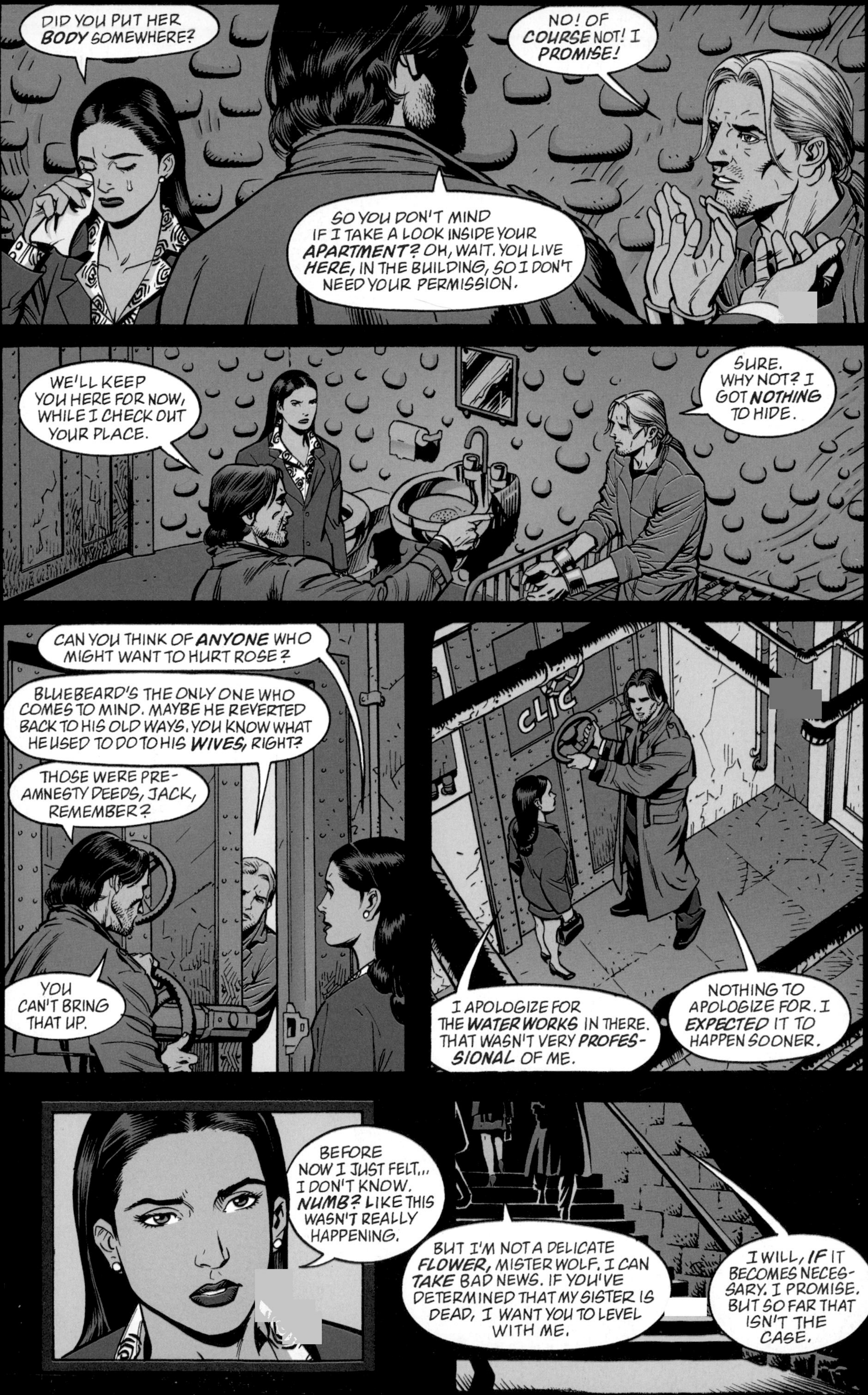

DID YOU PUT HER BODY SOMEWHERE?
NO! OF COURSE NOT! I PROMISE!
SO YOU DON'T MIND IF I TAKE A LOOK INSIDE YOUR APARTMENT? OH, WAIT. YOU LIVE HERE, IN THE BUILDING, SO I DON'T NEED YOUR PERMISSION.
WE'LL KEEP YOU HERE FOR NOW, WHILE I CHECK OUT YOUR PLACE.
SURE. WHY NOT? I GOT NOTHING TO HIDE.
CAN YOU THINK OF ANYONE WHO MIGHT WANT TO HURT ROSE?
BLUEBEARD'S THE ONLY ONE WHO COMES TO MIND. MAYBE HE REVERTED BACK TO HIS OLD WAYS. YOU KNOW WHAT HE USED TO DO TO HIS WIVES, RIGHT?
THOSE WERE PRE-AMNESTY DEEDS, JACK, REMEMBER?
YOU CAN'T BRING THAT UP.
CLIC
I APOLOGIZE FOR THE WATERWORKS IN THERE. THAT WASN'T VERY PROFES-SIONAL OF ME.
NOTHING TO APOLOGIZE FOR. I EXPECTED IT TO HAPPEN SOONER.
BEFORE NOW I JUST FELT... I DON'T KNOW. NUMB? LIKE THIS WASN'T REALLY HAPPENING.
BUT I'M NOT A DELICATE FLOWER, MISTER WOLF. I CAN TAKE BAD NEWS. IF YOU'VE DETERMINED THAT MY SISTER IS DEAD, I WANT YOU TO LEVEL WITH ME.
I WILL, IF IT BECOMES NECES-SARY. I PROMISE. BUT SO FAR THAT ISN'T THE CASE.

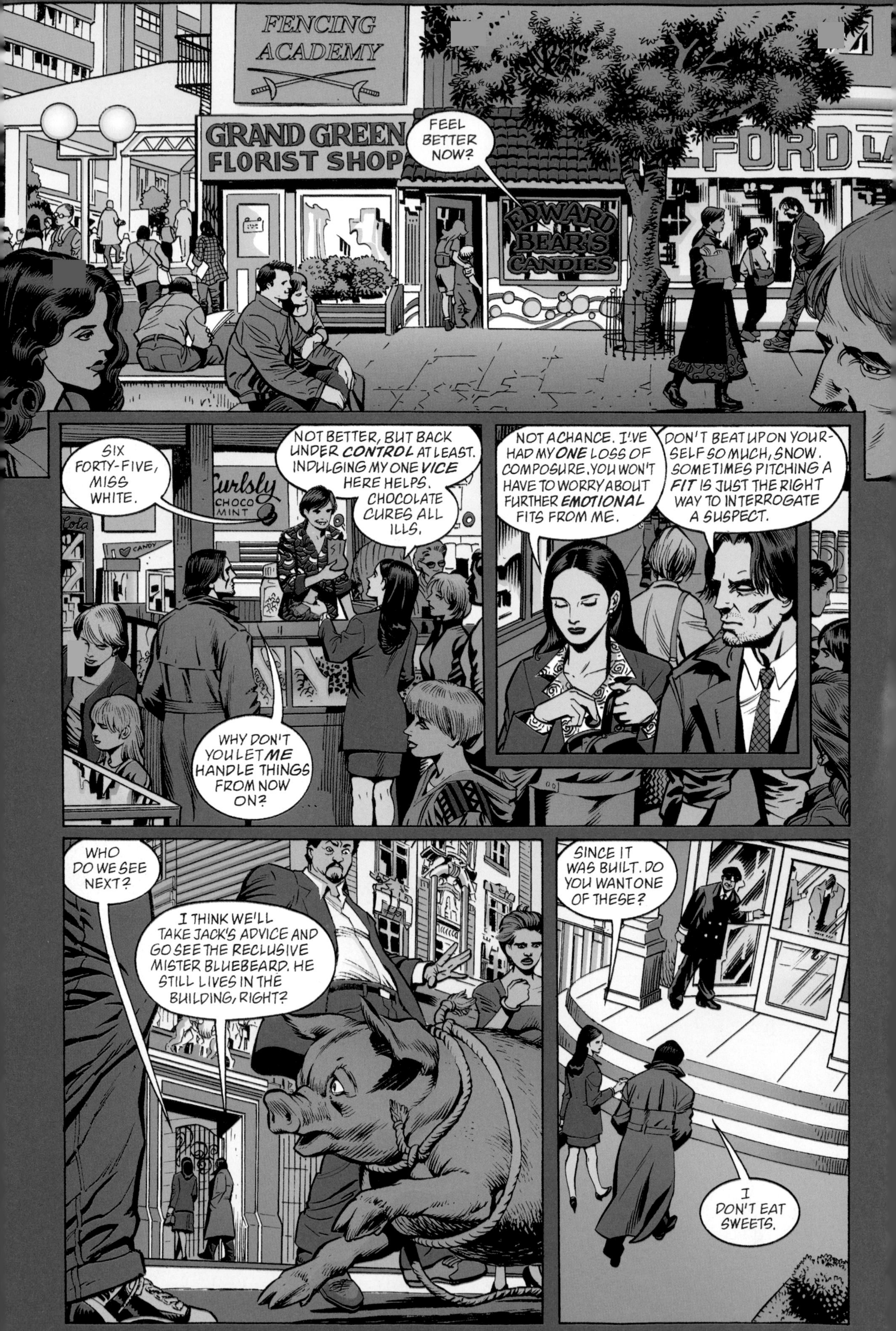
FENCING ACADEMY
GRAND GREEN FLORIST SHOP
FEEL BETTER NOW?
EDWARD BEAR'S CANDIES
SIX FORTY-FIVE, MISS WHITE.
NOT BETTER, BUT BACK UNDER **CONTROL** AT LEAST. INDULGING MY ONE **VICE** HERE HELPS. CHOCOLATE CURES ALL ILLS.
Curlsly CHOCO MINT
CANDY
WHY DON'T YOU LET **ME** HANDLE THINGS FROM NOW ON?
NOT A CHANCE. I'VE HAD MY **ONE** LOSS OF COMPOSURE. YOU WON'T HAVE TO WORRY ABOUT FURTHER **EMOTIONAL** FITS FROM ME.
DON'T BEAT UP ON YOURSELF SO MUCH, SNOW. SOMETIMES PITCHING A **FIT** IS JUST THE RIGHT WAY TO INTERROGATE A SUSPECT.
WHO DO WE SEE NEXT?
I THINK WE'LL TAKE JACK'S ADVICE AND GO SEE THE RECLUSIVE MISTER BLUEBEARD. HE STILL LIVES IN THE BUILDING, RIGHT?
SINCE IT WAS BUILT. DO YOU WANT ONE OF THESE?
I DON'T EAT SWEETS.

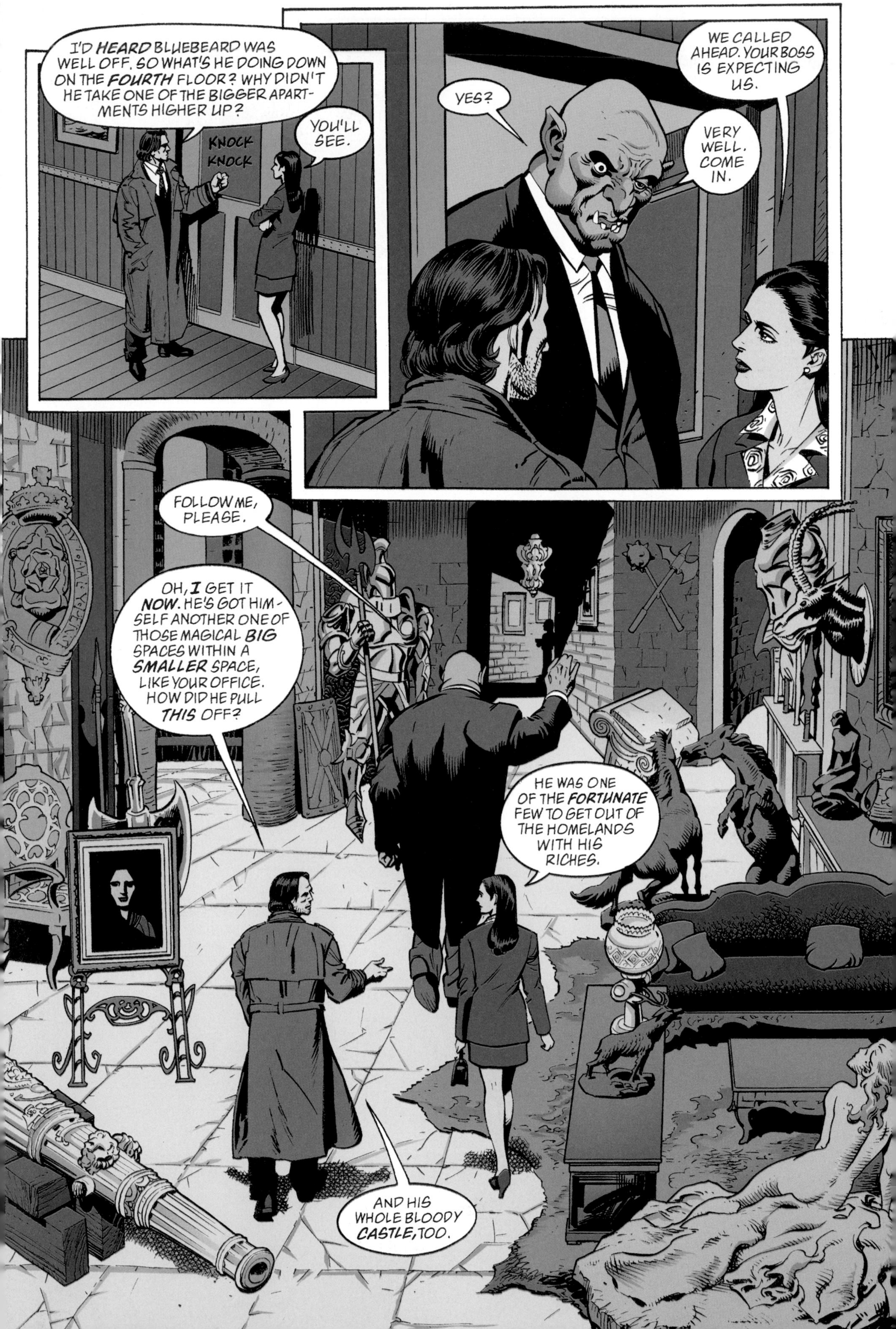
I'D HEARD BLUEBEARD WAS WELL OFF. SO WHAT'S HE DOING DOWN ON THE FOURTH FLOOR? WHY DIDN'T HE TAKE ONE OF THE BIGGER APARTMENTS HIGHER UP?
KNOCK KNOCK
YOU'LL SEE.
YES?
WE CALLED AHEAD. YOUR BOSS IS EXPECTING US.
VERY WELL. COME IN.
FOLLOW ME, PLEASE.
OH, I GET IT NOW. HE'S GOT HIMSELF ANOTHER ONE OF THOSE MAGICAL BIG SPACES WITHIN A SMALLER SPACE, LIKE YOUR OFFICE. HOW DID HE PULL THIS OFF?
HE WAS ONE OF THE FORTUNATE FEW TO GET OUT OF THE HOMELANDS WITH HIS RICHES.
AND HIS WHOLE BLOODY CASTLE, TOO.

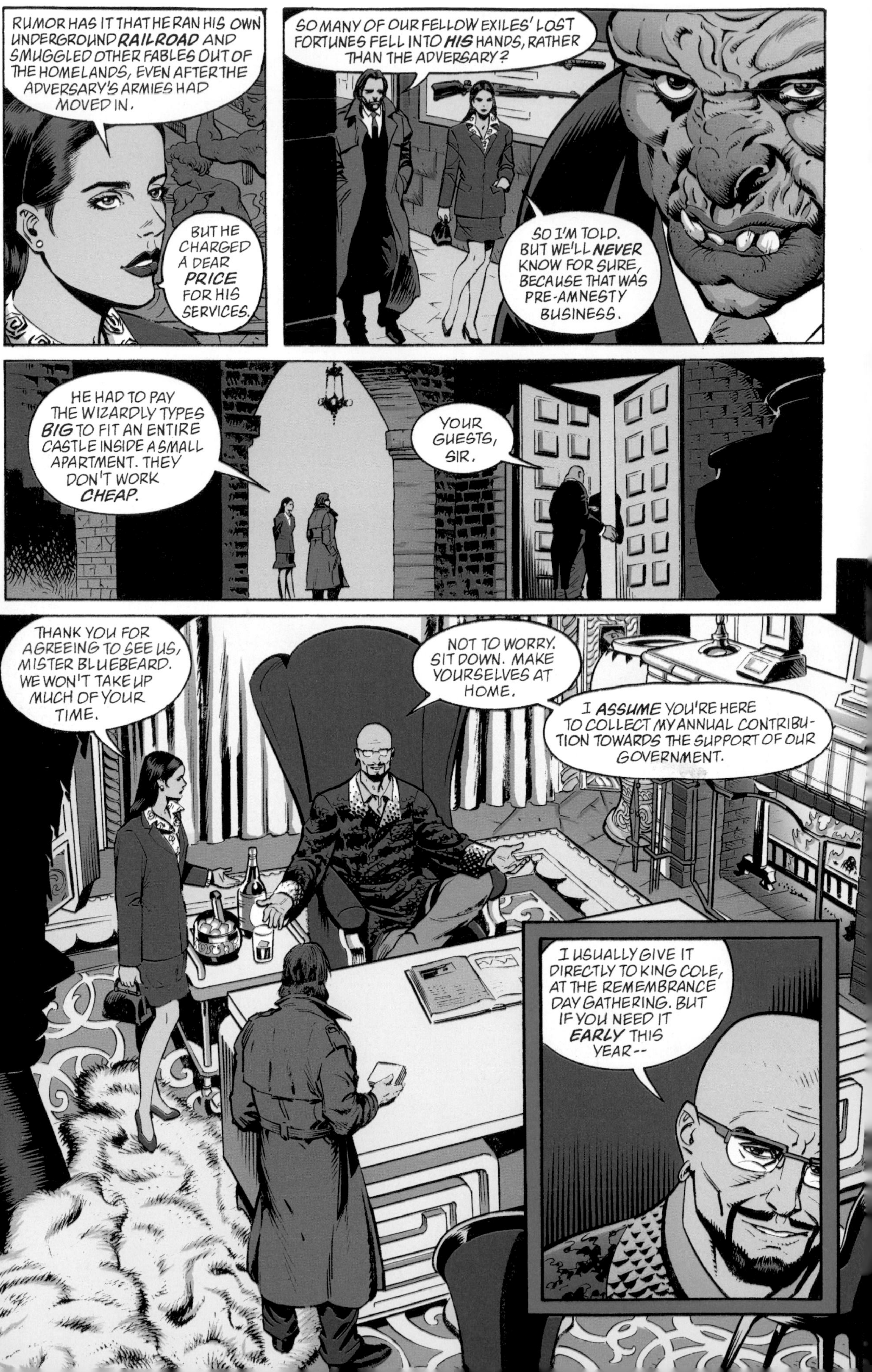
RUMOR HAS IT THAT HE RAN HIS OWN UNDERGROUND **RAILROAD** AND SMUGGLED OTHER FABLES OUT OF THE HOMELANDS, EVEN AFTER THE ADVERSARY'S ARMIES HAD MOVED IN.
BUT HE CHARGED A DEAR **PRICE** FOR HIS SERVICES.
SO MANY OF OUR FELLOW EXILES' LOST FORTUNES FELL INTO **HIS** HANDS, RATHER THAN THE ADVERSARY?
SO I'M TOLD. BUT WE'LL **NEVER** KNOW FOR SURE, BECAUSE THAT WAS PRE-AMNESTY BUSINESS.
HE HAD TO PAY THE WIZARDLY TYPES **BIG** TO FIT AN ENTIRE CASTLE INSIDE A SMALL APARTMENT. THEY DON'T WORK **CHEAP**.
YOUR GUESTS, SIR.
THANK YOU FOR AGREEING TO SEE US, MISTER BLUEBEARD. WE WON'T TAKE UP MUCH OF YOUR TIME.
NOT TO WORRY. SIT DOWN. MAKE YOURSELVES AT HOME.
I **ASSUME** YOU'RE HERE TO COLLECT MY ANNUAL CONTRIBUTION TOWARDS THE SUPPORT OF OUR GOVERNMENT.
I USUALLY GIVE IT DIRECTLY TO KING COLE, AT THE REMEMBRANCE DAY GATHERING. BUT IF YOU NEED IT **EARLY** THIS YEAR--

THAT'S *NOT* WHY WE'RE HERE.

TAKE A LOOK AT THESE PHOTOS. THEY WERE TAKEN IN ROSE RED'S APARTMENT LAST NIGHT, AND ALL THAT BLOOD IS *HERS*.

OH DEAR.

ALL WE NEED TO KNOW IS *WHY* YOU KILLED HER.

WHAT? HOW *DARE* YOU!

WOLF!

HOW DARE I *WHAT*? SPEAK RUDELY TO A MASS MURDERER?

THAT'S WHAT YOU DO, RIGHT? YOU MARRY THEM AND THEN *GUT* THEM?

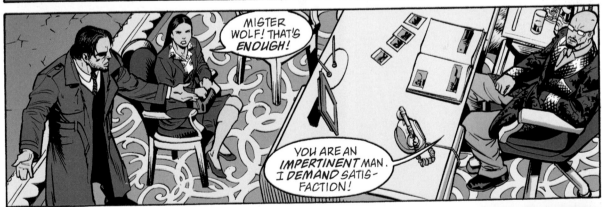

MISTER *WOLF*! THAT'S *ENOUGH*!

YOU ARE AN *IMPERTINENT* MAN. I DEMAND SATIS-FACTION!

FUCK YOUR SATISFACTION. I THINK YOU *KILLED* HER AND I'M READY TO *ARREST* YOU FOR IT *NOW*.

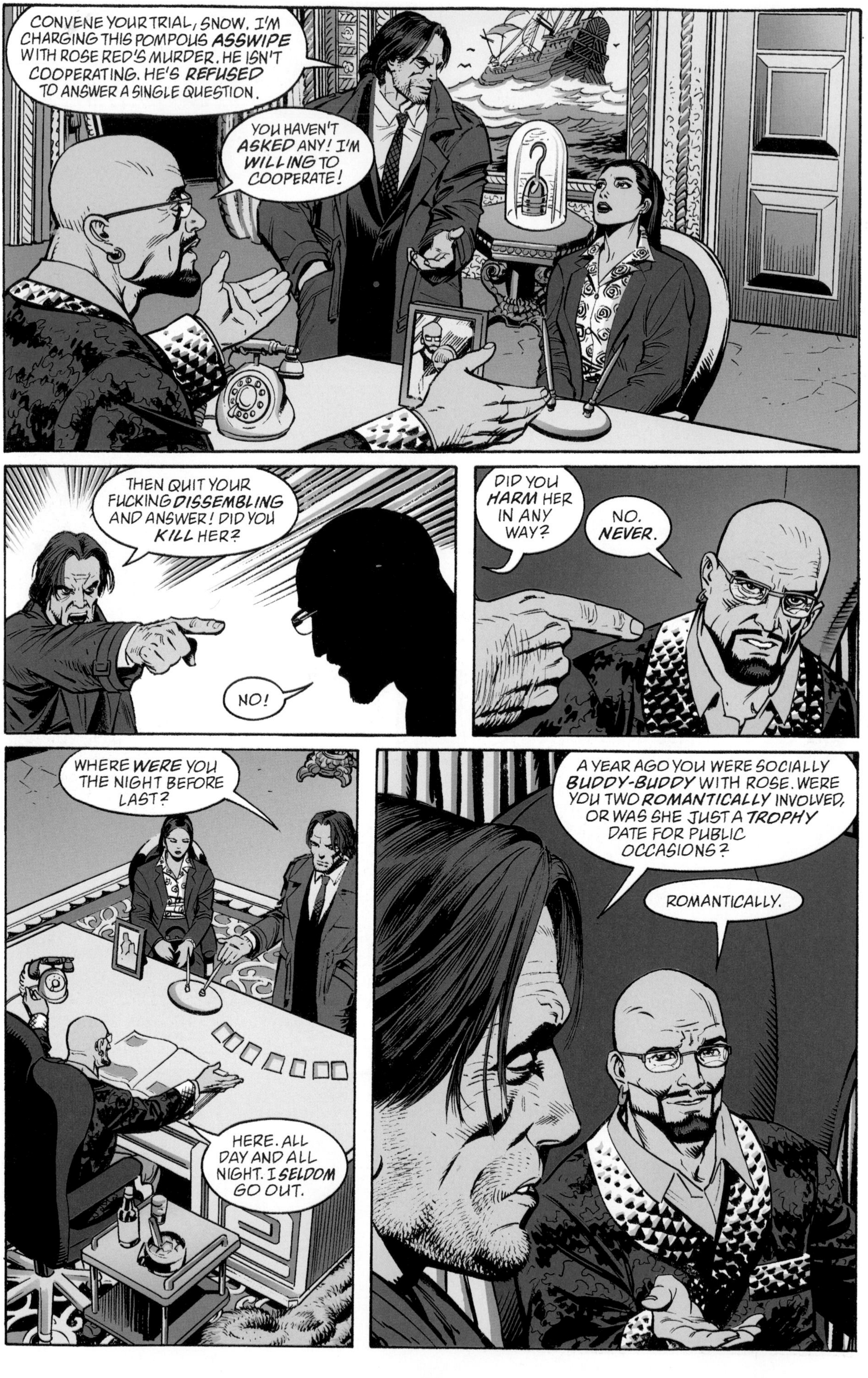
CONVENE YOUR TRIAL, SNOW. I'M CHARGING THIS POMPOUS ASSWIPE WITH ROSE RED'S MURDER. HE ISN'T COOPERATING. HE'S REFUSED TO ANSWER A SINGLE QUESTION.
YOU HAVEN'T ASKED ANY! I'M WILLING TO COOPERATE!
THEN QUIT YOUR FUCKING DISSEMBLING AND ANSWER! DID YOU KILL HER?
NO!
DID YOU HARM HER IN ANY WAY?
NO. NEVER.
WHERE WERE YOU THE NIGHT BEFORE LAST?
HERE. ALL DAY AND ALL NIGHT. I SELDOM GO OUT.
A YEAR AGO YOU WERE SOCIALLY BUDDY-BUDDY WITH ROSE. WERE YOU TWO ROMANTICALLY INVOLVED, OR WAS SHE JUST A TROPHY DATE FOR PUBLIC OCCASIONS?
ROMANTICALLY.

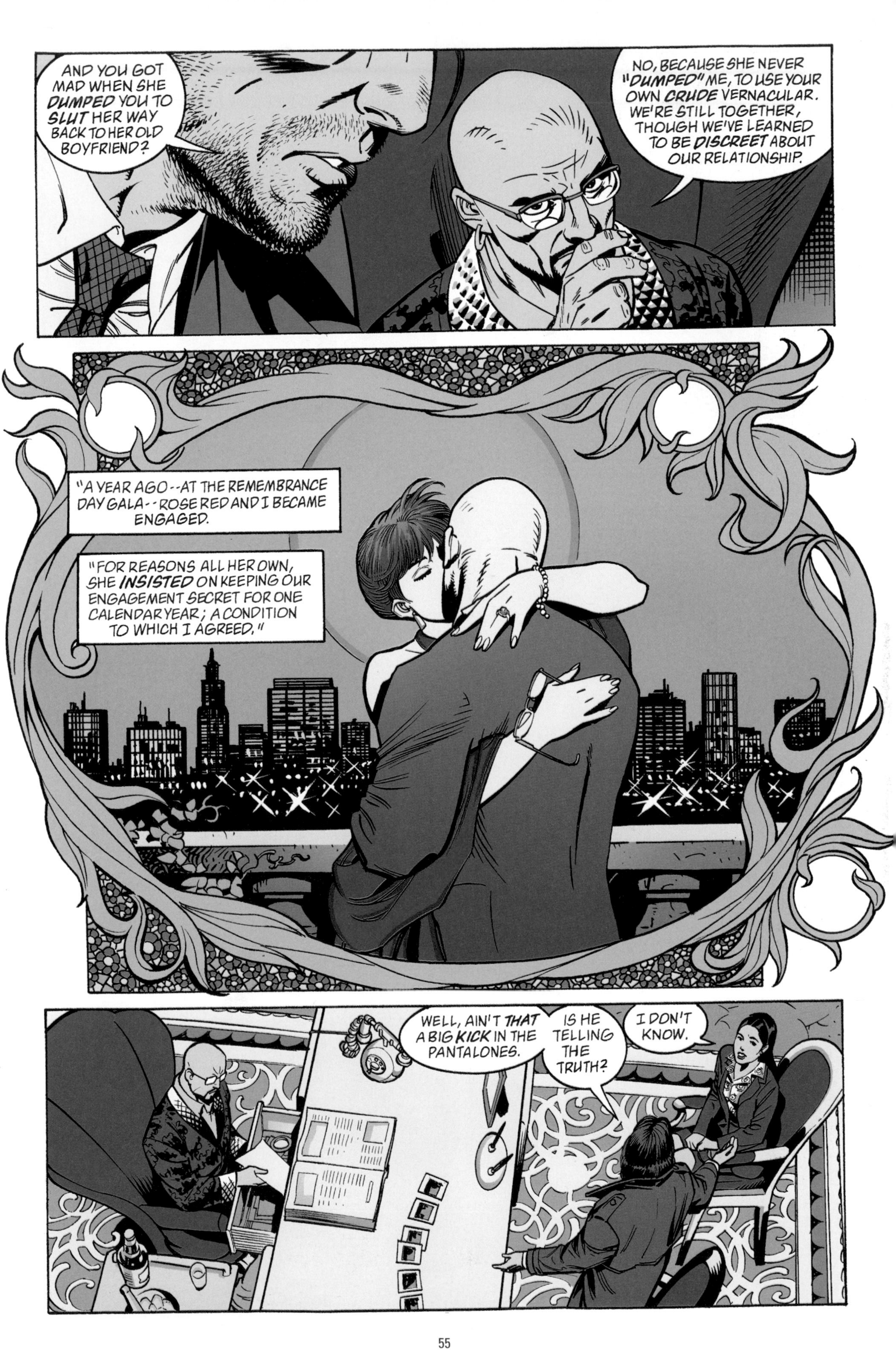
AND YOU GOT MAD WHEN SHE DUMPED YOU TO SLUT HER WAY BACK TO HER OLD BOYFRIEND?
NO, BECAUSE SHE NEVER "DUMPED" ME, TO USE YOUR OWN CRUDE VERNACULAR. WE'RE STILL TOGETHER, THOUGH WE'VE LEARNED TO BE DISCREET ABOUT OUR RELATIONSHIP.
"A YEAR AGO--AT THE REMEMBRANCE DAY GALA--ROSE RED AND I BECAME ENGAGED.
"FOR REASONS ALL HER OWN, SHE INSISTED ON KEEPING OUR ENGAGEMENT SECRET FOR ONE CALENDAR YEAR; A CONDITION TO WHICH I AGREED."
WELL, AIN'T THAT A BIG KICK IN THE PANTALONES.
IS HE TELLING THE TRUTH?
I DON'T KNOW.

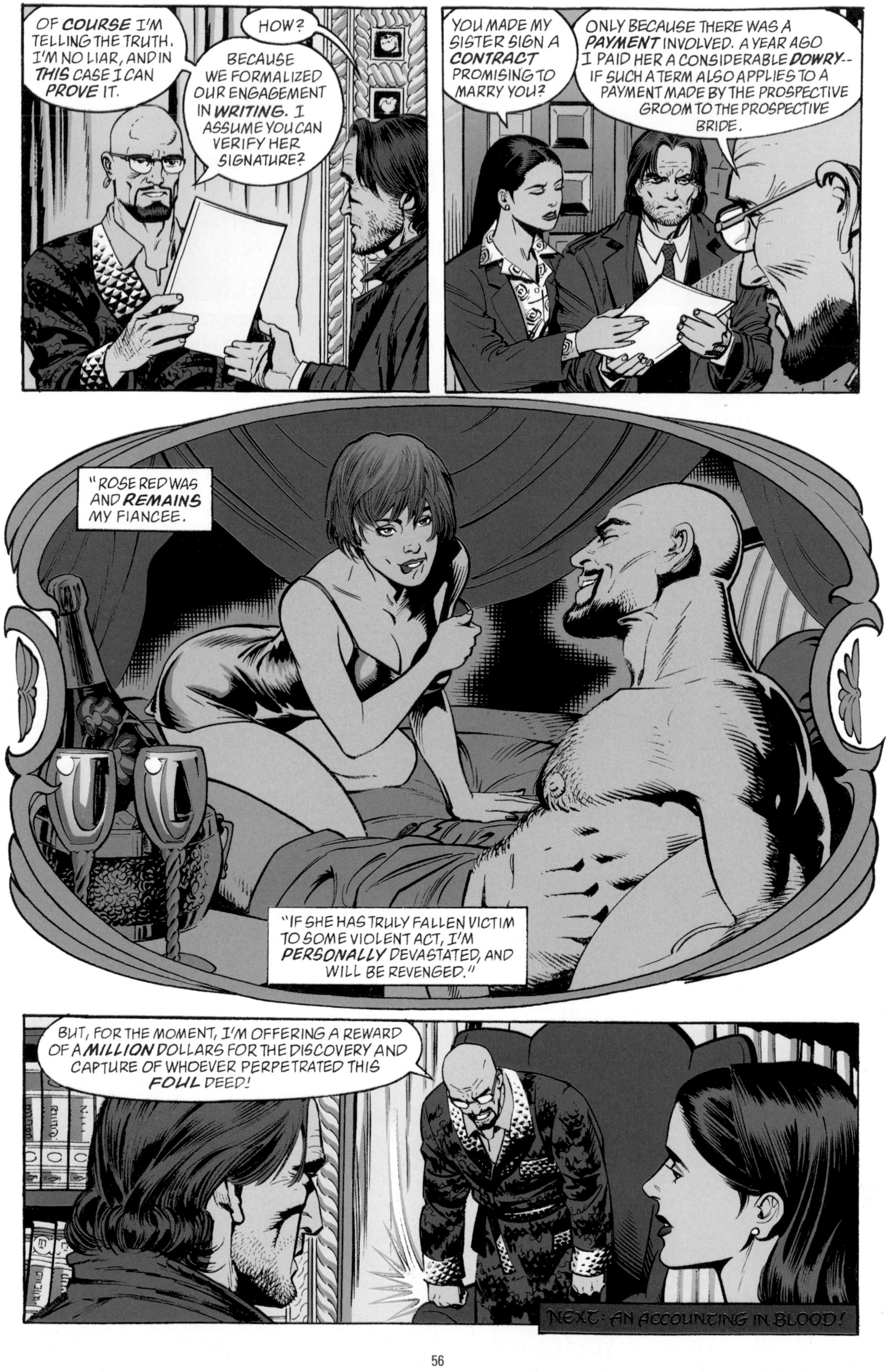

OF COURSE I'M TELLING THE TRUTH. I'M NO LIAR, AND IN THIS CASE I CAN PROVE IT.
HOW?
BECAUSE WE FORMALIZED OUR ENGAGEMENT IN WRITING. I ASSUME YOU CAN VERIFY HER SIGNATURE?
YOU MADE MY SISTER SIGN A CONTRACT PROMISING TO MARRY YOU?
ONLY BECAUSE THERE WAS A PAYMENT INVOLVED. A YEAR AGO I PAID HER A CONSIDERABLE DOWRY-- IF SUCH A TERM ALSO APPLIES TO A PAYMENT MADE BY THE PROSPECTIVE GROOM TO THE PROSPECTIVE BRIDE.
"ROSE RED WAS AND REMAINS MY FIANCEE.
"IF SHE HAS TRULY FALLEN VICTIM TO SOME VIOLENT ACT, I'M PERSONALLY DEVASTATED, AND WILL BE REVENGED."
BUT, FOR THE MOMENT, I'M OFFERING A REWARD OF A MILLION DOLLARS FOR THE DISCOVERY AND CAPTURE OF WHOEVER PERPETRATED THIS FOUL DEED!
NEXT: AN ACCOUNTING IN BLOOD!

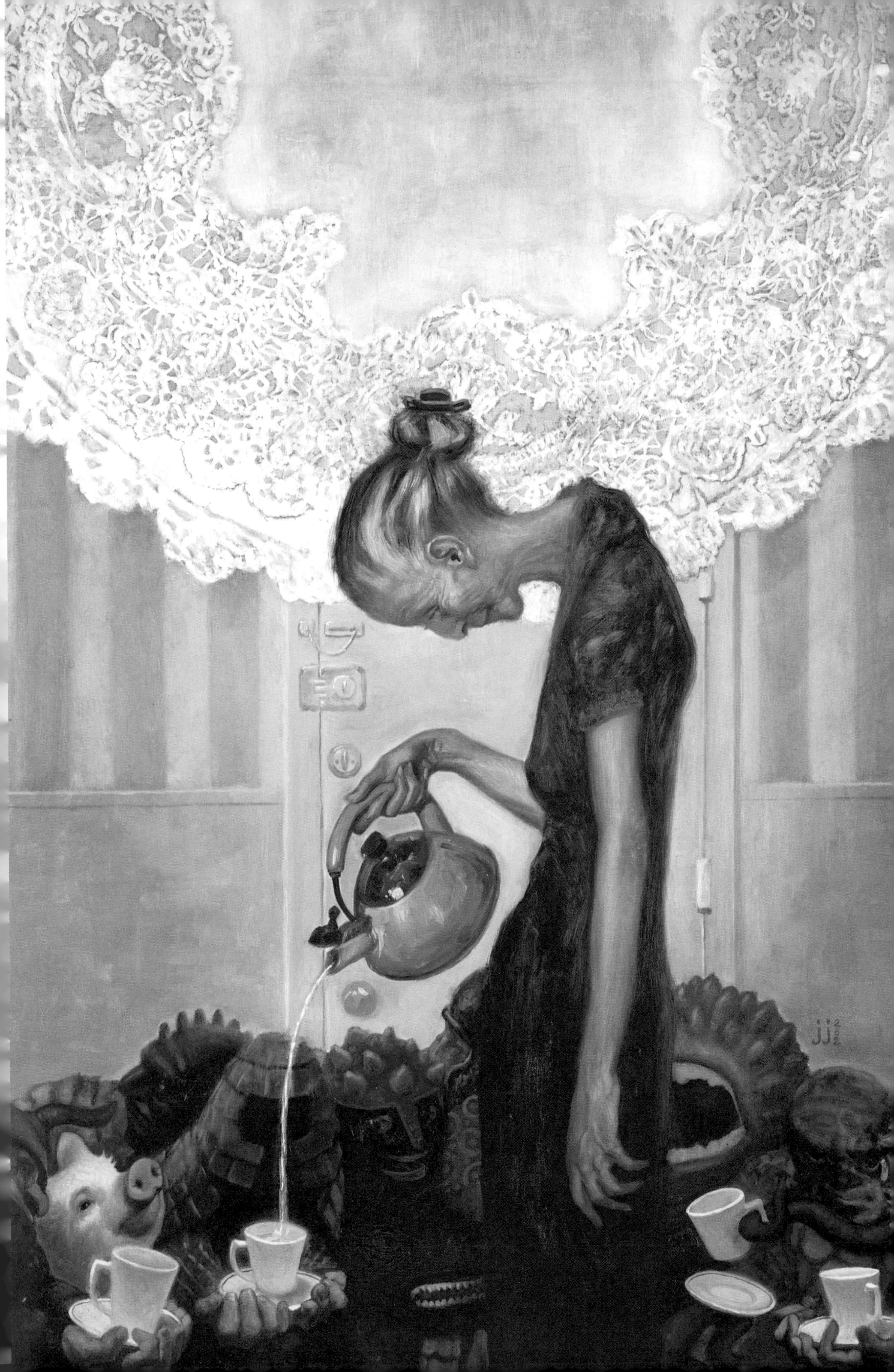

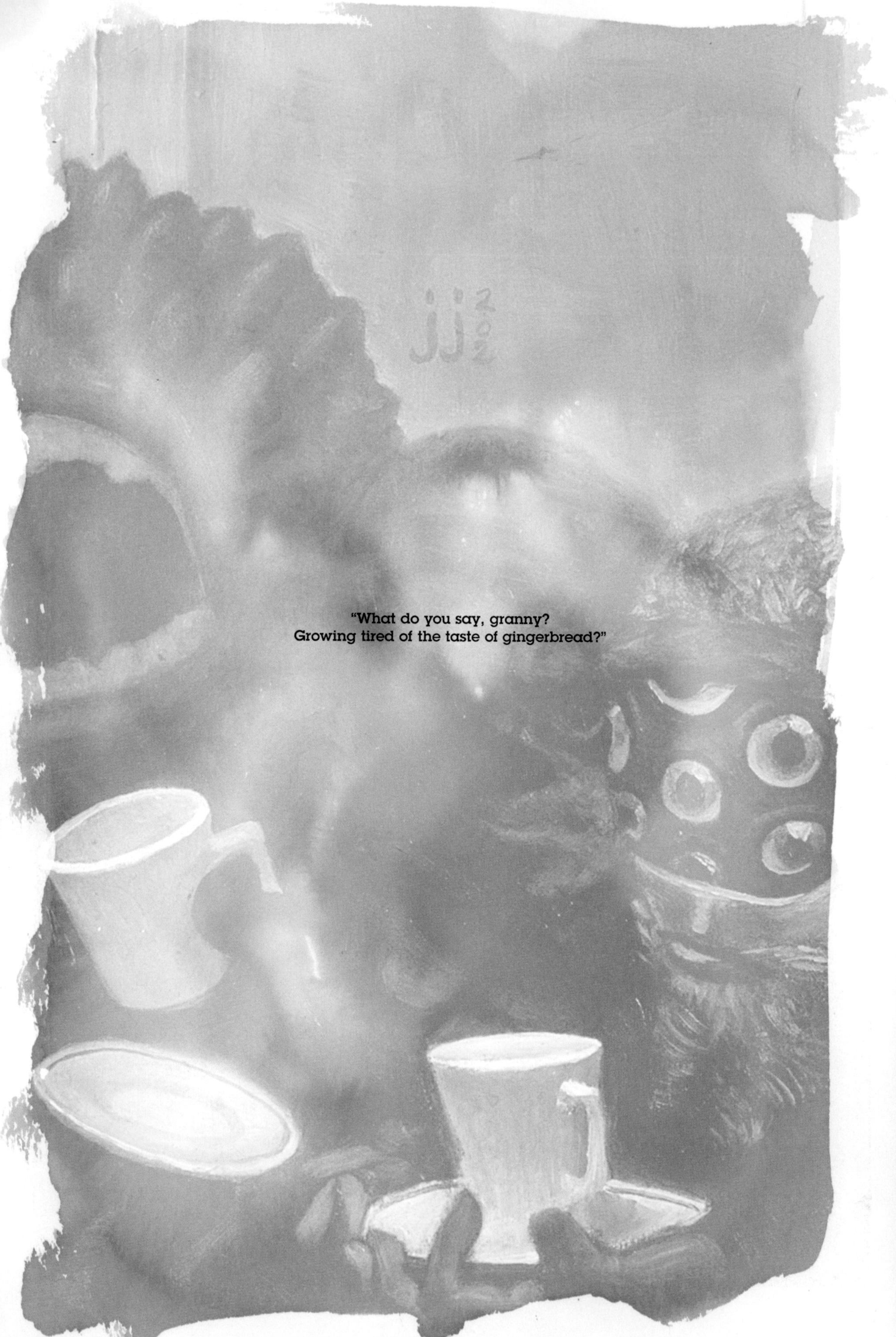
"What do you say, granny?
Growing tired of the taste of gingerbread?"

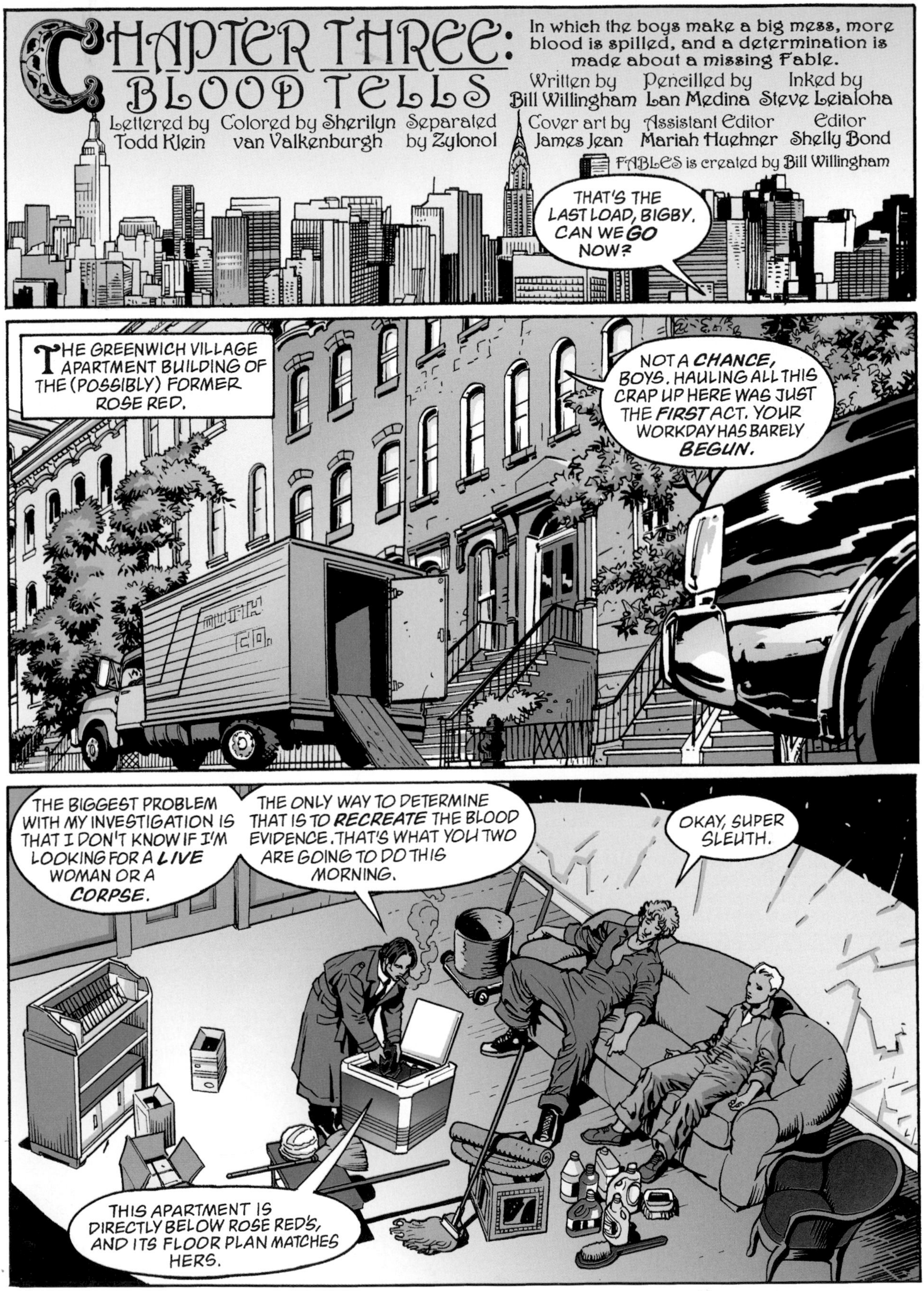
CHAPTER THREE:
BLOOD TELLS
In which the boys make a big mess, more blood is spilled, and a determination is made about a missing Fable.
Written by Bill Willingham
Pencilled by Lan Medina
Inked by Steve Leialoha
Lettered by Todd Klein
Colored by Sherilyn van Valkenburgh
Separated by Zylonol
Cover art by James Jean
Assistant Editor Mariah Huehner
Editor Shelly Bond
FABLES is created by Bill Willingham
THAT'S THE LAST LOAD, BIGBY. CAN WE GO NOW?
THE GREENWICH VILLAGE APARTMENT BUILDING OF THE (POSSIBLY) FORMER ROSE RED.
NOT A CHANCE, BOYS. HAULING ALL THIS CRAP UP HERE WAS JUST THE FIRST ACT. YOUR WORKDAY HAS BARELY BEGUN.
THE BIGGEST PROBLEM WITH MY INVESTIGATION IS THAT I DON'T KNOW IF I'M LOOKING FOR A LIVE WOMAN OR A CORPSE.
THE ONLY WAY TO DETERMINE THAT IS TO RECREATE THE BLOOD EVIDENCE. THAT'S WHAT YOU TWO ARE GOING TO DO THIS MORNING.
OKAY, SUPER SLEUTH.
THIS APARTMENT IS DIRECTLY BELOW ROSE RED'S, AND ITS FLOOR PLAN MATCHES HERS.

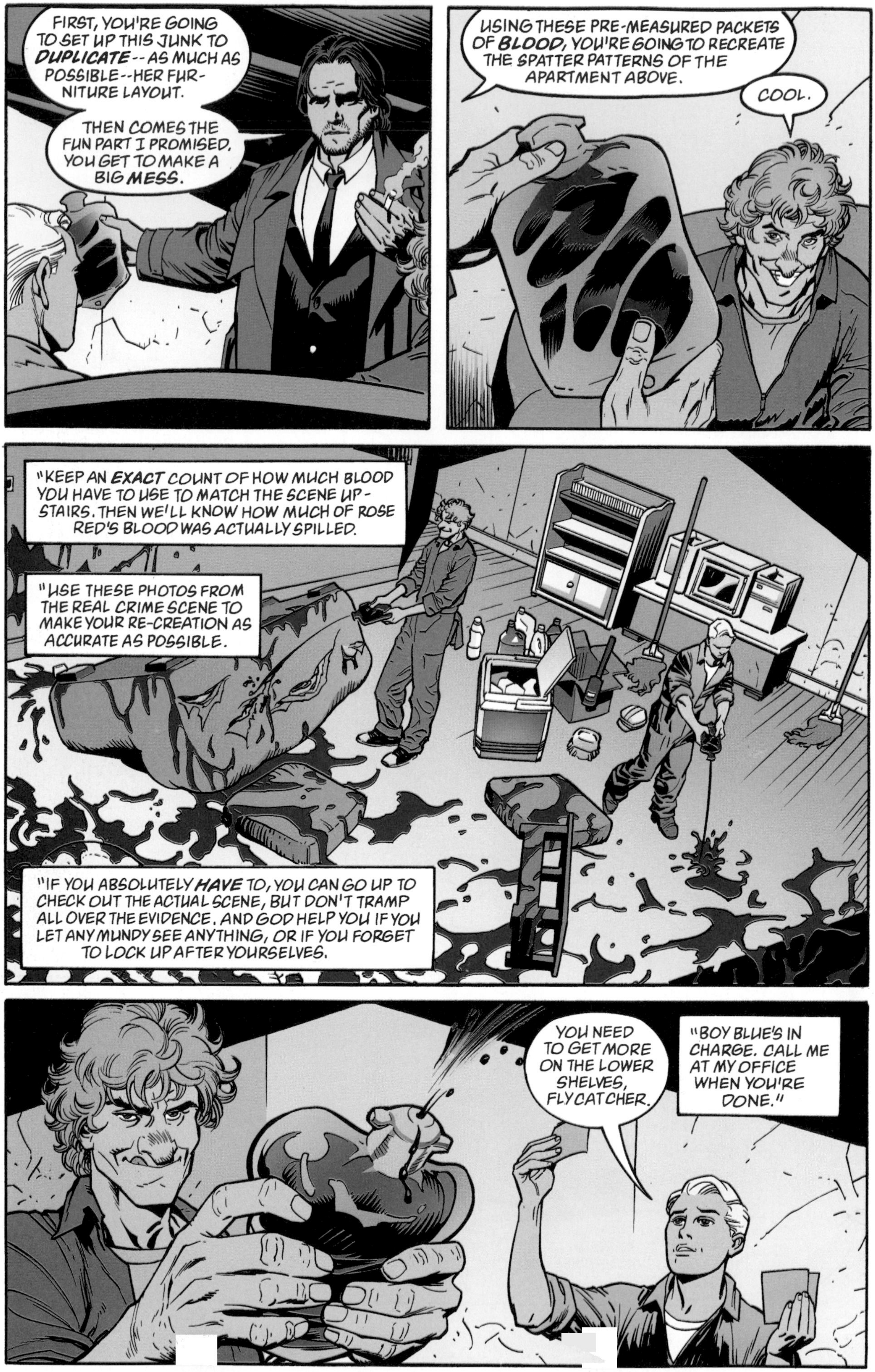
FIRST, YOU'RE GOING TO SET UP THIS JUNK TO DUPLICATE--AS MUCH AS POSSIBLE--HER FURNITURE LAYOUT.
THEN COMES THE FUN PART I PROMISED. YOU GET TO MAKE A BIG MESS.
USING THESE PRE-MEASURED PACKETS OF BLOOD, YOU'RE GOING TO RECREATE THE SPATTER PATTERNS OF THE APARTMENT ABOVE.
COOL.
"KEEP AN EXACT COUNT OF HOW MUCH BLOOD YOU HAVE TO USE TO MATCH THE SCENE UPSTAIRS. THEN WE'LL KNOW HOW MUCH OF ROSE RED'S BLOOD WAS ACTUALLY SPILLED.
"USE THESE PHOTOS FROM THE REAL CRIME SCENE TO MAKE YOUR RE-CREATION AS ACCURATE AS POSSIBLE.
"IF YOU ABSOLUTELY HAVE TO, YOU CAN GO UP TO CHECK OUT THE ACTUAL SCENE, BUT DON'T TRAMP ALL OVER THE EVIDENCE. AND GOD HELP YOU IF YOU LET ANY MUNDY SEE ANYTHING, OR IF YOU FORGET TO LOCK UP AFTER YOURSELVES.
YOU NEED TO GET MORE ON THE LOWER SHELVES, FLYCATCHER.
"BOY BLUE'S IN CHARGE. CALL ME AT MY OFFICE WHEN YOU'RE DONE."

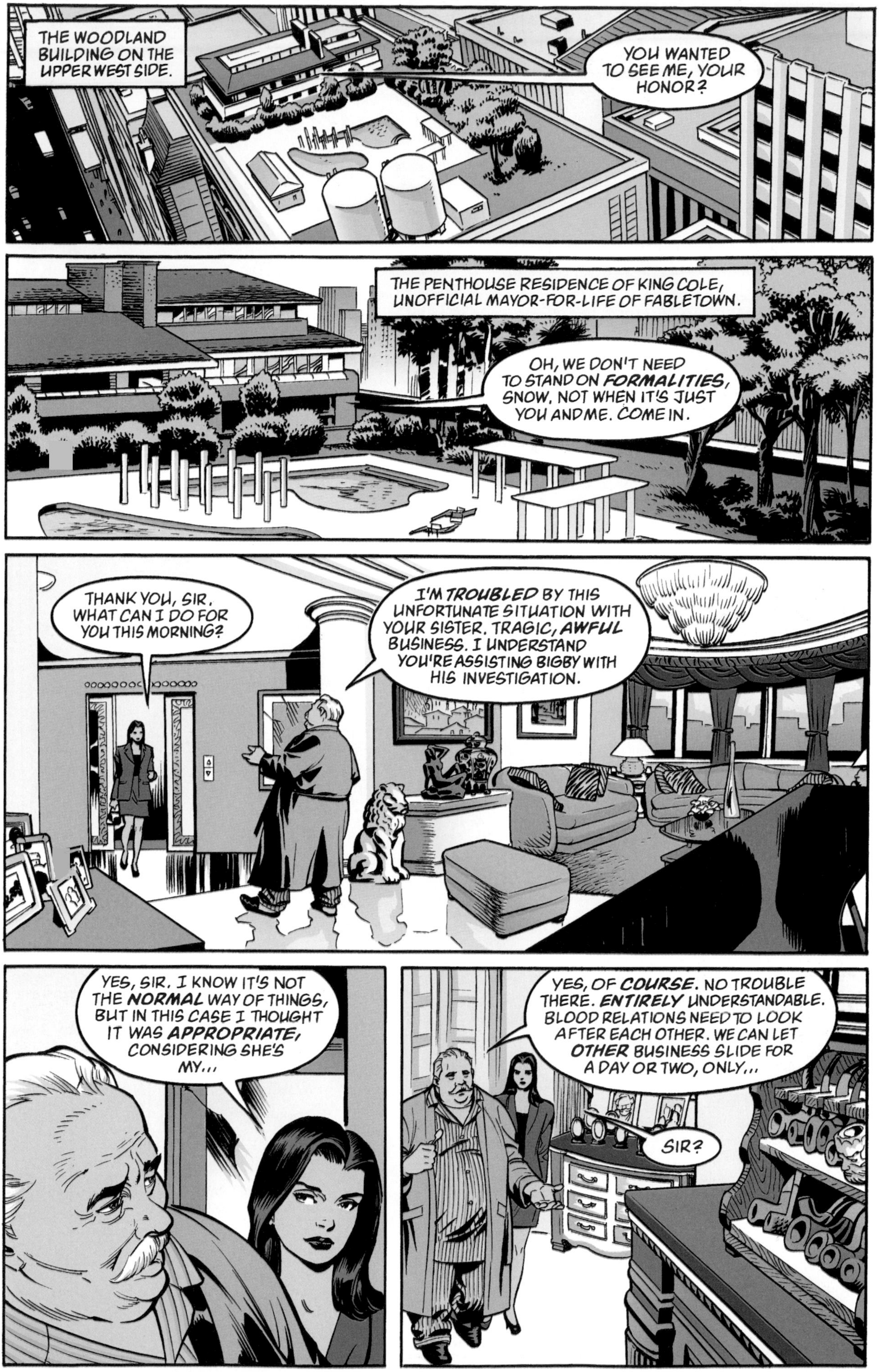
THE WOODLAND BUILDING ON THE UPPER WEST SIDE.
YOU WANTED TO SEE ME, YOUR HONOR?
THE PENTHOUSE RESIDENCE OF KING COLE, UNOFFICIAL MAYOR-FOR-LIFE OF FABLETOWN.
OH, WE DON'T NEED TO STAND ON FORMALITIES, SNOW, NOT WHEN IT'S JUST YOU AND ME. COME IN.
THANK YOU, SIR. WHAT CAN I DO FOR YOU THIS MORNING?
I'M TROUBLED BY THIS UNFORTUNATE SITUATION WITH YOUR SISTER. TRAGIC, AWFUL BUSINESS. I UNDERSTAND YOU'RE ASSISTING BIGBY WITH HIS INVESTIGATION.
YES, SIR. I KNOW IT'S NOT THE NORMAL WAY OF THINGS, BUT IN THIS CASE I THOUGHT IT WAS APPROPRIATE, CONSIDERING SHE'S MY...
YES, OF COURSE. NO TROUBLE THERE. ENTIRELY UNDERSTANDABLE. BLOOD RELATIONS NEED TO LOOK AFTER EACH OTHER. WE CAN LET OTHER BUSINESS SLIDE FOR A DAY OR TWO, ONLY...
SIR?

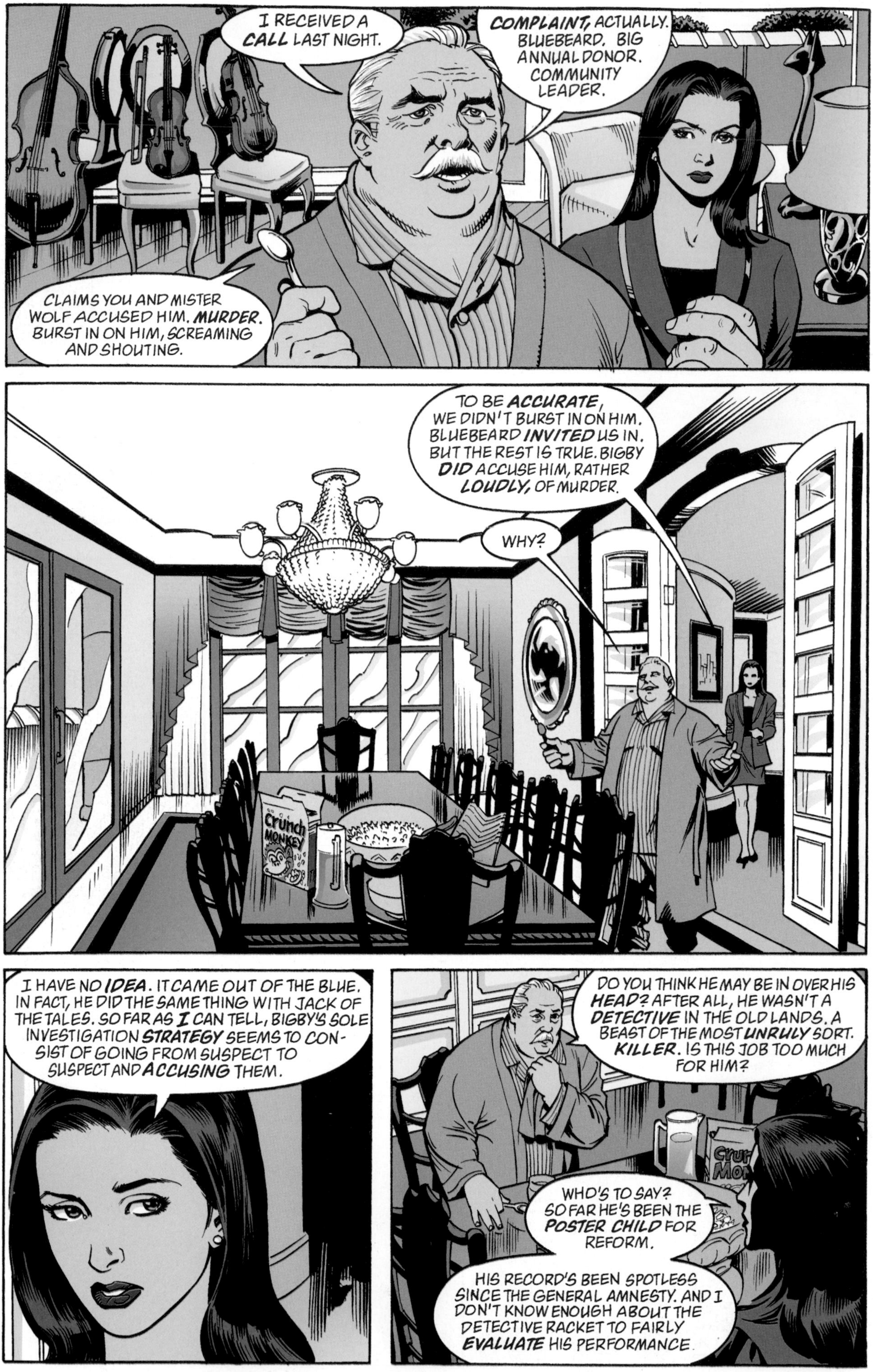
I RECEIVED A CALL LAST NIGHT.
COMPLAINT, ACTUALLY. BLUEBEARD. BIG ANNUAL DONOR. COMMUNITY LEADER.
CLAIMS YOU AND MISTER WOLF ACCUSED HIM. MURDER. BURST IN ON HIM, SCREAMING AND SHOUTING.
TO BE ACCURATE, WE DIDN'T BURST IN ON HIM. BLUEBEARD INVITED US IN. BUT THE REST IS TRUE. BIGBY DID ACCUSE HIM, RATHER LOUDLY, OF MURDER.
WHY?
Crunch MONKEY
I HAVE NO IDEA. IT CAME OUT OF THE BLUE. IN FACT, HE DID THE SAME THING WITH JACK OF THE TALES. SO FAR AS I CAN TELL, BIGBY'S SOLE INVESTIGATION STRATEGY SEEMS TO CONSIST OF GOING FROM SUSPECT TO SUSPECT AND ACCUSING THEM.
DO YOU THINK HE MAY BE IN OVER HIS HEAD? AFTER ALL, HE WASN'T A DETECTIVE IN THE OLD LANDS. A BEAST OF THE MOST UNRULY SORT. KILLER. IS THIS JOB TOO MUCH FOR HIM?
WHO'S TO SAY? SO FAR HE'S BEEN THE POSTER CHILD FOR REFORM.
HIS RECORD'S BEEN SPOTLESS SINCE THE GENERAL AMNESTY. AND I DON'T KNOW ENOUGH ABOUT THE DETECTIVE RACKET TO FAIRLY EVALUATE HIS PERFORMANCE.

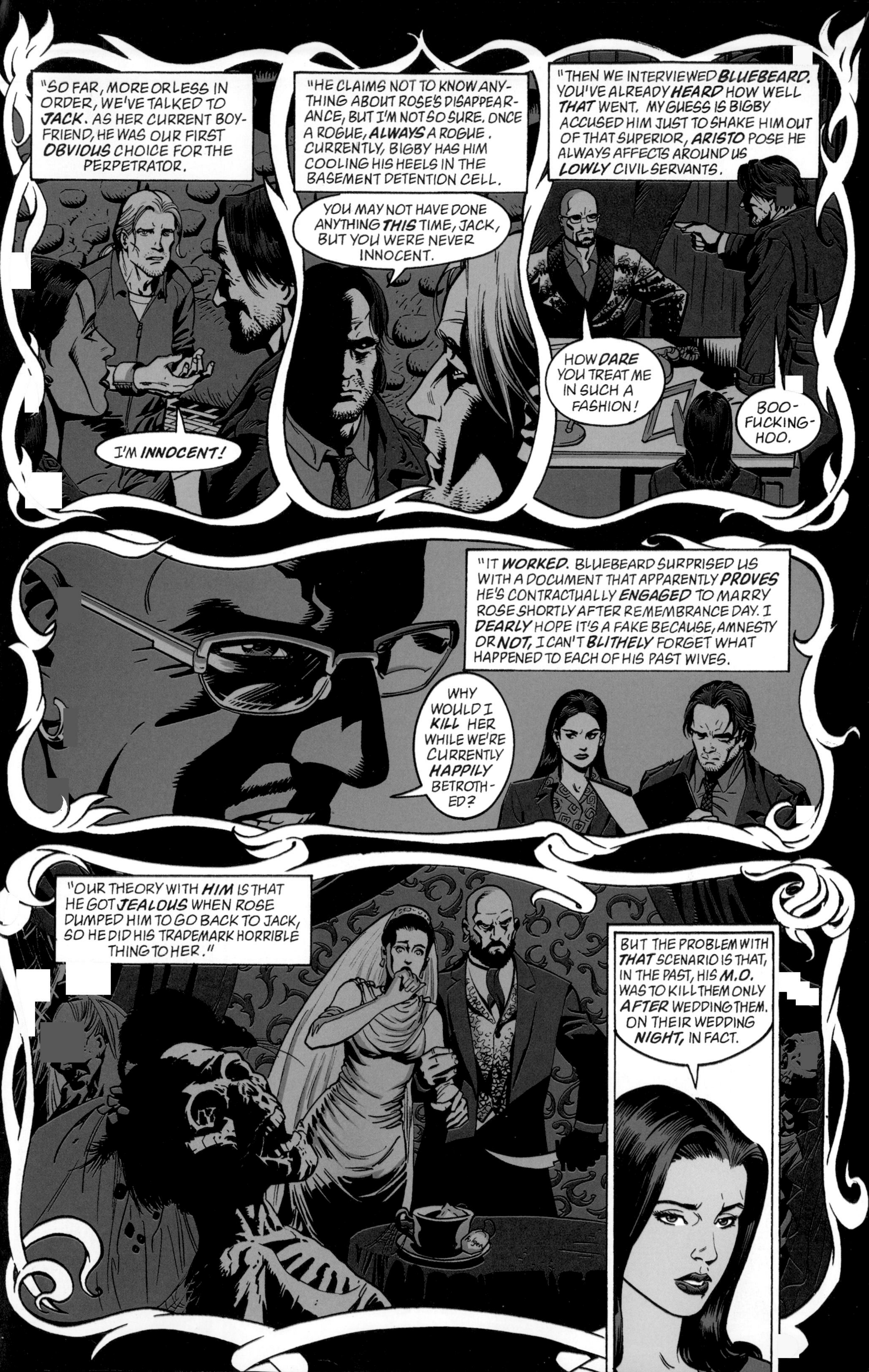
"SO FAR, MORE OR LESS IN ORDER, WE'VE TALKED TO JACK. AS HER CURRENT BOY-FRIEND, HE WAS OUR FIRST OBVIOUS CHOICE FOR THE PERPETRATOR.
I'M INNOCENT!
"HE CLAIMS NOT TO KNOW ANY-THING ABOUT ROSE'S DISAPPEAR-ANCE, BUT I'M NOT SO SURE. ONCE A ROGUE, ALWAYS A ROGUE. CURRENTLY, BIGBY HAS HIM COOLING HIS HEELS IN THE BASEMENT DETENTION CELL.
YOU MAY NOT HAVE DONE ANYTHING THIS TIME, JACK, BUT YOU WERE NEVER INNOCENT.
"THEN WE INTERVIEWED BLUEBEARD. YOU'VE ALREADY HEARD HOW WELL THAT WENT. MY GUESS IS BIGBY ACCUSED HIM JUST TO SHAKE HIM OUT OF THAT SUPERIOR, ARISTO POSE HE ALWAYS AFFECTS AROUND US LOWLY CIVIL SERVANTS.
HOW DARE YOU TREAT ME IN SUCH A FASHION!
BOO-FUCKING-HOO.
"IT WORKED. BLUEBEARD SURPRISED US WITH A DOCUMENT THAT APPARENTLY PROVES HE'S CONTRACTUALLY ENGAGED TO MARRY ROSE SHORTLY AFTER REMEMBRANCE DAY. I DEARLY HOPE IT'S A FAKE BECAUSE, AMNESTY OR NOT, I CAN'T BLITHELY FORGET WHAT HAPPENED TO EACH OF HIS PAST WIVES.
WHY WOULD I KILL HER WHILE WE'RE CURRENTLY HAPPILY BETROTH-ED?
"OUR THEORY WITH HIM IS THAT HE GOT JEALOUS WHEN ROSE DUMPED HIM TO GO BACK TO JACK, SO HE DID HIS TRADEMARK HORRIBLE THING TO HER."
BUT THE PROBLEM WITH THAT SCENARIO IS THAT, IN THE PAST, HIS M.O. WAS TO KILL THEM ONLY AFTER WEDDING THEM. ON THEIR WEDDING NIGHT, IN FACT.

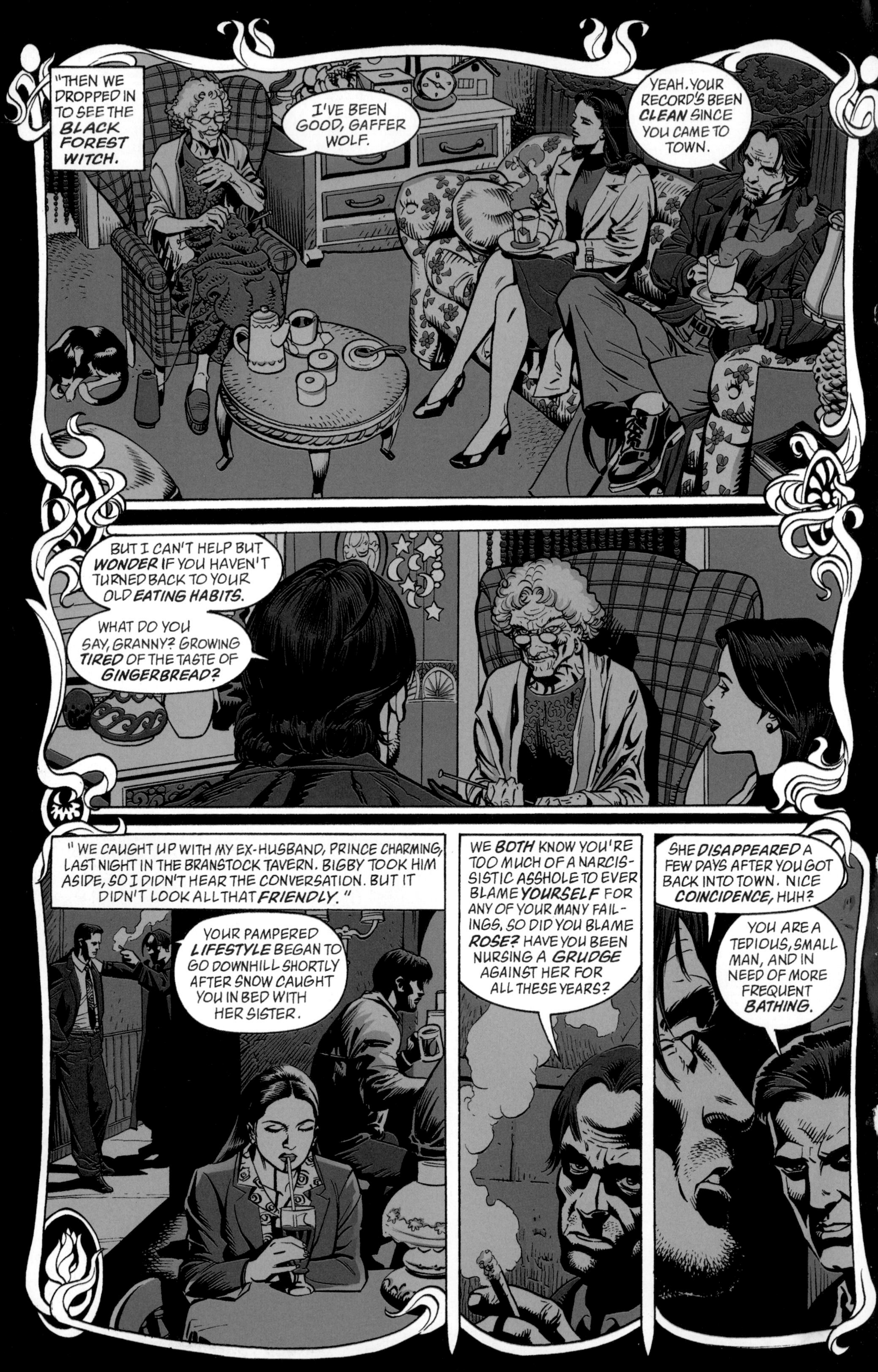
"THEN WE DROPPED IN TO SEE THE BLACK FOREST WITCH.
I'VE BEEN GOOD, GAFFER WOLF.
YEAH. YOUR RECORD'S BEEN CLEAN SINCE YOU CAME TO TOWN.
BUT I CAN'T HELP BUT WONDER IF YOU HAVEN'T TURNED BACK TO YOUR OLD EATING HABITS.
WHAT DO YOU SAY, GRANNY? GROWING TIRED OF THE TASTE OF GINGERBREAD?
" WE CAUGHT UP WITH MY EX-HUSBAND, PRINCE CHARMING, LAST NIGHT IN THE BRANSTOCK TAVERN. BIGBY TOOK HIM ASIDE, SO I DIDN'T HEAR THE CONVERSATION. BUT IT DIDN'T LOOK ALL THAT FRIENDLY."
YOUR PAMPERED LIFESTYLE BEGAN TO GO DOWNHILL SHORTLY AFTER SNOW CAUGHT YOU IN BED WITH HER SISTER.
WE BOTH KNOW YOU'RE TOO MUCH OF A NARCISSISTIC ASSHOLE TO EVER BLAME YOURSELF FOR ANY OF YOUR MANY FAILINGS, SO DID YOU BLAME ROSE? HAVE YOU BEEN NURSING A GRUDGE AGAINST HER FOR ALL THESE YEARS?
SHE DISAPPEARED A FEW DAYS AFTER YOU GOT BACK INTO TOWN. NICE COINCIDENCE, HUH?
YOU ARE A TEDIOUS, SMALL MAN, AND IN NEED OF MORE FREQUENT BATHING.

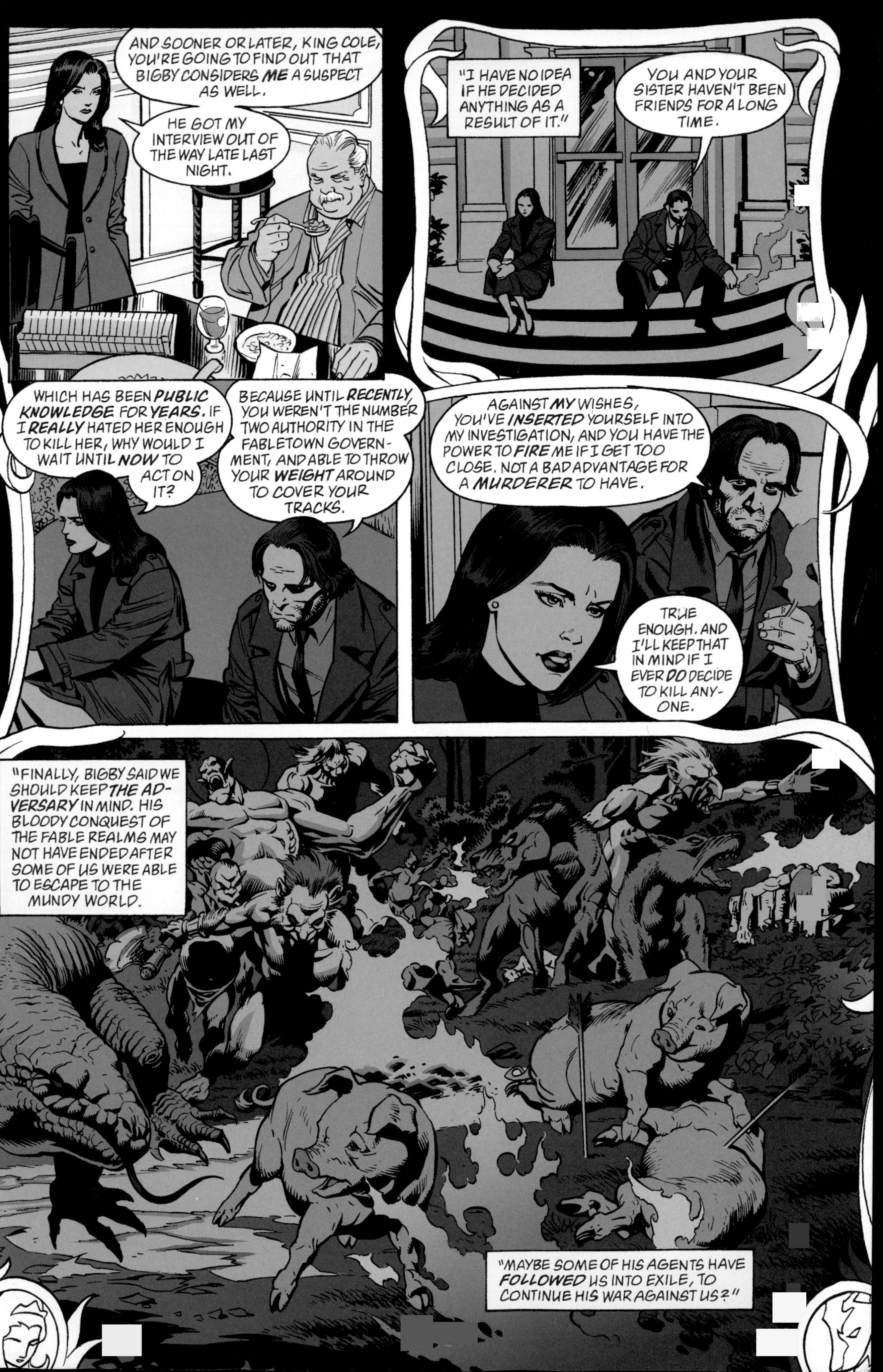
AND SOONER OR LATER, KING COLE, YOU'RE GOING TO FIND OUT THAT BIGBY CONSIDERS ME A SUSPECT AS WELL.
HE GOT MY INTERVIEW OUT OF THE WAY LATE LAST NIGHT.
"I HAVE NO IDEA IF HE DECIDED ANYTHING AS A RESULT OF IT."
YOU AND YOUR SISTER HAVEN'T BEEN FRIENDS FOR A LONG TIME.
WHICH HAS BEEN PUBLIC KNOWLEDGE FOR YEARS. IF I REALLY HATED HER ENOUGH TO KILL HER, WHY WOULD I WAIT UNTIL NOW TO ACT ON IT?
BECAUSE UNTIL RECENTLY, YOU WEREN'T THE NUMBER TWO AUTHORITY IN THE FABLETOWN GOVERN-MENT, AND ABLE TO THROW YOUR WEIGHT AROUND TO COVER YOUR TRACKS.
AGAINST MY WISHES, YOU'VE INSERTED YOURSELF INTO MY INVESTIGATION, AND YOU HAVE THE POWER TO FIRE ME IF I GET TOO CLOSE. NOT A BAD ADVANTAGE FOR A MURDERER TO HAVE.
TRUE ENOUGH. AND I'LL KEEP THAT IN MIND IF I EVER DO DECIDE TO KILL ANY-ONE.
"FINALLY, BIGBY SAID WE SHOULD KEEP THE AD-VERSARY IN MIND. HIS BLOODY CONQUEST OF THE FABLE REALMS MAY NOT HAVE ENDED AFTER SOME OF US WERE ABLE TO ESCAPE TO THE MUNDY WORLD.
"MAYBE SOME OF HIS AGENTS HAVE FOLLOWED US INTO EXILE, TO CONTINUE HIS WAR AGAINST US?"

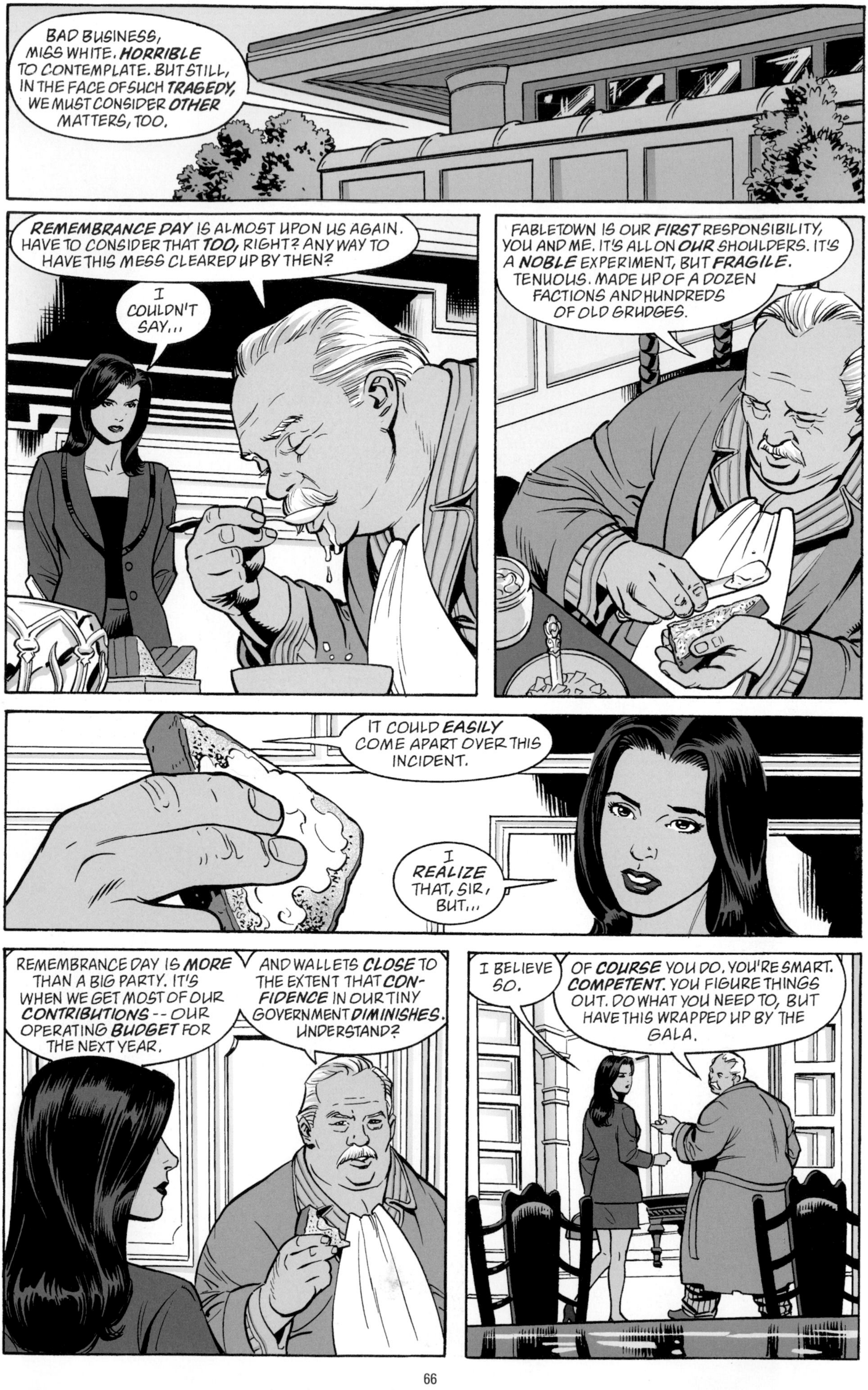
BAD BUSINESS, MISS WHITE. HORRIBLE TO CONTEMPLATE. BUT STILL, IN THE FACE OF SUCH TRAGEDY, WE MUST CONSIDER OTHER MATTERS, TOO.
REMEMBRANCE DAY IS ALMOST UPON US AGAIN. HAVE TO CONSIDER THAT TOO, RIGHT? ANY WAY TO HAVE THIS MESS CLEARED UP BY THEN?
I COULDN'T SAY...
FABLETOWN IS OUR FIRST RESPONSIBILITY, YOU AND ME. IT'S ALL ON OUR SHOULDERS. IT'S A NOBLE EXPERIMENT, BUT FRAGILE. TENUOUS. MADE UP OF A DOZEN FACTIONS AND HUNDREDS OF OLD GRUDGES.
IT COULD EASILY COME APART OVER THIS INCIDENT.
I REALIZE THAT, SIR, BUT...
REMEMBRANCE DAY IS MORE THAN A BIG PARTY. IT'S WHEN WE GET MOST OF OUR CONTRIBUTIONS -- OUR OPERATING BUDGET FOR THE NEXT YEAR.
AND WALLETS CLOSE TO THE EXTENT THAT CON-FIDENCE IN OUR TINY GOVERNMENT DIMINISHES. UNDERSTAND?
I BELIEVE SO.
OF COURSE YOU DO. YOU'RE SMART. COMPETENT. YOU FIGURE THINGS OUT. DO WHAT YOU NEED TO, BUT HAVE THIS WRAPPED UP BY THE GALA.

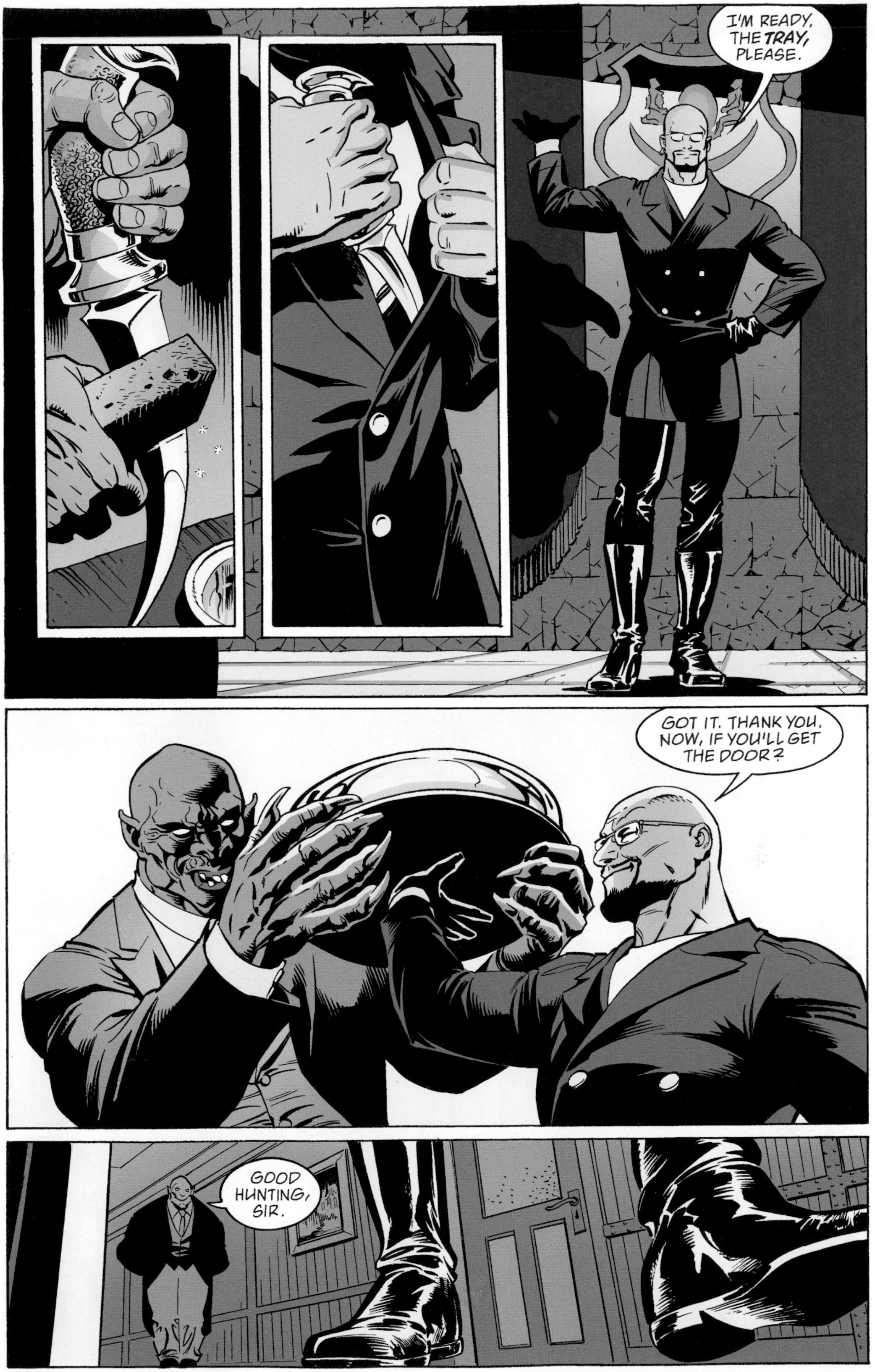
I'M READY, THE TRAY, PLEASE.
GOT IT. THANK YOU. NOW, IF YOU'LL GET THE DOOR?
GOOD HUNTING, SIR.

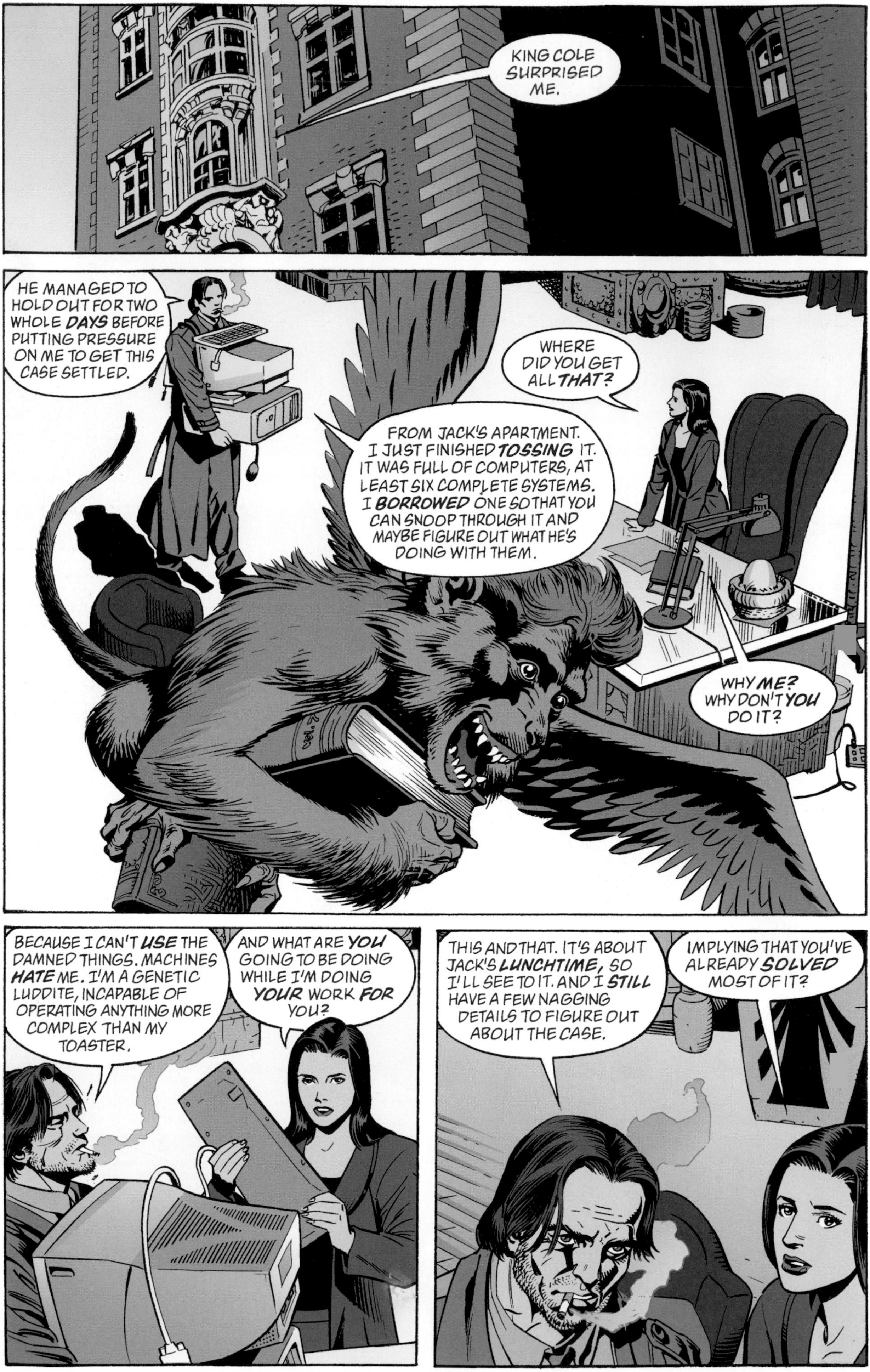
KING COLE SURPRISED ME.
HE MANAGED TO HOLD OUT FOR TWO WHOLE DAYS BEFORE PUTTING PRESSURE ON ME TO GET THIS CASE SETTLED.
WHERE DID YOU GET ALL THAT?
FROM JACK'S APARTMENT. I JUST FINISHED TOSSING IT. IT WAS FULL OF COMPUTERS, AT LEAST SIX COMPLETE SYSTEMS. I BORROWED ONE SO THAT YOU CAN SNOOP THROUGH IT AND MAYBE FIGURE OUT WHAT HE'S DOING WITH THEM.
WHY ME? WHY DON'T YOU DO IT?
BECAUSE I CAN'T USE THE DAMNED THINGS. MACHINES HATE ME. I'M A GENETIC LUDDITE, INCAPABLE OF OPERATING ANYTHING MORE COMPLEX THAN MY TOASTER.
AND WHAT ARE YOU GOING TO BE DOING WHILE I'M DOING YOUR WORK FOR YOU?
THIS AND THAT. IT'S ABOUT JACK'S LUNCHTIME, SO I'LL SEE TO IT. AND I STILL HAVE A FEW NAGGING DETAILS TO FIGURE OUT ABOUT THE CASE.
IMPLYING THAT YOU'VE ALREADY SOLVED MOST OF IT?

YUP. I SOLVED THE BULK OF IT WITHIN THE FIRST *HOUR.* I PRETTY MUCH KNOW *WHAT* HAPPENED, AND MOST OF *HOW,* BUT I'M STILL SHORT ON SOME OF THE *WHO* AND *WHY.*

AND WHEN *EXACTLY* ARE YOU PLANNING TO CLUE *ME* IN?

THE VERY MOMENT I'M CONVINCED YOU AREN'T THE *VILLAIN* IN THIS MYSTERY.

AT *LEAST* TELL ME IF SHE'S DEAD OR ALIVE.

WE'LL SEE.

YOU CAN BE ONE *FRUSTRATING* SON OF A BITCH!

LITERALLY, IN *MY* CASE, BUT SHE WAS NEVER LESS THAN LOVING AND NURTURING. THE BEST *MOTHER* ANY BOY COULD WANT.

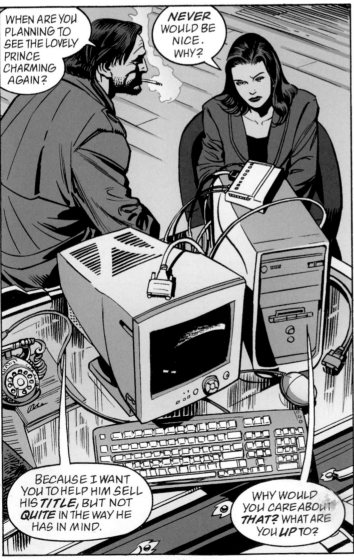

WHEN ARE YOU PLANNING TO SEE THE LOVELY PRINCE CHARMING AGAIN?

NEVER WOULD BE NICE. WHY?

BECAUSE I WANT YOU TO HELP HIM SELL HIS *TITLE,* BUT NOT *QUITE* IN THE WAY HE HAS IN MIND.

WHY WOULD YOU CARE ABOUT *THAT?* WHAT ARE YOU *UP* TO?

A MAD BUT *IMPROBABLE* SCHEME TO MAKE EVERYTHING COME OUT RIGHT IN THE END, WITHOUT ANY *FURTHER* BLOODSHED. AND JUST *MAYBE* THE FABLE COMMUNITY DOESN'T DISINTEGRATE IN THE PROCESS.

PROBABLY WON'T WORK, THOUGH.

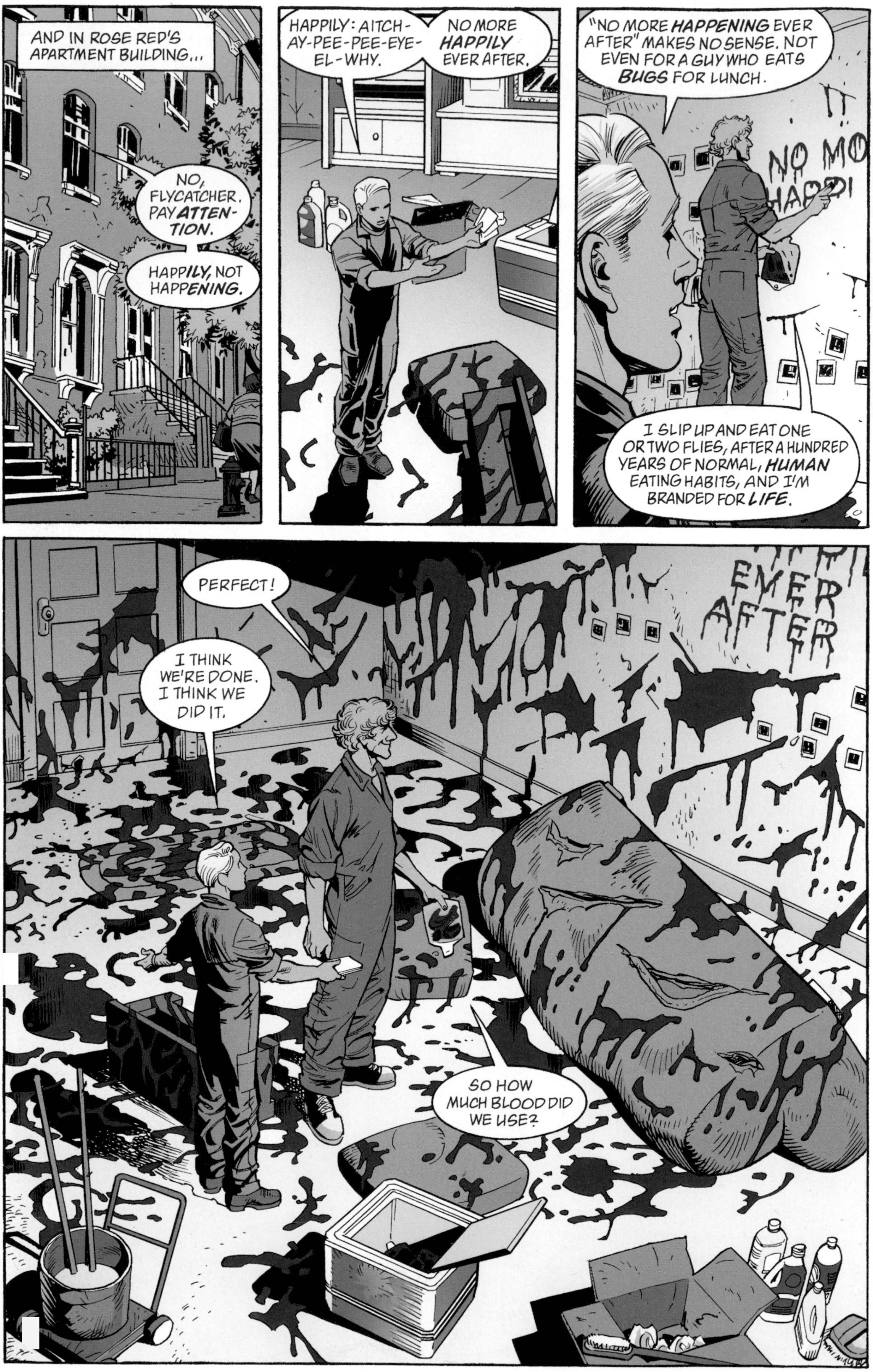
AND IN ROSE RED'S APARTMENT BUILDING...
NO, FLYCATCHER. PAY ATTENTION.
HAPPILY, NOT HAPPENING.
HAPPILY: AITCH-AY-PEE-PEE-EYE-EL-WHY.
NO MORE HAPPILY EVER AFTER.
"NO MORE HAPPENING EVER AFTER" MAKES NO SENSE. NOT EVEN FOR A GUY WHO EATS BUGS FOR LUNCH.
NO MO HAPPI
I SLIP UP AND EAT ONE OR TWO FLIES, AFTER A HUNDRED YEARS OF NORMAL, HUMAN EATING HABITS, AND I'M BRANDED FOR LIFE.
PERFECT!
EVER AFTER
I THINK WE'RE DONE. I THINK WE DID IT.
SO HOW MUCH BLOOD DID WE USE?

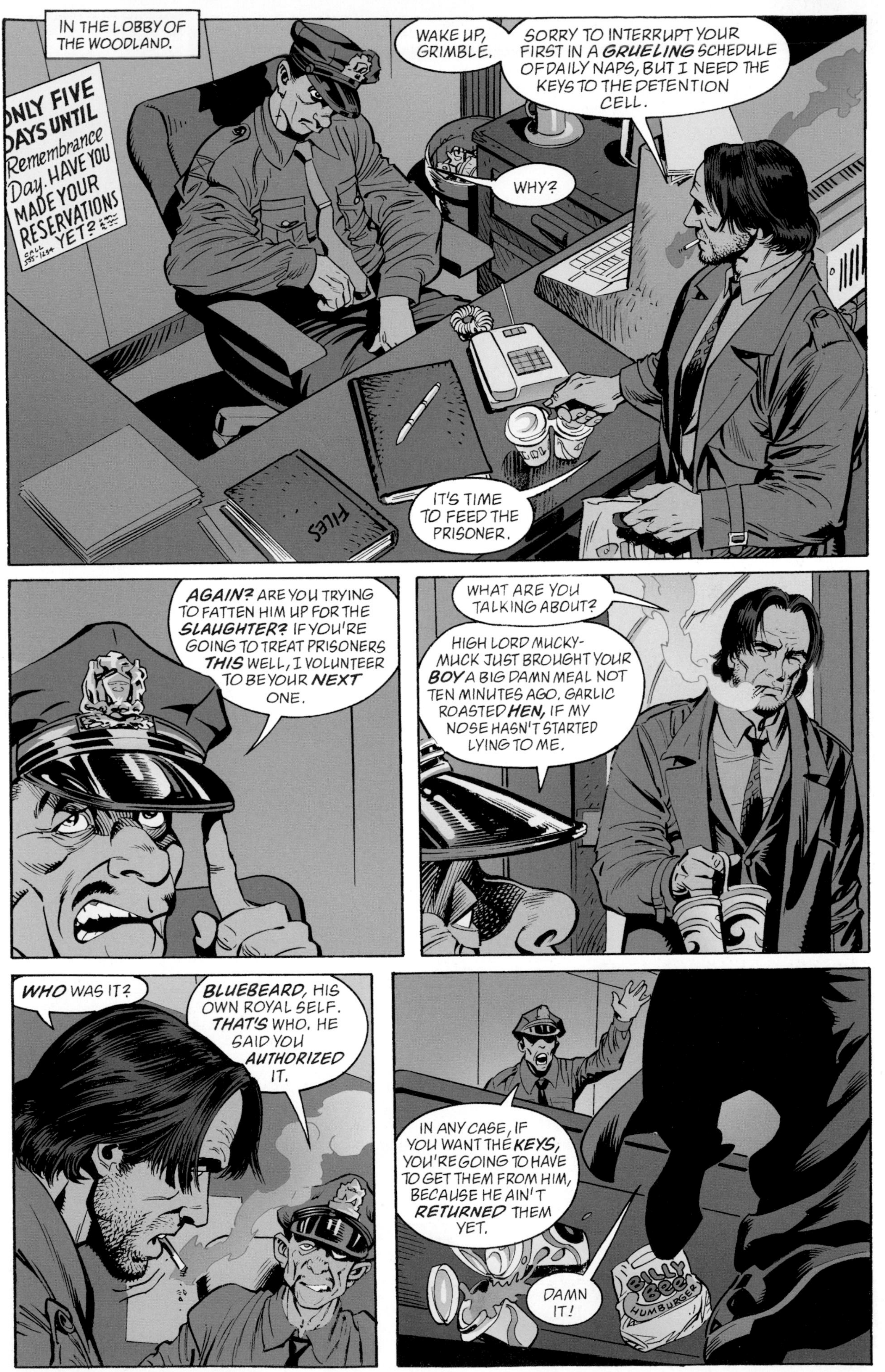

IN THE LOBBY OF THE WOODLAND.
ONLY FIVE DAYS UNTIL Remembrance Day. HAVE YOU MADE YOUR RESERVATIONS YET?
WAKE UP, GRIMBLE.
SORRY TO INTERRUPT YOUR FIRST IN A GRUELING SCHEDULE OF DAILY NAPS, BUT I NEED THE KEYS TO THE DETENTION CELL.
WHY?
IT'S TIME TO FEED THE PRISONER.
FILES
AGAIN? ARE YOU TRYING TO FATTEN HIM UP FOR THE SLAUGHTER? IF YOU'RE GOING TO TREAT PRISONERS THIS WELL, I VOLUNTEER TO BE YOUR NEXT ONE.
WHAT ARE YOU TALKING ABOUT?
HIGH LORD MUCKY-MUCK JUST BROUGHT YOUR BOY A BIG DAMN MEAL NOT TEN MINUTES AGO. GARLIC ROASTED HEN, IF MY NOSE HASN'T STARTED LYING TO ME.
WHO WAS IT?
BLUEBEARD, HIS OWN ROYAL SELF. THAT'S WHO. HE SAID YOU AUTHORIZED IT.
IN ANY CASE, IF YOU WANT THE KEYS, YOU'RE GOING TO HAVE TO GET THEM FROM HIM, BECAUSE HE AIN'T RETURNED THEM YET.
DAMN IT!
BILLY BEE HUMBURGER

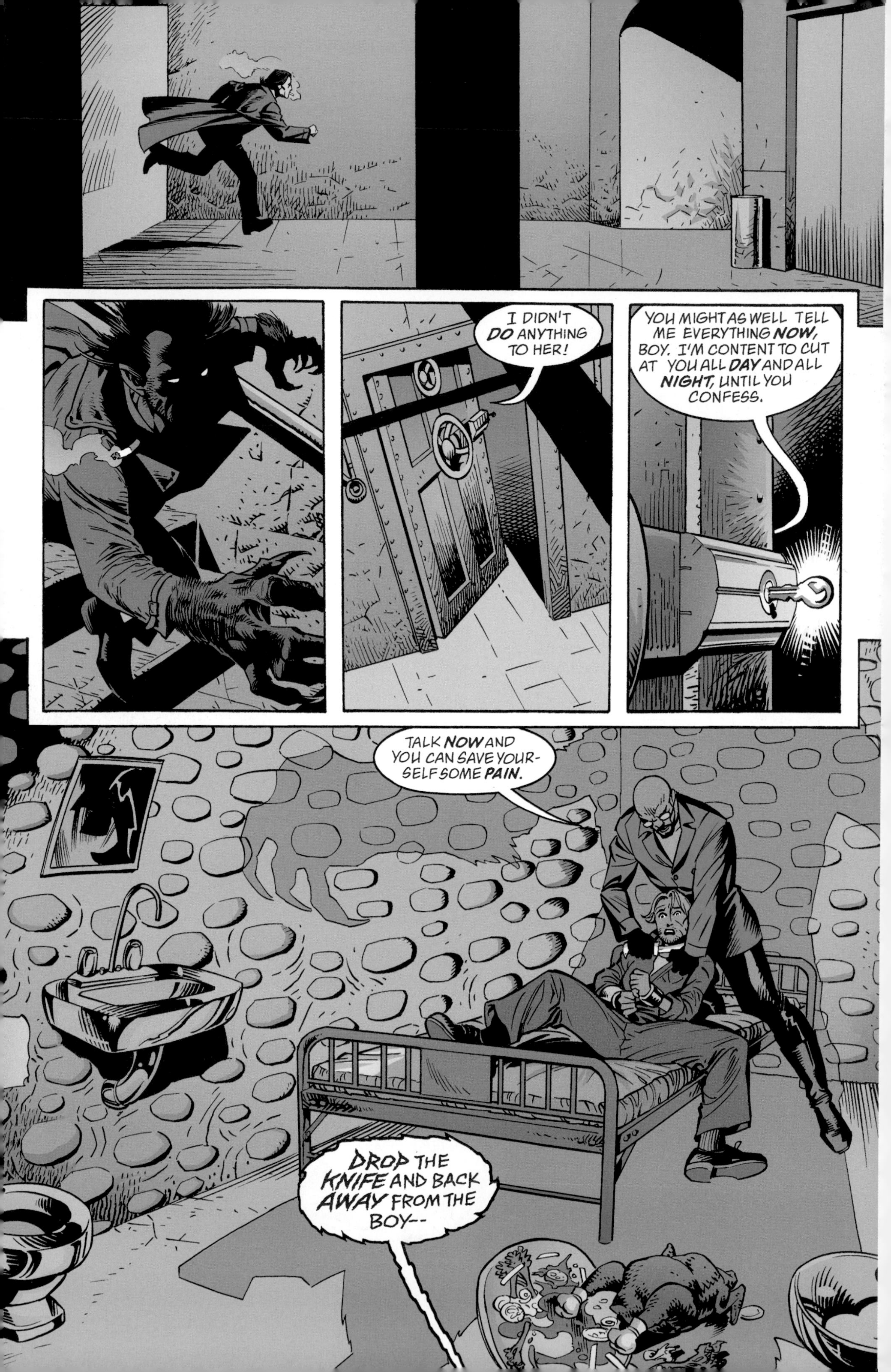

I DIDN'T DO ANYTHING TO HER!
YOU MIGHT AS WELL TELL ME EVERYTHING NOW, BOY. I'M CONTENT TO CUT AT YOU ALL DAY AND ALL NIGHT, UNTIL YOU CONFESS.
TALK NOW AND YOU CAN SAVE YOURSELF SOME PAIN.
DROP THE KNIFE AND BACK AWAY FROM THE BOY--

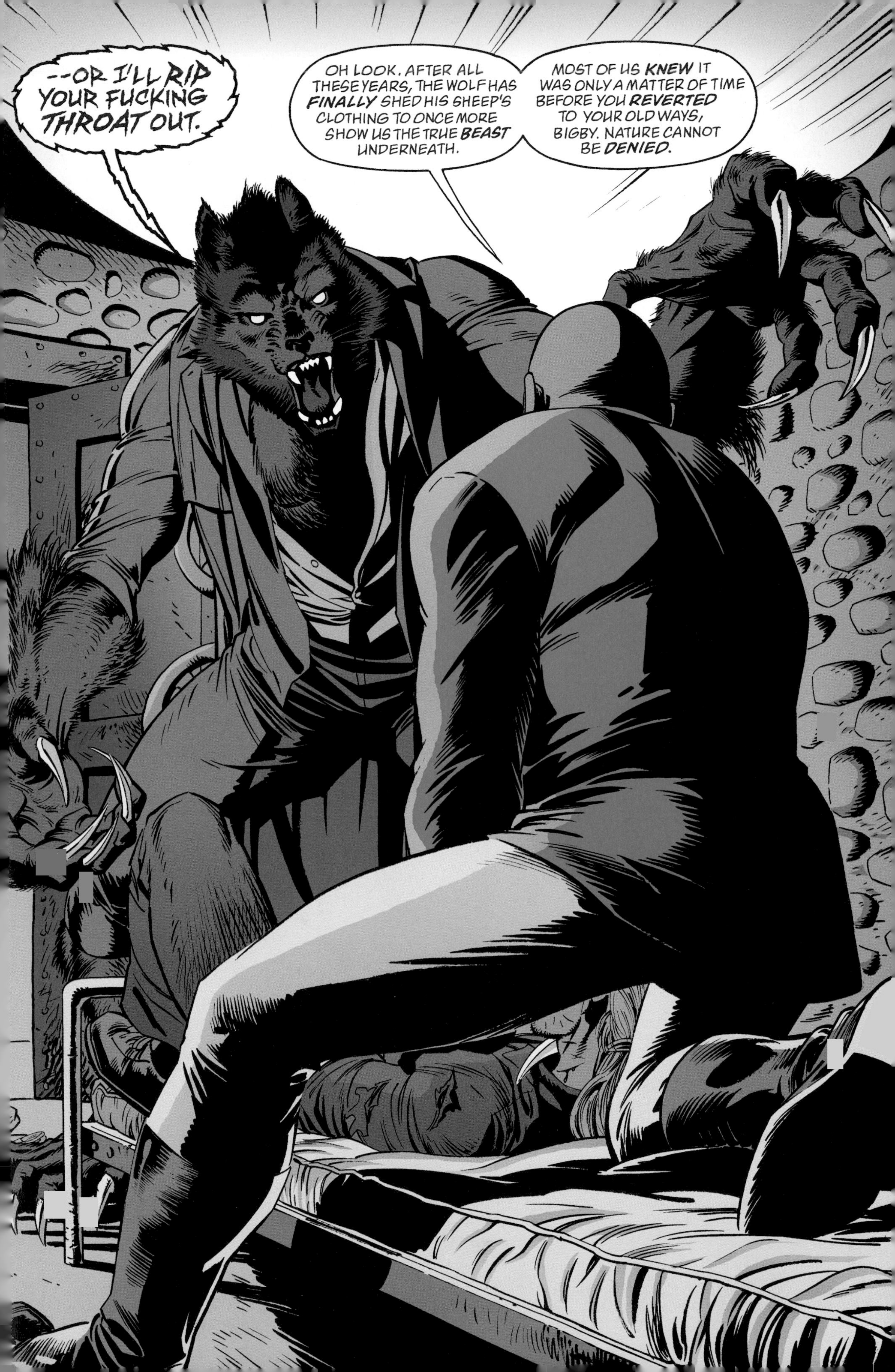
--OR I'LL RIP YOUR FUCKING THROAT OUT.
OH LOOK. AFTER ALL THESE YEARS, THE WOLF HAS FINALLY SHED HIS SHEEP'S CLOTHING TO ONCE MORE SHOW US THE TRUE BEAST UNDERNEATH.
MOST OF US KNEW IT WAS ONLY A MATTER OF TIME BEFORE YOU REVERTED TO YOUR OLD WAYS, BIGBY. NATURE CANNOT BE DENIED.

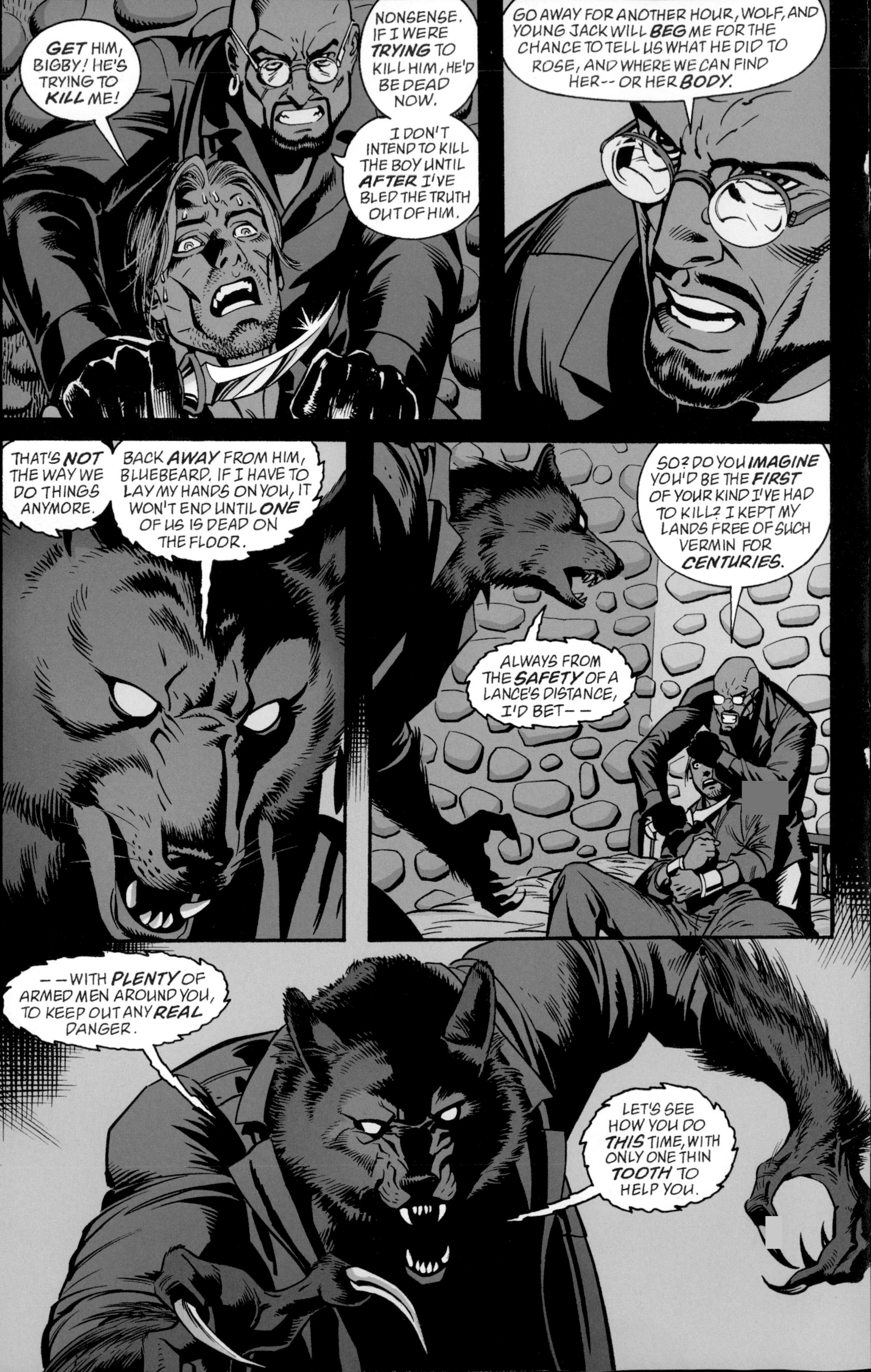
GET HIM, BIGBY! HE'S TRYING TO KILL ME!
NONSENSE. IF I WERE TRYING TO KILL HIM, HE'D BE DEAD NOW.
I DON'T INTEND TO KILL THE BOY UNTIL AFTER I'VE BLED THE TRUTH OUT OF HIM.
GO AWAY FOR ANOTHER HOUR, WOLF, AND YOUNG JACK WILL BEG ME FOR THE CHANCE TO TELL US WHAT HE DID TO ROSE, AND WHERE WE CAN FIND HER-- OR HER BODY.
THAT'S NOT THE WAY WE DO THINGS ANYMORE.
BACK AWAY FROM HIM, BLUEBEARD. IF I HAVE TO LAY MY HANDS ON YOU, IT WON'T END UNTIL ONE OF US IS DEAD ON THE FLOOR.
SO? DO YOU IMAGINE YOU'D BE THE FIRST OF YOUR KIND I'VE HAD TO KILL? I KEPT MY LANDS FREE OF SUCH VERMIN FOR CENTURIES.
ALWAYS FROM THE SAFETY OF A LANCE'S DISTANCE, I'D BET--
--WITH PLENTY OF ARMED MEN AROUND YOU, TO KEEP OUT ANY REAL DANGER.
LET'S SEE HOW YOU DO THIS TIME, WITH ONLY ONE THIN TOOTH TO HELP YOU.

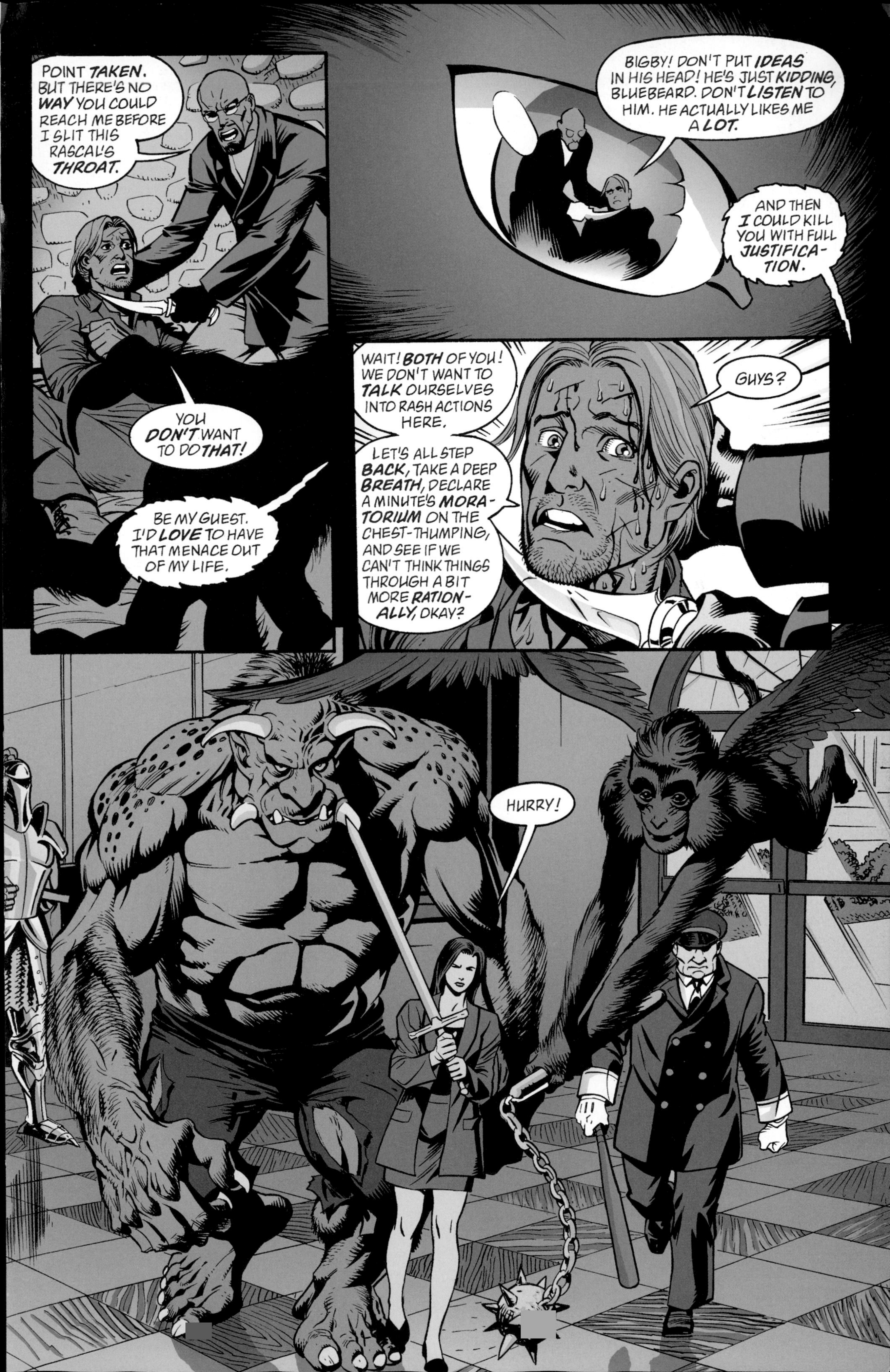
POINT TAKEN. BUT THERE'S NO WAY YOU COULD REACH ME BEFORE I SLIT THIS RASCAL'S THROAT.
BIGBY! DON'T PUT IDEAS IN HIS HEAD! HE'S JUST KIDDING, BLUEBEARD. DON'T LISTEN TO HIM. HE ACTUALLY LIKES ME A LOT.
AND THEN I COULD KILL YOU WITH FULL JUSTIFICATION.
YOU DON'T WANT TO DO THAT!
BE MY GUEST. I'D LOVE TO HAVE THAT MENACE OUT OF MY LIFE.
WAIT! BOTH OF YOU! WE DON'T WANT TO TALK OURSELVES INTO RASH ACTIONS HERE.
LET'S ALL STEP BACK, TAKE A DEEP BREATH, DECLARE A MINUTE'S MORATORIUM ON THE CHEST-THUMPING, AND SEE IF WE CAN'T THINK THINGS THROUGH A BIT MORE RATIONALLY, OKAY?
GUYS?
HURRY!

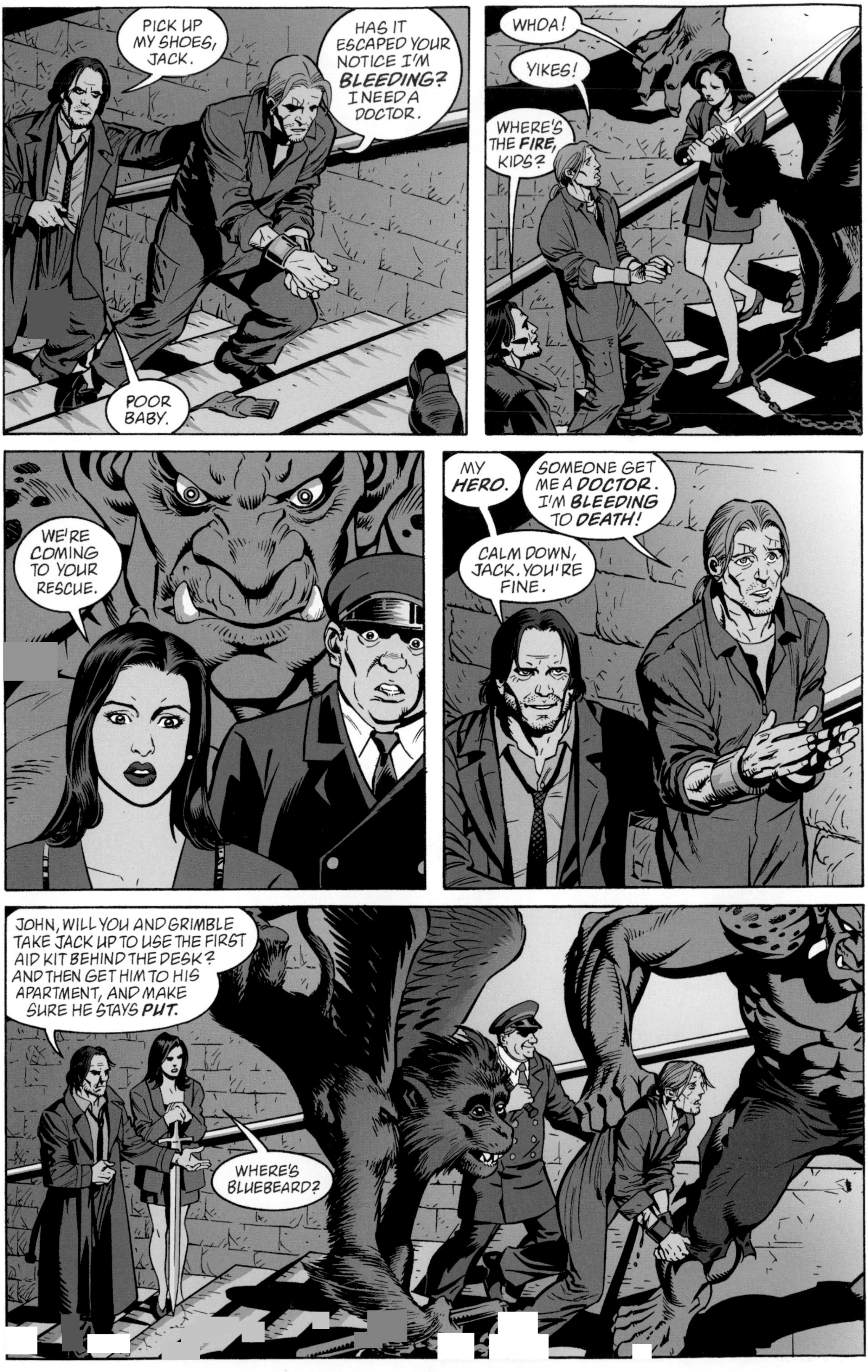
PICK UP MY SHOES, JACK.
HAS IT ESCAPED YOUR NOTICE I'M BLEEDING? I NEED A DOCTOR.
POOR BABY.
WHOA!
YIKES!
WHERE'S THE FIRE, KIDS?
WE'RE COMING TO YOUR RESCUE.
MY HERO.
SOMEONE GET ME A DOCTOR. I'M BLEEDING TO DEATH!
CALM DOWN, JACK. YOU'RE FINE.
JOHN, WILL YOU AND GRIMBLE TAKE JACK UP TO USE THE FIRST AID KIT BEHIND THE DESK? AND THEN GET HIM TO HIS APARTMENT, AND MAKE SURE HE STAYS PUT.
WHERE'S BLUEBEARD?

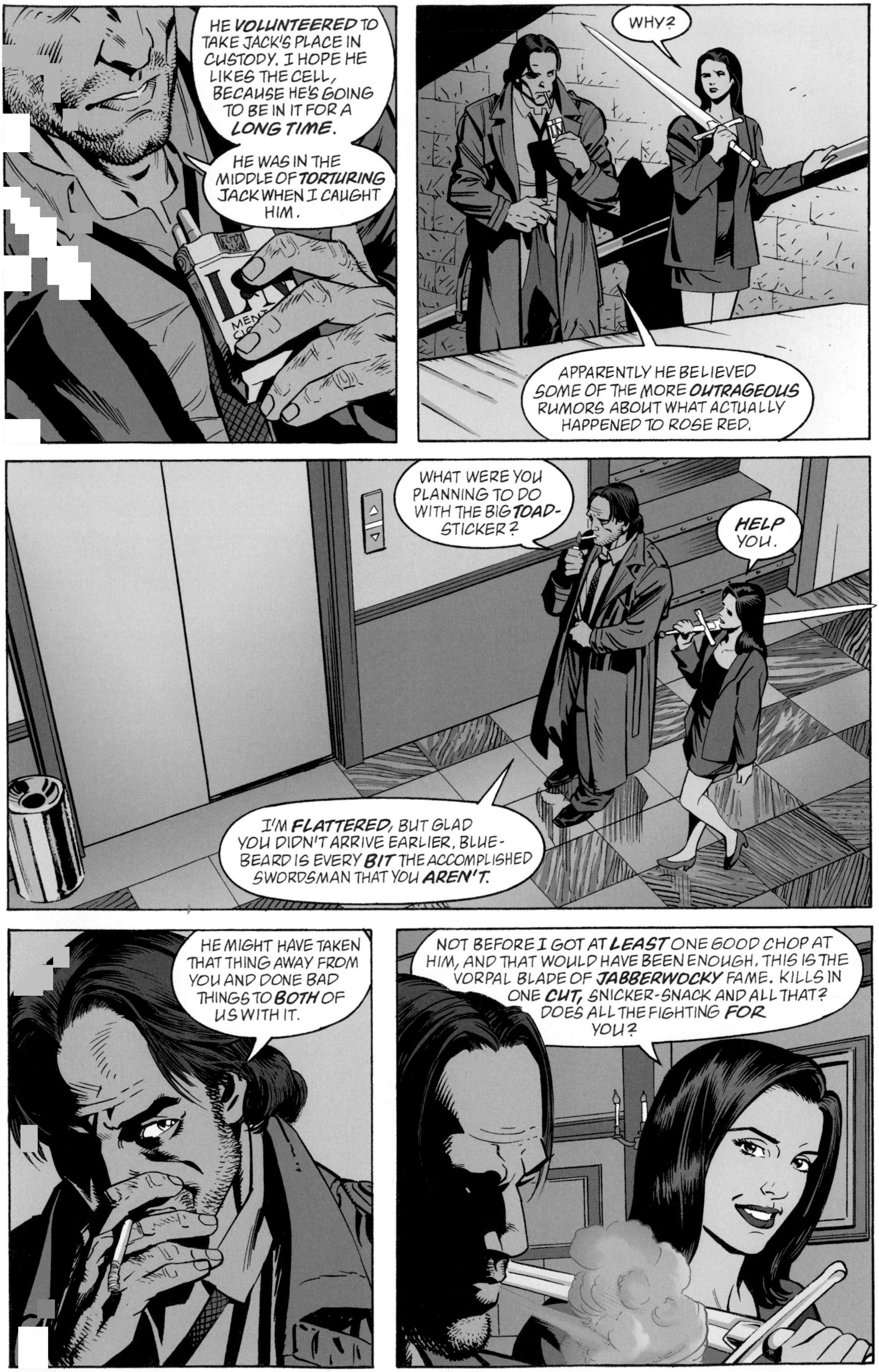
HE VOLUNTEERED TO TAKE JACK'S PLACE IN CUSTODY. I HOPE HE LIKES THE CELL, BECAUSE HE'S GOING TO BE IN IT FOR A LONG TIME.
HE WAS IN THE MIDDLE OF TORTURING JACK WHEN I CAUGHT HIM.
WHY?
APPARENTLY HE BELIEVED SOME OF THE MORE OUTRAGEOUS RUMORS ABOUT WHAT ACTUALLY HAPPENED TO ROSE RED.
WHAT WERE YOU PLANNING TO DO WITH THE BIG TOAD-STICKER?
HELP YOU.
I'M FLATTERED, BUT GLAD YOU DIDN'T ARRIVE EARLIER. BLUE-BEARD IS EVERY BIT THE ACCOMPLISHED SWORDSMAN THAT YOU AREN'T.
HE MIGHT HAVE TAKEN THAT THING AWAY FROM YOU AND DONE BAD THINGS TO BOTH OF US WITH IT.
NOT BEFORE I GOT AT LEAST ONE GOOD CHOP AT HIM, AND THAT WOULD HAVE BEEN ENOUGH. THIS IS THE VORPAL BLADE OF JABBERWOCKY FAME. KILLS IN ONE CUT, SNICKER-SNACK AND ALL THAT? DOES ALL THE FIGHTING FOR YOU?

OH JOY, THEN DON'T *CARRY* IT THAT WAY, OR YOU'RE LIKELY TO CUT YOUR *OWN* HEAD OFF. I NEED YOU TO BE IN ONE PIECE FOR THE BIG PARTY NEXT WEEK.

EXCUSE ME?

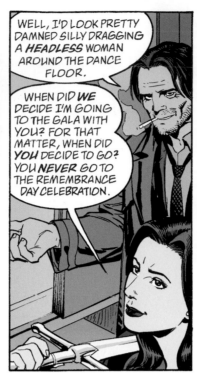

WELL, I'D LOOK PRETTY DAMNED SILLY DRAGGING A *HEADLESS* WOMAN AROUND THE DANCE FLOOR.

WHEN DID *WE* DECIDE I'M GOING TO THE GALA WITH YOU? FOR THAT MATTER, WHEN DID *YOU* DECIDE TO GO? YOU *NEVER* GO TO THE REMEMBRANCE DAY CELEBRATION.

I CAN'T AVOID IT THIS YEAR. IF THERE'S *ANY* CHANCE TO WORK EVERYTHING OUT, I NEED TO BE THERE AND *YOU* HAVE TO GO AS MY *DATE*.

IT'S ALL VERY COMPLICATED AND I CAN'T EXPLAIN IT YET, SO JUST GO ALONG.

NOW, IF YOU'LL *EXCUSE* ME, I HAVE TO GO HOME AND CHANGE.

RINNNG RINNNG

KEEP YOUR *PANTS* ON! I'M *COMING!*

HELLO?

ZZZZZ

WHAT? OH YEAH. SORRY. I'VE BEEN OUT OF TOUCH FOR MOST OF THE DAY.

WHAT DID YOU FIND OUT? OH. OKAY.

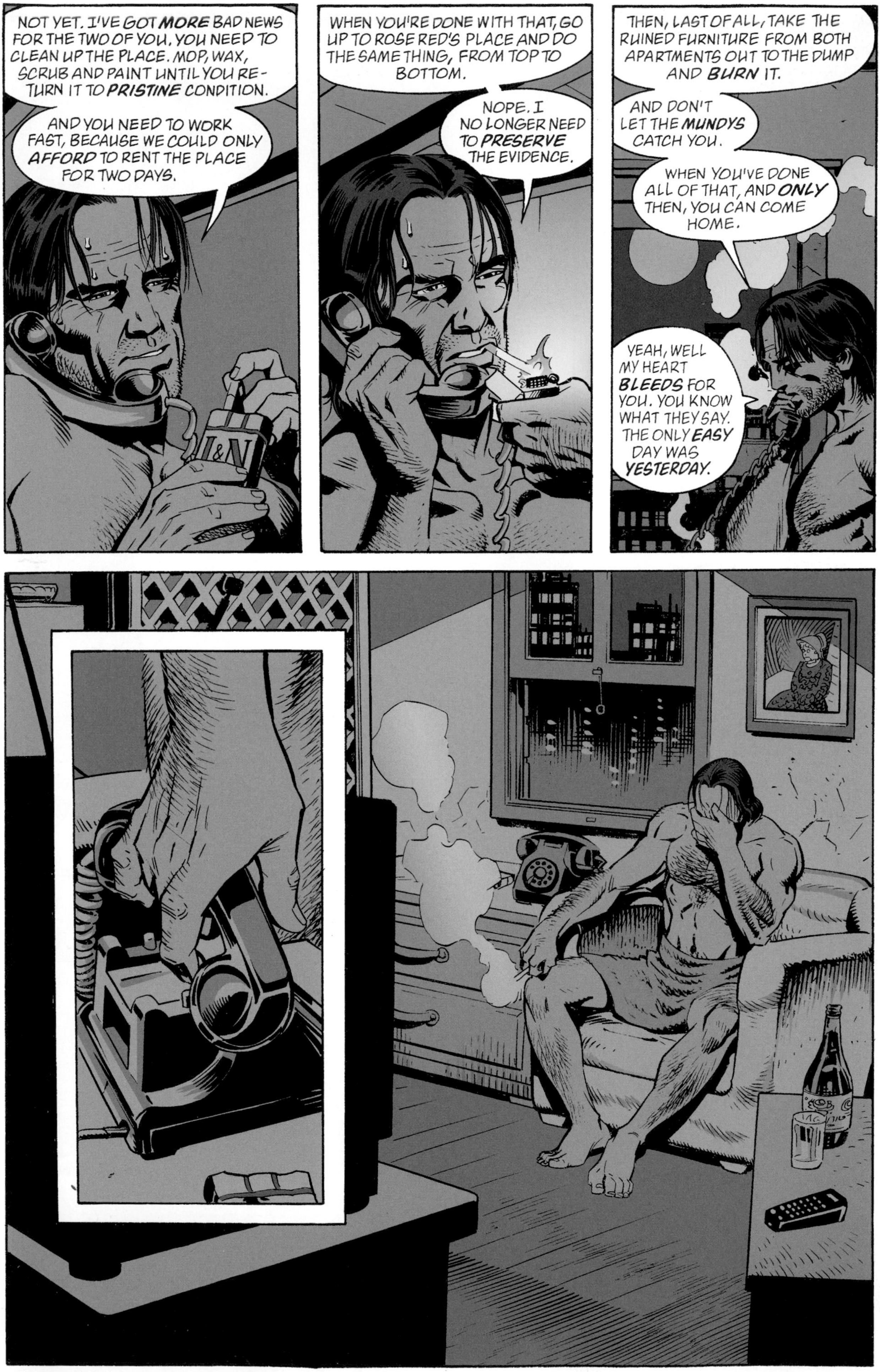
NOT YET. I'VE GOT MORE BAD NEWS FOR THE TWO OF YOU. YOU NEED TO CLEAN UP THE PLACE. MOP, WAX, SCRUB AND PAINT UNTIL YOU RETURN IT TO PRISTINE CONDITION.
AND YOU NEED TO WORK FAST, BECAUSE WE COULD ONLY AFFORD TO RENT THE PLACE FOR TWO DAYS.
WHEN YOU'RE DONE WITH THAT, GO UP TO ROSE RED'S PLACE AND DO THE SAME THING, FROM TOP TO BOTTOM.
NOPE. I NO LONGER NEED TO PRESERVE THE EVIDENCE.
THEN, LAST OF ALL, TAKE THE RUINED FURNITURE FROM BOTH APARTMENTS OUT TO THE DUMP AND BURN IT.
AND DON'T LET THE MUNDYS CATCH YOU.
WHEN YOU'VE DONE ALL OF THAT, AND ONLY THEN, YOU CAN COME HOME.
YEAH, WELL MY HEART BLEEDS FOR YOU. YOU KNOW WHAT THEY SAY. THE ONLY EASY DAY WAS YESTERDAY.

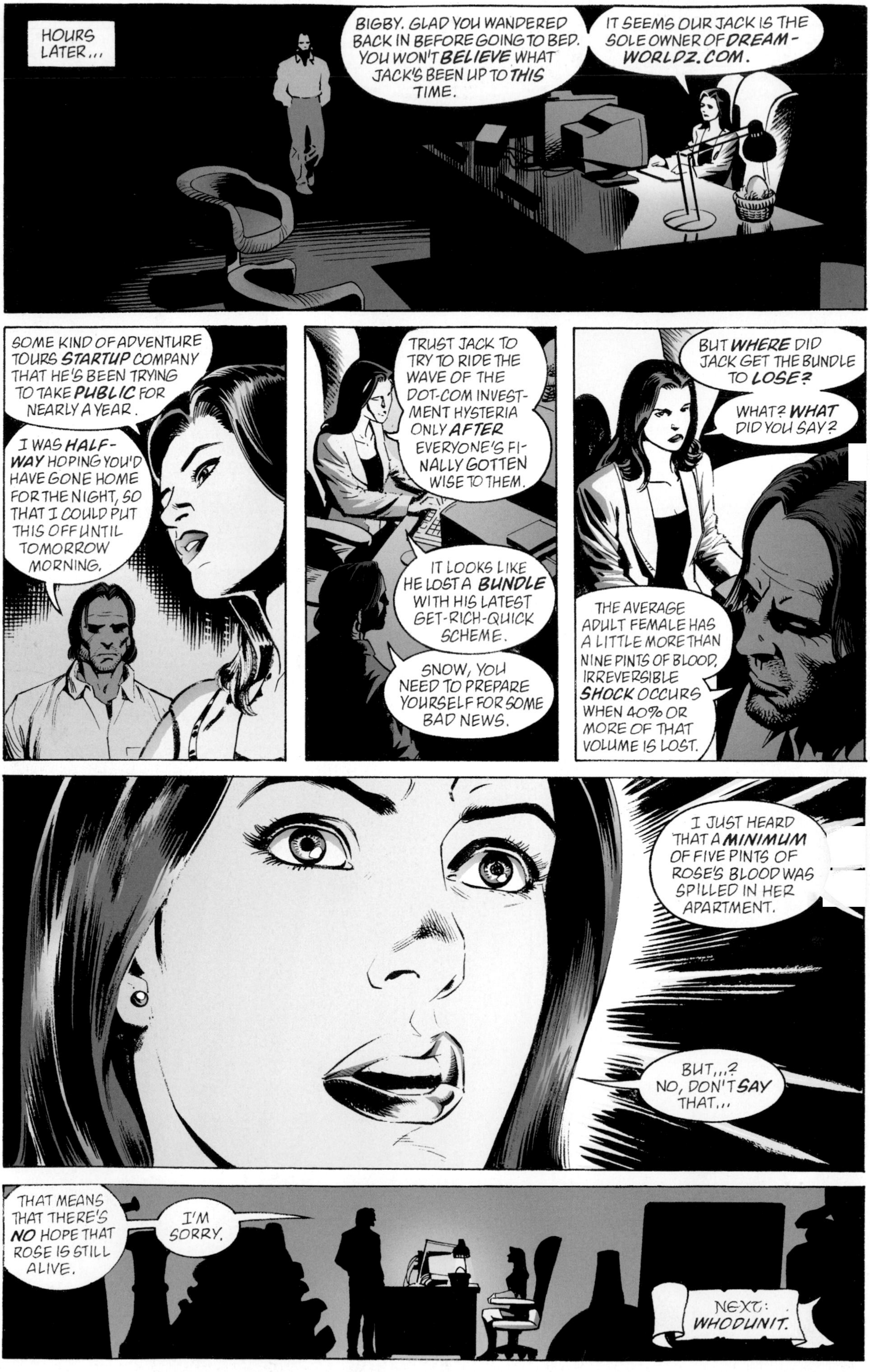
HOURS LATER...
BIGBY. GLAD YOU WANDERED BACK IN BEFORE GOING TO BED. YOU WON'T BELIEVE WHAT JACK'S BEEN UP TO THIS TIME.
IT SEEMS OUR JACK IS THE SOLE OWNER OF DREAM-WORLDZ.COM.
SOME KIND OF ADVENTURE TOURS STARTUP COMPANY THAT HE'S BEEN TRYING TO TAKE PUBLIC FOR NEARLY A YEAR.
I WAS HALF-WAY HOPING YOU'D HAVE GONE HOME FOR THE NIGHT, SO THAT I COULD PUT THIS OFF UNTIL TOMORROW MORNING.
TRUST JACK TO TRY TO RIDE THE WAVE OF THE DOT-COM INVEST-MENT HYSTERIA ONLY AFTER EVERYONE'S FI-NALLY GOTTEN WISE TO THEM.
IT LOOKS LIKE HE LOST A BUNDLE WITH HIS LATEST GET-RICH-QUICK SCHEME.
SNOW, YOU NEED TO PREPARE YOURSELF FOR SOME BAD NEWS.
BUT WHERE DID JACK GET THE BUNDLE TO LOSE?
WHAT? WHAT DID YOU SAY?
THE AVERAGE ADULT FEMALE HAS A LITTLE MORE THAN NINE PINTS OF BLOOD. IRREVERSIBLE SHOCK OCCURS WHEN 40% OR MORE OF THAT VOLUME IS LOST.
I JUST HEARD THAT A MINIMUM OF FIVE PINTS OF ROSE'S BLOOD WAS SPILLED IN HER APARTMENT.
BUT...? NO, DON'T SAY THAT...
THAT MEANS THAT THERE'S NO HOPE THAT ROSE IS STILL ALIVE.
I'M SORRY.
NEXT: WHODUNIT.

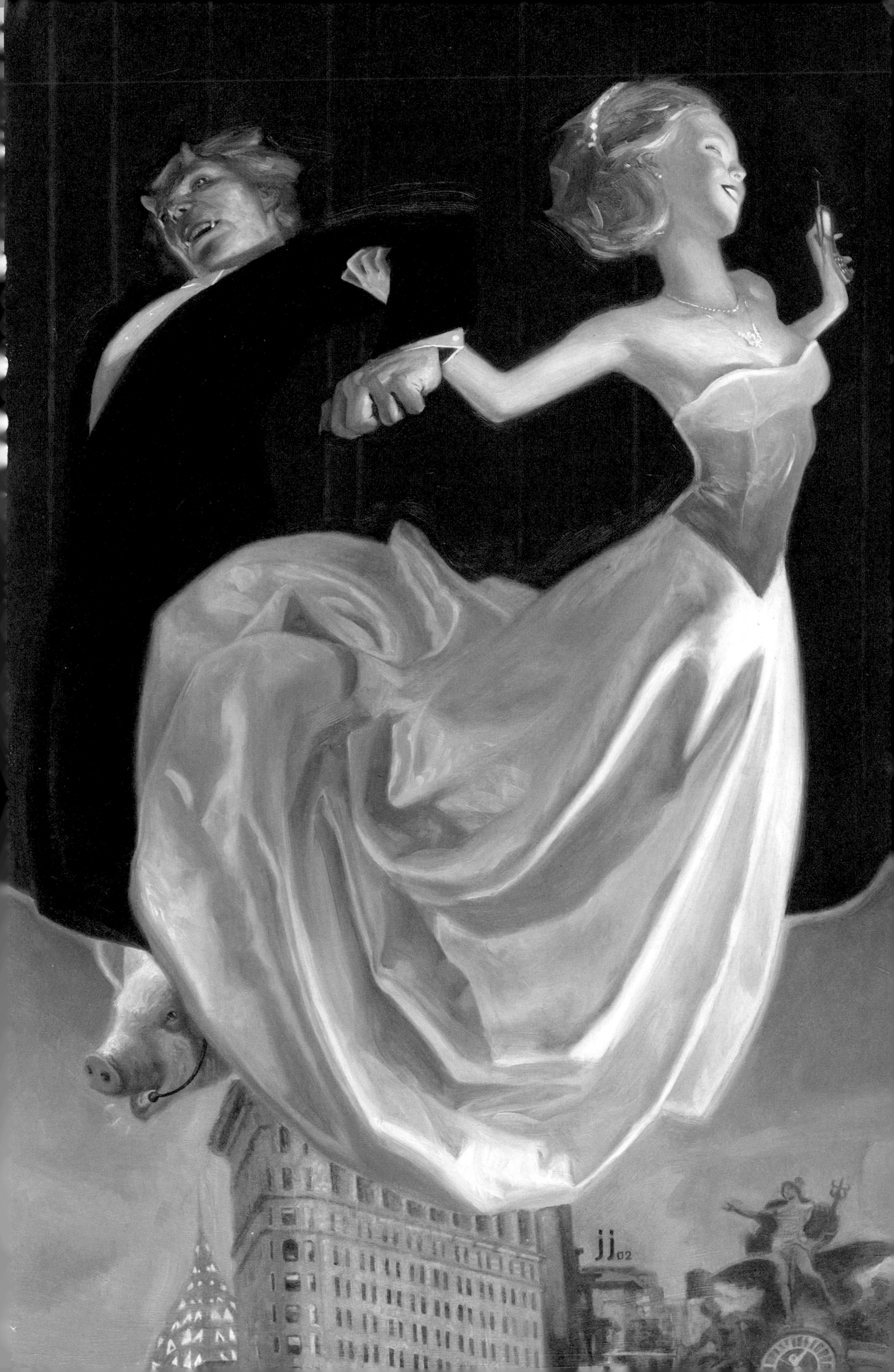

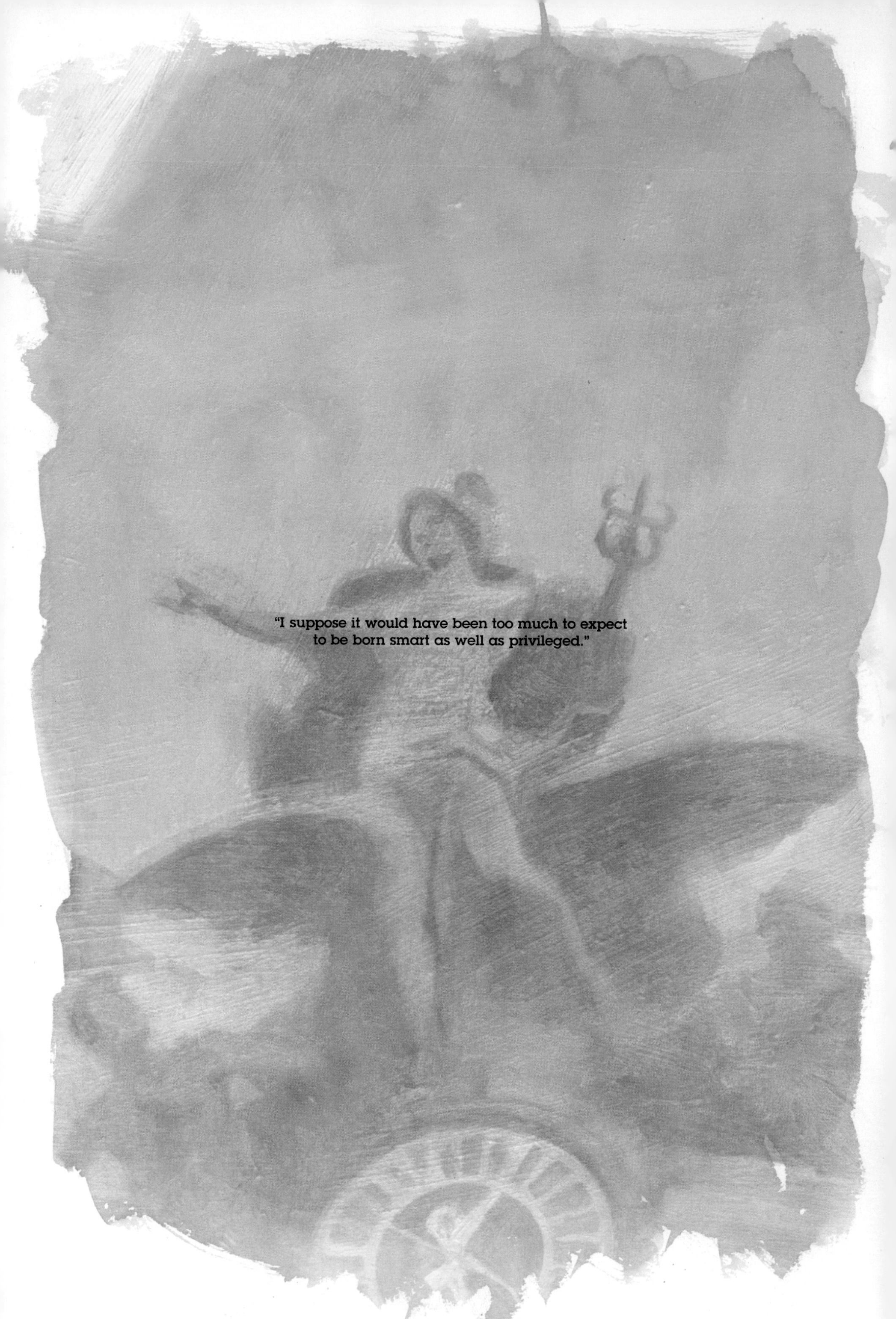
"I suppose it would have been too much to expect to be born smart as well as privileged."

AND JUST LIKE THAT, THE BIG DAY ARRIVED.

FABLETOWN'S GRANDEST EVENT OF THE YEAR, LIKE CHRISTMAS AND FOURTH OF JULY MULTIPLIED MANY TIMES OVER.

CHAPTER FOUR: REMEMBRANCE DAY

In which everyone dresses up to the nines, old stories are retold and the wolf takes a swim.

| Written by | Pencilled by | Inked by |
| Bill Willingham | Lan Medina | Craig Hamilton |

| Lettered by | Colored by Sherilyn | Separated |
| Todd Klein | van Valkenburgh | by Zylonol |

| Cover art by | Assistant Editor | Editor |
| James Jean | Mariah Huehner | Shelly Bond |

FABLES is created by Bill Willingham

AT THE FRONT DOOR BY TWILIGHT.

AS **PROMISED,** MY LOVE.

LADY BEAUTY, LORD BEAST, HOW **GRAND** YOU BOTH LOOK TONIGHT. AND I'LL BE A ROGUE IF YOU DON'T LOOK COMPLETELY **HUMAN** AGAIN, SIR. CONGRATULATIONS.

IT'S MY WIFE'S FAULT. SHE LOVES EVERYTHING ABOUT THIS DAY--INCLUDING **ME,** IT SEEMS--ENOUGH TO MAKE ME **HANDSOME** AGAIN.

DON'T START.

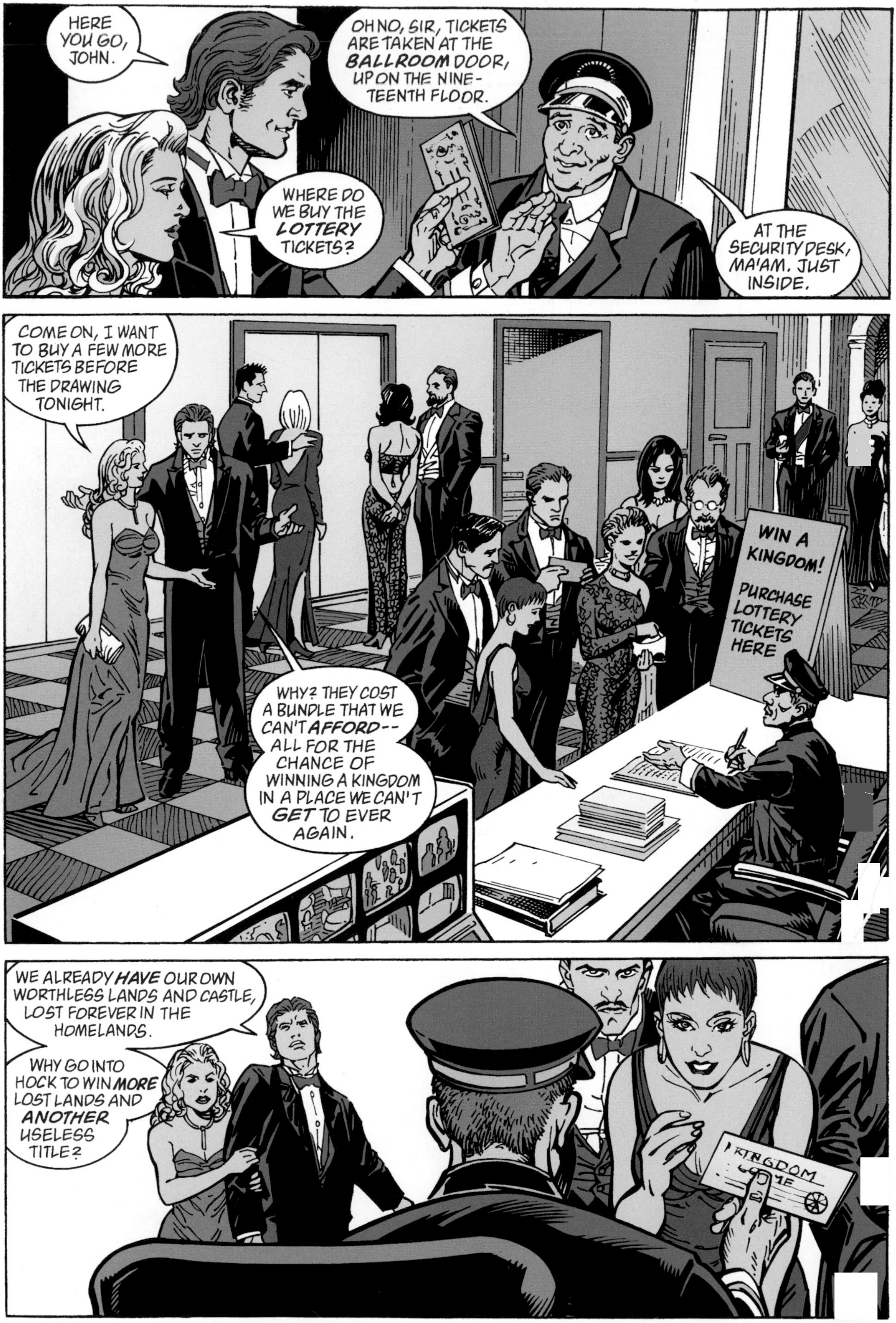
HERE YOU GO, JOHN.
OH NO, SIR, TICKETS ARE TAKEN AT THE BALLROOM DOOR, UP ON THE NINE-TEENTH FLOOR.
WHERE DO WE BUY THE LOTTERY TICKETS?
AT THE SECURITY DESK, MA'AM. JUST INSIDE.
COME ON, I WANT TO BUY A FEW MORE TICKETS BEFORE THE DRAWING TONIGHT.
WIN A KINGDOM!
PURCHASE LOTTERY TICKETS HERE
WHY? THEY COST A BUNDLE THAT WE CAN'T AFFORD-- ALL FOR THE CHANCE OF WINNING A KINGDOM IN A PLACE WE CAN'T GET TO EVER AGAIN.
WE ALREADY HAVE OUR OWN WORTHLESS LANDS AND CASTLE, LOST FOREVER IN THE HOMELANDS.
WHY GO INTO HOCK TO WIN MORE LOST LANDS AND ANOTHER USELESS TITLE?

BECAUSE THEY WERE *YOUR* LANDS AND *YOUR* TITLE. I WAS JUST A PEASANT GIRL WHO *MARRIED* INTO MONEY. I WANT SOMETHING OF MY *OWN*.

IF I WIN, I'LL BE A PRINCESS IN MY OWN RIGHT.

BUT STILL WORKING FOR MINIMUM WAGE IN A *BOOKSTORE*.

DON'T *SPOIL* THE EVENING, DARLING.

A HUNDRED DOLLARS A TICKET, BUT FIFTY DOLLARS *OFF* IF YOU BUY FIVE AT A TIME.

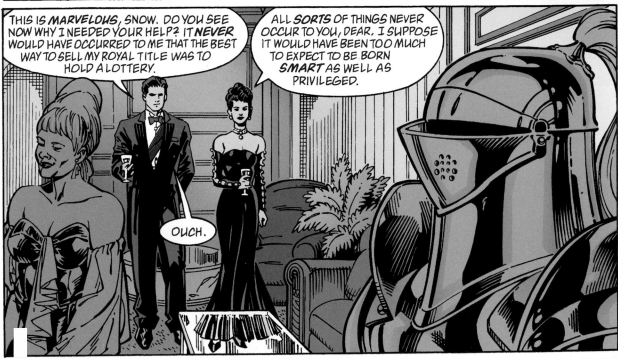

THIS IS *MARVELOUS*, SNOW. DO YOU SEE NOW WHY I NEEDED YOUR HELP? IT *NEVER* WOULD HAVE OCCURRED TO ME THAT THE BEST WAY TO SELL MY ROYAL TITLE WAS TO HOLD A LOTTERY.

ALL *SORTS* OF THINGS NEVER OCCUR TO YOU, DEAR. I SUPPOSE IT WOULD HAVE BEEN TOO MUCH TO EXPECT TO BE BORN *SMART* AS WELL AS PRIVILEGED.

OUCH.

HOW MUCH HAVE WE MADE SO FAR?

AS OF THIS MORNING, WE WERE CLOSING IN ON THREE HUNDRED *GRAND*, BUT SALES HAVE PICKED UP TODAY. I'D BE SURPRISED IF WE HAVEN'T *DOUBLED* THAT AMOUNT BY NOW.

LOVELY. WHO WOULD HAVE THOUGHT THAT SO *MANY* WOULD WILLINGLY SPEND SO *MUCH* FOR A SLIGHT CHANCE TO WIN ABSOLUTELY *NOTHING* OF SUBSTANCE?

NO WONDER THEY CALL LOTTERIES *TAXES* ON STUPID PEOPLE.

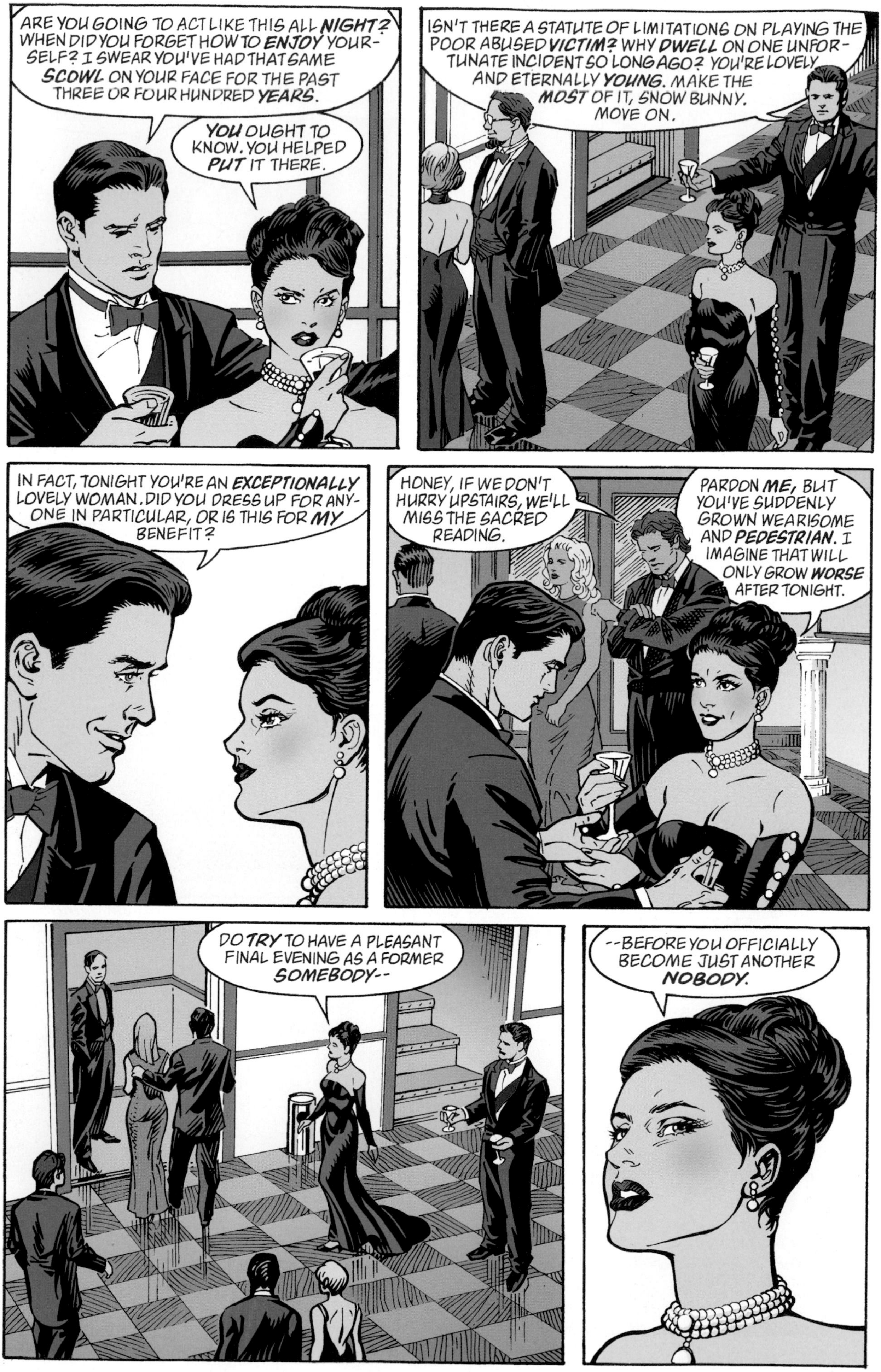
ARE YOU GOING TO ACT LIKE THIS ALL NIGHT? WHEN DID YOU FORGET HOW TO ENJOY YOURSELF? I SWEAR YOU'VE HAD THAT SAME SCOWL ON YOUR FACE FOR THE PAST THREE OR FOUR HUNDRED YEARS.
YOU OUGHT TO KNOW. YOU HELPED PUT IT THERE.
ISN'T THERE A STATUTE OF LIMITATIONS ON PLAYING THE POOR ABUSED VICTIM? WHY DWELL ON ONE UNFORTUNATE INCIDENT SO LONG AGO? YOU'RE LOVELY AND ETERNALLY YOUNG. MAKE THE MOST OF IT, SNOW BUNNY. MOVE ON.
IN FACT, TONIGHT YOU'RE AN EXCEPTIONALLY LOVELY WOMAN. DID YOU DRESS UP FOR ANYONE IN PARTICULAR, OR IS THIS FOR MY BENEFIT?
HONEY, IF WE DON'T HURRY UPSTAIRS, WE'LL MISS THE SACRED READING.
PARDON ME, BUT YOU'VE SUDDENLY GROWN WEARISOME AND PEDESTRIAN. I IMAGINE THAT WILL ONLY GROW WORSE AFTER TONIGHT.
DO TRY TO HAVE A PLEASANT FINAL EVENING AS A FORMER SOMEBODY--
--BEFORE YOU OFFICIALLY BECOME JUST ANOTHER NOBODY.

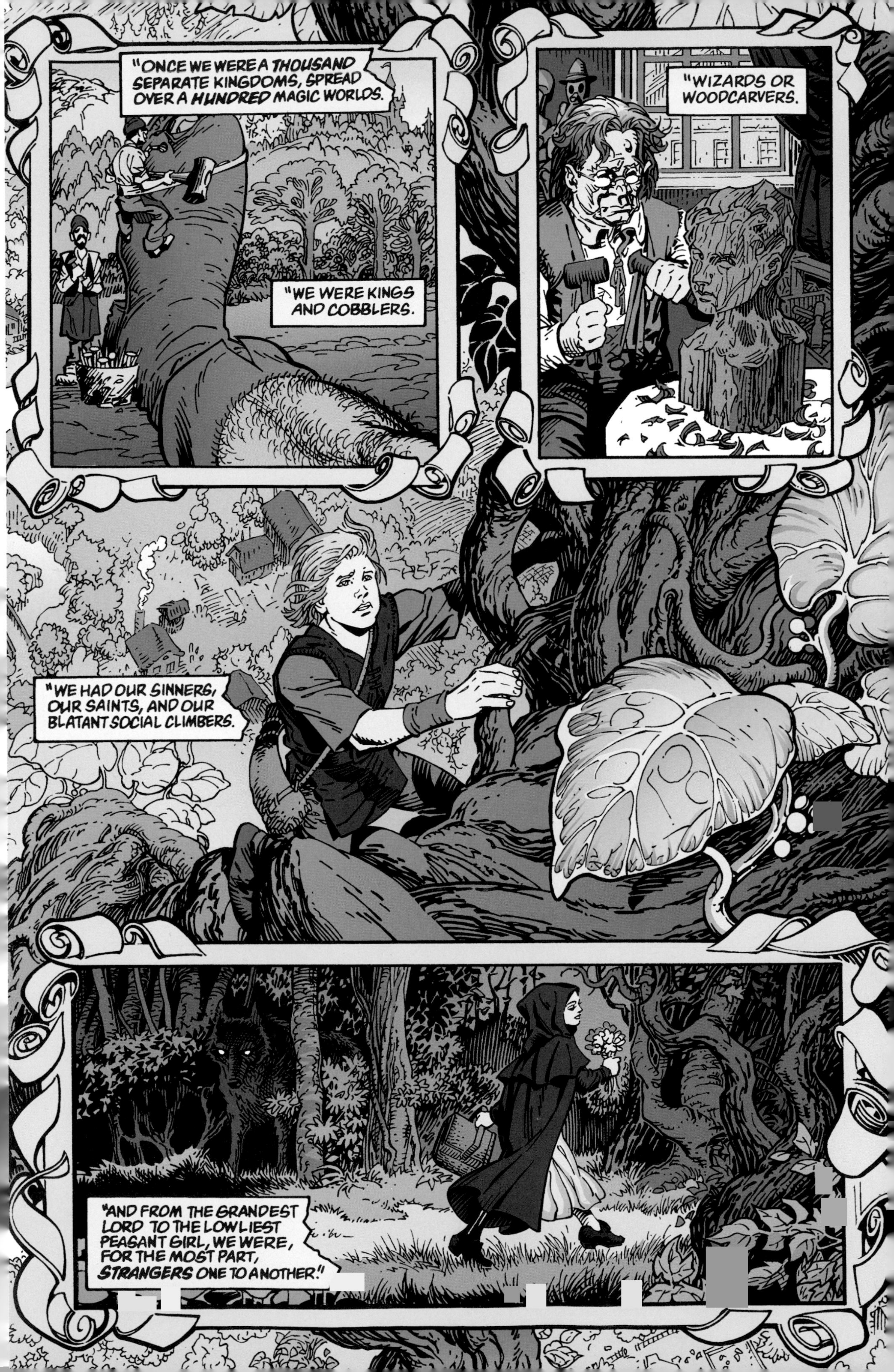

"ONCE WE WERE A THOUSAND SEPARATE KINGDOMS, SPREAD OVER A HUNDRED MAGIC WORLDS.
"WE WERE KINGS AND COBBLERS.
"WIZARDS OR WOODCARVERS.
"WE HAD OUR SINNERS, OUR SAINTS, AND OUR BLATANT SOCIAL CLIMBERS.
"AND FROM THE GRANDEST LORD TO THE LOWLIEST PEASANT GIRL, WE WERE, FOR THE MOST PART, STRANGERS ONE TO ANOTHER."

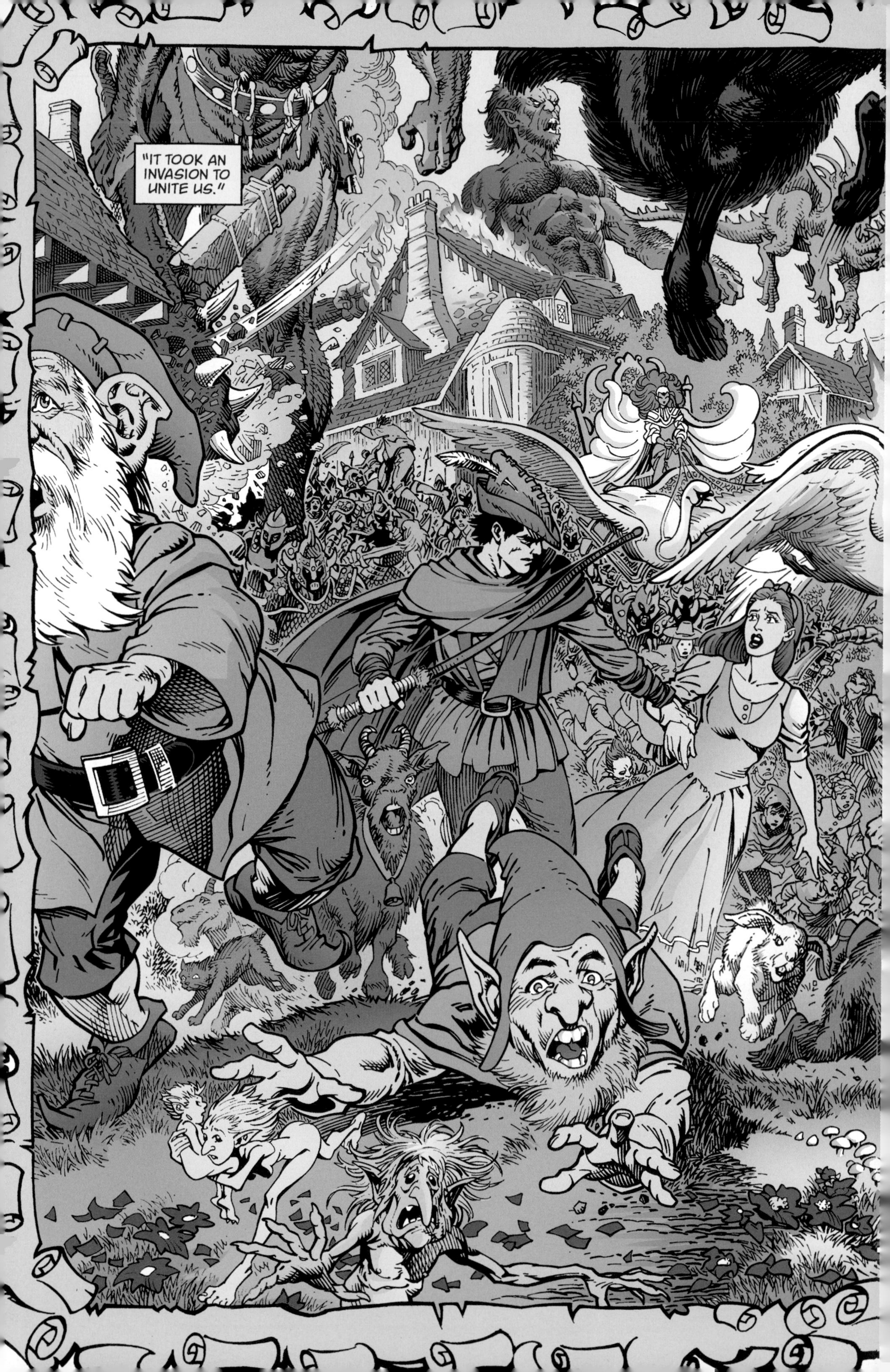
"IT TOOK AN INVASION TO UNITE US."

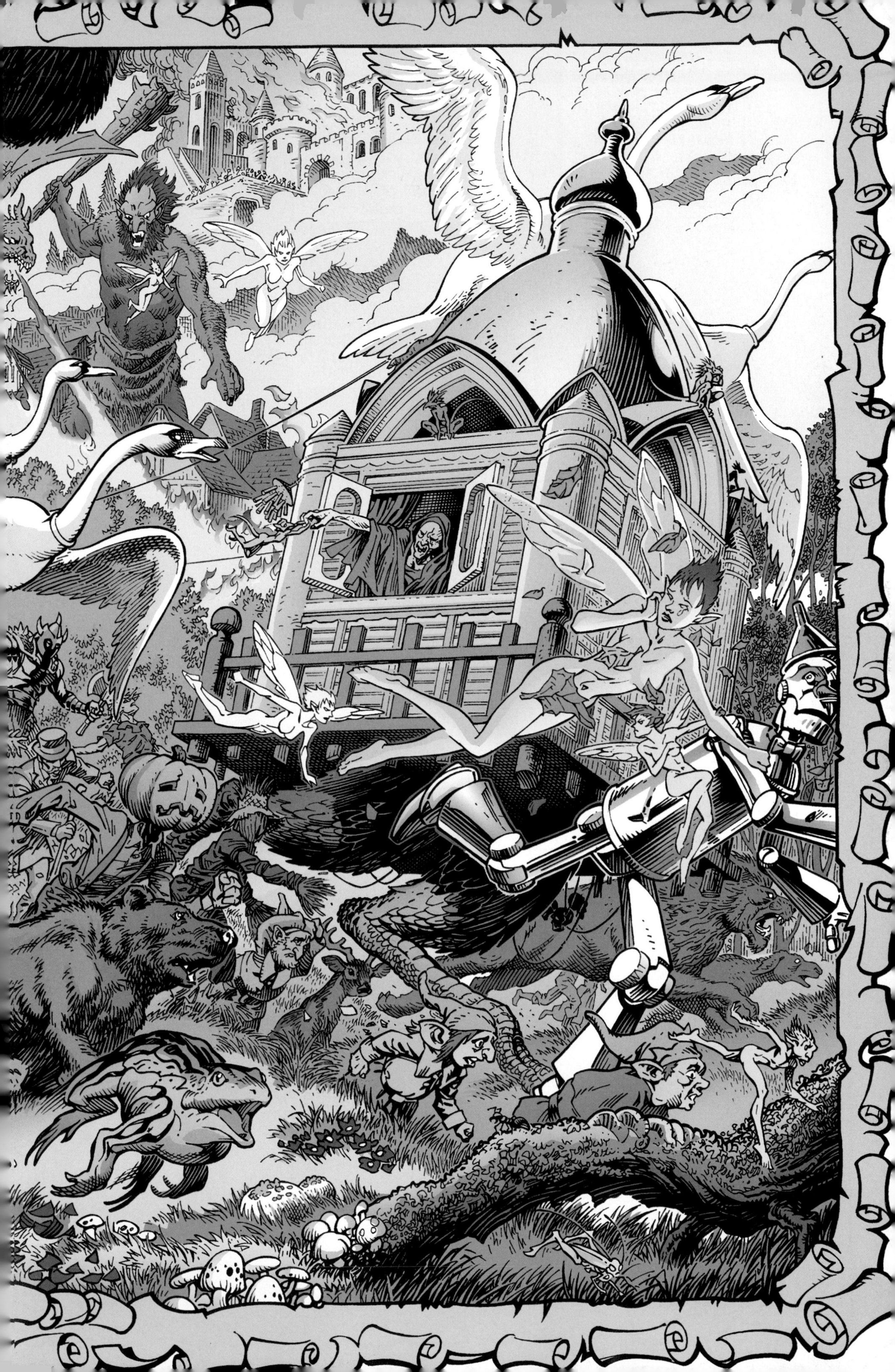

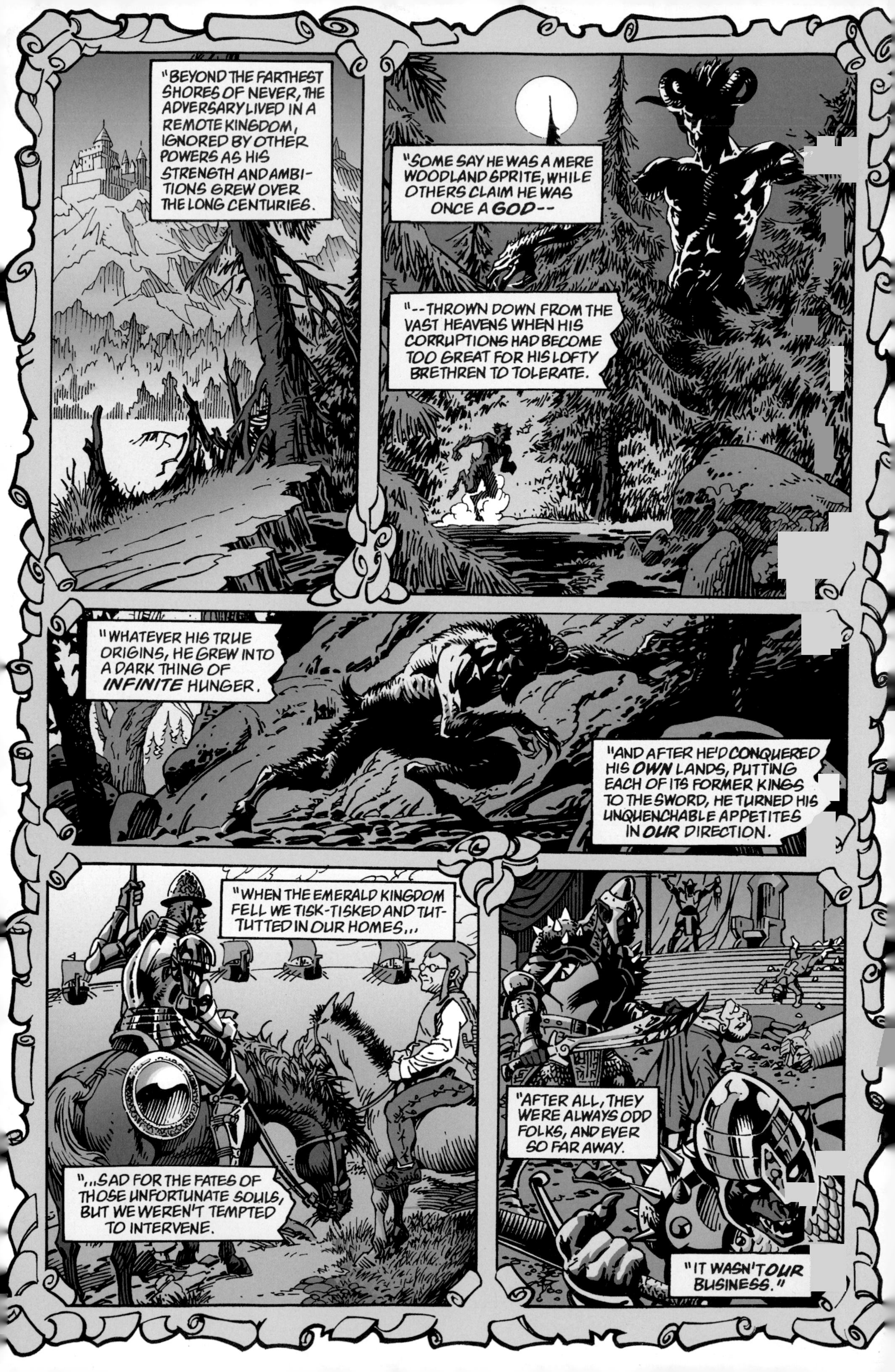
"BEYOND THE FARTHEST SHORES OF NEVER, THE ADVERSARY LIVED IN A REMOTE KINGDOM, IGNORED BY OTHER POWERS AS HIS STRENGTH AND AMBITIONS GREW OVER THE LONG CENTURIES.
"SOME SAY HE WAS A MERE WOODLAND SPRITE, WHILE OTHERS CLAIM HE WAS ONCE A GOD--
"--THROWN DOWN FROM THE VAST HEAVENS WHEN HIS CORRUPTIONS HAD BECOME TOO GREAT FOR HIS LOFTY BRETHREN TO TOLERATE.
"WHATEVER HIS TRUE ORIGINS, HE GREW INTO A DARK THING OF INFINITE HUNGER.
"AND AFTER HE'D CONQUERED HIS OWN LANDS, PUTTING EACH OF ITS FORMER KINGS TO THE SWORD, HE TURNED HIS UNQUENCHABLE APPETITES IN OUR DIRECTION.
"WHEN THE EMERALD KINGDOM FELL WE TISK-TISKED AND TUT-TUTTED IN OUR HOMES...
"...SAD FOR THE FATES OF THOSE UNFORTUNATE SOULS, BUT WE WEREN'T TEMPTED TO INTERVENE.
"AFTER ALL, THEY WERE ALWAYS ODD FOLKS, AND EVER SO FAR AWAY.
"IT WASN'T OUR BUSINESS."

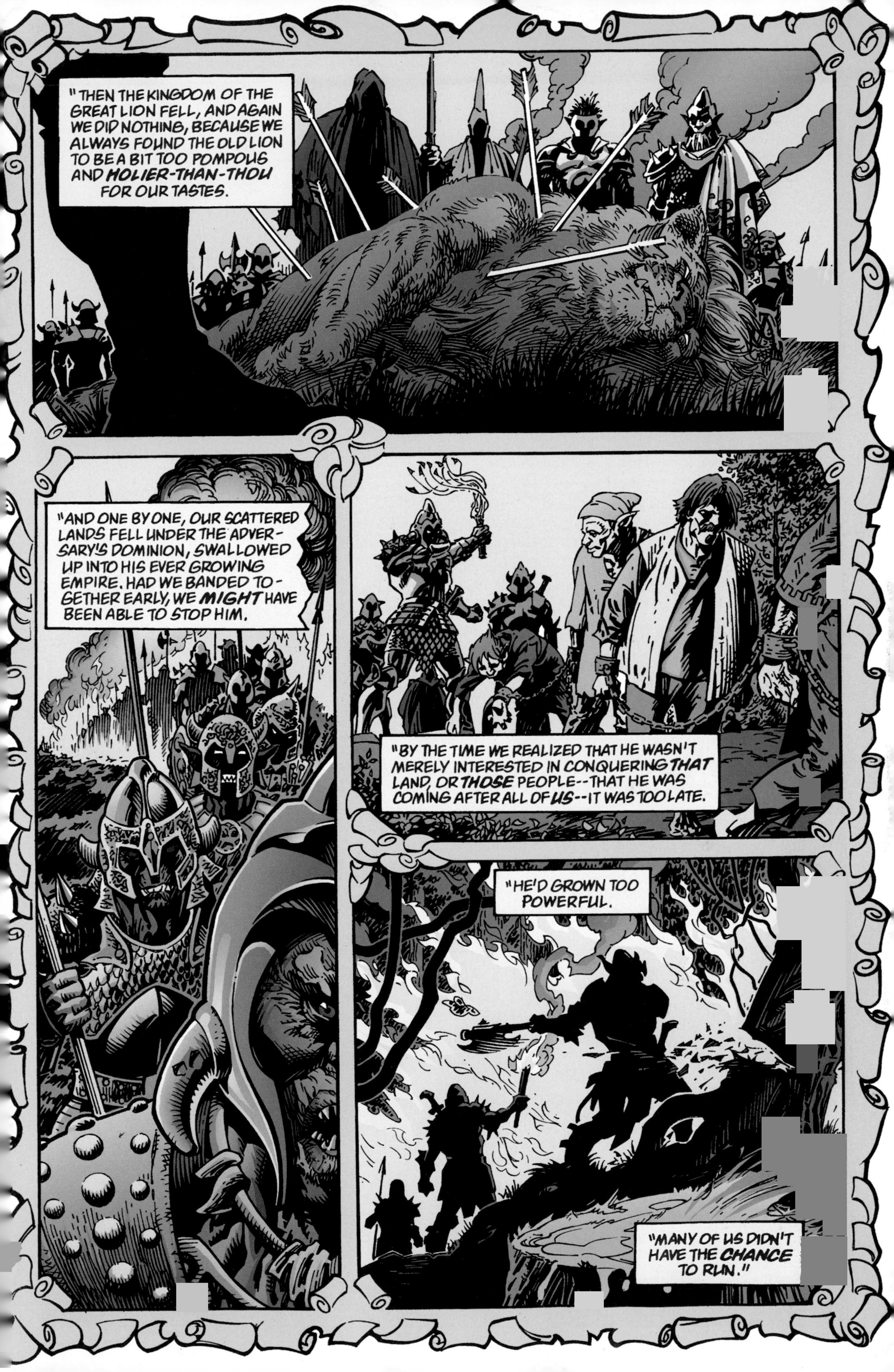
"THEN THE KINGDOM OF THE GREAT LION FELL, AND AGAIN WE DID NOTHING, BECAUSE WE ALWAYS FOUND THE OLD LION TO BE A BIT TOO POMPOUS AND HOLIER-THAN-THOU FOR OUR TASTES.
"AND ONE BY ONE, OUR SCATTERED LANDS FELL UNDER THE ADVERSARY'S DOMINION, SWALLOWED UP INTO HIS EVER GROWING EMPIRE. HAD WE BANDED TOGETHER EARLY, WE MIGHT HAVE BEEN ABLE TO STOP HIM.
"BY THE TIME WE REALIZED THAT HE WASN'T MERELY INTERESTED IN CONQUERING THAT LAND, OR THOSE PEOPLE--THAT HE WAS COMING AFTER ALL OF US--IT WAS TOO LATE.
"HE'D GROWN TOO POWERFUL.
"MANY OF US DIDN'T HAVE THE CHANCE TO RUN."

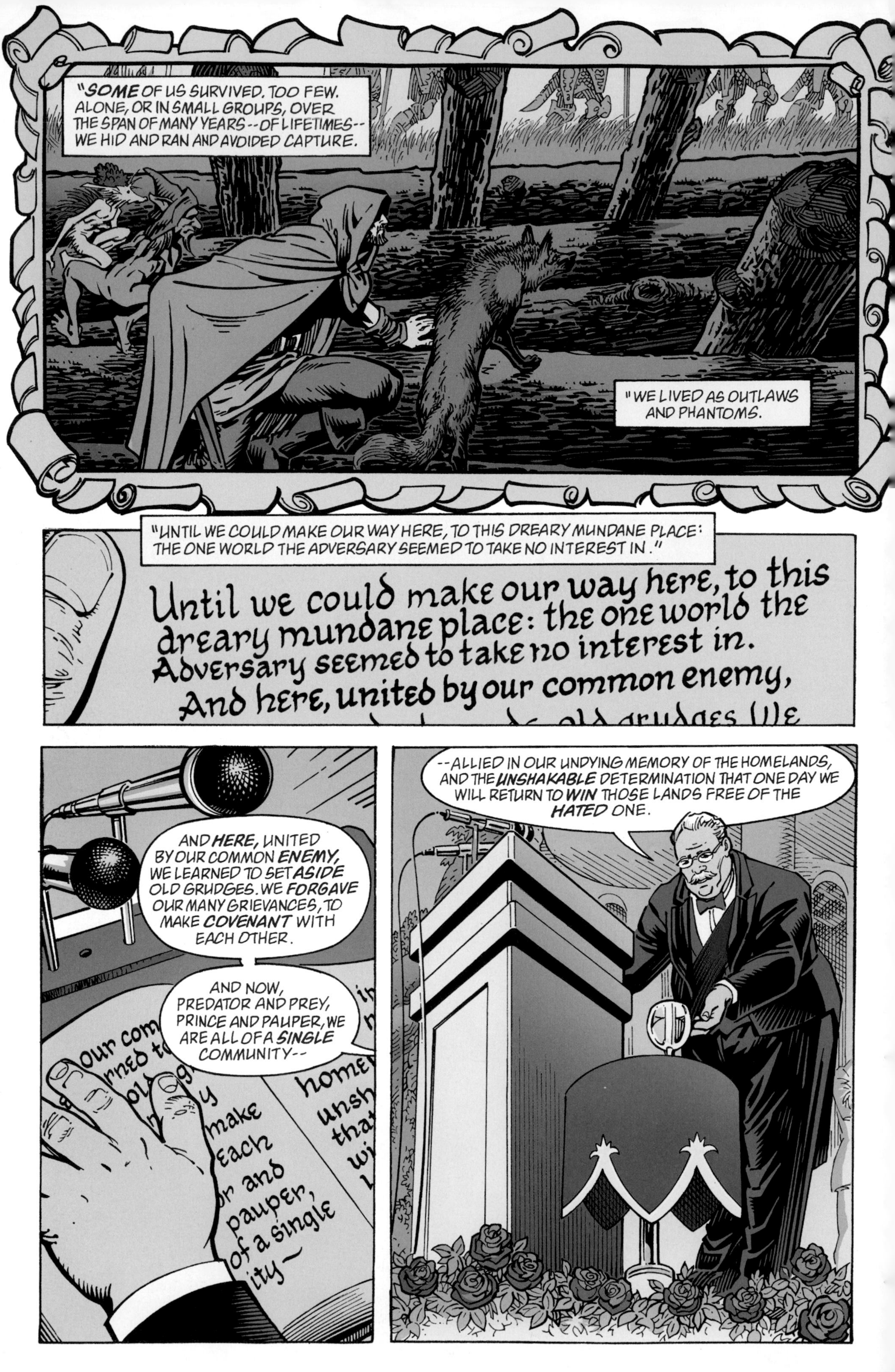
"SOME OF US SURVIVED. TOO FEW. ALONE, OR IN SMALL GROUPS, OVER THE SPAN OF MANY YEARS--OF LIFETIMES--WE HID AND RAN AND AVOIDED CAPTURE.
"WE LIVED AS OUTLAWS AND PHANTOMS.
"UNTIL WE COULD MAKE OUR WAY HERE, TO THIS DREARY MUNDANE PLACE: THE ONE WORLD THE ADVERSARY SEEMED TO TAKE NO INTEREST IN."
Until we could make our way here, to this dreary mundane place: the one world the Adversary seemed to take no interest in.
And here, united by our common enemy,
AND HERE, UNITED BY OUR COMMON ENEMY, WE LEARNED TO SET ASIDE OLD GRUDGES. WE FORGAVE OUR MANY GRIEVANCES, TO MAKE COVENANT WITH EACH OTHER.
AND NOW, PREDATOR AND PREY, PRINCE AND PAUPER, WE ARE ALL OF A SINGLE COMMUNITY--
--ALLIED IN OUR UNDYING MEMORY OF THE HOMELANDS, AND THE UNSHAKABLE DETERMINATION THAT ONE DAY WE WILL RETURN TO WIN THOSE LANDS FREE OF THE HATED ONE.

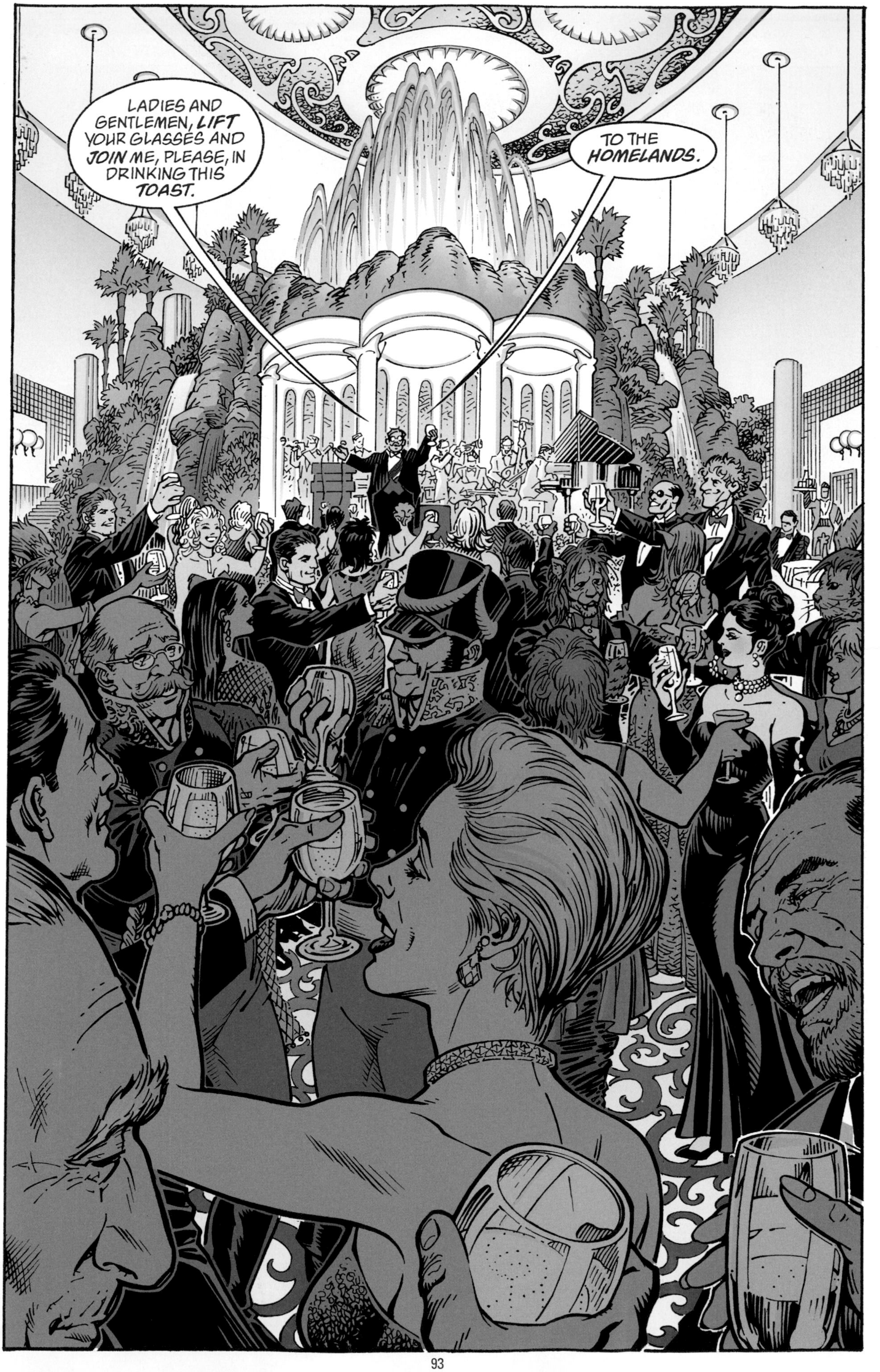
LADIES AND GENTLEMEN, LIFT YOUR GLASSES AND JOIN ME, PLEASE, IN DRINKING THIS TOAST.
TO THE HOMELANDS.

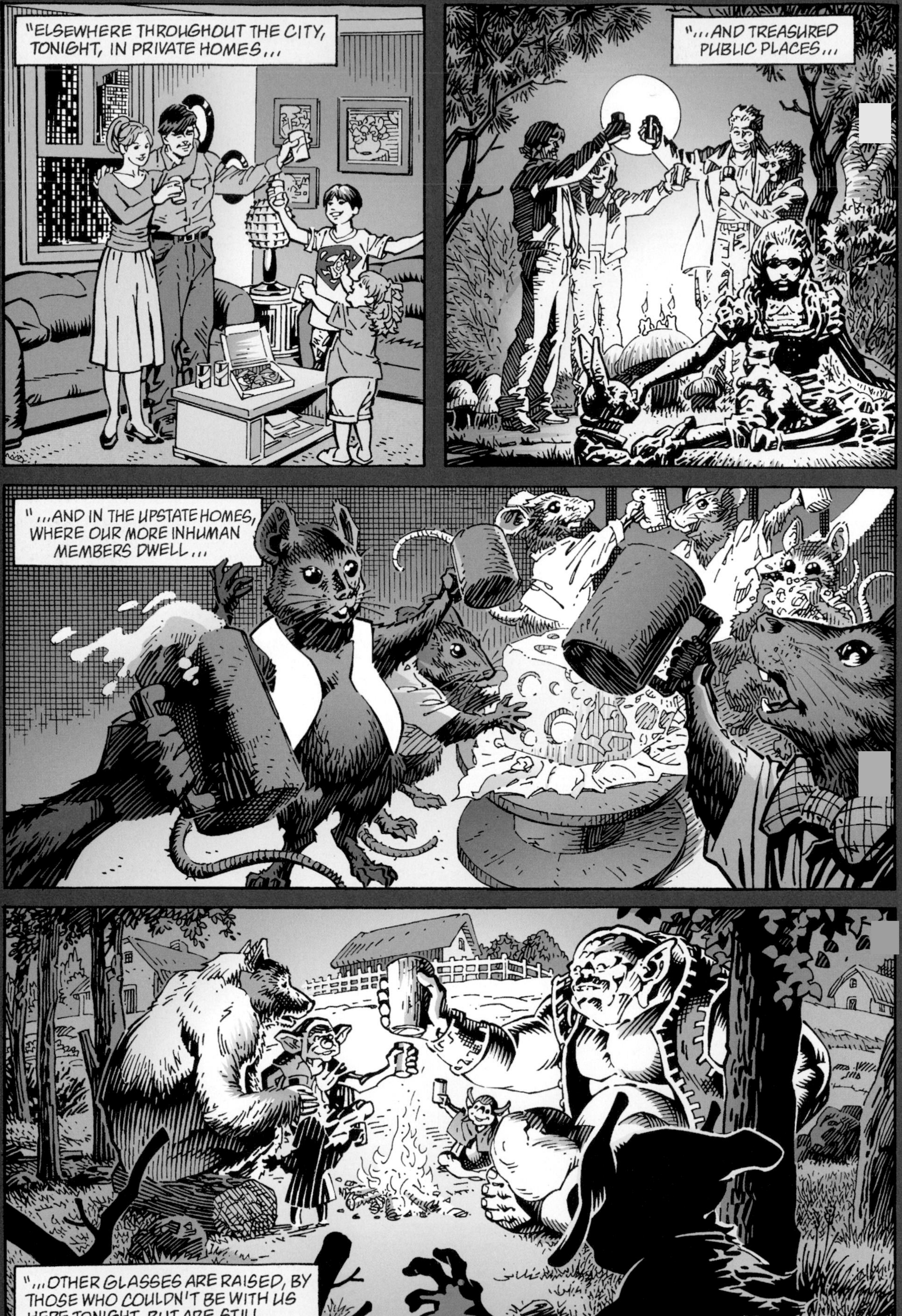
"ELSEWHERE THROUGHOUT THE CITY, TONIGHT, IN PRIVATE HOMES...
"...AND TREASURED PUBLIC PLACES...
"...AND IN THE UPSTATE HOMES, WHERE OUR MORE INHUMAN MEMBERS DWELL...
"...OTHER GLASSES ARE RAISED, BY THOSE WHO COULDN'T BE WITH US HERE TONIGHT BUT ARE STILL CITIZENS OF FABLETOWN, AND ARE *EQUALLY* DETERMINED NEVER TO FORGET."

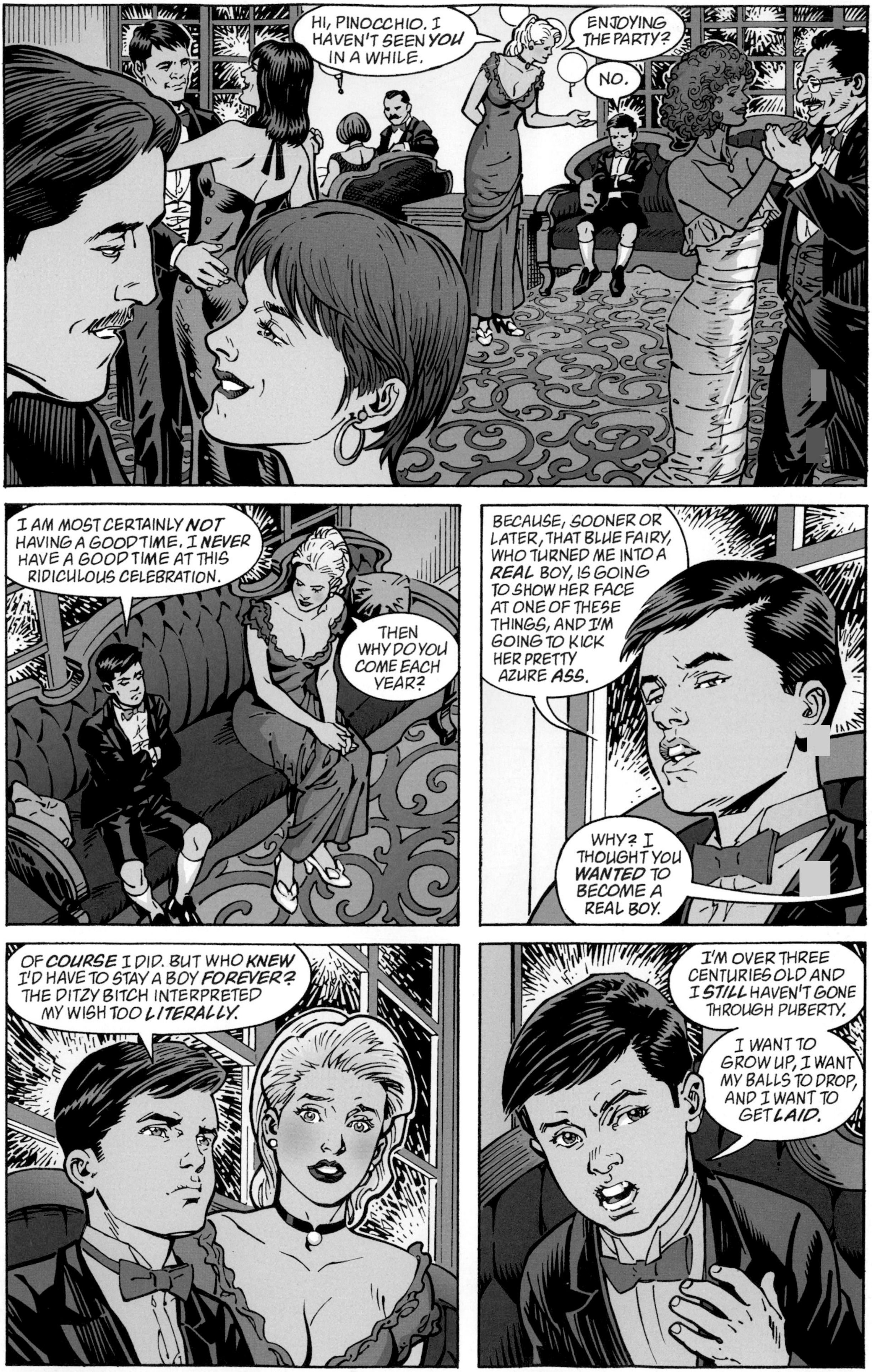
HI, PINOCCHIO. I HAVEN'T SEEN YOU IN A WHILE.
ENJOYING THE PARTY?
NO.
I AM MOST CERTAINLY NOT HAVING A GOOD TIME. I NEVER HAVE A GOOD TIME AT THIS RIDICULOUS CELEBRATION.
THEN WHY DO YOU COME EACH YEAR?
BECAUSE, SOONER OR LATER, THAT BLUE FAIRY, WHO TURNED ME INTO A REAL BOY, IS GOING TO SHOW HER FACE AT ONE OF THESE THINGS, AND I'M GOING TO KICK HER PRETTY AZURE ASS.
WHY? I THOUGHT YOU WANTED TO BECOME A REAL BOY.
OF COURSE I DID. BUT WHO KNEW I'D HAVE TO STAY A BOY FOREVER? THE DITZY BITCH INTERPRETED MY WISH TOO LITERALLY.
I'M OVER THREE CENTURIES OLD AND I STILL HAVEN'T GONE THROUGH PUBERTY.
I WANT TO GROW UP, I WANT MY BALLS TO DROP, AND I WANT TO GET LAID.

SECURITY
OFFICE
B. WOLF

BOTH OF YOU, QUIT YOUR DAMNED BITCHING AND CRYING.

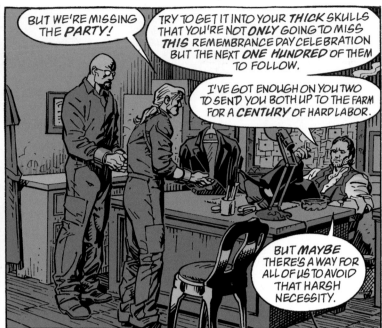

BUT WE'RE MISSING THE *PARTY!*

TRY TO GET IT INTO YOUR *THICK* SKULLS THAT YOU'RE NOT *ONLY* GOING TO MISS *THIS* REMEMBRANCE DAY CELEBRATION BUT THE NEXT *ONE HUNDRED* OF THEM TO FOLLOW.

I'VE GOT ENOUGH ON YOU TWO TO SEND YOU BOTH UP TO THE FARM FOR A *CENTURY* OF HARD LABOR.

BUT *MAYBE* THERE'S A WAY FOR ALL OF US TO AVOID THAT HARSH NECESSITY.

BULLSHIT, BIGBY! SURE, YOU GOT BLUE-BEARD HERE BECAUSE YOU CAUGHT HIM RED-HANDED TORTURING ME...

SHUT UP, YOU PATHETIC, BLEATING *CHILD.*

...BUT YOU'VE GOT NOTHING ON ME -- NOTHING YOU CAN *PROVE,* ANYWAY.

YOU'RE ABOUT TO FIND OUT EXACTLY HOW *MUCH* I CAN PROVE. BUT UNTIL I BRING THE *HAMMER* DOWN, YOU CAN BOTH GO TO WHAT'S *LEFT* OF THE PARTY -- PROVIDED YOU STAY AT LEAST A DOZEN YARDS AWAY FROM EACH OTHER AT ALL TIMES.

BLUEBEARD, YOU'VE GOT JUST ENOUGH TIME TO CLEAN UP AND GET YOUR ANNUAL *DONATION* INTO OUR BELOVED MAYOR'S POCKET -- WHICH WILL REMIND US WHAT A GOOD AND *SUPPORT-IVE* CITIZEN YOU ARE.

AND *THIS* TIME LEAVE THE GUNS, DAGGERS AND BATTLE AXES AT HOME, PLEASE.

AND JACK, WE'RE GOING TO TALK *PRIVATELY* FOR A BIT. THEN YOU'RE GOING TO DEMONSTRATE YOUR *HELPFUL* NATURE BY DELIVERING A MESSAGE FROM ME TO ONE OF THE PARTY GUESTS.

WHY DON'T YOU RUN YOUR *OWN* DAMNED ERRANDS?

"PARTLY BECAUSE I'VE *ALREADY* MISSED TOO MUCH OF THE PARTY, BUT *MOSTLY* BECAUSE THIS IS WHAT YOU HAVE TO DO IF YOU WANT TO KEEP YOUR FREEDOM."

NO NO *NO!* TOO MUCH *STIRRING!* THE SAUCE MUST BE *ALLOWED* TO CARMELIZE.

WHERE ARE MY CORNISH HENS? WHO *TOOK* THEM?

SHALLOTS? BUT YOU *CLEARLY* SAID RED ONIONS!

ARE WE STILL SERVING SOUP?

WE'RE ALMOST OUT OF THE GOOSE LIVER. SHOULD WE PUT OUT MORE OR--?

BETTER PUT OUT MORE OF SOMETHING *FAST.* THIS CROWD'S EATING ANYTHING IN SIGHT.

YOU HURRY UP AND YOU SLOW DOWN! *EVERYTHING* MUST BE COORDINATED TO ARRIVE AT THE *PROPER* TIME!

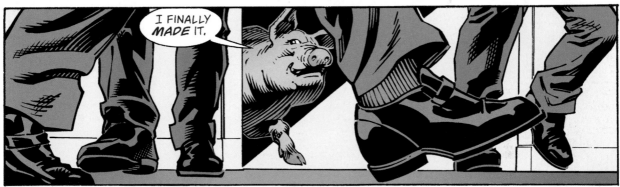

I FINALLY *MADE* IT.

BACKSTAGE AT THE *GRANDEST* EVENT OF THE YEAR.

YUM.

ARE YOU ON THE MENU?

OH GOSH. I SURE *HOPE* NOT.

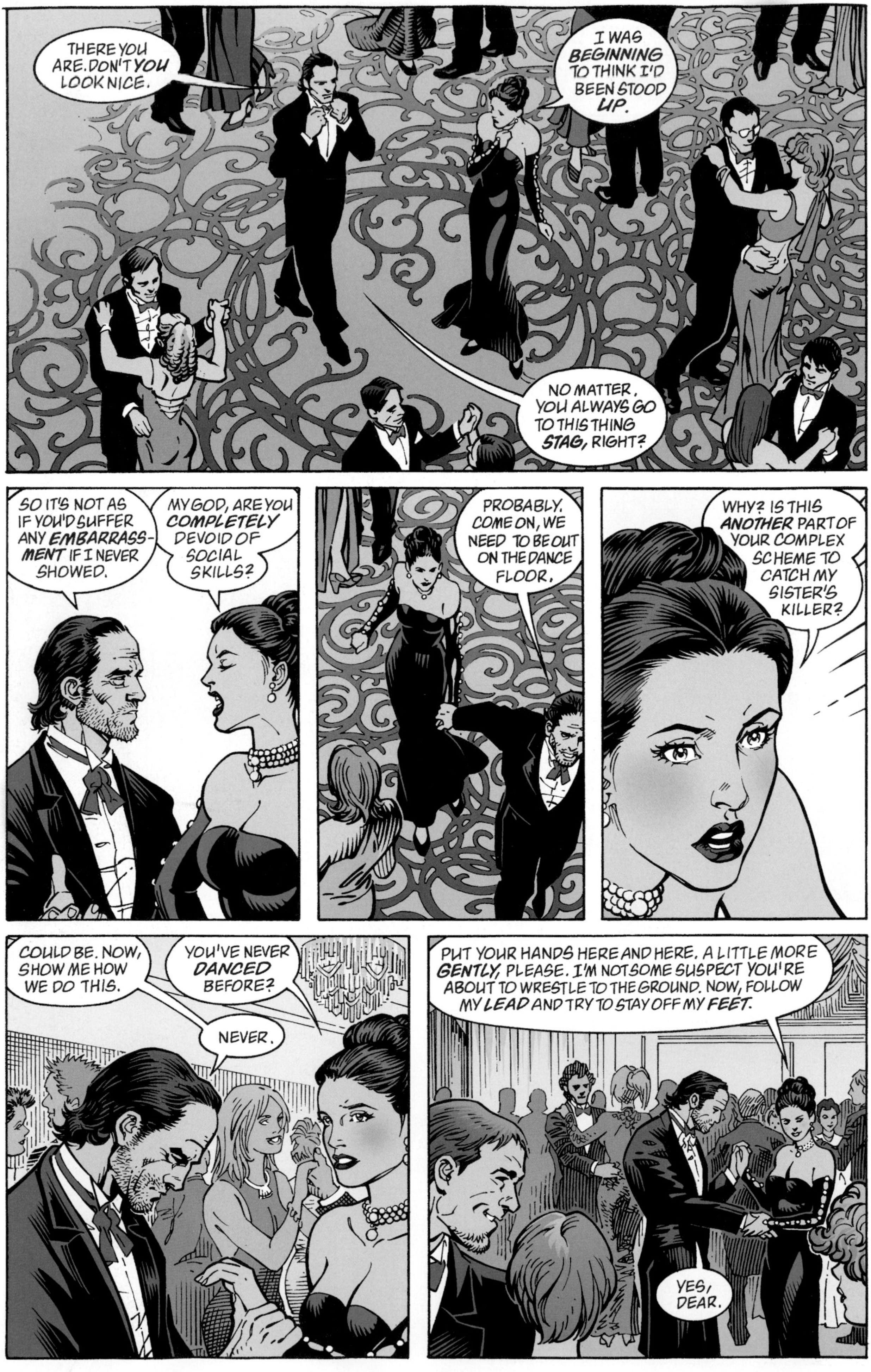
THERE YOU ARE. DON'T YOU LOOK NICE.
I WAS BEGINNING TO THINK I'D BEEN STOOD UP.
NO MATTER. YOU ALWAYS GO TO THIS THING STAG, RIGHT?
SO IT'S NOT AS IF YOU'D SUFFER ANY EMBARRASSMENT IF I NEVER SHOWED.
MY GOD, ARE YOU COMPLETELY DEVOID OF SOCIAL SKILLS?
PROBABLY. COME ON, WE NEED TO BE OUT ON THE DANCE FLOOR.
WHY? IS THIS ANOTHER PART OF YOUR COMPLEX SCHEME TO CATCH MY SISTER'S KILLER?
COULD BE. NOW, SHOW ME HOW WE DO THIS.
YOU'VE NEVER DANCED BEFORE?
NEVER.
PUT YOUR HANDS HERE AND HERE. A LITTLE MORE GENTLY, PLEASE. I'M NOT SOME SUSPECT YOU'RE ABOUT TO WRESTLE TO THE GROUND. NOW, FOLLOW MY LEAD AND TRY TO STAY OFF MY FEET.
YES, DEAR.

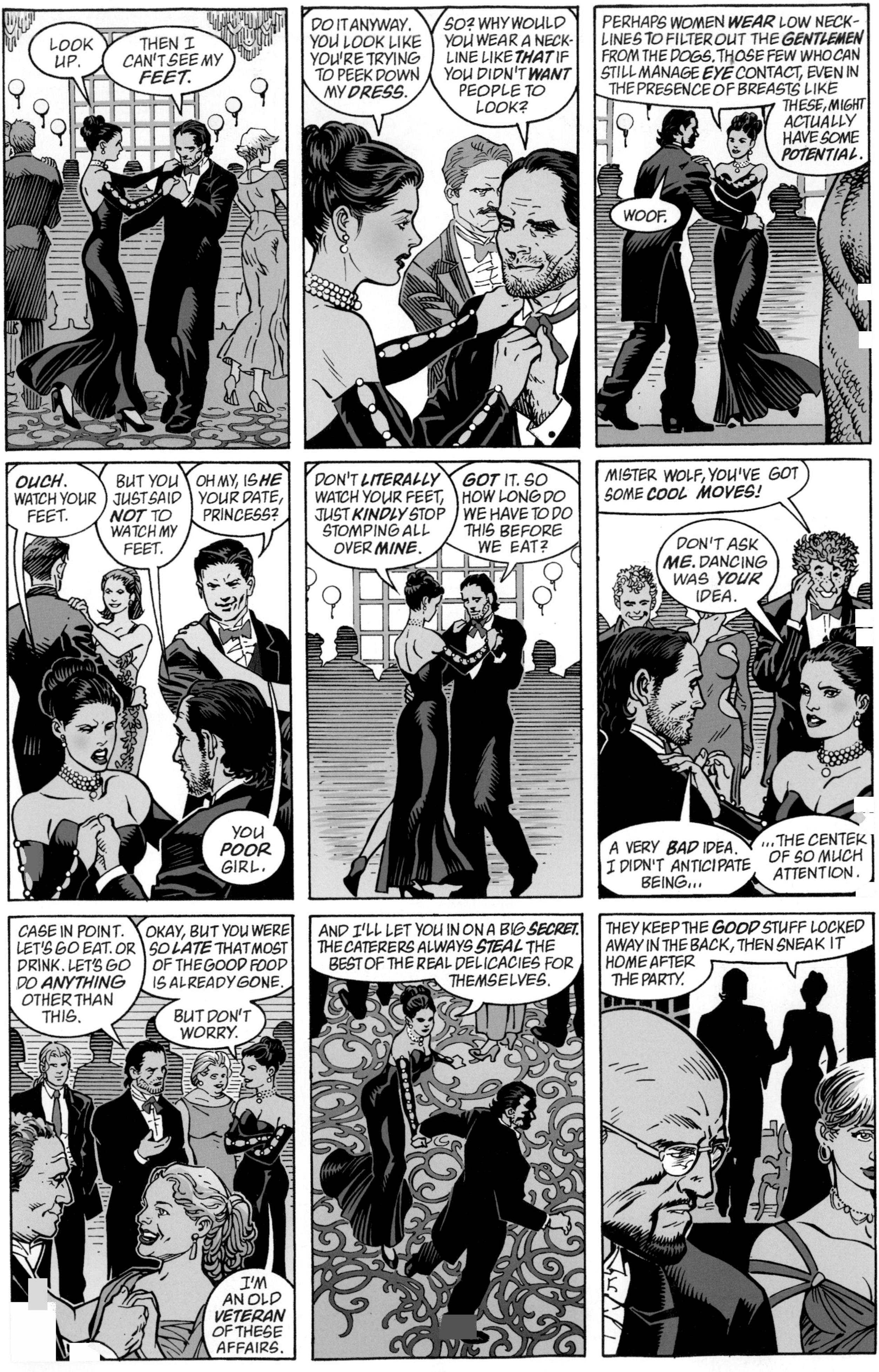

LOOK UP.
THEN I CAN'T SEE MY FEET.
DO IT ANYWAY. YOU LOOK LIKE YOU'RE TRYING TO PEEK DOWN MY DRESS.
SO? WHY WOULD YOU WEAR A NECKLINE LIKE THAT IF YOU DIDN'T WANT PEOPLE TO LOOK?
PERHAPS WOMEN WEAR LOW NECKLINES TO FILTER OUT THE GENTLEMEN FROM THE DOGS. THOSE FEW WHO CAN STILL MANAGE EYE CONTACT, EVEN IN THE PRESENCE OF BREASTS LIKE THESE, MIGHT ACTUALLY HAVE SOME POTENTIAL.
WOOF.
OUCH. WATCH YOUR FEET.
BUT YOU JUST SAID NOT TO WATCH MY FEET.
OH MY, IS HE YOUR DATE, PRINCESS?
YOU POOR GIRL.
DON'T LITERALLY WATCH YOUR FEET, JUST KINDLY STOP STOMPING ALL OVER MINE.
GOT IT. SO HOW LONG DO WE HAVE TO DO THIS BEFORE WE EAT?
MISTER WOLF, YOU'VE GOT SOME COOL MOVES!
DON'T ASK ME. DANCING WAS YOUR IDEA.
A VERY BAD IDEA. I DIDN'T ANTICIPATE BEING...
...THE CENTER OF SO MUCH ATTENTION.
CASE IN POINT. LET'S GO EAT. OR DRINK. LET'S GO DO ANYTHING OTHER THAN THIS.
OKAY, BUT YOU WERE SO LATE THAT MOST OF THE GOOD FOOD IS ALREADY GONE.
BUT DON'T WORRY.
I'M AN OLD VETERAN OF THESE AFFAIRS.
AND I'LL LET YOU IN ON A BIG SECRET. THE CATERERS ALWAYS STEAL THE BEST OF THE REAL DELICACIES FOR THEMSELVES.
THEY KEEP THE GOOD STUFF LOCKED AWAY IN THE BACK, THEN SNEAK IT HOME AFTER THE PARTY.

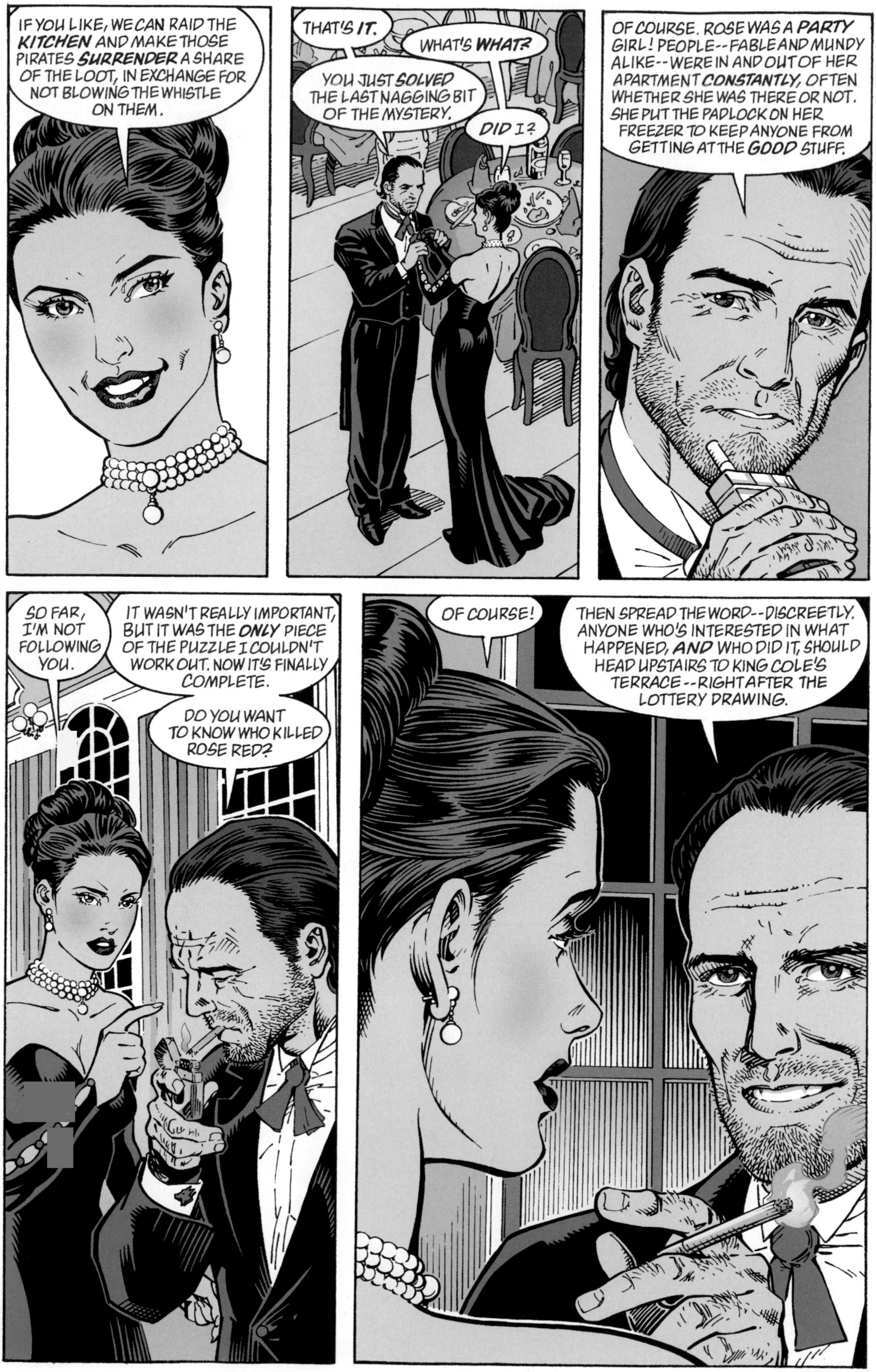

IF YOU LIKE, WE CAN RAID THE KITCHEN AND MAKE THOSE PIRATES SURRENDER A SHARE OF THE LOOT, IN EXCHANGE FOR NOT BLOWING THE WHISTLE ON THEM.
THAT'S IT.
WHAT'S WHAT?
YOU JUST SOLVED THE LAST NAGGING BIT OF THE MYSTERY.
DID I?
OF COURSE. ROSE WAS A PARTY GIRL! PEOPLE--FABLE AND MUNDY ALIKE--WERE IN AND OUT OF HER APARTMENT CONSTANTLY, OFTEN WHETHER SHE WAS THERE OR NOT. SHE PUT THE PADLOCK ON HER FREEZER TO KEEP ANYONE FROM GETTING AT THE GOOD STUFF.
SO FAR, I'M NOT FOLLOWING YOU.
IT WASN'T REALLY IMPORTANT, BUT IT WAS THE ONLY PIECE OF THE PUZZLE I COULDN'T WORK OUT. NOW IT'S FINALLY COMPLETE.
DO YOU WANT TO KNOW WHO KILLED ROSE RED?
OF COURSE!
THEN SPREAD THE WORD--DISCREETLY. ANYONE WHO'S INTERESTED IN WHAT HAPPENED, AND WHO DID IT, SHOULD HEAD UPSTAIRS TO KING COLE'S TERRACE--RIGHT AFTER THE LOTTERY DRAWING.

AND THE **WINNING** TICKET IS...

DOES HIS **ROYAL NIBS** KNOW YOU SNEAK UP HERE TO USE HIS **POOL** WHEN HE'S NOT AROUND?

WHO KNOWS?

IF HE **DOES**, HE'S NEVER COMPLAINED.

MIND IF I BUM A SMOKE?

I GUESS NOT.

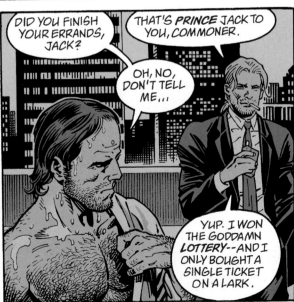

DID YOU FINISH YOUR ERRANDS, JACK?

THAT'S **PRINCE** JACK TO YOU, COMMONER.

OH, NO, DON'T TELL ME...

YUP. I WON THE GODDAMN **LOTTERY**--AND I ONLY BOUGHT A SINGLE TICKET ON A LARK.

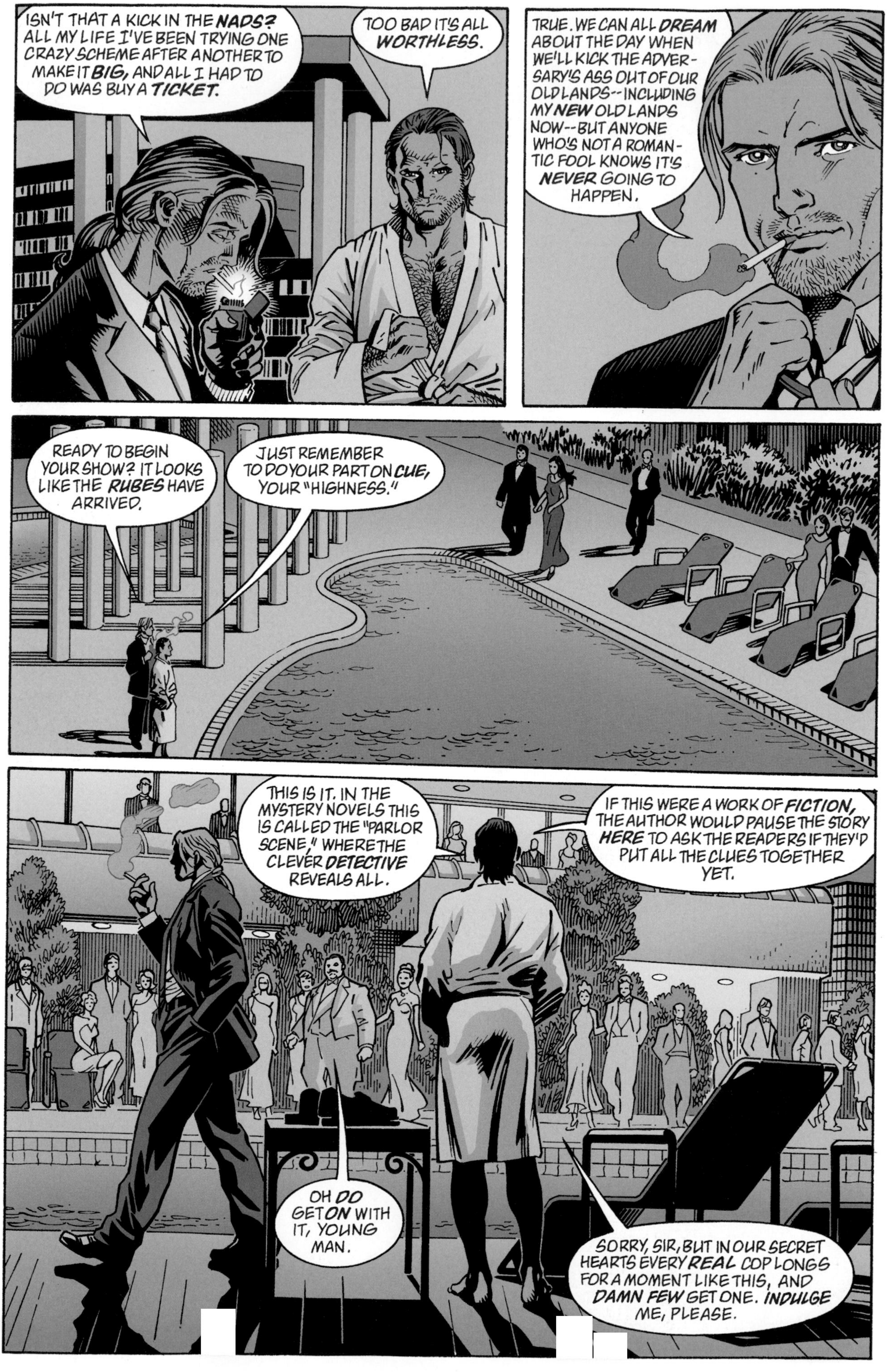

ISN'T THAT A KICK IN THE NADS? ALL MY LIFE I'VE BEEN TRYING ONE CRAZY SCHEME AFTER ANOTHER TO MAKE IT BIG, AND ALL I HAD TO DO WAS BUY A TICKET.
TOO BAD IT'S ALL WORTHLESS.
TRUE. WE CAN ALL DREAM ABOUT THE DAY WHEN WE'LL KICK THE ADVERSARY'S ASS OUT OF OUR OLD LANDS--INCLUDING MY NEW OLD LANDS NOW--BUT ANYONE WHO'S NOT A ROMANTIC FOOL KNOWS IT'S NEVER GOING TO HAPPEN.
READY TO BEGIN YOUR SHOW? IT LOOKS LIKE THE RUBES HAVE ARRIVED.
JUST REMEMBER TO DO YOUR PART ON CUE, YOUR "HIGHNESS."
THIS IS IT. IN THE MYSTERY NOVELS THIS IS CALLED THE "PARLOR SCENE," WHERE THE CLEVER DETECTIVE REVEALS ALL.
IF THIS WERE A WORK OF FICTION, THE AUTHOR WOULD PAUSE THE STORY HERE TO ASK THE READERS IF THEY'D PUT ALL THE CLUES TOGETHER YET.
OH DO GET ON WITH IT, YOUNG MAN.
SORRY, SIR, BUT IN OUR SECRET HEARTS EVERY REAL COP LONGS FOR A MOMENT LIKE THIS, AND DAMN FEW GET ONE. INDULGE ME, PLEASE.

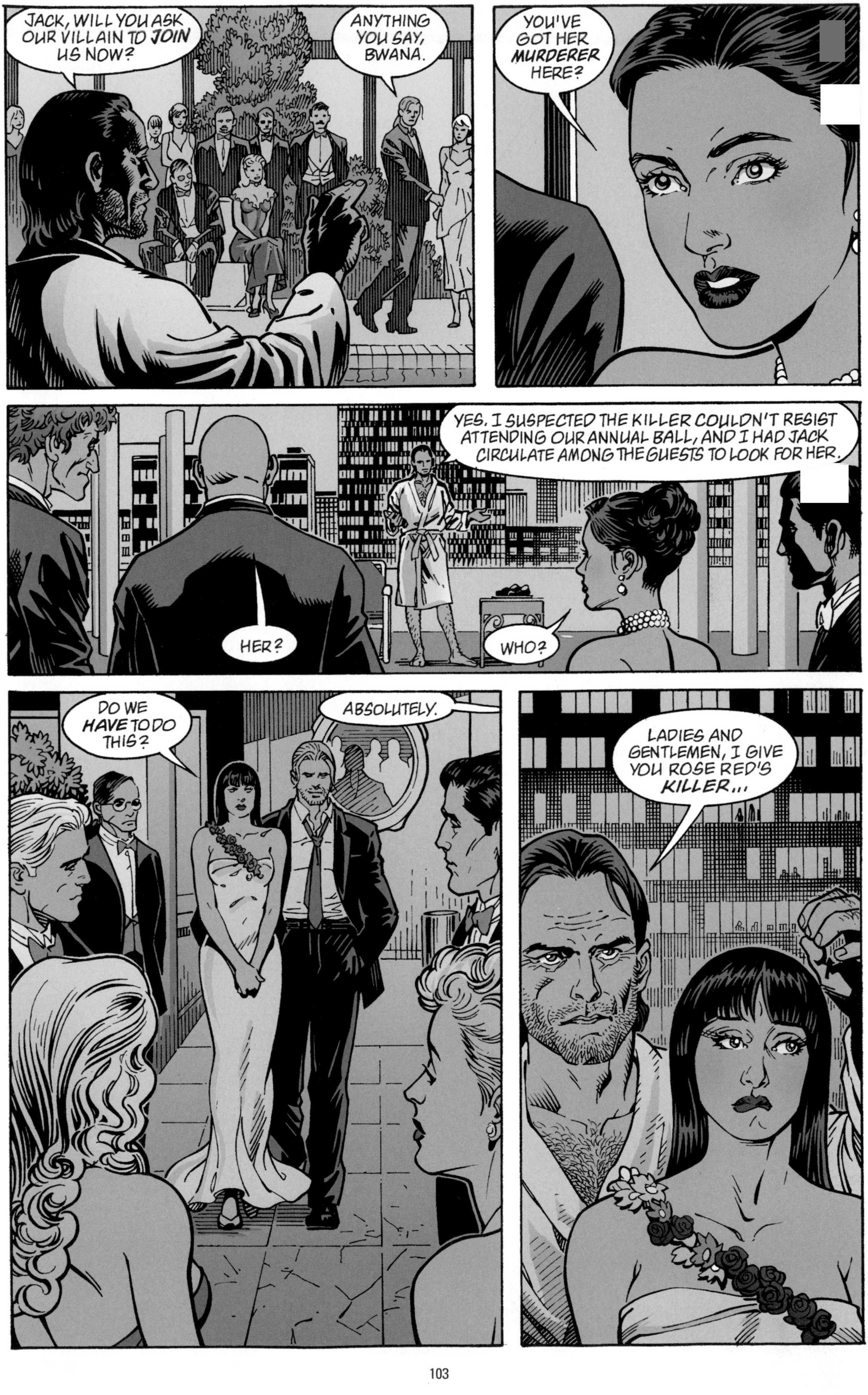
JACK, WILL YOU ASK OUR VILLAIN TO JOIN US NOW?
ANYTHING YOU SAY, BWANA.
YOU'VE GOT HER MURDERER HERE?
YES. I SUSPECTED THE KILLER COULDN'T RESIST ATTENDING OUR ANNUAL BALL, AND I HAD JACK CIRCULATE AMONG THE GUESTS TO LOOK FOR HER.
HER?
WHO?
DO WE HAVE TO DO THIS?
ABSOLUTELY.
LADIES AND GENTLEMEN, I GIVE YOU ROSE RED'S KILLER...

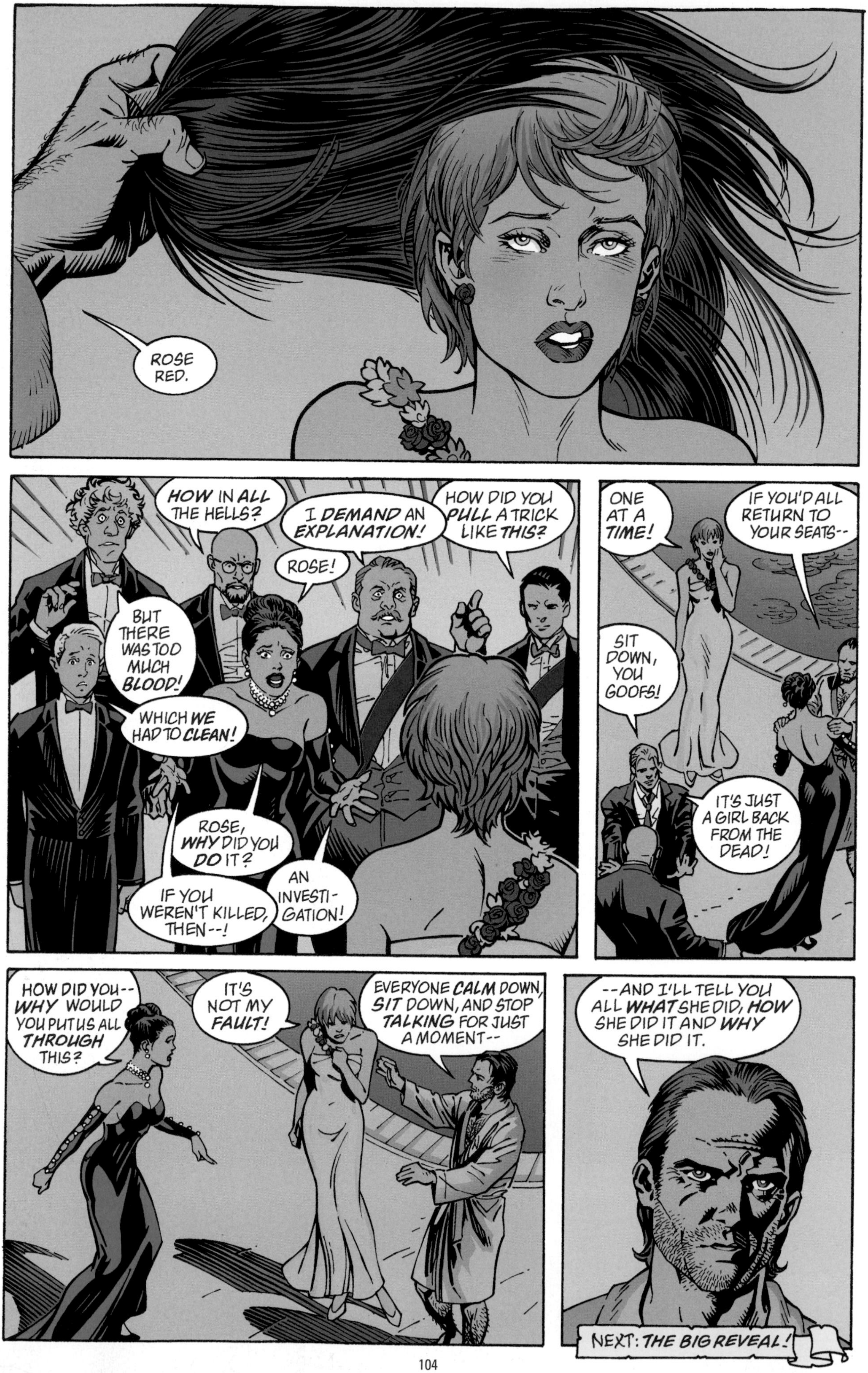
ROSE RED.
HOW IN ALL THE HELLS?
I DEMAND AN EXPLANATION!
HOW DID YOU PULL A TRICK LIKE THIS?
ROSE!
BUT THERE WAS TOO MUCH BLOOD!
WHICH WE HAD TO CLEAN!
ROSE, WHY DID YOU DO IT?
AN INVESTI-GATION!
IF YOU WEREN'T KILLED, THEN--!
ONE AT A TIME!
IF YOU'D ALL RETURN TO YOUR SEATS--
SIT DOWN, YOU GOOFS!
IT'S JUST A GIRL BACK FROM THE DEAD!
HOW DID YOU-- WHY WOULD YOU PUT US ALL THROUGH THIS?
IT'S NOT MY FAULT!
EVERYONE CALM DOWN, SIT DOWN, AND STOP TALKING FOR JUST A MOMENT--
--AND I'LL TELL YOU ALL WHAT SHE DID, HOW SHE DID IT AND WHY SHE DID IT.
NEXT: THE BIG REVEAL!

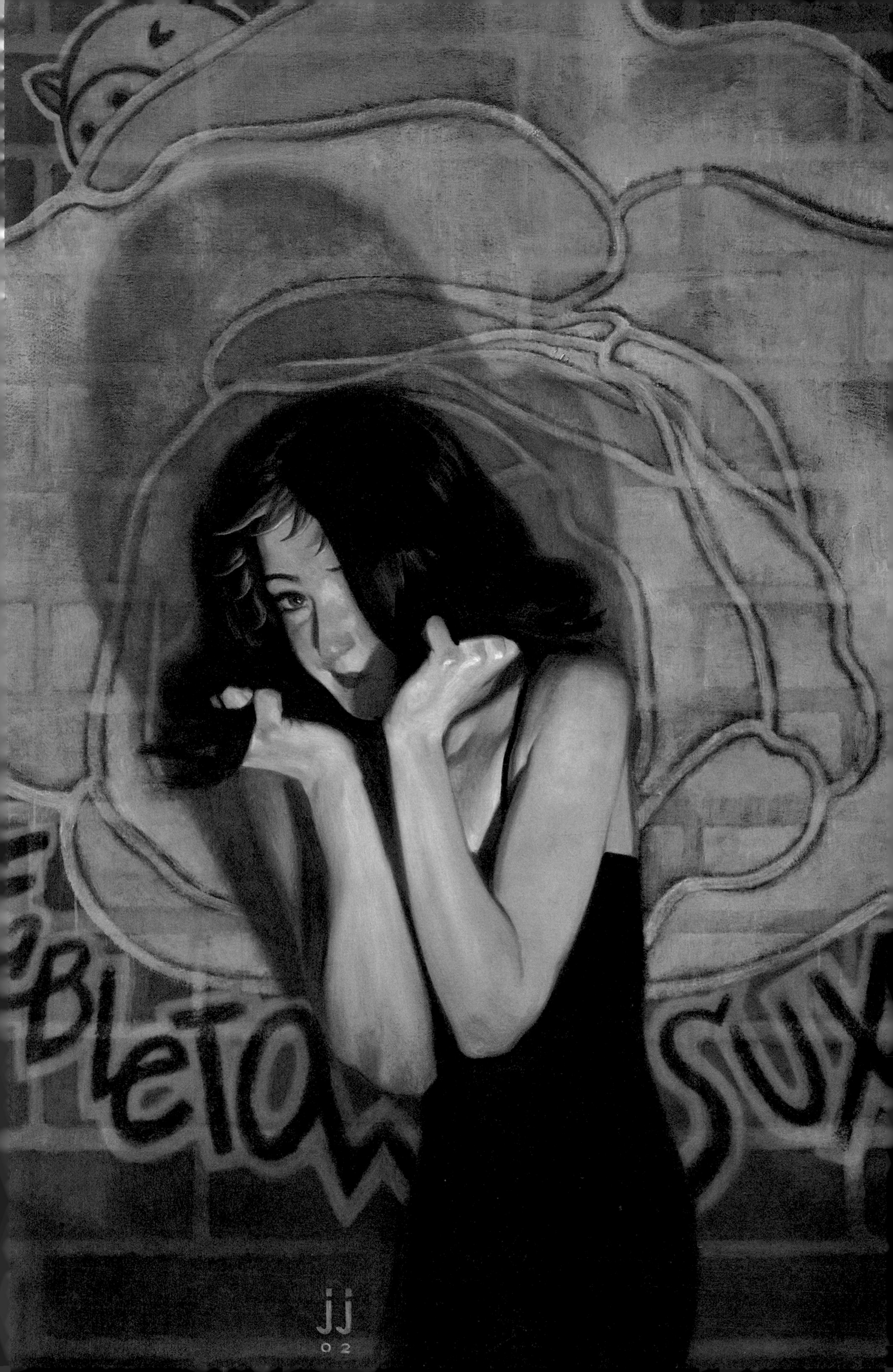

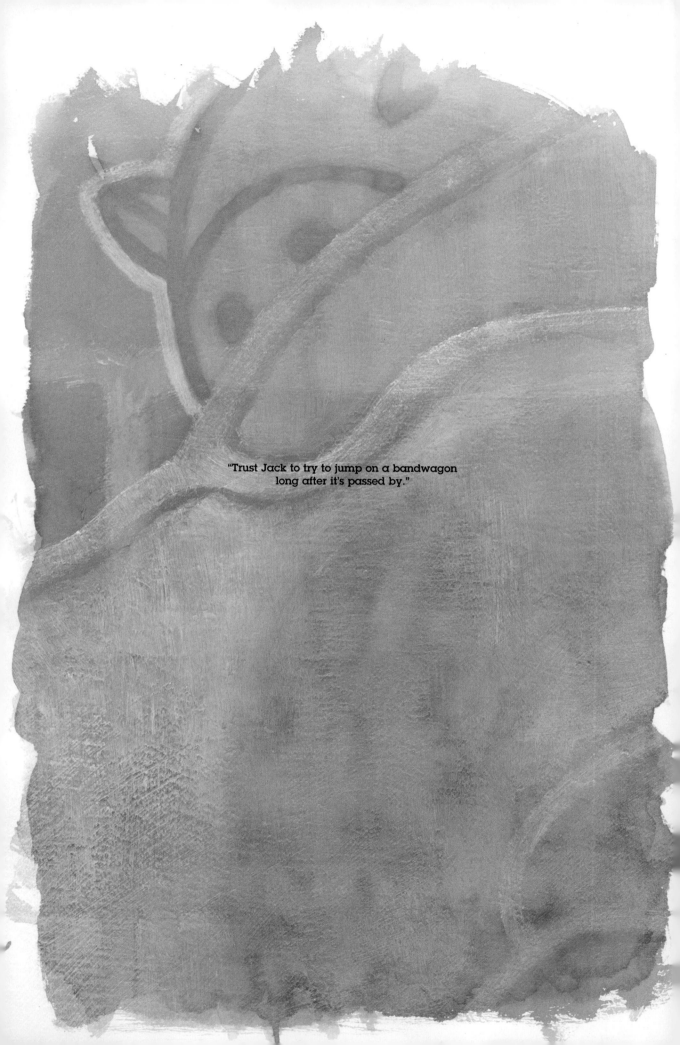

"Trust Jack to try to jump on a bandwagon
long after it's passed by."

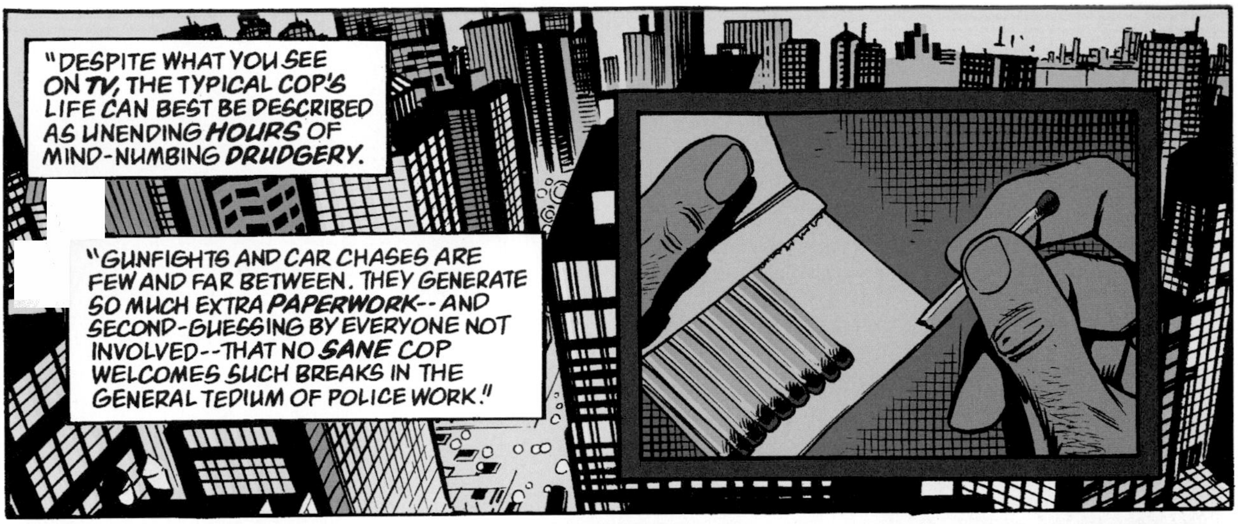
"DESPITE WHAT YOU SEE ON TV, THE TYPICAL COP'S LIFE CAN BEST BE DESCRIBED AS UNENDING HOURS OF MIND-NUMBING DRUDGERY.
"GUNFIGHTS AND CAR CHASES ARE FEW AND FAR BETWEEN. THEY GENERATE SO MUCH EXTRA PAPERWORK--AND SECOND-GUESSING BY EVERYONE NOT INVOLVED--THAT NO SANE COP WELCOMES SUCH BREAKS IN THE GENERAL TEDIUM OF POLICE WORK."

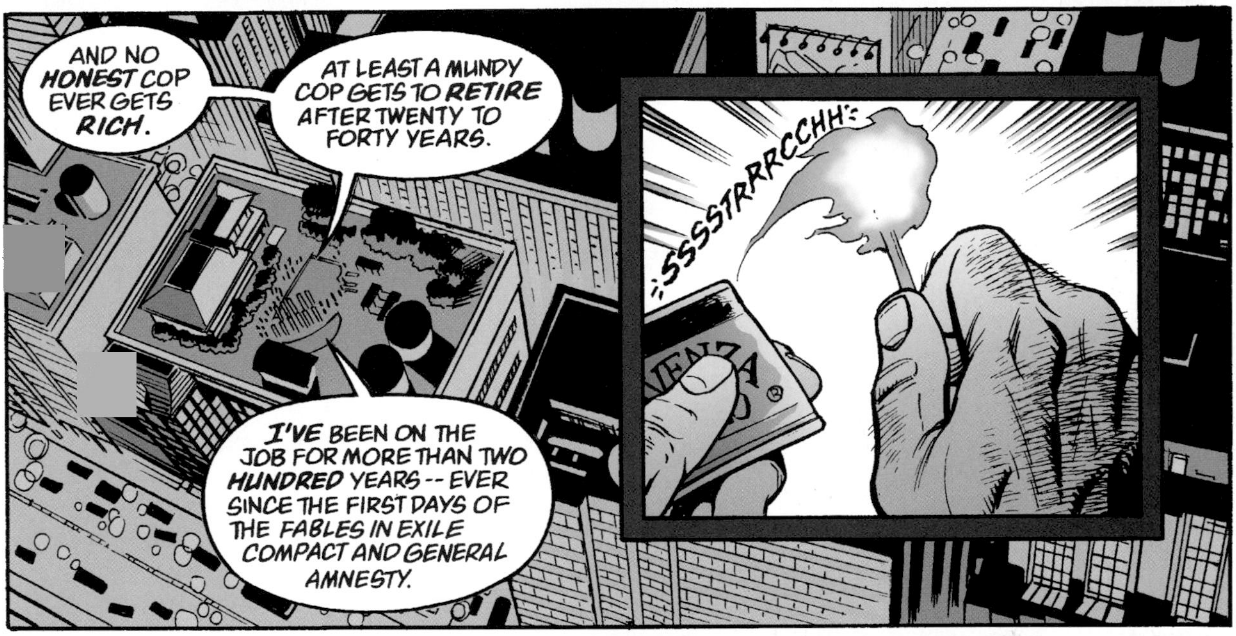
AND NO HONEST COP EVER GETS RICH.
AT LEAST A MUNDY COP GETS TO RETIRE AFTER TWENTY TO FORTY YEARS.
SSSSTRRRCCHH
I'VE BEEN ON THE JOB FOR MORE THAN TWO HUNDRED YEARS--EVER SINCE THE FIRST DAYS OF THE FABLES IN EXILE COMPACT AND GENERAL AMNESTY.

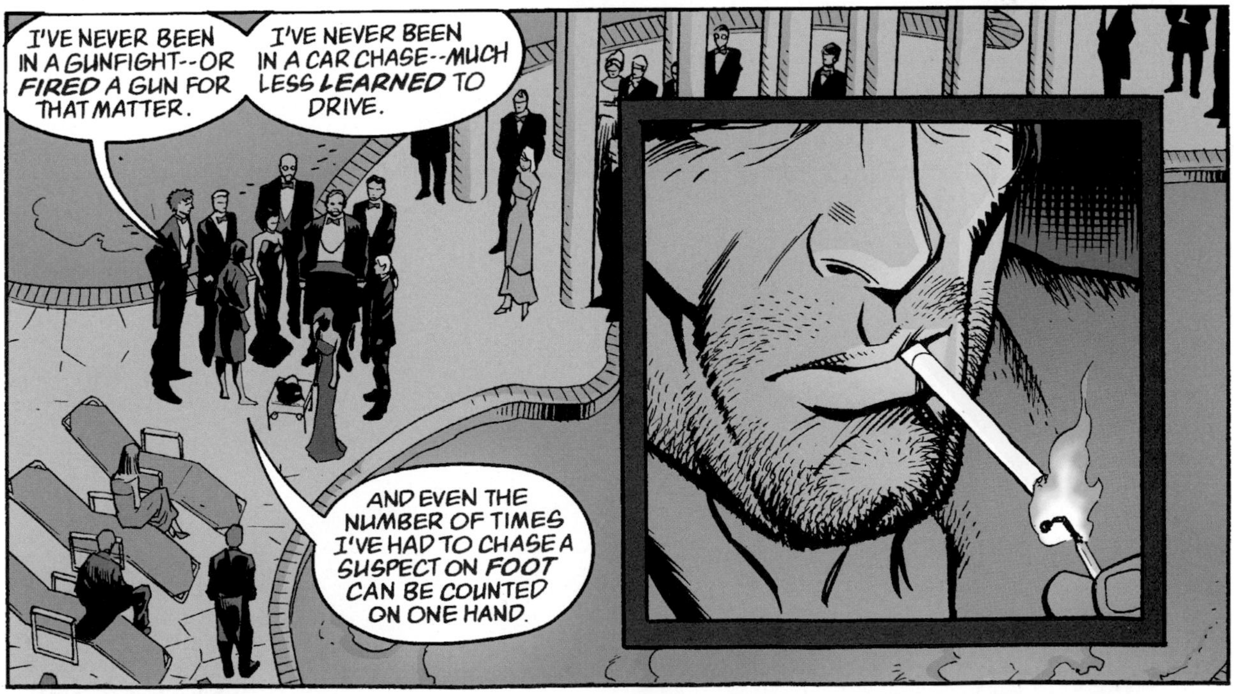
I'VE NEVER BEEN IN A GUNFIGHT--OR FIRED A GUN FOR THAT MATTER.
I'VE NEVER BEEN IN A CAR CHASE--MUCH LESS LEARNED TO DRIVE.
AND EVEN THE NUMBER OF TIMES I'VE HAD TO CHASE A SUSPECT ON FOOT CAN BE COUNTED ON ONE HAND.

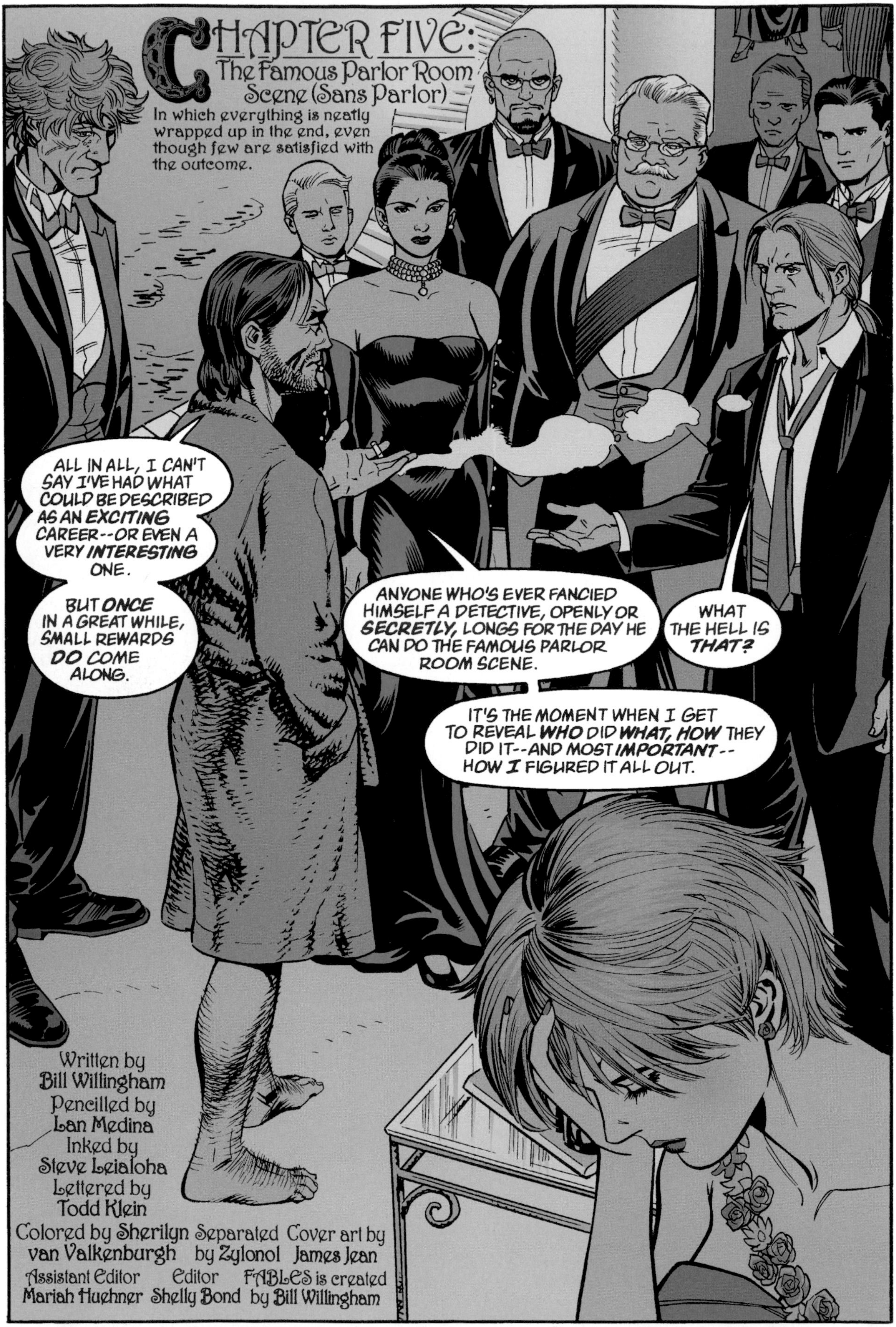
CHAPTER FIVE:
The Famous Parlor Room Scene (Sans Parlor)
In which everything is neatly wrapped up in the end, even though few are satisfied with the outcome.
ALL IN ALL, I CAN'T SAY I'VE HAD WHAT COULD BE DESCRIBED AS AN EXCITING CAREER--OR EVEN A VERY INTERESTING ONE.
BUT ONCE IN A GREAT WHILE, SMALL REWARDS DO COME ALONG.
ANYONE WHO'S EVER FANCIED HIMSELF A DETECTIVE, OPENLY OR SECRETLY, LONGS FOR THE DAY HE CAN DO THE FAMOUS PARLOR ROOM SCENE.
WHAT THE HELL IS THAT?
IT'S THE MOMENT WHEN I GET TO REVEAL WHO DID WHAT, HOW THEY DID IT--AND MOST IMPORTANT--HOW I FIGURED IT ALL OUT.
Written by Bill Willingham
Pencilled by Lan Medina
Inked by Steve Leialoha
Lettered by Todd Klein
Colored by Sherilyn van Valkenburgh
Separated by Zylonol
Cover art by James Jean
Assistant Editor Mariah Huehner
Editor Shelly Bond
FABLES is created by Bill Willingham

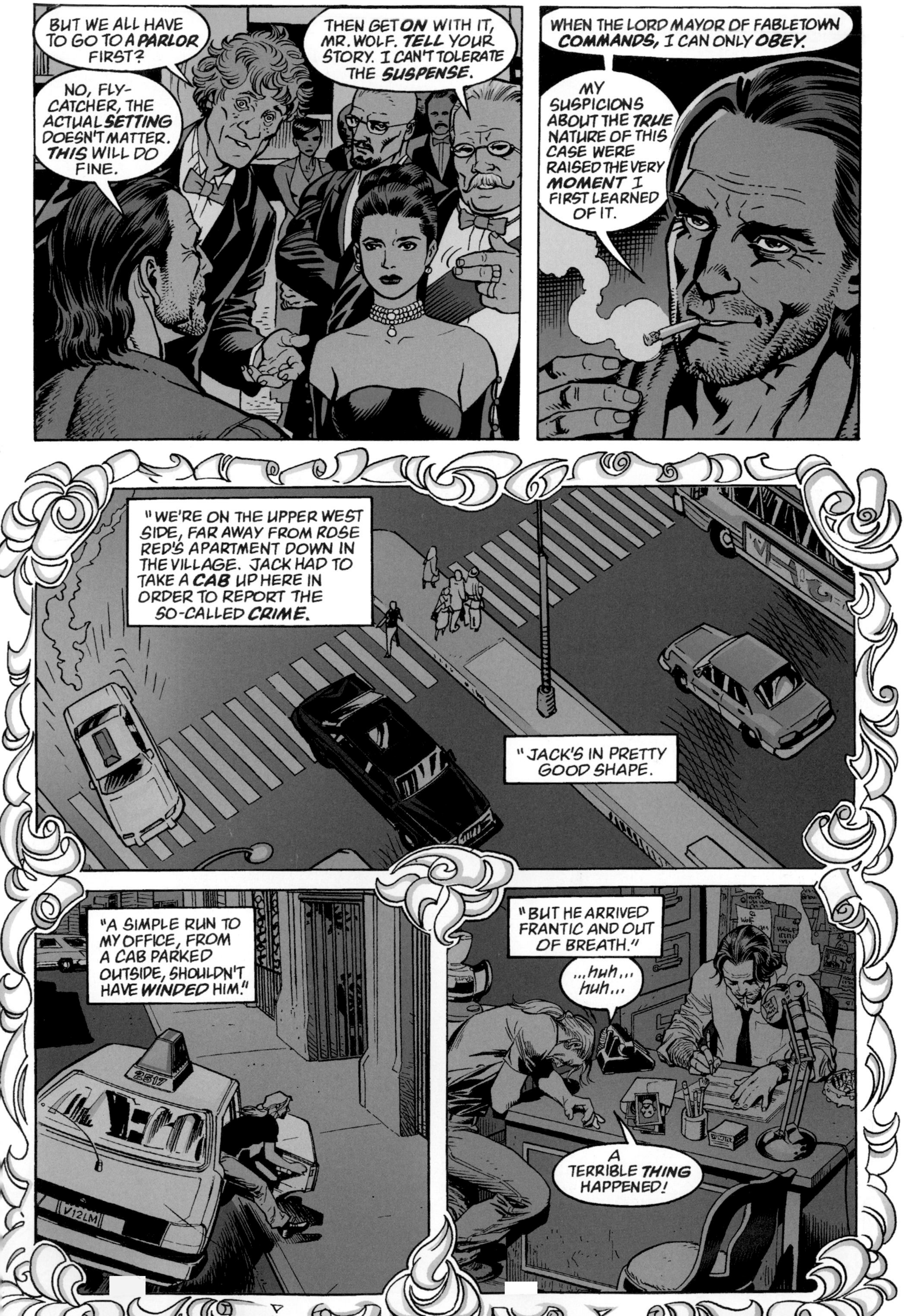
BUT WE ALL HAVE TO GO TO A PARLOR FIRST?
NO, FLY-CATCHER, THE ACTUAL SETTING DOESN'T MATTER. THIS WILL DO FINE.
THEN GET ON WITH IT, MR. WOLF. TELL YOUR STORY. I CAN'T TOLERATE THE SUSPENSE.
WHEN THE LORD MAYOR OF FABLETOWN COMMANDS, I CAN ONLY OBEY.
MY SUSPICIONS ABOUT THE TRUE NATURE OF THIS CASE WERE RAISED THE VERY MOMENT I FIRST LEARNED OF IT.
"WE'RE ON THE UPPER WEST SIDE, FAR AWAY FROM ROSE RED'S APARTMENT DOWN IN THE VILLAGE. JACK HAD TO TAKE A CAB UP HERE IN ORDER TO REPORT THE SO-CALLED CRIME.
"JACK'S IN PRETTY GOOD SHAPE.
"A SIMPLE RUN TO MY OFFICE, FROM A CAB PARKED OUTSIDE, SHOULDN'T HAVE WINDED HIM."
2517
V12LM
"BUT HE ARRIVED FRANTIC AND OUT OF BREATH."
...huh... huh...
A TERRIBLE THING HAPPENED!

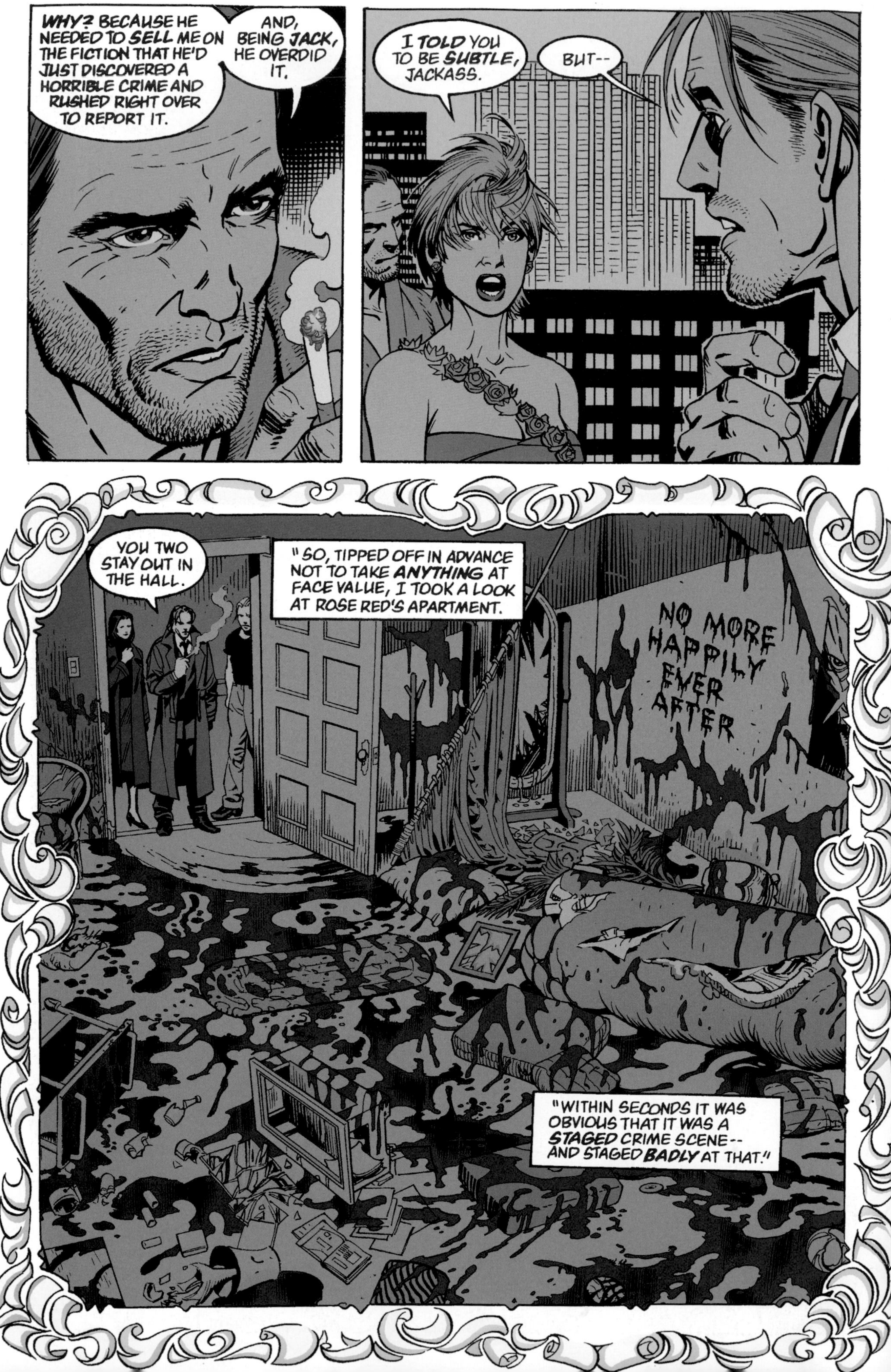
WHY? BECAUSE HE NEEDED TO SELL ME ON THE FICTION THAT HE'D JUST DISCOVERED A HORRIBLE CRIME AND RUSHED RIGHT OVER TO REPORT IT.
AND, BEING JACK, HE OVERDID IT.
I TOLD YOU TO BE SUBTLE, JACKASS.
BUT--
YOU TWO STAY OUT IN THE HALL.
"SO, TIPPED OFF IN ADVANCE NOT TO TAKE ANYTHING AT FACE VALUE, I TOOK A LOOK AT ROSE RED'S APARTMENT.
NO MORE HAPPILY EVER AFTER
"WITHIN SECONDS IT WAS OBVIOUS THAT IT WAS A STAGED CRIME SCENE-- AND STAGED BADLY AT THAT."

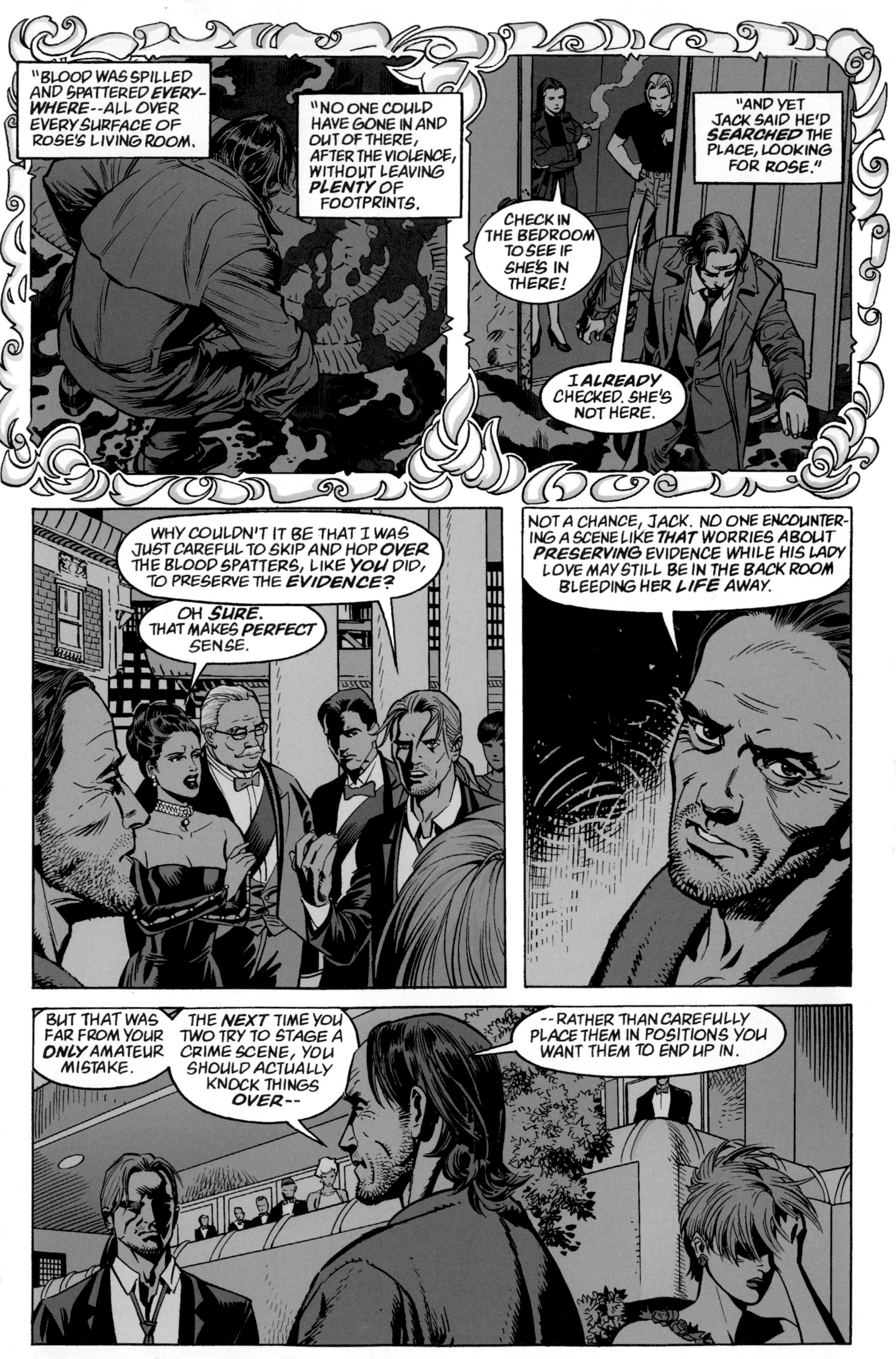
"BLOOD WAS SPILLED AND SPATTERED EVERY-WHERE--ALL OVER EVERY SURFACE OF ROSE'S LIVING ROOM.
"NO ONE COULD HAVE GONE IN AND OUT OF THERE, AFTER THE VIOLENCE, WITHOUT LEAVING PLENTY OF FOOTPRINTS.
"AND YET JACK SAID HE'D SEARCHED THE PLACE, LOOKING FOR ROSE."
CHECK IN THE BEDROOM TO SEE IF SHE'S IN THERE!
I ALREADY CHECKED. SHE'S NOT HERE.
WHY COULDN'T IT BE THAT I WAS JUST CAREFUL TO SKIP AND HOP OVER THE BLOOD SPATTERS, LIKE YOU DID, TO PRESERVE THE EVIDENCE?
OH SURE. THAT MAKES PERFECT SENSE.
NOT A CHANCE, JACK. NO ONE ENCOUNTERING A SCENE LIKE THAT WORRIES ABOUT PRESERVING EVIDENCE WHILE HIS LADY LOVE MAY STILL BE IN THE BACK ROOM BLEEDING HER LIFE AWAY.
BUT THAT WAS FAR FROM YOUR ONLY AMATEUR MISTAKE.
THE NEXT TIME YOU TWO TRY TO STAGE A CRIME SCENE, YOU SHOULD ACTUALLY KNOCK THINGS OVER--
--RATHER THAN CAREFULLY PLACE THEM IN POSITIONS YOU WANT THEM TO END UP IN.

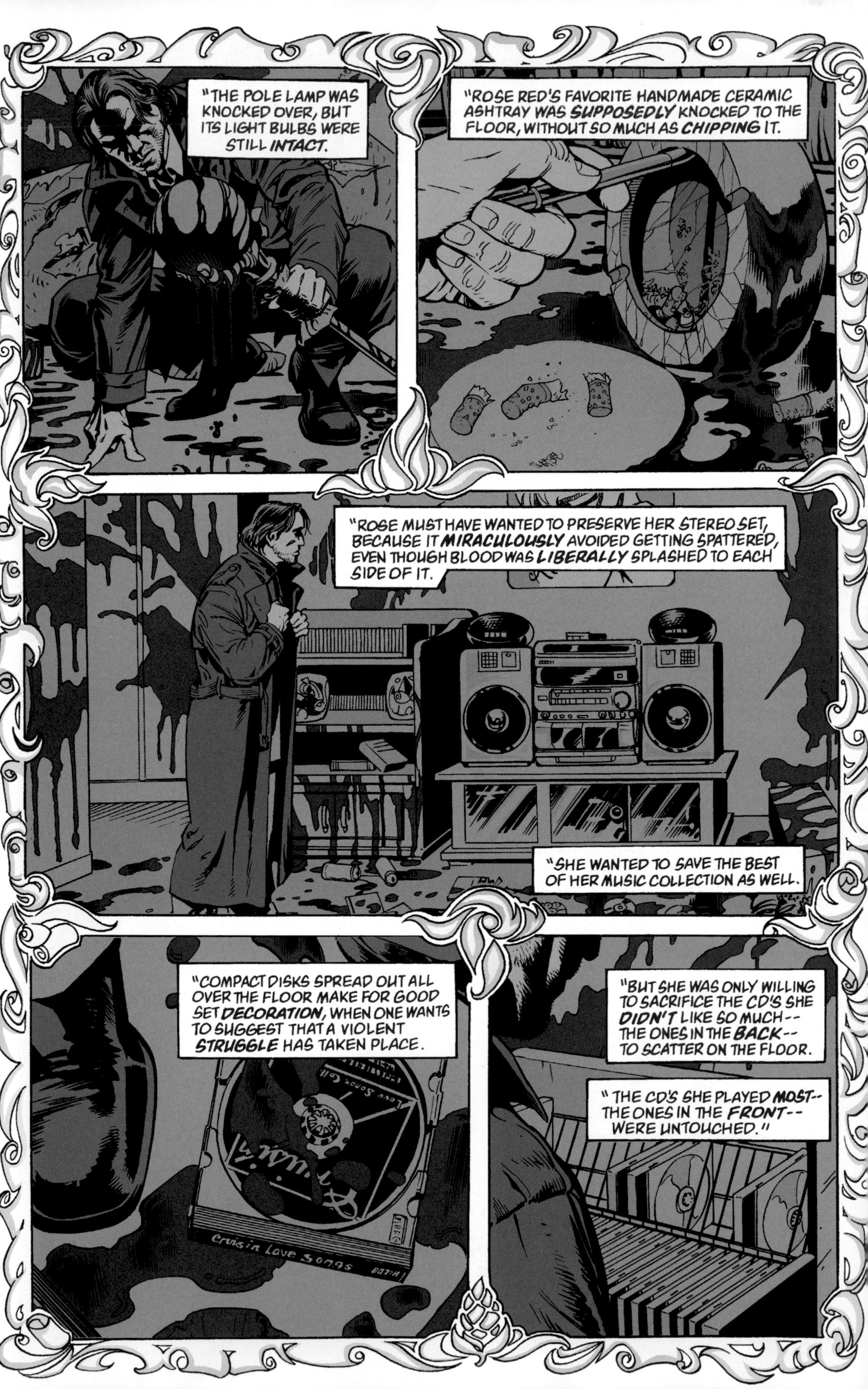
"THE POLE LAMP WAS KNOCKED OVER, BUT ITS LIGHT BULBS WERE STILL INTACT.
"ROSE RED'S FAVORITE HANDMADE CERAMIC ASHTRAY WAS SUPPOSEDLY KNOCKED TO THE FLOOR, WITHOUT SO MUCH AS CHIPPING IT.
"ROSE MUST HAVE WANTED TO PRESERVE HER STEREO SET, BECAUSE IT MIRACULOUSLY AVOIDED GETTING SPATTERED, EVEN THOUGH BLOOD WAS LIBERALLY SPLASHED TO EACH SIDE OF IT.
"SHE WANTED TO SAVE THE BEST OF HER MUSIC COLLECTION AS WELL.
"COMPACT DISKS SPREAD OUT ALL OVER THE FLOOR MAKE FOR GOOD SET DECORATION, WHEN ONE WANTS TO SUGGEST THAT A VIOLENT STRUGGLE HAS TAKEN PLACE.
Cruisin Love Songs
"BUT SHE WAS ONLY WILLING TO SACRIFICE THE CD'S SHE DIDN'T LIKE SO MUCH-- THE ONES IN THE BACK-- TO SCATTER ON THE FLOOR.
"THE CD'S SHE PLAYED MOST-- THE ONES IN THE FRONT-- WERE UNTOUCHED."

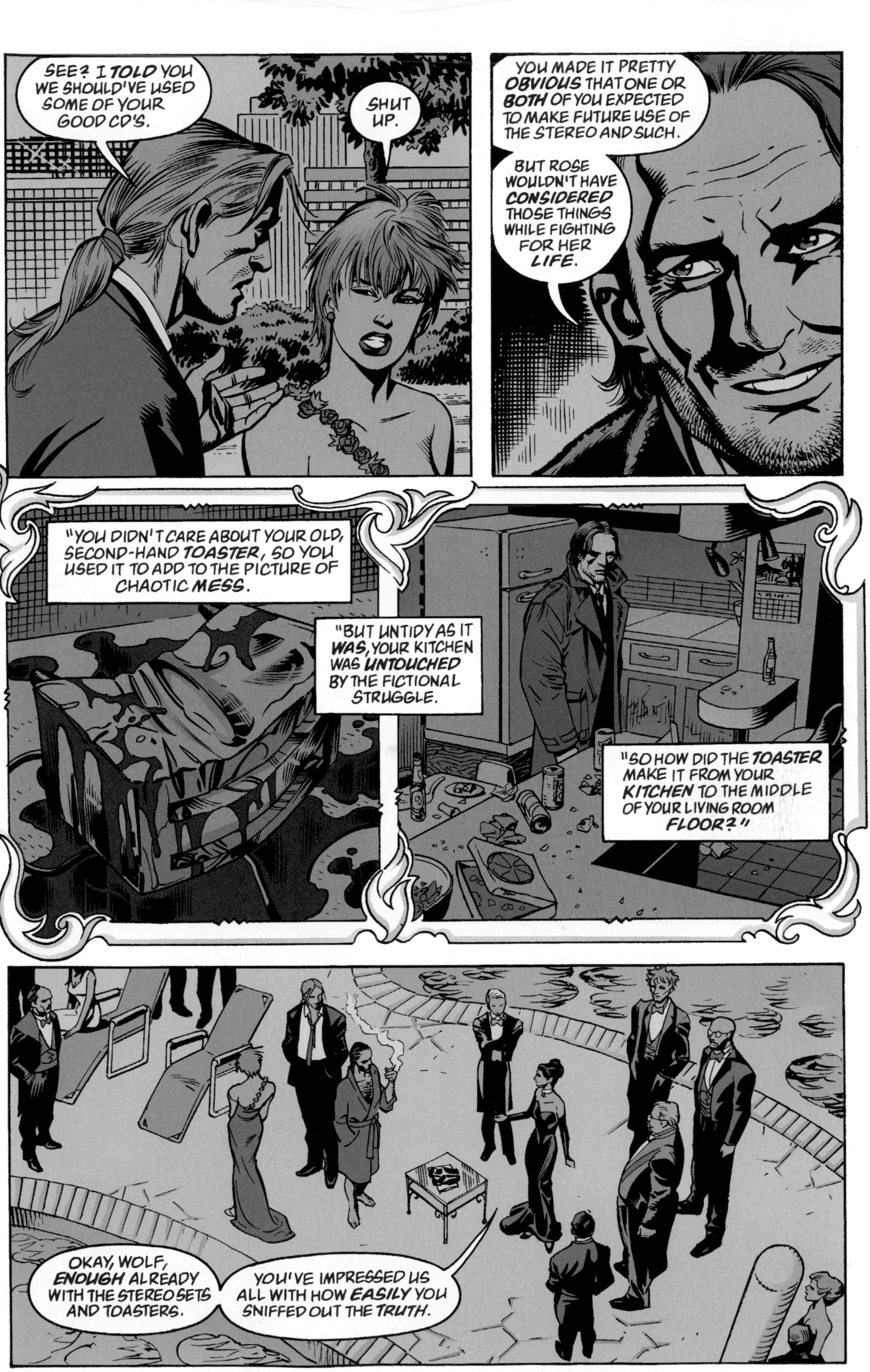

SEE? I TOLD YOU WE SHOULD'VE USED SOME OF YOUR GOOD CD'S.
SHUT UP.
YOU MADE IT PRETTY OBVIOUS THAT ONE OR BOTH OF YOU EXPECTED TO MAKE FUTURE USE OF THE STEREO AND SUCH.
BUT ROSE WOULDN'T HAVE CONSIDERED THOSE THINGS WHILE FIGHTING FOR HER LIFE.
"YOU DIDN'T CARE ABOUT YOUR OLD, SECOND-HAND TOASTER, SO YOU USED IT TO ADD TO THE PICTURE OF CHAOTIC MESS.
"BUT UNTIDY AS IT WAS, YOUR KITCHEN WAS UNTOUCHED BY THE FICTIONAL STRUGGLE.
"SO HOW DID THE TOASTER MAKE IT FROM YOUR KITCHEN TO THE MIDDLE OF YOUR LIVING ROOM FLOOR?"
OKAY, WOLF, ENOUGH ALREADY WITH THE STEREO SETS AND TOASTERS.
YOU'VE IMPRESSED US ALL WITH HOW EASILY YOU SNIFFED OUT THE TRUTH.

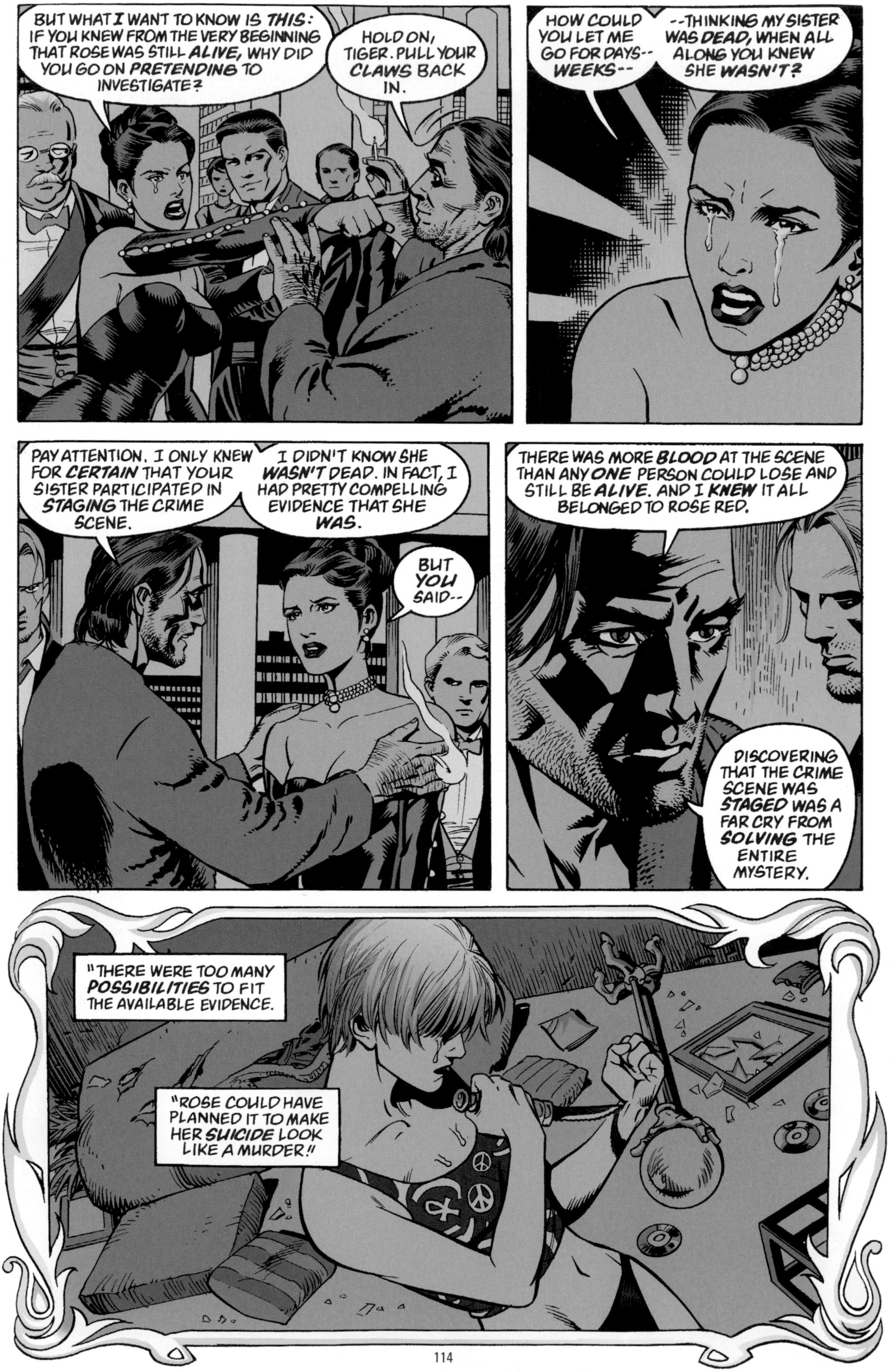
BUT WHAT I WANT TO KNOW IS THIS: IF YOU KNEW FROM THE VERY BEGINNING THAT ROSE WAS STILL ALIVE, WHY DID YOU GO ON PRETENDING TO INVESTIGATE?
HOLD ON, TIGER. PULL YOUR CLAWS BACK IN.
HOW COULD YOU LET ME GO FOR DAYS-- WEEKS--
--THINKING MY SISTER WAS DEAD, WHEN ALL ALONG YOU KNEW SHE WASN'T?
PAY ATTENTION. I ONLY KNEW FOR CERTAIN THAT YOUR SISTER PARTICIPATED IN STAGING THE CRIME SCENE.
I DIDN'T KNOW SHE WASN'T DEAD. IN FACT, I HAD PRETTY COMPELLING EVIDENCE THAT SHE WAS.
BUT YOU SAID--
THERE WAS MORE BLOOD AT THE SCENE THAN ANY ONE PERSON COULD LOSE AND STILL BE ALIVE. AND I KNEW IT ALL BELONGED TO ROSE RED.
DISCOVERING THAT THE CRIME SCENE WAS STAGED WAS A FAR CRY FROM SOLVING THE ENTIRE MYSTERY.
"THERE WERE TOO MANY POSSIBILITIES TO FIT THE AVAILABLE EVIDENCE.
"ROSE COULD HAVE PLANNED IT TO MAKE HER SUICIDE LOOK LIKE A MURDER!"

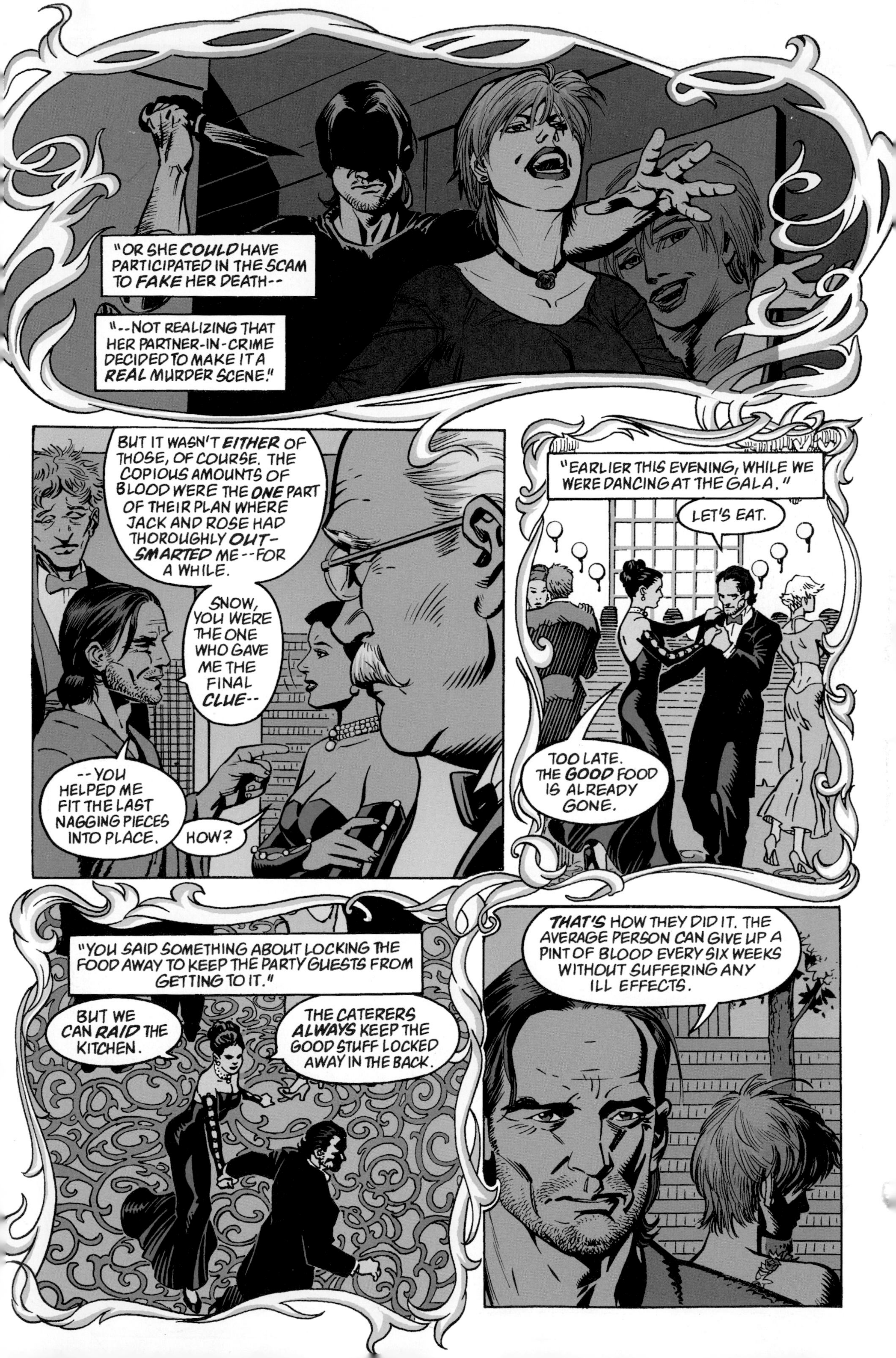
"OR SHE COULD HAVE PARTICIPATED IN THE SCAM TO FAKE HER DEATH--
"--NOT REALIZING THAT HER PARTNER-IN-CRIME DECIDED TO MAKE IT A REAL MURDER SCENE."
BUT IT WASN'T EITHER OF THOSE, OF COURSE. THE COPIOUS AMOUNTS OF BLOOD WERE THE ONE PART OF THEIR PLAN WHERE JACK AND ROSE HAD THOROUGHLY OUT-SMARTED ME--FOR A WHILE.
SNOW, YOU WERE THE ONE WHO GAVE ME THE FINAL CLUE--
--YOU HELPED ME FIT THE LAST NAGGING PIECES INTO PLACE.
HOW?
"EARLIER THIS EVENING, WHILE WE WERE DANCING AT THE GALA."
LET'S EAT.
TOO LATE. THE GOOD FOOD IS ALREADY GONE.
"YOU SAID SOMETHING ABOUT LOCKING THE FOOD AWAY TO KEEP THE PARTY GUESTS FROM GETTING TO IT."
BUT WE CAN RAID THE KITCHEN.
THE CATERERS ALWAYS KEEP THE GOOD STUFF LOCKED AWAY IN THE BACK.
THAT'S HOW THEY DID IT. THE AVERAGE PERSON CAN GIVE UP A PINT OF BLOOD EVERY SIX WEEKS WITHOUT SUFFERING ANY ILL EFFECTS.

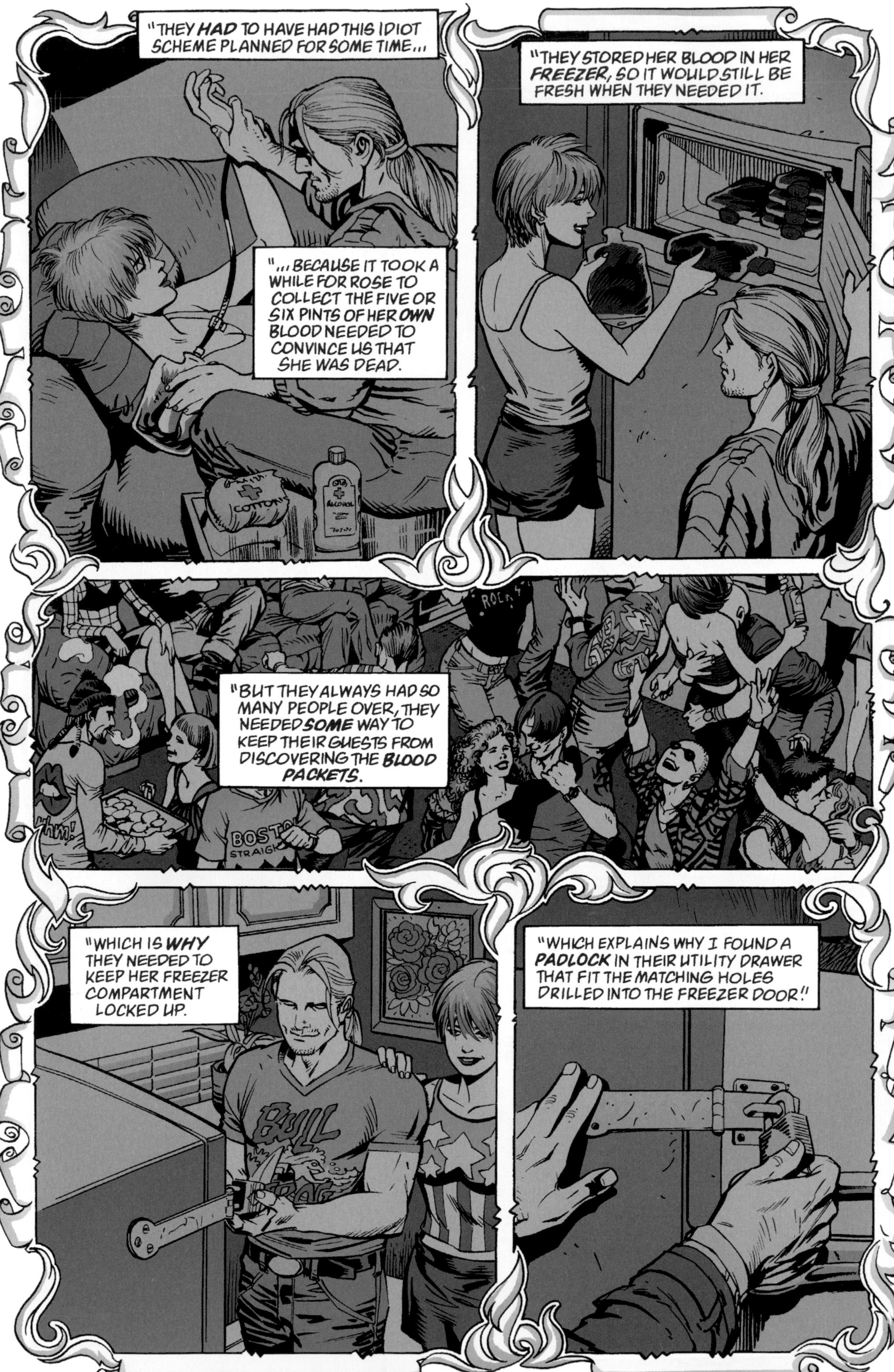
"THEY HAD TO HAVE HAD THIS IDIOT SCHEME PLANNED FOR SOME TIME...
"...BECAUSE IT TOOK A WHILE FOR ROSE TO COLLECT THE FIVE OR SIX PINTS OF HER OWN BLOOD NEEDED TO CONVINCE US THAT SHE WAS DEAD.
COTTON
ALCOHOL
"THEY STORED HER BLOOD IN HER FREEZER, SO IT WOULD STILL BE FRESH WHEN THEY NEEDED IT.
"BUT THEY ALWAYS HAD SO MANY PEOPLE OVER, THEY NEEDED SOME WAY TO KEEP THEIR GUESTS FROM DISCOVERING THE BLOOD PACKETS.
"WHICH IS WHY THEY NEEDED TO KEEP HER FREEZER COMPARTMENT LOCKED UP.
BULL
"WHICH EXPLAINS WHY I FOUND A PADLOCK IN THEIR UTILITY DRAWER THAT FIT THE MATCHING HOLES DRILLED INTO THE FREEZER DOOR!"

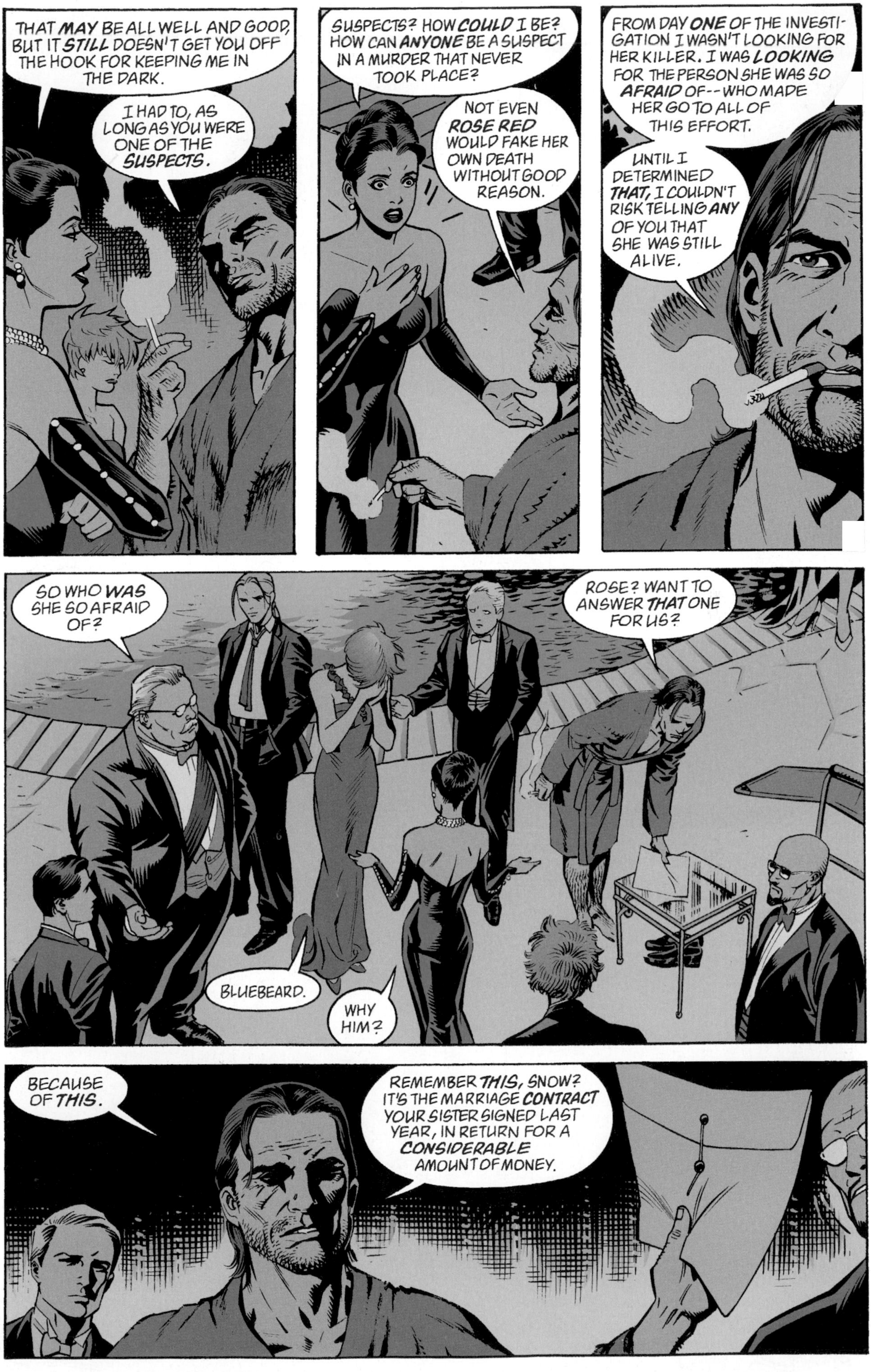

THAT MAY BE ALL WELL AND GOOD, BUT IT STILL DOESN'T GET YOU OFF THE HOOK FOR KEEPING ME IN THE DARK.
I HAD TO, AS LONG AS YOU WERE ONE OF THE SUSPECTS.
SUSPECTS? HOW COULD I BE? HOW CAN ANYONE BE A SUSPECT IN A MURDER THAT NEVER TOOK PLACE?
NOT EVEN ROSE RED WOULD FAKE HER OWN DEATH WITHOUT GOOD REASON.
FROM DAY ONE OF THE INVESTIGATION I WASN'T LOOKING FOR HER KILLER. I WAS LOOKING FOR THE PERSON SHE WAS SO AFRAID OF--WHO MADE HER GO TO ALL OF THIS EFFORT.
UNTIL I DETERMINED THAT, I COULDN'T RISK TELLING ANY OF YOU THAT SHE WAS STILL ALIVE.
SO WHO WAS SHE SO AFRAID OF?
ROSE? WANT TO ANSWER THAT ONE FOR US?
BLUEBEARD.
WHY HIM?
BECAUSE OF THIS.
REMEMBER THIS, SNOW? IT'S THE MARRIAGE CONTRACT YOUR SISTER SIGNED LAST YEAR, IN RETURN FOR A CONSIDERABLE AMOUNT OF MONEY.

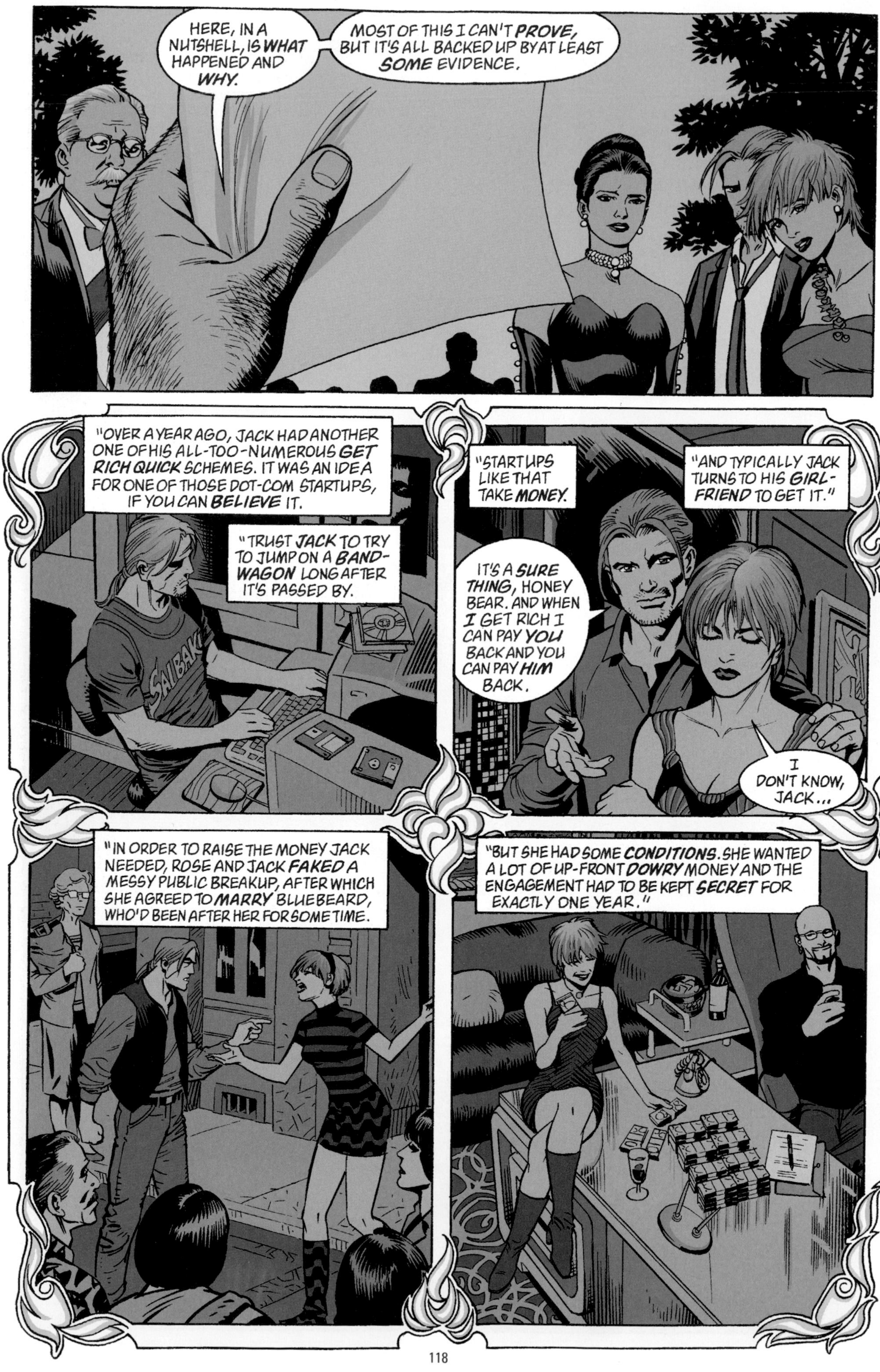
HERE, IN A NUTSHELL, IS WHAT HAPPENED AND WHY.
MOST OF THIS I CAN'T PROVE, BUT IT'S ALL BACKED UP BY AT LEAST SOME EVIDENCE.
"OVER A YEAR AGO, JACK HAD ANOTHER ONE OF HIS ALL-TOO-NUMEROUS GET RICH QUICK SCHEMES. IT WAS AN IDEA FOR ONE OF THOSE DOT-COM STARTUPS, IF YOU CAN BELIEVE IT.
"TRUST JACK TO TRY TO JUMP ON A BAND-WAGON LONG AFTER IT'S PASSED BY.
SAIBAK
"STARTUPS LIKE THAT TAKE MONEY.
"AND TYPICALLY JACK TURNS TO HIS GIRL-FRIEND TO GET IT."
IT'S A SURE THING, HONEY BEAR. AND WHEN I GET RICH I CAN PAY YOU BACK AND YOU CAN PAY HIM BACK.
I DON'T KNOW, JACK...
"IN ORDER TO RAISE THE MONEY JACK NEEDED, ROSE AND JACK FAKED A MESSY PUBLIC BREAKUP, AFTER WHICH SHE AGREED TO MARRY BLUEBEARD, WHO'D BEEN AFTER HER FOR SOME TIME.
"BUT SHE HAD SOME CONDITIONS. SHE WANTED A LOT OF UP-FRONT DOWRY MONEY AND THE ENGAGEMENT HAD TO BE KEPT SECRET FOR EXACTLY ONE YEAR."

THAT GAVE JACK ENOUGH TIME TO MAKE HIS *FORTUNE,* AND THEN ROSE WOULD PAY BLUEBEARD BACK AND-- RELUCTANTLY-- BREAK OFF THEIR SECRET ENGAGEMENT.

UNFORTUNATELY JACK LOST ALL THAT MONEY, DOWN THE SAME *BLACK HOLE* WHERE EVERYONE ELSE LOST THEIR DOT-COM INVESTMENTS.

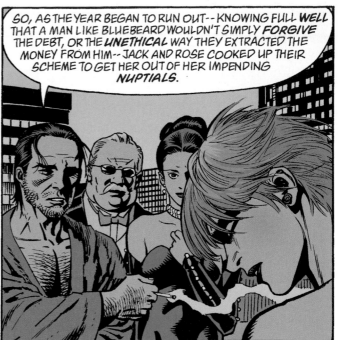

SO, AS THE YEAR BEGAN TO RUN OUT-- KNOWING FULL *WELL* THAT A MAN LIKE BLUEBEARD WOULDN'T SIMPLY *FORGIVE* THE DEBT, OR THE *UNETHICAL* WAY THEY EXTRACTED THE MONEY FROM HIM-- JACK AND ROSE COOKED UP THEIR SCHEME TO GET HER OUT OF HER IMPENDING *NUPTIALS.*

FAKING YOUR *DEATH?* ARE YOU FUCKING *KIDDING* ME, ROSE?

HOW LONG DID YOU IMAGINE *THAT* WOULD WORK?

WE NEEDED A WAY TO BUY MORE *TIME*-- JUST UNTIL WE FIGURED OUT ANOTHER WAY TO...

TO LAND YOURSELF IN *MUCH* MORE TROUBLE THAN YOU WERE IN *ORIGINALLY?*

NEITHER ROSE NOR JACK EARNED RENOWN FOR THEIR *INTELLIGENCE.* WORKING TOGETHER, THEY COULDN'T *HELP* BUT REACH NEW LOWS OF IMBECILITY.

OH YEAH, PEASANT SCUM? IF *I'M* SO DUMB AND *YOU'RE* SO SMART, HOW IS IT I *NOW* HAVE THE TITLES AND LANDS *YOU* USED TO *OWN?*

WHY DO YOU THINK THEY CALL IT DUMB *LUCK,* PRINCE KNUCKLE-DRAGGER?

ENOUGH OF THIS! *STOP* IT, BOTH OF YOU! *ALL* OF YOU!

119

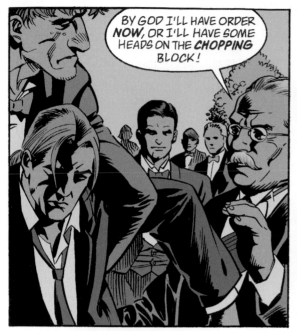

BY GOD I'LL HAVE ORDER **NOW**, OR I'LL HAVE SOME HEADS ON THE **CHOPPING** BLOCK!

MISTER WOLF, IS THERE ANYTHING **ELSE** YOU'VE YET TO REVEAL?

NO, I'VE PRETTY MUCH TOLD **ALL** OF IT.

THEN WHAT ARE WE TO DO **NOW**?

WHO KNOWS? I'VE DONE **MY** JOB BY FIGURING EVERYTHING OUT. IT'S UP TO **YOU** AND **SNOW** TO WORK OUT WHAT TO **DO** ABOUT IT.

BUT I HAVE SOME **SUGGESTIONS**, IF YOU'D CARE TO HEAR ABOUT THEM -- IN **PRIVATE**.

I'M THE INJURED PARTY HERE. I'VE BEEN CHEATED OUT OF MY MONEY **AND** A BRIDE. I'LL HAVE SATISFACTION FROM THESE TWO. **HIS** BLOOD ON MY BLADE, AND **HER** HAND IN MARRIAGE -- AS SHE IS **CONTRACTED** TO DO.

AND **I** HAVE SOME MONEY COMING TOO.

YOU'VE YET TO **PAY** ME THE GLORIOUS **MILLIONS** I'VE EARNED FOR THE RAFFLE OF MY TITLE AND ESTATES.

WE'LL SETTLE ALL OF THAT **LATER**. FOR NOW, IT'S LATE. EVERYONE GO HOME, AND **STAY** THERE.

THE MAYOR, THE SHERIFF AND I WILL MEET TO WORK THINGS OUT -- AND **SUMMON** YOU AS YOU'RE NEEDED -- SO DON'T ANYONE WANDER OFF.

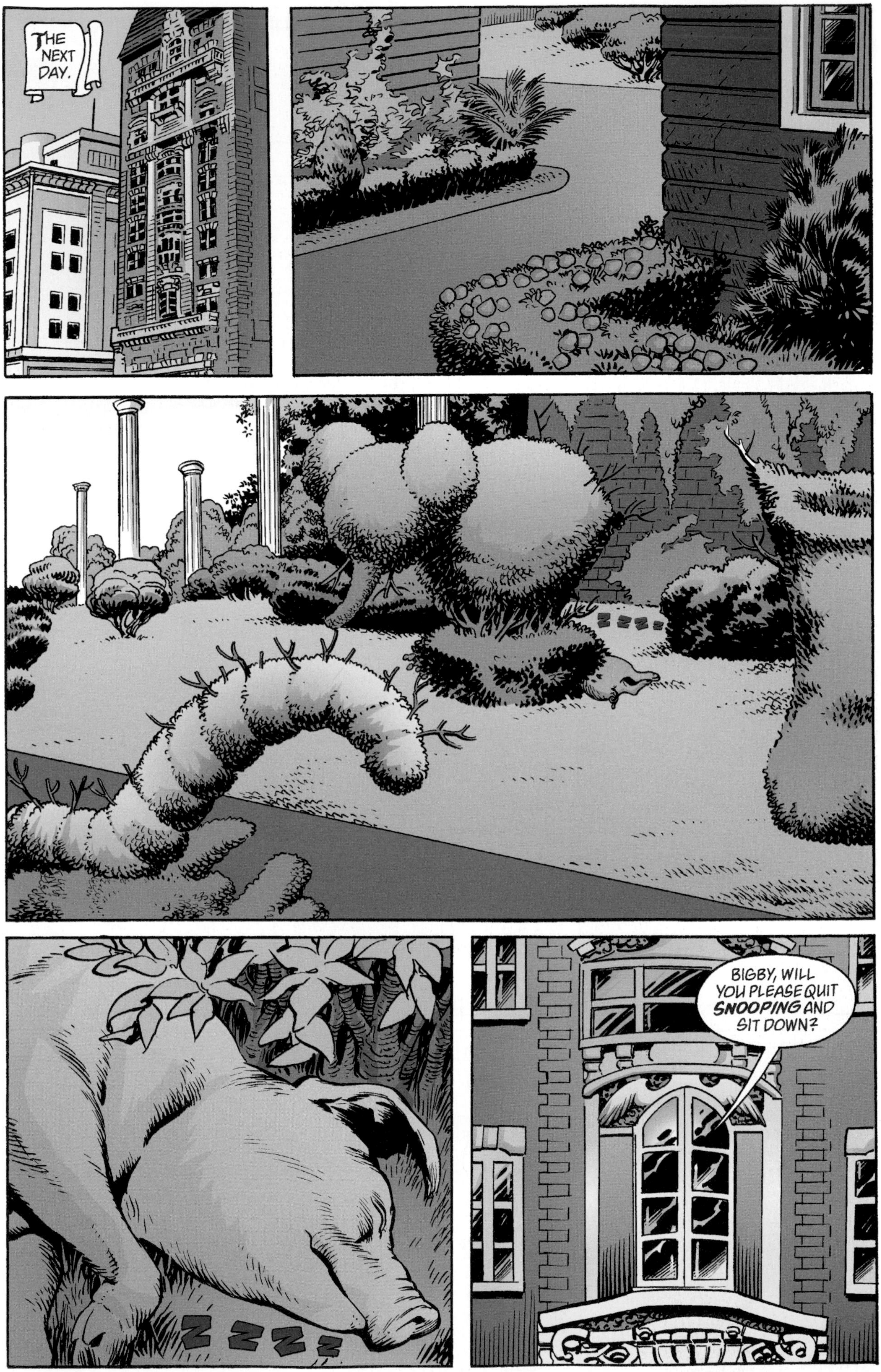
THE NEXT DAY.
ZZZZ
ZZZZ
BIGBY, WILL YOU PLEASE QUIT SNOOPING AND SIT DOWN?

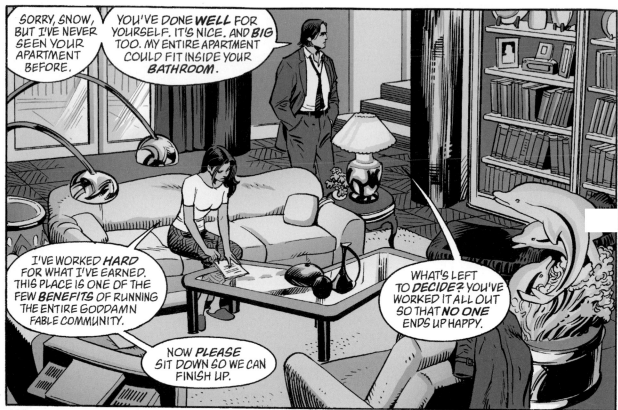

SORRY, SNOW, BUT I'VE NEVER SEEN YOUR APARTMENT BEFORE.

YOU'VE DONE **WELL** FOR YOURSELF. IT'S NICE. AND **BIG** TOO. MY ENTIRE APARTMENT COULD FIT INSIDE YOUR **BATHROOM.**

I'VE WORKED **HARD** FOR WHAT I'VE EARNED. THIS PLACE IS ONE OF THE FEW **BENEFITS** OF RUNNING THE ENTIRE GODDAMN FABLE COMMUNITY.

NOW **PLEASE** SIT DOWN SO WE CAN FINISH UP.

WHAT'S LEFT TO **DECIDE?** YOU'VE WORKED IT ALL OUT SO THAT **NO ONE** ENDS UP HAPPY.

BUT AT LEAST THE MISERY IS SPREAD **OUT** AS MUCH AS POSSIBLE.

AND KING COLE WILL GO **ALONG** WITH THIS?

THE MAYOR'S JOB IS TO **GLAD-HAND** AND SET GENERAL POLICY. IT'S **MY** JOB TO WORK OUT THE DIRTY **DETAILS.**

HE'LL GO ALONG WITH WHAT I DECIDE.

NO ONE'S GOING TO BE VERY HAPPY WITH YOU AFTER TODAY.

BOO FUCKING HOO. I'LL TRY TO **LIVE** WITH THE LOSS.

WHEN DID **YOU** START CUSSING SO MUCH?

NOW LET'S GET **TO** IT. BRING THEM TO ME IN **THIS** ORDER, AT **THESE** PLACES, AND **I'LL** HANDLE THE ACTUAL **BLOODLETTING.**

DON'T YOU **DARE** LIGHT THAT UNTIL YOU LEAVE.

SO HERE WE ARE, MY *SWEET*, BACK AT THE SAME TABLE, IN THE SAME *PLACE* WHERE WE ORIGINALLY KICKED OFF THE PLAN THAT MADE ME *RICH* AGAIN. *FULL CIRCLE*, YOU MIGHT SAY.

DO YOU *HAVE* MY MONEY?

HERE YOU GO.

I AM THE EGG MAN DINER

DON'T SPEND IT ALL IN ONE PLACE, *DARLING*.

WHERE'S THE *REST*?

THAT'S ALL OF IT--LESS THE *PRE-AGREED* FEES AND *EXPENSES* OF COURSE.

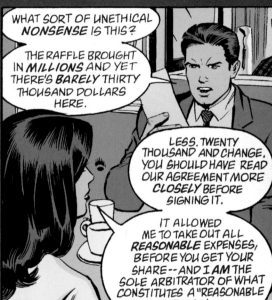

WHAT SORT OF UNETHICAL *NONSENSE* IS THIS?

THE RAFFLE BROUGHT IN *MILLIONS* AND YET THERE'S *BARELY* THIRTY THOUSAND DOLLARS HERE.

LESS. TWENTY THOUSAND AND CHANGE. YOU SHOULD HAVE READ OUR AGREEMENT MORE *CLOSELY* BEFORE SIGNING IT.

IT ALLOWED ME TO TAKE OUT ALL *REASONABLE* EXPENSES, BEFORE YOU GET YOUR SHARE-- AND I AM THE SOLE ARBITRATOR OF WHAT CONSTITUTES A "REASONABLE" EXPENSE!

THE MONEY WE RAISED IS NEEDED TO PAY OFF *BLUEBEARD*, AND THE COST OF THE *INVESTIGATION*. YOU'RE *LUCKY* I GAVE YOU THE LEFTOVERS.

BUT *NONE* OF THAT IS *MY* RESPONSIBILITY!

TOO *BAD*. YOU SHOULD *NEVER* HAVE SLEPT WITH MY SISTER.

NOW, IF I WERE *YOU*, I'D USE WHAT'S *LEFT* TO BUY YOUR TITLE *BACK* FROM JACK. I BET HE CAN BE BOUGHT *CHEAP*, AND YOU'D NEVER MAKE IT AS A *POOR* COMMONER.

BYE, LOVE. YOU'LL PICK UP THE *CHECK*?

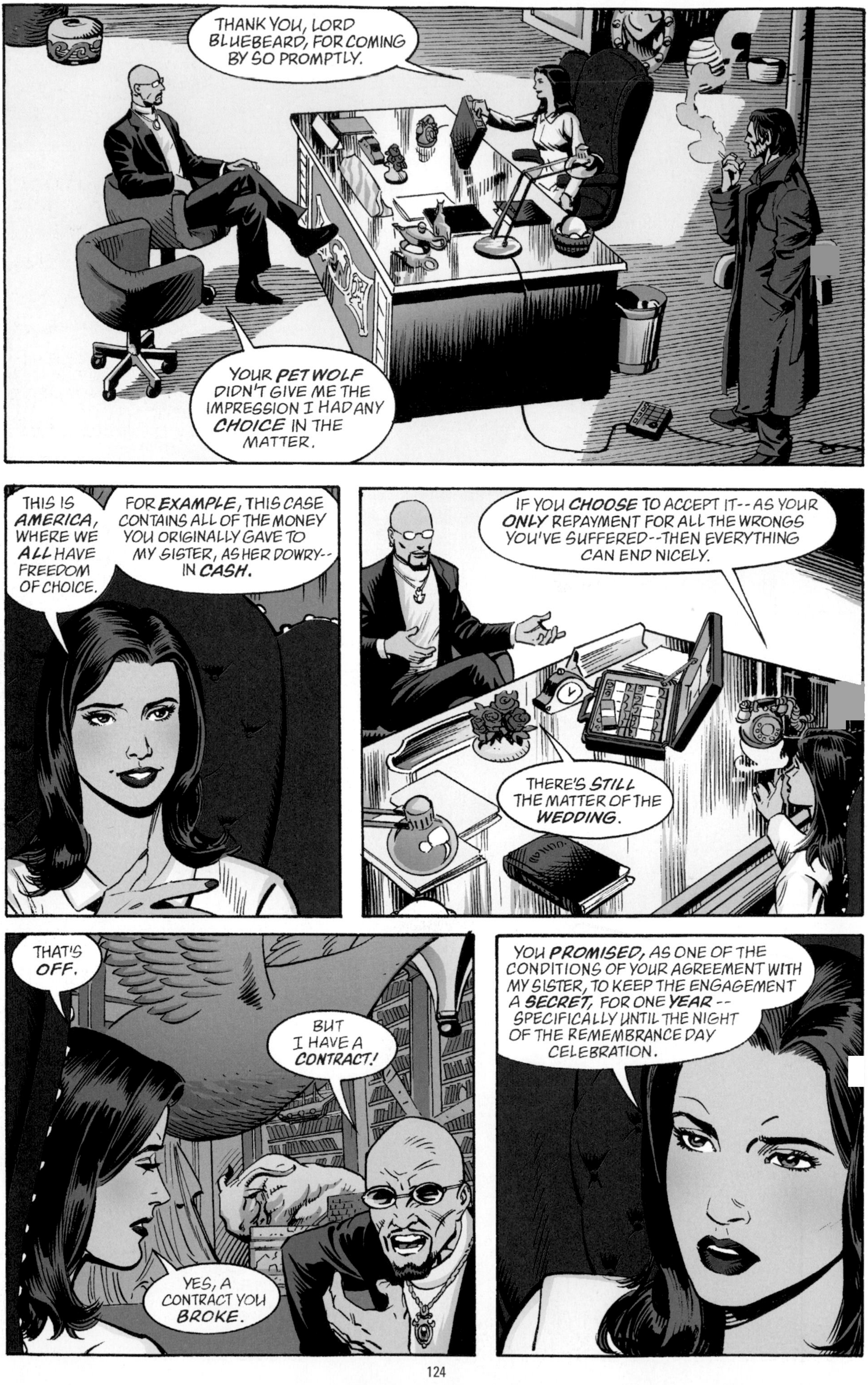
THANK YOU, LORD BLUEBEARD, FOR COMING BY SO PROMPTLY.
YOUR PET WOLF DIDN'T GIVE ME THE IMPRESSION I HAD ANY CHOICE IN THE MATTER.
THIS IS AMERICA, WHERE WE ALL HAVE FREEDOM OF CHOICE.
FOR EXAMPLE, THIS CASE CONTAINS ALL OF THE MONEY YOU ORIGINALLY GAVE TO MY SISTER, AS HER DOWRY-- IN CASH.
IF YOU CHOOSE TO ACCEPT IT--AS YOUR ONLY REPAYMENT FOR ALL THE WRONGS YOU'VE SUFFERED--THEN EVERYTHING CAN END NICELY.
THERE'S STILL THE MATTER OF THE WEDDING.
THAT'S OFF.
BUT I HAVE A CONTRACT!
YES, A CONTRACT YOU BROKE.
YOU PROMISED, AS ONE OF THE CONDITIONS OF YOUR AGREEMENT WITH MY SISTER, TO KEEP THE ENGAGEMENT A SECRET, FOR ONE YEAR -- SPECIFICALLY UNTIL THE NIGHT OF THE REMEMBRANCE DAY CELEBRATION.

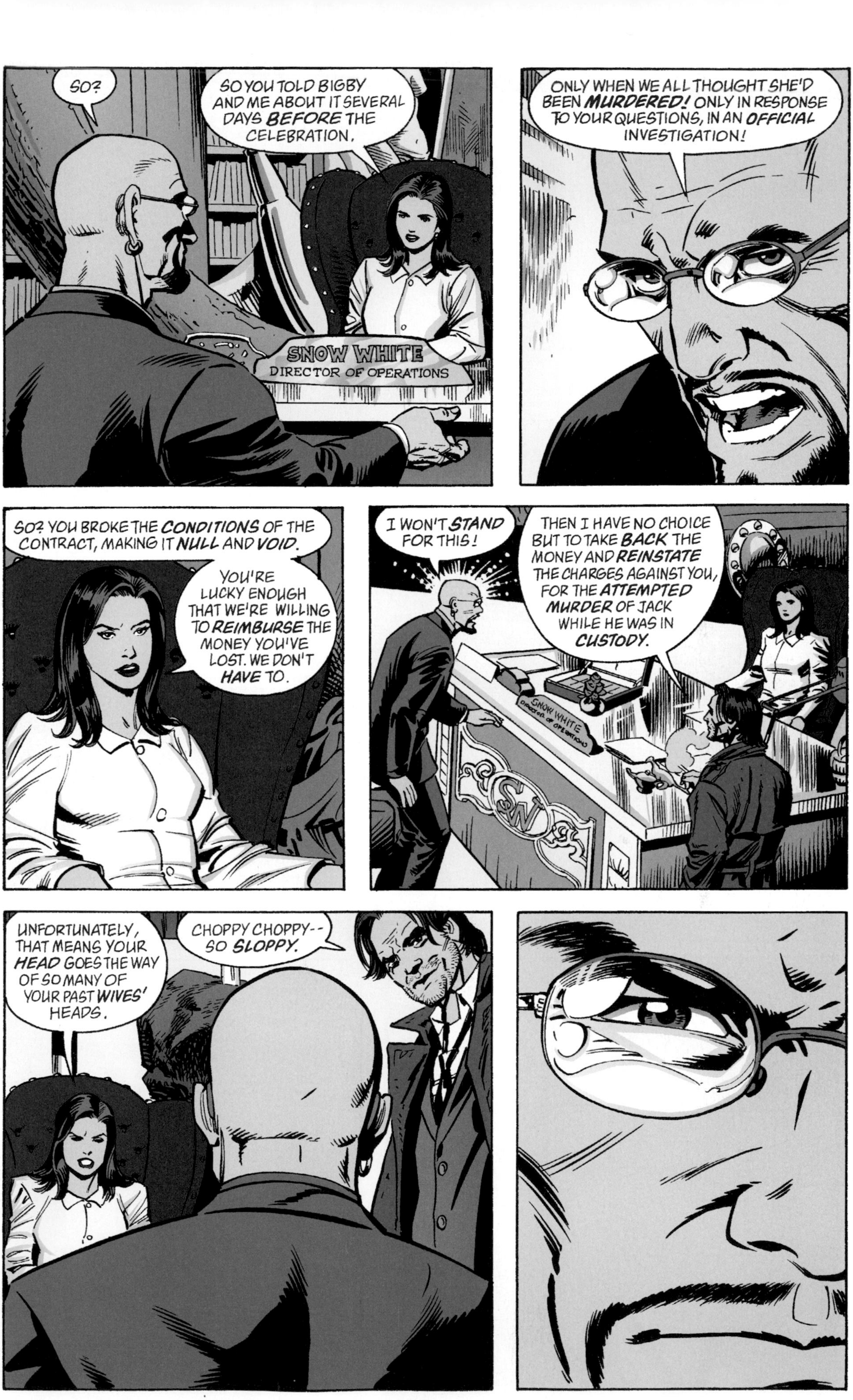
SO?
SO YOU TOLD BIGBY AND ME ABOUT IT SEVERAL DAYS BEFORE THE CELEBRATION.
SNOW WHITE
DIRECTOR OF OPERATIONS
ONLY WHEN WE ALL THOUGHT SHE'D BEEN MURDERED! ONLY IN RESPONSE TO YOUR QUESTIONS, IN AN OFFICIAL INVESTIGATION!
SO? YOU BROKE THE CONDITIONS OF THE CONTRACT, MAKING IT NULL AND VOID.
YOU'RE LUCKY ENOUGH THAT WE'RE WILLING TO REIMBURSE THE MONEY YOU'VE LOST. WE DON'T HAVE TO.
I WON'T STAND FOR THIS!
THEN I HAVE NO CHOICE BUT TO TAKE BACK THE MONEY AND REINSTATE THE CHARGES AGAINST YOU, FOR THE ATTEMPTED MURDER OF JACK WHILE HE WAS IN CUSTODY.
SNOW WHITE
DIRECTOR OF OPERATIONS
UNFORTUNATELY, THAT MEANS YOUR HEAD GOES THE WAY OF SO MANY OF YOUR PAST WIVES' HEADS.
CHOPPY CHOPPY--
SO SLOPPY.

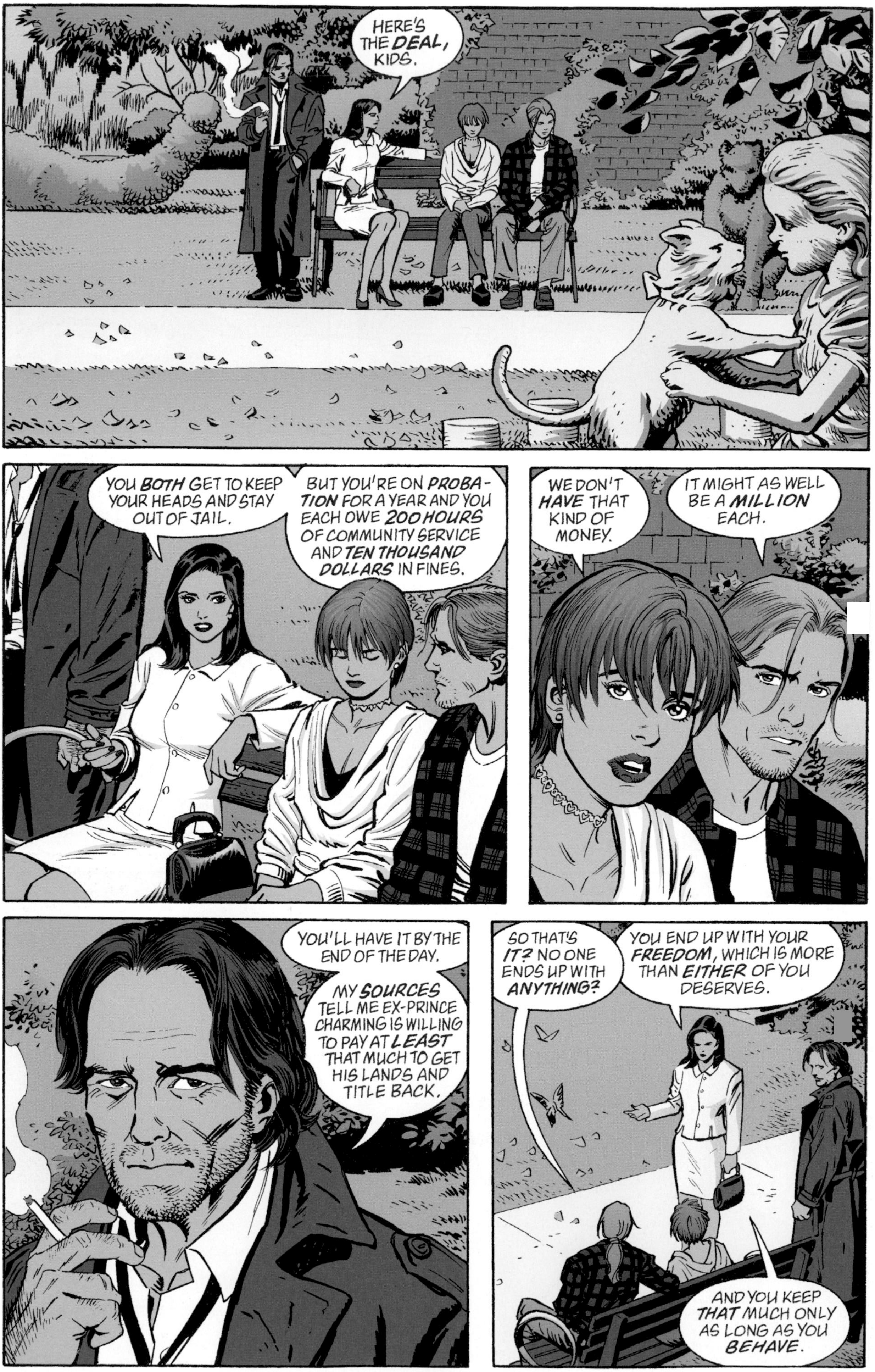
HERE'S THE DEAL, KIDS.
YOU BOTH GET TO KEEP YOUR HEADS AND STAY OUT OF JAIL.
BUT YOU'RE ON PROBATION FOR A YEAR AND YOU EACH OWE 200 HOURS OF COMMUNITY SERVICE AND TEN THOUSAND DOLLARS IN FINES.
WE DON'T HAVE THAT KIND OF MONEY.
IT MIGHT AS WELL BE A MILLION EACH.
YOU'LL HAVE IT BY THE END OF THE DAY.
MY SOURCES TELL ME EX-PRINCE CHARMING IS WILLING TO PAY AT LEAST THAT MUCH TO GET HIS LANDS AND TITLE BACK.
SO THAT'S IT? NO ONE ENDS UP WITH ANYTHING?
YOU END UP WITH YOUR FREEDOM, WHICH IS MORE THAN EITHER OF YOU DESERVES.
AND YOU KEEP THAT MUCH ONLY AS LONG AS YOU BEHAVE.

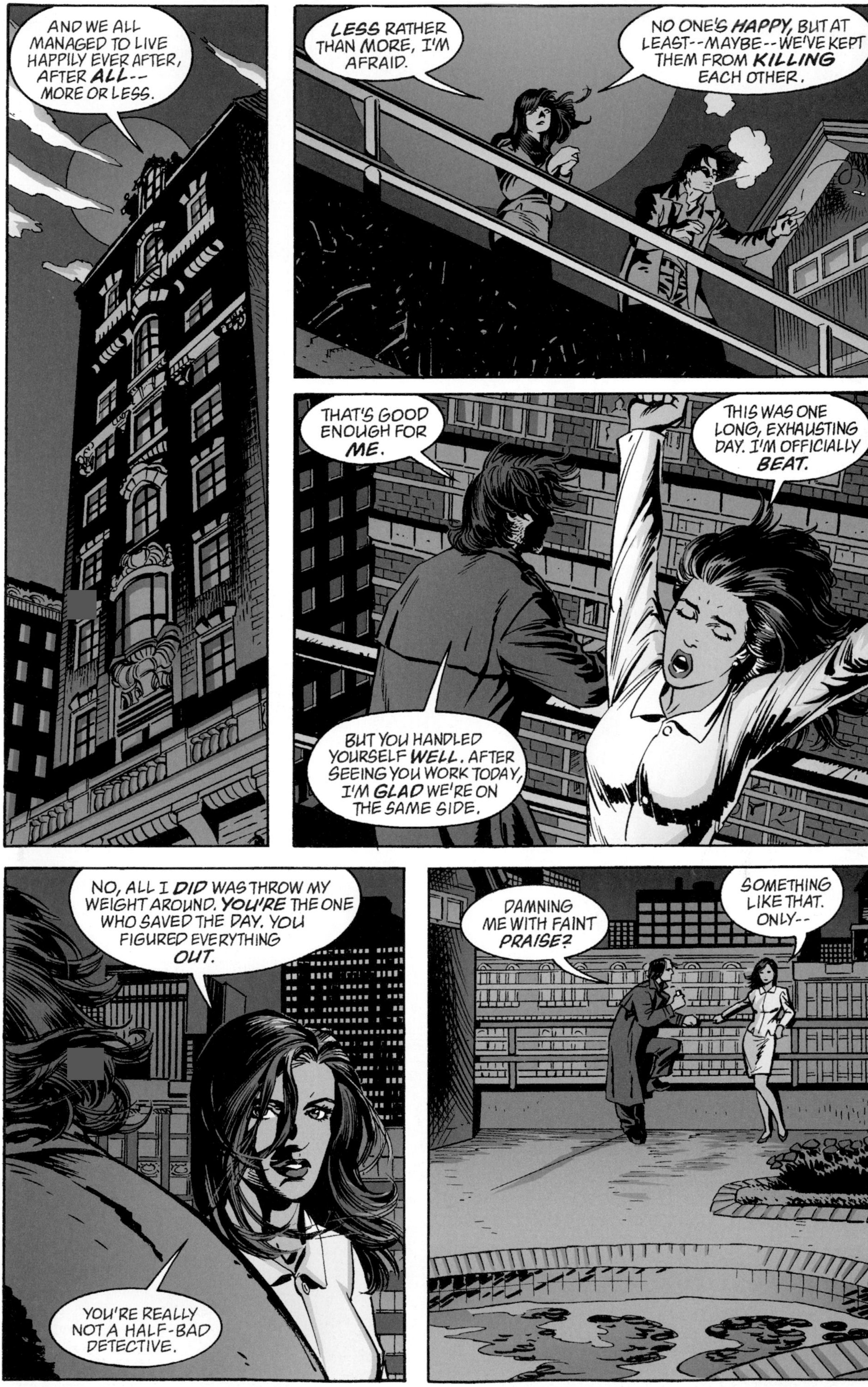
AND WE ALL MANAGED TO LIVE HAPPILY EVER AFTER, AFTER ALL-- MORE OR LESS.
LESS RATHER THAN MORE, I'M AFRAID.
NO ONE'S HAPPY, BUT AT LEAST--MAYBE--WE'VE KEPT THEM FROM KILLING EACH OTHER.
THAT'S GOOD ENOUGH FOR ME.
THIS WAS ONE LONG, EXHAUSTING DAY. I'M OFFICIALLY BEAT.
BUT YOU HANDLED YOURSELF WELL. AFTER SEEING YOU WORK TODAY, I'M GLAD WE'RE ON THE SAME SIDE.
NO, ALL I DID WAS THROW MY WEIGHT AROUND. YOU'RE THE ONE WHO SAVED THE DAY. YOU FIGURED EVERYTHING OUT.
YOU'RE REALLY NOT A HALF-BAD DETECTIVE.
DAMNING ME WITH FAINT PRAISE?
SOMETHING LIKE THAT. ONLY--

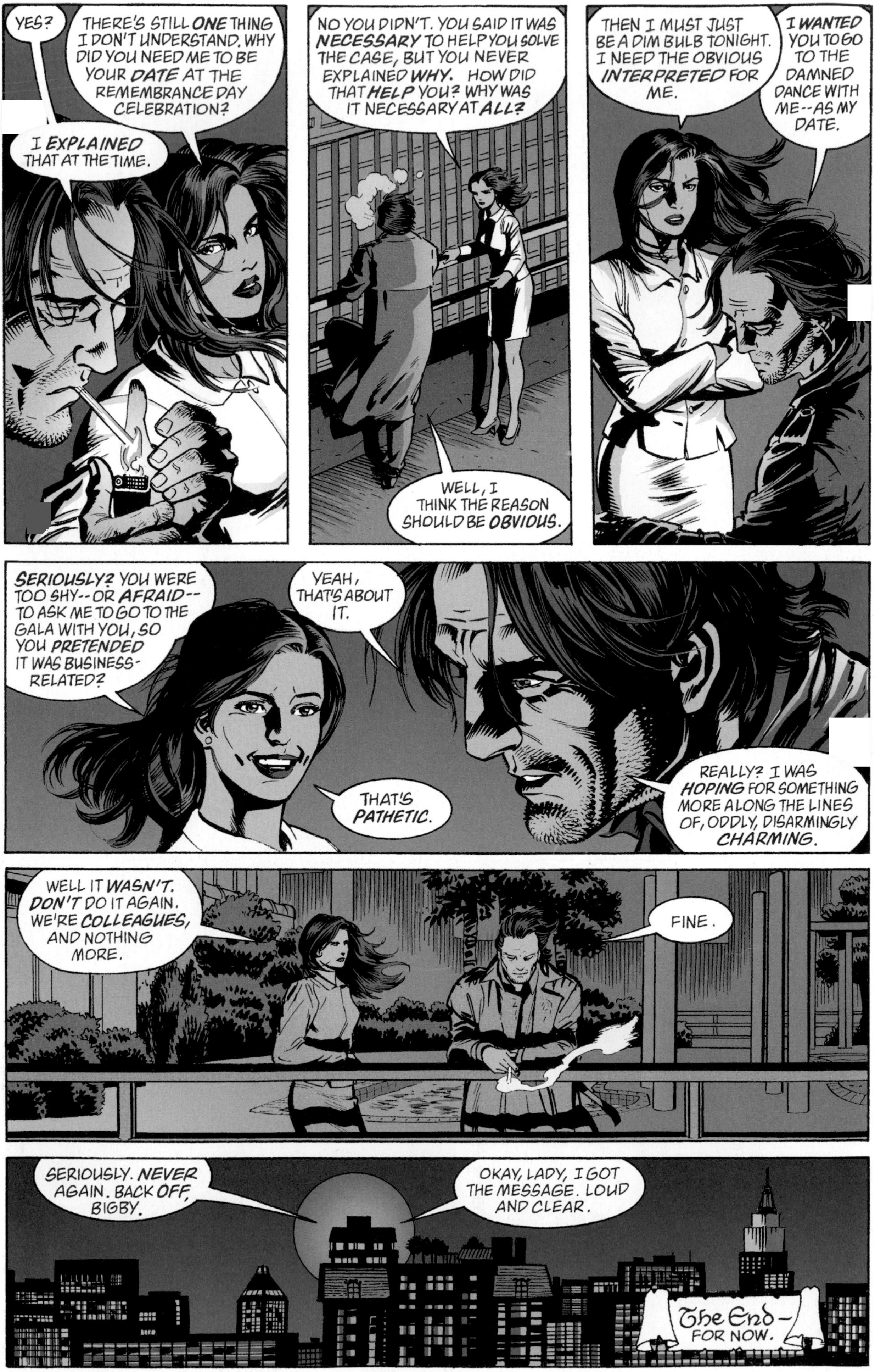
YES?
THERE'S STILL ONE THING I DON'T UNDERSTAND. WHY DID YOU NEED ME TO BE YOUR DATE AT THE REMEMBRANCE DAY CELEBRATION?
I EXPLAINED THAT AT THE TIME.
NO YOU DIDN'T. YOU SAID IT WAS NECESSARY TO HELP YOU SOLVE THE CASE, BUT YOU NEVER EXPLAINED WHY. HOW DID THAT HELP YOU? WHY WAS IT NECESSARY AT ALL?
WELL, I THINK THE REASON SHOULD BE OBVIOUS.
THEN I MUST JUST BE A DIM BULB TONIGHT. I NEED THE OBVIOUS INTERPRETED FOR ME.
I WANTED YOU TO GO TO THE DAMNED DANCE WITH ME--AS MY DATE.
SERIOUSLY? YOU WERE TOO SHY--OR AFRAID--TO ASK ME TO GO TO THE GALA WITH YOU, SO YOU PRETENDED IT WAS BUSINESS-RELATED?
YEAH, THAT'S ABOUT IT.
THAT'S PATHETIC.
REALLY? I WAS HOPING FOR SOMETHING MORE ALONG THE LINES OF, ODDLY, DISARMINGLY CHARMING.
WELL IT WASN'T. DON'T DO IT AGAIN. WE'RE COLLEAGUES, AND NOTHING MORE.
FINE.
SERIOUSLY. NEVER AGAIN. BACK OFF, BIGBY.
OKAY, LADY, I GOT THE MESSAGE. LOUD AND CLEAR.
The End— FOR NOW.

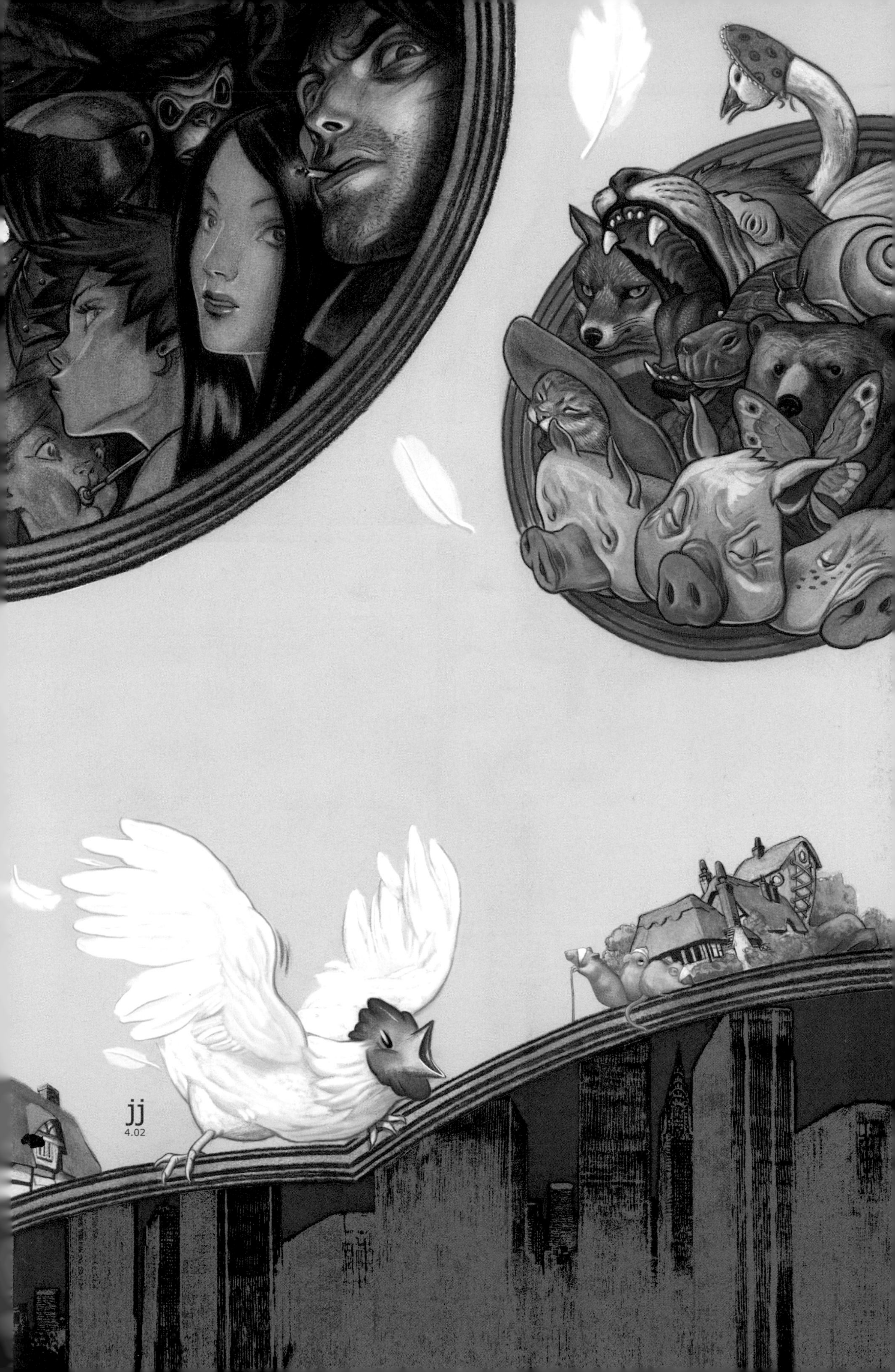
jj
4.02

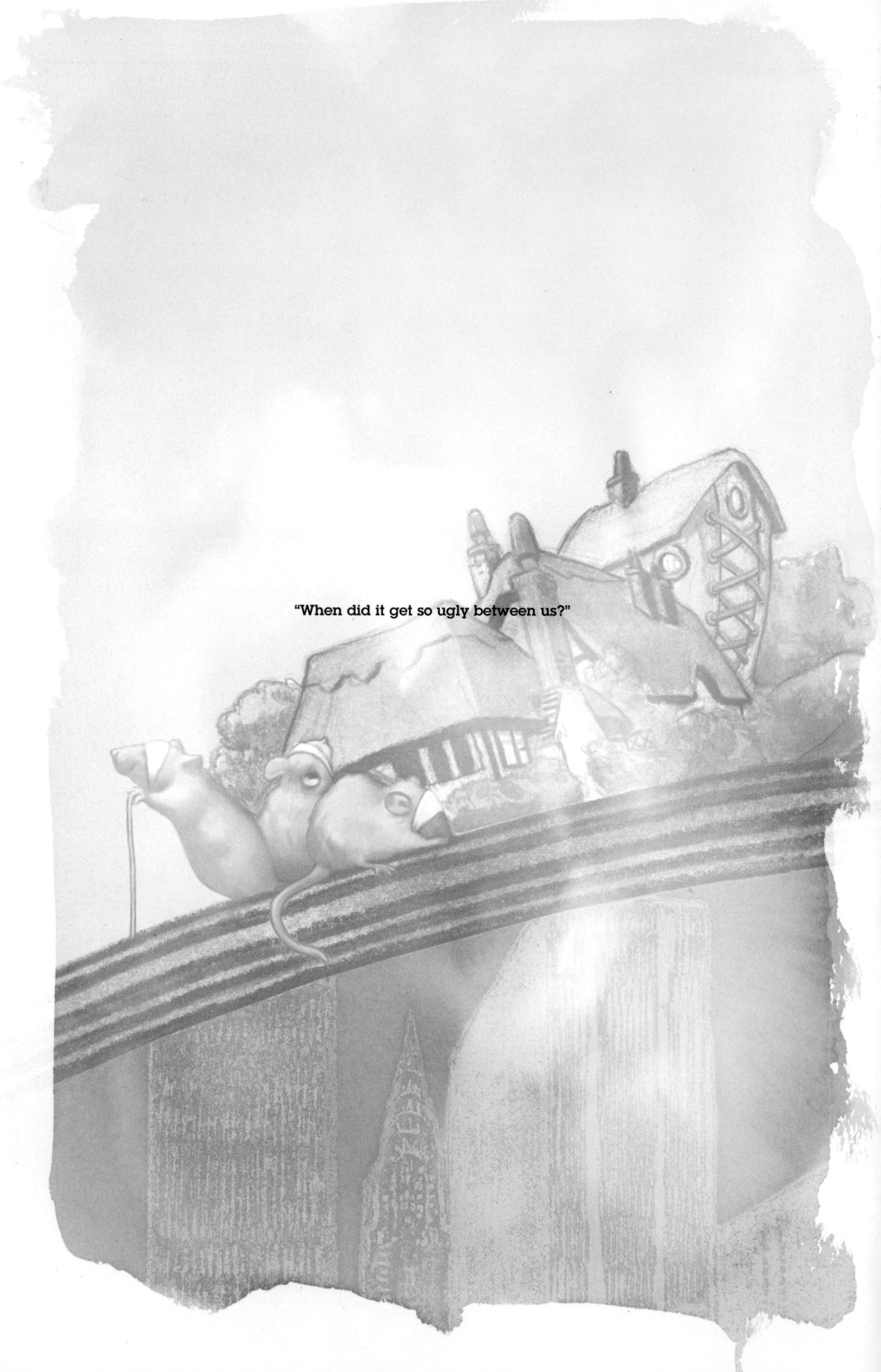
"When did it get so ugly between us?"

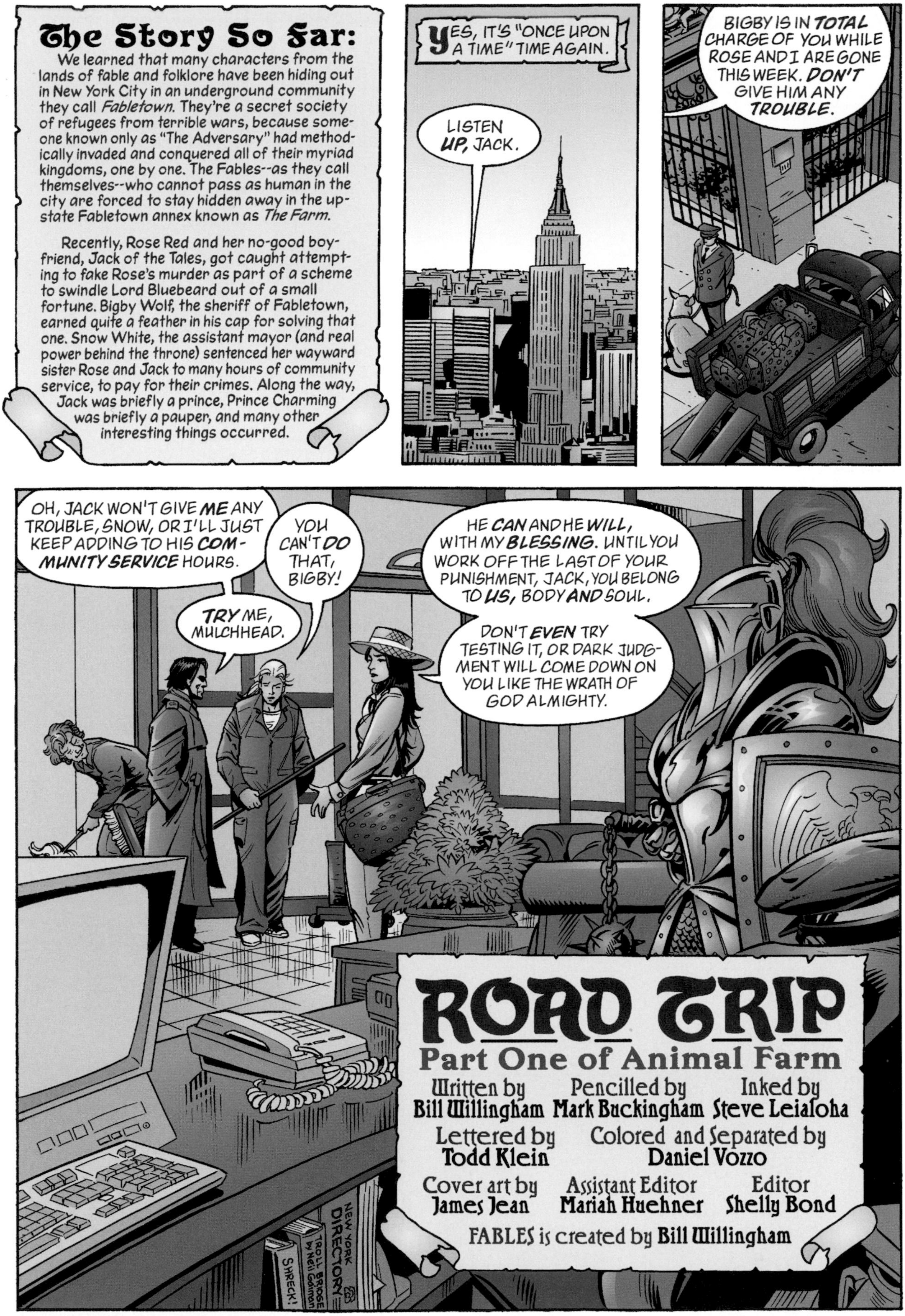
The Story So Far:
We learned that many characters from the lands of fable and folklore have been hiding out in New York City in an underground community they call Fabletown. They're a secret society of refugees from terrible wars, because someone known only as "The Adversary" had methodically invaded and conquered all of their myriad kingdoms, one by one. The Fables--as they call themselves--who cannot pass as human in the city are forced to stay hidden away in the upstate Fabletown annex known as The Farm.
Recently, Rose Red and her no-good boyfriend, Jack of the Tales, got caught attempting to fake Rose's murder as part of a scheme to swindle Lord Bluebeard out of a small fortune. Bigby Wolf, the sheriff of Fabletown, earned quite a feather in his cap for solving that one. Snow White, the assistant mayor (and real power behind the throne) sentenced her wayward sister Rose and Jack to many hours of community service, to pay for their crimes. Along the way, Jack was briefly a prince, Prince Charming was briefly a pauper, and many other interesting things occurred.
YES, IT'S "ONCE UPON A TIME" TIME AGAIN.
LISTEN UP, JACK.
BIGBY IS IN TOTAL CHARGE OF YOU WHILE ROSE AND I ARE GONE THIS WEEK. DON'T GIVE HIM ANY TROUBLE.
OH, JACK WON'T GIVE ME ANY TROUBLE, SNOW, OR I'LL JUST KEEP ADDING TO HIS COMMUNITY SERVICE HOURS.
YOU CAN'T DO THAT, BIGBY!
TRY ME, MULCHHEAD.
HE CAN AND HE WILL, WITH MY BLESSING. UNTIL YOU WORK OFF THE LAST OF YOUR PUNISHMENT, JACK, YOU BELONG TO US, BODY AND SOUL.
DON'T EVEN TRY TESTING IT, OR DARK JUDGMENT WILL COME DOWN ON YOU LIKE THE WRATH OF GOD ALMIGHTY.
ROAD TRIP
Part One of Animal Farm
Written by Bill Willingham
Pencilled by Mark Buckingham
Inked by Steve Leialoha
Lettered by Todd Klein
Colored and Separated by Daniel Vozzo
Cover art by James Jean
Assistant Editor Mariah Huehner
Editor Shelly Bond
FABLES is created by Bill Willingham
NEW YORK DIRECTORY
TROLL BRIDGE by Neil Gaiman
SHRECK!

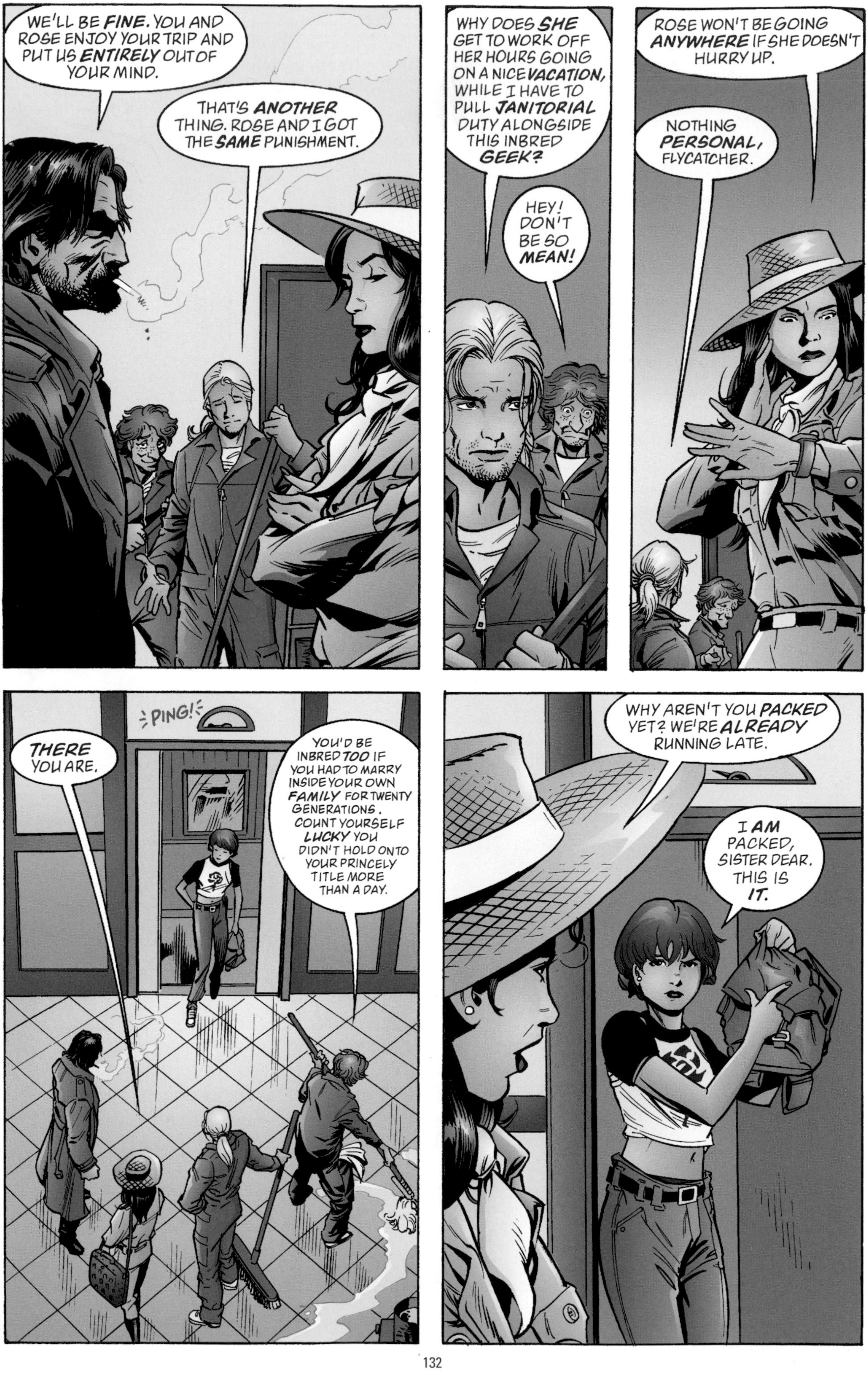
WE'LL BE FINE. YOU AND ROSE ENJOY YOUR TRIP AND PUT US ENTIRELY OUT OF YOUR MIND.
THAT'S ANOTHER THING. ROSE AND I GOT THE SAME PUNISHMENT.
WHY DOES SHE GET TO WORK OFF HER HOURS GOING ON A NICE VACATION, WHILE I HAVE TO PULL JANITORIAL DUTY ALONGSIDE THIS INBRED GEEK?
HEY! DON'T BE SO MEAN!
ROSE WON'T BE GOING ANYWHERE IF SHE DOESN'T HURRY UP.
NOTHING PERSONAL, FLYCATCHER.
PING!
THERE YOU ARE.
YOU'D BE INBRED TOO IF YOU HAD TO MARRY INSIDE YOUR OWN FAMILY FOR TWENTY GENERATIONS. COUNT YOURSELF LUCKY YOU DIDN'T HOLD ONTO YOUR PRINCELY TITLE MORE THAN A DAY.
WHY AREN'T YOU PACKED YET? WE'RE ALREADY RUNNING LATE.
I AM PACKED, SISTER DEAR. THIS IS IT.

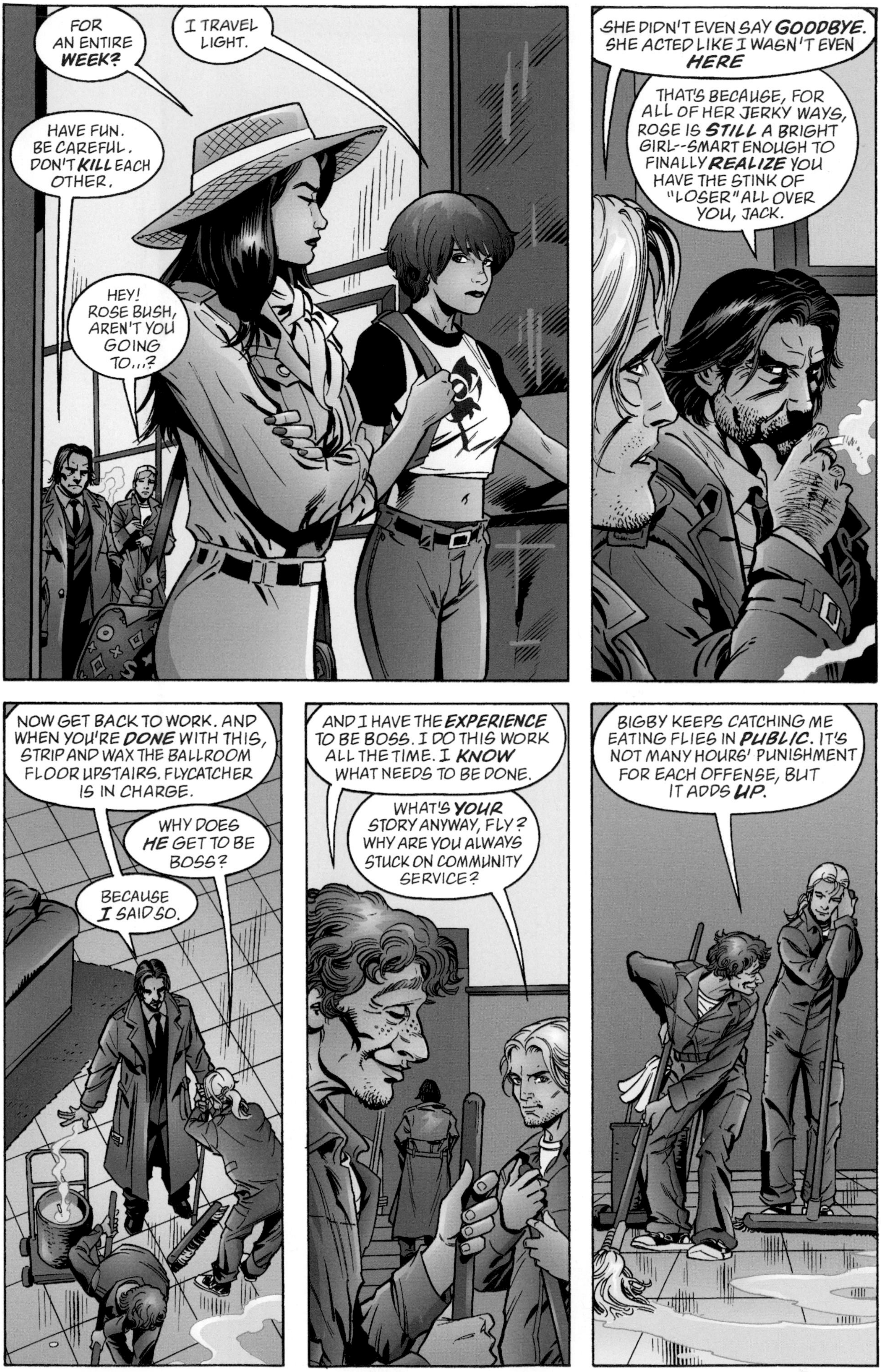
FOR AN ENTIRE WEEK?
I TRAVEL LIGHT.
HAVE FUN. BE CAREFUL. DON'T KILL EACH OTHER.
HEY! ROSE BUSH, AREN'T YOU GOING TO...?
SHE DIDN'T EVEN SAY GOODBYE. SHE ACTED LIKE I WASN'T EVEN HERE
THAT'S BECAUSE, FOR ALL OF HER JERKY WAYS, ROSE IS STILL A BRIGHT GIRL--SMART ENOUGH TO FINALLY REALIZE YOU HAVE THE STINK OF "LOSER" ALL OVER YOU, JACK.
NOW GET BACK TO WORK. AND WHEN YOU'RE DONE WITH THIS, STRIP AND WAX THE BALLROOM FLOOR UPSTAIRS. FLYCATCHER IS IN CHARGE.
WHY DOES HE GET TO BE BOSS?
BECAUSE I SAID SO.
AND I HAVE THE EXPERIENCE TO BE BOSS. I DO THIS WORK ALL THE TIME. I KNOW WHAT NEEDS TO BE DONE.
WHAT'S YOUR STORY ANYWAY, FLY? WHY ARE YOU ALWAYS STUCK ON COMMUNITY SERVICE?
BIGBY KEEPS CATCHING ME EATING FLIES IN PUBLIC. IT'S NOT MANY HOURS' PUNISHMENT FOR EACH OFFENSE, BUT IT ADDS UP.

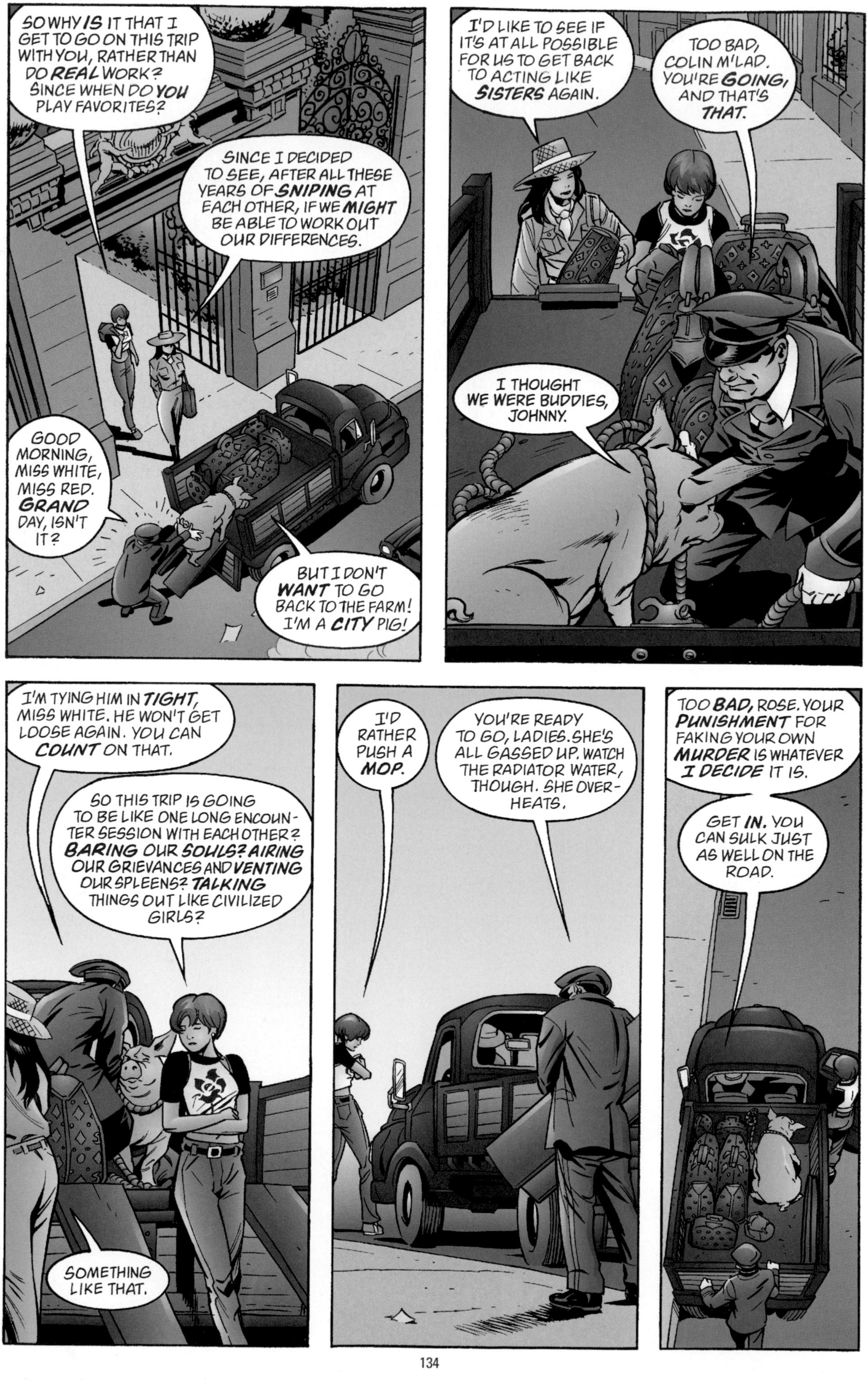
SO WHY IS IT THAT I GET TO GO ON THIS TRIP WITH YOU, RATHER THAN DO REAL WORK? SINCE WHEN DO YOU PLAY FAVORITES?
SINCE I DECIDED TO SEE, AFTER ALL THESE YEARS OF SNIPING AT EACH OTHER, IF WE MIGHT BE ABLE TO WORK OUT OUR DIFFERENCES.
GOOD MORNING, MISS WHITE, MISS RED. GRAND DAY, ISN'T IT?
BUT I DON'T WANT TO GO BACK TO THE FARM! I'M A CITY PIG!
I'D LIKE TO SEE IF IT'S AT ALL POSSIBLE FOR US TO GET BACK TO ACTING LIKE SISTERS AGAIN.
TOO BAD, COLIN M'LAD. YOU'RE GOING, AND THAT'S THAT.
I THOUGHT WE WERE BUDDIES, JOHNNY.
I'M TYING HIM IN TIGHT, MISS WHITE. HE WON'T GET LOOSE AGAIN. YOU CAN COUNT ON THAT.
SO THIS TRIP IS GOING TO BE LIKE ONE LONG ENCOUNTER SESSION WITH EACH OTHER? BARING OUR SOULS? AIRING OUR GRIEVANCES AND VENTING OUR SPLEENS? TALKING THINGS OUT LIKE CIVILIZED GIRLS?
SOMETHING LIKE THAT.
I'D RATHER PUSH A MOP.
YOU'RE READY TO GO, LADIES. SHE'S ALL GASSED UP. WATCH THE RADIATOR WATER, THOUGH. SHE OVERHEATS.
TOO BAD, ROSE. YOUR PUNISHMENT FOR FAKING YOUR OWN MURDER IS WHATEVER I DECIDE IT IS.
GET IN. YOU CAN SULK JUST AS WELL ON THE ROAD.

HAVE A GOOD TIME!

THIS IS GOING TO *SUCK*.

YOU MIGHT AS WELL *TRY* TO ENJOY THIS, ROSE, BECAUSE YOU'RE *NOT* GETTING OUT OF IT. TWICE A YEAR I HAVE TO GO UPSTATE TO CHECK ON THE FABLE COMMUNITY AT THE FARM. IT'S NOT A VACATION. IT'S *WORK*. AND *YOU'RE* GOING TO HELP.

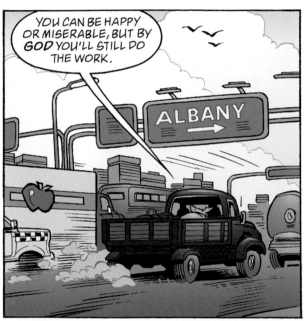

YOU CAN BE HAPPY OR MISERABLE, BUT BY *GOD* YOU'LL STILL DO THE WORK.

ALBANY

WHERE *ARE* WE?

ARE WE *THERE* YET?

PLEASE DON'T SMOKE IN HERE. I *MEAN* IT. DON'T YOU *DARE* LIGHT THAT!

TOO LATE.

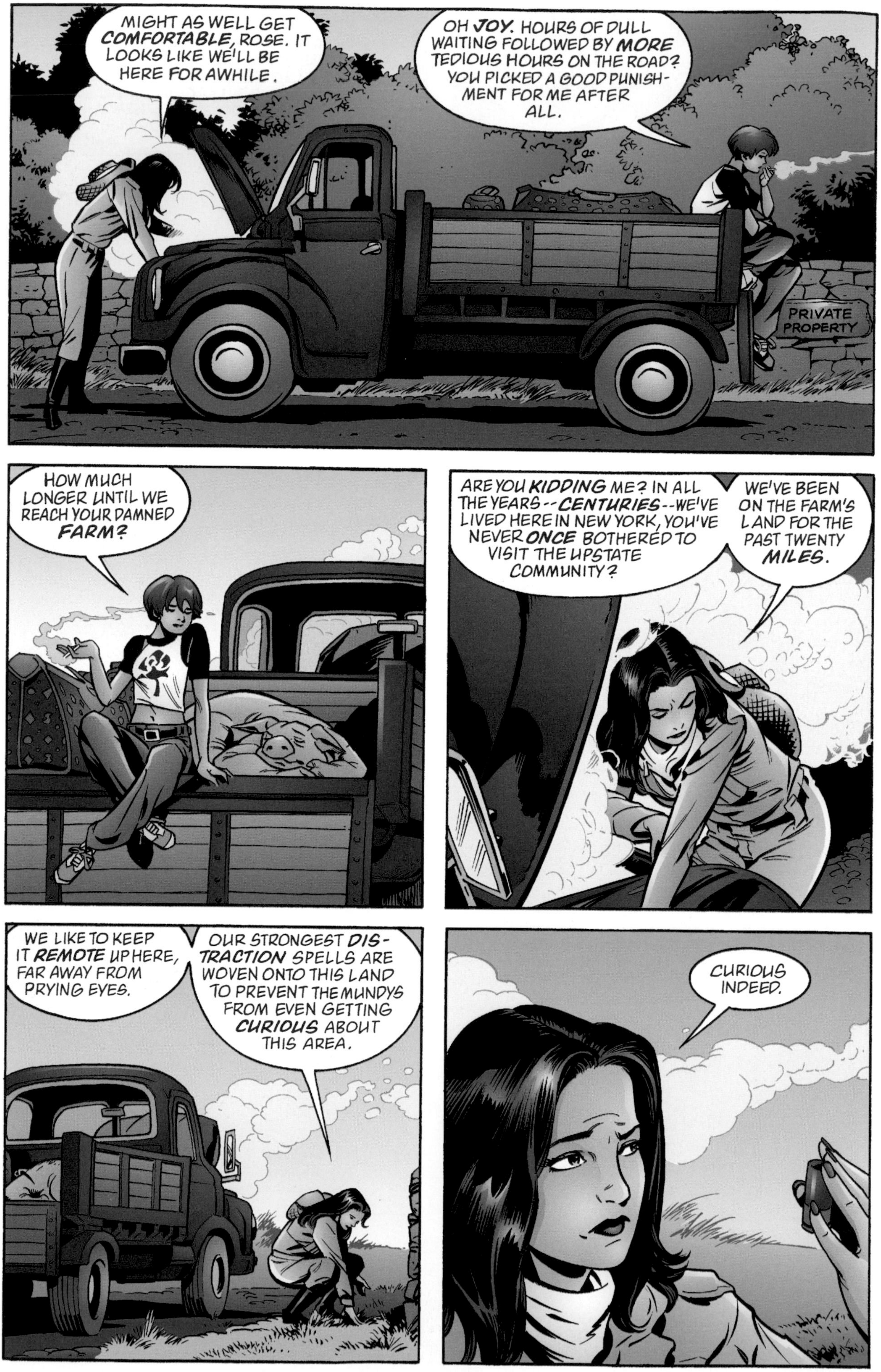
MIGHT AS WELL GET COMFORTABLE, ROSE. IT LOOKS LIKE WE'LL BE HERE FOR AWHILE.
OH JOY. HOURS OF DULL WAITING FOLLOWED BY MORE TEDIOUS HOURS ON THE ROAD? YOU PICKED A GOOD PUNISHMENT FOR ME AFTER ALL.
PRIVATE PROPERTY
HOW MUCH LONGER UNTIL WE REACH YOUR DAMNED FARM?
ARE YOU KIDDING ME? IN ALL THE YEARS--CENTURIES--WE'VE LIVED HERE IN NEW YORK, YOU'VE NEVER ONCE BOTHERED TO VISIT THE UPSTATE COMMUNITY?
WE'VE BEEN ON THE FARM'S LAND FOR THE PAST TWENTY MILES.
WE LIKE TO KEEP IT REMOTE UP HERE, FAR AWAY FROM PRYING EYES.
OUR STRONGEST DISTRACTION SPELLS ARE WOVEN ONTO THIS LAND TO PREVENT THE MUNDYS FROM EVEN GETTING CURIOUS ABOUT THIS AREA.
CURIOUS INDEED.

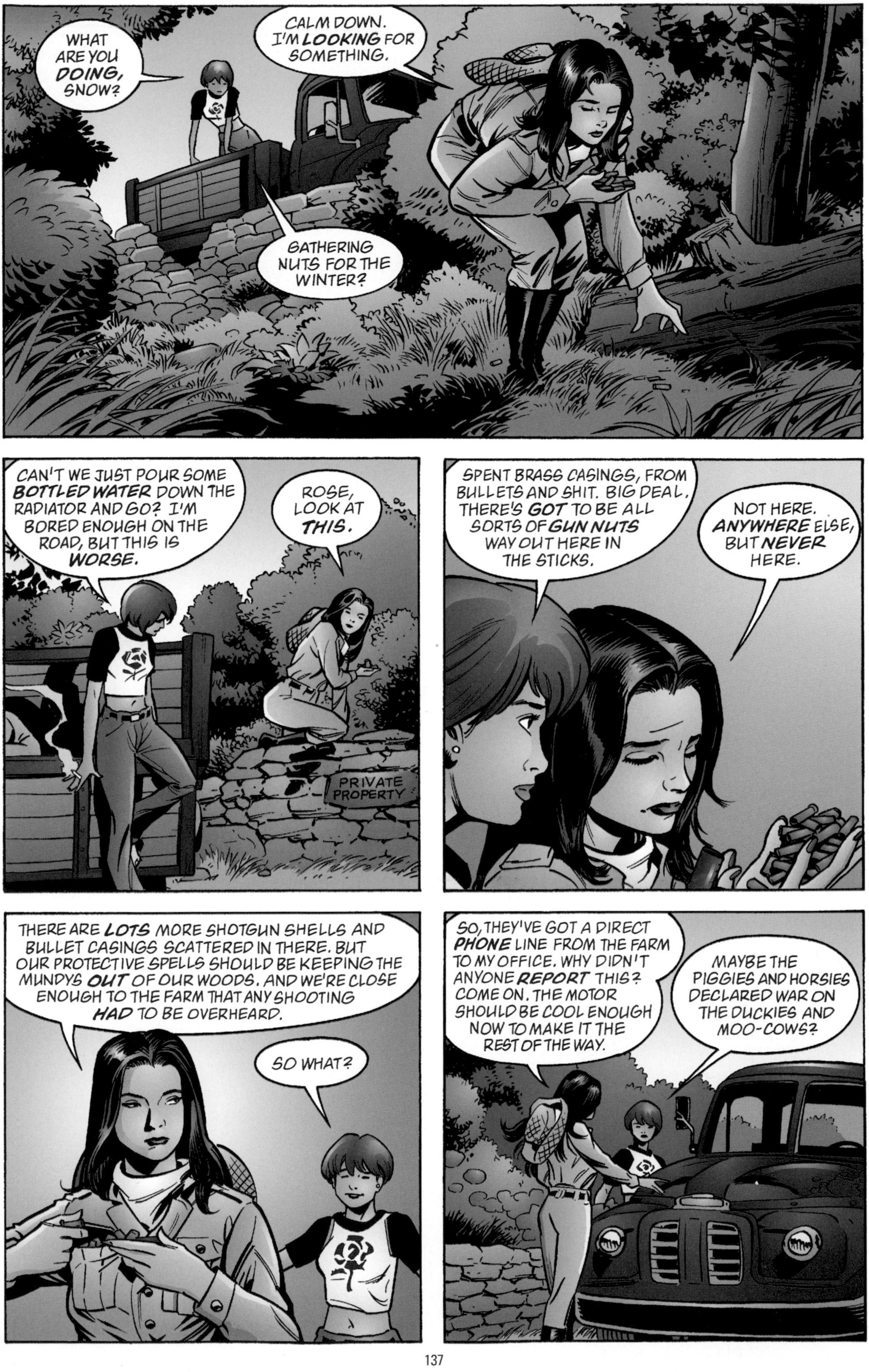

WHAT ARE YOU DOING, SNOW?
CALM DOWN. I'M LOOKING FOR SOMETHING.
GATHERING NUTS FOR THE WINTER?
CAN'T WE JUST POUR SOME BOTTLED WATER DOWN THE RADIATOR AND GO? I'M BORED ENOUGH ON THE ROAD, BUT THIS IS WORSE.
ROSE, LOOK AT THIS.
PRIVATE PROPERTY
SPENT BRASS CASINGS, FROM BULLETS AND SHIT. BIG DEAL. THERE'S GOT TO BE ALL SORTS OF GUN NUTS WAY OUT HERE IN THE STICKS.
NOT HERE. ANYWHERE ELSE, BUT NEVER HERE.
THERE ARE LOTS MORE SHOTGUN SHELLS AND BULLET CASINGS SCATTERED IN THERE. BUT OUR PROTECTIVE SPELLS SHOULD BE KEEPING THE MUNDYS OUT OF OUR WOODS. AND WE'RE CLOSE ENOUGH TO THE FARM THAT ANY SHOOTING HAD TO BE OVERHEARD.
SO WHAT?
SO, THEY'VE GOT A DIRECT PHONE LINE FROM THE FARM TO MY OFFICE. WHY DIDN'T ANYONE REPORT THIS? COME ON. THE MOTOR SHOULD BE COOL ENOUGH NOW TO MAKE IT THE REST OF THE WAY.
MAYBE THE PIGGIES AND HORSIES DECLARED WAR ON THE DUCKIES AND MOO-COWS?

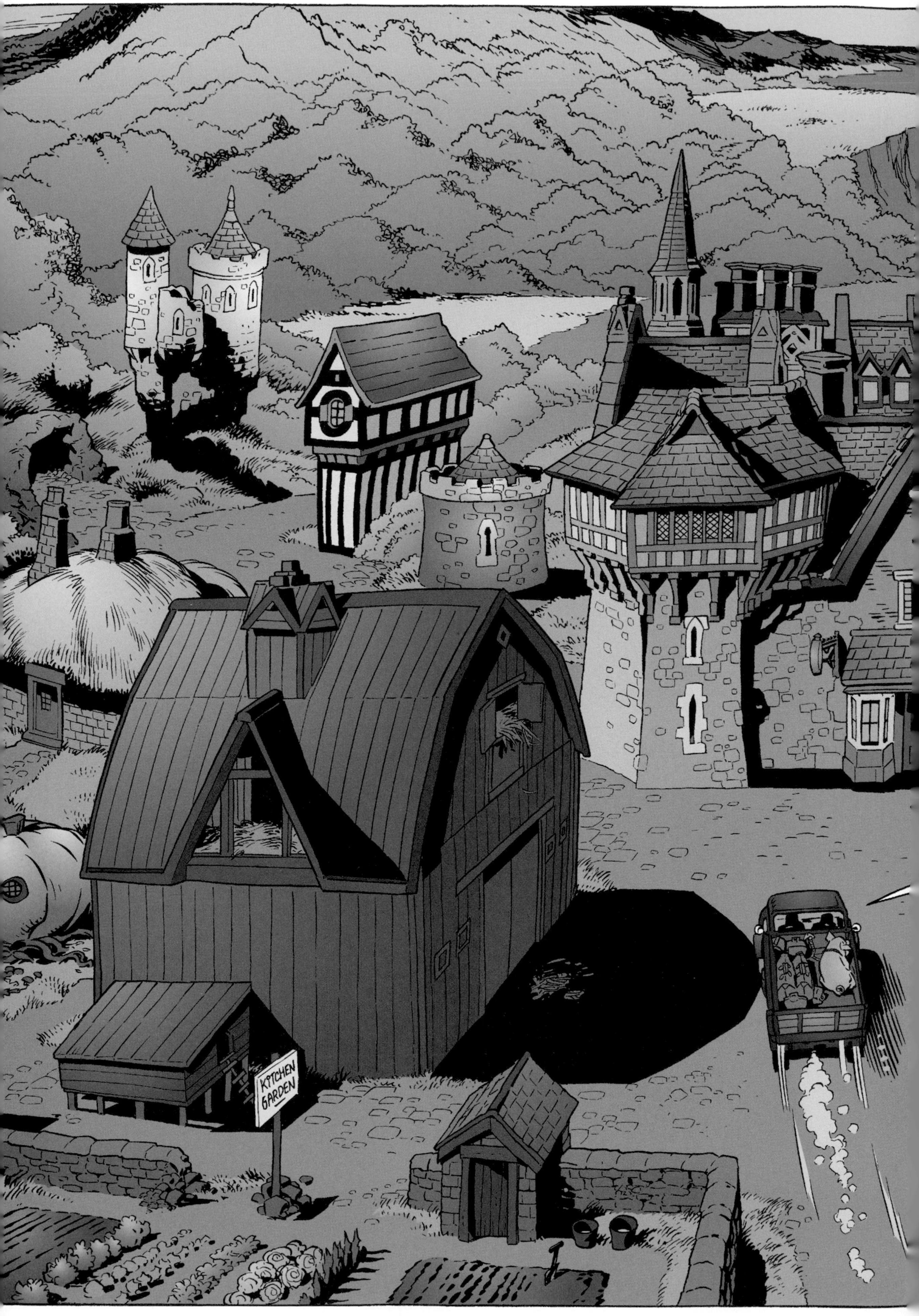
KITCHEN GARDEN

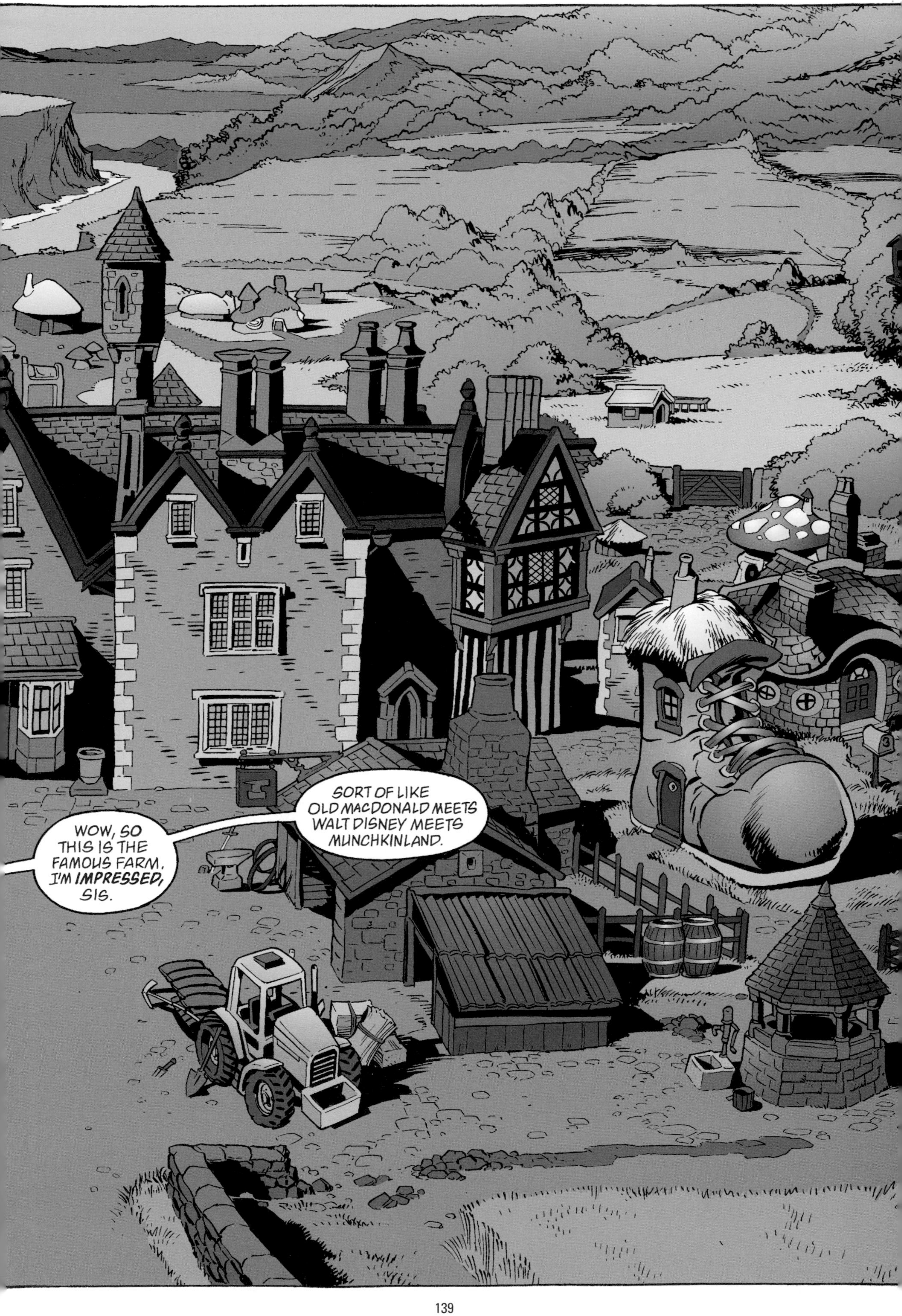
WOW, SO THIS IS THE FAMOUS FARM. I'M IMPRESSED, SIS.
SORT OF LIKE OLD MACDONALD MEETS WALT DISNEY MEETS MUNCHKINLAND.

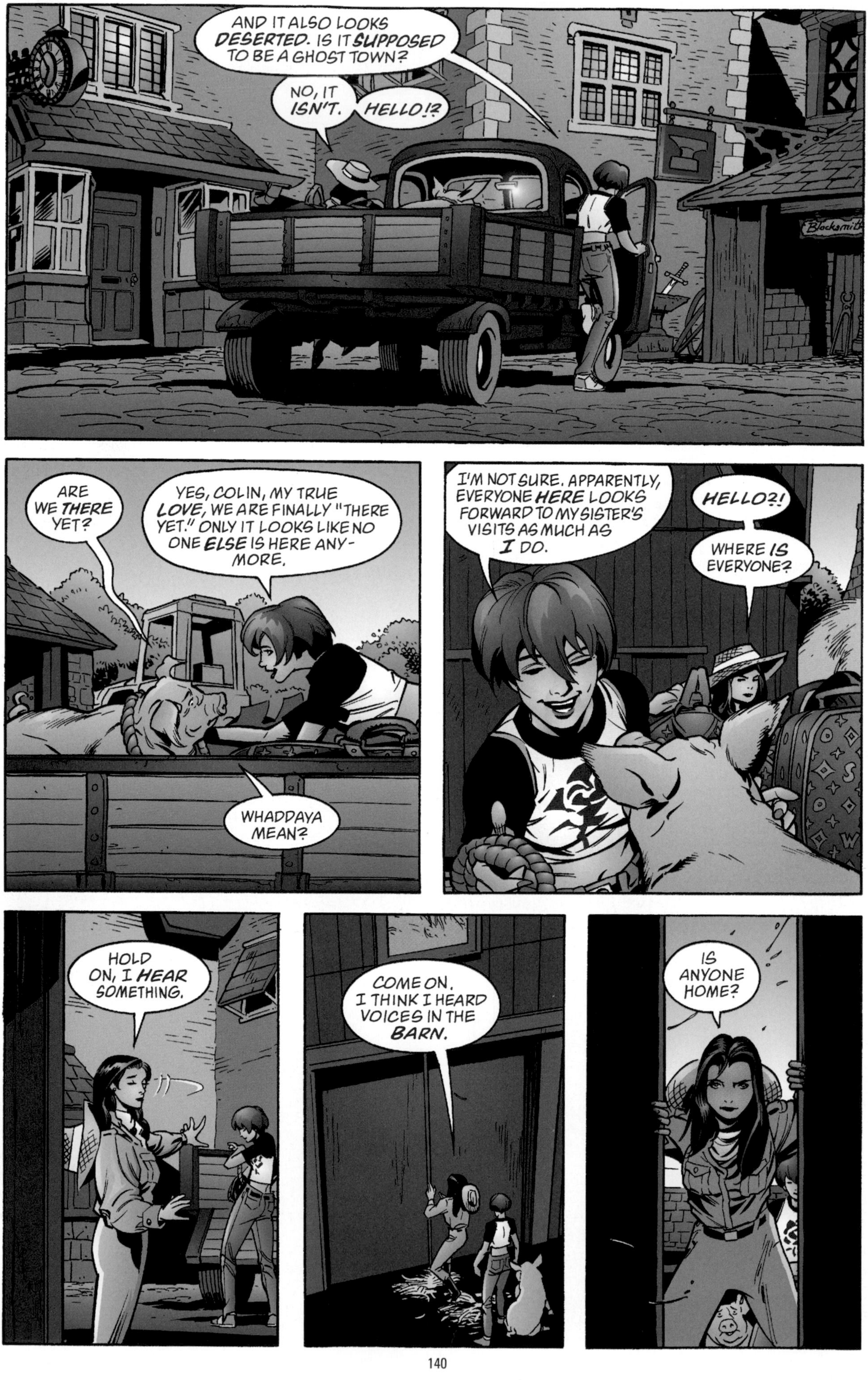
AND IT ALSO LOOKS DESERTED. IS IT SUPPOSED TO BE A GHOST TOWN?
NO, IT ISN'T.
HELLO!?
Blacksmith
ARE WE THERE YET?
YES, COLIN, MY TRUE LOVE, WE ARE FINALLY "THERE YET." ONLY IT LOOKS LIKE NO ONE ELSE IS HERE ANYMORE.
WHADDAYA MEAN?
I'M NOT SURE. APPARENTLY, EVERYONE HERE LOOKS FORWARD TO MY SISTER'S VISITS AS MUCH AS I DO.
HELLO?!
WHERE IS EVERYONE?
HOLD ON, I HEAR SOMETHING.
COME ON. I THINK I HEARD VOICES IN THE BARN.
IS ANYONE HOME?

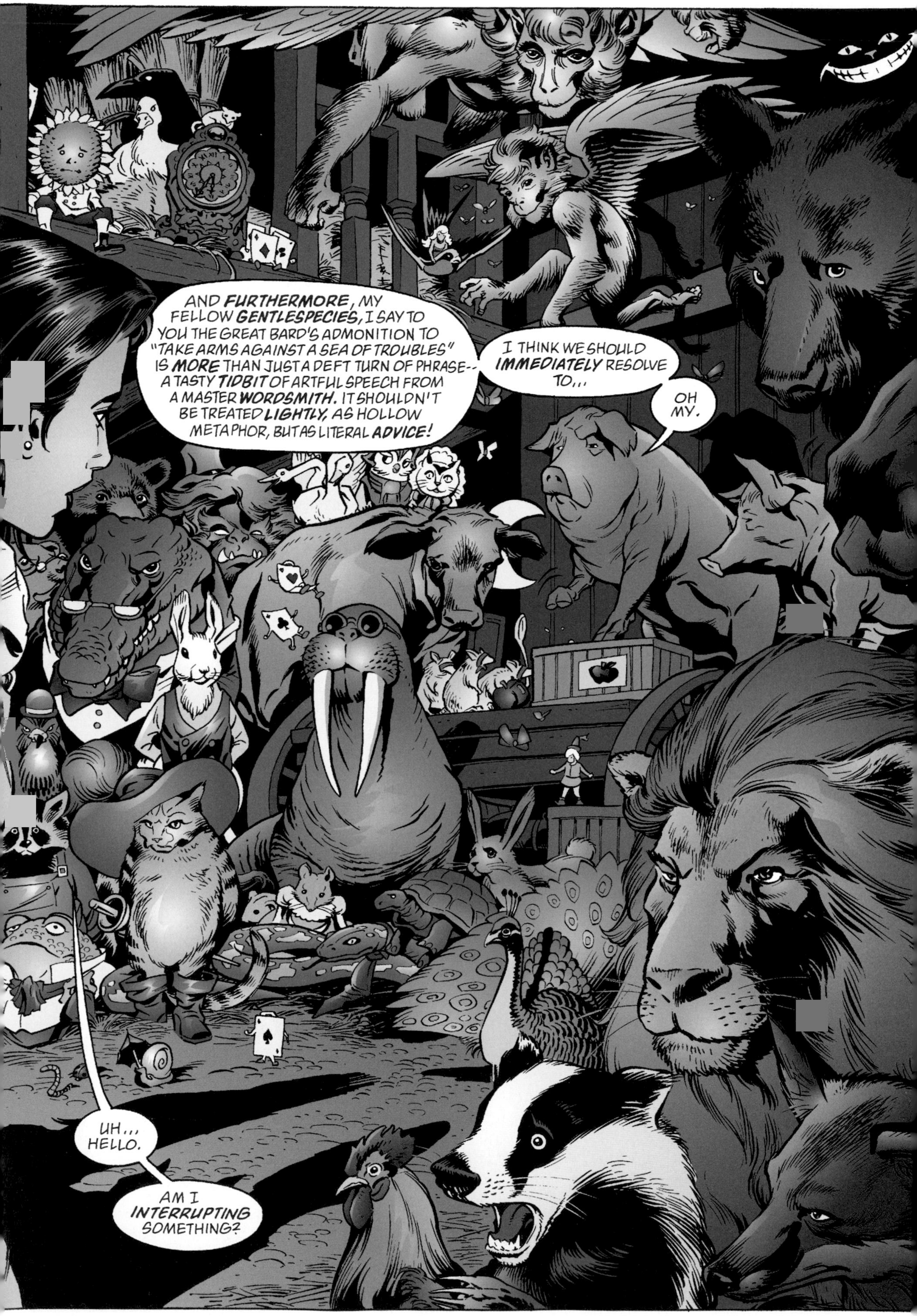
AND FURTHERMORE, MY FELLOW GENTLESPECIES, I SAY TO YOU THE GREAT BARD'S ADMONITION TO "TAKE ARMS AGAINST A SEA OF TROUBLES" IS MORE THAN JUST A DEFT TURN OF PHRASE-- A TASTY TIDBIT OF ARTFUL SPEECH FROM A MASTER WORDSMITH. IT SHOULDN'T BE TREATED LIGHTLY, AS HOLLOW METAPHOR, BUT AS LITERAL ADVICE!
I THINK WE SHOULD IMMEDIATELY RESOLVE TO...
OH MY.
UH... HELLO.
AM I INTERRUPTING SOMETHING?

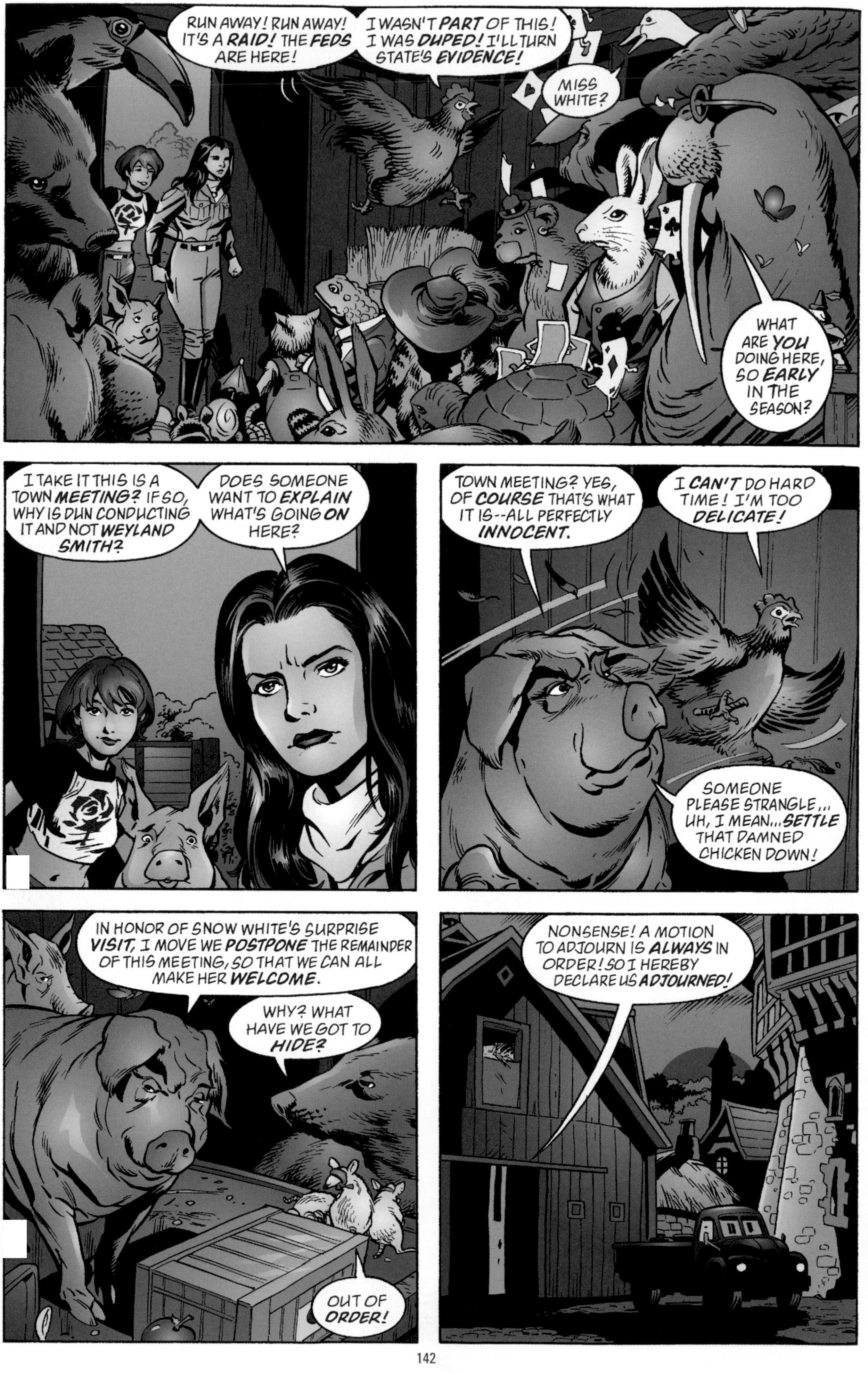
RUN AWAY! RUN AWAY! IT'S A RAID! THE FEDS ARE HERE!
I WASN'T PART OF THIS! I WAS DUPED! I'LL TURN STATE'S EVIDENCE!
MISS WHITE?
WHAT ARE YOU DOING HERE, SO EARLY IN THE SEASON?
I TAKE IT THIS IS A TOWN MEETING? IF SO, WHY IS DUN CONDUCTING IT AND NOT WEYLAND SMITH?
DOES SOMEONE WANT TO EXPLAIN WHAT'S GOING ON HERE?
TOWN MEETING? YES, OF COURSE THAT'S WHAT IT IS--ALL PERFECTLY INNOCENT.
I CAN'T DO HARD TIME! I'M TOO DELICATE!
SOMEONE PLEASE STRANGLE... UH, I MEAN...SETTLE THAT DAMNED CHICKEN DOWN!
IN HONOR OF SNOW WHITE'S SURPRISE VISIT, I MOVE WE POSTPONE THE REMAINDER OF THIS MEETING, SO THAT WE CAN ALL MAKE HER WELCOME.
WHY? WHAT HAVE WE GOT TO HIDE?
OUT OF ORDER!
NONSENSE! A MOTION TO ADJOURN IS ALWAYS IN ORDER! SO I HEREBY DECLARE US ADJOURNED!

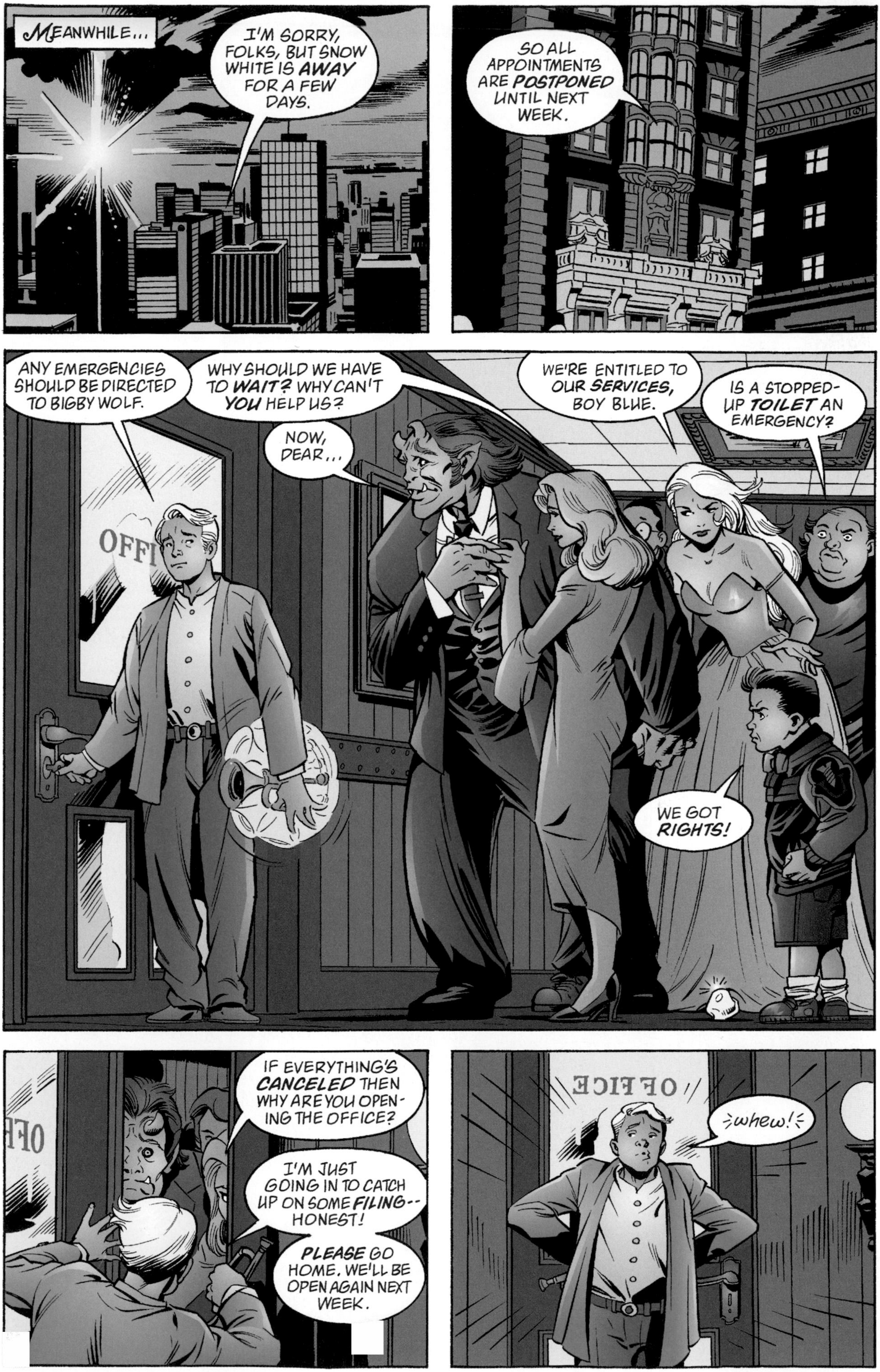
MEANWHILE...
I'M SORRY, FOLKS, BUT SNOW WHITE IS AWAY FOR A FEW DAYS.
SO ALL APPOINTMENTS ARE POSTPONED UNTIL NEXT WEEK.
ANY EMERGENCIES SHOULD BE DIRECTED TO BIGBY WOLF.
WHY SHOULD WE HAVE TO WAIT? WHY CAN'T YOU HELP US?
NOW, DEAR...
WE'RE ENTITLED TO OUR SERVICES, BOY BLUE.
IS A STOPPED-UP TOILET AN EMERGENCY?
OFFI
WE GOT RIGHTS!
IF EVERYTHING'S CANCELED THEN WHY ARE YOU OPENING THE OFFICE?
I'M JUST GOING IN TO CATCH UP ON SOME FILING-- HONEST!
PLEASE GO HOME. WE'LL BE OPEN AGAIN NEXT WEEK.
OFFICE
whew!

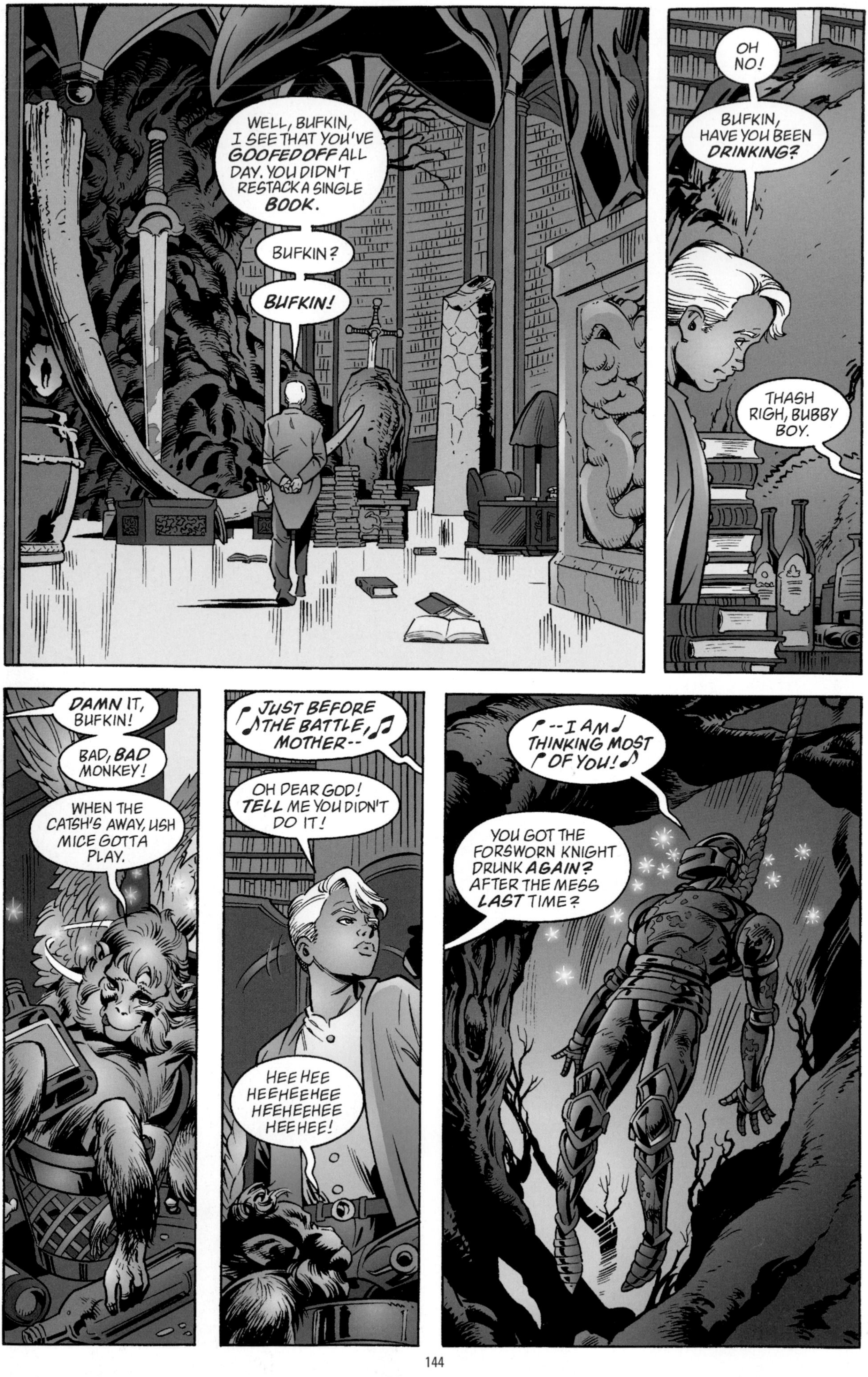
WELL, BUFKIN, I SEE THAT YOU'VE GOOFED OFF ALL DAY. YOU DIDN'T RESTACK A SINGLE BOOK.
BUFKIN?
BUFKIN!
OH NO!
BUFKIN, HAVE YOU BEEN DRINKING?
THASH RIGH, BUBBY BOY.
DAMN IT, BUFKIN!
BAD, BAD MONKEY!
WHEN THE CATSH'S AWAY, USH MICE GOTTA PLAY.
JUST BEFORE THE BATTLE, MOTHER--
OH DEAR GOD! TELL ME YOU DIDN'T DO IT!
HEE HEE HEEHEEHEE HEEHEEHEE HEE HEE!
--I AM THINKING MOST OF YOU!
YOU GOT THE FORSWORN KNIGHT DRUNK AGAIN? AFTER THE MESS LAST TIME?

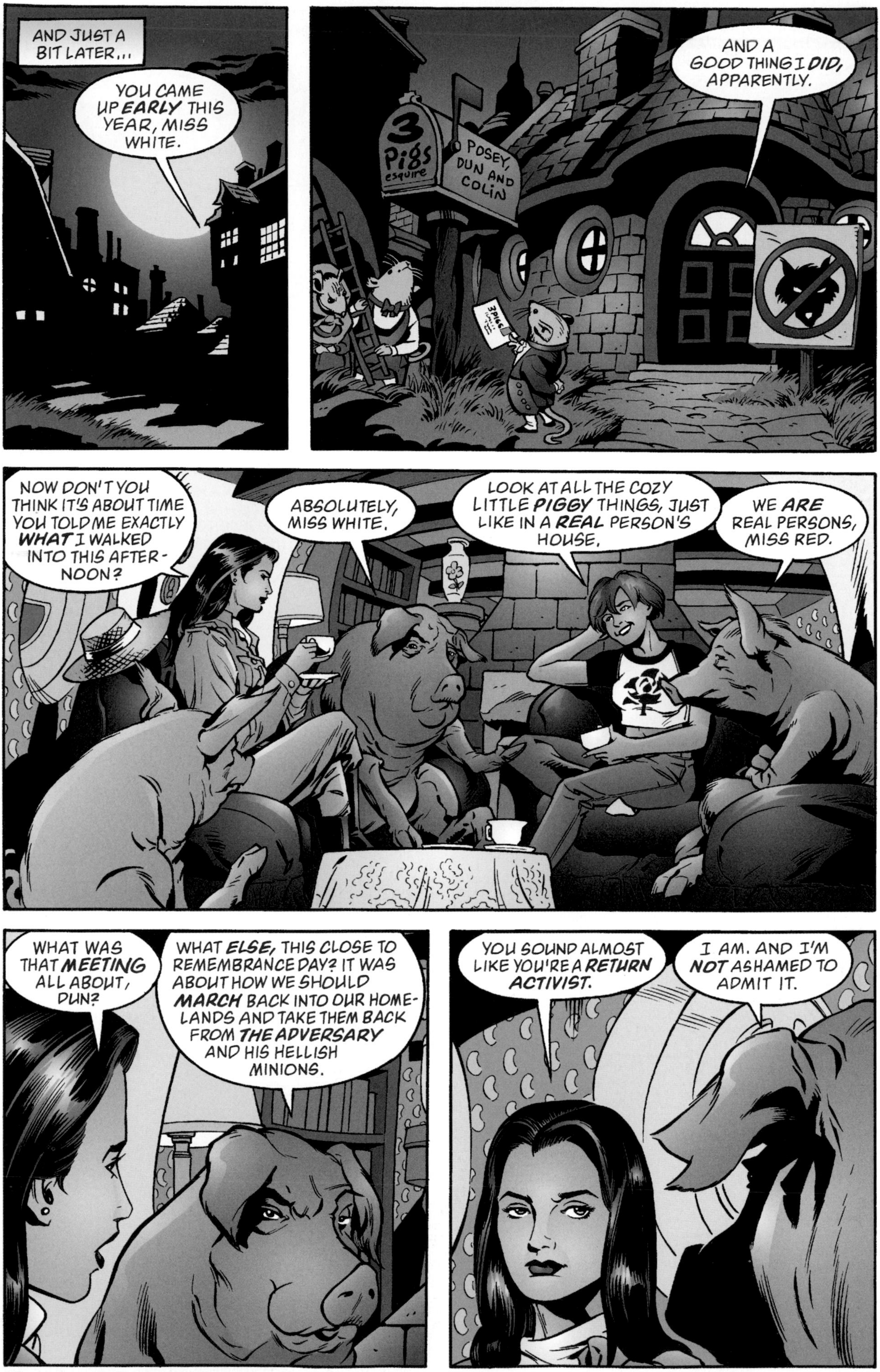
AND JUST A BIT LATER...
YOU CAME UP EARLY THIS YEAR, MISS WHITE.
3 Pigs esquire
POSEY, DUN AND COLIN
AND A GOOD THING I DID, APPARENTLY.
NOW DON'T YOU THINK IT'S ABOUT TIME YOU TOLD ME EXACTLY WHAT I WALKED INTO THIS AFTER-NOON?
ABSOLUTELY, MISS WHITE.
LOOK AT ALL THE COZY LITTLE PIGGY THINGS, JUST LIKE IN A REAL PERSON'S HOUSE.
WE ARE REAL PERSONS, MISS RED.
WHAT WAS THAT MEETING ALL ABOUT, DUN?
WHAT ELSE, THIS CLOSE TO REMEMBRANCE DAY? IT WAS ABOUT HOW WE SHOULD MARCH BACK INTO OUR HOME-LANDS AND TAKE THEM BACK FROM THE ADVERSARY AND HIS HELLISH MINIONS.
YOU SOUND ALMOST LIKE YOU'RE A RETURN ACTIVIST.
I AM. AND I'M NOT ASHAMED TO ADMIT IT.

I'LL BE DAMNED. AND THERE ARE *OTHERS* HERE AT THE FARM?

HUNDREDS.

A LARGE MAJORITY OF US, IN FACT.

SINCE *WHEN?*

SINCE BEFORE THERE WAS AN OFFICIAL *NAME* FOR IT.

WHY, DUN? POSEY? HOW CAN YOU SERIOUSLY *ADVOCATE* THROWING YOUR LIVES AWAY ON A SENSELESS *BID* TO RETAKE THE OLD FABLE LANDS?

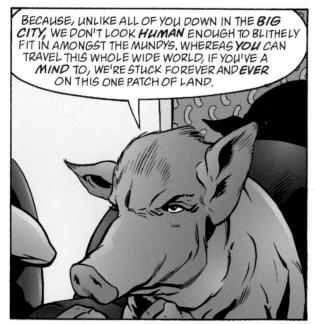

BECAUSE, UNLIKE ALL OF YOU DOWN IN THE *BIG CITY,* WE DON'T LOOK *HUMAN* ENOUGH TO BLITHELY FIT IN AMONGST THE MUNDYS. WHEREAS *YOU* CAN TRAVEL THIS WHOLE WIDE WORLD, IF YOU'VE A *MIND* TO, WE'RE STUCK FOREVER AND *EVER* ON THIS ONE PATCH OF LAND.

AS LONG AS YOU *INSIST* ON THE LAWS KEEPING OUR TRUE NATURES HIDDEN FROM THE MUNDYS, WE CAN'T SET ONE *FOOT* OUTSIDE OF THIS PRISON CAMP, FOR FEAR A *TALKING* PIG OR REAL, LIVING *GIANT* WOULD LET THE CAT OUT OF THE BAG--SO TO SPEAK.

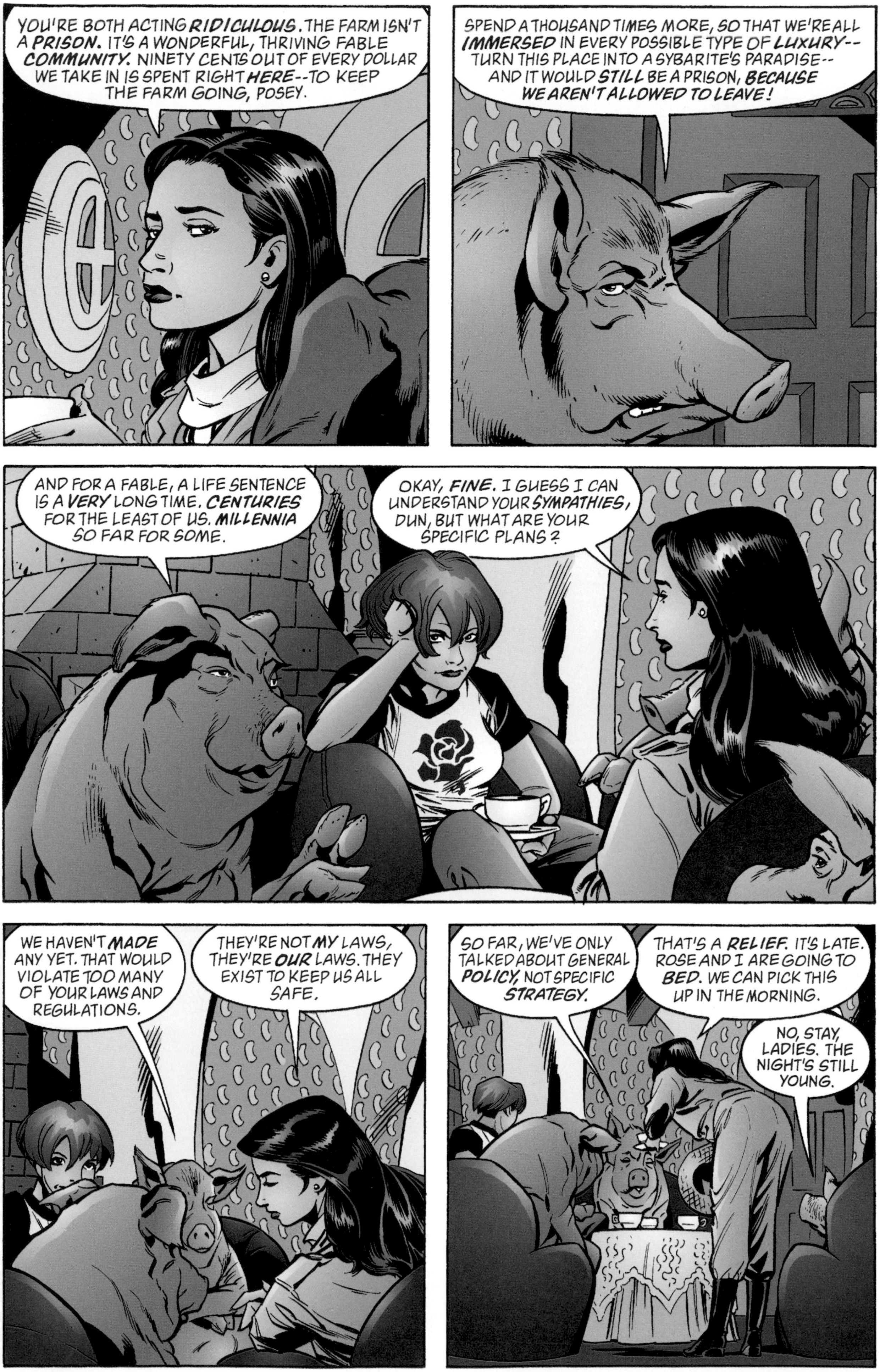
YOU'RE BOTH ACTING RIDICULOUS. THE FARM ISN'T A PRISON. IT'S A WONDERFUL, THRIVING FABLE COMMUNITY. NINETY CENTS OUT OF EVERY DOLLAR WE TAKE IN IS SPENT RIGHT HERE--TO KEEP THE FARM GOING, POSEY.
SPEND A THOUSAND TIMES MORE, SO THAT WE'RE ALL IMMERSED IN EVERY POSSIBLE TYPE OF LUXURY-- TURN THIS PLACE INTO A SYBARITE'S PARADISE-- AND IT WOULD STILL BE A PRISON, BECAUSE WE AREN'T ALLOWED TO LEAVE!
AND FOR A FABLE, A LIFE SENTENCE IS A VERY LONG TIME. CENTURIES FOR THE LEAST OF US. MILLENNIA SO FAR FOR SOME.
OKAY, FINE. I GUESS I CAN UNDERSTAND YOUR SYMPATHIES, DUN, BUT WHAT ARE YOUR SPECIFIC PLANS?
WE HAVEN'T MADE ANY YET. THAT WOULD VIOLATE TOO MANY OF YOUR LAWS AND REGULATIONS.
THEY'RE NOT MY LAWS, THEY'RE OUR LAWS. THEY EXIST TO KEEP US ALL SAFE.
SO FAR, WE'VE ONLY TALKED ABOUT GENERAL POLICY, NOT SPECIFIC STRATEGY.
THAT'S A RELIEF. IT'S LATE. ROSE AND I ARE GOING TO BED. WE CAN PICK THIS UP IN THE MORNING.
NO, STAY, LADIES. THE NIGHT'S STILL YOUNG.

HAVE A PLEASANT NIGHT'S REST. THE GUEST ROOM IS ALL READY FOR YOU.

THANKS, POSEY. GOOD NIGHT.

OH, BUT JUST ONE LAST THING.

WHERE IS WEYLAND SMITH?

HE LEFT.

RESIGNED.

SUDDENLY.

IT TOOK US ALL BY SURPRISE.

I'M SURE IT DID. WELL, THAT'S ANOTHER THING WE'LL HAVE TO DISCUSS TOMORROW.

COMING, ROSE?

WHAT WAS THAT ALL ABOUT? WHO'S WEYLAND SMITH?

MY OPPOSITE NUMBER UP HERE. THE MAN WHO RUNS THE FARM. OR WHO USED TO, APPARENTLY.

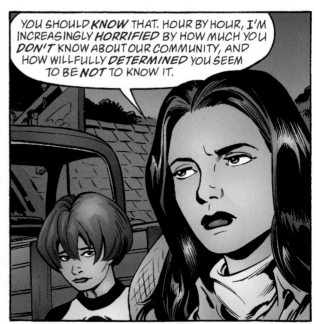

YOU SHOULD KNOW THAT. HOUR BY HOUR, I'M INCREASINGLY HORRIFIED BY HOW MUCH YOU DON'T KNOW ABOUT OUR COMMUNITY, AND HOW WILLFULLY DETERMINED YOU SEEM TO BE NOT TO KNOW IT.

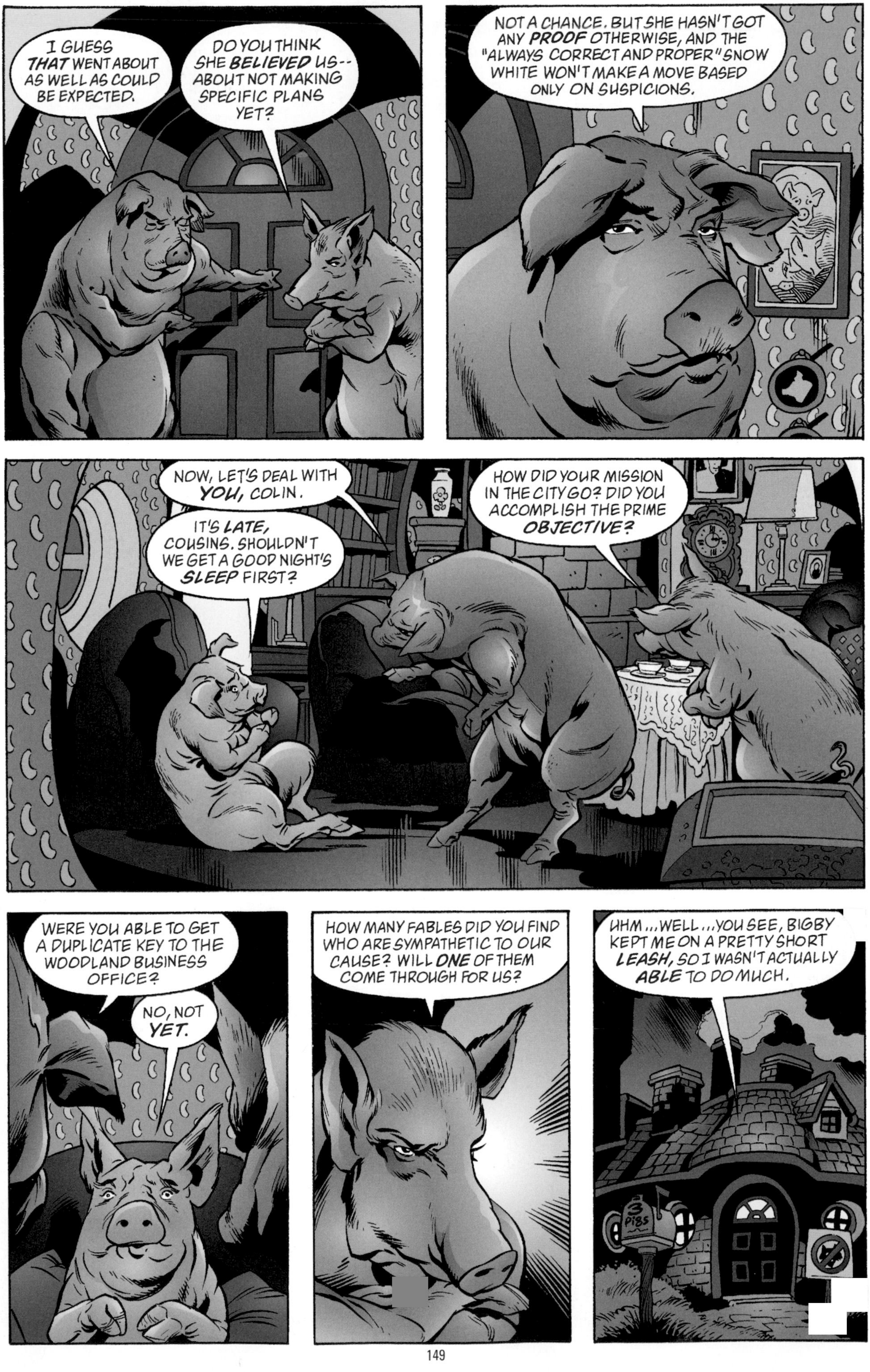
I GUESS THAT WENT ABOUT AS WELL AS COULD BE EXPECTED.
DO YOU THINK SHE BELIEVED US-- ABOUT NOT MAKING SPECIFIC PLANS YET?
NOT A CHANCE. BUT SHE HASN'T GOT ANY PROOF OTHERWISE, AND THE "ALWAYS CORRECT AND PROPER" SNOW WHITE WON'T MAKE A MOVE BASED ONLY ON SUSPICIONS.
NOW, LET'S DEAL WITH YOU, COLIN.
IT'S LATE, COUSINS. SHOULDN'T WE GET A GOOD NIGHT'S SLEEP FIRST?
HOW DID YOUR MISSION IN THE CITY GO? DID YOU ACCOMPLISH THE PRIME OBJECTIVE?
WERE YOU ABLE TO GET A DUPLICATE KEY TO THE WOODLAND BUSINESS OFFICE?
NO, NOT YET.
HOW MANY FABLES DID YOU FIND WHO ARE SYMPATHETIC TO OUR CAUSE? WILL ONE OF THEM COME THROUGH FOR US?
UHM ... WELL ... YOU SEE, BIGBY KEPT ME ON A PRETTY SHORT LEASH, SO I WASN'T ACTUALLY ABLE TO DO MUCH.
3 PIGS

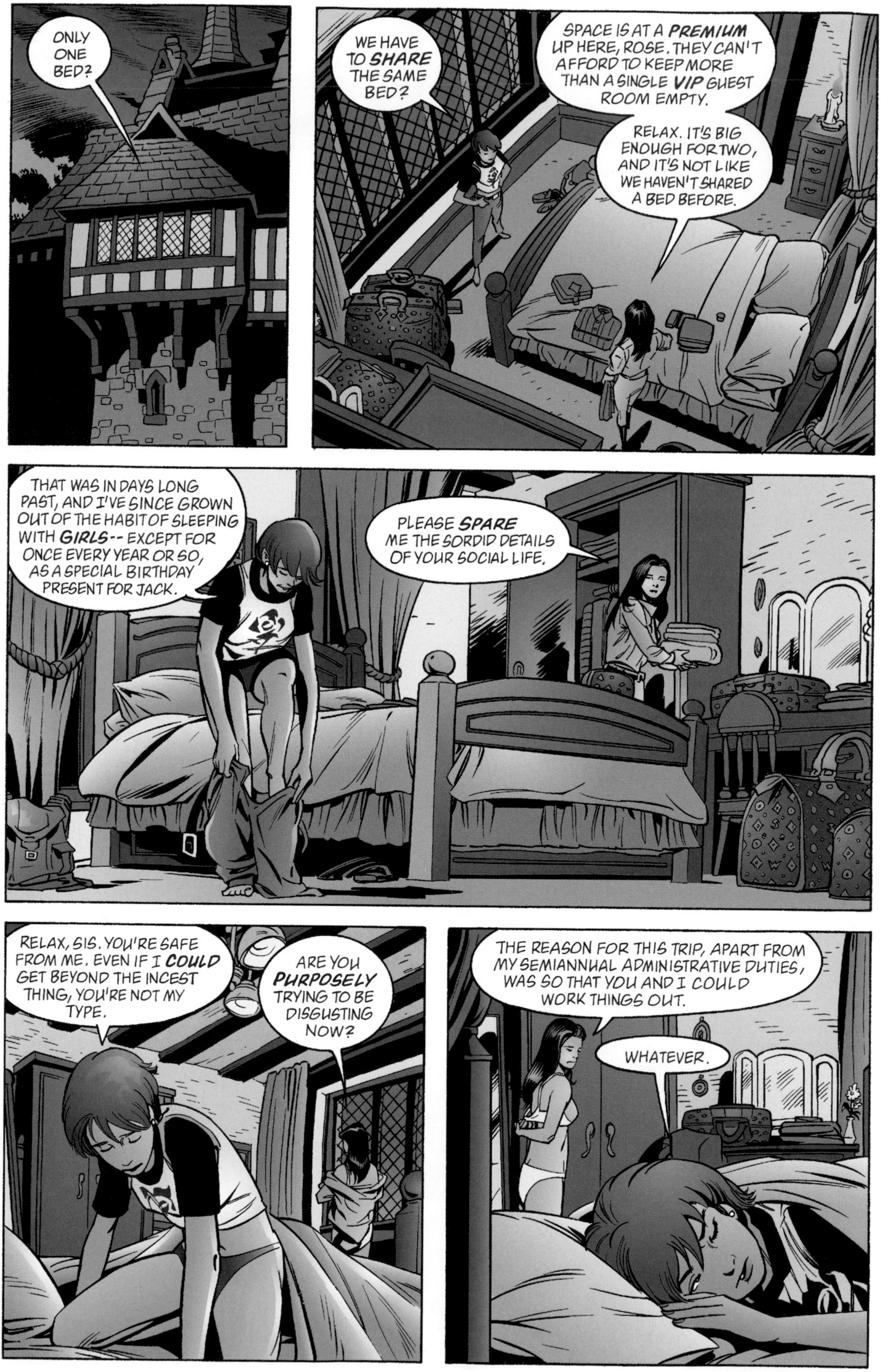

ONLY ONE BED?
WE HAVE TO SHARE THE SAME BED?
SPACE IS AT A PREMIUM UP HERE, ROSE. THEY CAN'T AFFORD TO KEEP MORE THAN A SINGLE VIP GUEST ROOM EMPTY.
RELAX. IT'S BIG ENOUGH FOR TWO, AND IT'S NOT LIKE WE HAVEN'T SHARED A BED BEFORE.
THAT WAS IN DAYS LONG PAST, AND I'VE SINCE GROWN OUT OF THE HABIT OF SLEEPING WITH GIRLS-- EXCEPT FOR ONCE EVERY YEAR OR SO, AS A SPECIAL BIRTHDAY PRESENT FOR JACK.
PLEASE SPARE ME THE SORDID DETAILS OF YOUR SOCIAL LIFE.
RELAX, SIS. YOU'RE SAFE FROM ME. EVEN IF I COULD GET BEYOND THE INCEST THING, YOU'RE NOT MY TYPE.
ARE YOU PURPOSELY TRYING TO BE DISGUSTING NOW?
THE REASON FOR THIS TRIP, APART FROM MY SEMIANNUAL ADMINISTRATIVE DUTIES, WAS SO THAT YOU AND I COULD WORK THINGS OUT.
WHATEVER.

"HOW COULD WE HAVE BEEN SO CLOSE AND LOVING TO EACH OTHER WHEN WE WERE CHILDREN...

WILL WE BE BEST FRIENDS **ALWAYS?**

OF COURSE. FOREVER AND EVER.

"...ONLY TO END UP HATING THE VERY **SIGHT** OF EACH OTHER AS ADULTS?"

MY SISTER HAS THE WORLD'S BIGGEST **STICK** UP HER ASS!

WHEN DID IT GET SO **UGLY** BETWEEN US?

WHEN YOU CAUGHT ME IN BED WITH YOUR HUSBAND, **REMEMBER?**

OF **COURSE** I DO, BUT I THINK IT STARTED BEFORE THAT.

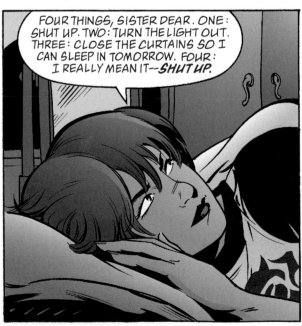

FOUR THINGS, SISTER DEAR. ONE: SHUT UP. TWO: TURN THE LIGHT OUT. THREE: CLOSE THE CURTAINS SO I CAN SLEEP IN TOMORROW. FOUR: I REALLY MEAN IT--**SHUT UP.**

FINE, WE CAN FINISH THIS IN THE --HEY, WHAT'S **THAT?**

WHAT'S **WHAT?**

THAT **THING** OUT THERE BY OUR TRUCK.

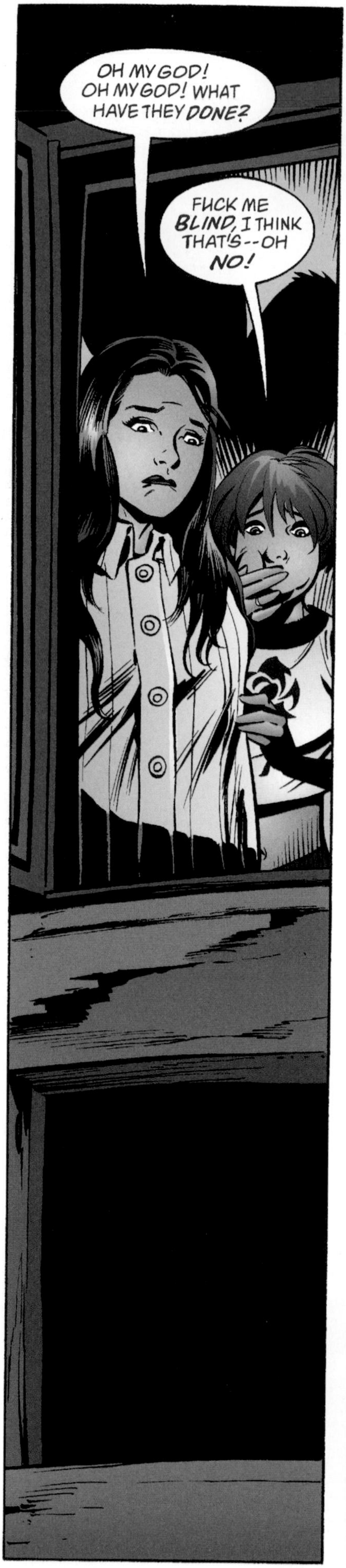
OH MY GOD! OH MY GOD! WHAT HAVE THEY DONE?
FUCK ME BLIND, I THINK THAT'S--OH NO!

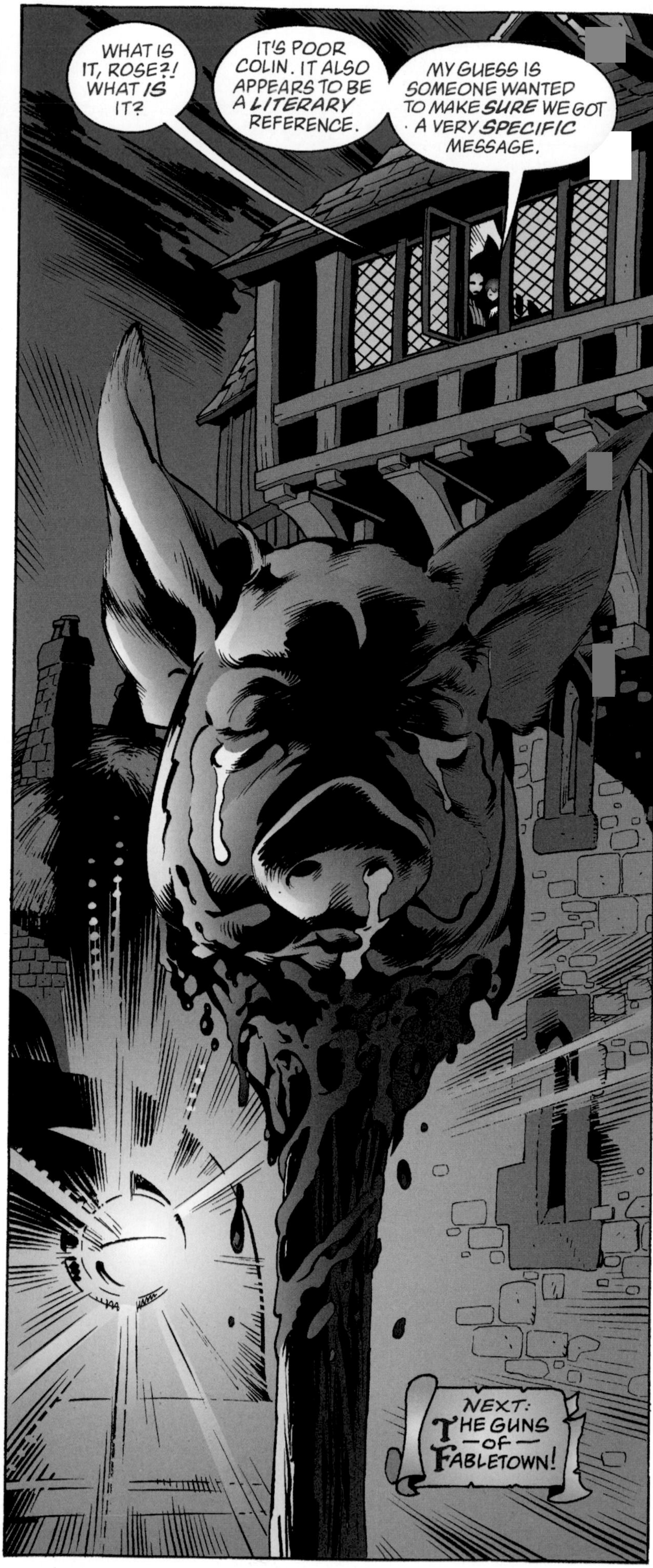
WHAT IS IT, ROSE?! WHAT IS IT?
IT'S POOR COLIN. IT ALSO APPEARS TO BE A LITERARY REFERENCE.
MY GUESS IS SOMEONE WANTED TO MAKE SURE WE GOT A VERY SPECIFIC MESSAGE.
NEXT: THE GUNS —OF— FABLETOWN!

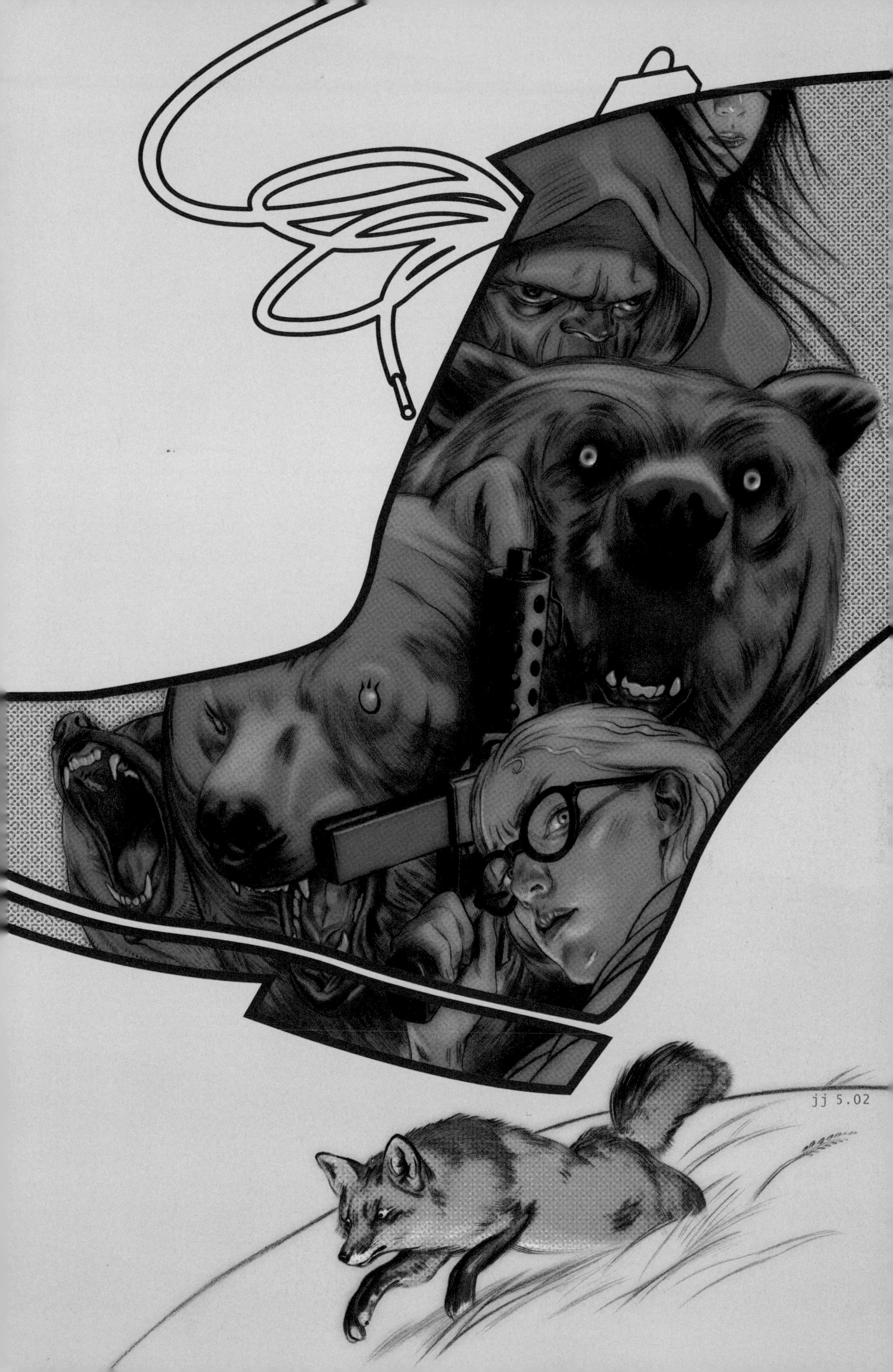
jj 5.02

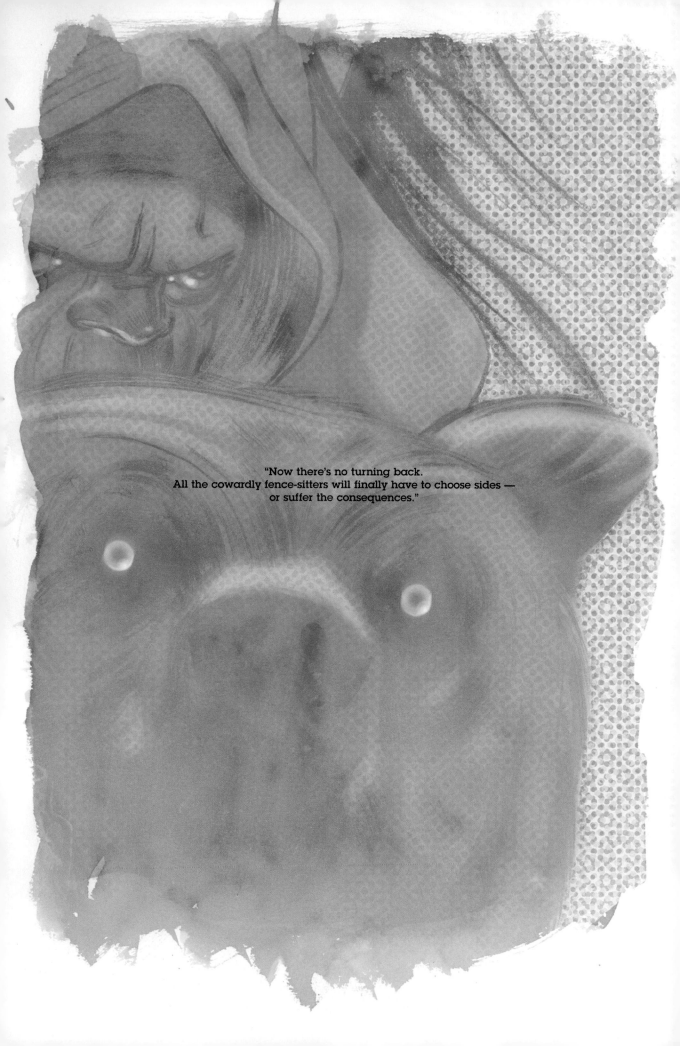

"Now there's no turning back.
All the cowardly fence-sitters will finally have to choose sides —
or suffer the consequences."

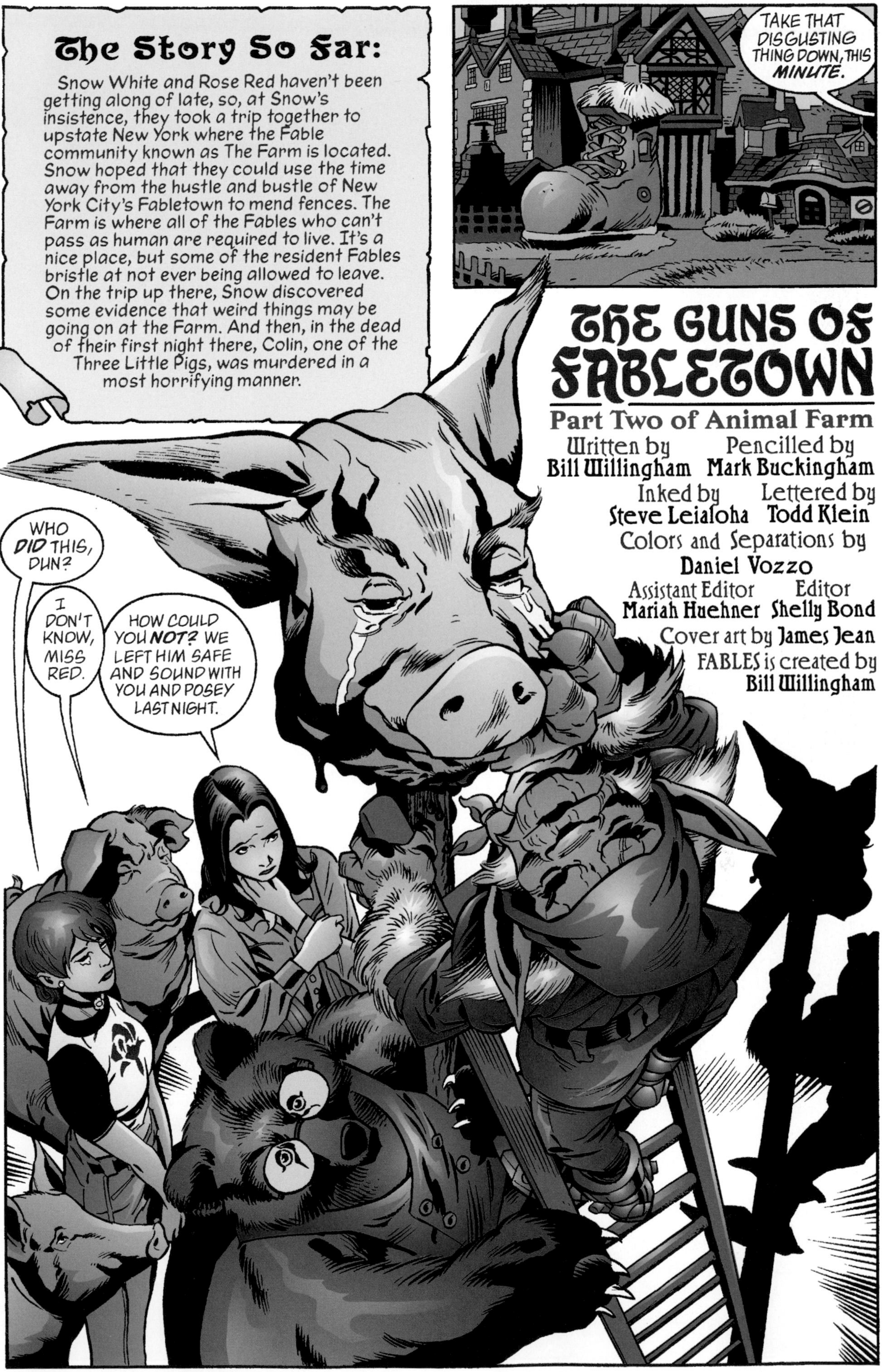
The Story So Far:
Snow White and Rose Red haven't been getting along of late, so, at Snow's insistence, they took a trip together to upstate New York where the Fable community known as The Farm is located. Snow hoped that they could use the time away from the hustle and bustle of New York City's Fabletown to mend fences. The Farm is where all of the Fables who can't pass as human are required to live. It's a nice place, but some of the resident Fables bristle at not ever being allowed to leave. On the trip up there, Snow discovered some evidence that weird things may be going on at the Farm. And then, in the dead of their first night there, Colin, one of the Three Little Pigs, was murdered in a most horrifying manner.
TAKE THAT DISGUSTING THING DOWN, THIS MINUTE.
THE GUNS OF FABLETOWN
Part Two of Animal Farm
Written by Bill Willingham
Pencilled by Mark Buckingham
Inked by Steve Leialoha
Lettered by Todd Klein
Colors and Separations by Daniel Vozzo
Assistant Editor Mariah Huehner
Editor Shelly Bond
Cover art by James Jean
FABLES is created by Bill Willingham
WHO DID THIS, DUN?
I DON'T KNOW, MISS RED.
HOW COULD YOU NOT? WE LEFT HIM SAFE AND SOUND WITH YOU AND POSEY LAST NIGHT.

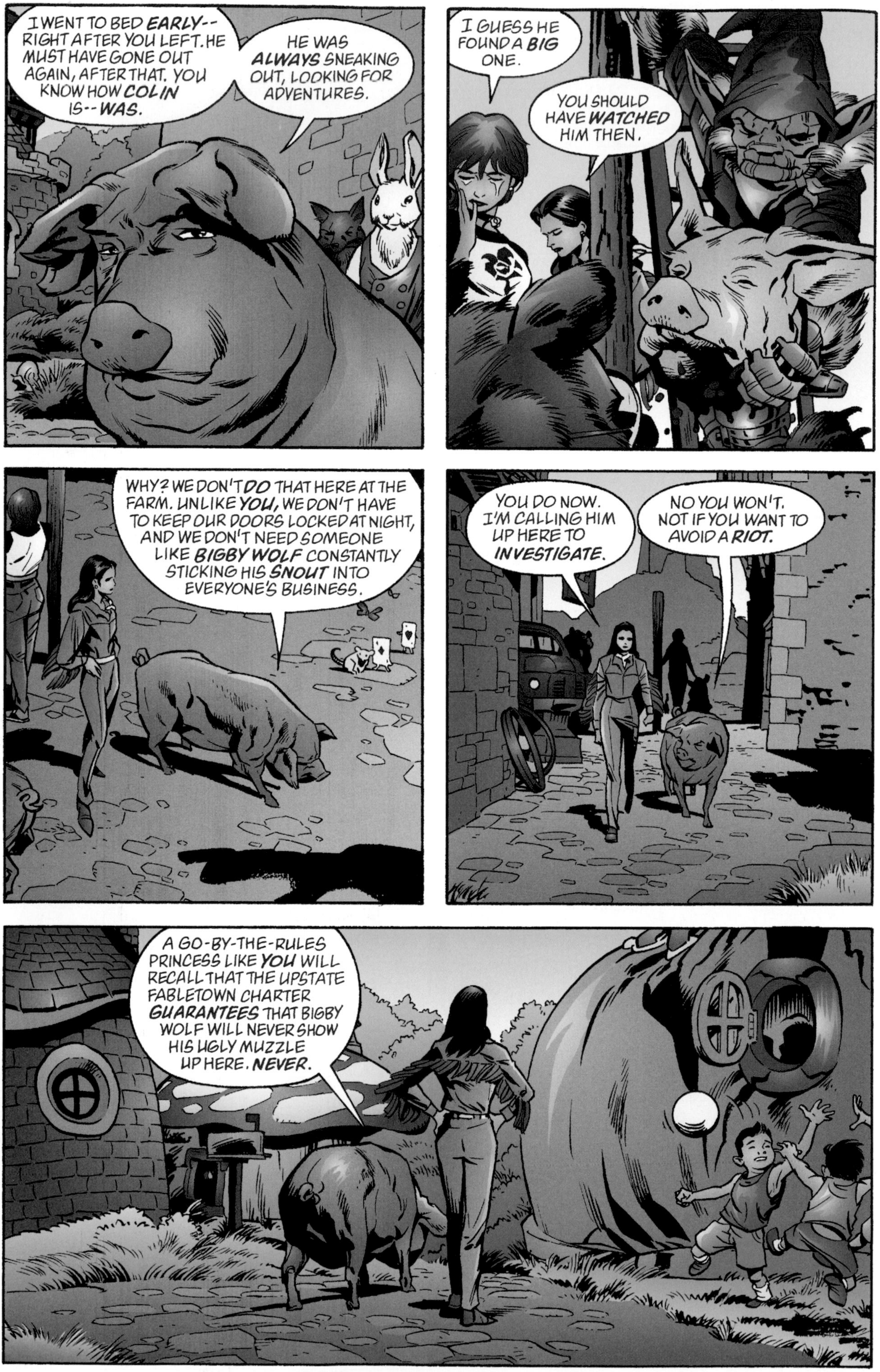
I WENT TO BED EARLY-- RIGHT AFTER YOU LEFT. HE MUST HAVE GONE OUT AGAIN, AFTER THAT. YOU KNOW HOW COLIN IS--WAS.
HE WAS ALWAYS SNEAKING OUT, LOOKING FOR ADVENTURES.
I GUESS HE FOUND A BIG ONE.
YOU SHOULD HAVE WATCHED HIM THEN.
WHY? WE DON'T DO THAT HERE AT THE FARM. UNLIKE YOU, WE DON'T HAVE TO KEEP OUR DOORS LOCKED AT NIGHT, AND WE DON'T NEED SOMEONE LIKE BIGBY WOLF CONSTANTLY STICKING HIS SNOUT INTO EVERYONE'S BUSINESS.
YOU DO NOW. I'M CALLING HIM UP HERE TO INVESTIGATE.
NO YOU WON'T. NOT IF YOU WANT TO AVOID A RIOT.
A GO-BY-THE-RULES PRINCESS LIKE YOU WILL RECALL THAT THE UPSTATE FABLETOWN CHARTER GUARANTEES THAT BIGBY WOLF WILL NEVER SHOW HIS UGLY MUZZLE UP HERE. NEVER.

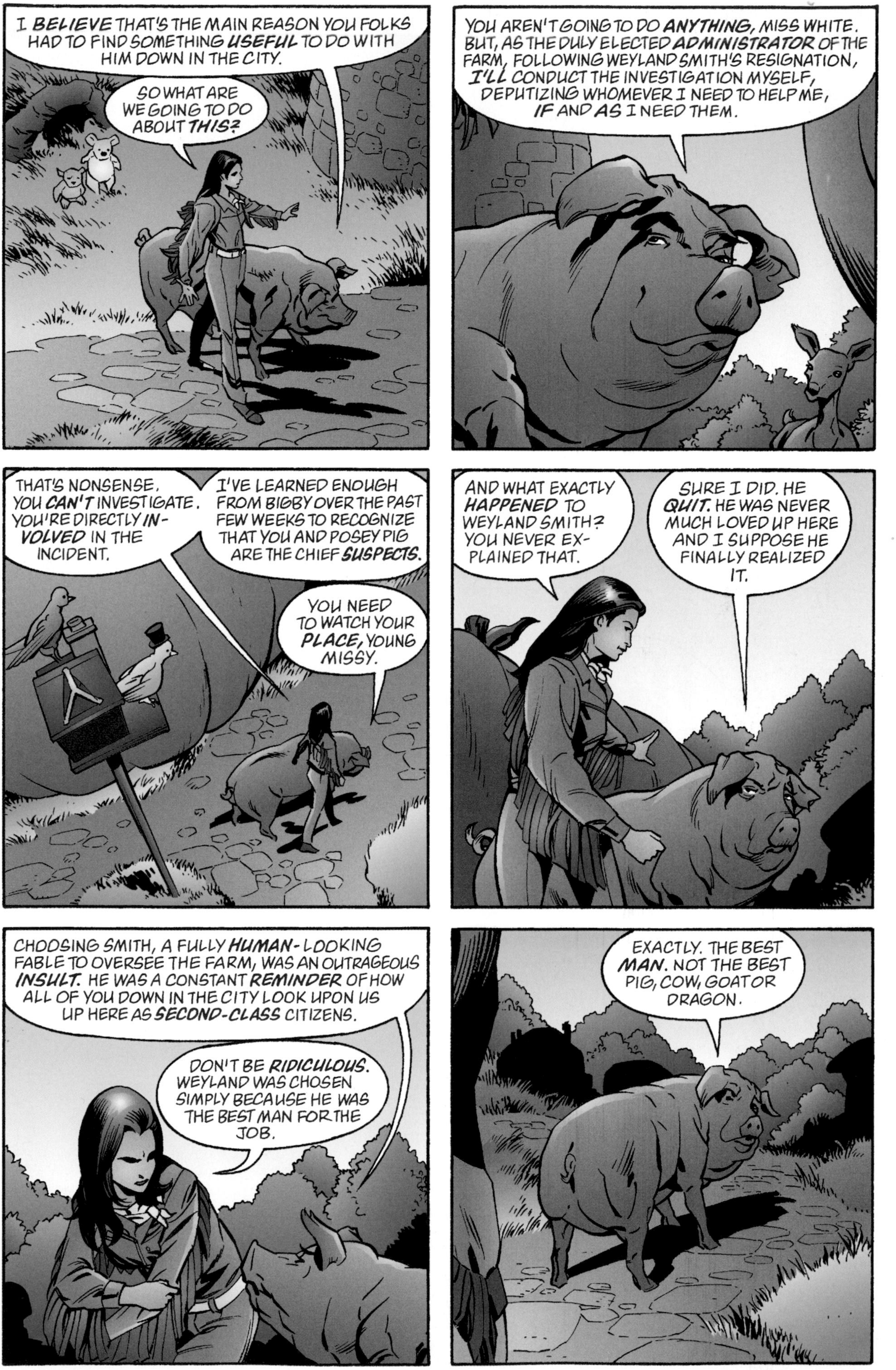
I BELIEVE THAT'S THE MAIN REASON YOU FOLKS HAD TO FIND SOMETHING USEFUL TO DO WITH HIM DOWN IN THE CITY.
SO WHAT ARE WE GOING TO DO ABOUT THIS?
YOU AREN'T GOING TO DO ANYTHING, MISS WHITE. BUT, AS THE DULY ELECTED ADMINISTRATOR OF THE FARM, FOLLOWING WEYLAND SMITH'S RESIGNATION, I'LL CONDUCT THE INVESTIGATION MYSELF, DEPUTIZING WHOMEVER I NEED TO HELP ME, IF AND AS I NEED THEM.
THAT'S NONSENSE. YOU CAN'T INVESTIGATE. YOU'RE DIRECTLY INVOLVED IN THE INCIDENT.
I'VE LEARNED ENOUGH FROM BIGBY OVER THE PAST FEW WEEKS TO RECOGNIZE THAT YOU AND POSEY PIG ARE THE CHIEF SUSPECTS.
YOU NEED TO WATCH YOUR PLACE, YOUNG MISSY.
AND WHAT EXACTLY HAPPENED TO WEYLAND SMITH? YOU NEVER EXPLAINED THAT.
SURE I DID. HE QUIT. HE WAS NEVER MUCH LOVED UP HERE AND I SUPPOSE HE FINALLY REALIZED IT.
CHOOSING SMITH, A FULLY HUMAN-LOOKING FABLE TO OVERSEE THE FARM, WAS AN OUTRAGEOUS INSULT. HE WAS A CONSTANT REMINDER OF HOW ALL OF YOU DOWN IN THE CITY LOOK UPON US UP HERE AS SECOND-CLASS CITIZENS.
DON'T BE RIDICULOUS. WEYLAND WAS CHOSEN SIMPLY BECAUSE HE WAS THE BEST MAN FOR THE JOB.
EXACTLY. THE BEST MAN. NOT THE BEST PIG, COW, GOAT OR DRAGON.

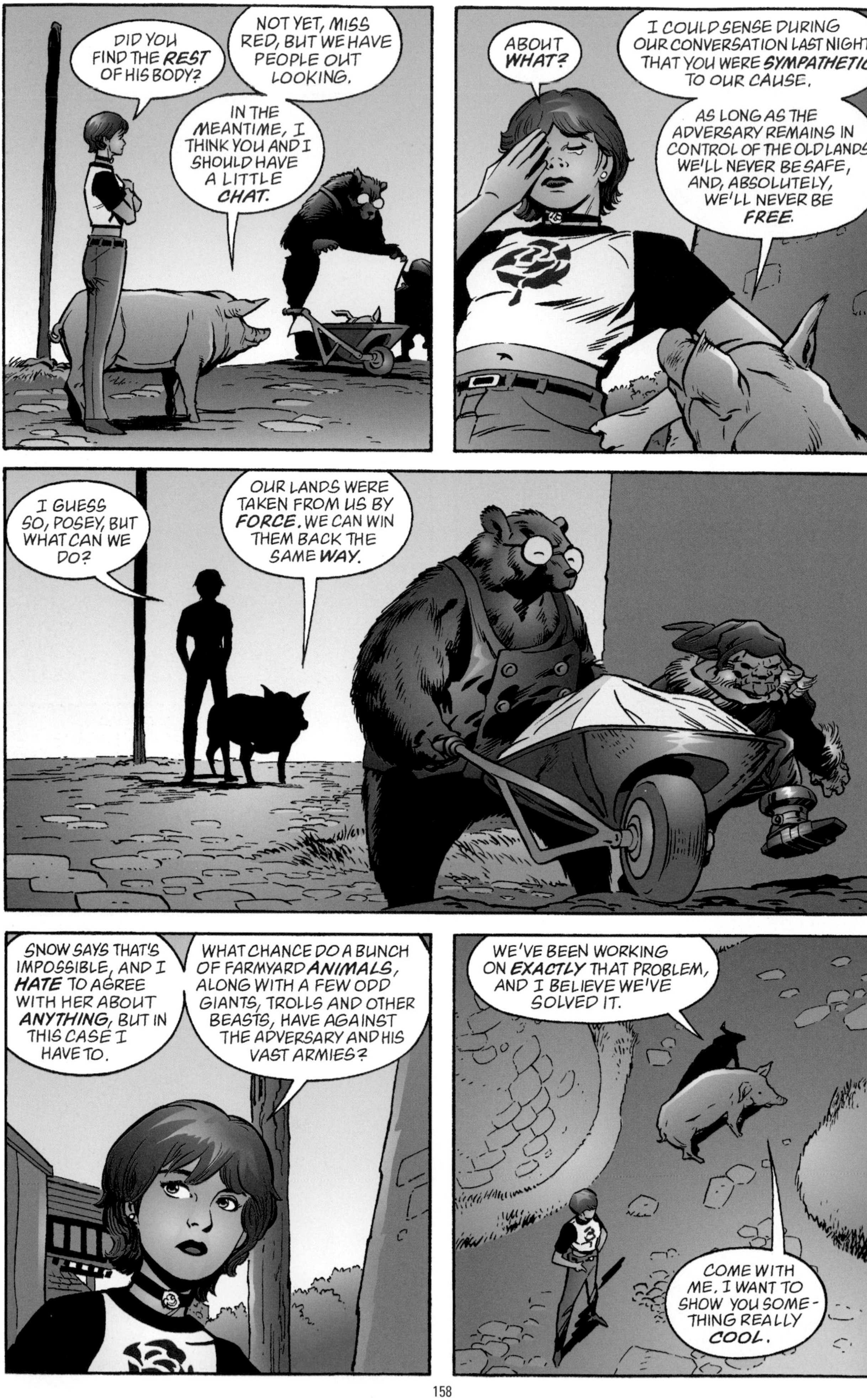

DID YOU FIND THE REST OF HIS BODY?
NOT YET, MISS RED, BUT WE HAVE PEOPLE OUT LOOKING.
IN THE MEANTIME, I THINK YOU AND I SHOULD HAVE A LITTLE CHAT.
ABOUT WHAT?
I COULD SENSE DURING OUR CONVERSATION LAST NIGHT, THAT YOU WERE SYMPATHETIC TO OUR CAUSE.
AS LONG AS THE ADVERSARY REMAINS IN CONTROL OF THE OLD LANDS, WE'LL NEVER BE SAFE, AND, ABSOLUTELY, WE'LL NEVER BE FREE.
I GUESS SO, POSEY, BUT WHAT CAN WE DO?
OUR LANDS WERE TAKEN FROM US BY FORCE. WE CAN WIN THEM BACK THE SAME WAY.
SNOW SAYS THAT'S IMPOSSIBLE, AND I HATE TO AGREE WITH HER ABOUT ANYTHING, BUT IN THIS CASE I HAVE TO.
WHAT CHANCE DO A BUNCH OF FARMYARD ANIMALS, ALONG WITH A FEW ODD GIANTS, TROLLS AND OTHER BEASTS, HAVE AGAINST THE ADVERSARY AND HIS VAST ARMIES?
WE'VE BEEN WORKING ON EXACTLY THAT PROBLEM, AND I BELIEVE WE'VE SOLVED IT.
COME WITH ME. I WANT TO SHOW YOU SOME-THING REALLY COOL.

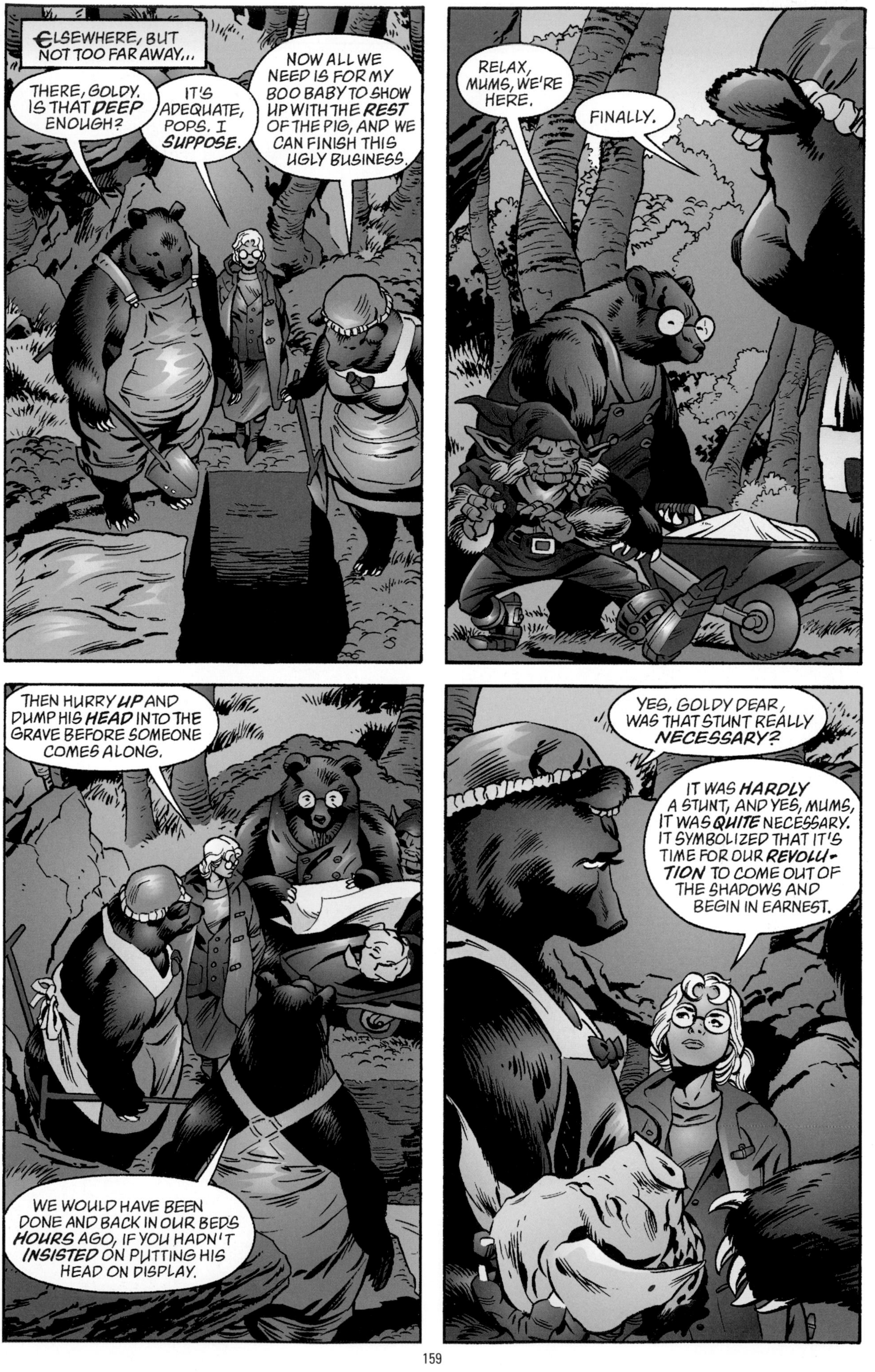
ELSEWHERE, BUT NOT TOO FAR AWAY...
THERE, GOLDY. IS THAT DEEP ENOUGH?
IT'S ADEQUATE, POPS. I SUPPOSE.
NOW ALL WE NEED IS FOR MY BOO BABY TO SHOW UP WITH THE REST OF THE PIG, AND WE CAN FINISH THIS UGLY BUSINESS.
RELAX, MUMS, WE'RE HERE.
FINALLY.
THEN HURRY UP AND DUMP HIS HEAD INTO THE GRAVE BEFORE SOMEONE COMES ALONG.
WE WOULD HAVE BEEN DONE AND BACK IN OUR BEDS HOURS AGO, IF YOU HADN'T INSISTED ON PUTTING HIS HEAD ON DISPLAY.
YES, GOLDY DEAR, WAS THAT STUNT REALLY NECESSARY?
IT WAS HARDLY A STUNT, AND YES, MUMS, IT WAS QUITE NECESSARY. IT SYMBOLIZED THAT IT'S TIME FOR OUR REVOLUTION TO COME OUT OF THE SHADOWS AND BEGIN IN EARNEST.

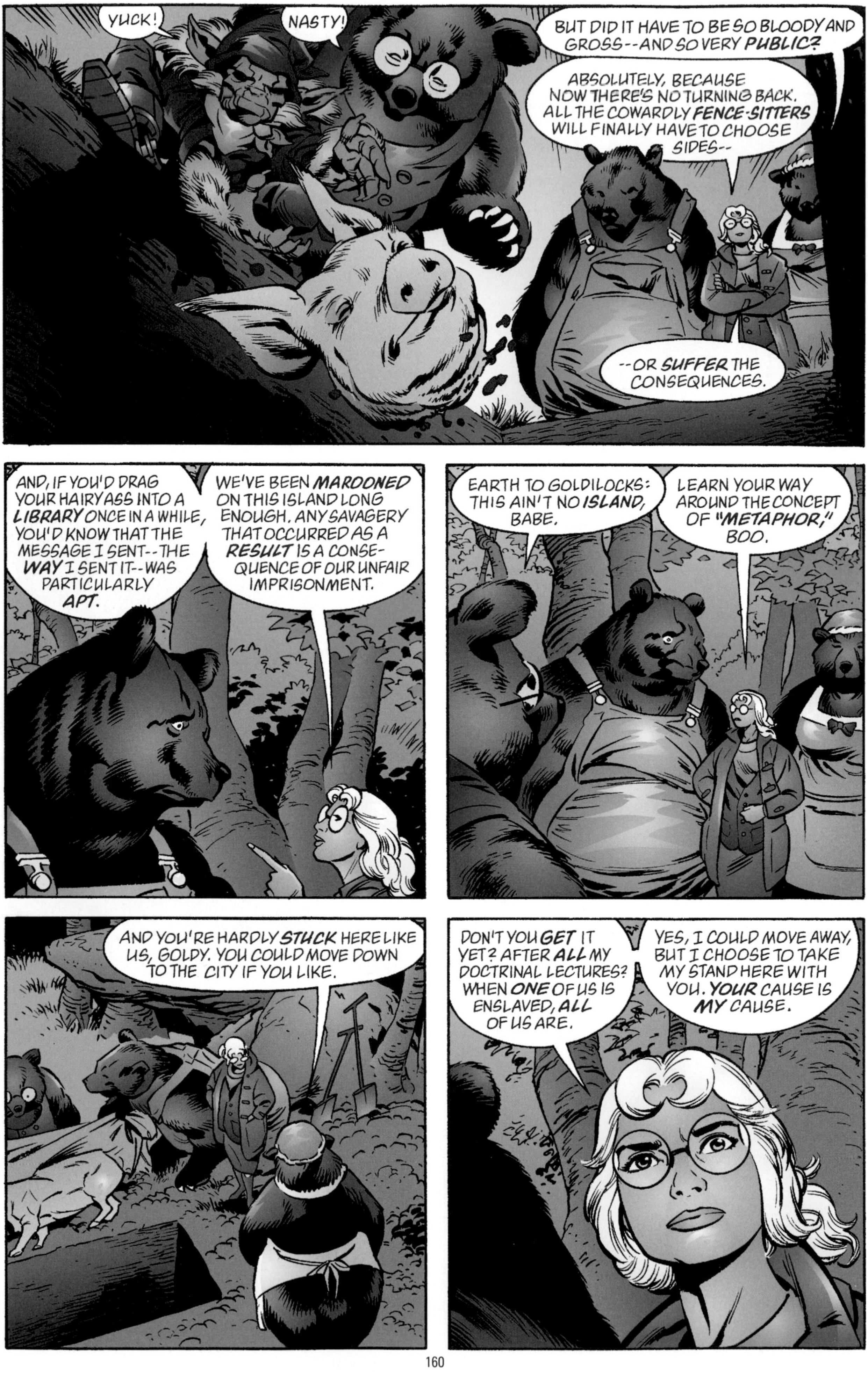
YUCK!
NASTY!
BUT DID IT HAVE TO BE SO BLOODY AND GROSS--AND SO VERY PUBLIC?
ABSOLUTELY, BECAUSE NOW THERE'S NO TURNING BACK. ALL THE COWARDLY FENCE-SITTERS WILL FINALLY HAVE TO CHOOSE SIDES--
--OR SUFFER THE CONSEQUENCES.
AND, IF YOU'D DRAG YOUR HAIRY ASS INTO A LIBRARY ONCE IN A WHILE, YOU'D KNOW THAT THE MESSAGE I SENT--THE WAY I SENT IT--WAS PARTICULARLY APT.
WE'VE BEEN MAROONED ON THIS ISLAND LONG ENOUGH. ANY SAVAGERY THAT OCCURRED AS A RESULT IS A CONSEQUENCE OF OUR UNFAIR IMPRISONMENT.
EARTH TO GOLDILOCKS: THIS AIN'T NO ISLAND, BABE.
LEARN YOUR WAY AROUND THE CONCEPT OF "METAPHOR," BOO.
AND YOU'RE HARDLY STUCK HERE LIKE US, GOLDY. YOU COULD MOVE DOWN TO THE CITY IF YOU LIKE.
DON'T YOU GET IT YET? AFTER ALL MY DOCTRINAL LECTURES? WHEN ONE OF US IS ENSLAVED, ALL OF US ARE.
YES, I COULD MOVE AWAY, BUT I CHOOSE TO TAKE MY STAND HERE WITH YOU. YOUR CAUSE IS MY CAUSE.

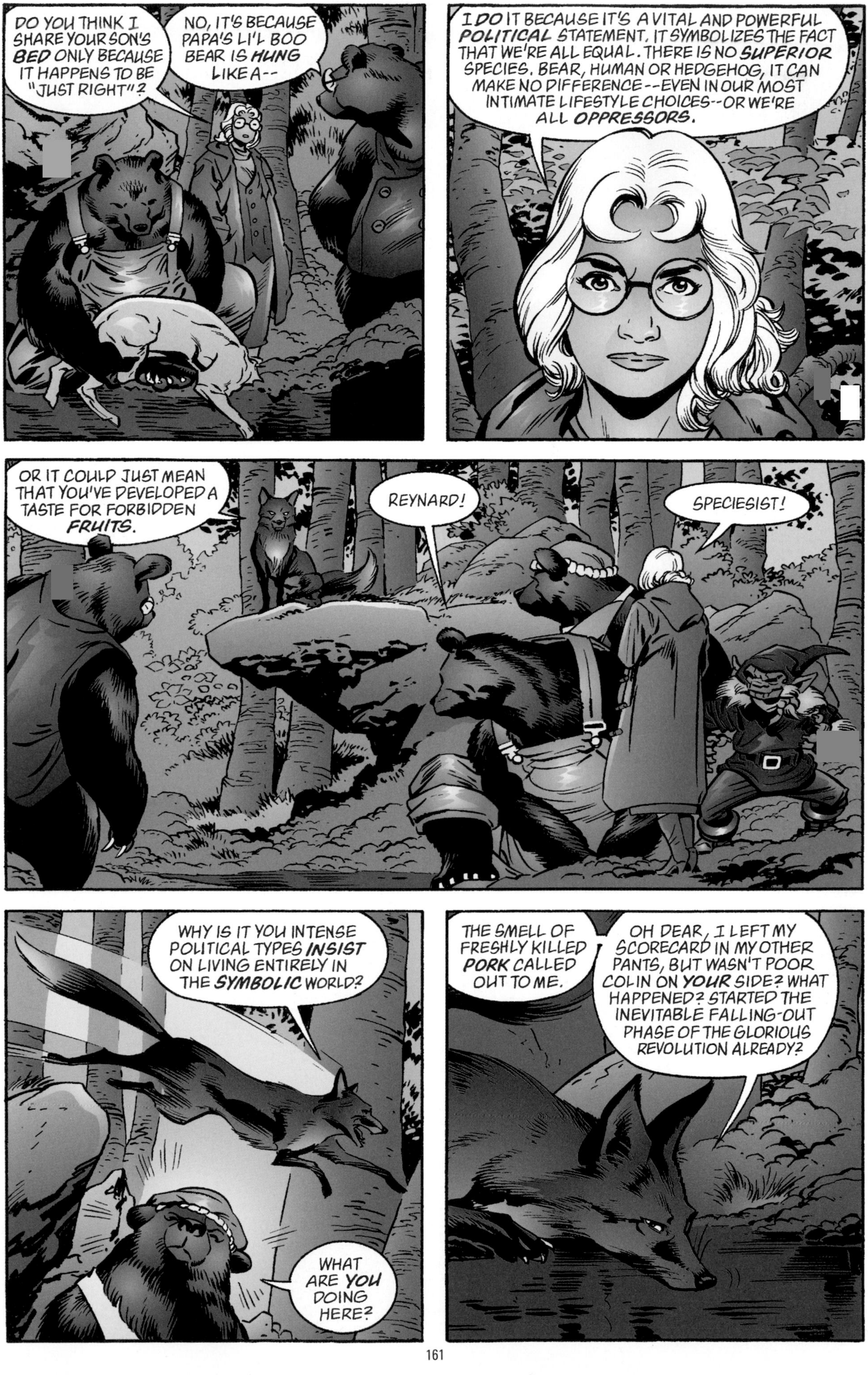
DO YOU THINK I SHARE YOUR SON'S BED ONLY BECAUSE IT HAPPENS TO BE "JUST RIGHT"?
NO, IT'S BECAUSE PAPA'S LI'L BOO BEAR IS HUNG LIKE A--
I DO IT BECAUSE IT'S A VITAL AND POWERFUL POLITICAL STATEMENT. IT SYMBOLIZES THE FACT THAT WE'RE ALL EQUAL. THERE IS NO SUPERIOR SPECIES. BEAR, HUMAN OR HEDGEHOG, IT CAN MAKE NO DIFFERENCE--EVEN IN OUR MOST INTIMATE LIFESTYLE CHOICES--OR WE'RE ALL OPPRESSORS.
OR IT COULD JUST MEAN THAT YOU'VE DEVELOPED A TASTE FOR FORBIDDEN FRUITS.
REYNARD!
SPECIESIST!
WHY IS IT YOU INTENSE POLITICAL TYPES INSIST ON LIVING ENTIRELY IN THE SYMBOLIC WORLD?
WHAT ARE YOU DOING HERE?
THE SMELL OF FRESHLY KILLED PORK CALLED OUT TO ME.
OH DEAR, I LEFT MY SCORECARD IN MY OTHER PANTS, BUT WASN'T POOR COLIN ON YOUR SIDE? WHAT HAPPENED? STARTED THE INEVITABLE FALLING-OUT PHASE OF THE GLORIOUS REVOLUTION ALREADY?

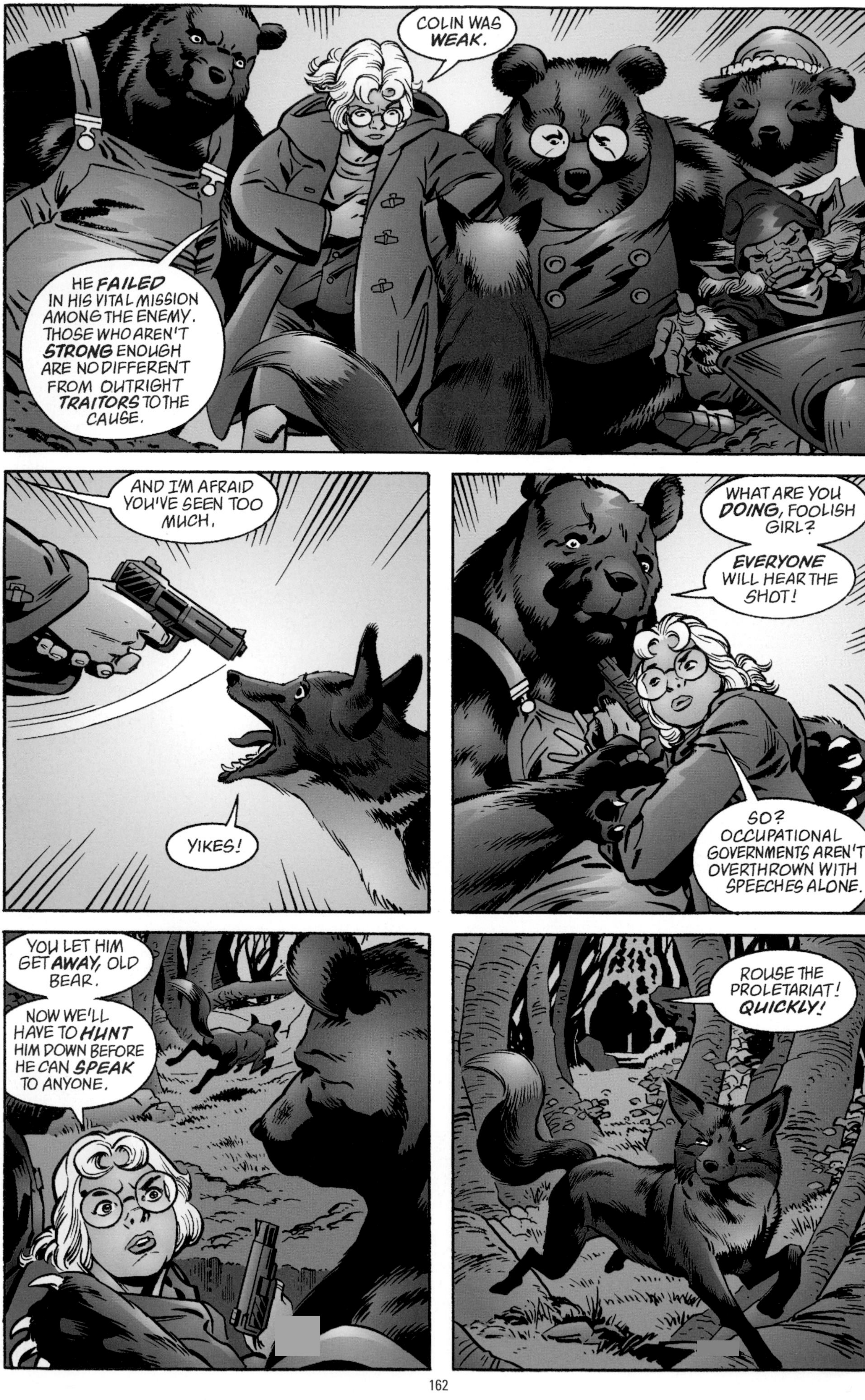
COLIN WAS WEAK.
HE FAILED IN HIS VITAL MISSION AMONG THE ENEMY. THOSE WHO AREN'T STRONG ENOUGH ARE NO DIFFERENT FROM OUTRIGHT TRAITORS TO THE CAUSE.
AND I'M AFRAID YOU'VE SEEN TOO MUCH.
YIKES!
WHAT ARE YOU DOING, FOOLISH GIRL?
EVERYONE WILL HEAR THE SHOT!
SO? OCCUPATIONAL GOVERNMENTS AREN'T OVERTHROWN WITH SPEECHES ALONE.
YOU LET HIM GET AWAY, OLD BEAR.
NOW WE'LL HAVE TO HUNT HIM DOWN BEFORE HE CAN SPEAK TO ANYONE.
ROUSE THE PROLETARIAT! QUICKLY!

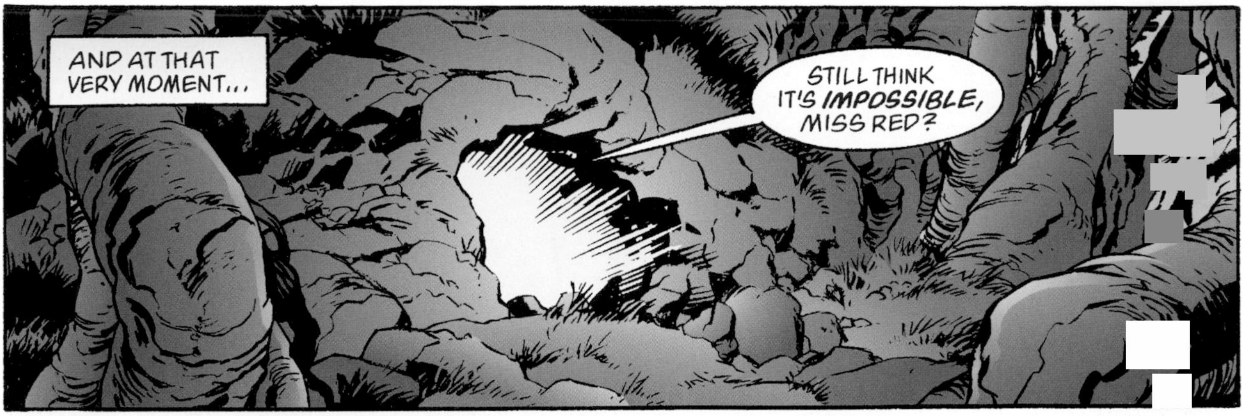
AND AT THAT VERY MOMENT...
STILL THINK IT'S *IMPOSSIBLE,* MISS RED?

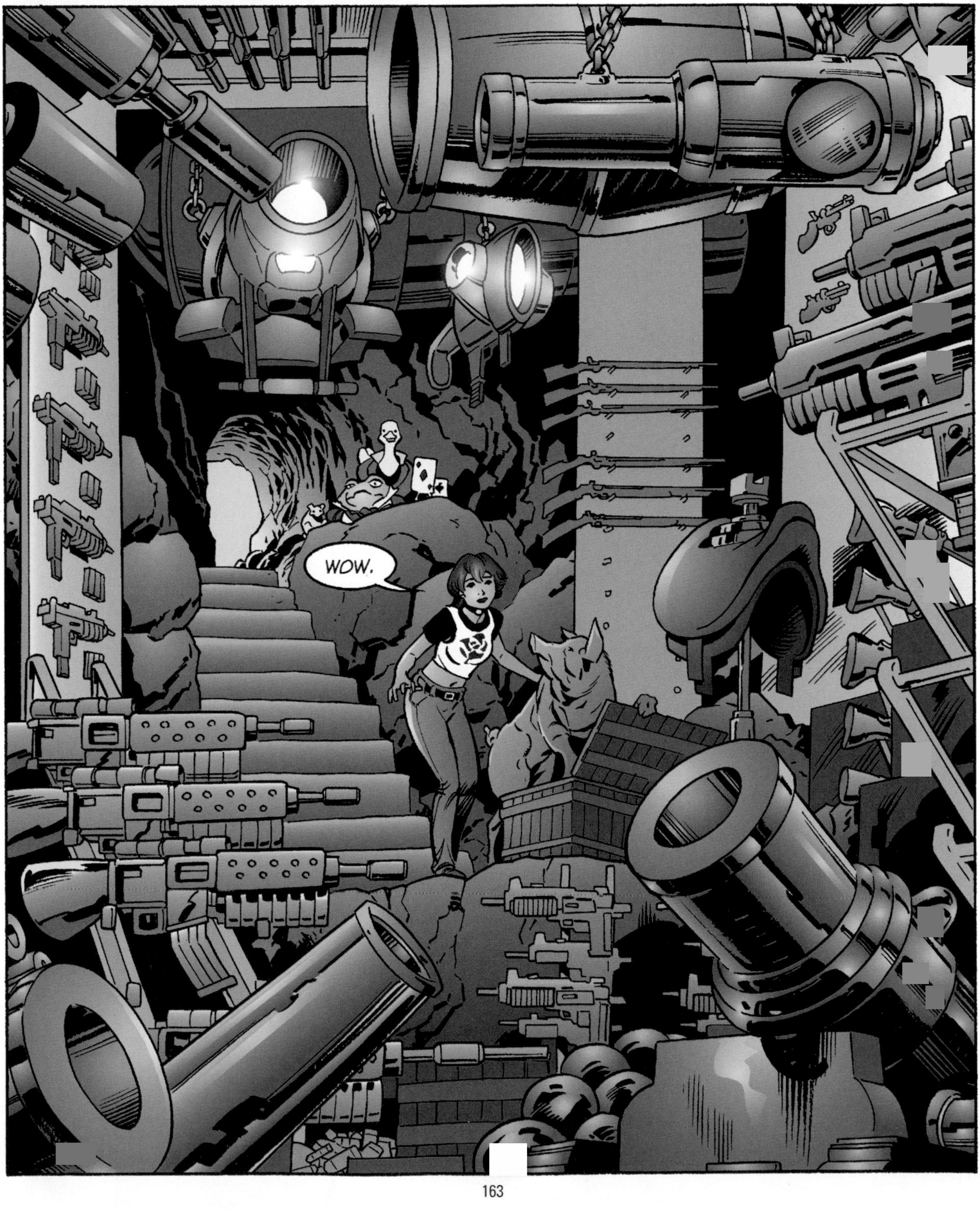
WOW.

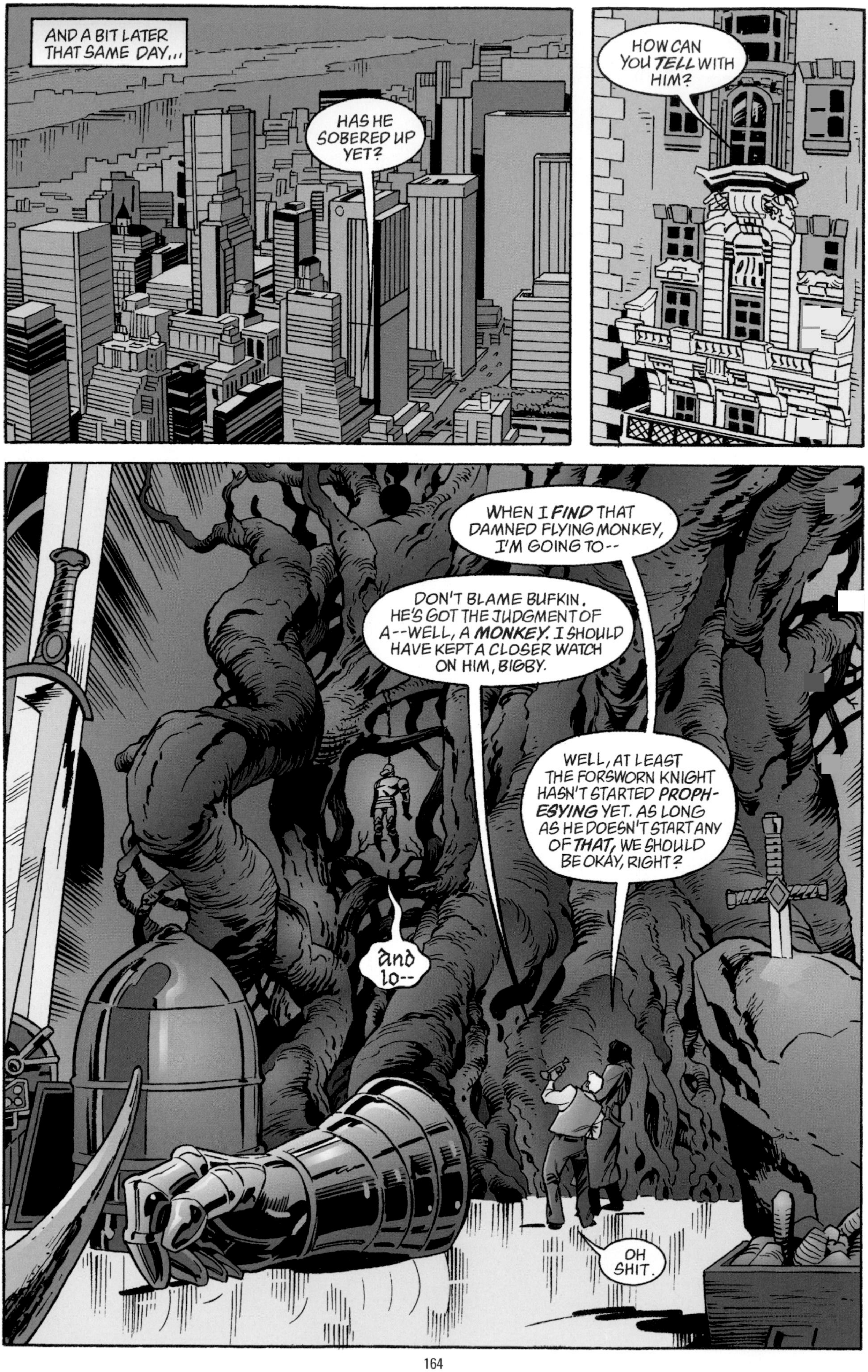
AND A BIT LATER THAT SAME DAY...
HAS HE SOBERED UP YET?
HOW CAN YOU TELL WITH HIM?
WHEN I FIND THAT DAMNED FLYING MONKEY, I'M GOING TO--
DON'T BLAME BUFKIN. HE'S GOT THE JUDGMENT OF A--WELL, A MONKEY. I SHOULD HAVE KEPT A CLOSER WATCH ON HIM, BIGBY.
WELL, AT LEAST THE FORSWORN KNIGHT HASN'T STARTED PROPH-ESYING YET. AS LONG AS HE DOESN'T START ANY OF THAT, WE SHOULD BE OKAY, RIGHT?
and lo--
OH SHIT.

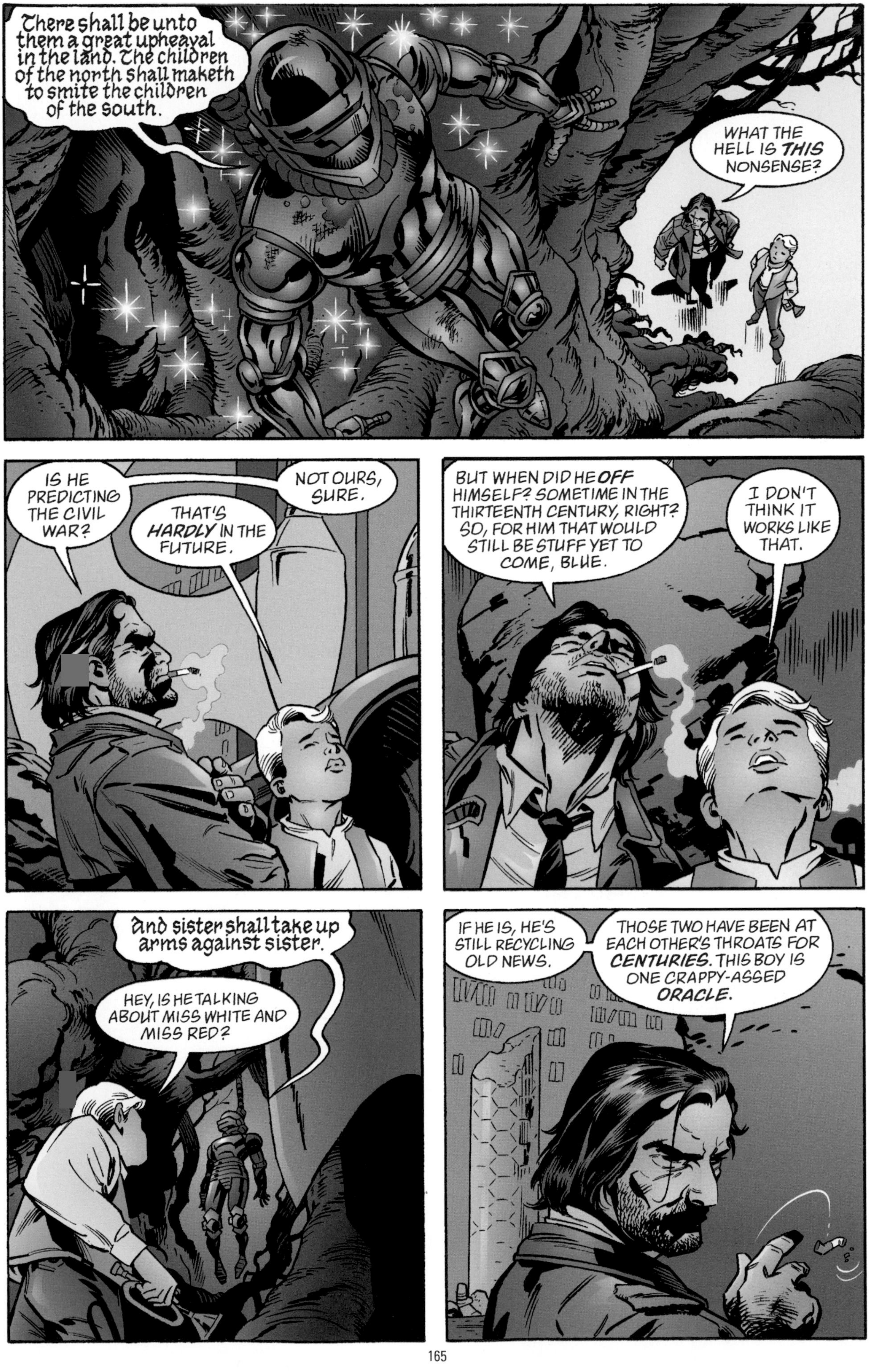
There shall be unto them a great upheaval in the land. The children of the north shall maketh to smite the children of the south.
WHAT THE HELL IS THIS NONSENSE?
IS HE PREDICTING THE CIVIL WAR?
NOT OURS, SURE.
THAT'S HARDLY IN THE FUTURE.
BUT WHEN DID HE OFF HIMSELF? SOMETIME IN THE THIRTEENTH CENTURY, RIGHT? SO, FOR HIM THAT WOULD STILL BE STUFF YET TO COME, BLUE.
I DON'T THINK IT WORKS LIKE THAT.
And sister shall take up arms against sister.
HEY, IS HE TALKING ABOUT MISS WHITE AND MISS RED?
IF HE IS, HE'S STILL RECYCLING OLD NEWS.
THOSE TWO HAVE BEEN AT EACH OTHER'S THROATS FOR CENTURIES. THIS BOY IS ONE CRAPPY-ASSED ORACLE.

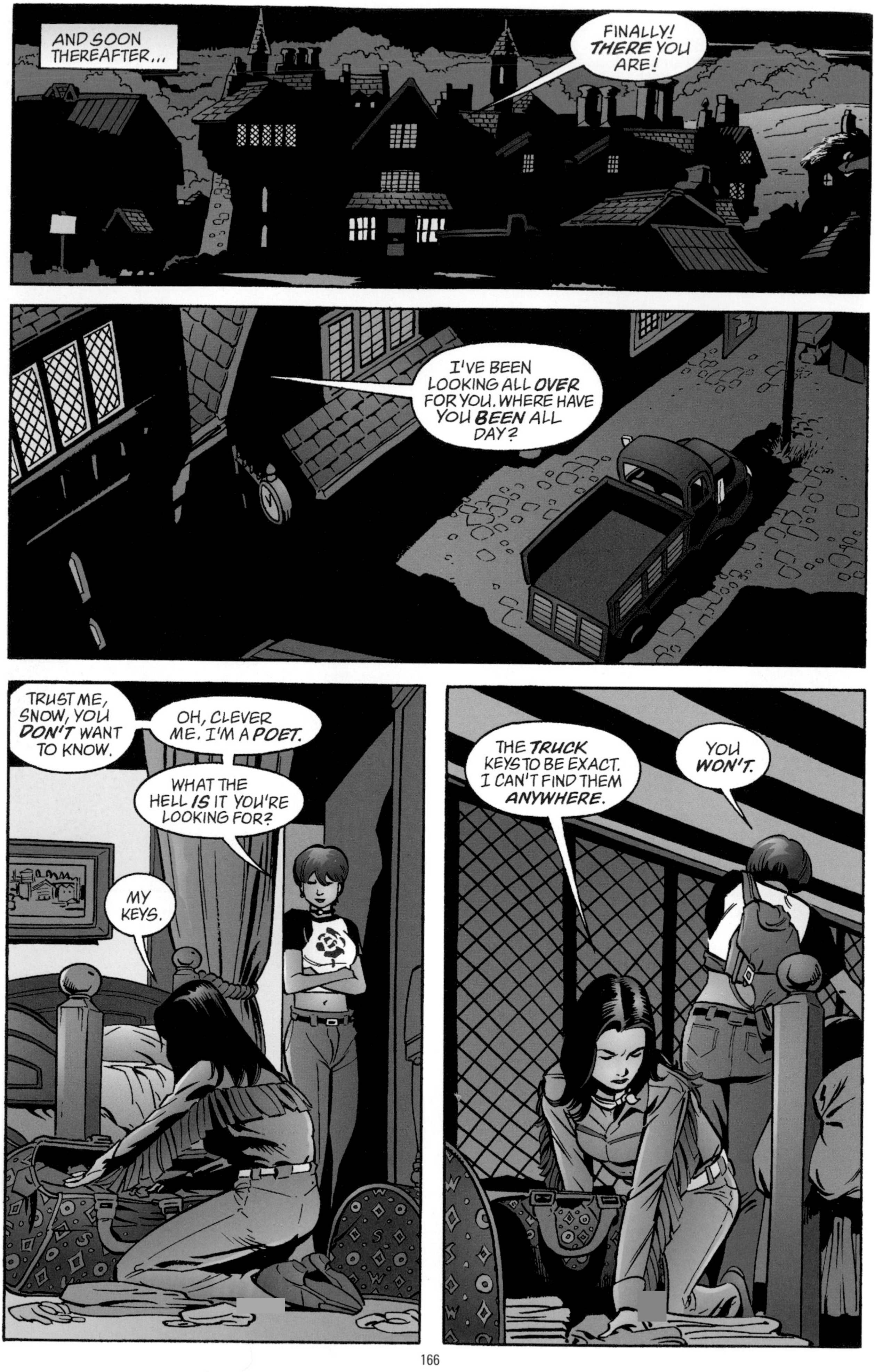
AND SOON THEREAFTER...
FINALLY! THERE YOU ARE!
I'VE BEEN LOOKING ALL OVER FOR YOU. WHERE HAVE YOU BEEN ALL DAY?
TRUST ME, SNOW, YOU DON'T WANT TO KNOW.
OH, CLEVER ME. I'M A POET.
WHAT THE HELL IS IT YOU'RE LOOKING FOR?
MY KEYS.
THE TRUCK KEYS TO BE EXACT. I CAN'T FIND THEM ANYWHERE.
YOU WON'T.

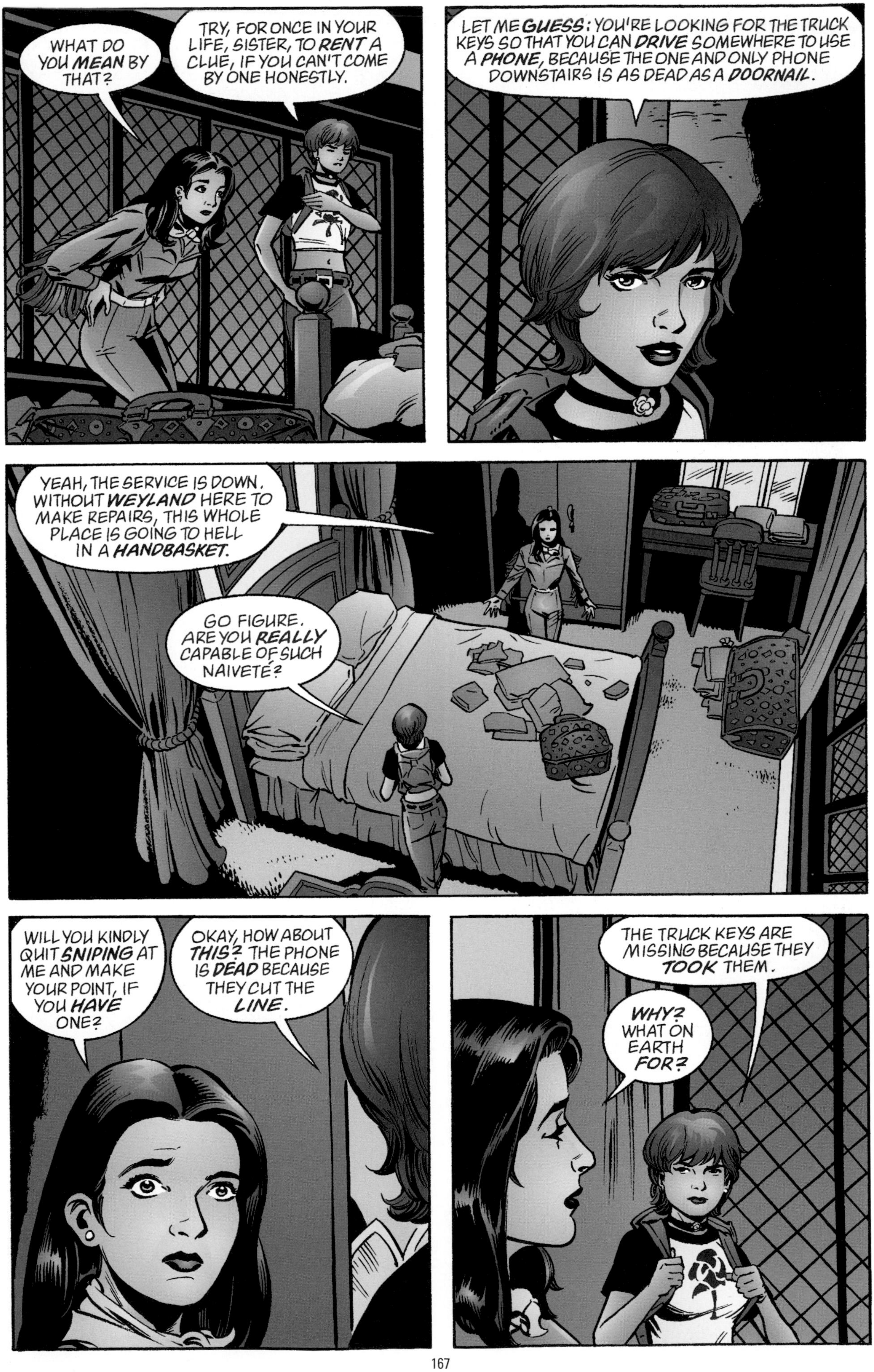
WHAT DO YOU MEAN BY THAT?
TRY, FOR ONCE IN YOUR LIFE, SISTER, TO RENT A CLUE, IF YOU CAN'T COME BY ONE HONESTLY.
LET ME GUESS: YOU'RE LOOKING FOR THE TRUCK KEYS SO THAT YOU CAN DRIVE SOMEWHERE TO USE A PHONE, BECAUSE THE ONE AND ONLY PHONE DOWNSTAIRS IS AS DEAD AS A DOORNAIL.
YEAH, THE SERVICE IS DOWN. WITHOUT WEYLAND HERE TO MAKE REPAIRS, THIS WHOLE PLACE IS GOING TO HELL IN A HANDBASKET.
GO FIGURE. ARE YOU REALLY CAPABLE OF SUCH NAIVETÉ?
WILL YOU KINDLY QUIT SNIPING AT ME AND MAKE YOUR POINT, IF YOU HAVE ONE?
OKAY, HOW ABOUT THIS? THE PHONE IS DEAD BECAUSE THEY CUT THE LINE.
THE TRUCK KEYS ARE MISSING BECAUSE THEY TOOK THEM.
WHY? WHAT ON EARTH FOR?

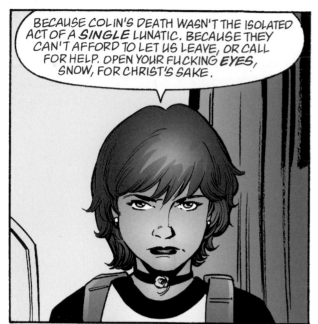

BECAUSE COLIN'S DEATH WASN'T THE ISOLATED ACT OF A *SINGLE* LUNATIC. BECAUSE THEY CAN'T AFFORD TO LET US LEAVE, OR CALL FOR HELP. OPEN YOUR FUCKING *EYES*, SNOW, FOR CHRIST'S SAKE.

ACTUALLY, *FORGET* I SAID THAT. YOU'LL PROBABLY BE SAFER THE MORE YOU *DON'T* NOTICE THINGS. DO YOUR-SELF A FAVOR AND CON-TINUE PLAYING THE DULLARD FOR A FEW DAYS.

IT SHOULD BE RIDICULOUSLY *EASY* FOR YOU.

WHAT ARE YOU *UP* TO? WHERE ARE YOU *GOING*?

AWAY. I'LL BE GONE FOR AWHILE. AND DON'T RAISE A FUSS *LOOKING* FOR ME, EITHER.

WAIT JUST A GODDAMN *MINUTE*! COME *BACK* HERE!

CAN'T, HON, GOTTA SCOOT. PEOPLE WAITING ON ME. REMEMBER WHAT I SAID.

LET'S GO, KIDS. I'M ALL *YOURS*.

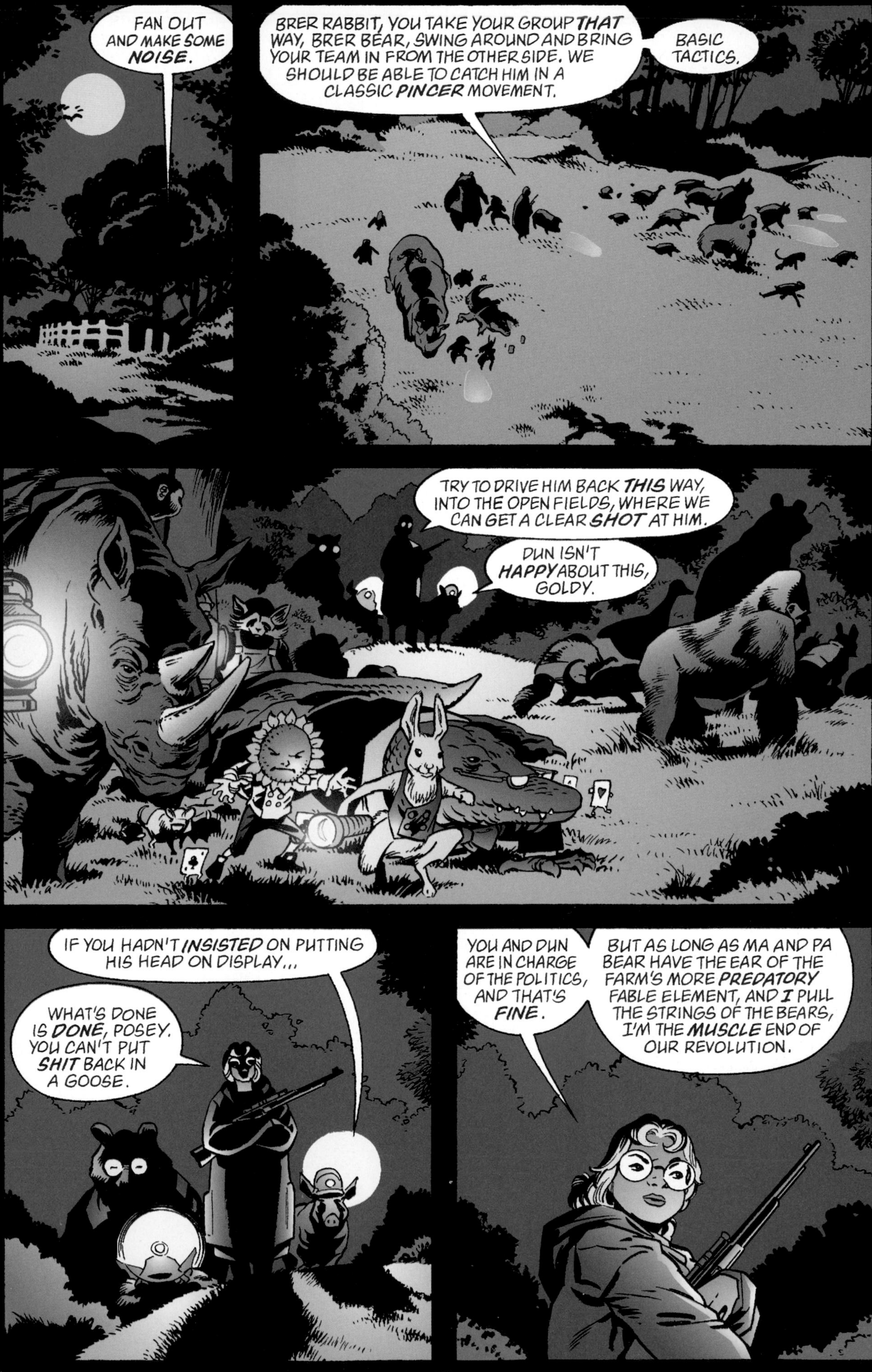
FAN OUT AND MAKE SOME NOISE.
BRER RABBIT, YOU TAKE YOUR GROUP THAT WAY, BRER BEAR, SWING AROUND AND BRING YOUR TEAM IN FROM THE OTHER SIDE. WE SHOULD BE ABLE TO CATCH HIM IN A CLASSIC PINCER MOVEMENT.
BASIC TACTICS.
TRY TO DRIVE HIM BACK THIS WAY, INTO THE OPEN FIELDS, WHERE WE CAN GET A CLEAR SHOT AT HIM.
DUN ISN'T HAPPY ABOUT THIS, GOLDY.
IF YOU HADN'T INSISTED ON PUTTING HIS HEAD ON DISPLAY...
WHAT'S DONE IS DONE, POSEY. YOU CAN'T PUT SHIT BACK IN A GOOSE.
YOU AND DUN ARE IN CHARGE OF THE POLITICS, AND THAT'S FINE.
BUT AS LONG AS MA AND PA BEAR HAVE THE EAR OF THE FARM'S MORE PREDATORY FABLE ELEMENT, AND I PULL THE STRINGS OF THE BEARS, I'M THE MUSCLE END OF OUR REVOLUTION.

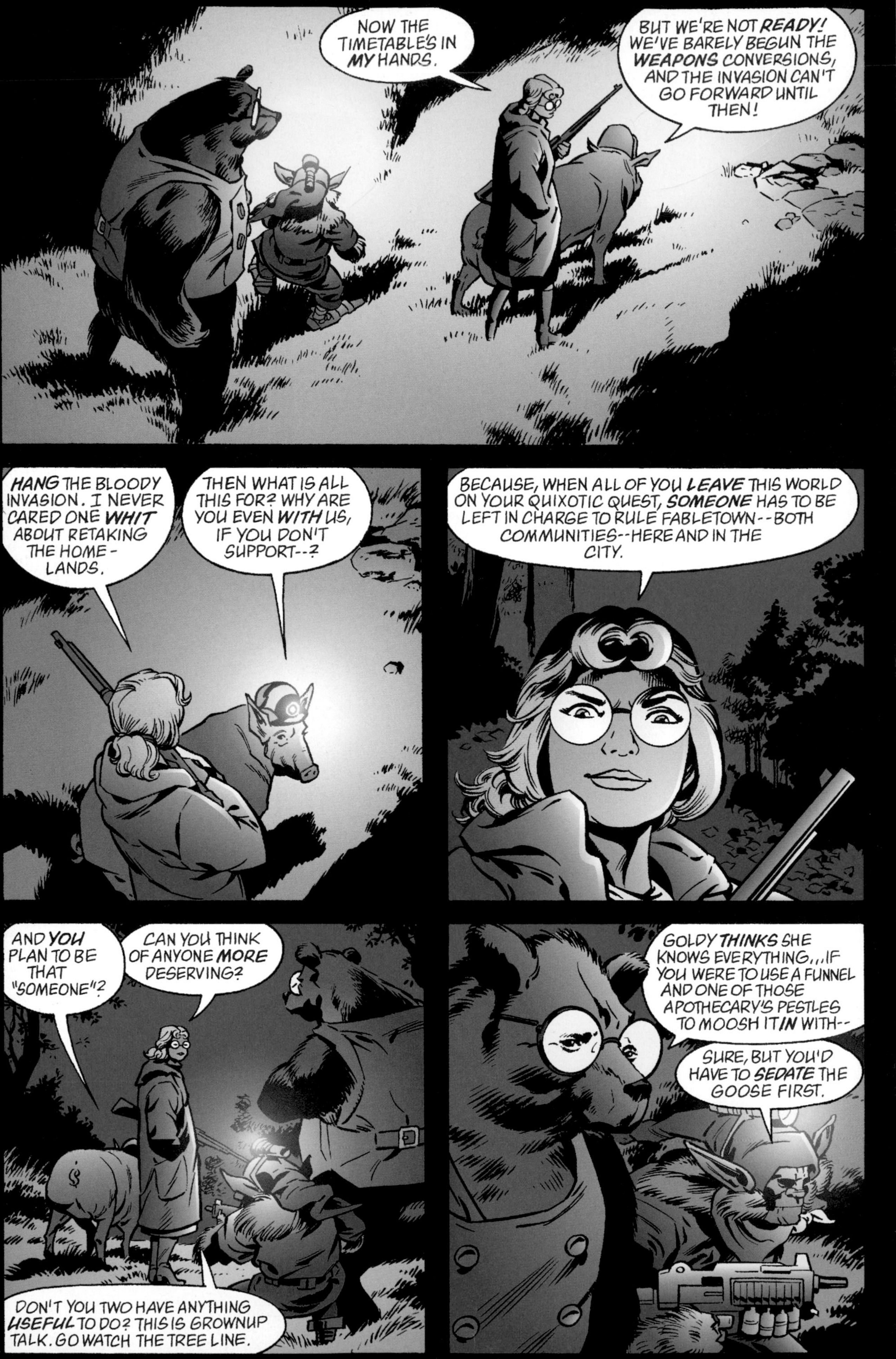
NOW THE TIMETABLE'S IN MY HANDS.
BUT WE'RE NOT READY! WE'VE BARELY BEGUN THE WEAPONS CONVERSIONS, AND THE INVASION CAN'T GO FORWARD UNTIL THEN!
HANG THE BLOODY INVASION. I NEVER CARED ONE WHIT ABOUT RETAKING THE HOME-LANDS.
THEN WHAT IS ALL THIS FOR? WHY ARE YOU EVEN WITH US, IF YOU DON'T SUPPORT--?
BECAUSE, WHEN ALL OF YOU LEAVE THIS WORLD ON YOUR QUIXOTIC QUEST, SOMEONE HAS TO BE LEFT IN CHARGE TO RULE FABLETOWN--BOTH COMMUNITIES--HERE AND IN THE CITY.
AND YOU PLAN TO BE THAT "SOMEONE"?
CAN YOU THINK OF ANYONE MORE DESERVING?
DON'T YOU TWO HAVE ANYTHING USEFUL TO DO? THIS IS GROWNUP TALK. GO WATCH THE TREE LINE.
GOLDY THINKS SHE KNOWS EVERYTHING... IF YOU WERE TO USE A FUNNEL AND ONE OF THOSE APOTHECARY'S PESTLES TO MOOSH IT IN WITH--
SURE, BUT YOU'D HAVE TO SEDATE THE GOOSE FIRST.

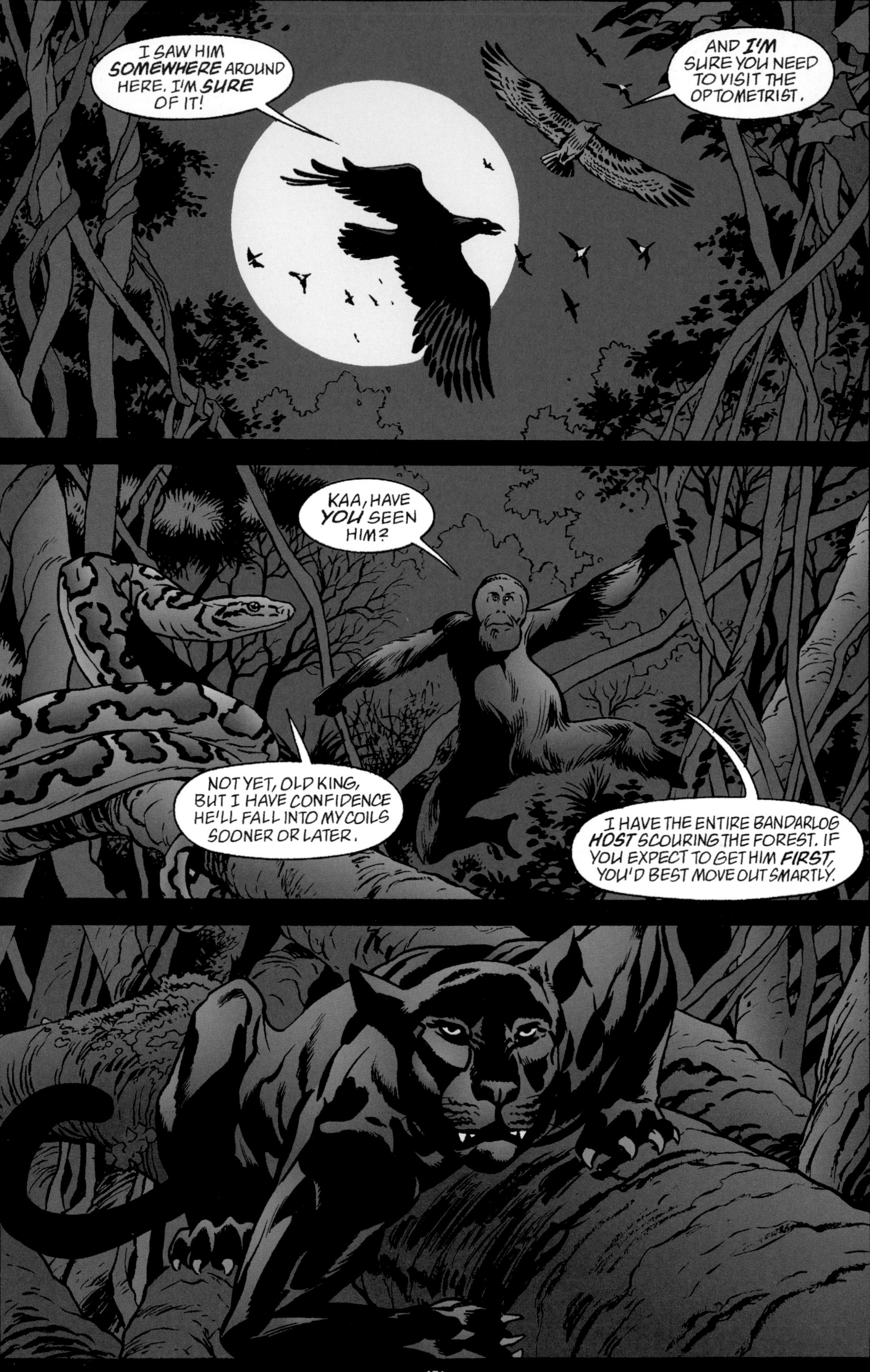
I SAW HIM SOMEWHERE AROUND HERE. I'M SURE OF IT!
AND I'M SURE YOU NEED TO VISIT THE OPTOMETRIST.
KAA, HAVE YOU SEEN HIM?
NOT YET, OLD KING, BUT I HAVE CONFIDENCE HE'LL FALL INTO MY COILS SOONER OR LATER.
I HAVE THE ENTIRE BANDARLOG HOST SCOURING THE FOREST. IF YOU EXPECT TO GET HIM FIRST, YOU'D BEST MOVE OUT SMARTLY.

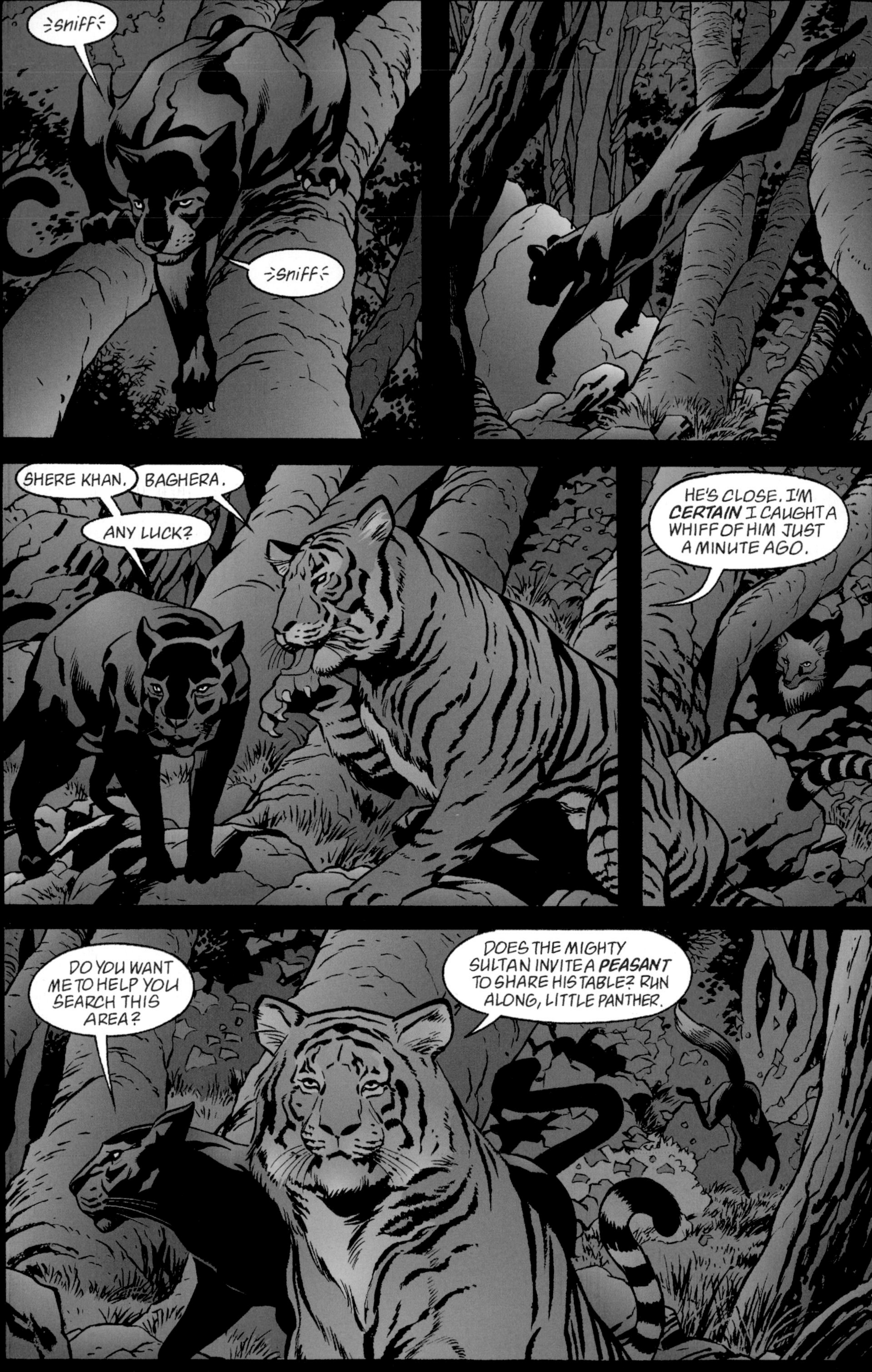

SNIFF
SNIFF
SHERE KHAN.
BAGHERA.
ANY LUCK?
HE'S CLOSE. I'M CERTAIN I CAUGHT A WHIFF OF HIM JUST A MINUTE AGO.
DO YOU WANT ME TO HELP YOU SEARCH THIS AREA?
DOES THE MIGHTY SULTAN INVITE A PEASANT TO SHARE HIS TABLE? RUN ALONG, LITTLE PANTHER.

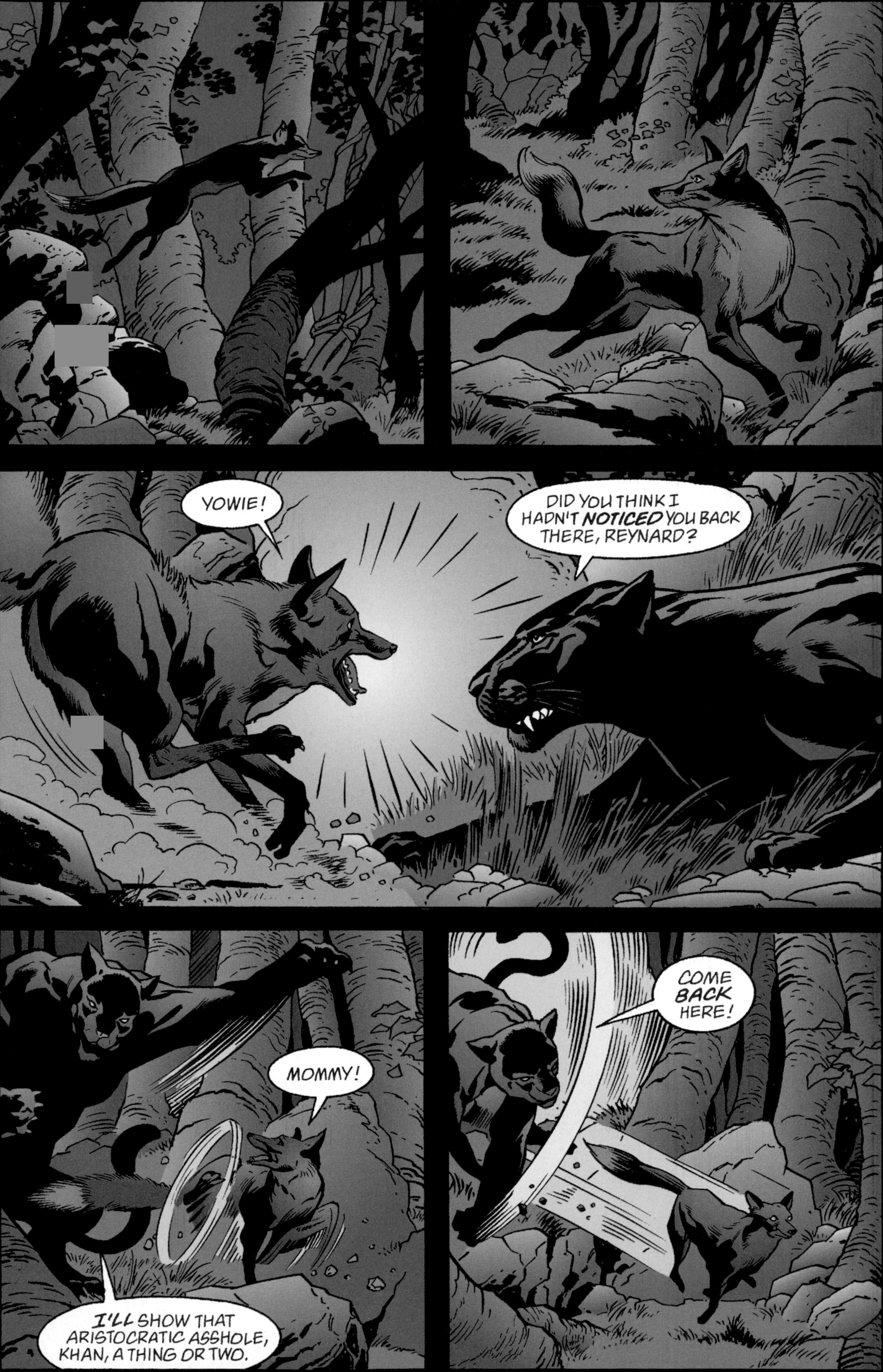
YOWIE!
DID YOU THINK I HADN'T NOTICED YOU BACK THERE, REYNARD?
MOMMY!
I'LL SHOW THAT ARISTOCRATIC ASSHOLE, KHAN, A THING OR TWO.
COME BACK HERE!

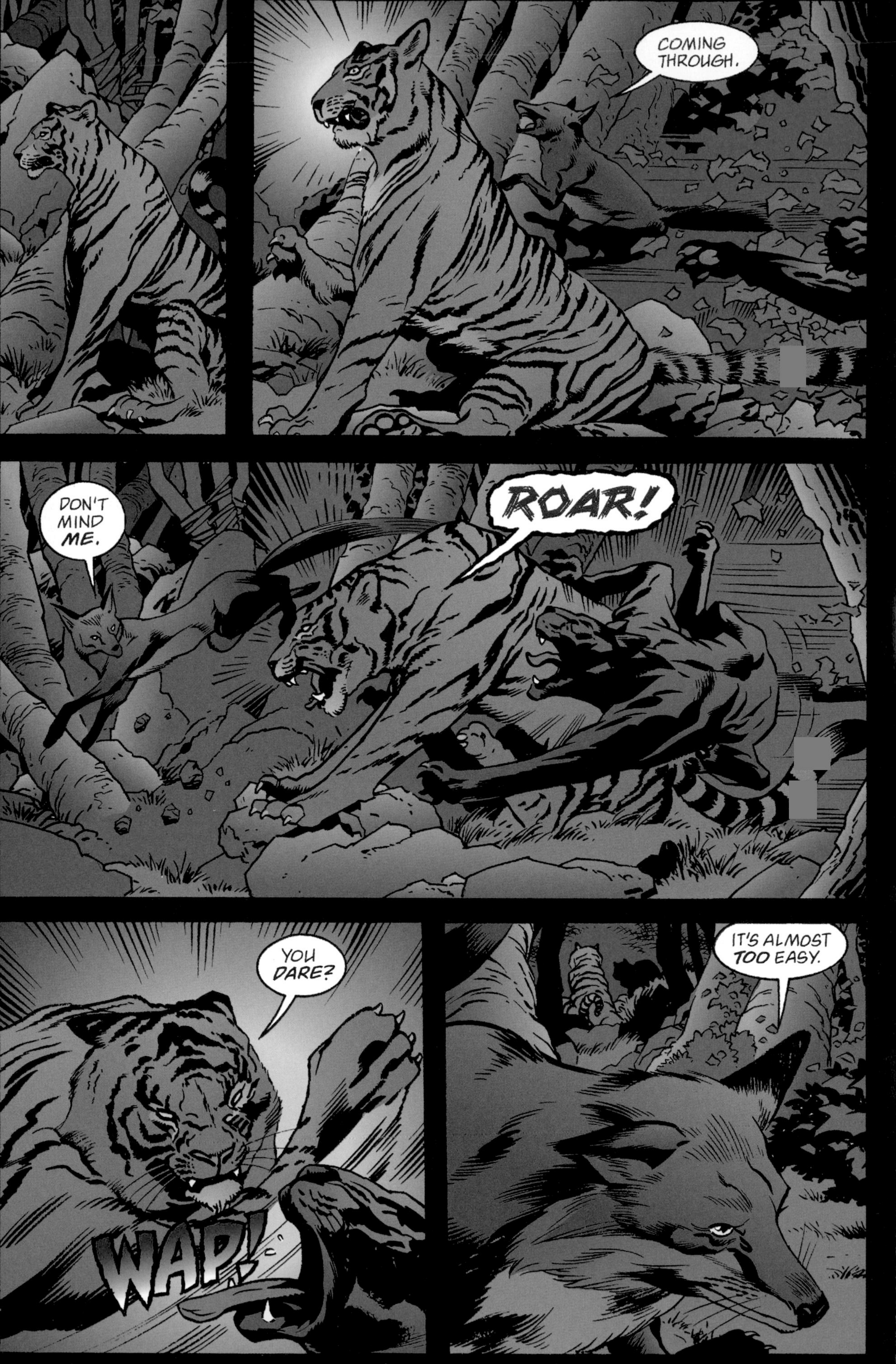
COMING THROUGH.
DON'T MIND ME.
ROAR!
YOU DARE?
WAP!
IT'S ALMOST TOO EASY.

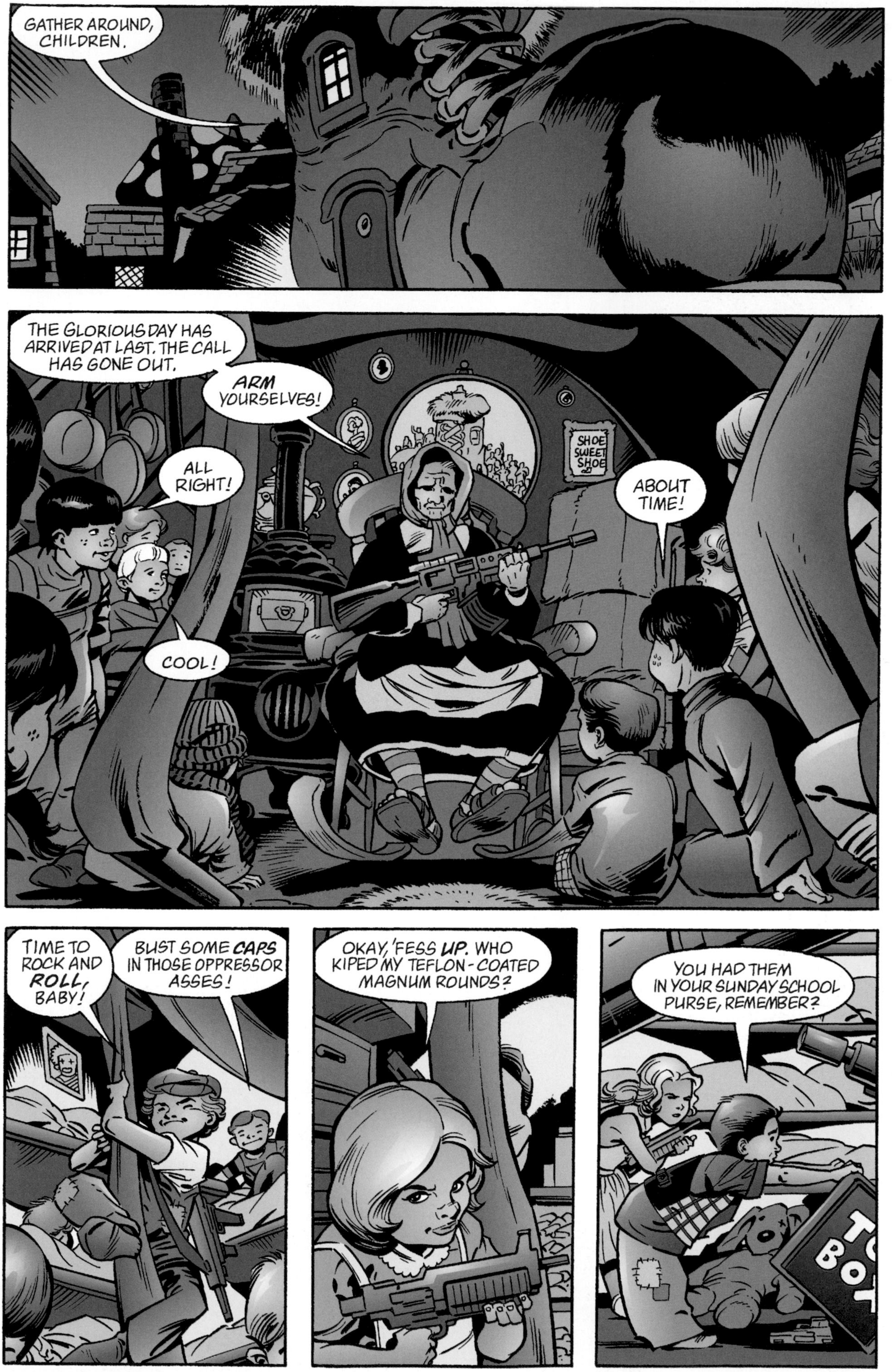
GATHER AROUND, CHILDREN.
THE GLORIOUS DAY HAS ARRIVED AT LAST. THE CALL HAS GONE OUT.
ARM YOURSELVES!
SHOE SWEET SHOE
ALL RIGHT!
ABOUT TIME!
COOL!
TIME TO ROCK AND ROLL, BABY!
BUST SOME CAPS IN THOSE OPPRESSOR ASSES!
OKAY, 'FESS UP. WHO KIPED MY TEFLON-COATED MAGNUM ROUNDS?
YOU HAD THEM IN YOUR SUNDAY SCHOOL PURSE, REMEMBER?

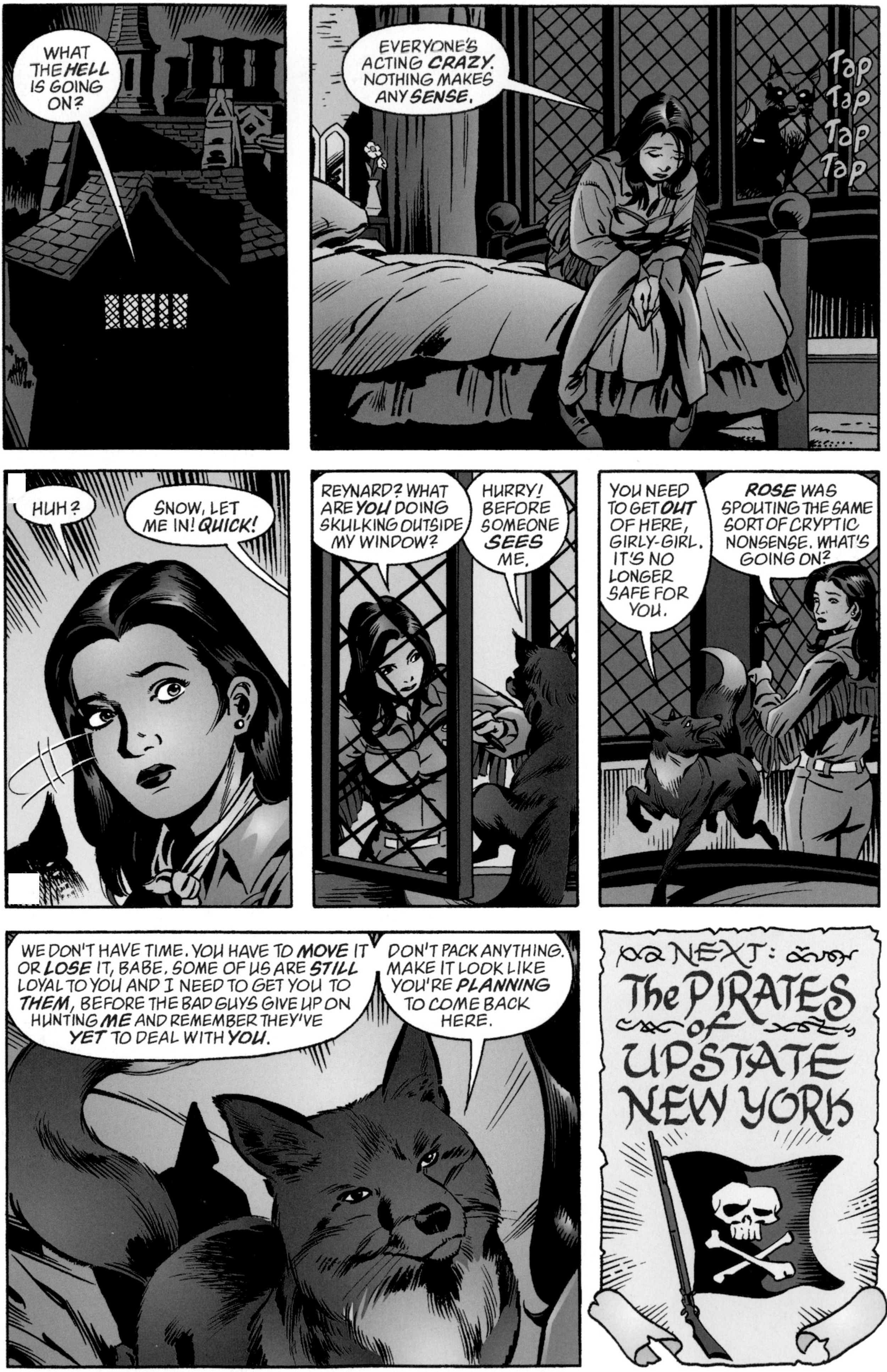
WHAT THE HELL IS GOING ON?
EVERYONE'S ACTING CRAZY. NOTHING MAKES ANY SENSE.
Tap Tap Tap Tap
HUH?
SNOW, LET ME IN! QUICK!
REYNARD? WHAT ARE YOU DOING SKULKING OUTSIDE MY WINDOW?
HURRY! BEFORE SOMEONE SEES ME.
YOU NEED TO GET OUT OF HERE, GIRLY-GIRL. IT'S NO LONGER SAFE FOR YOU.
ROSE WAS SPOUTING THE SAME SORT OF CRYPTIC NONSENSE. WHAT'S GOING ON?
WE DON'T HAVE TIME. YOU HAVE TO MOVE IT OR LOSE IT, BABE. SOME OF US ARE STILL LOYAL TO YOU AND I NEED TO GET YOU TO THEM, BEFORE THE BAD GUYS GIVE UP ON HUNTING ME AND REMEMBER THEY'VE YET TO DEAL WITH YOU.
DON'T PACK ANYTHING. MAKE IT LOOK LIKE YOU'RE PLANNING TO COME BACK HERE.
NEXT: The PIRATES of UPSTATE NEW YORK

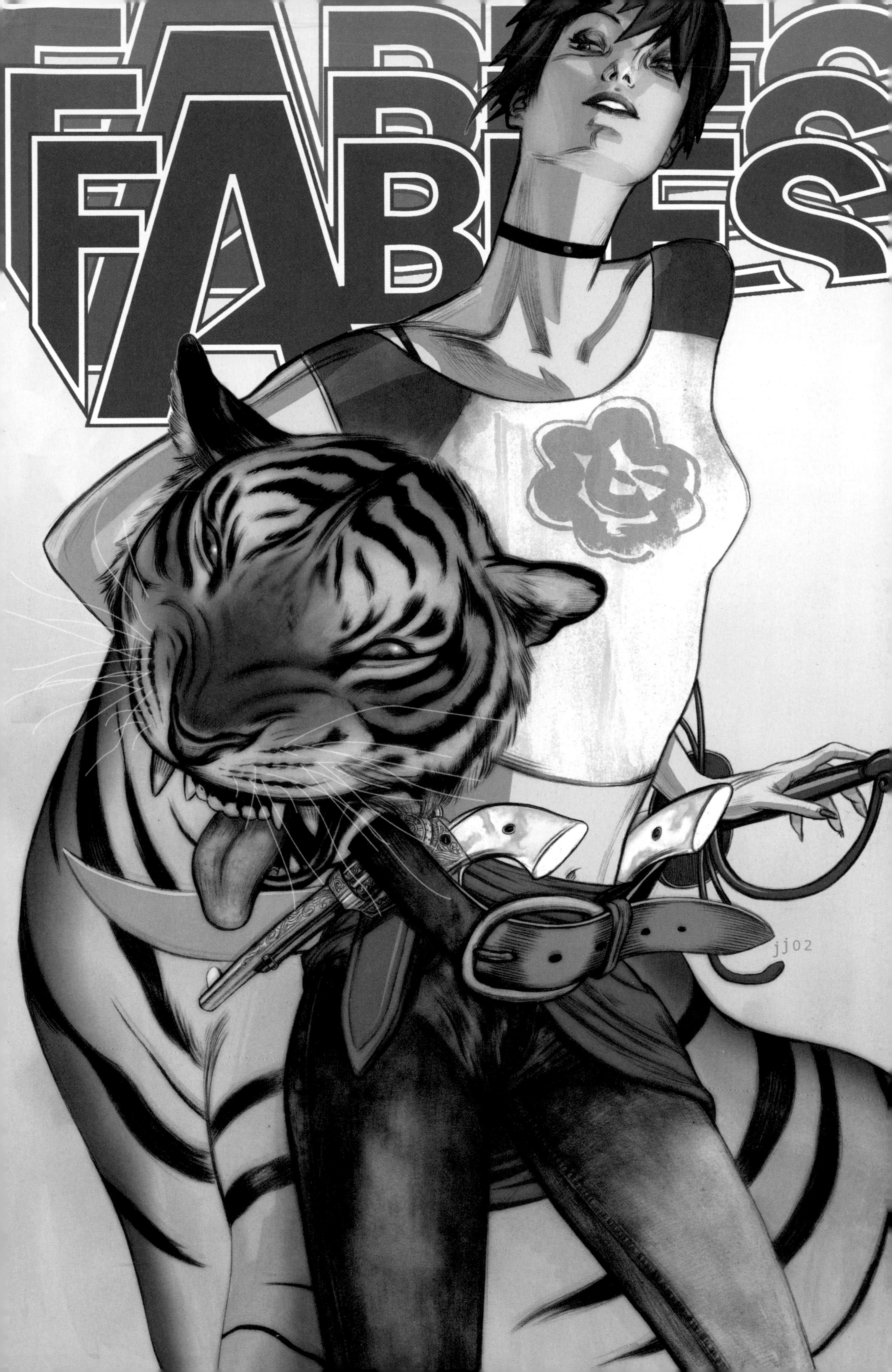
FABLES
jj02

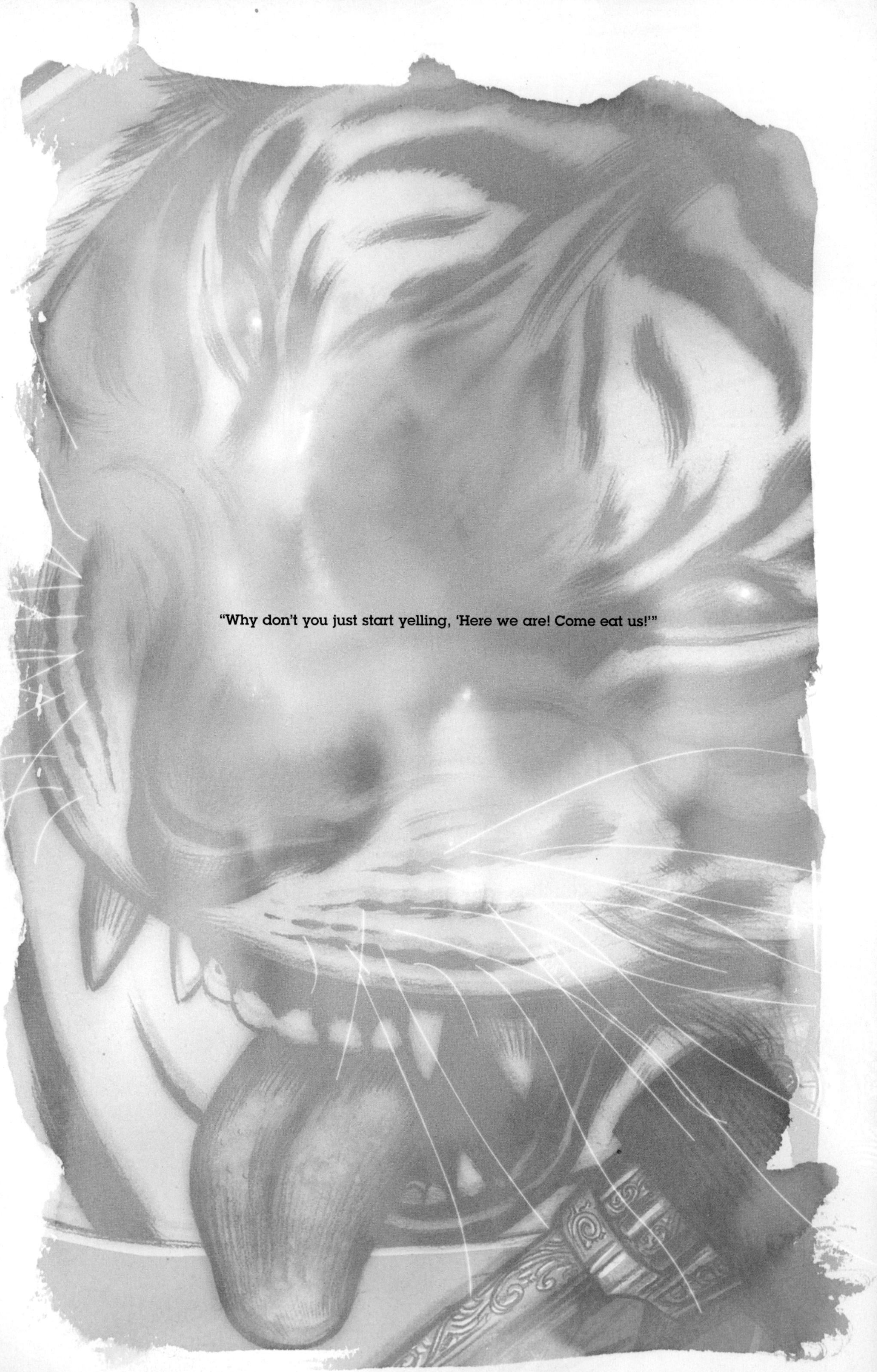

"Why don't you just start yelling, 'Here we are! Come eat us!'"

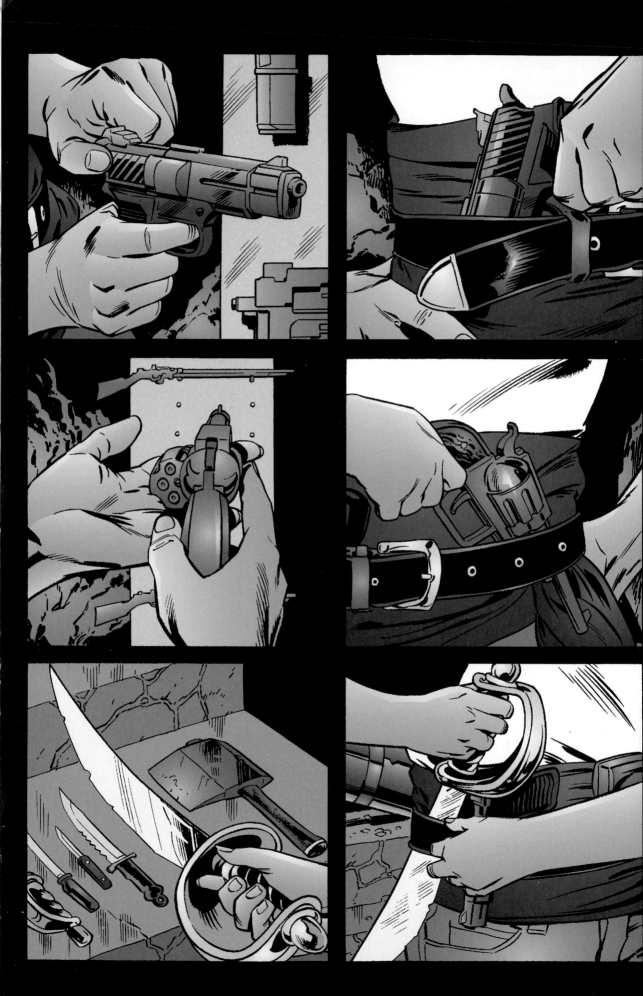

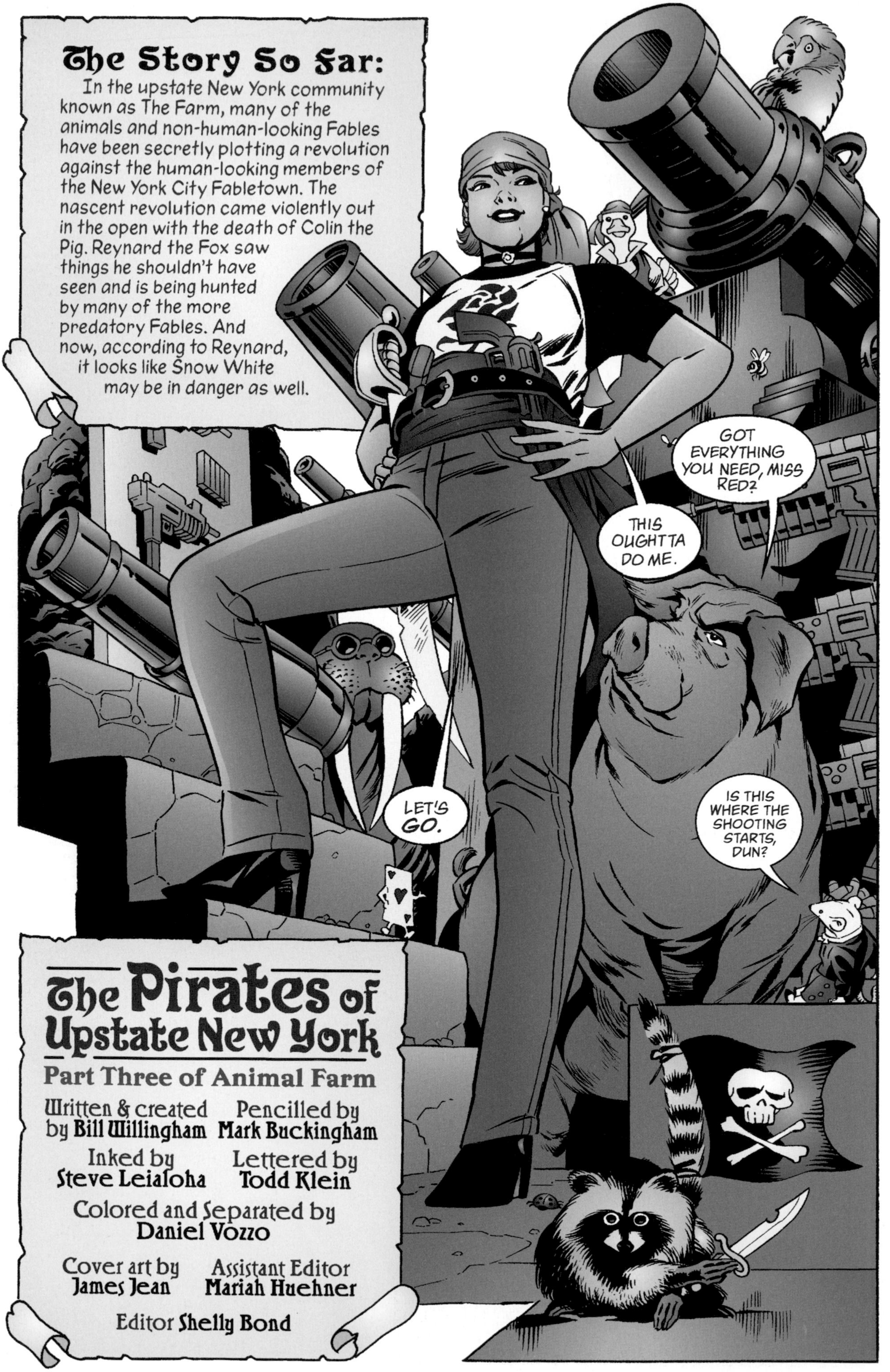

The Story So Far:
In the upstate New York community known as The Farm, many of the animals and non-human-looking Fables have been secretly plotting a revolution against the human-looking members of the New York City Fabletown. The nascent revolution came violently out in the open with the death of Colin the Pig. Reynard the Fox saw things he shouldn't have seen and is being hunted by many of the more predatory Fables. And now, according to Reynard, it looks like Snow White may be in danger as well.
GOT EVERYTHING YOU NEED, MISS RED?
THIS OUGHTTA DO ME.
LET'S GO.
IS THIS WHERE THE SHOOTING STARTS, DUN?
The Pirates of Upstate New York
Part Three of Animal Farm
Written & created by Bill Willingham
Pencilled by Mark Buckingham
Inked by Steve Leialoha
Lettered by Todd Klein
Colored and Separated by Daniel Vozzo
Cover art by James Jean
Assistant Editor Mariah Huehner
Editor Shelly Bond

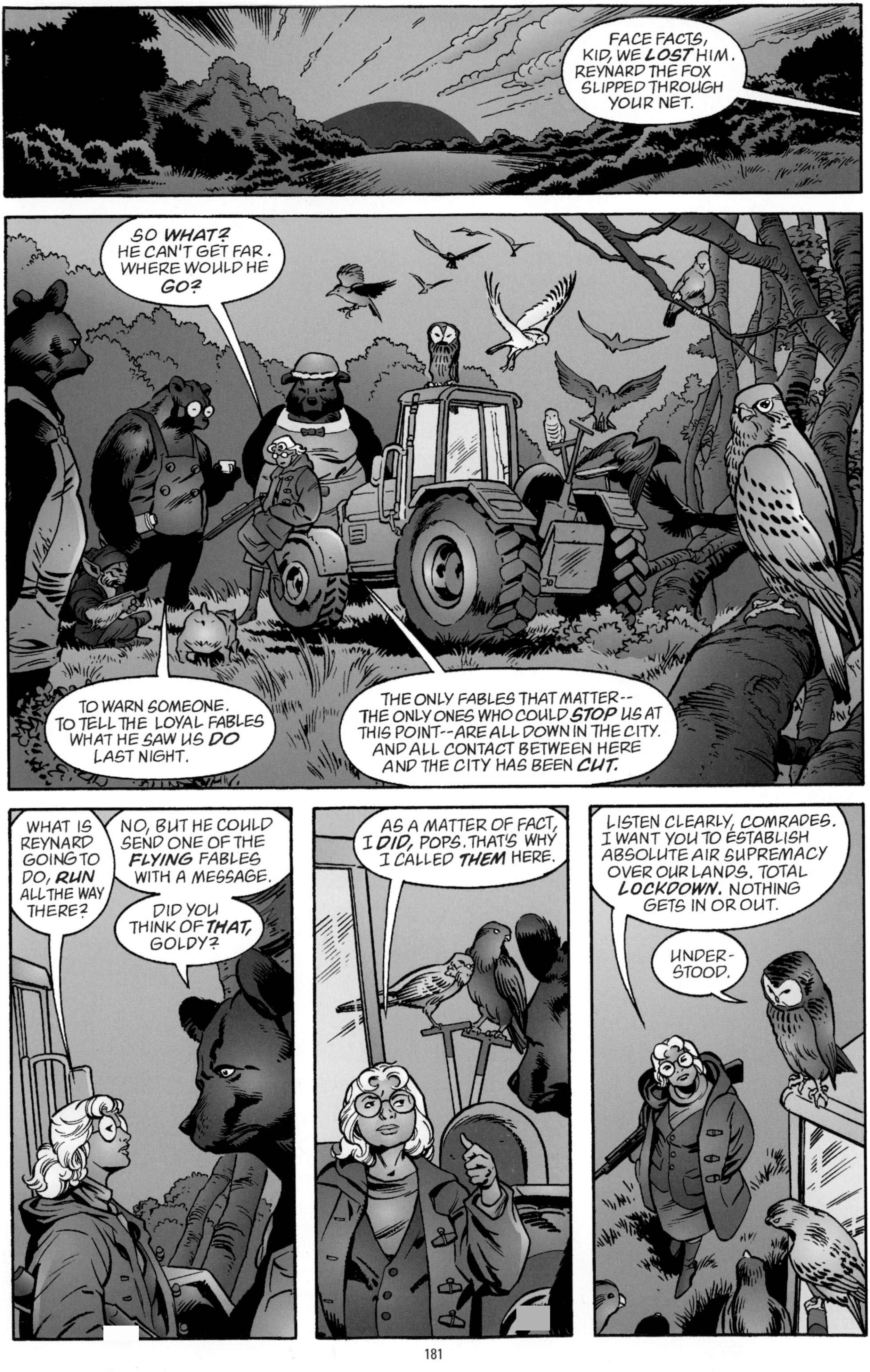
FACE FACTS, KID, WE LOST HIM. REYNARD THE FOX SLIPPED THROUGH YOUR NET.
SO WHAT? HE CAN'T GET FAR. WHERE WOULD HE GO?
TO WARN SOMEONE. TO TELL THE LOYAL FABLES WHAT HE SAW US DO LAST NIGHT.
THE ONLY FABLES THAT MATTER-- THE ONLY ONES WHO COULD STOP US AT THIS POINT--ARE ALL DOWN IN THE CITY. AND ALL CONTACT BETWEEN HERE AND THE CITY HAS BEEN CUT.
WHAT IS REYNARD GOING TO DO, RUN ALL THE WAY THERE?
NO, BUT HE COULD SEND ONE OF THE FLYING FABLES WITH A MESSAGE.
DID YOU THINK OF THAT, GOLDY?
AS A MATTER OF FACT, I DID, POPS. THAT'S WHY I CALLED THEM HERE.
LISTEN CLEARLY, COMRADES. I WANT YOU TO ESTABLISH ABSOLUTE AIR SUPREMACY OVER OUR LANDS. TOTAL LOCKDOWN. NOTHING GETS IN OR OUT.
UNDER-STOOD.

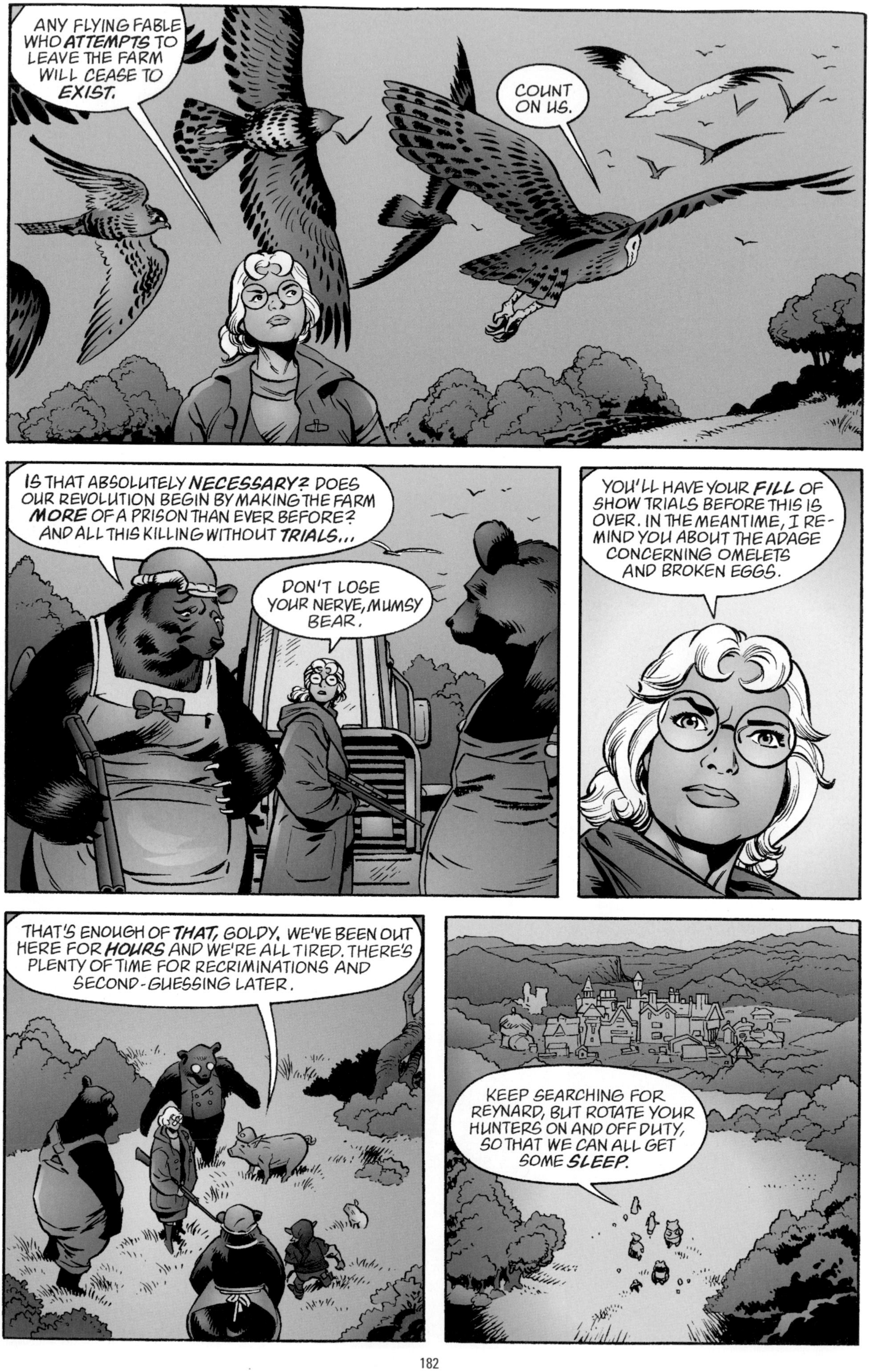
ANY FLYING FABLE WHO ATTEMPTS TO LEAVE THE FARM WILL CEASE TO EXIST.
COUNT ON US.
IS THAT ABSOLUTELY NECESSARY? DOES OUR REVOLUTION BEGIN BY MAKING THE FARM MORE OF A PRISON THAN EVER BEFORE? AND ALL THIS KILLING WITHOUT TRIALS...
DON'T LOSE YOUR NERVE, MUMSY BEAR.
YOU'LL HAVE YOUR FILL OF SHOW TRIALS BEFORE THIS IS OVER. IN THE MEANTIME, I REMIND YOU ABOUT THE ADAGE CONCERNING OMELETS AND BROKEN EGGS.
THAT'S ENOUGH OF THAT, GOLDY. WE'VE BEEN OUT HERE FOR HOURS AND WE'RE ALL TIRED. THERE'S PLENTY OF TIME FOR RECRIMINATIONS AND SECOND-GUESSING LATER.
KEEP SEARCHING FOR REYNARD, BUT ROTATE YOUR HUNTERS ON AND OFF DUTY, SO THAT WE CAN ALL GET SOME SLEEP.

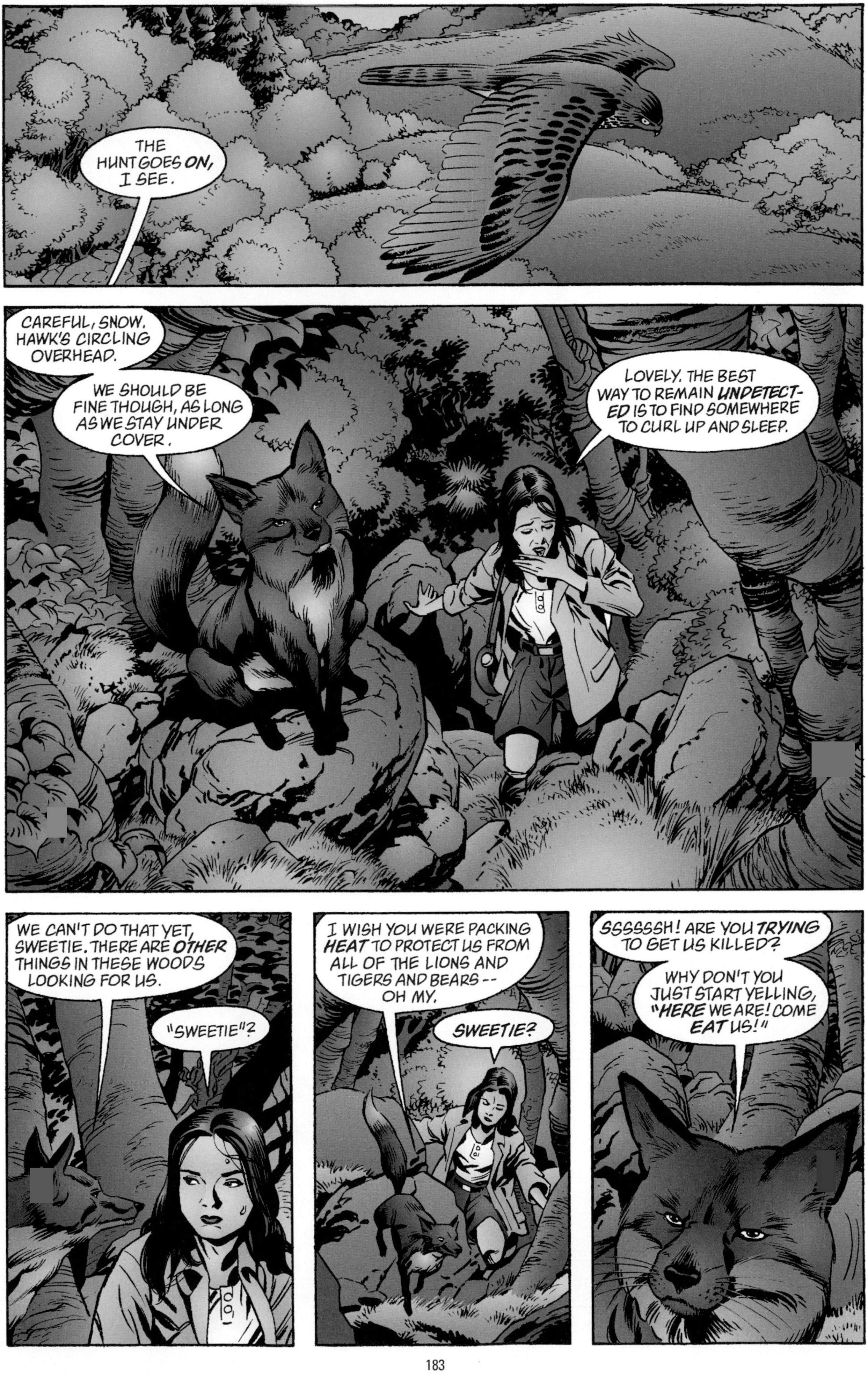
THE HUNT GOES ON, I SEE.
CAREFUL, SNOW. HAWK'S CIRCLING OVERHEAD.
WE SHOULD BE FINE THOUGH, AS LONG AS WE STAY UNDER COVER.
LOVELY. THE BEST WAY TO REMAIN UNDETECTED IS TO FIND SOMEWHERE TO CURL UP AND SLEEP.
WE CAN'T DO THAT YET, SWEETIE. THERE ARE OTHER THINGS IN THESE WOODS LOOKING FOR US.
"SWEETIE"?
I WISH YOU WERE PACKING HEAT TO PROTECT US FROM ALL OF THE LIONS AND TIGERS AND BEARS -- OH MY.
SWEETIE?
SSSSSSH! ARE YOU TRYING TO GET US KILLED?
WHY DON'T YOU JUST START YELLING, "HERE WE ARE! COME EAT US!"

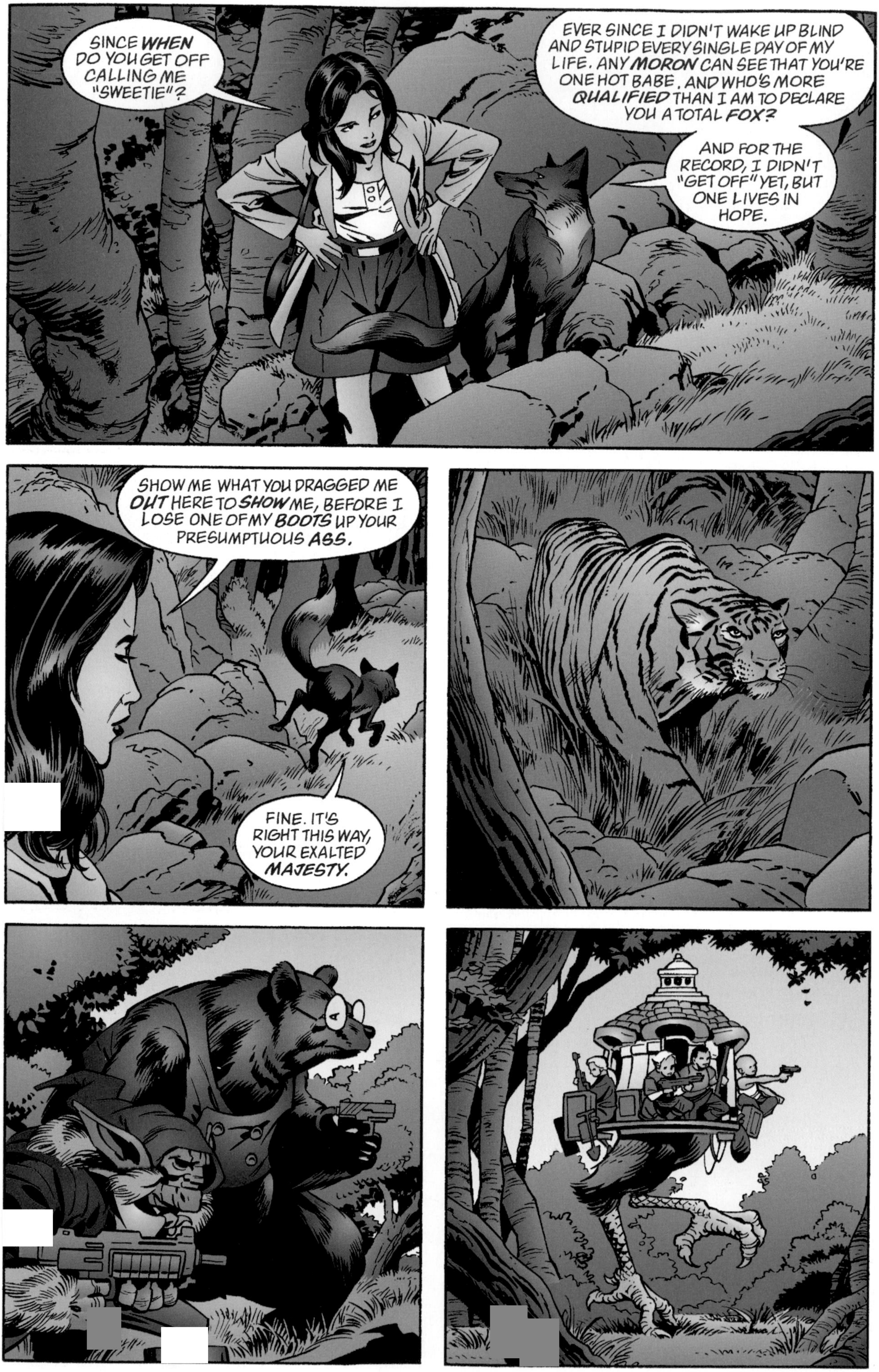
SINCE WHEN DO YOU GET OFF CALLING ME "SWEETIE"?
EVER SINCE I DIDN'T WAKE UP BLIND AND STUPID EVERY SINGLE DAY OF MY LIFE. ANY MORON CAN SEE THAT YOU'RE ONE HOT BABE. AND WHO'S MORE QUALIFIED THAN I AM TO DECLARE YOU A TOTAL FOX?
AND FOR THE RECORD, I DIDN'T "GET OFF" YET, BUT ONE LIVES IN HOPE.
SHOW ME WHAT YOU DRAGGED ME OUT HERE TO SHOW ME, BEFORE I LOSE ONE OF MY BOOTS UP YOUR PRESUMPTUOUS ASS.
FINE. IT'S RIGHT THIS WAY, YOUR EXALTED MAJESTY.

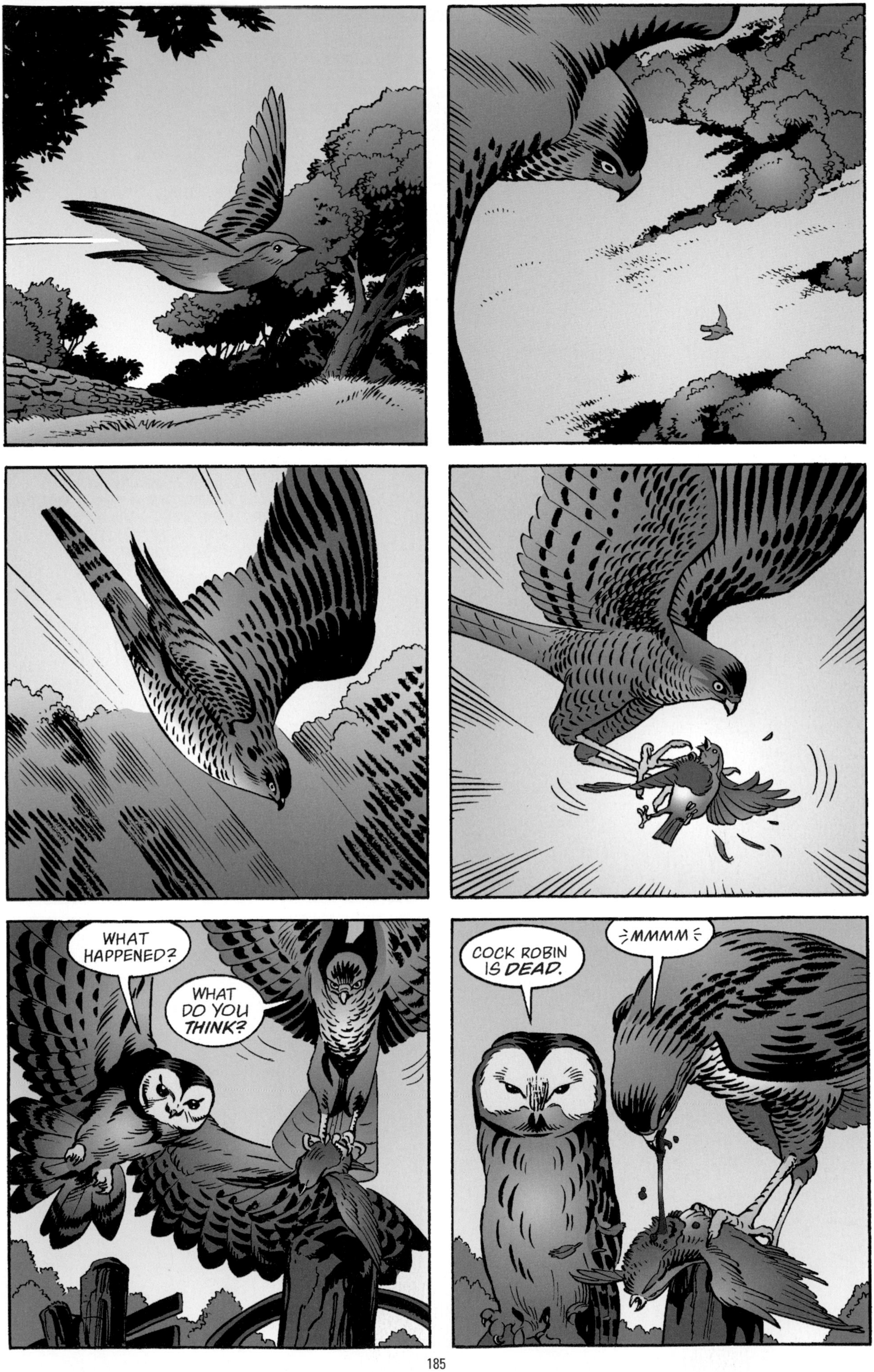
WHAT HAPPENED?
WHAT DO YOU THINK?
COCK ROBIN IS DEAD.
MMMM

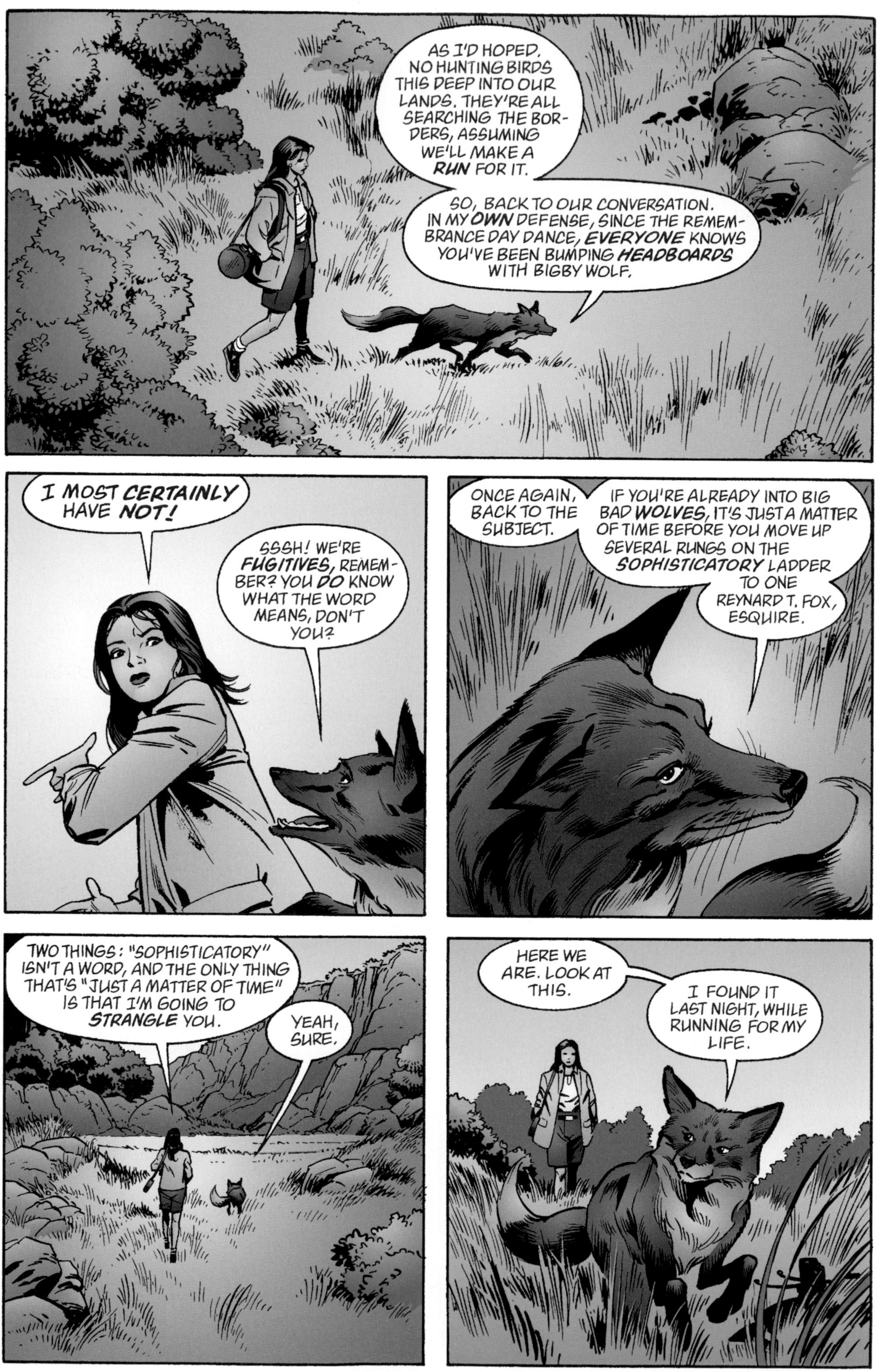

AS I'D HOPED, NO HUNTING BIRDS THIS DEEP INTO OUR LANDS. THEY'RE ALL SEARCHING THE BORDERS, ASSUMING WE'LL MAKE A RUN FOR IT.
SO, BACK TO OUR CONVERSATION. IN MY OWN DEFENSE, SINCE THE REMEMBRANCE DAY DANCE, EVERYONE KNOWS YOU'VE BEEN BUMPING HEADBOARDS WITH BIGBY WOLF.
I MOST CERTAINLY HAVE NOT!
SSSH! WE'RE FUGITIVES, REMEMBER? YOU DO KNOW WHAT THE WORD MEANS, DON'T YOU?
ONCE AGAIN, BACK TO THE SUBJECT.
IF YOU'RE ALREADY INTO BIG BAD WOLVES, IT'S JUST A MATTER OF TIME BEFORE YOU MOVE UP SEVERAL RUNGS ON THE SOPHISTICATORY LADDER TO ONE REYNARD T. FOX, ESQUIRE.
TWO THINGS: "SOPHISTICATORY" ISN'T A WORD, AND THE ONLY THING THAT'S "JUST A MATTER OF TIME" IS THAT I'M GOING TO STRANGLE YOU.
YEAH, SURE.
HERE WE ARE. LOOK AT THIS.
I FOUND IT LAST NIGHT, WHILE RUNNING FOR MY LIFE.

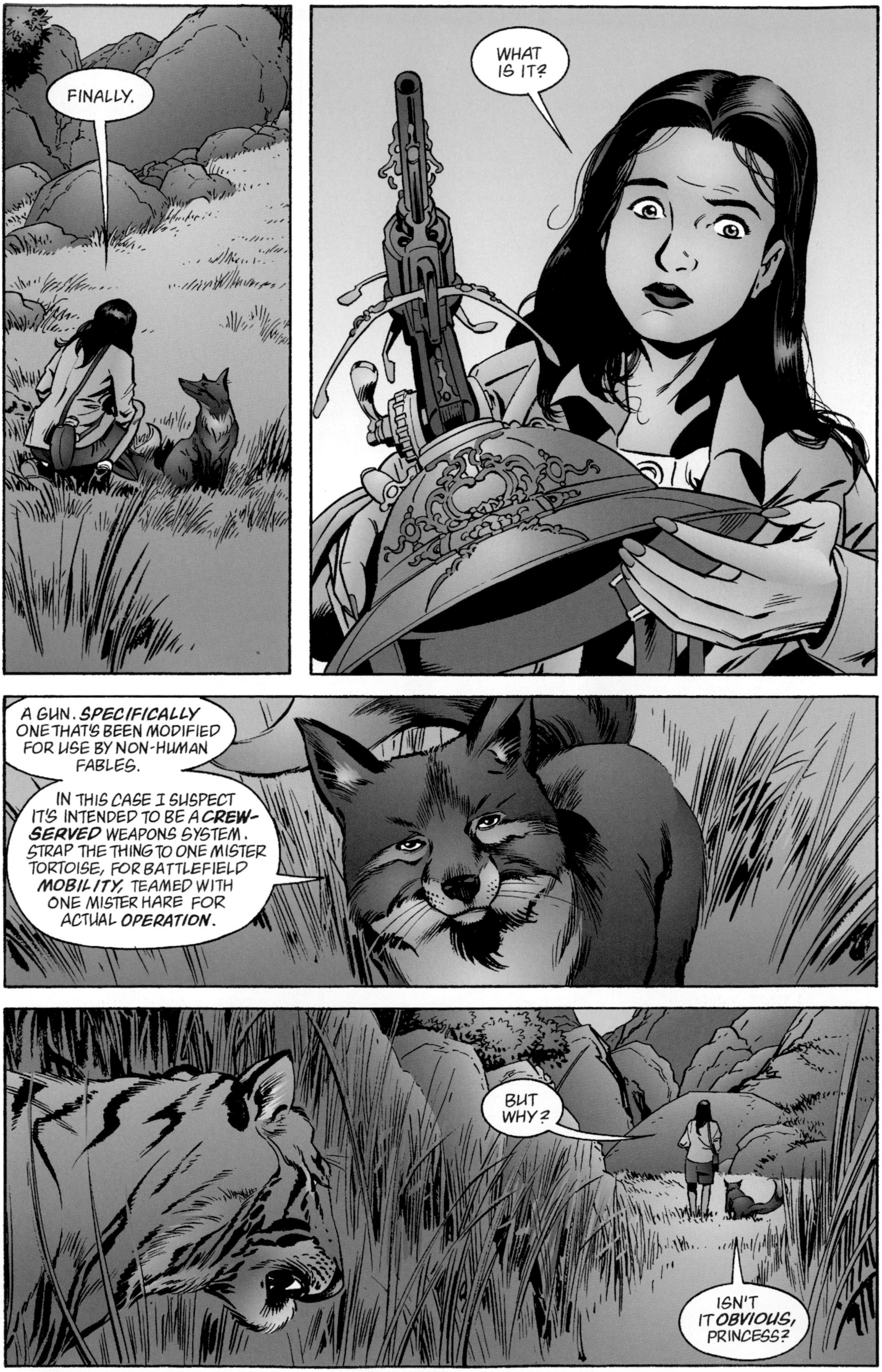
FINALLY.
WHAT IS IT?
A GUN. SPECIFICALLY ONE THAT'S BEEN MODIFIED FOR USE BY NON-HUMAN FABLES.
IN THIS CASE I SUSPECT IT'S INTENDED TO BE A CREW-SERVED WEAPONS SYSTEM. STRAP THE THING TO ONE MISTER TORTOISE, FOR BATTLEFIELD MOBILITY, TEAMED WITH ONE MISTER HARE FOR ACTUAL OPERATION.
BUT WHY?
ISN'T IT OBVIOUS, PRINCESS?

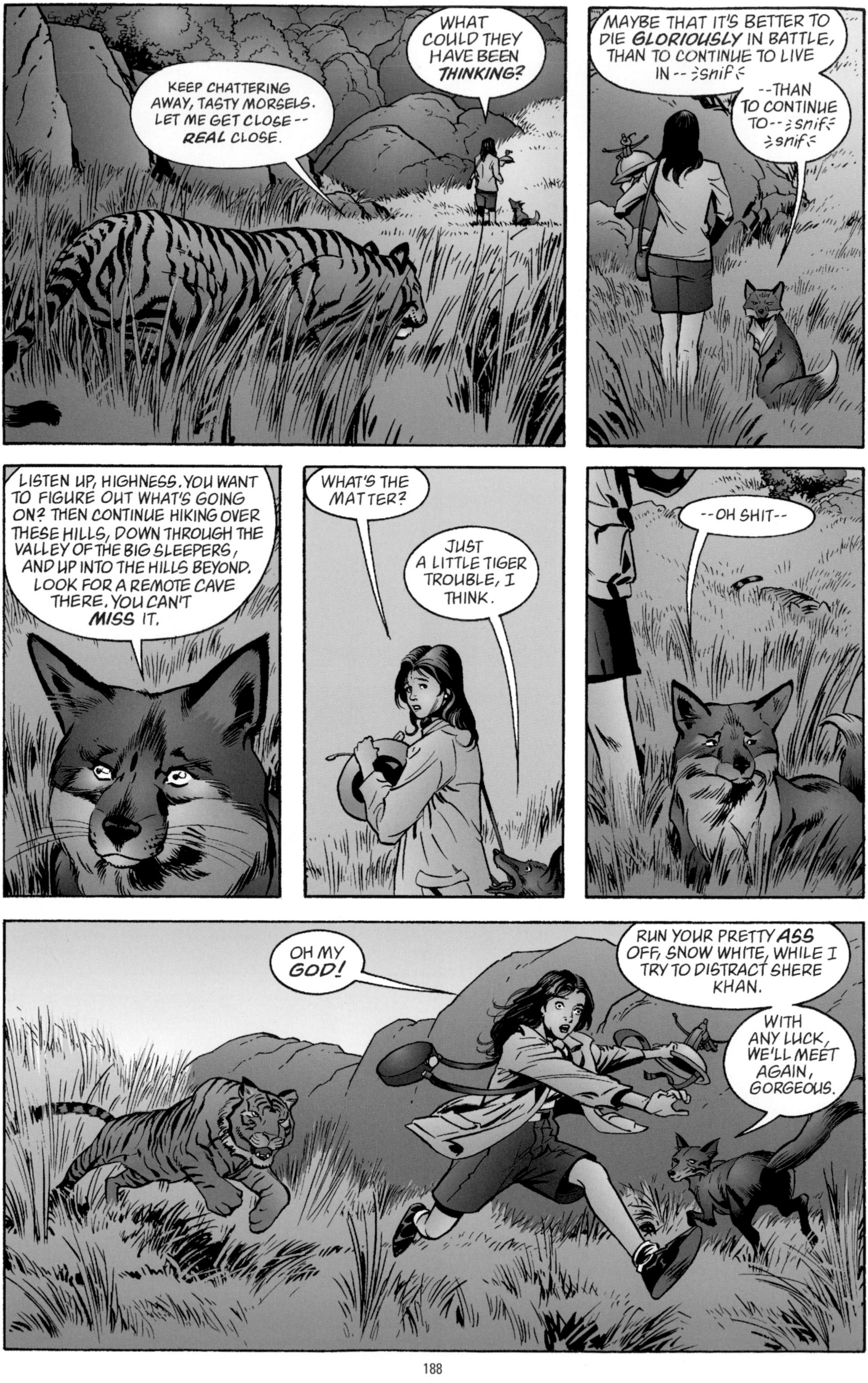
KEEP CHATTERING AWAY, TASTY MORSELS. LET ME GET CLOSE-- REAL CLOSE.
WHAT COULD THEY HAVE BEEN THINKING?
MAYBE THAT IT'S BETTER TO DIE GLORIOUSLY IN BATTLE, THAN TO CONTINUE TO LIVE IN-- snif
--THAN TO CONTINUE TO-- snif snif
LISTEN UP, HIGHNESS. YOU WANT TO FIGURE OUT WHAT'S GOING ON? THEN CONTINUE HIKING OVER THESE HILLS, DOWN THROUGH THE VALLEY OF THE BIG SLEEPERS, AND UP INTO THE HILLS BEYOND. LOOK FOR A REMOTE CAVE THERE. YOU CAN'T MISS IT.
WHAT'S THE MATTER?
JUST A LITTLE TIGER TROUBLE, I THINK.
--OH SHIT--
OH MY GOD!
RUN YOUR PRETTY ASS OFF, SNOW WHITE, WHILE I TRY TO DISTRACT SHERE KHAN.
WITH ANY LUCK, WE'LL MEET AGAIN, GORGEOUS.

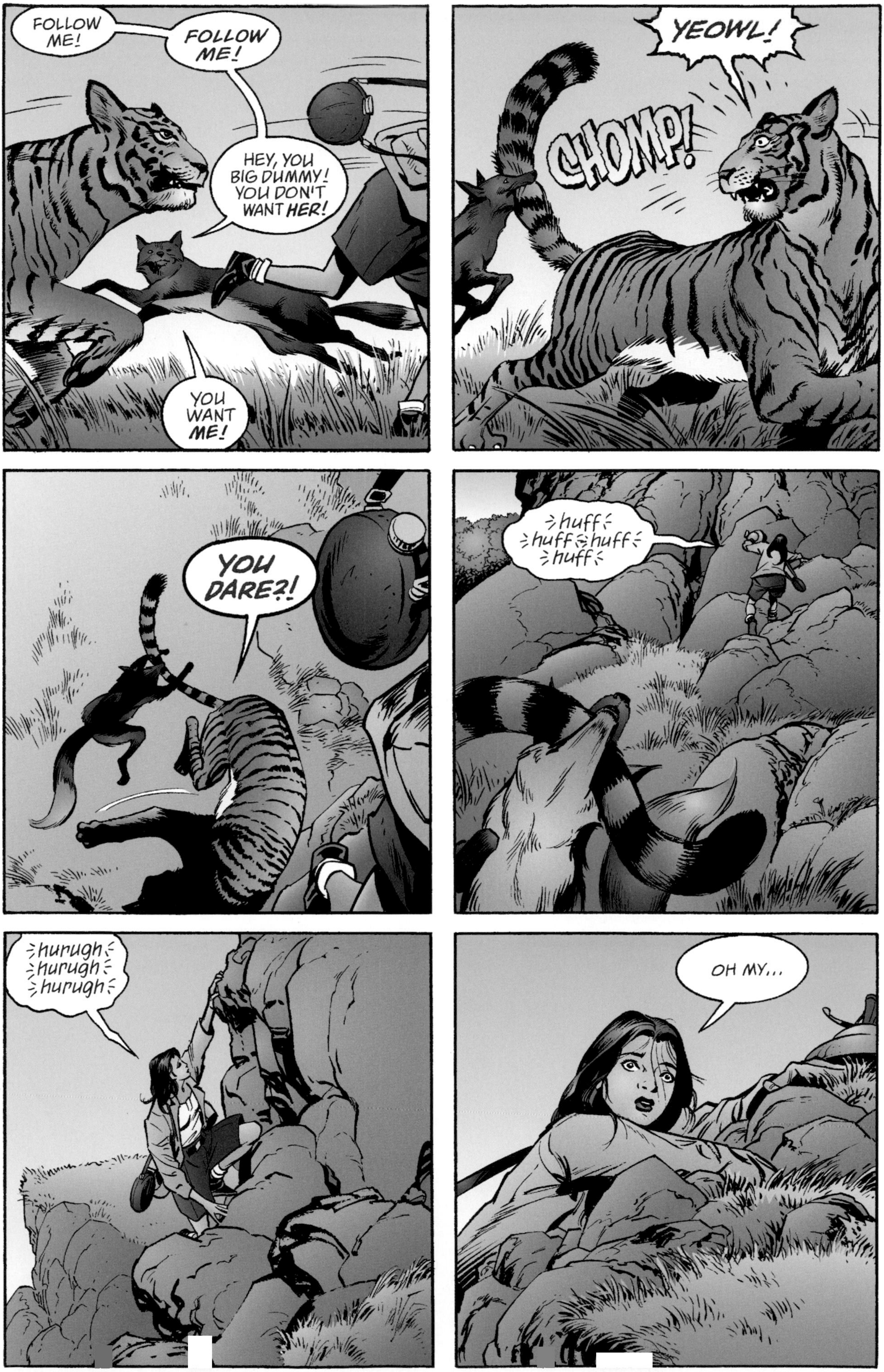
FOLLOW ME!
FOLLOW ME!
HEY, YOU BIG DUMMY! YOU DON'T WANT HER!
YOU WANT ME!
YEOWL!
CHOMP!
YOU DARE?!
huff huff huff huff
hurugh hurugh hurugh
OH MY...

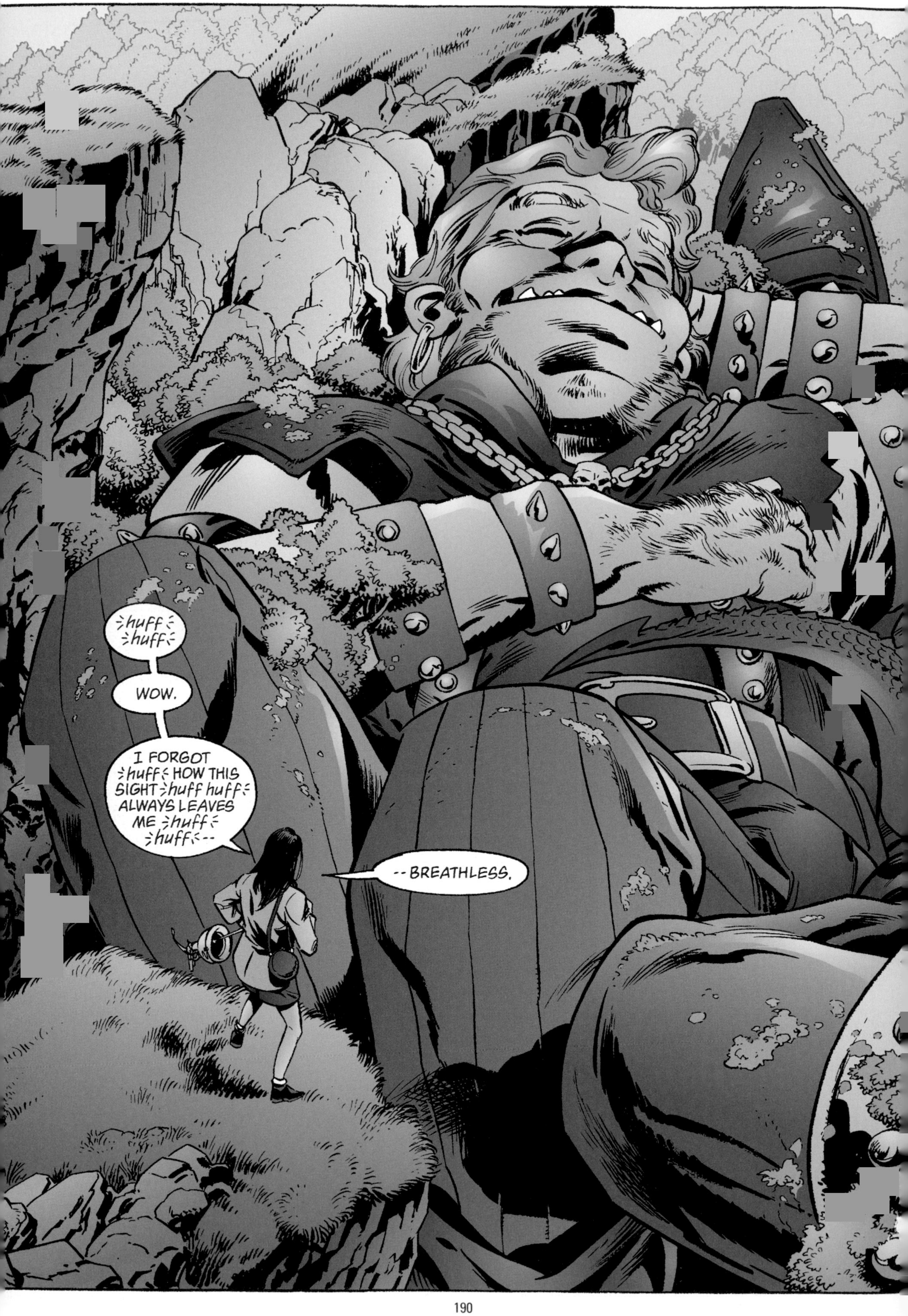

huff huff
WOW.
I FORGOT huff HOW THIS SIGHT huff huff ALWAYS LEAVES ME huff huff--
--BREATHLESS.

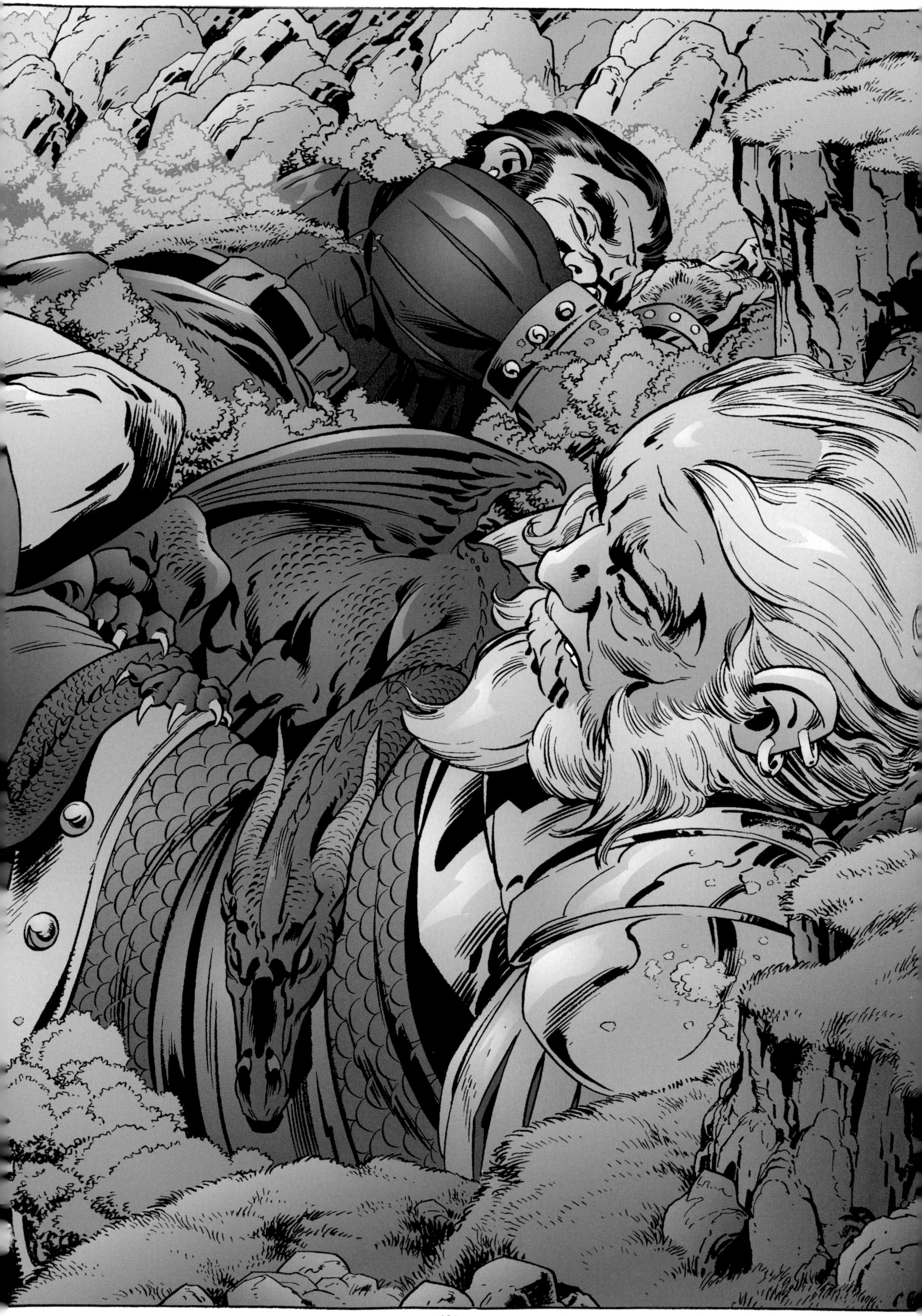

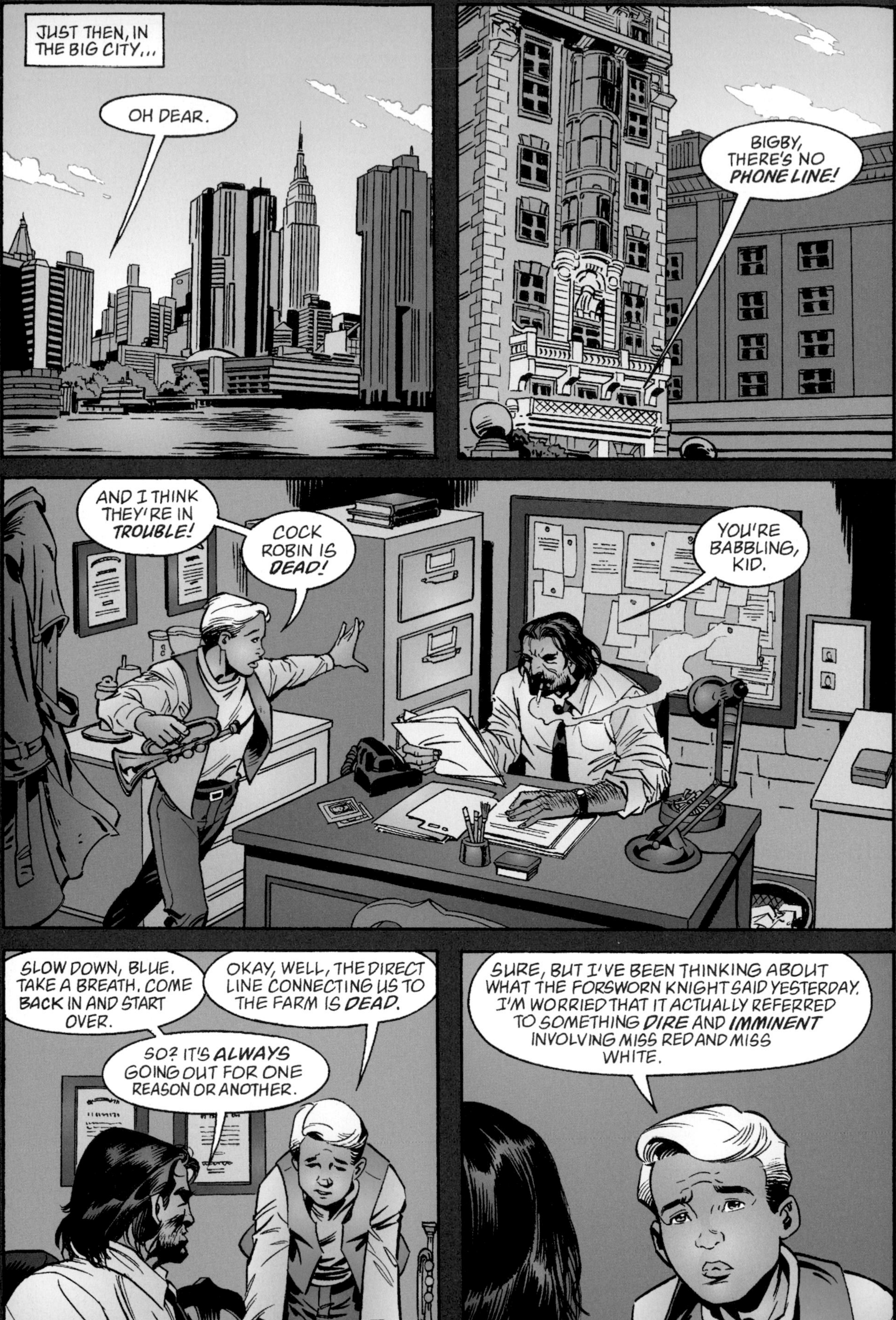
JUST THEN, IN THE BIG CITY...
OH DEAR.
BIGBY, THERE'S NO PHONE LINE!
AND I THINK THEY'RE IN TROUBLE!
COCK ROBIN IS DEAD!
YOU'RE BABBLING, KID.
SLOW DOWN, BLUE. TAKE A BREATH. COME BACK IN AND START OVER.
OKAY, WELL, THE DIRECT LINE CONNECTING US TO THE FARM IS DEAD.
SO? IT'S ALWAYS GOING OUT FOR ONE REASON OR ANOTHER.
SURE, BUT I'VE BEEN THINKING ABOUT WHAT THE FORSWORN KNIGHT SAID YESTERDAY. I'M WORRIED THAT IT ACTUALLY REFERRED TO SOMETHING DIRE AND IMMINENT INVOLVING MISS RED AND MISS WHITE.

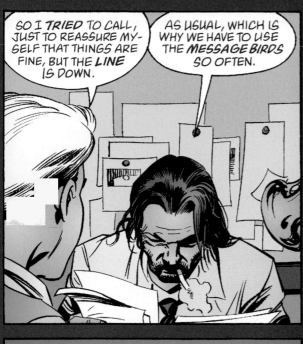

SO I **TRIED** TO CALL, JUST TO REASSURE MY-SELF THAT THINGS ARE FINE, BUT THE **LINE** IS DOWN.

AS USUAL, WHICH IS WHY WE HAVE TO USE THE **MESSAGE BIRDS** SO OFTEN.

RIGHT, SO THAT WAS MY **NEXT** STEP. COCK ROBIN WAS IN THE DOCK FOR THE **NEXT FLIGHT**, AND HE'S AWFUL **RELIABLE**. BUT NOW HE'S **DEAD!** HE WAS KILLED THIS MORNING, ALMOST THE VERY **MOMENT** HE REACHED THE FARM.

HOW THE HELL DO YOU KNOW **THAT?**

I HAD THE BLACK FOREST WITCH PUT A **WATCHING** WARD ON HIM BEFORE HE LEFT.

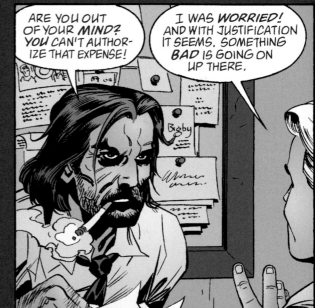

ARE YOU OUT OF YOUR **MIND?** **YOU** CAN'T AUTHOR-IZE THAT EXPENSE!

I WAS **WORRIED!** AND WITH JUSTIFICATION IT SEEMS. SOMETHING **BAD** IS GOING ON UP THERE.

OKAY, KID, YOU'VE **CONVINCED** ME. SINCE I CAN'T GO UP THERE MYSELF, I'LL HELP YOU ROUND UP A **POSSE.**

NOW WE'RE TALKING!

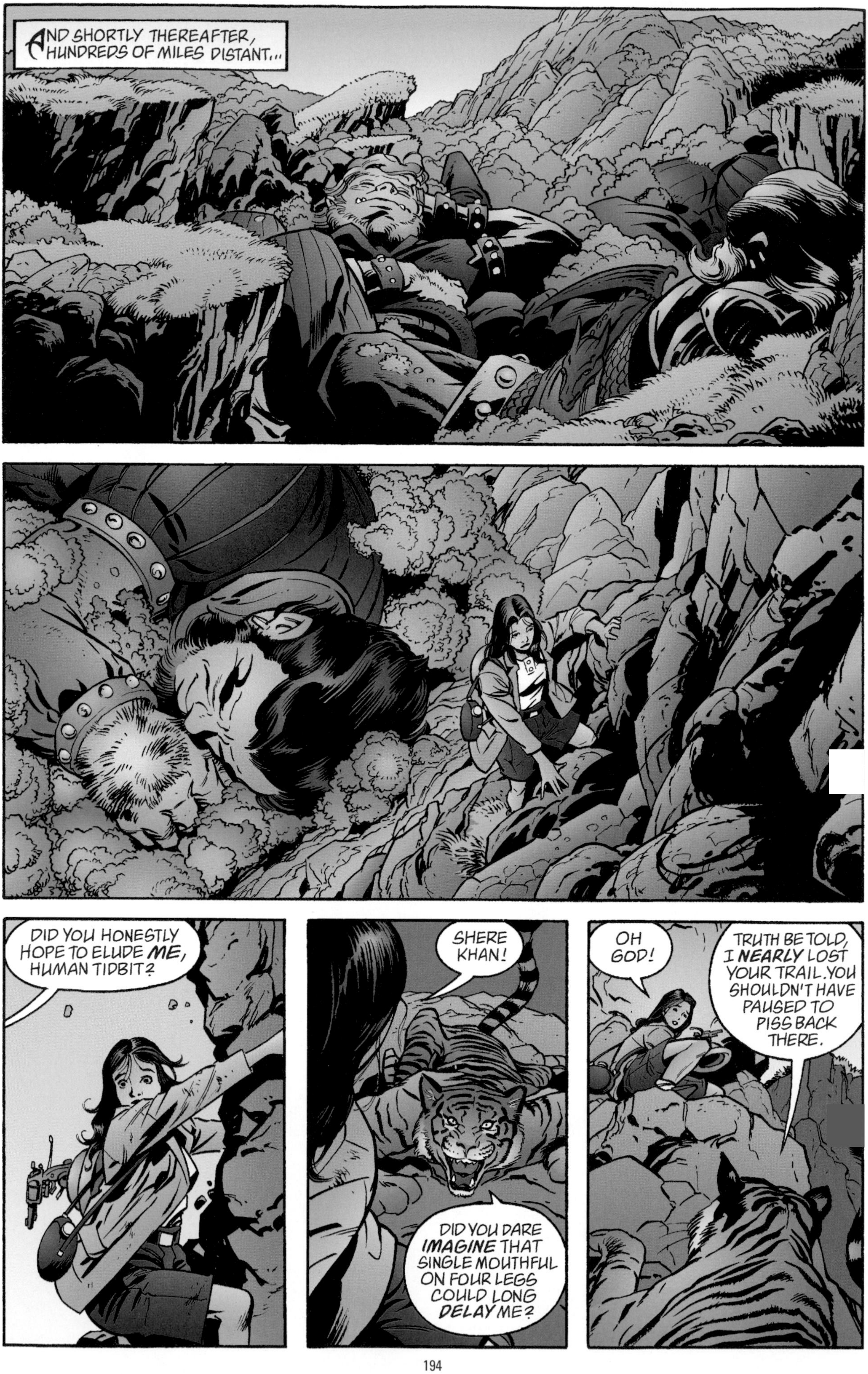
AND SHORTLY THEREAFTER, HUNDREDS OF MILES DISTANT...
DID YOU HONESTLY HOPE TO ELUDE ME, HUMAN TIDBIT?
SHERE KHAN!
DID YOU DARE IMAGINE THAT SINGLE MOUTHFUL ON FOUR LEGS COULD LONG DELAY ME?
OH GOD!
TRUTH BE TOLD, I NEARLY LOST YOUR TRAIL. YOU SHOULDN'T HAVE PAUSED TO PISS BACK THERE.

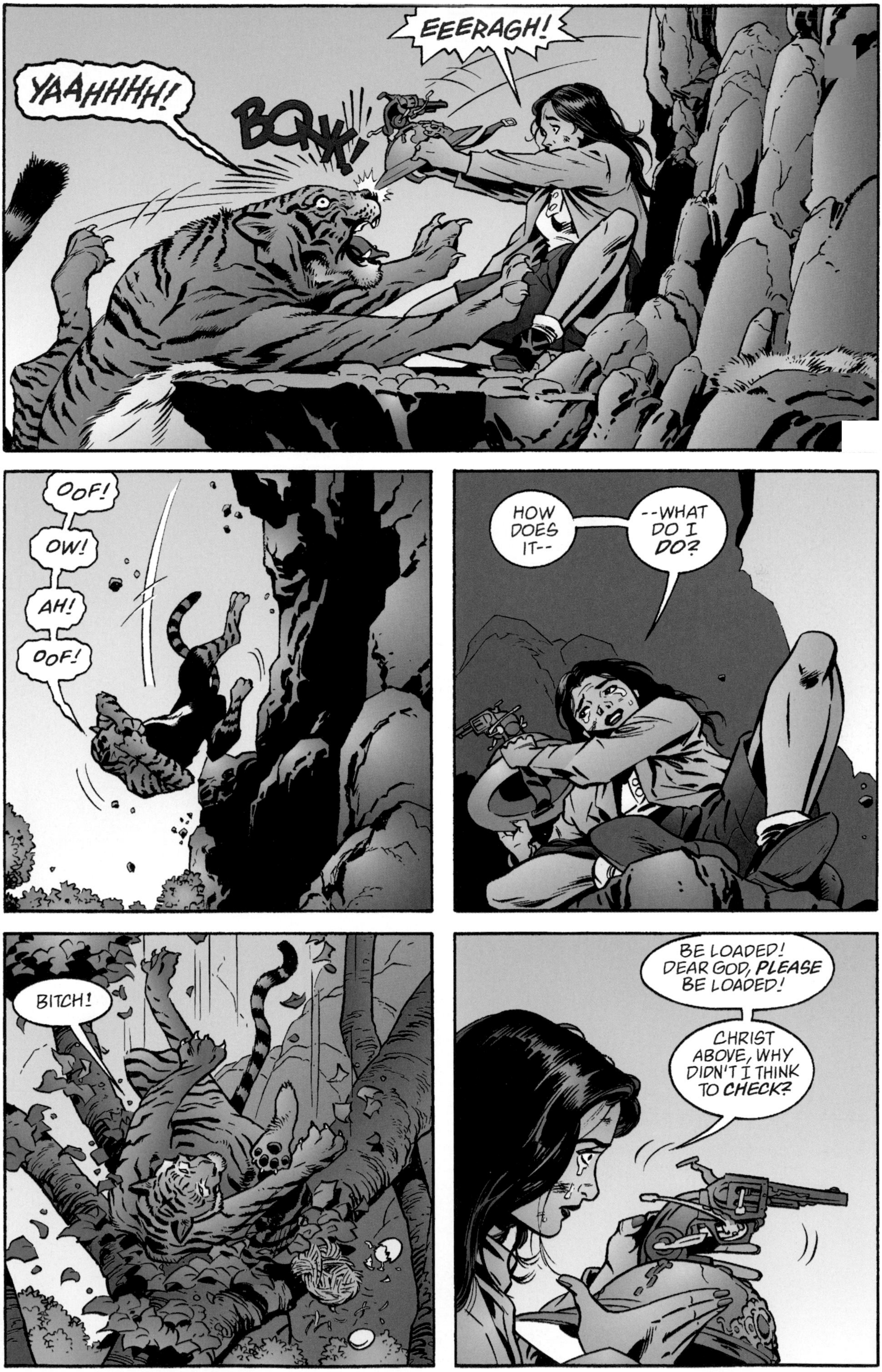
EEERAGH!
YAAHHHH!
BONK!
OOF!
OW!
AH!
OOF!
HOW DOES IT--
--WHAT DO I DO?
BITCH!
BE LOADED! DEAR GOD, PLEASE BE LOADED!
CHRIST ABOVE, WHY DIDN'T I THINK TO CHECK?

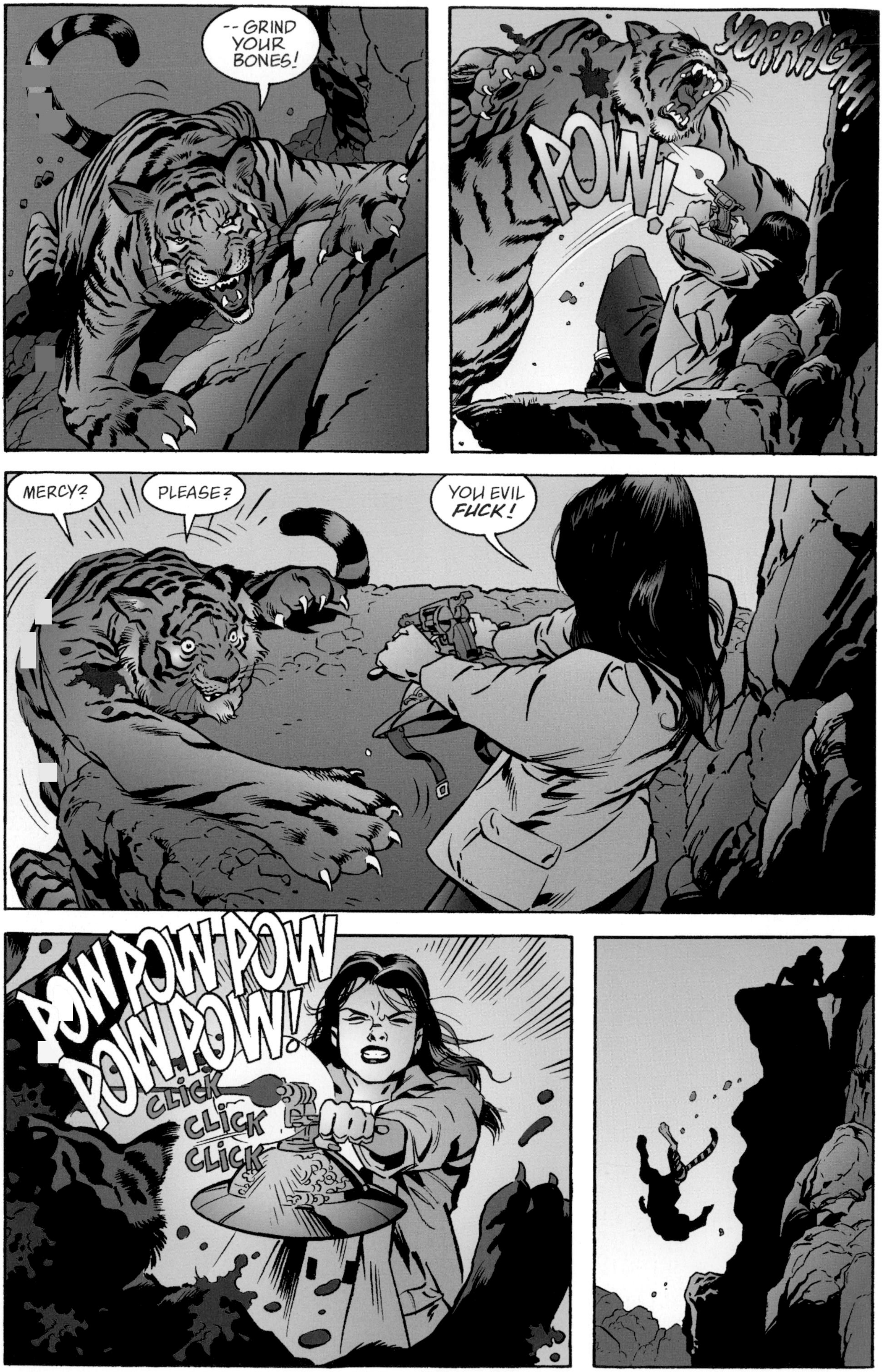
-- GRIND YOUR BONES!
YORRAGH!
POW!
MERCY?
PLEASE?
YOU EVIL FUCK!
POW POW POW POW POW!
CLICK
CLICK
CLICK

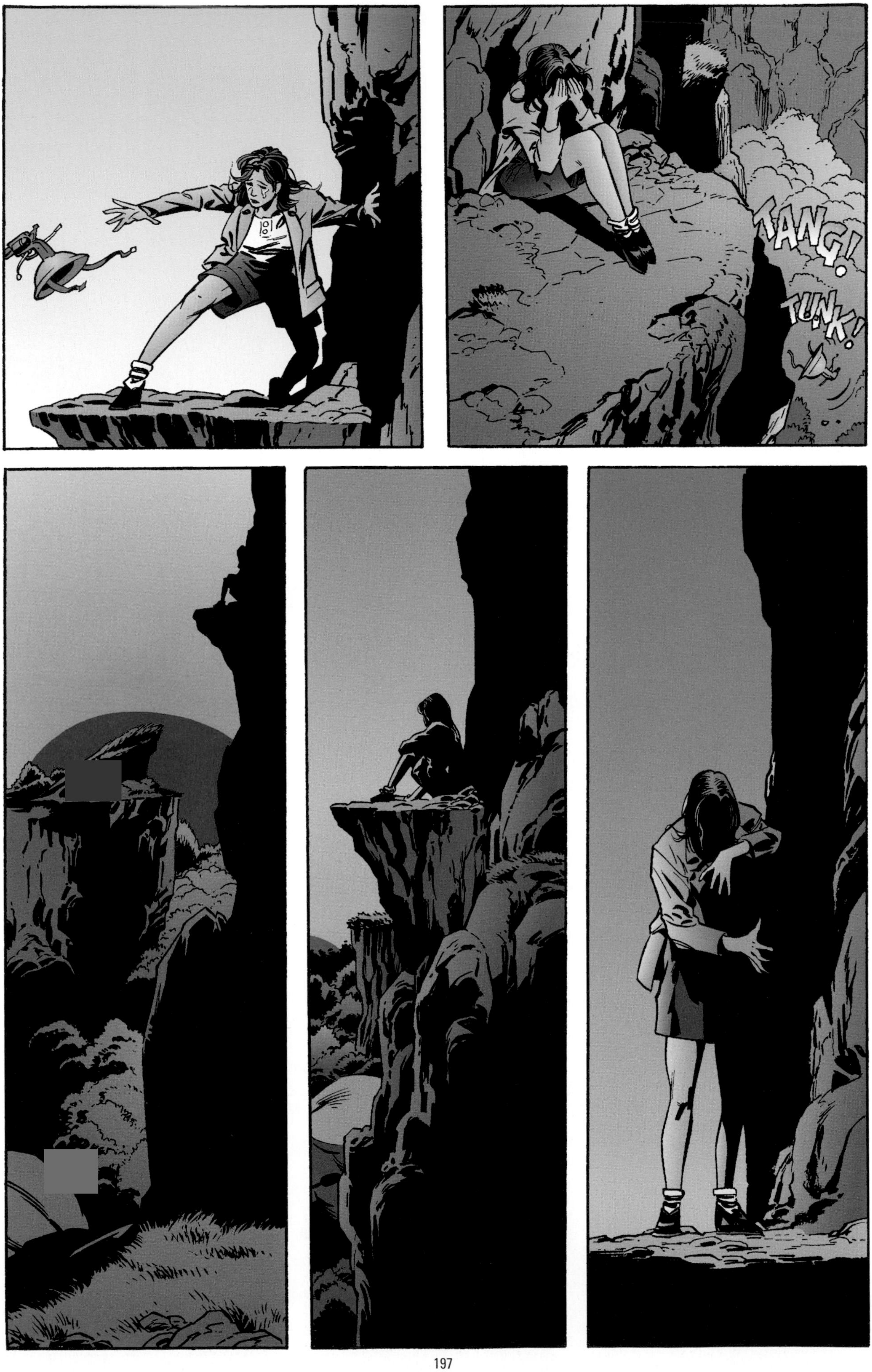
TANG!
TUNK!

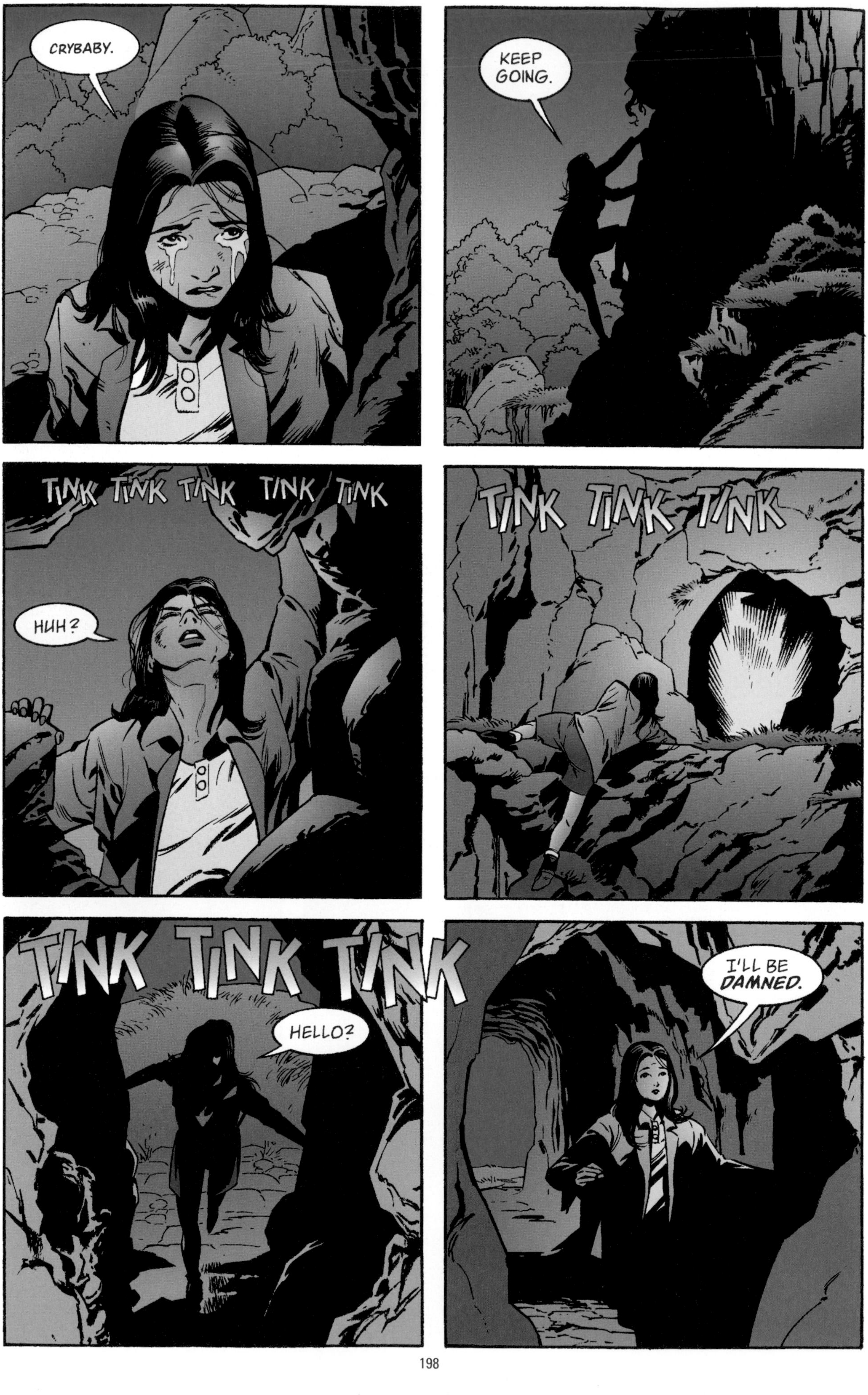
CRYBABY.
KEEP GOING.
TINK TINK TINK TINK TINK
HUH?
TINK TINK TINK
TINK TINK TINK
HELLO?
I'LL BE DAMNED.

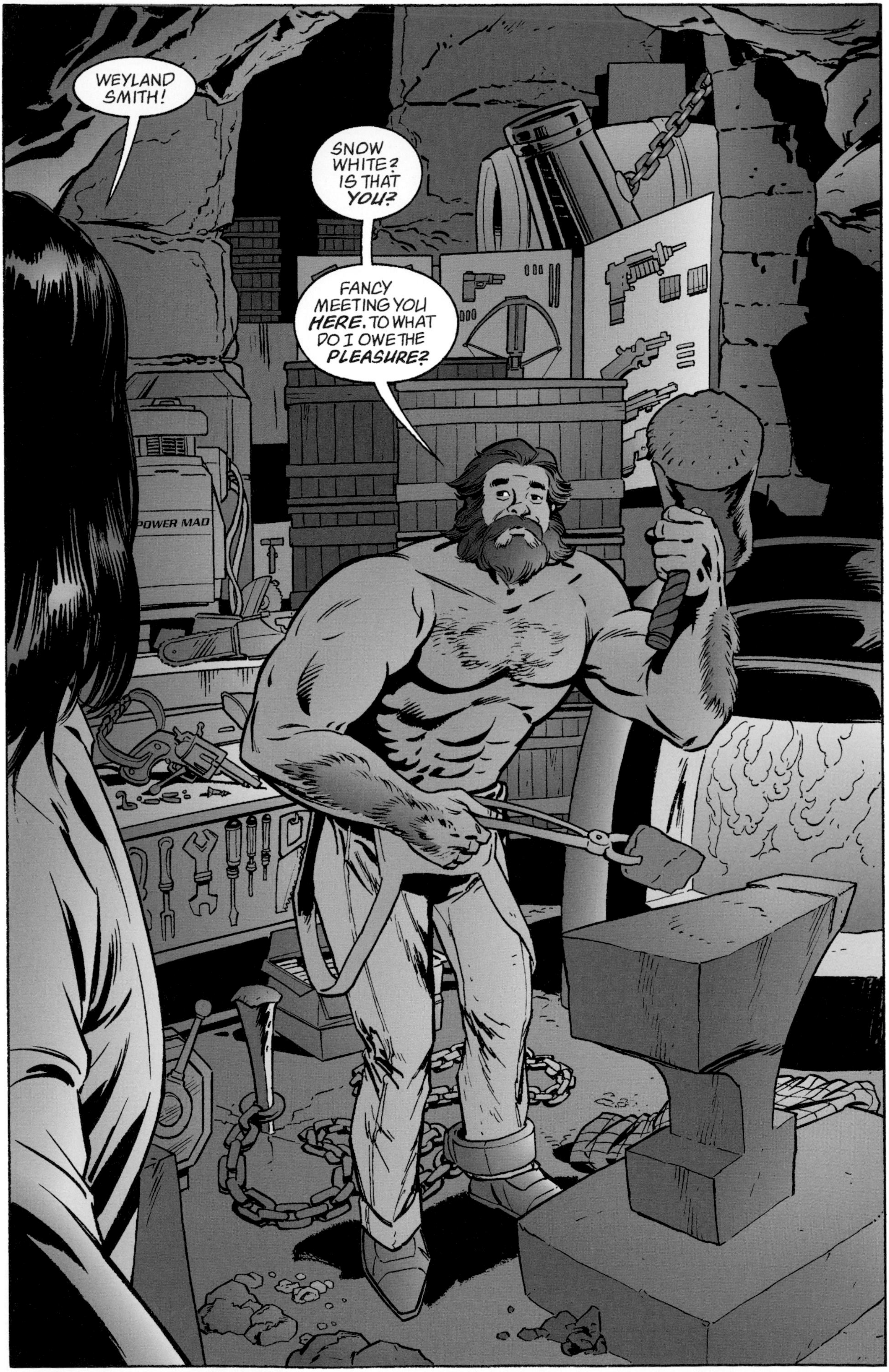
WEYLAND SMITH!
SNOW WHITE? IS THAT YOU?
FANCY MEETING YOU HERE. TO WHAT DO I OWE THE PLEASURE?
POWER MAD

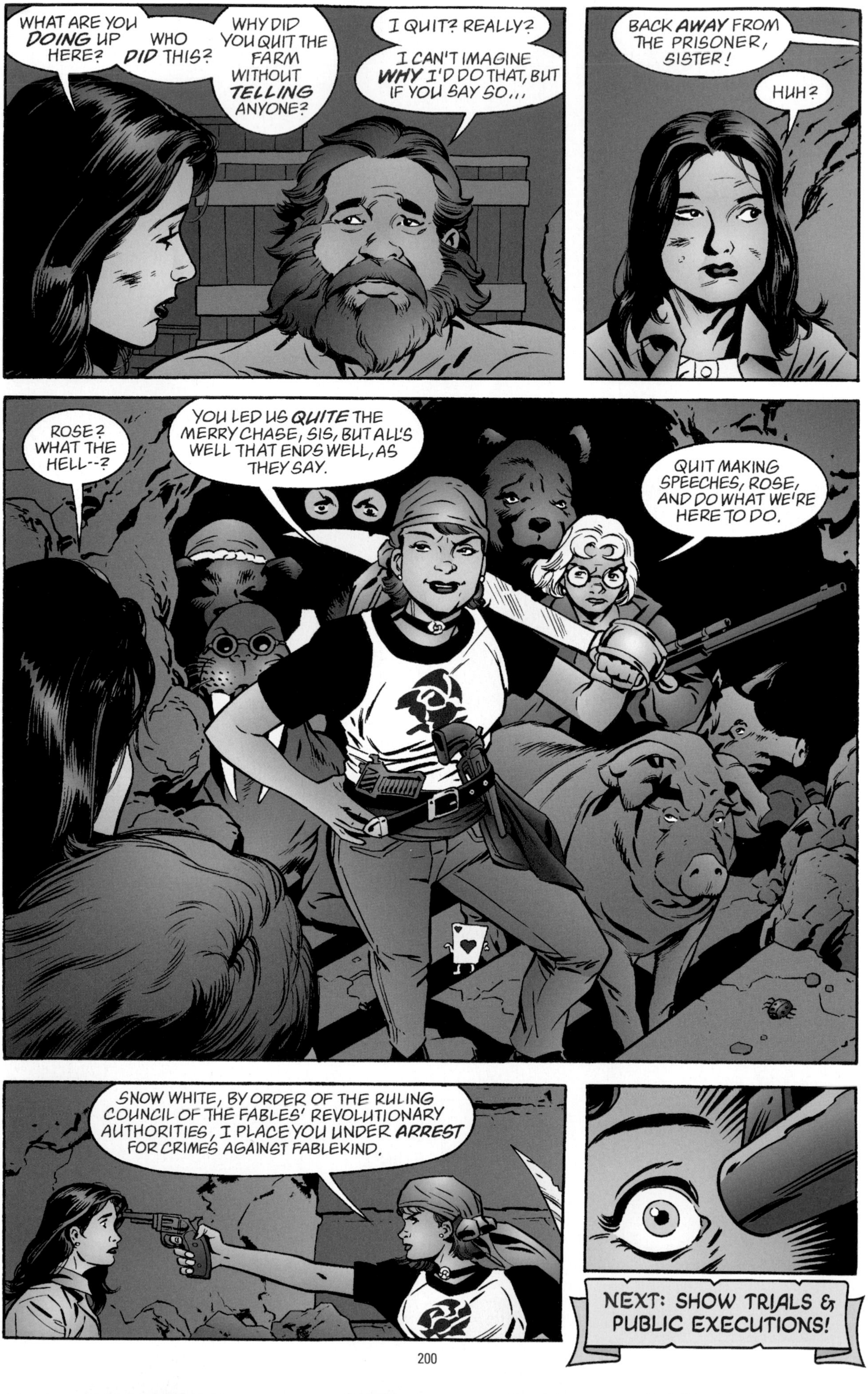
WHAT ARE YOU DOING UP HERE?
WHO DID THIS?
WHY DID YOU QUIT THE FARM WITHOUT TELLING ANYONE?
I QUIT? REALLY?
I CAN'T IMAGINE WHY I'D DO THAT, BUT IF YOU SAY SO...
BACK AWAY FROM THE PRISONER, SISTER!
HUH?
ROSE? WHAT THE HELL--?
YOU LED US QUITE THE MERRY CHASE, SIS, BUT ALL'S WELL THAT ENDS WELL, AS THEY SAY.
QUIT MAKING SPEECHES, ROSE, AND DO WHAT WE'RE HERE TO DO.
SNOW WHITE, BY ORDER OF THE RULING COUNCIL OF THE FABLES' REVOLUTIONARY AUTHORITIES, I PLACE YOU UNDER ARREST FOR CRIMES AGAINST FABLEKIND.
NEXT: SHOW TRIALS & PUBLIC EXECUTIONS!

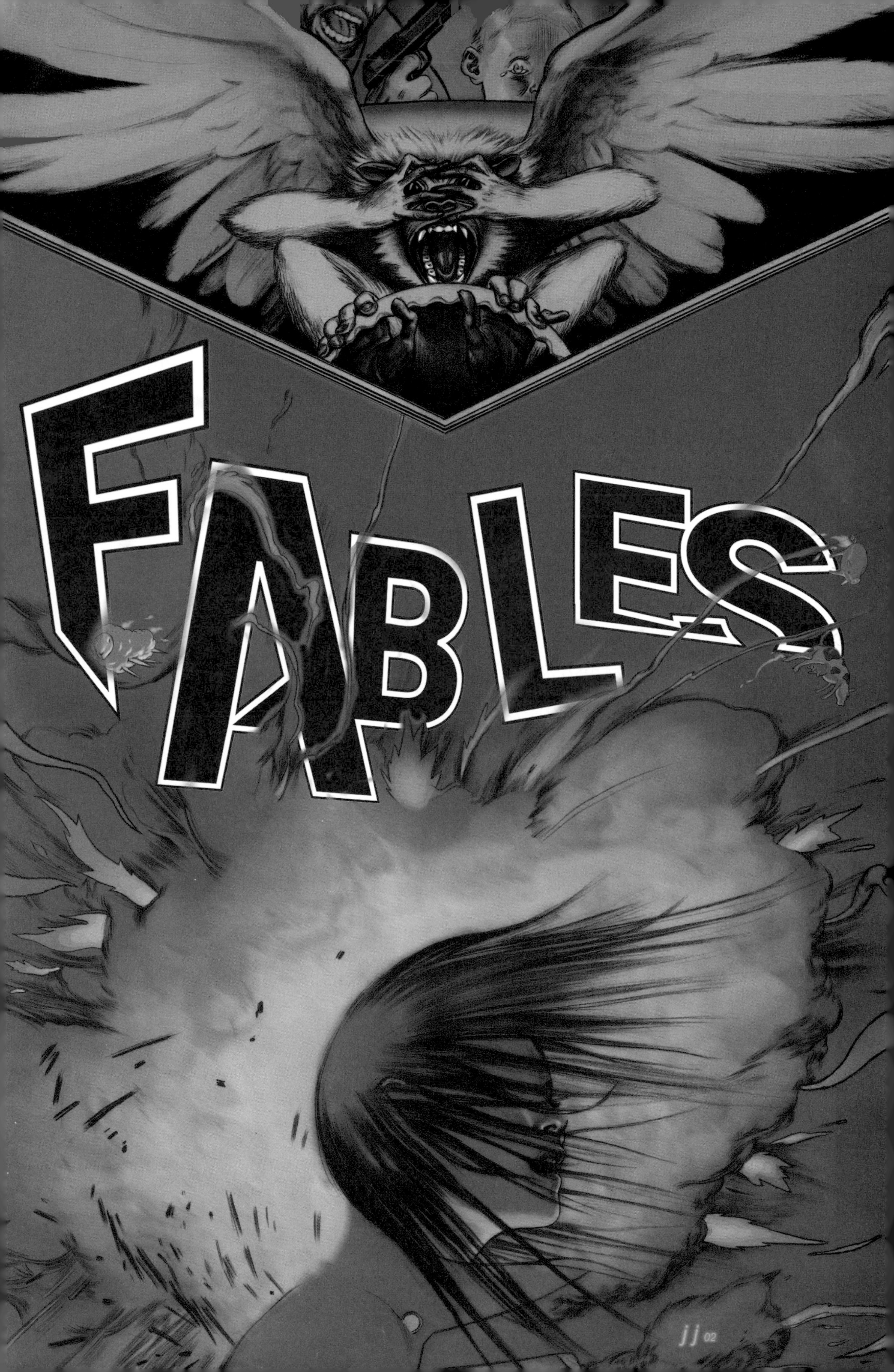
FABLES
jj 02

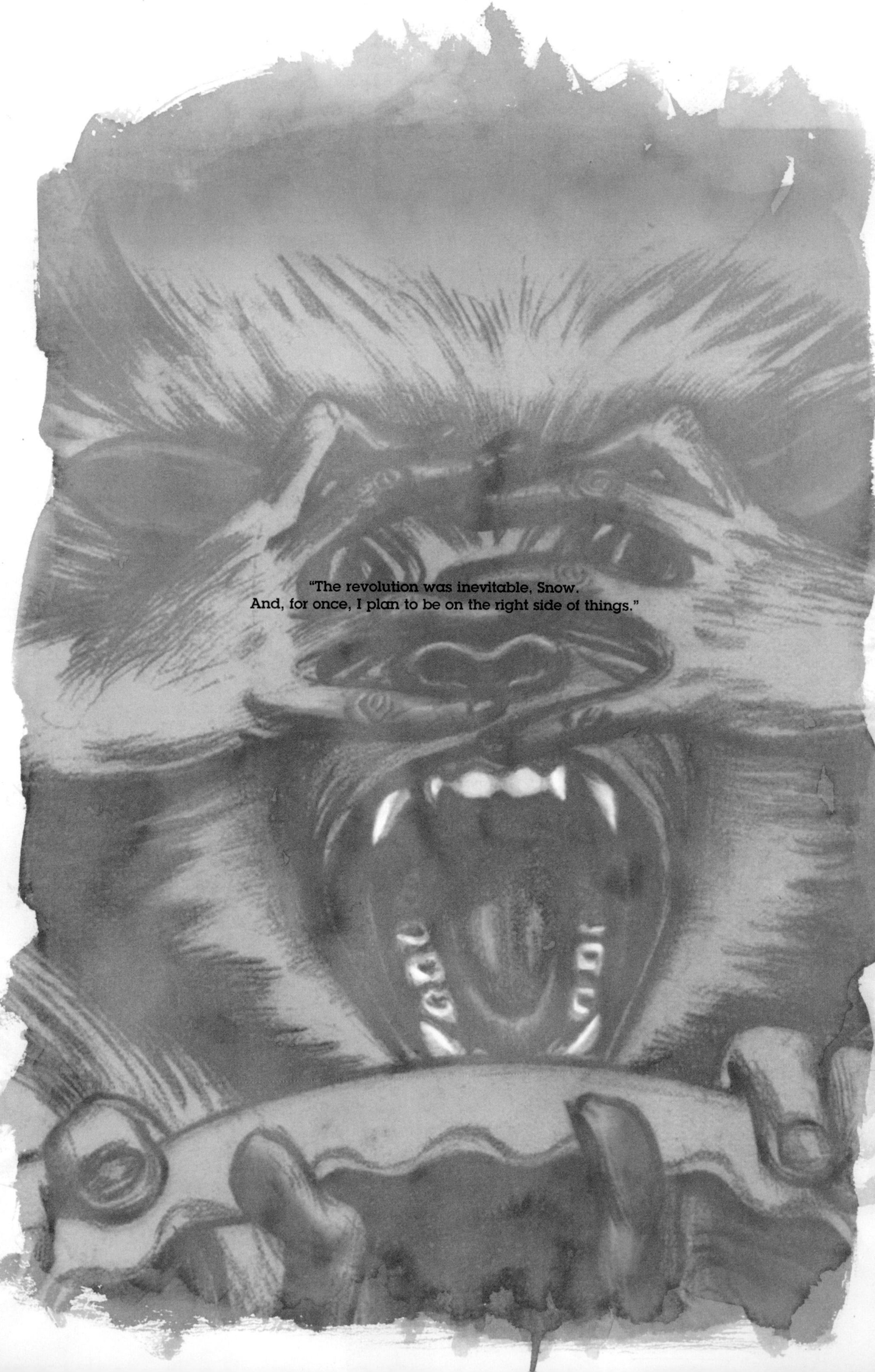
"The revolution was inevitable, Snow.
And, for once, I plan to be on the right side of things."

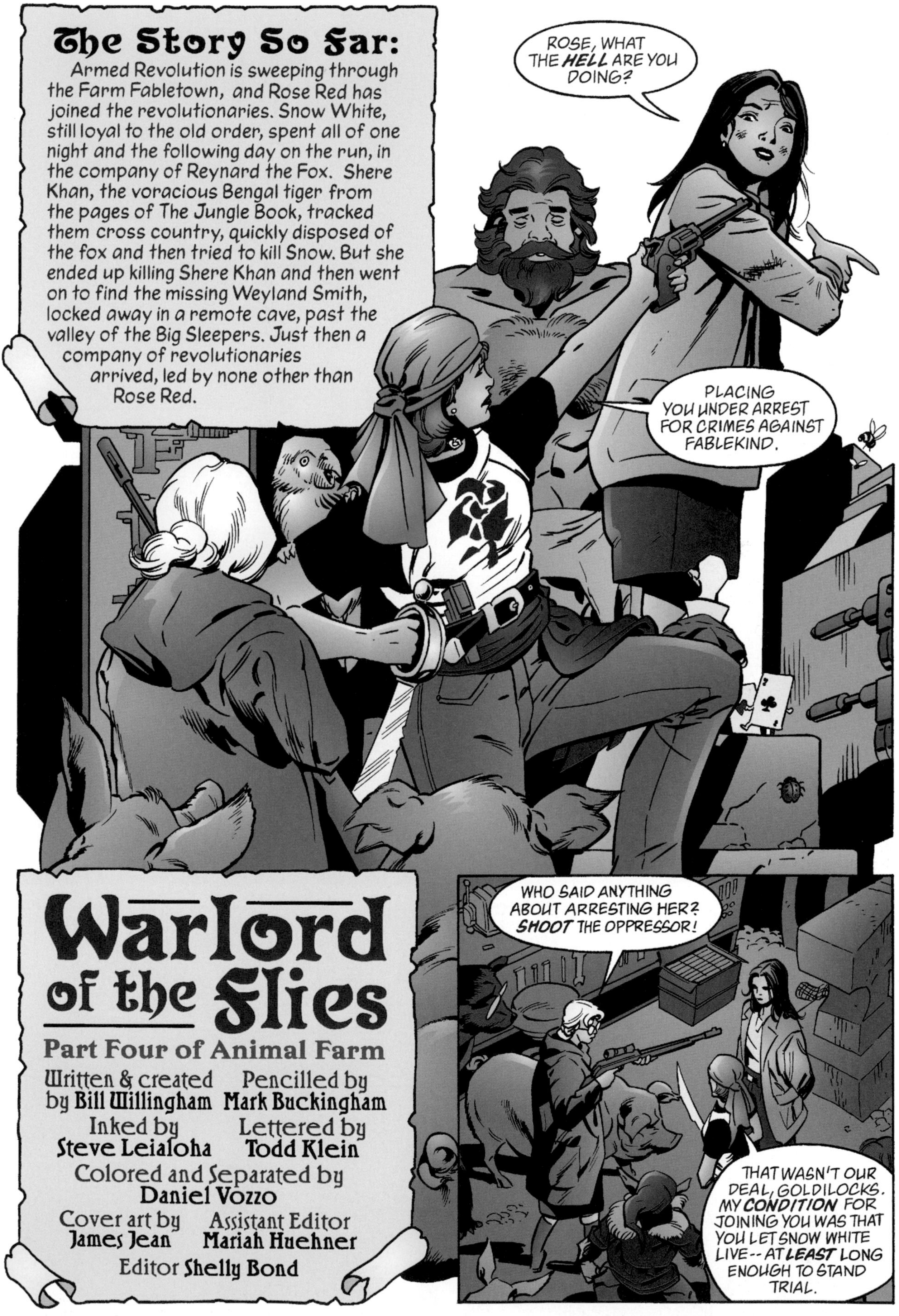
The Story So Far:
Armed Revolution is sweeping through the Farm Fabletown, and Rose Red has joined the revolutionaries. Snow White, still loyal to the old order, spent all of one night and the following day on the run, in the company of Reynard the Fox. Shere Khan, the voracious Bengal tiger from the pages of The Jungle Book, tracked them cross country, quickly disposed of the fox and then tried to kill Snow. But she ended up killing Shere Khan and then went on to find the missing Weyland Smith, locked away in a remote cave, past the valley of the Big Sleepers. Just then a company of revolutionaries arrived, led by none other than Rose Red.
ROSE, WHAT THE HELL ARE YOU DOING?
PLACING YOU UNDER ARREST FOR CRIMES AGAINST FABLEKIND.
Warlord of the Flies
Part Four of Animal Farm
Written & created by Bill Willingham
Pencilled by Mark Buckingham
Inked by Steve Leialoha
Lettered by Todd Klein
Colored and Separated by Daniel Vozzo
Cover art by James Jean
Assistant Editor Mariah Huehner
Editor Shelly Bond
WHO SAID ANYTHING ABOUT ARRESTING HER? SHOOT THE OPPRESSOR!
THAT WASN'T OUR DEAL, GOLDILOCKS. MY CONDITION FOR JOINING YOU WAS THAT YOU LET SNOW WHITE LIVE-- AT LEAST LONG ENOUGH TO STAND TRIAL.

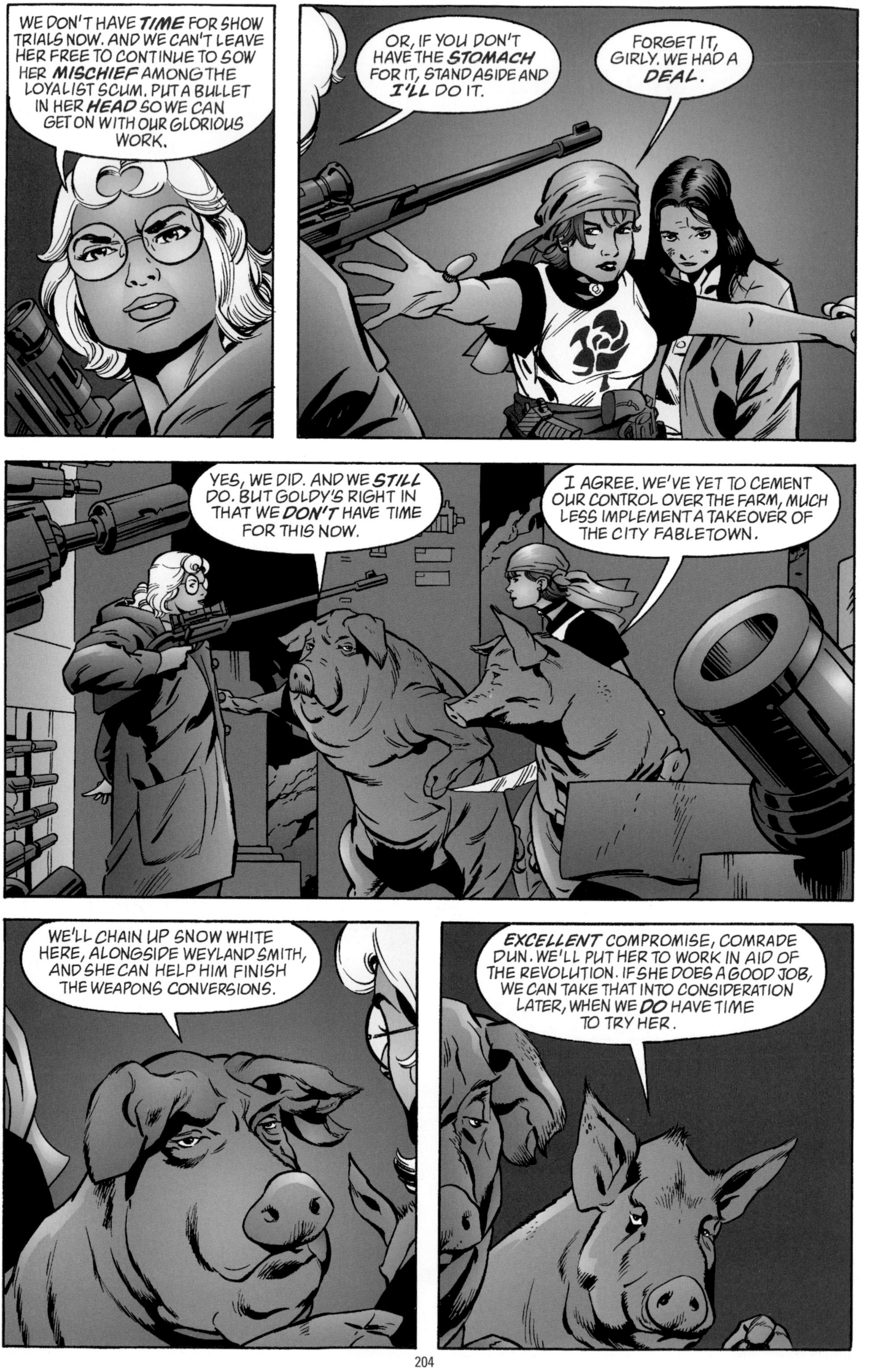
WE DON'T HAVE TIME FOR SHOW TRIALS NOW. AND WE CAN'T LEAVE HER FREE TO CONTINUE TO SOW HER MISCHIEF AMONG THE LOYALIST SCUM. PUT A BULLET IN HER HEAD SO WE CAN GET ON WITH OUR GLORIOUS WORK.
OR, IF YOU DON'T HAVE THE STOMACH FOR IT, STAND ASIDE AND I'LL DO IT.
FORGET IT, GIRLY. WE HAD A DEAL.
YES, WE DID. AND WE STILL DO. BUT GOLDY'S RIGHT IN THAT WE DON'T HAVE TIME FOR THIS NOW.
I AGREE. WE'VE YET TO CEMENT OUR CONTROL OVER THE FARM, MUCH LESS IMPLEMENT A TAKEOVER OF THE CITY FABLETOWN.
WE'LL CHAIN UP SNOW WHITE HERE, ALONGSIDE WEYLAND SMITH, AND SHE CAN HELP HIM FINISH THE WEAPONS CONVERSIONS.
EXCELLENT COMPROMISE, COMRADE DUN. WE'LL PUT HER TO WORK IN AID OF THE REVOLUTION. IF SHE DOES A GOOD JOB, WE CAN TAKE THAT INTO CONSIDERATION LATER, WHEN WE DO HAVE TIME TO TRY HER.

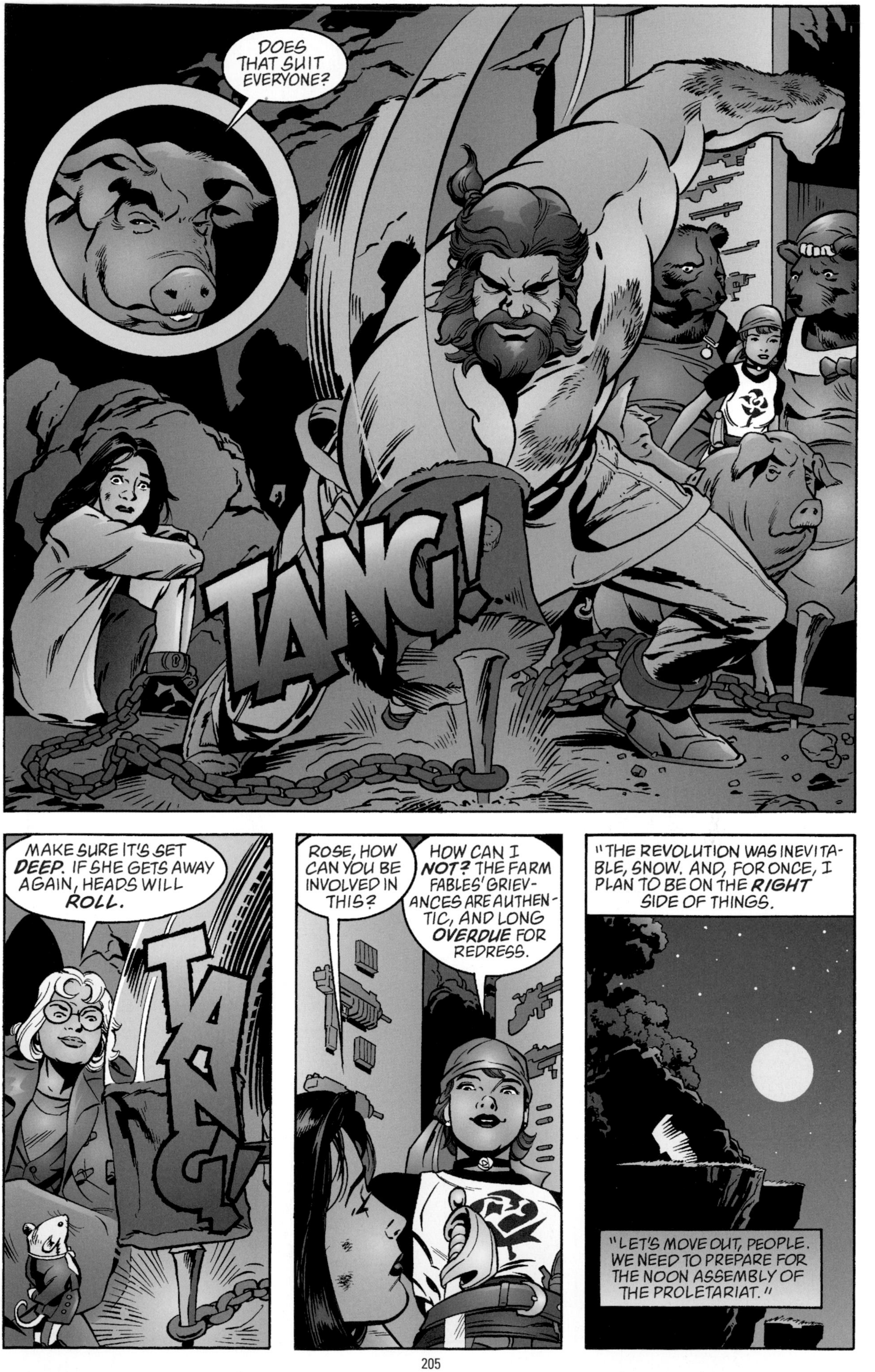
DOES THAT SUIT EVERYONE?
TANG!
MAKE SURE IT'S SET DEEP. IF SHE GETS AWAY AGAIN, HEADS WILL ROLL.
TANG!
ROSE, HOW CAN YOU BE INVOLVED IN THIS?
HOW CAN I NOT? THE FARM FABLES' GRIEVANCES ARE AUTHENTIC, AND LONG OVERDUE FOR REDRESS.
"THE REVOLUTION WAS INEVITABLE, SNOW. AND, FOR ONCE, I PLAN TO BE ON THE RIGHT SIDE OF THINGS.
"LET'S MOVE OUT, PEOPLE. WE NEED TO PREPARE FOR THE NOON ASSEMBLY OF THE PROLETARIAT."

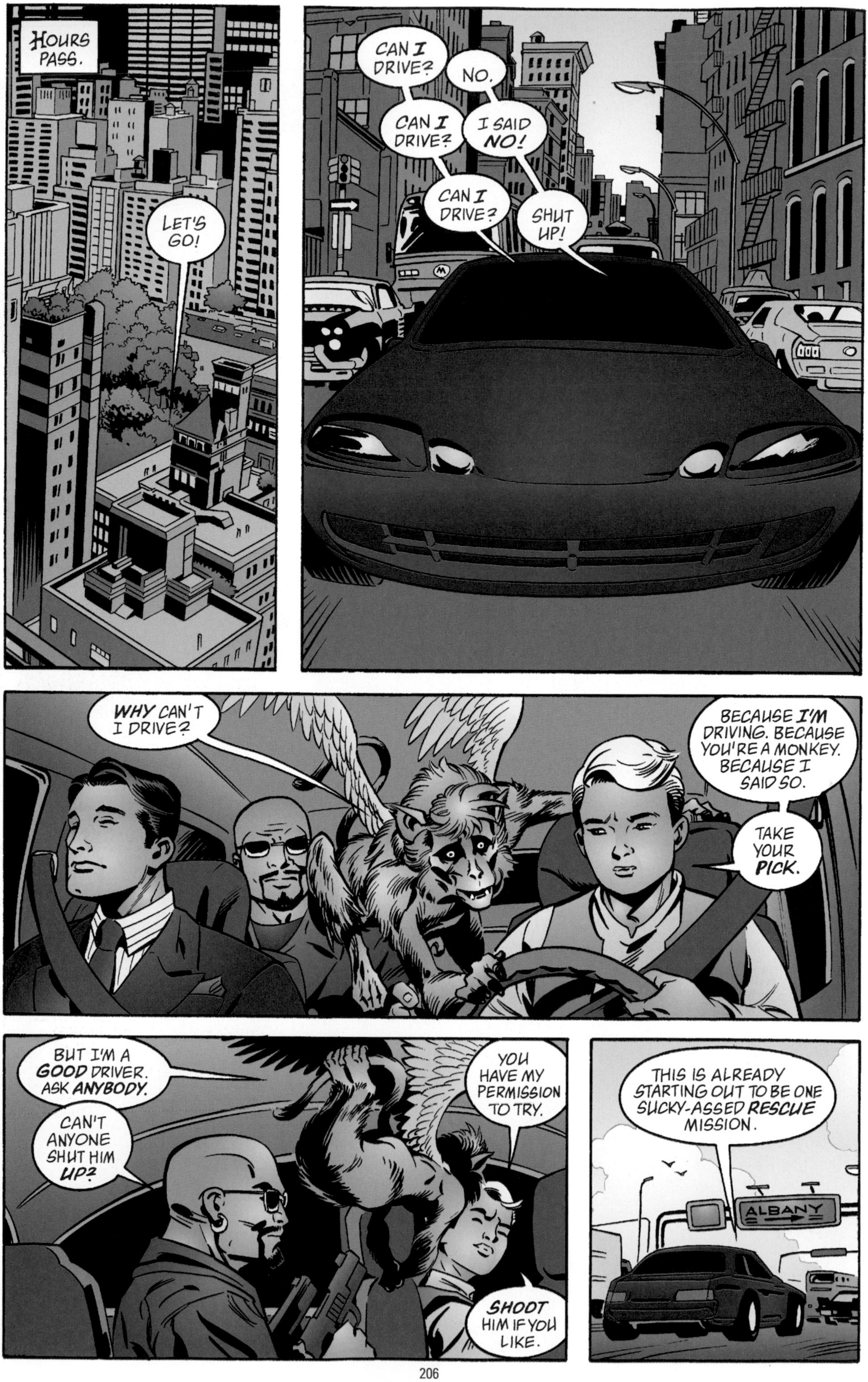
HOURS PASS.
LET'S GO!
CAN I DRIVE?
NO.
CAN I DRIVE?
I SAID NO!
CAN I DRIVE?
SHUT UP!
WHY CAN'T I DRIVE?
BECAUSE I'M DRIVING. BECAUSE YOU'RE A MONKEY. BECAUSE I SAID SO.
TAKE YOUR PICK.
BUT I'M A GOOD DRIVER. ASK ANYBODY.
CAN'T ANYONE SHUT HIM UP?
YOU HAVE MY PERMISSION TO TRY.
SHOOT HIM IF YOU LIKE.
THIS IS ALREADY STARTING OUT TO BE ONE SUCKY-ASSED RESCUE MISSION.
ALBANY

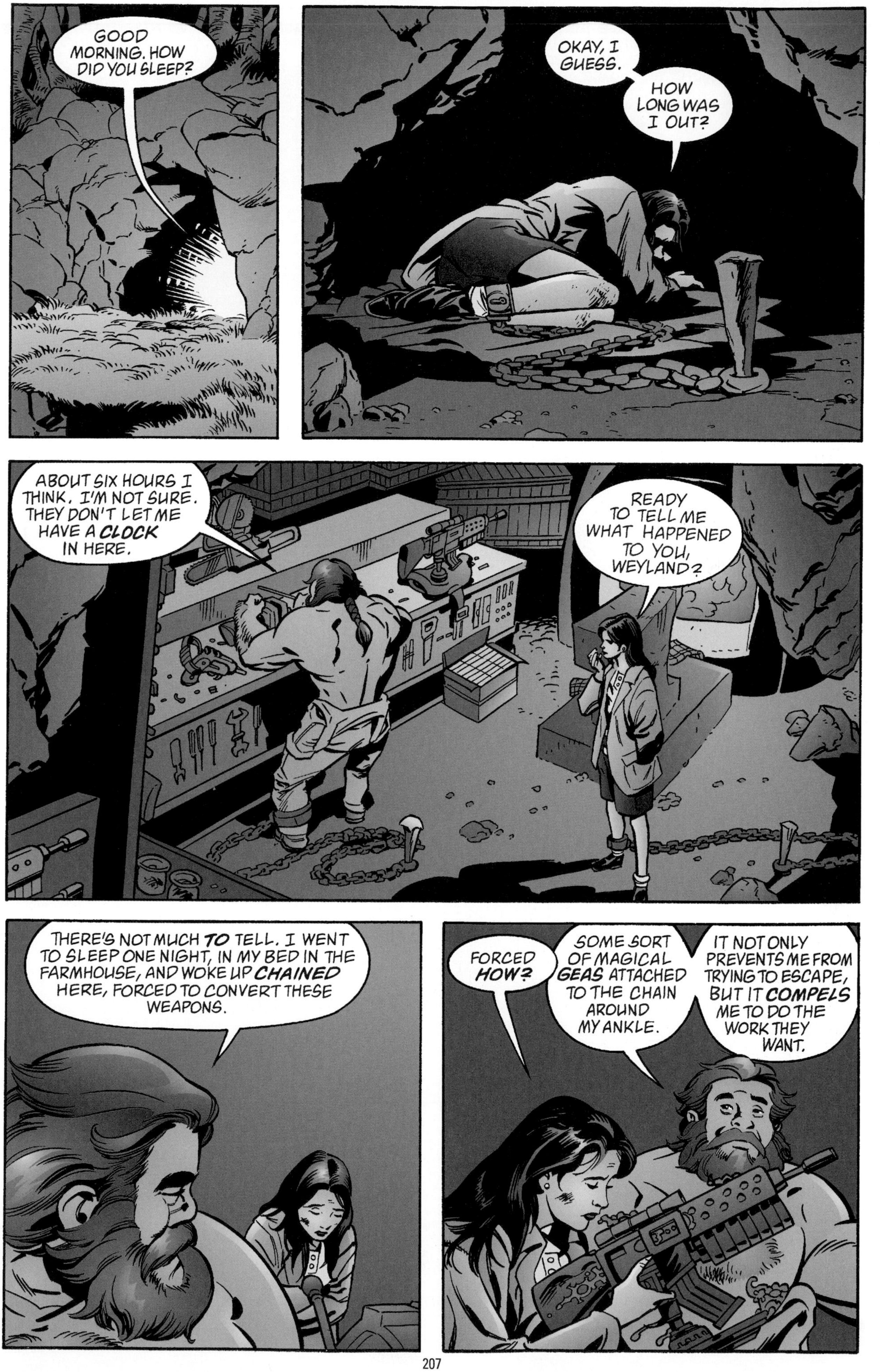
GOOD MORNING. HOW DID YOU SLEEP?
OKAY, I GUESS.
HOW LONG WAS I OUT?
ABOUT SIX HOURS I THINK. I'M NOT SURE. THEY DON'T LET ME HAVE A **CLOCK** IN HERE.
READY TO TELL ME WHAT HAPPENED TO YOU, WEYLAND?
THERE'S NOT MUCH **TO** TELL. I WENT TO SLEEP ONE NIGHT, IN MY BED IN THE FARMHOUSE, AND WOKE UP **CHAINED** HERE, FORCED TO CONVERT THESE WEAPONS.
FORCED **HOW?**
SOME SORT OF MAGICAL **GEAS** ATTACHED TO THE CHAIN AROUND MY ANKLE.
IT NOT ONLY PREVENTS ME FROM TRYING TO ESCAPE, BUT IT **COMPELS** ME TO DO THE WORK THEY WANT.

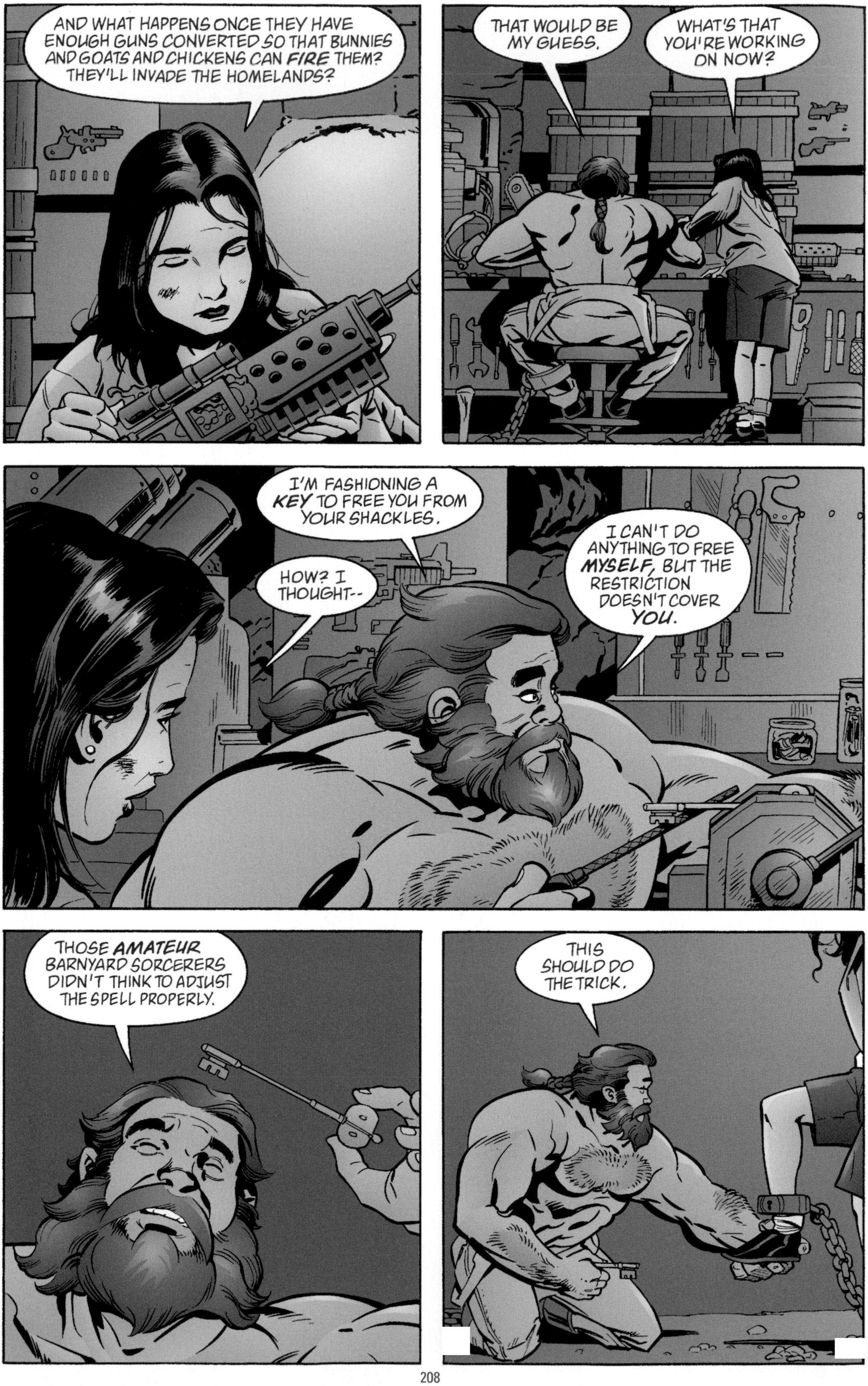
AND WHAT HAPPENS ONCE THEY HAVE ENOUGH GUNS CONVERTED SO THAT BUNNIES AND GOATS AND CHICKENS CAN FIRE THEM? THEY'LL INVADE THE HOMELANDS?
THAT WOULD BE MY GUESS.
WHAT'S THAT YOU'RE WORKING ON NOW?
I'M FASHIONING A KEY TO FREE YOU FROM YOUR SHACKLES.
HOW? I THOUGHT--
I CAN'T DO ANYTHING TO FREE MYSELF, BUT THE RESTRICTION DOESN'T COVER YOU.
THOSE AMATEUR BARNYARD SORCERERS DIDN'T THINK TO ADJUST THE SPELL PROPERLY.
THIS SHOULD DO THE TRICK.

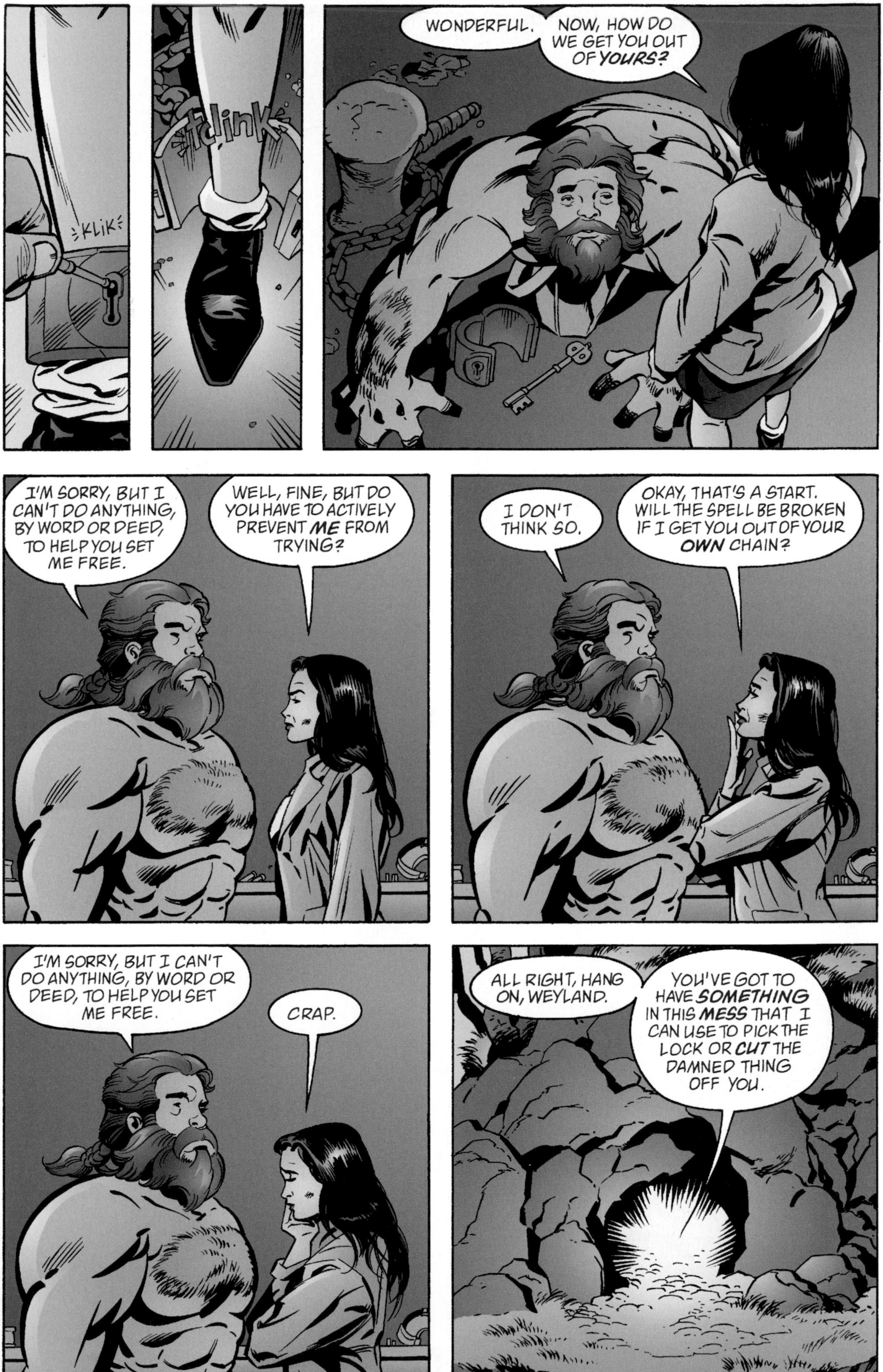
KLIK
fdink
WONDERFUL.
NOW, HOW DO WE GET YOU OUT OF YOURS?
I'M SORRY, BUT I CAN'T DO ANYTHING, BY WORD OR DEED, TO HELP YOU SET ME FREE.
WELL, FINE, BUT DO YOU HAVE TO ACTIVELY PREVENT ME FROM TRYING?
I DON'T THINK SO.
OKAY, THAT'S A START. WILL THE SPELL BE BROKEN IF I GET YOU OUT OF YOUR OWN CHAIN?
I'M SORRY, BUT I CAN'T DO ANYTHING, BY WORD OR DEED, TO HELP YOU SET ME FREE.
CRAP.
ALL RIGHT, HANG ON, WEYLAND.
YOU'VE GOT TO HAVE SOMETHING IN THIS MESS THAT I CAN USE TO PICK THE LOCK OR CUT THE DAMNED THING OFF YOU.

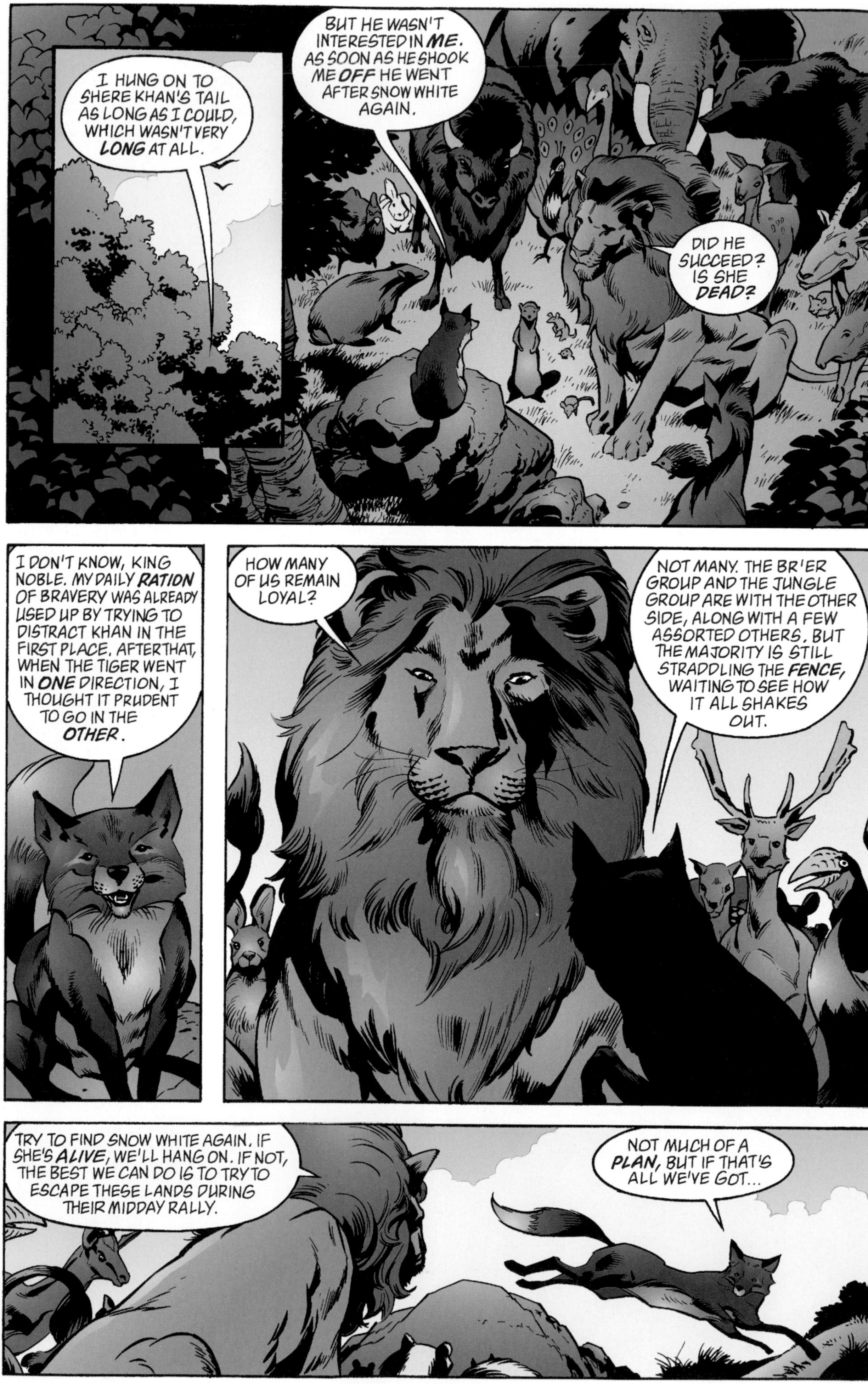
I HUNG ON TO SHERE KHAN'S TAIL AS LONG AS I COULD, WHICH WASN'T VERY LONG AT ALL.
BUT HE WASN'T INTERESTED IN ME. AS SOON AS HE SHOOK ME OFF HE WENT AFTER SNOW WHITE AGAIN.
DID HE SUCCEED? IS SHE DEAD?
I DON'T KNOW, KING NOBLE. MY DAILY RATION OF BRAVERY WAS ALREADY USED UP BY TRYING TO DISTRACT KHAN IN THE FIRST PLACE. AFTER THAT, WHEN THE TIGER WENT IN ONE DIRECTION, I THOUGHT IT PRUDENT TO GO IN THE OTHER.
HOW MANY OF US REMAIN LOYAL?
NOT MANY. THE BR'ER GROUP AND THE JUNGLE GROUP ARE WITH THE OTHER SIDE, ALONG WITH A FEW ASSORTED OTHERS. BUT THE MAJORITY IS STILL STRADDLING THE FENCE, WAITING TO SEE HOW IT ALL SHAKES OUT.
TRY TO FIND SNOW WHITE AGAIN. IF SHE'S ALIVE, WE'LL HANG ON. IF NOT, THE BEST WE CAN DO IS TO TRY TO ESCAPE THESE LANDS DURING THEIR MIDDAY RALLY.
NOT MUCH OF A PLAN, BUT IF THAT'S ALL WE'VE GOT...

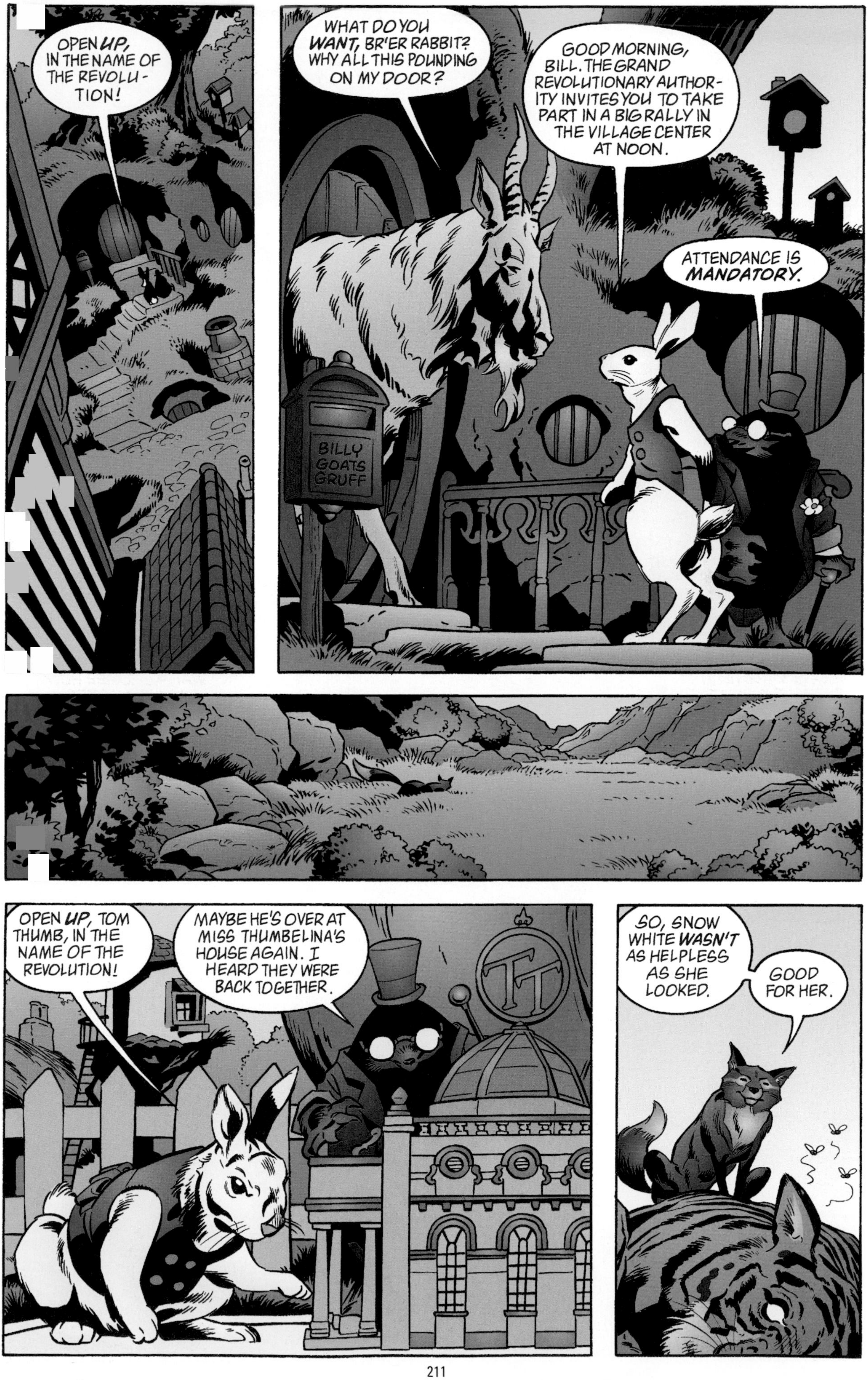
OPEN UP, IN THE NAME OF THE REVOLU-TION!
WHAT DO YOU WANT, BR'ER RABBIT? WHY ALL THIS POUNDING ON MY DOOR?
GOOD MORNING, BILL. THE GRAND REVOLUTIONARY AUTHOR-ITY INVITES YOU TO TAKE PART IN A BIG RALLY IN THE VILLAGE CENTER AT NOON.
ATTENDANCE IS MANDATORY.
BILLY GOATS GRUFF
OPEN UP, TOM THUMB, IN THE NAME OF THE REVOLUTION!
MAYBE HE'S OVER AT MISS THUMBELINA'S HOUSE AGAIN. I HEARD THEY WERE BACK TOGETHER.
TT
SO, SNOW WHITE WASN'T AS HELPLESS AS SHE LOOKED.
GOOD FOR HER.

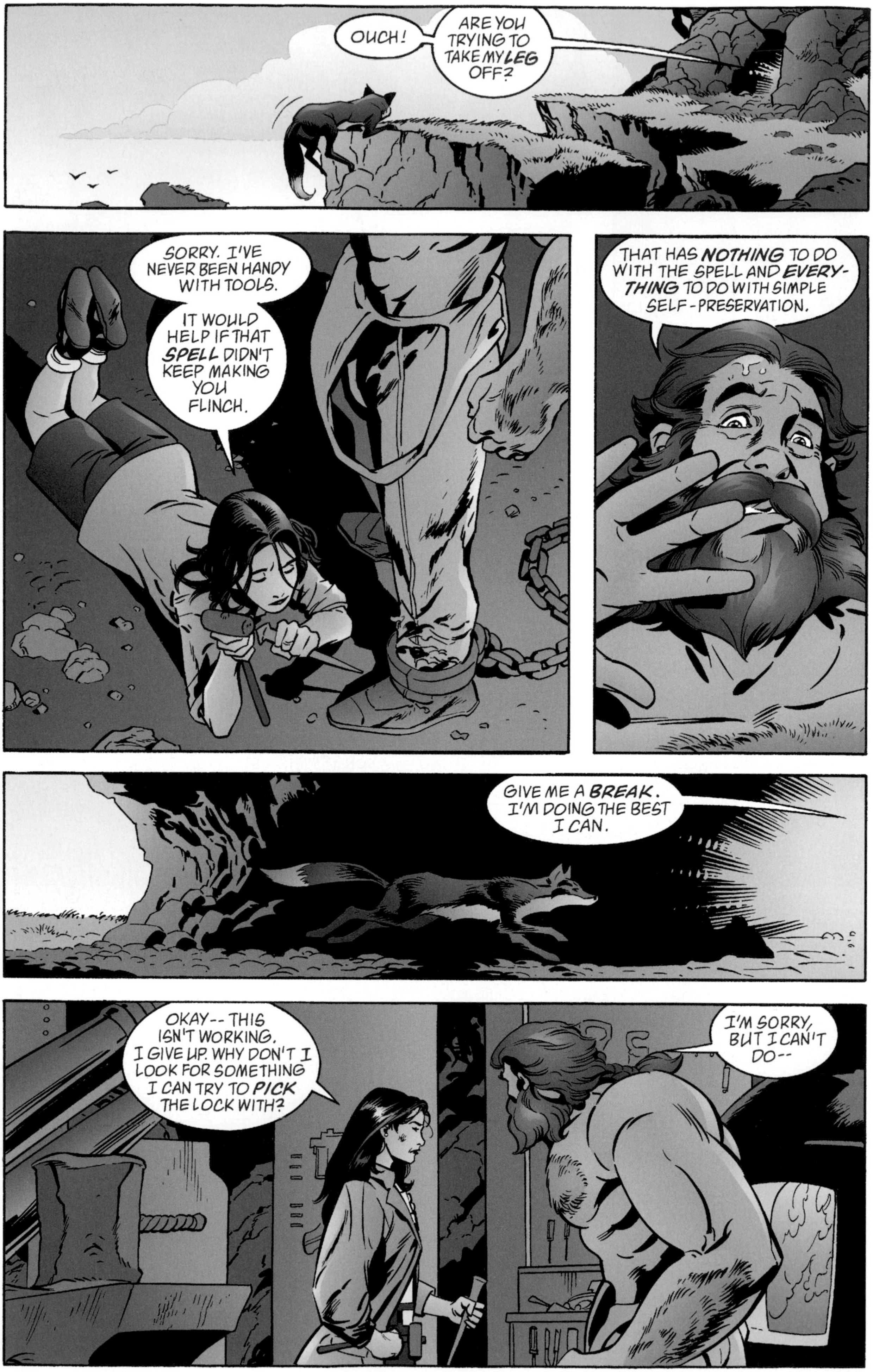
OUCH!
ARE YOU TRYING TO TAKE MY LEG OFF?
SORRY. I'VE NEVER BEEN HANDY WITH TOOLS.
IT WOULD HELP IF THAT SPELL DIDN'T KEEP MAKING YOU FLINCH.
THAT HAS NOTHING TO DO WITH THE SPELL AND EVERY-THING TO DO WITH SIMPLE SELF-PRESERVATION.
GIVE ME A BREAK. I'M DOING THE BEST I CAN.
OKAY-- THIS ISN'T WORKING. I GIVE UP. WHY DON'T I LOOK FOR SOMETHING I CAN TRY TO PICK THE LOCK WITH?
I'M SORRY, BUT I CAN'T DO--

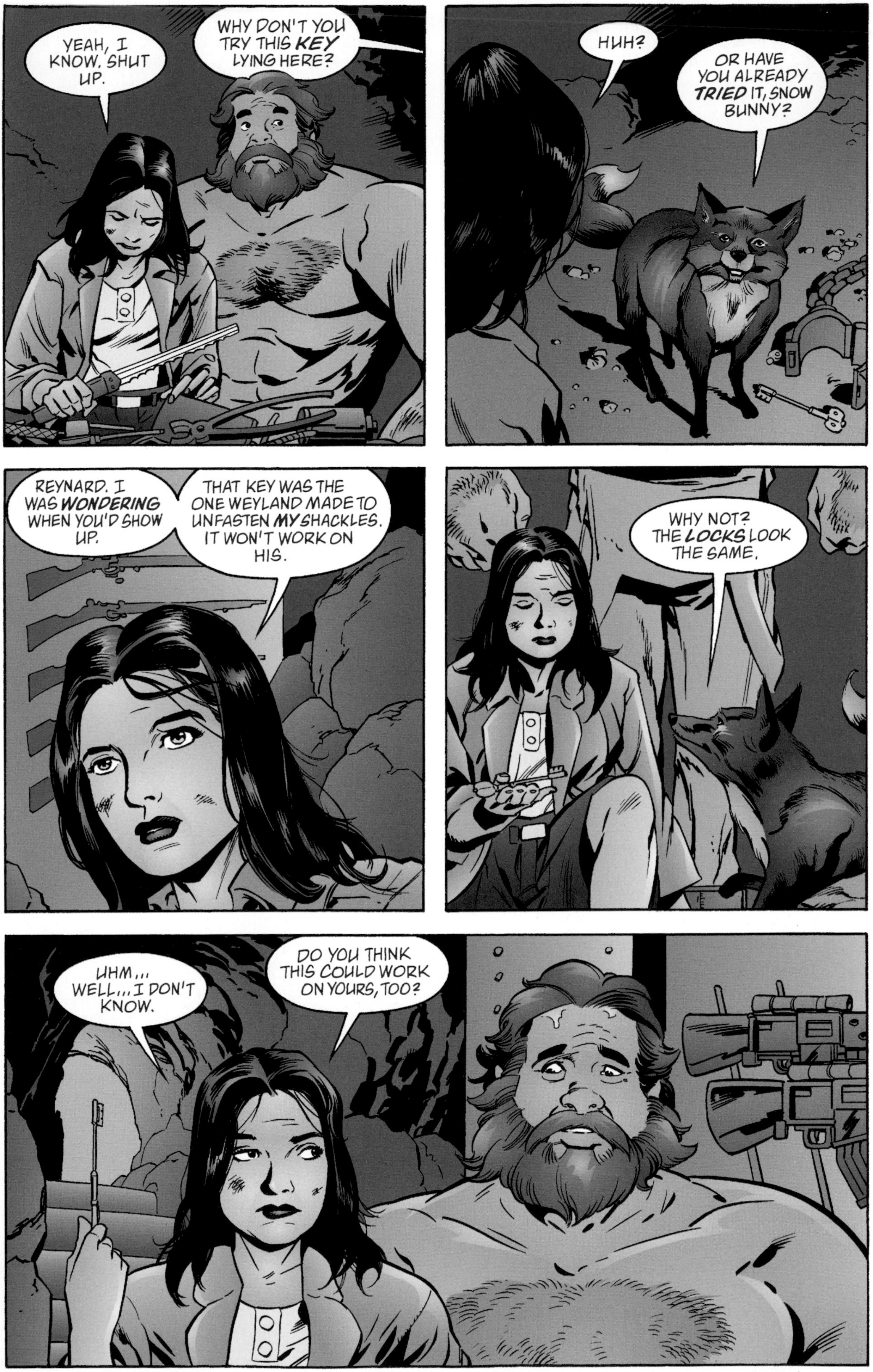
YEAH, I KNOW. SHUT UP.
WHY DON'T YOU TRY THIS KEY LYING HERE?
HUH?
OR HAVE YOU ALREADY TRIED IT, SNOW BUNNY?
REYNARD. I WAS WONDERING WHEN YOU'D SHOW UP.
THAT KEY WAS THE ONE WEYLAND MADE TO UNFASTEN MY SHACKLES. IT WON'T WORK ON HIS.
WHY NOT? THE LOCKS LOOK THE SAME.
UHM... WELL... I DON'T KNOW.
DO YOU THINK THIS COULD WORK ON YOURS, TOO?

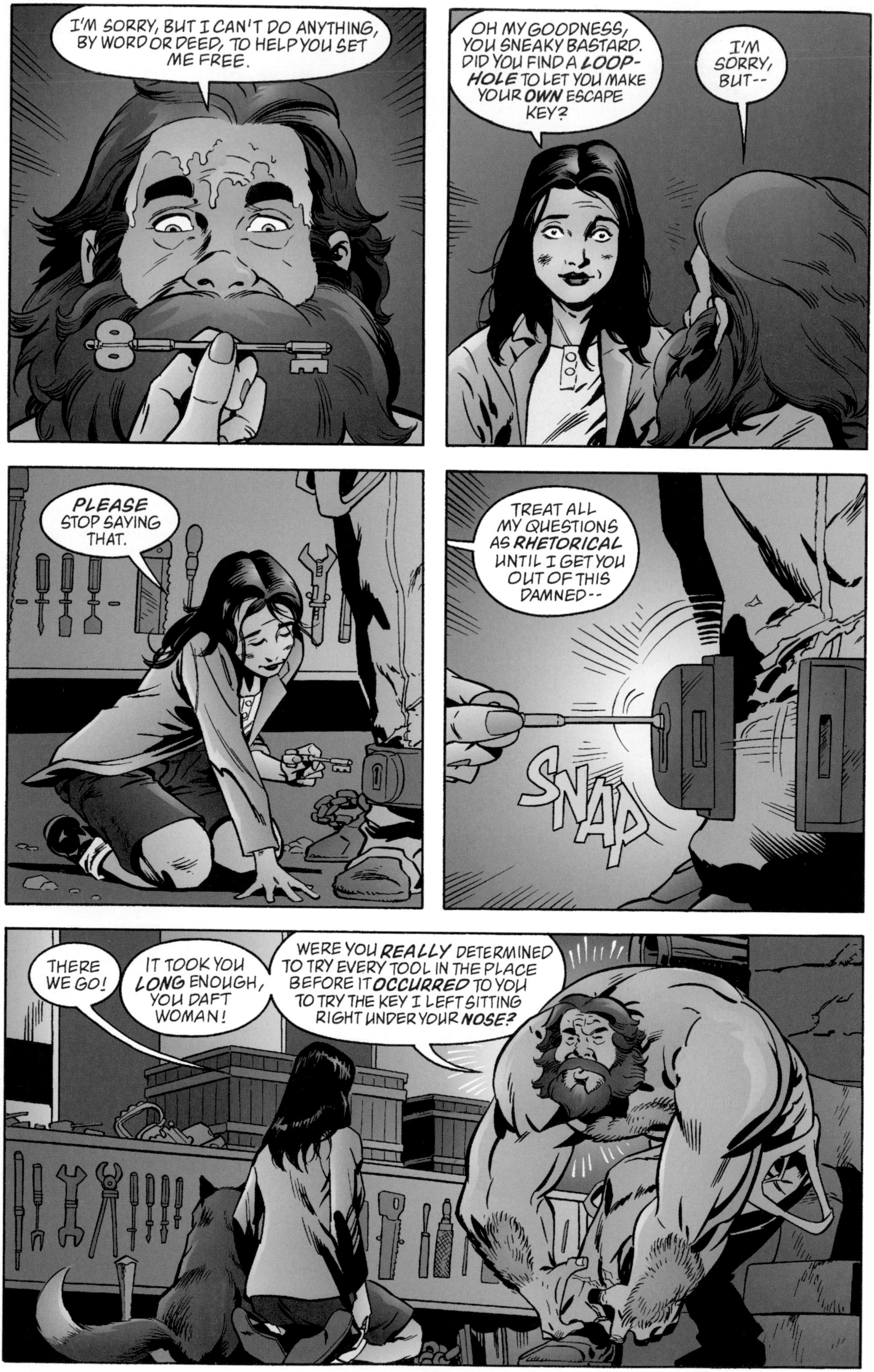

I'M SORRY, BUT I CAN'T DO ANYTHING, BY WORD OR DEED, TO HELP YOU SET ME FREE.
OH MY GOODNESS, YOU SNEAKY BASTARD. DID YOU FIND A LOOP-HOLE TO LET YOU MAKE YOUR OWN ESCAPE KEY?
I'M SORRY, BUT--
PLEASE STOP SAYING THAT.
TREAT ALL MY QUESTIONS AS RHETORICAL UNTIL I GET YOU OUT OF THIS DAMNED--
SNAP
THERE WE GO!
IT TOOK YOU LONG ENOUGH, YOU DAFT WOMAN!
WERE YOU REALLY DETERMINED TO TRY EVERY TOOL IN THE PLACE BEFORE IT OCCURRED TO YOU TO TRY THE KEY I LEFT SITTING RIGHT UNDER YOUR NOSE?

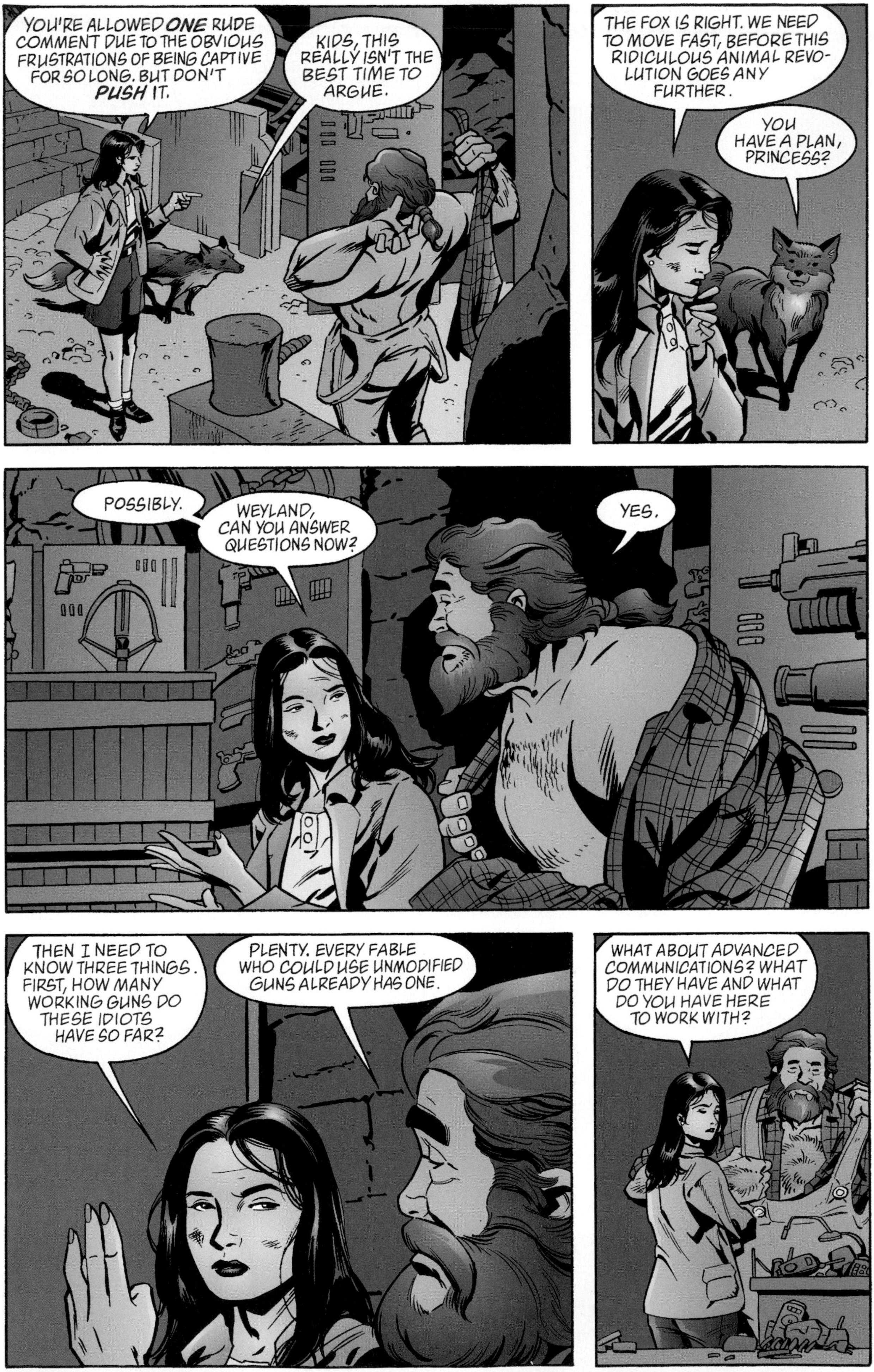
YOU'RE ALLOWED ONE RUDE COMMENT DUE TO THE OBVIOUS FRUSTRATIONS OF BEING CAPTIVE FOR SO LONG. BUT DON'T PUSH IT.
KIDS, THIS REALLY ISN'T THE BEST TIME TO ARGUE.
THE FOX IS RIGHT. WE NEED TO MOVE FAST, BEFORE THIS RIDICULOUS ANIMAL REVOLUTION GOES ANY FURTHER.
YOU HAVE A PLAN, PRINCESS?
POSSIBLY.
WEYLAND, CAN YOU ANSWER QUESTIONS NOW?
YES.
THEN I NEED TO KNOW THREE THINGS. FIRST, HOW MANY WORKING GUNS DO THESE IDIOTS HAVE SO FAR?
PLENTY. EVERY FABLE WHO COULD USE UNMODIFIED GUNS ALREADY HAS ONE.
WHAT ABOUT ADVANCED COMMUNICATIONS? WHAT DO THEY HAVE AND WHAT DO YOU HAVE HERE TO WORK WITH?

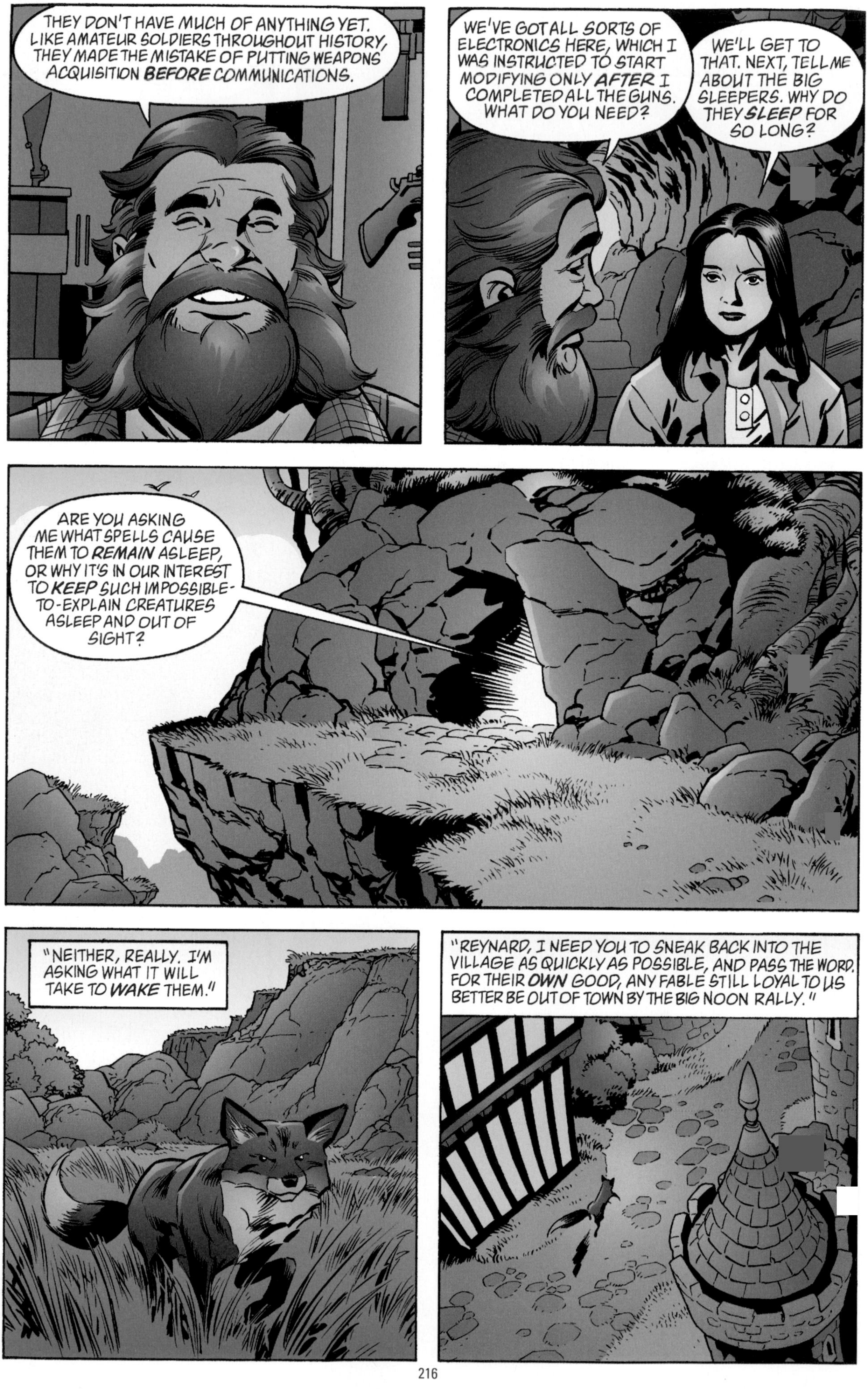
THEY DON'T HAVE MUCH OF ANYTHING YET. LIKE AMATEUR SOLDIERS THROUGHOUT HISTORY, THEY MADE THE MISTAKE OF PUTTING WEAPONS ACQUISITION BEFORE COMMUNICATIONS.
WE'VE GOT ALL SORTS OF ELECTRONICS HERE, WHICH I WAS INSTRUCTED TO START MODIFYING ONLY AFTER I COMPLETED ALL THE GUNS. WHAT DO YOU NEED?
WE'LL GET TO THAT. NEXT, TELL ME ABOUT THE BIG SLEEPERS. WHY DO THEY SLEEP FOR SO LONG?
ARE YOU ASKING ME WHAT SPELLS CAUSE THEM TO REMAIN ASLEEP, OR WHY IT'S IN OUR INTEREST TO KEEP SUCH IMPOSSIBLE-TO-EXPLAIN CREATURES ASLEEP AND OUT OF SIGHT?
"NEITHER, REALLY. I'M ASKING WHAT IT WILL TAKE TO WAKE THEM."
"REYNARD, I NEED YOU TO SNEAK BACK INTO THE VILLAGE AS QUICKLY AS POSSIBLE, AND PASS THE WORD. FOR THEIR OWN GOOD, ANY FABLE STILL LOYAL TO US BETTER BE OUT OF TOWN BY THE BIG NOON RALLY."

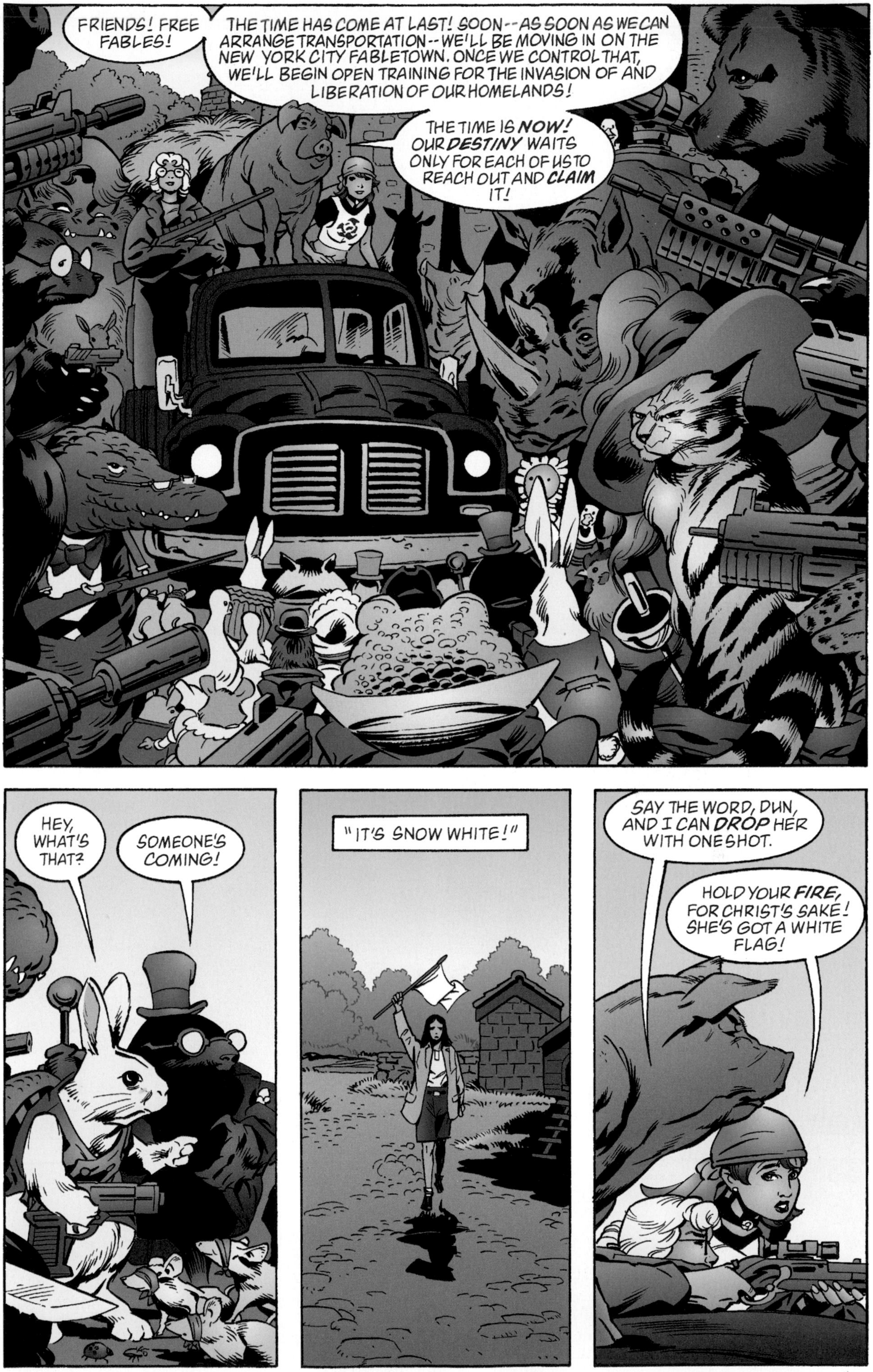
FRIENDS! FREE FABLES!
THE TIME HAS COME AT LAST! SOON--AS SOON AS WE CAN ARRANGE TRANSPORTATION--WE'LL BE MOVING IN ON THE NEW YORK CITY FABLETOWN. ONCE WE CONTROL THAT, WE'LL BEGIN OPEN TRAINING FOR THE INVASION OF AND LIBERATION OF OUR HOMELANDS!
THE TIME IS NOW! OUR DESTINY WAITS ONLY FOR EACH OF US TO REACH OUT AND CLAIM IT!
HEY, WHAT'S THAT?
SOMEONE'S COMING!
"IT'S SNOW WHITE!"
SAY THE WORD, DUN, AND I CAN DROP HER WITH ONE SHOT.
HOLD YOUR FIRE, FOR CHRIST'S SAKE! SHE'S GOT A WHITE FLAG!

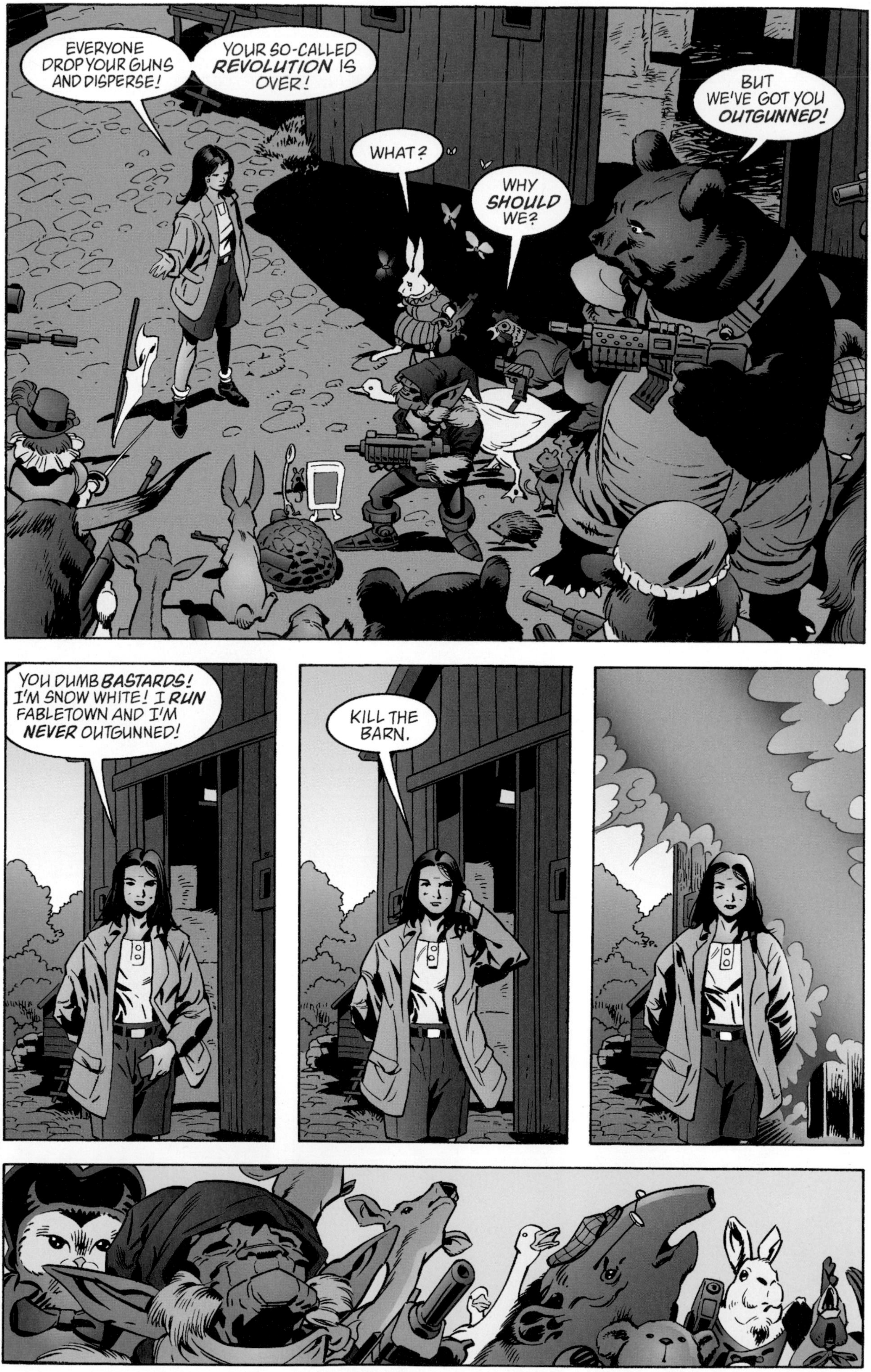
EVERYONE DROP YOUR GUNS AND DISPERSE!
YOUR SO-CALLED REVOLUTION IS OVER!
WHAT?
WHY SHOULD WE?
BUT WE'VE GOT YOU OUTGUNNED!
YOU DUMB BASTARDS! I'M SNOW WHITE! I RUN FABLETOWN AND I'M NEVER OUTGUNNED!
KILL THE BARN.

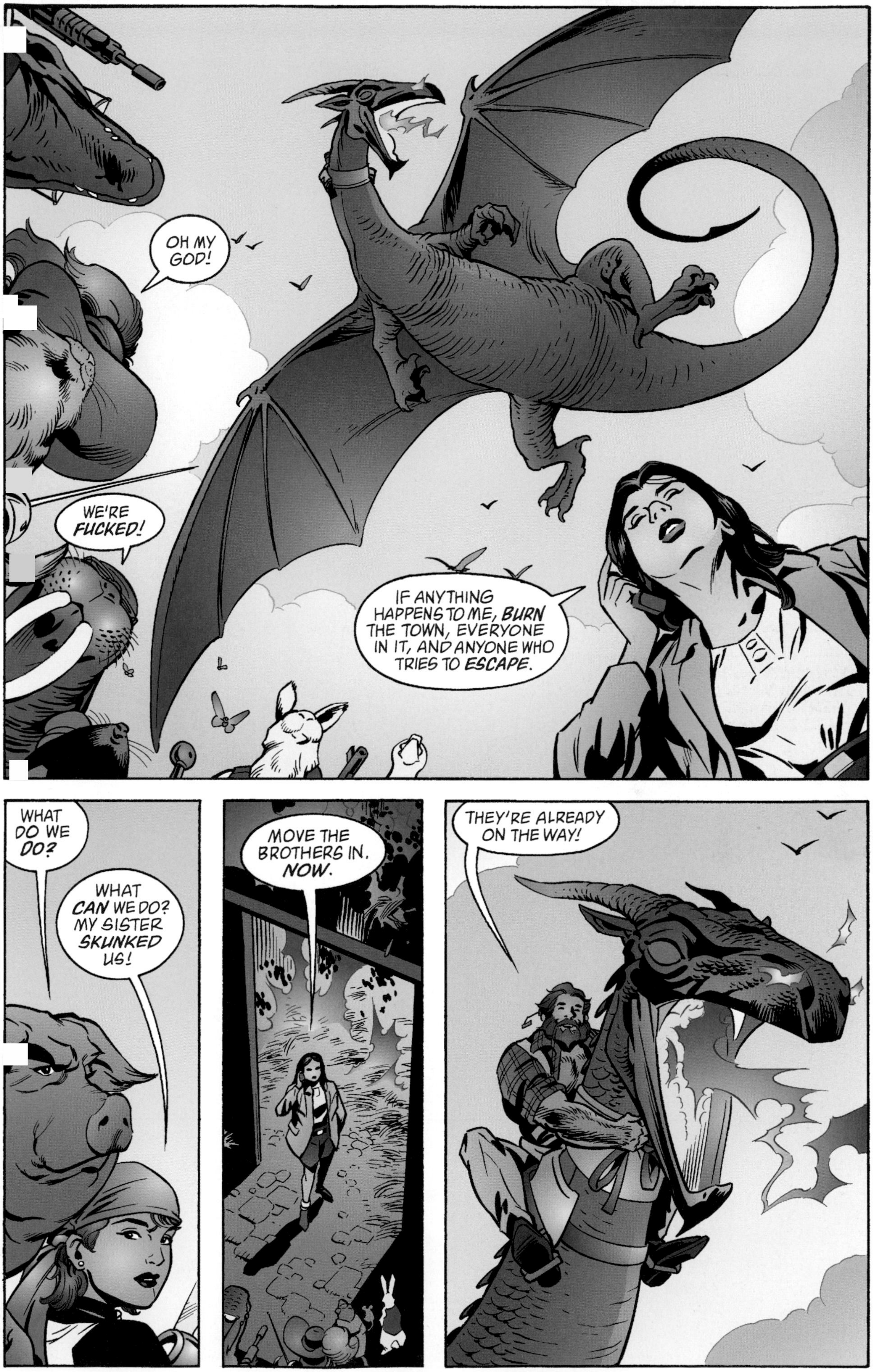
OH MY GOD!
WE'RE FUCKED!
IF ANYTHING HAPPENS TO ME, BURN THE TOWN, EVERYONE IN IT, AND ANYONE WHO TRIES TO ESCAPE.
WHAT DO WE DO?
WHAT CAN WE DO? MY SISTER SKUNKED US!
MOVE THE BROTHERS IN. NOW.
THEY'RE ALREADY ON THE WAY!

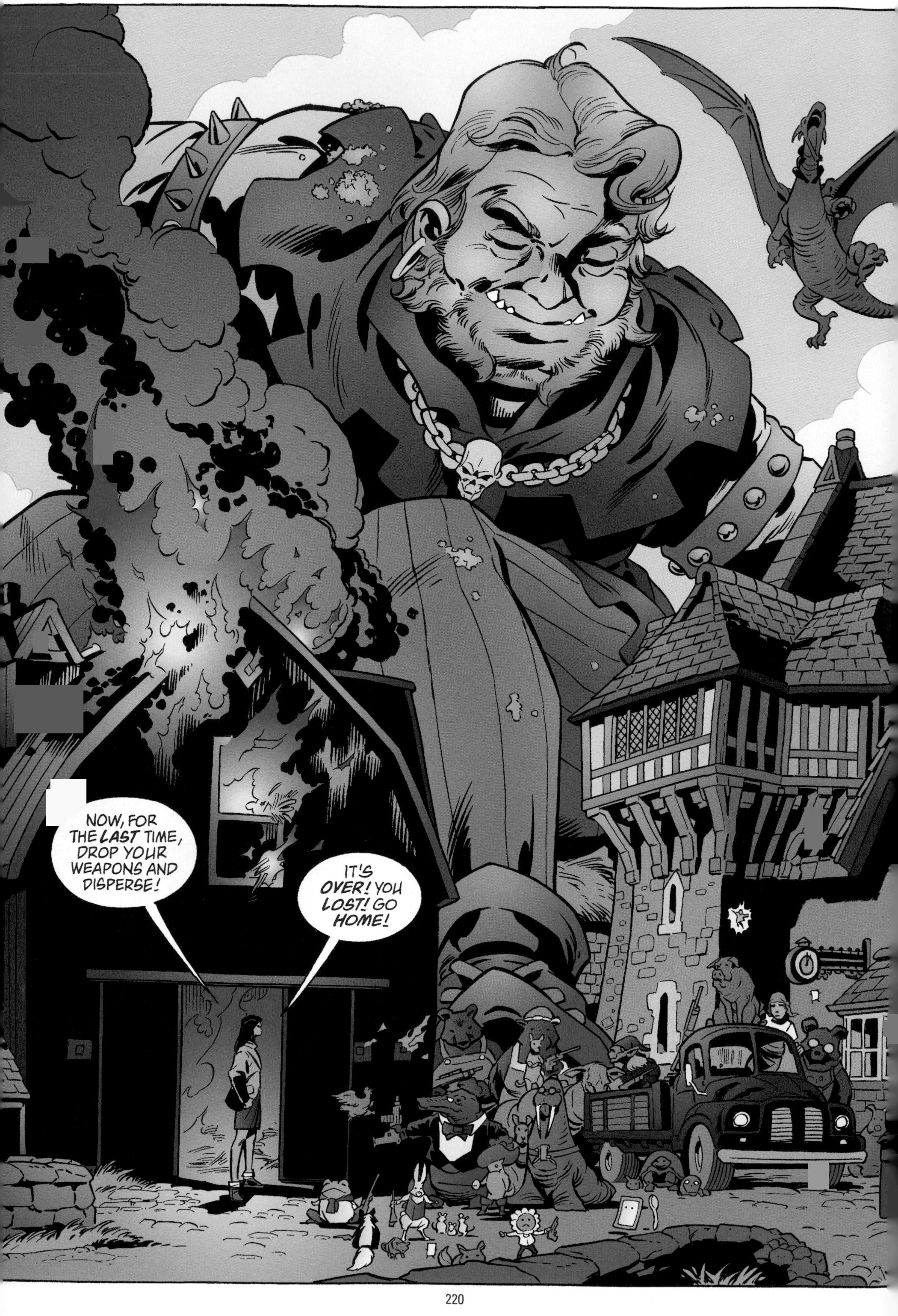
NOW, FOR THE LAST TIME, DROP YOUR WEAPONS AND DISPERSE!
IT'S OVER! YOU LOST! GO HOME!

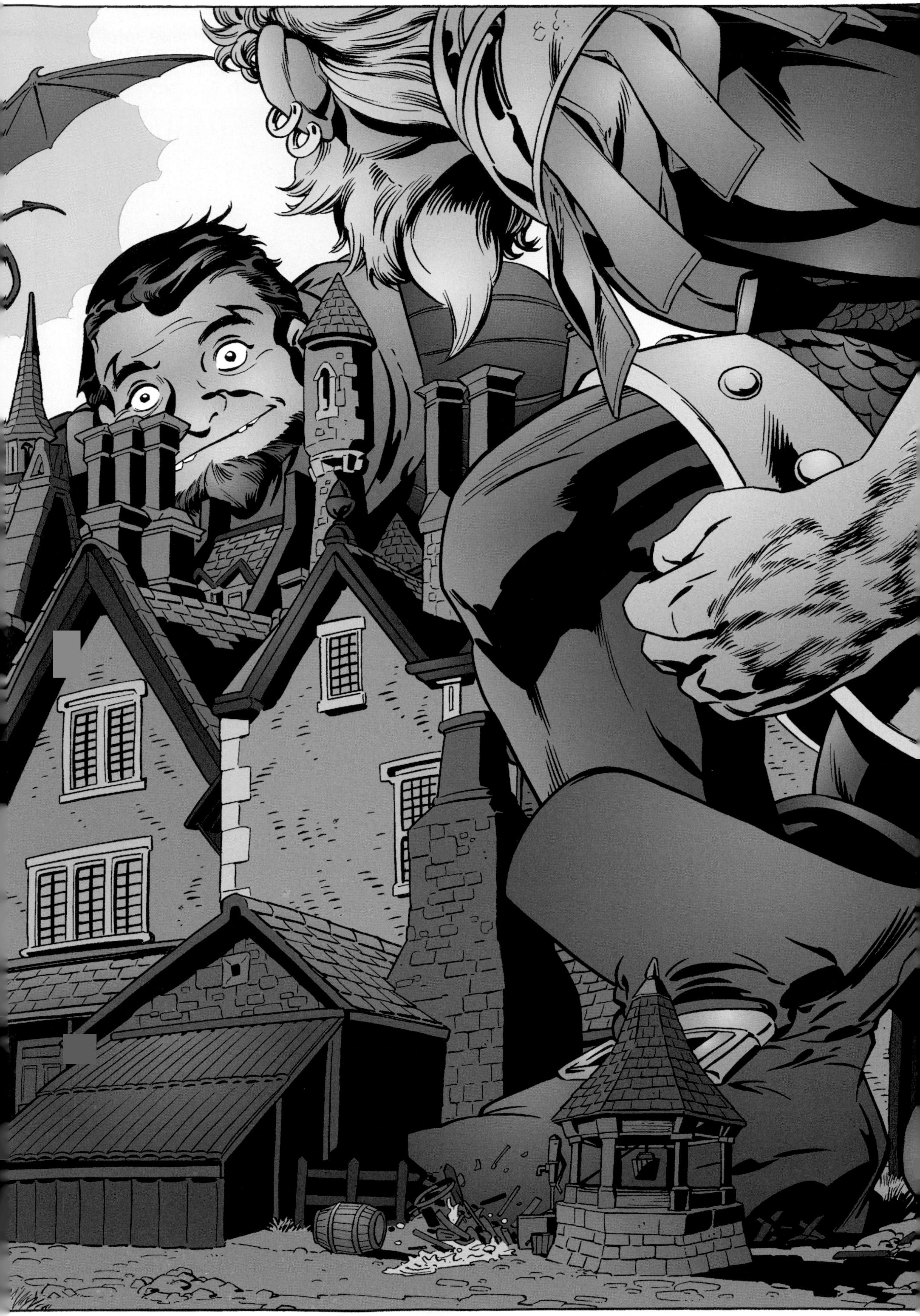

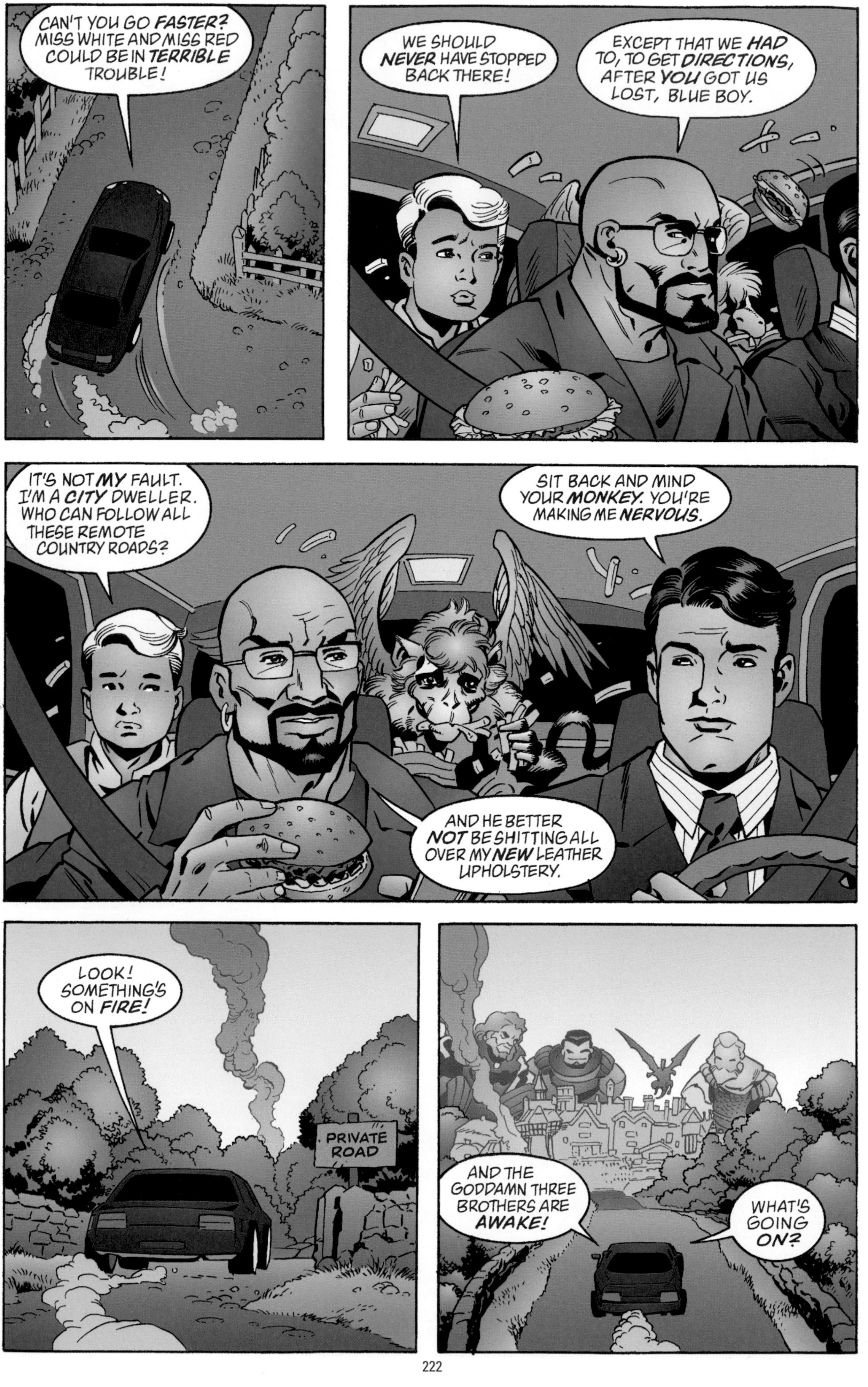
CAN'T YOU GO FASTER? MISS WHITE AND MISS RED COULD BE IN TERRIBLE TROUBLE!
WE SHOULD NEVER HAVE STOPPED BACK THERE!
EXCEPT THAT WE HAD TO, TO GET DIRECTIONS, AFTER YOU GOT US LOST, BLUE BOY.
IT'S NOT MY FAULT. I'M A CITY DWELLER. WHO CAN FOLLOW ALL THESE REMOTE COUNTRY ROADS?
SIT BACK AND MIND YOUR MONKEY. YOU'RE MAKING ME NERVOUS.
AND HE BETTER NOT BE SHITTING ALL OVER MY NEW LEATHER UPHOLSTERY.
LOOK! SOMETHING'S ON FIRE!
PRIVATE ROAD
AND THE GODDAMN THREE BROTHERS ARE AWAKE!
WHAT'S GOING ON?

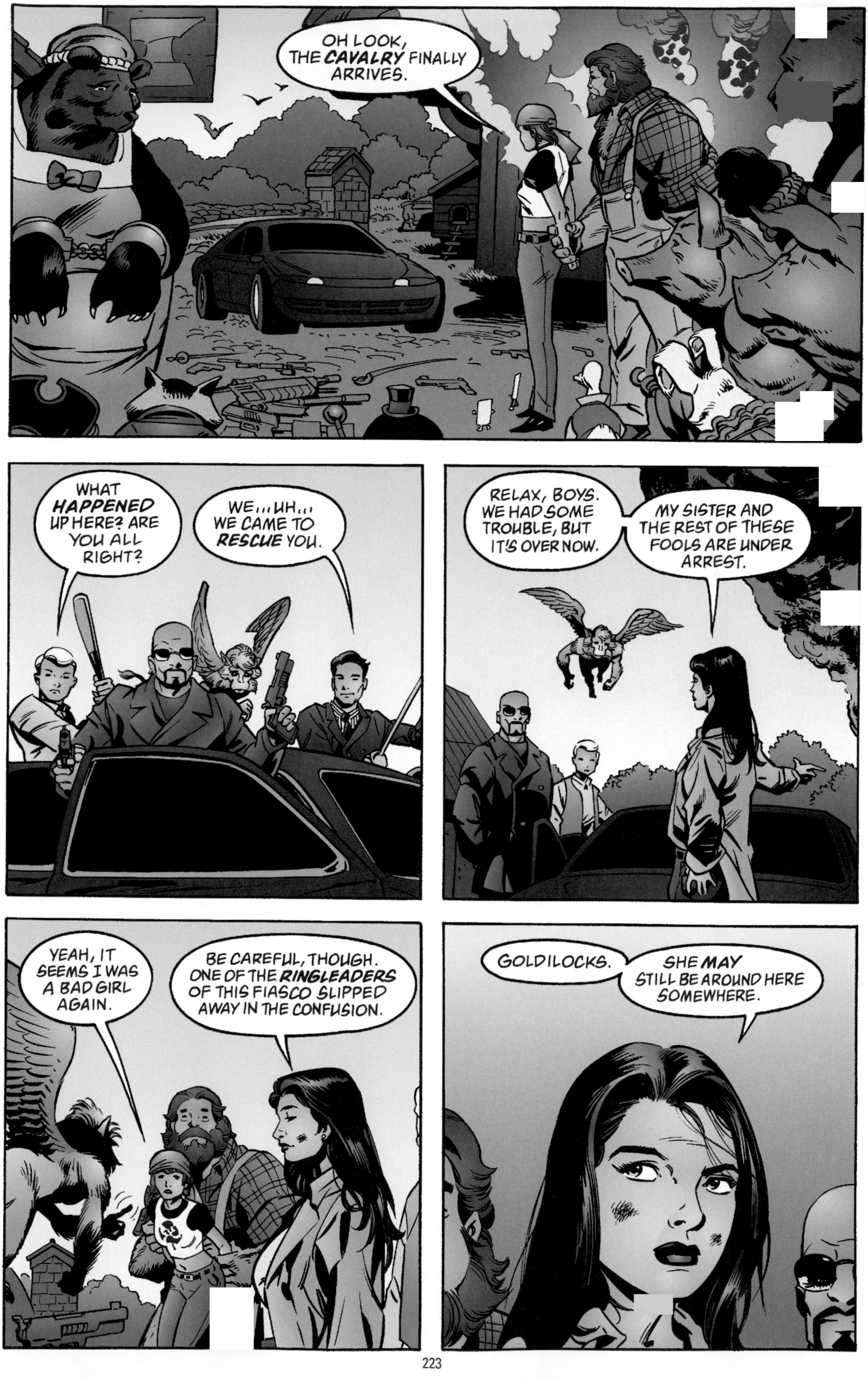
OH LOOK, THE CAVALRY FINALLY ARRIVES.
WHAT HAPPENED UP HERE? ARE YOU ALL RIGHT?
WE...UH... WE CAME TO RESCUE YOU.
RELAX, BOYS. WE HAD SOME TROUBLE, BUT IT'S OVER NOW.
MY SISTER AND THE REST OF THESE FOOLS ARE UNDER ARREST.
YEAH, IT SEEMS I WAS A BAD GIRL AGAIN.
BE CAREFUL, THOUGH. ONE OF THE RINGLEADERS OF THIS FIASCO SLIPPED AWAY IN THE CONFUSION.
GOLDILOCKS.
SHE MAY STILL BE AROUND HERE SOMEWHERE.

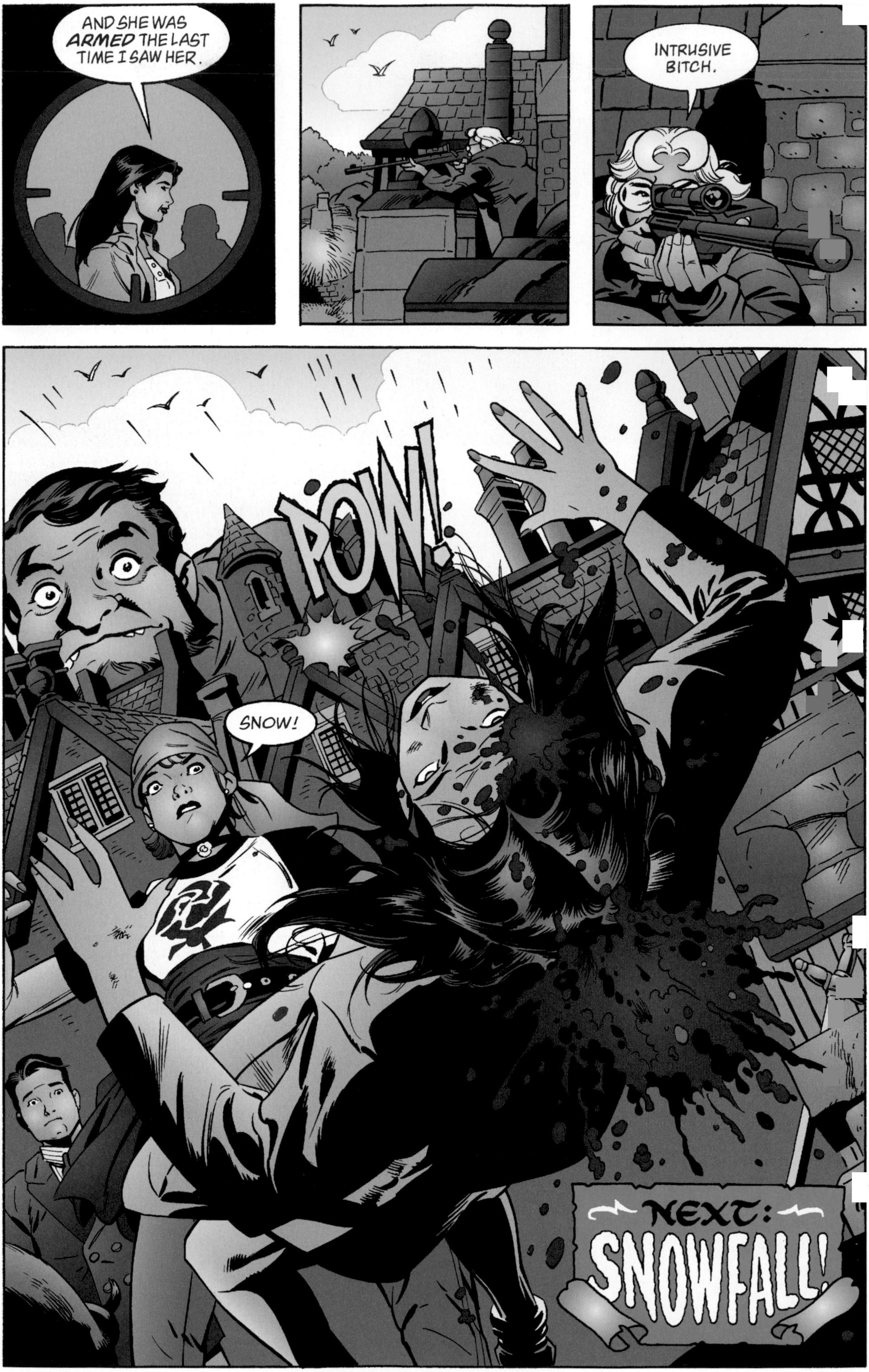
AND SHE WAS ARMED THE LAST TIME I SAW HER.
INTRUSIVE BITCH.
POW!
SNOW!
NEXT: SNOWFALL!

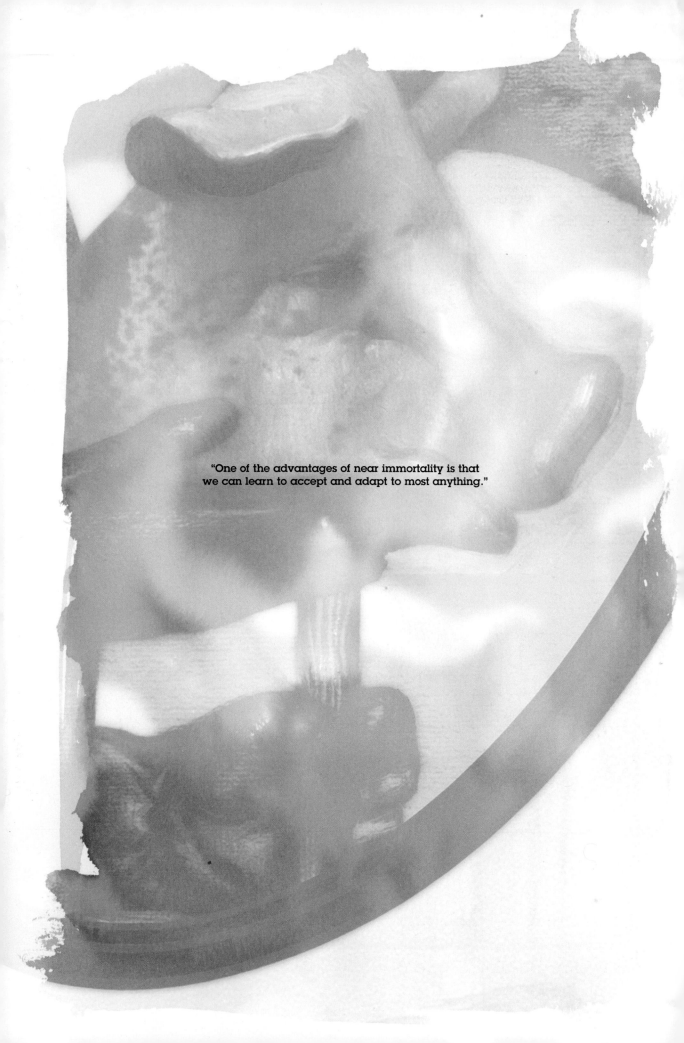

"One of the advantages of near immortality is that
we can learn to accept and adapt to most anything."

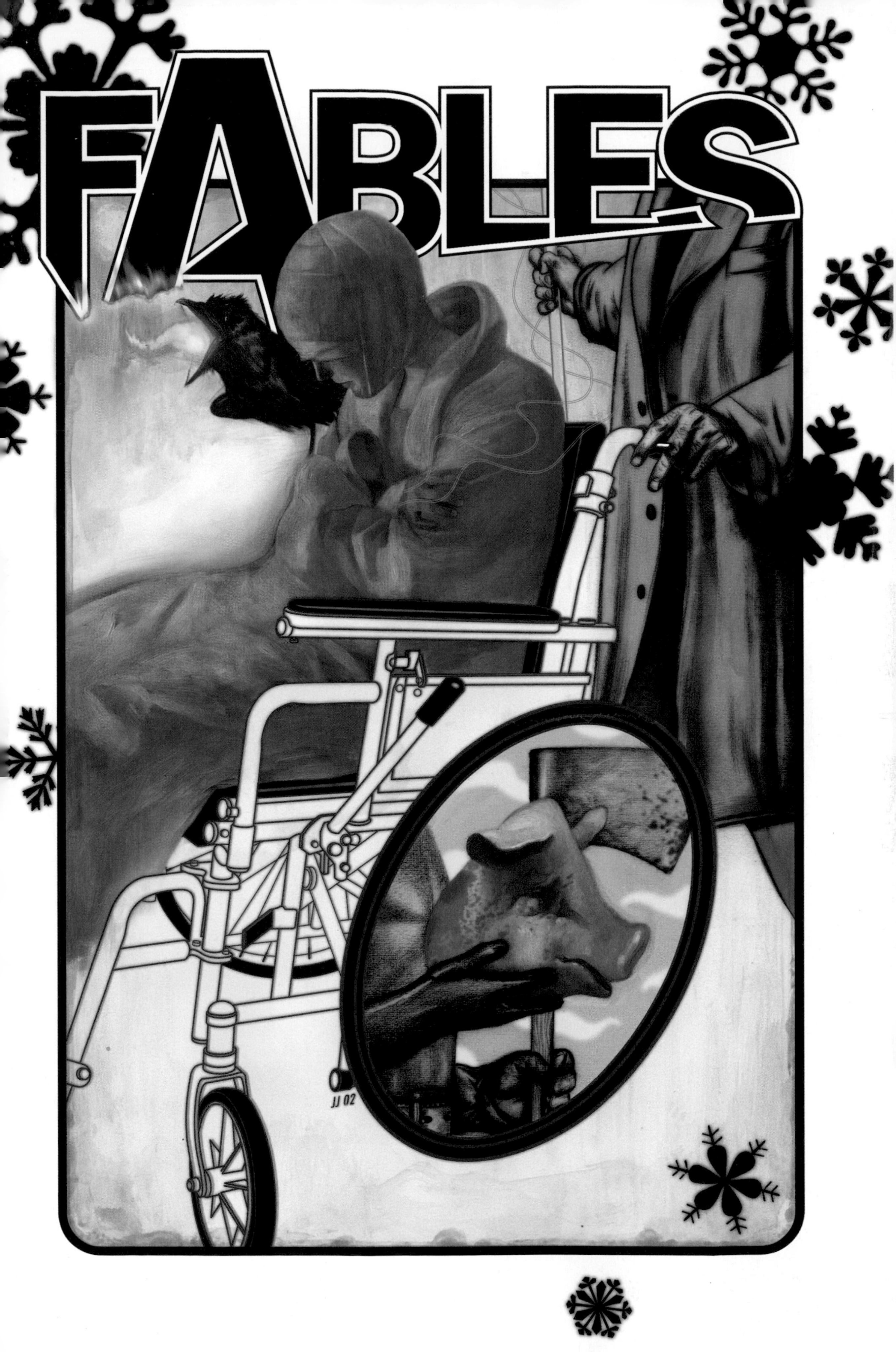
FABLES
JJ 02

Twilight of the Dogs
Part Five of Animal Farm

| Written & created by **Bill Willingham** | Pencilled by **Mark Buckingham** | Inked by **Steve Leialoha** | Lettered by **Todd Klein** | Colored and Separated by **Daniel Vozzo** | Cover art by **James Jean** | Assistant Ed. **Mariah Huehner** | Editor **Shelly Bond** |

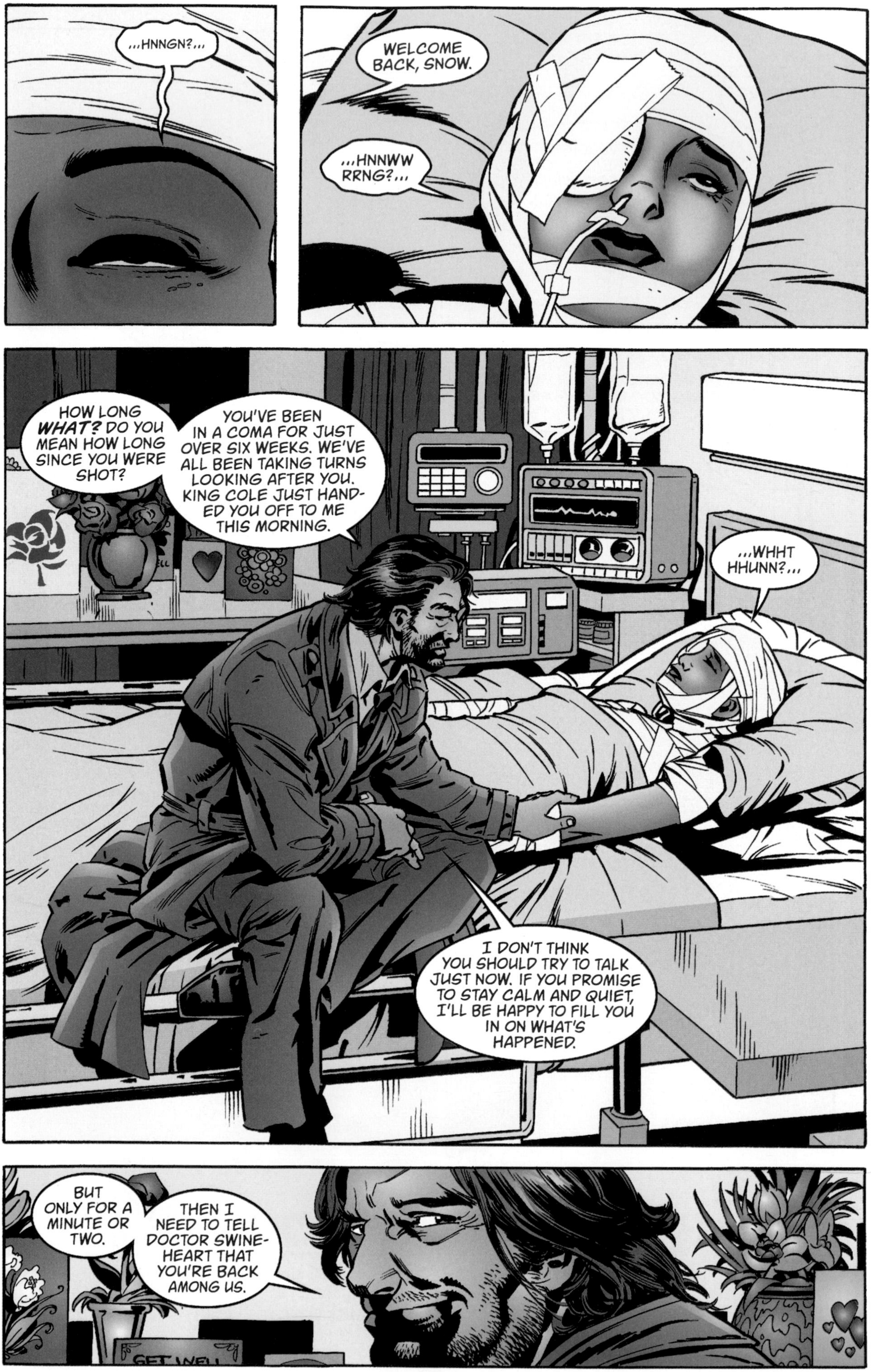
...HNNGN?...
WELCOME BACK, SNOW.
...HNNWW RRNG?...
HOW LONG *WHAT?* DO YOU MEAN HOW LONG SINCE YOU WERE SHOT?
YOU'VE BEEN IN A COMA FOR JUST OVER SIX WEEKS. WE'VE ALL BEEN TAKING TURNS LOOKING AFTER YOU. KING COLE JUST HANDED YOU OFF TO ME THIS MORNING.
...WHHT HHUNN?...
I DON'T THINK YOU SHOULD TRY TO TALK JUST NOW. IF YOU PROMISE TO STAY CALM AND QUIET, I'LL BE HAPPY TO FILL YOU IN ON WHAT'S HAPPENED.
BUT ONLY FOR A MINUTE OR TWO.
THEN I NEED TO TELL DOCTOR SWINEHEART THAT YOU'RE BACK AMONG US.
GET WELL

"UNDERSTAND THOUGH THAT I GET **MOST** OF THIS SECONDHAND, SINCE I'M STILL NOT ALLOWED UP AT THE FARM.

MOVE **BACK**, DAMN YOU ALL!

"THE FOILED REVOLUTION THREATENED TO FLARE UP AGAIN, IN THE CHAOS THAT IMMEDIATELY FOLLOWED YOUR SHOOTING.

♪♪ da-**TA!** da-**TA!** da-**TA!**

SETTLE DOWN, EVERY GOD-CURSED ONE OF YOU, OR I'LL GUN THE **LOT** OF YOU DOWN WHERE YOU STAND!

"BUT BOY BLUE, BLUEBEARD AND YOUR EX-HUSBAND QUICKLY TOOK CONTROL.

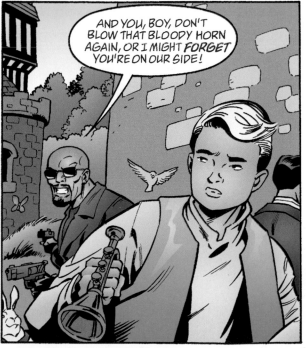

AND YOU, BOY, DON'T BLOW THAT BLOODY HORN AGAIN, OR I MIGHT **FORGET** YOU'RE ON OUR SIDE!

"I UNDERSTAND EVEN BOY BLUE'S **MONKEY** WAS OF SOME HELP, ALTHOUGH I CAN'T IMAGINE HOW."

HEAVE TO, CHICKEN LITTLE! YOU CAN'T ESCAPE OUR SWIFT, SURE **JUSTICE!**

BUT I'M **INNOCENT!** I WAS **FRAMED!** MY HEART WAS **ALWAYS** WITH YOU GUYS! **HONEST!**

"ONCE A SEMBLANCE OF ORDER WAS RESTORED, THE LOYAL FABLES WERE FANNED OUT ON A SEARCH FOR GOLDILOCKS.

DO YOU REALLY THINK THERE'S A CHANCE SHE'S *STILL* NEARBY?

SHE'S HAD MORE THAN AN *HOUR* TO MAKE HER GETAWAY.

"THEY FOUND HER WEAPON WHERE SHE'D ABANDONED IT, BUT BY THEN SHE WAS LONG GONE.

SHE CAN'T HIDE FROM US FOREVER. WHERE CAN SHE *GO?*

CERTAINLY NOT BACK TO THE HOMELANDS. I HEAR THE ADVERSARY WANTS HER DEAD AT *LEAST* AS MUCH AS WE DO.

"AND LOSING GOLDILOCKS WAS THE *LEAST* OF THEIR PROBLEMS.

"THEY STILL HAD TO WORK OUT WHAT TO DO WITH THE TREASON-OUS FABLES, AND WHAT TO DO WITH A WAKENED DRAGON AND THREE GIANTS."

I'M HUNGRY.

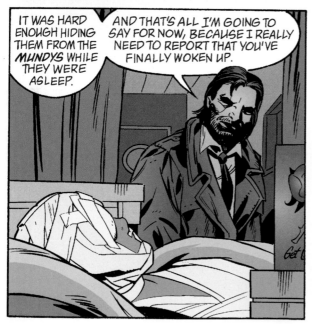

IT WAS HARD ENOUGH HIDING THEM FROM THE *MUNDYS* WHILE THEY WERE ASLEEP.

AND THAT'S ALL I'M GOING TO SAY FOR NOW, BECAUSE I REALLY NEED TO REPORT THAT YOU'VE FINALLY WOKEN UP.

AND I SUSPECT YOU NEED SOME *NON-COMA* REST.

KNIGHTS OF MALTA
HOSPITAL

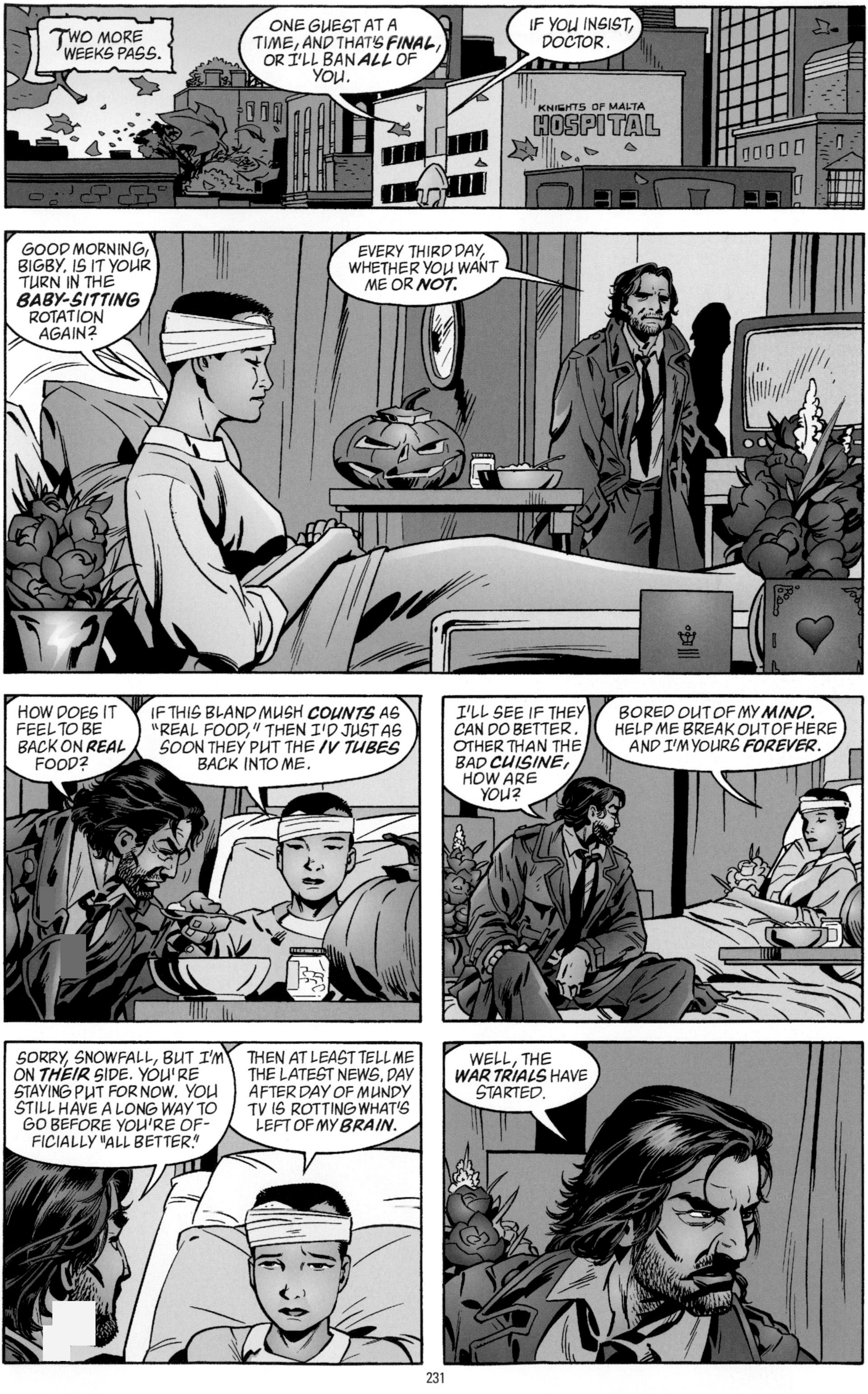
TWO MORE WEEKS PASS.
ONE GUEST AT A TIME, AND THAT'S FINAL, OR I'LL BAN ALL OF YOU.
IF YOU INSIST, DOCTOR.
KNIGHTS OF MALTA HOSPITAL
GOOD MORNING, BIGBY. IS IT YOUR TURN IN THE BABY-SITTING ROTATION AGAIN?
EVERY THIRD DAY, WHETHER YOU WANT ME OR NOT.
HOW DOES IT FEEL TO BE BACK ON REAL FOOD?
IF THIS BLAND MUSH COUNTS AS "REAL FOOD," THEN I'D JUST AS SOON THEY PUT THE IV TUBES BACK INTO ME.
I'LL SEE IF THEY CAN DO BETTER. OTHER THAN THE BAD CUISINE, HOW ARE YOU?
BORED OUT OF MY MIND. HELP ME BREAK OUT OF HERE AND I'M YOURS FOREVER.
SORRY, SNOWFALL, BUT I'M ON THEIR SIDE. YOU'RE STAYING PUT FOR NOW. YOU STILL HAVE A LONG WAY TO GO BEFORE YOU'RE OFFICIALLY "ALL BETTER."
THEN AT LEAST TELL ME THE LATEST NEWS. DAY AFTER DAY OF MUNDY TV IS ROTTING WHAT'S LEFT OF MY BRAIN.
WELL, THE WAR TRIALS HAVE STARTED.

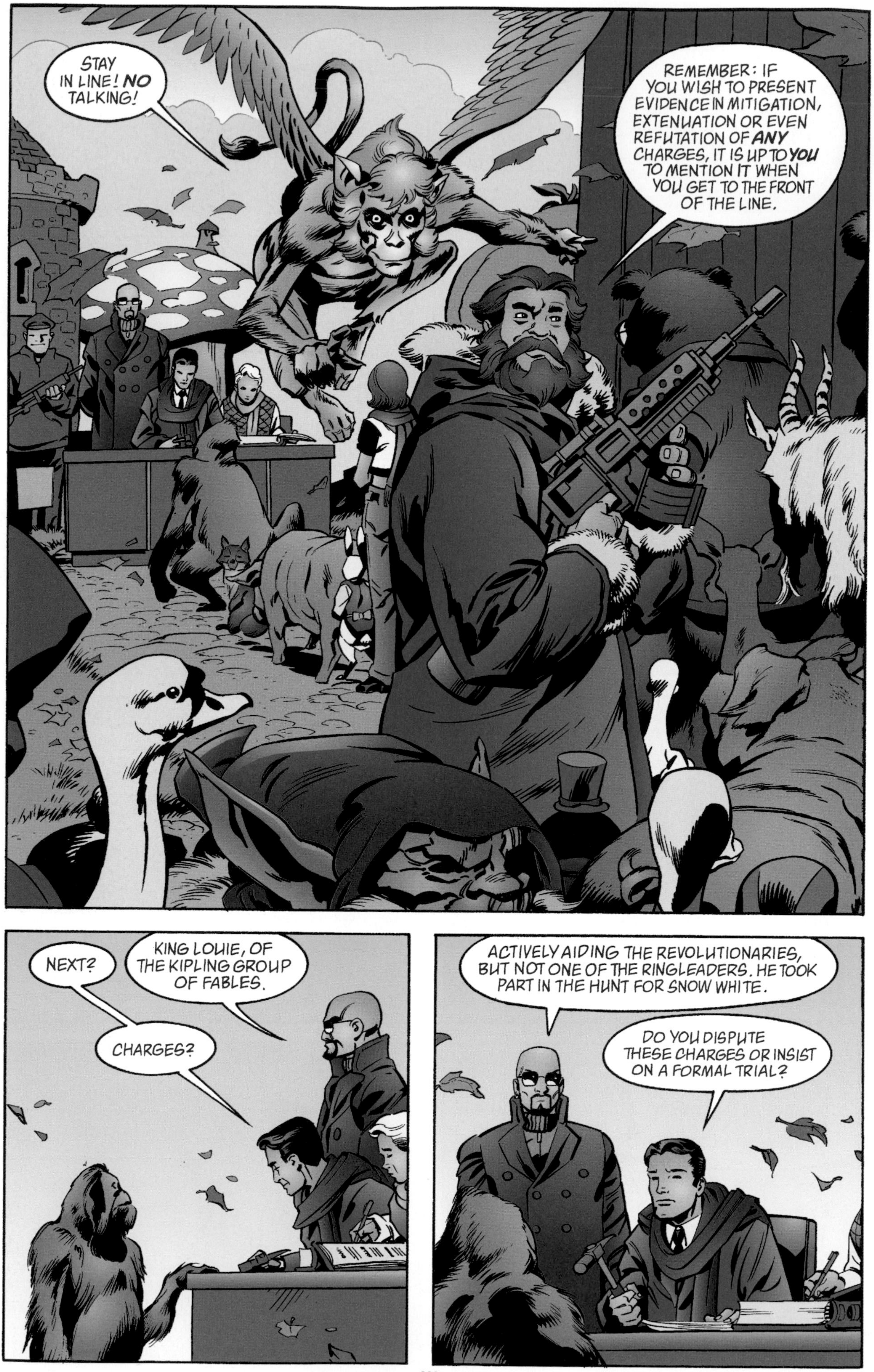
STAY IN LINE! NO TALKING!
REMEMBER: IF YOU WISH TO PRESENT EVIDENCE IN MITIGATION, EXTENUATION OR EVEN REFUTATION OF ANY CHARGES, IT IS UP TO YOU TO MENTION IT WHEN YOU GET TO THE FRONT OF THE LINE.
NEXT?
KING LOUIE, OF THE KIPLING GROUP OF FABLES.
CHARGES?
ACTIVELY AIDING THE REVOLUTIONARIES, BUT NOT ONE OF THE RINGLEADERS. HE TOOK PART IN THE HUNT FOR SNOW WHITE.
DO YOU DISPUTE THESE CHARGES OR INSIST ON A FORMAL TRIAL?

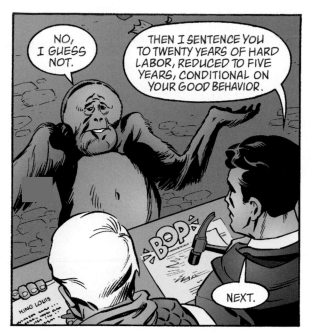

NO, I GUESS NOT.

THEN I SENTENCE YOU TO TWENTY YEARS OF HARD LABOR, REDUCED TO FIVE YEARS, CONDITIONAL ON YOUR GOOD BEHAVIOR.

BOP

KING LOUIS...

NEXT.

REYNARD THE FOX. NO CHARGES. HE ACTIVELY RESISTED THE REVOLUTIONARIES AND THEREBY SAVED SNOW WHITE'S LIFE.

FOR WHICH THE FABLE COMMUNITY OWES YOU A DEBT OF GRATITUDE.

I HOPE YOU'LL FORGIVE US FOR PUTTING OFF ANY FORMAL RECOGNITION OF YOUR INSPIRATIONAL ACTS OF HEROISM FOR ANOTHER OCCASION.

NO PROBLEM. GLAD TO HELP.

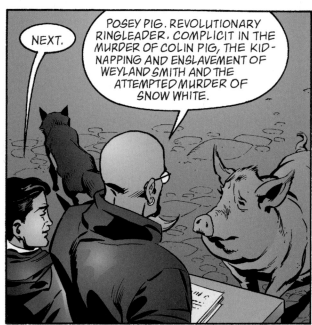

NEXT.

POSEY PIG. REVOLUTIONARY RINGLEADER. COMPLICIT IN THE MURDER OF COLIN PIG, THE KIDNAPPING AND ENSLAVEMENT OF WEYLAND SMITH AND THE ATTEMPTED MURDER OF SNOW WHITE.

IN MY OWN DEFENSE, I'D LIKE TO SAY THAT--

SAVE IT FOR LATER.

POSEY PIG IS ORDERED HELD OVER FOR FORMAL TRIBUNAL IN CONTEMPLATION OF CAPITAL PUNISHMENT.

BOP

TAKE THE PIG INTO CUSTODY.

NEXT.

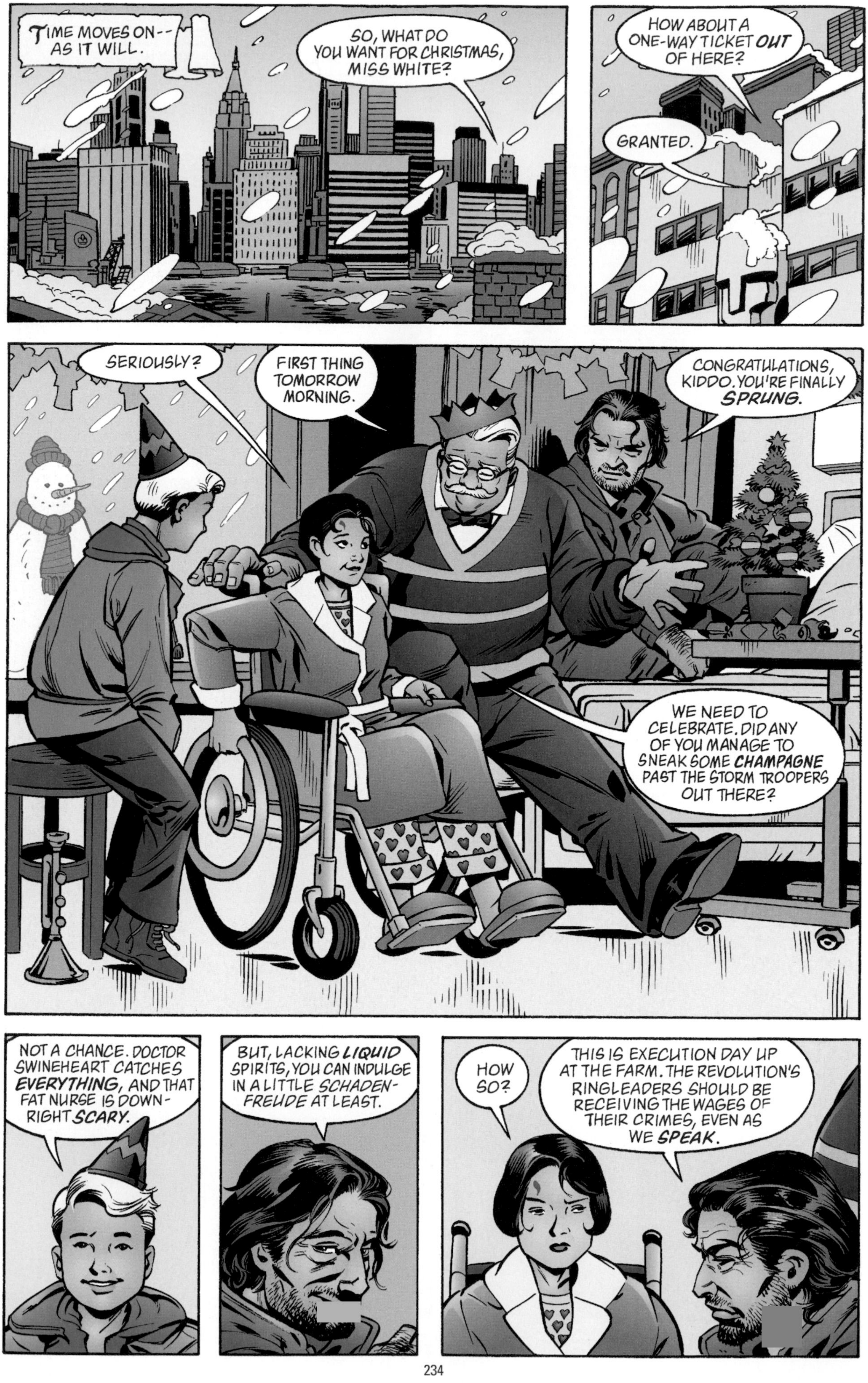
TIME MOVES ON-- AS IT WILL.
SO, WHAT DO YOU WANT FOR CHRISTMAS, MISS WHITE?
HOW ABOUT A ONE-WAY TICKET OUT OF HERE?
GRANTED.
SERIOUSLY?
FIRST THING TOMORROW MORNING.
CONGRATULATIONS, KIDDO. YOU'RE FINALLY SPRUNG.
WE NEED TO CELEBRATE. DID ANY OF YOU MANAGE TO SNEAK SOME CHAMPAGNE PAST THE STORM TROOPERS OUT THERE?
NOT A CHANCE. DOCTOR SWINEHEART CATCHES EVERYTHING, AND THAT FAT NURSE IS DOWN-RIGHT SCARY.
BUT, LACKING LIQUID SPIRITS, YOU CAN INDULGE IN A LITTLE SCHADEN-FREUDE AT LEAST.
HOW SO?
THIS IS EXECUTION DAY UP AT THE FARM. THE REVOLUTION'S RINGLEADERS SHOULD BE RECEIVING THE WAGES OF THEIR CRIMES, EVEN AS WE SPEAK.

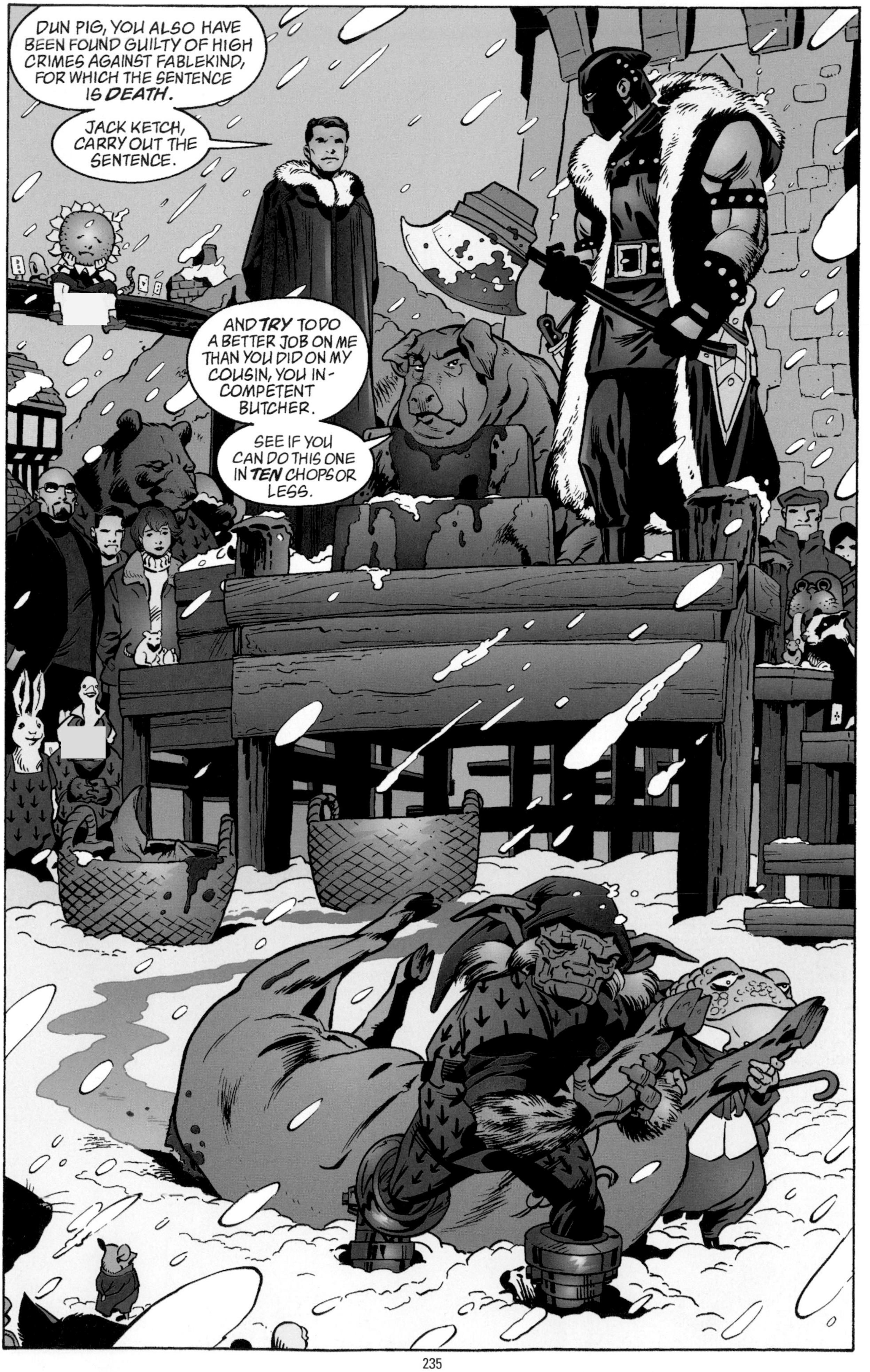
DUN PIG, YOU ALSO HAVE BEEN FOUND GUILTY OF HIGH CRIMES AGAINST FABLEKIND, FOR WHICH THE SENTENCE IS DEATH.
JACK KETCH, CARRY OUT THE SENTENCE.
AND TRY TO DO A BETTER JOB ON ME THAN YOU DID ON MY COUSIN, YOU INCOMPETENT BUTCHER.
SEE IF YOU CAN DO THIS ONE IN TEN CHOPS OR LESS.

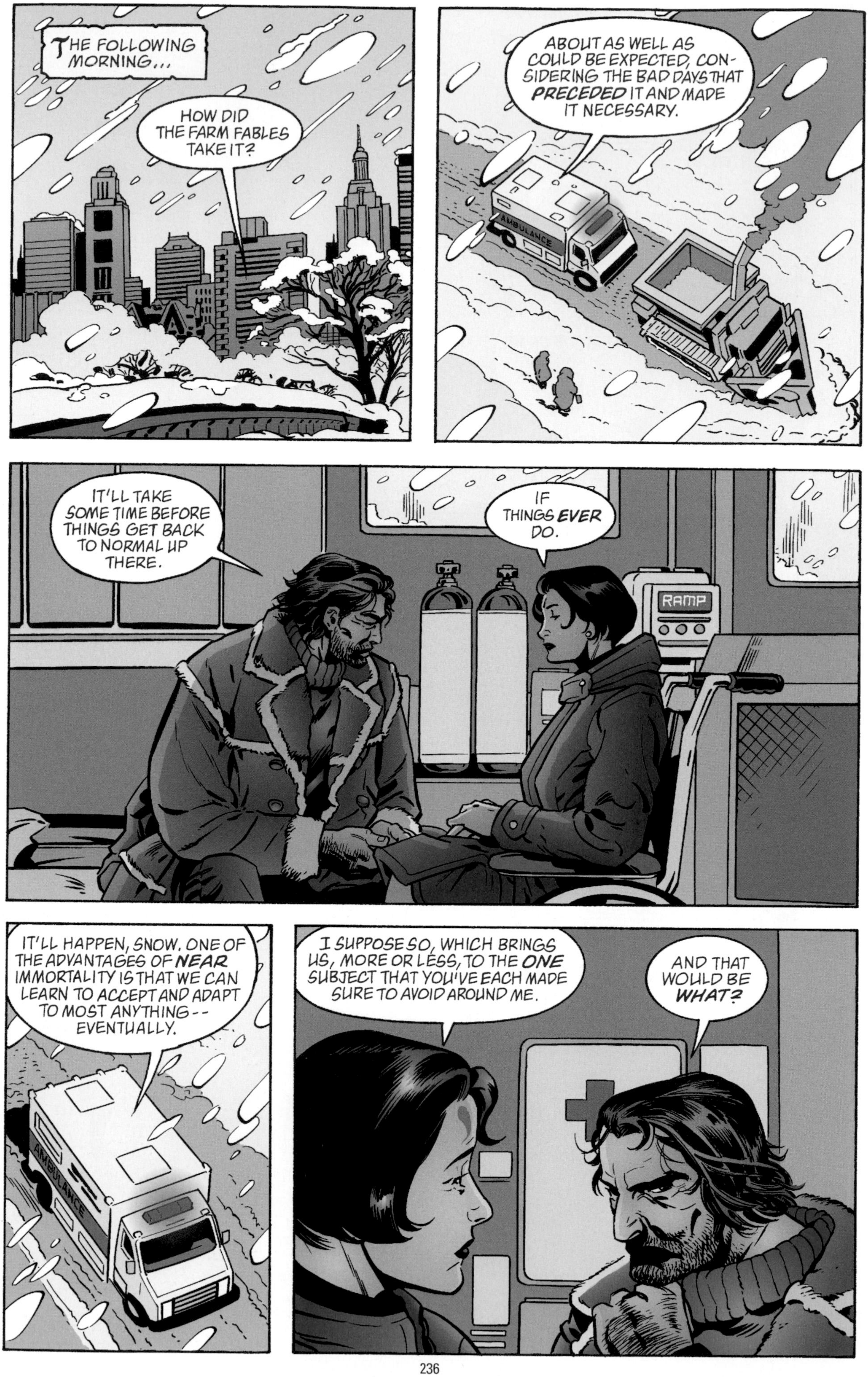
THE FOLLOWING MORNING...
HOW DID THE FARM FABLES TAKE IT?
ABOUT AS WELL AS COULD BE EXPECTED, CONSIDERING THE BAD DAYS THAT PRECEDED IT AND MADE IT NECESSARY.
AMBULANCE
IT'LL TAKE SOME TIME BEFORE THINGS GET BACK TO NORMAL UP THERE.
IF THINGS EVER DO.
RAMP
IT'LL HAPPEN, SNOW. ONE OF THE ADVANTAGES OF NEAR IMMORTALITY IS THAT WE CAN LEARN TO ACCEPT AND ADAPT TO MOST ANYTHING-- EVENTUALLY.
AMBULANCE
I SUPPOSE SO, WHICH BRINGS US, MORE OR LESS, TO THE ONE SUBJECT THAT YOU'VE EACH MADE SURE TO AVOID AROUND ME.
AND THAT WOULD BE WHAT?

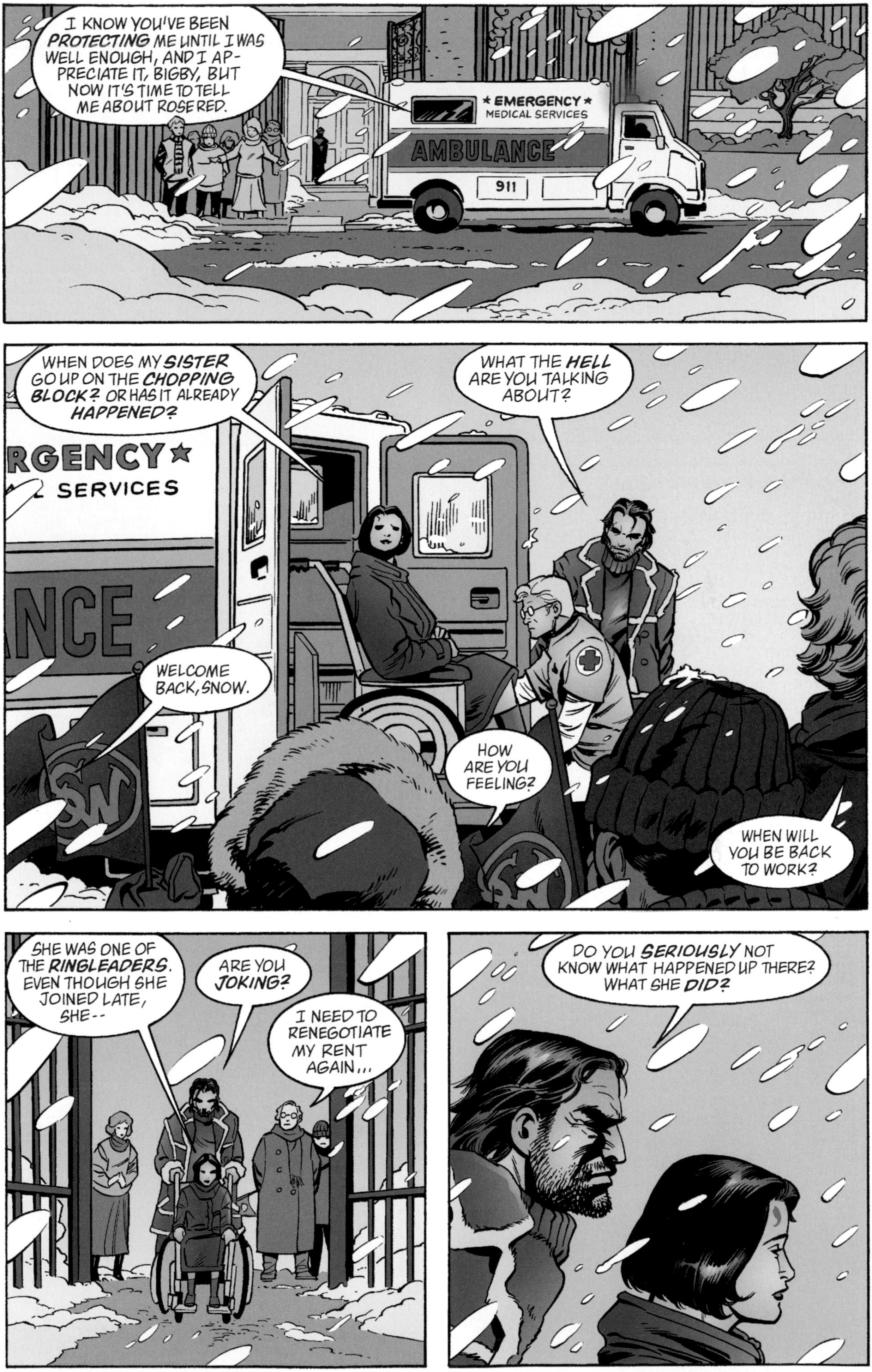
I KNOW YOU'VE BEEN PROTECTING ME UNTIL I WAS WELL ENOUGH, AND I APPRECIATE IT, BIGBY, BUT NOW IT'S TIME TO TELL ME ABOUT ROSE RED.
★ EMERGENCY ★
MEDICAL SERVICES
AMBULANCE
911
WHEN DOES MY SISTER GO UP ON THE CHOPPING BLOCK? OR HAS IT ALREADY HAPPENED?
WHAT THE HELL ARE YOU TALKING ABOUT?
RGENCY★
SERVICES
NCE
WELCOME BACK, SNOW.
HOW ARE YOU FEELING?
WHEN WILL YOU BE BACK TO WORK?
SHE WAS ONE OF THE RINGLEADERS. EVEN THOUGH SHE JOINED LATE, SHE--
ARE YOU JOKING?
I NEED TO RENEGOTIATE MY RENT AGAIN...
DO YOU SERIOUSLY NOT KNOW WHAT HAPPENED UP THERE? WHAT SHE DID?

I THOUGHT SO. SHE MADE IT PRETTY **CLEAR** TO ME AT THE TIME. WHAT DO YOU THINK NEEDS FURTHER EXPLANATION?

WELCOME **HOME**, MISS WHITE. WE MISSED YOU **DEARLY** THESE PAST MONTHS.

ARE YOU COMPLETELY **UNAWARE** THAT SHE SAVED YOUR LIFE?

EXCUSE ME?

IT ALL CAME OUT AT HER HEARING.

THE REVOLUTIONARIES HAD JUST KILLED COLIN AND AFTER CUTTING YOU **ENTIRELY** OFF FROM OUTSIDE CONTACT, IT WAS OBVIOUS TO HER --IF NOT **YOU**-- THAT THE TWO OF YOU WERE NEXT.

IT WAS UNLIKELY YOU'D SURVIVE THE **NIGHT**, IN FACT.

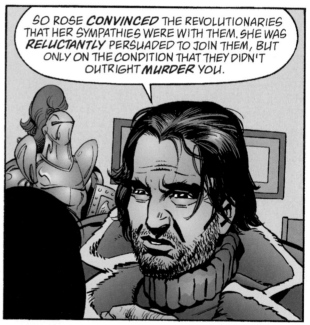

SO ROSE **CONVINCED** THE REVOLUTIONARIES THAT HER SYMPATHIES WERE WITH THEM. SHE WAS **RELUCTANTLY** PERSUADED TO JOIN THEM, BUT ONLY ON THE CONDITION THAT THEY DIDN'T OUTRIGHT **MURDER** YOU.

YEAH, OKAY, SHE SAID **SOMETHING** LIKE THAT, AT ONE POINT, BUT I THOUGHT--

SHE BOUGHT **ENOUGH** TIME FOR ONE OF YOU TO FIGURE A WAY OUT OF YOUR PREDICAMENT--WHICH **YOU** EVENTUALLY DID.

GOD STRIKE ME DOWN FOR A **FOOL**, BIGBY. I NEVER **REALIZED** --

238

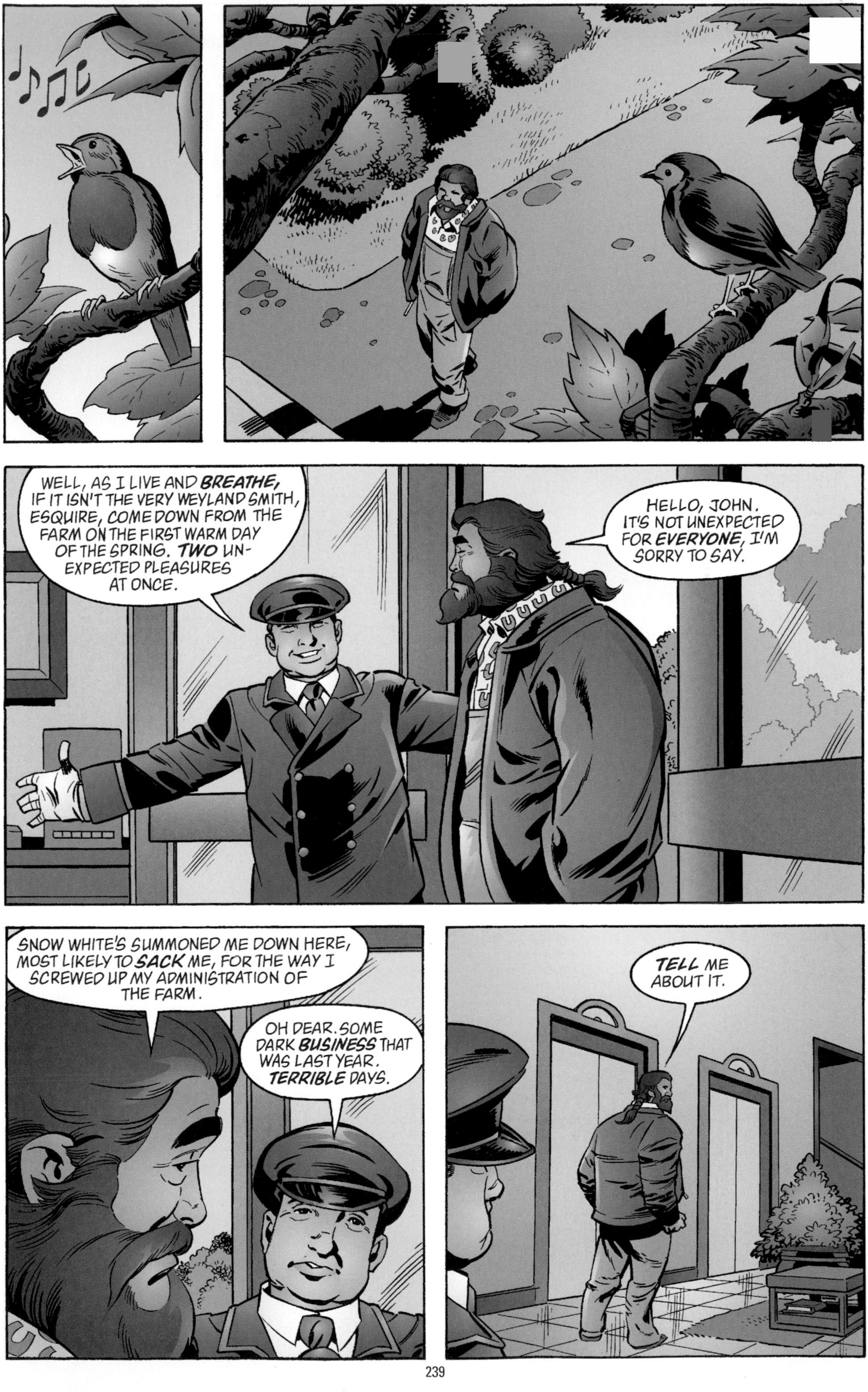
WELL, AS I LIVE AND BREATHE, IF IT ISN'T THE VERY WEYLAND SMITH, ESQUIRE, COME DOWN FROM THE FARM ON THE FIRST WARM DAY OF THE SPRING. TWO UN-EXPECTED PLEASURES AT ONCE.
HELLO, JOHN. IT'S NOT UNEXPECTED FOR EVERYONE, I'M SORRY TO SAY.
SNOW WHITE'S SUMMONED ME DOWN HERE, MOST LIKELY TO SACK ME, FOR THE WAY I SCREWED UP MY ADMINISTRATION OF THE FARM.
OH DEAR. SOME DARK BUSINESS THAT WAS LAST YEAR. TERRIBLE DAYS.
TELL ME ABOUT IT.

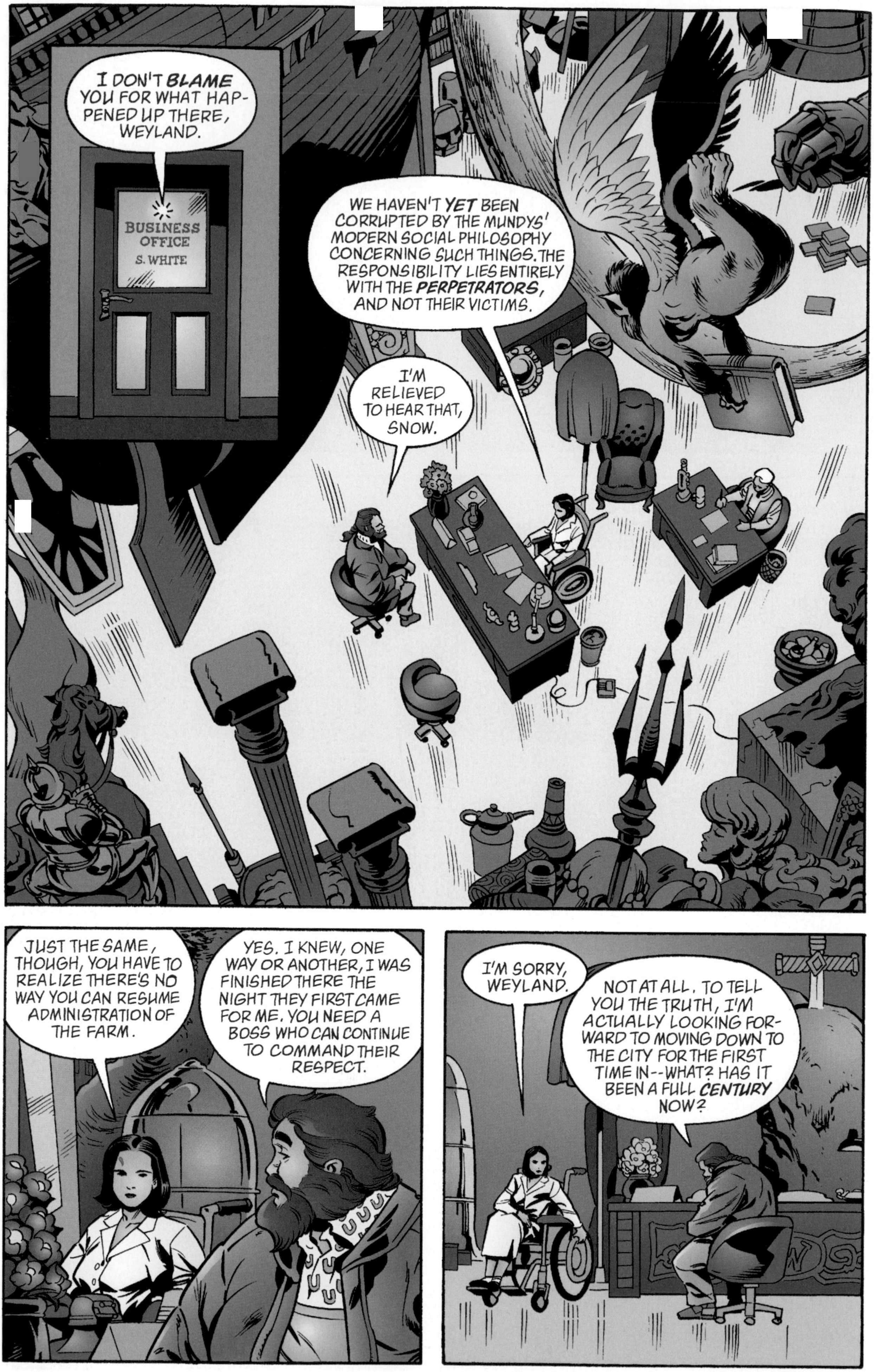

I DON'T BLAME YOU FOR WHAT HAPPENED UP THERE, WEYLAND.
BUSINESS OFFICE
S. WHITE
WE HAVEN'T YET BEEN CORRUPTED BY THE MUNDYS' MODERN SOCIAL PHILOSOPHY CONCERNING SUCH THINGS. THE RESPONSIBILITY LIES ENTIRELY WITH THE PERPETRATORS, AND NOT THEIR VICTIMS.
I'M RELIEVED TO HEAR THAT, SNOW.
JUST THE SAME, THOUGH, YOU HAVE TO REALIZE THERE'S NO WAY YOU CAN RESUME ADMINISTRATION OF THE FARM.
YES. I KNEW, ONE WAY OR ANOTHER, I WAS FINISHED THERE THE NIGHT THEY FIRST CAME FOR ME. YOU NEED A BOSS WHO CAN CONTINUE TO COMMAND THEIR RESPECT.
I'M SORRY, WEYLAND.
NOT AT ALL. TO TELL YOU THE TRUTH, I'M ACTUALLY LOOKING FORWARD TO MOVING DOWN TO THE CITY FOR THE FIRST TIME IN--WHAT? HAS IT BEEN A FULL CENTURY NOW?

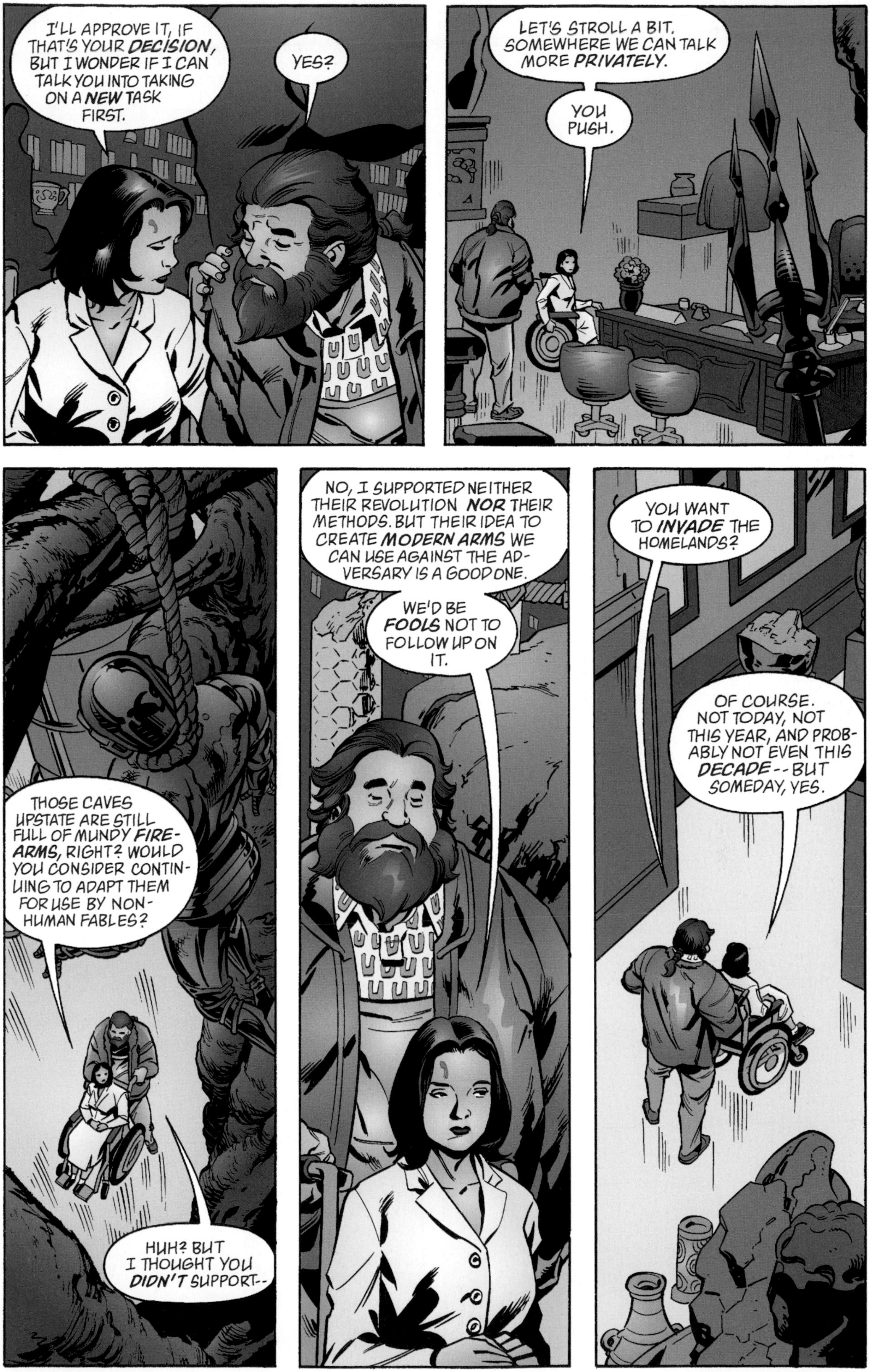
I'LL APPROVE IT, IF THAT'S YOUR DECISION, BUT I WONDER IF I CAN TALK YOU INTO TAKING ON A NEW TASK FIRST.
YES?
LET'S STROLL A BIT. SOMEWHERE WE CAN TALK MORE PRIVATELY.
YOU PUSH.
THOSE CAVES UPSTATE ARE STILL FULL OF MUNDY FIRE-ARMS, RIGHT? WOULD YOU CONSIDER CONTIN-UING TO ADAPT THEM FOR USE BY NON-HUMAN FABLES?
HUH? BUT I THOUGHT YOU DIDN'T SUPPORT--
NO, I SUPPORTED NEITHER THEIR REVOLUTION NOR THEIR METHODS. BUT THEIR IDEA TO CREATE MODERN ARMS WE CAN USE AGAINST THE AD-VERSARY IS A GOOD ONE.
WE'D BE FOOLS NOT TO FOLLOW UP ON IT.
YOU WANT TO INVADE THE HOMELANDS?
OF COURSE. NOT TODAY, NOT THIS YEAR, AND PROB-ABLY NOT EVEN THIS DECADE--BUT SOMEDAY, YES.

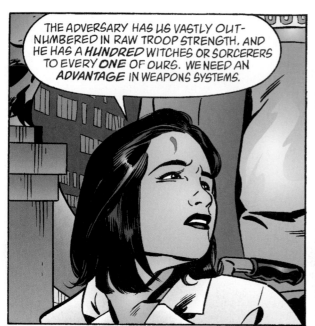

THE ADVERSARY HAS US VASTLY OUT-NUMBERED IN RAW TROOP STRENGTH. AND HE HAS A *HUNDRED* WITCHES OR SORCERERS TO EVERY *ONE* OF OURS. WE NEED AN *ADVANTAGE* IN WEAPONS SYSTEMS.

SO, WILL YOU CONTINUE PROVIDING IT TO US? ONLY NOT *CHAINED UP* THIS TIME, OF COURSE. YOU'D BE FREE TO WORK AT WHATEVER PACE SUITS YOU.

I'LL CONSIDER IT.

THANK YOU. LET'S GO THIS WAY.

IF YOU'LL PUT ME UP IN ONE OF THE WOOD-LAND'S GUEST ROOMS TONIGHT, WE CAN CONTINUE THIS TOMORROW.

IN THE MEANTIME, I'VE GOT A BIT OF A *SURPRISE* FOR YOU, THOUGH I HAVE NO CERTAINTY IF IT'S A GOOD ONE--OR OTHERWISE.

YES? WHAT IS IT?

ROSE RED RODE DOWN FROM THE FARM WITH ME. SHE'S BEEN DOING GREAT WORK UP THERE, BUT I THINK SHE'S FINALLY READY TO SEE YOU FACE-TO-FACE.

SHE'S WAITING OUT IN THE TRUCK, IN CASE YOU'RE NOT UP TO SEEING HER YET.

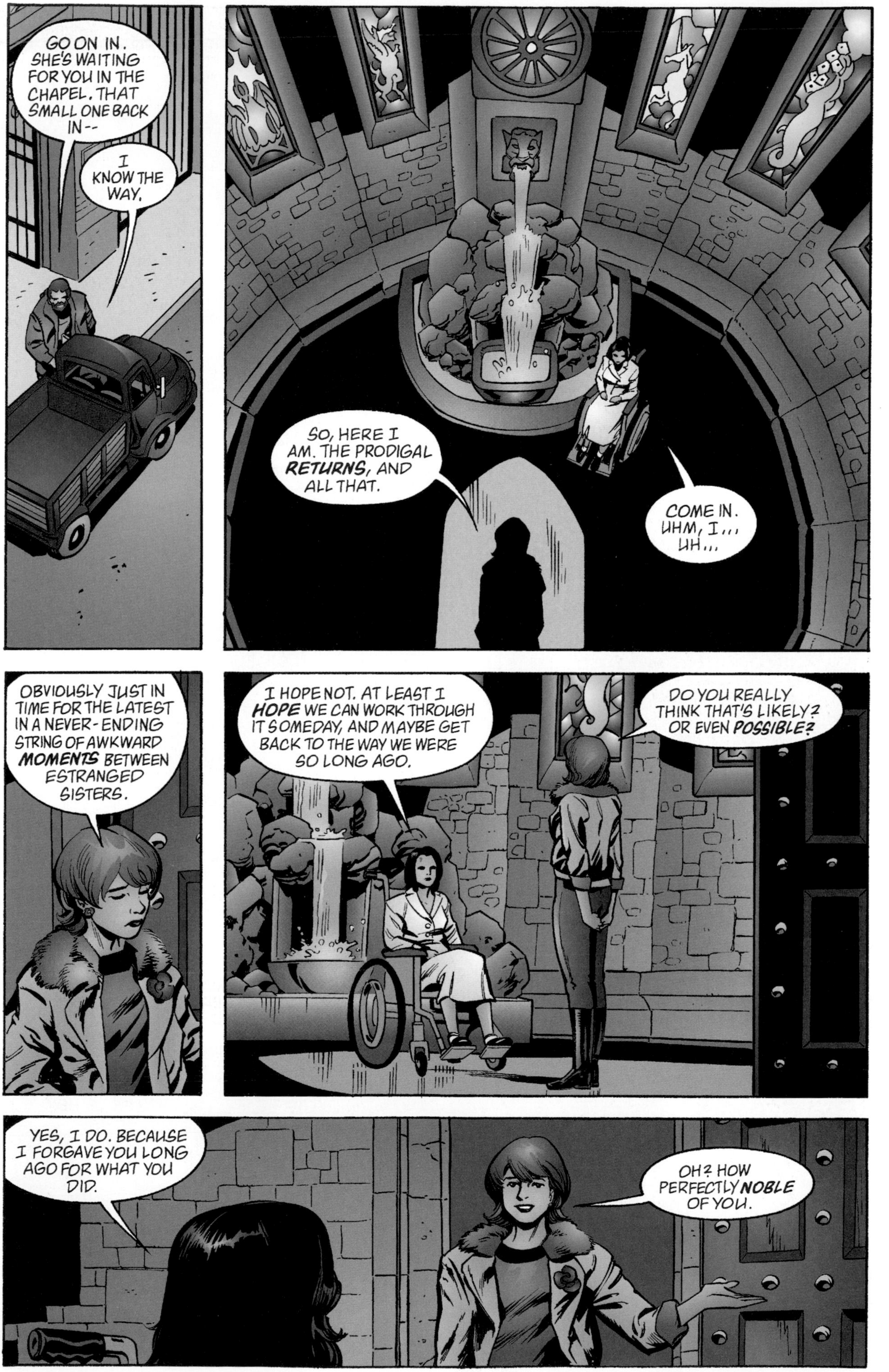
GO ON IN. SHE'S WAITING FOR YOU IN THE CHAPEL. THAT SMALL ONE BACK IN--
I KNOW THE WAY.
SO, HERE I AM. THE PRODIGAL RETURNS, AND ALL THAT.
COME IN. UHM, I... UH...
OBVIOUSLY JUST IN TIME FOR THE LATEST IN A NEVER-ENDING STRING OF AWKWARD MOMENTS BETWEEN ESTRANGED SISTERS.
I HOPE NOT. AT LEAST I HOPE WE CAN WORK THROUGH IT SOMEDAY, AND MAYBE GET BACK TO THE WAY WE WERE SO LONG AGO.
DO YOU REALLY THINK THAT'S LIKELY? OR EVEN POSSIBLE?
YES, I DO. BECAUSE I FORGAVE YOU LONG AGO FOR WHAT YOU DID.
OH? HOW PERFECTLY NOBLE OF YOU.

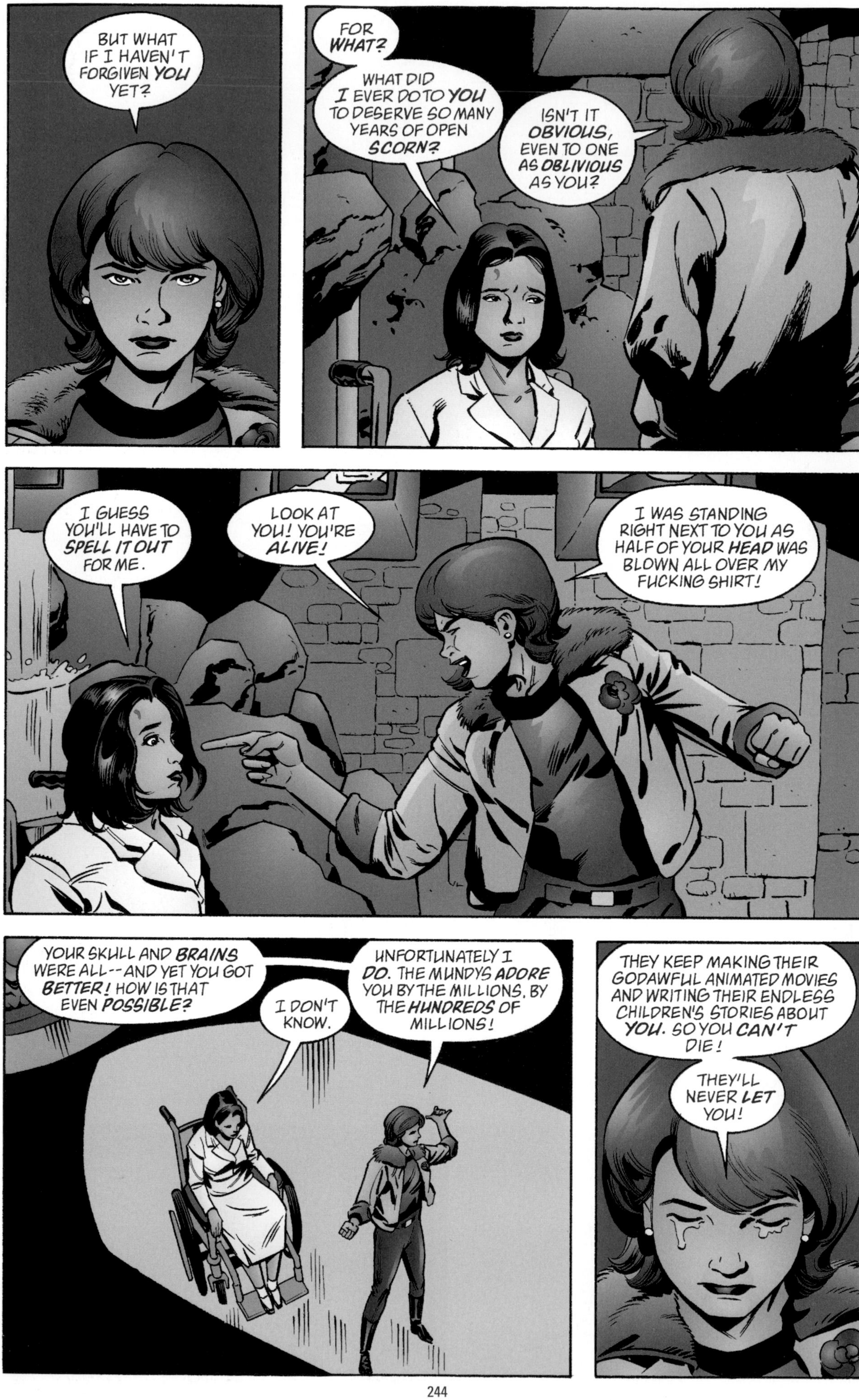
BUT WHAT IF I HAVEN'T FORGIVEN YOU YET?
FOR WHAT?
WHAT DID I EVER DO TO YOU TO DESERVE SO MANY YEARS OF OPEN SCORN?
ISN'T IT OBVIOUS, EVEN TO ONE AS OBLIVIOUS AS YOU?
I GUESS YOU'LL HAVE TO SPELL IT OUT FOR ME.
LOOK AT YOU! YOU'RE ALIVE!
I WAS STANDING RIGHT NEXT TO YOU AS HALF OF YOUR HEAD WAS BLOWN ALL OVER MY FUCKING SHIRT!
YOUR SKULL AND BRAINS WERE ALL--AND YET YOU GOT BETTER! HOW IS THAT EVEN POSSIBLE?
I DON'T KNOW.
UNFORTUNATELY I DO. THE MUNDYS ADORE YOU BY THE MILLIONS, BY THE HUNDREDS OF MILLIONS!
THEY KEEP MAKING THEIR GODAWFUL ANIMATED MOVIES AND WRITING THEIR ENDLESS CHILDREN'S STORIES ABOUT YOU. SO YOU CAN'T DIE!
THEY'LL NEVER LET YOU!

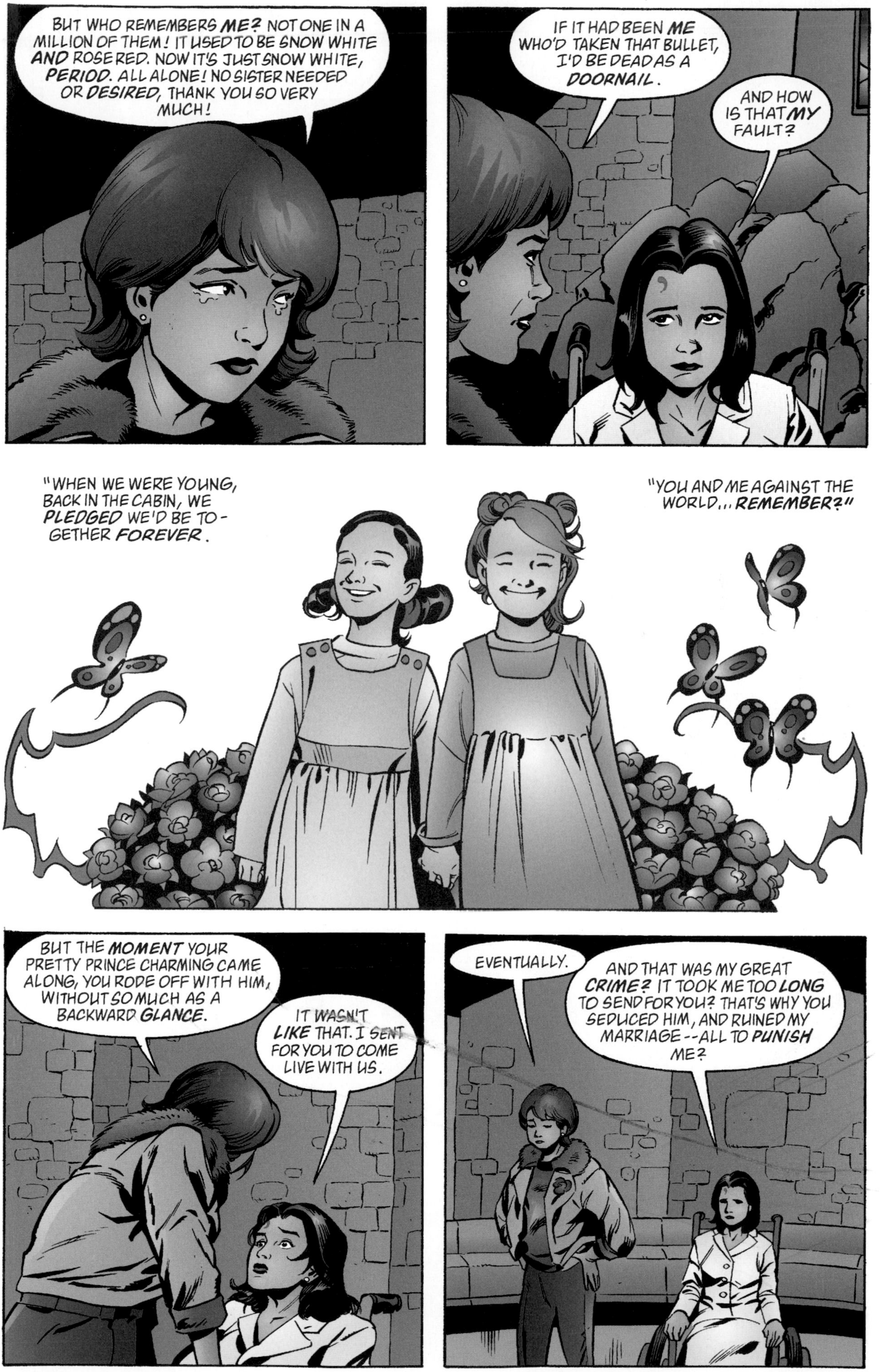

BUT WHO REMEMBERS ME? NOT ONE IN A MILLION OF THEM! IT USED TO BE SNOW WHITE AND ROSE RED. NOW IT'S JUST SNOW WHITE, PERIOD. ALL ALONE! NO SISTER NEEDED OR DESIRED, THANK YOU SO VERY MUCH!
IF IT HAD BEEN ME WHO'D TAKEN THAT BULLET, I'D BE DEAD AS A DOORNAIL.
AND HOW IS THAT MY FAULT?
"WHEN WE WERE YOUNG, BACK IN THE CABIN, WE PLEDGED WE'D BE TO-GETHER FOREVER.
"YOU AND ME AGAINST THE WORLD... REMEMBER?"
BUT THE MOMENT YOUR PRETTY PRINCE CHARMING CAME ALONG, YOU RODE OFF WITH HIM, WITHOUT SO MUCH AS A BACKWARD GLANCE.
IT WASN'T LIKE THAT. I SENT FOR YOU TO COME LIVE WITH US.
EVENTUALLY.
AND THAT WAS MY GREAT CRIME? IT TOOK ME TOO LONG TO SEND FOR YOU? THAT'S WHY YOU SEDUCED HIM, AND RUINED MY MARRIAGE--ALL TO PUNISH ME?

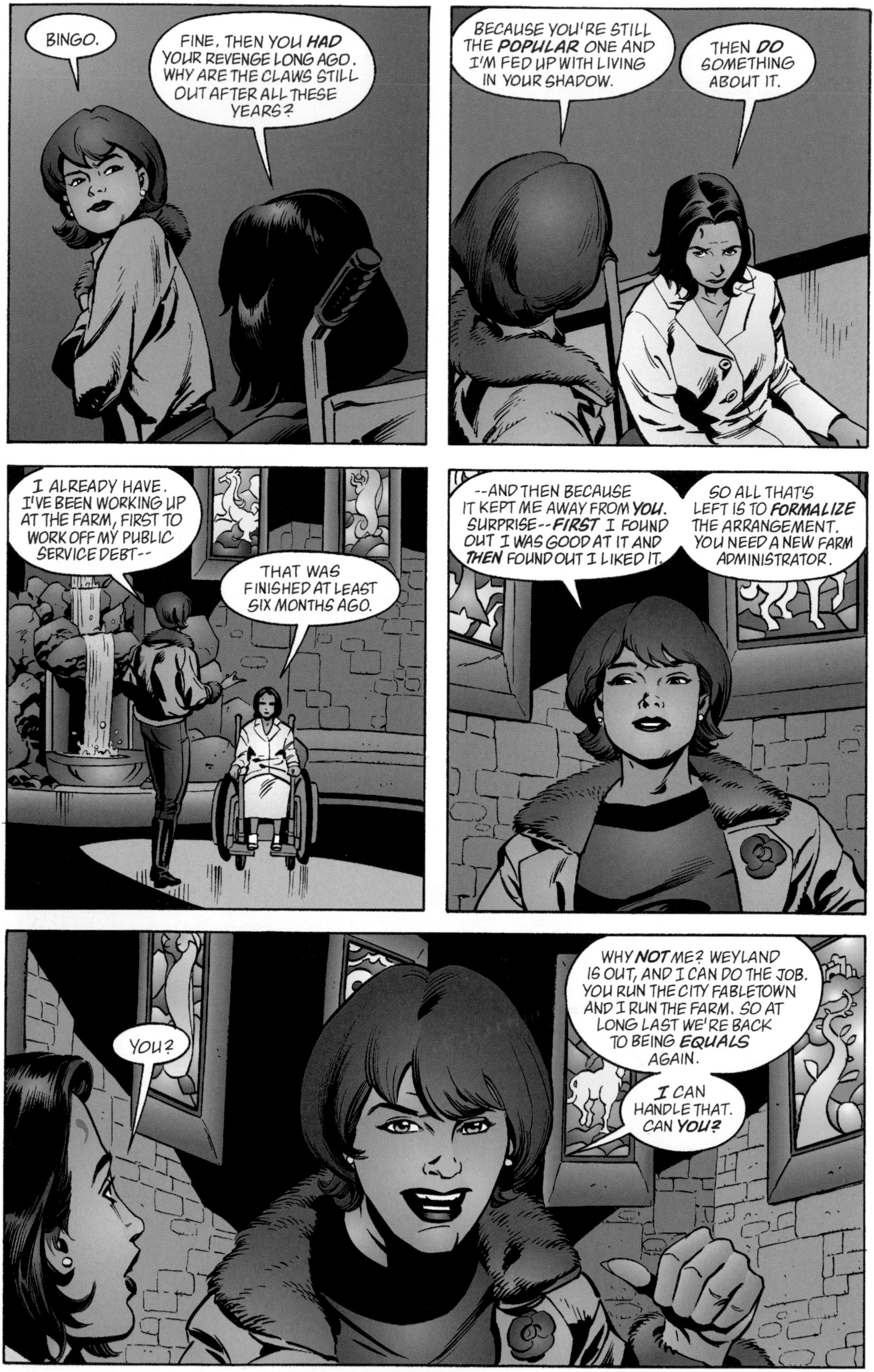
BINGO.
FINE. THEN YOU HAD YOUR REVENGE LONG AGO. WHY ARE THE CLAWS STILL OUT AFTER ALL THESE YEARS?
BECAUSE YOU'RE STILL THE POPULAR ONE AND I'M FED UP WITH LIVING IN YOUR SHADOW.
THEN DO SOMETHING ABOUT IT.
I ALREADY HAVE. I'VE BEEN WORKING UP AT THE FARM, FIRST TO WORK OFF MY PUBLIC SERVICE DEBT--
THAT WAS FINISHED AT LEAST SIX MONTHS AGO.
--AND THEN BECAUSE IT KEPT ME AWAY FROM YOU. SURPRISE--FIRST I FOUND OUT I WAS GOOD AT IT AND THEN FOUND OUT I LIKED IT.
SO ALL THAT'S LEFT IS TO FORMALIZE THE ARRANGEMENT. YOU NEED A NEW FARM ADMINISTRATOR.
YOU?
WHY NOT ME? WEYLAND IS OUT, AND I CAN DO THE JOB. YOU RUN THE CITY FABLETOWN AND I RUN THE FARM. SO AT LONG LAST WE'RE BACK TO BEING EQUALS AGAIN.
I CAN HANDLE THAT. CAN YOU?

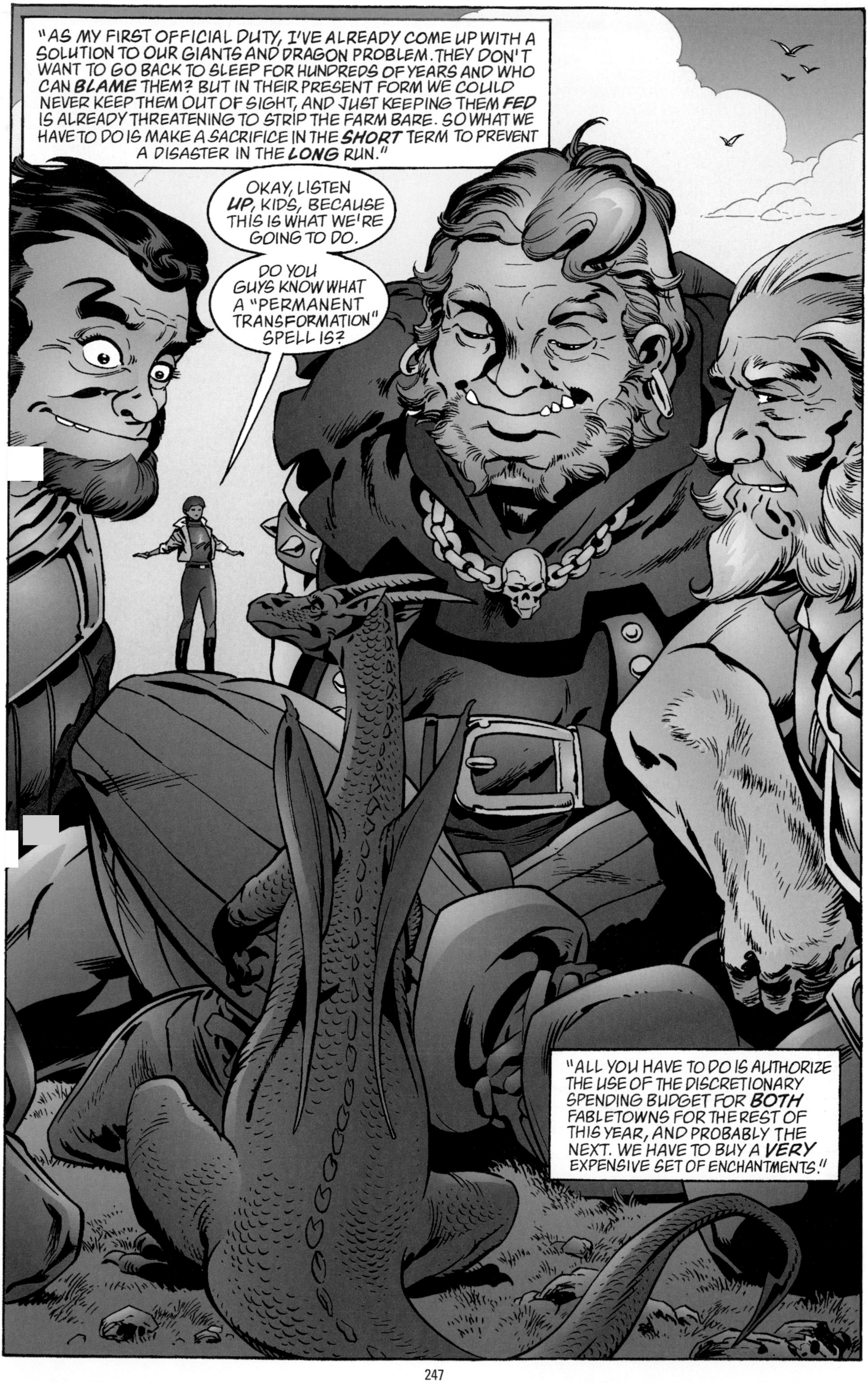
"AS MY FIRST OFFICIAL DUTY, I'VE ALREADY COME UP WITH A SOLUTION TO OUR GIANTS AND DRAGON PROBLEM. THEY DON'T WANT TO GO BACK TO SLEEP FOR HUNDREDS OF YEARS AND WHO CAN BLAME THEM? BUT IN THEIR PRESENT FORM WE COULD NEVER KEEP THEM OUT OF SIGHT, AND JUST KEEPING THEM FED IS ALREADY THREATENING TO STRIP THE FARM BARE. SO WHAT WE HAVE TO DO IS MAKE A SACRIFICE IN THE SHORT TERM TO PREVENT A DISASTER IN THE LONG RUN."
OKAY, LISTEN UP, KIDS, BECAUSE THIS IS WHAT WE'RE GOING TO DO.
DO YOU GUYS KNOW WHAT A "PERMANENT TRANSFORMATION" SPELL IS?
"ALL YOU HAVE TO DO IS AUTHORIZE THE USE OF THE DISCRETIONARY SPENDING BUDGET FOR BOTH FABLETOWNS FOR THE REST OF THIS YEAR, AND PROBABLY THE NEXT. WE HAVE TO BUY A VERY EXPENSIVE SET OF ENCHANTMENTS."

AND SOON ENOUGH...

LADIES AND GENTLEMEN-- IMPORTANT VISITING *INDIGNITARIES*-- SINCE THE ORIGINALS ARE *DEAD*, MEET THE "THREE LITTLE PIGS" PART *TWO.*

JOHNNY, DONNY AND LONNY: FORMERLY GIANTS OF RENOWN.

SO WHERE'S OUR NEW COTTAGE?

WONDERFUL.

YOU DID IT.

WELL DONE, ROSE.

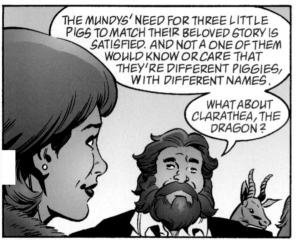

THE MUNDYS' NEED FOR THREE LITTLE PIGS TO MATCH THEIR BELOVED *STORY* IS SATISFIED. AND NOT A ONE OF THEM WOULD KNOW OR CARE THAT THEY'RE DIFFERENT PIGGIES, WITH DIFFERENT NAMES.

WHAT ABOUT CLARATHEA, THE DRAGON?

CLARA IS NOW MY NEW *BEST FRIEND* AND ENFORCER.

ENFORCER? HOW?

SHOW THEM, SWEETIE.

WE DECIDED TO HOLD ONTO ONE OF HER MORE *ADVANTAGEOUS* DRAGON QUALITIES. NO MORE REVOLUTIONS HERE.

WHOOOSH!

CHARMING.

And later, as soon as she could politely slip away-- when she could hold them back no longer--Snow White removed herself to a quiet, private place and let the tears out. She cried for all the killing and terror of the past year at the Farm. And she cried for the sister she had lost for so many years and, perhaps, found again. But most of all she cried for the loss of a true wise friend called Colin Piggy.

Treasures from the Woodland Vaults

Below: Cover art by Alex Maleev for the variant edition of FABLES #1.

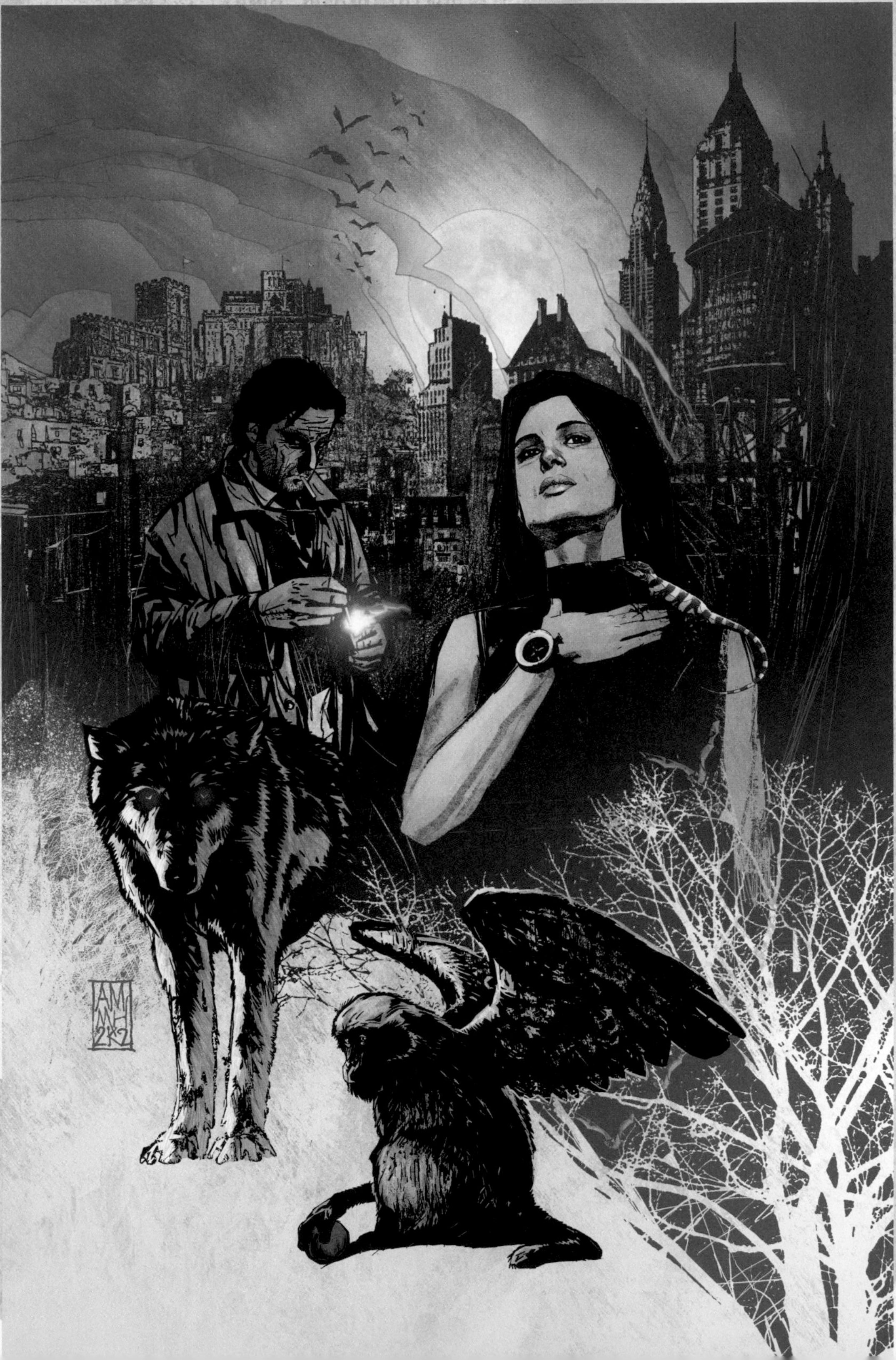

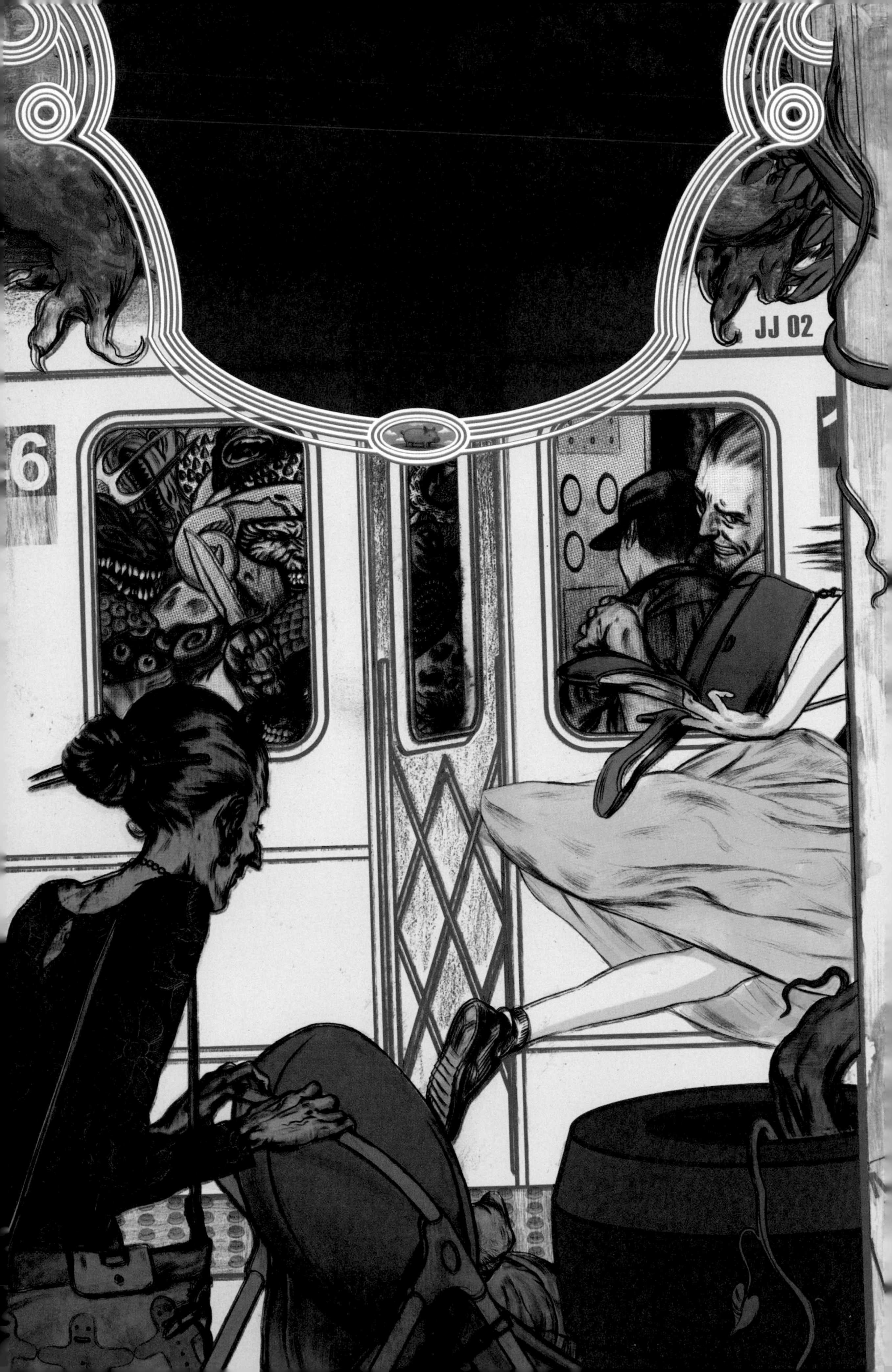

JJ 02
6

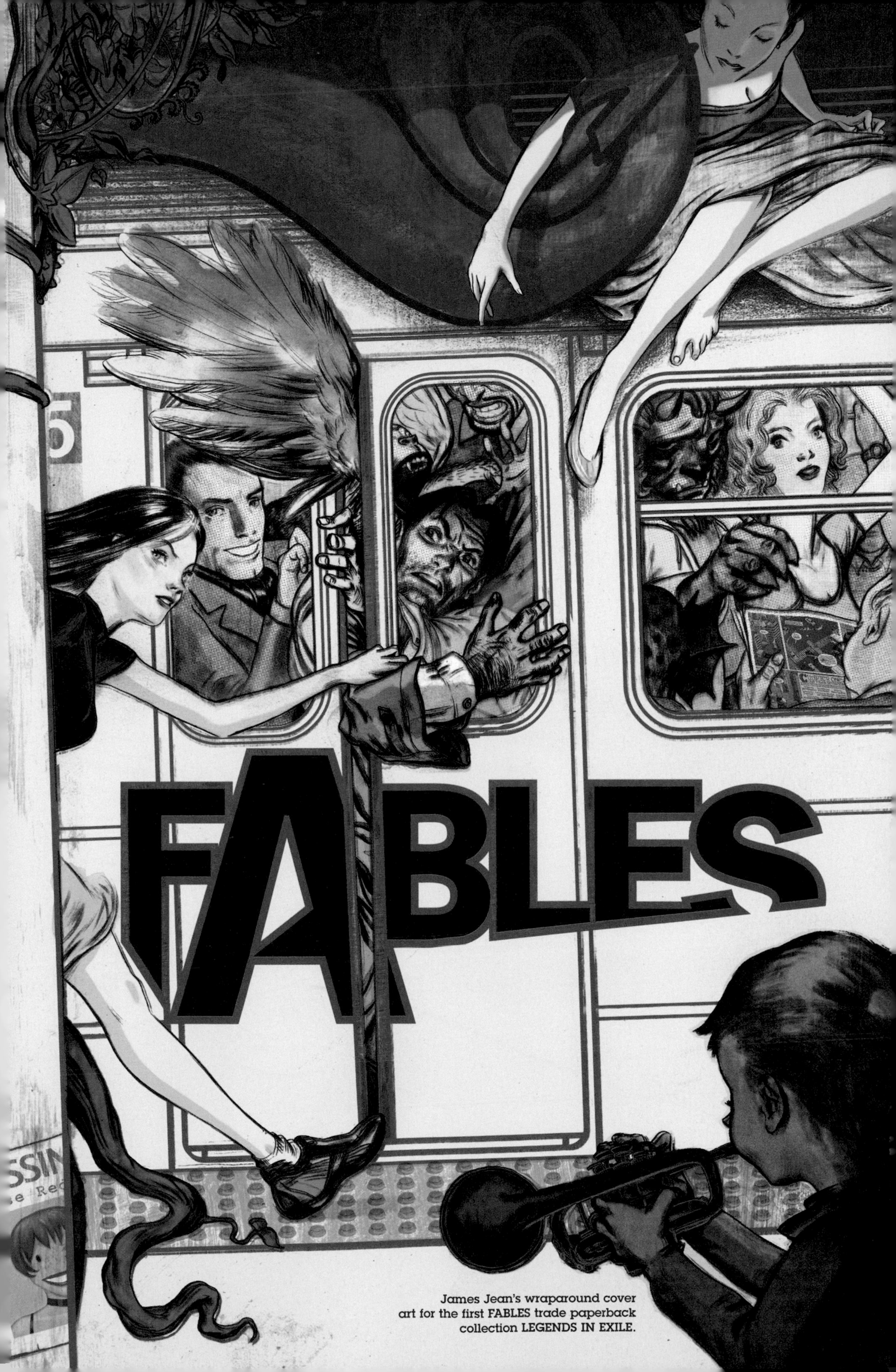
FABLES

James Jean's wraparound cover
art for the first FABLES trade paperback
collection LEGENDS IN EXILE.

Bigby Wolf

Bill Willingham's original character designs for the FABLES cast.

Bluebeard

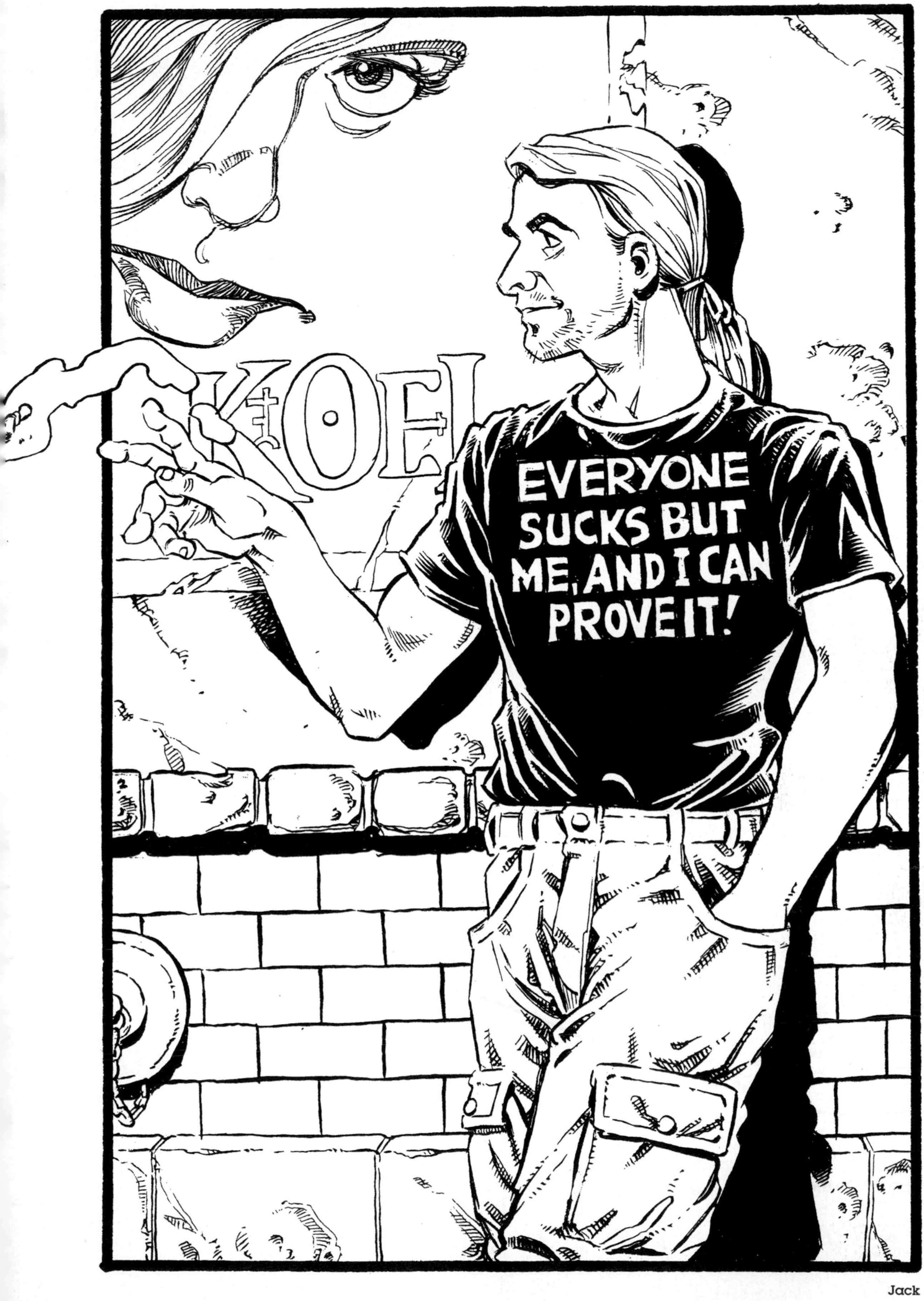

EVERYONE SUCKS BUT ME, AND I CAN PROVE IT!

Jack

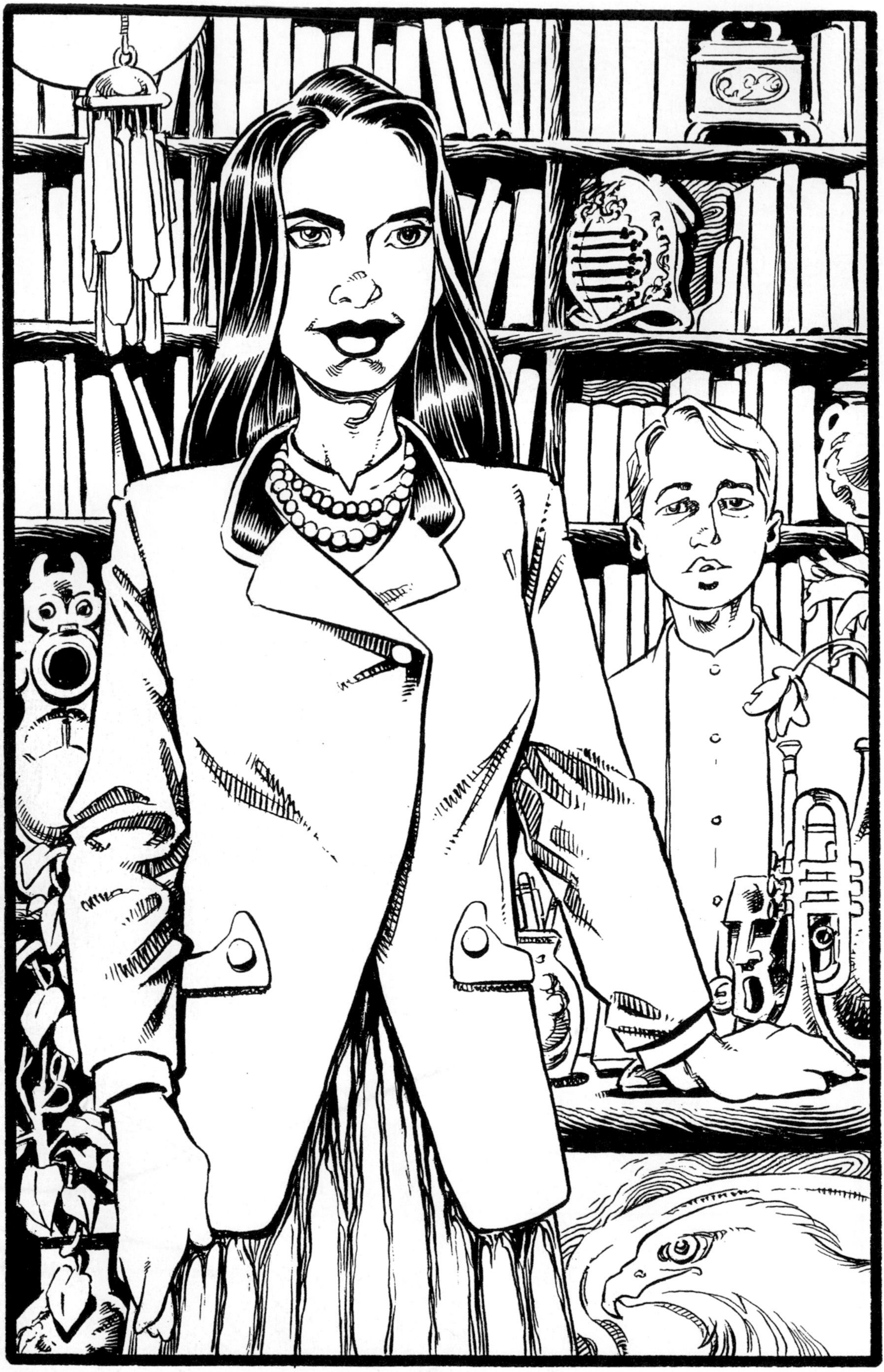

Snow White and Little Boy Blue

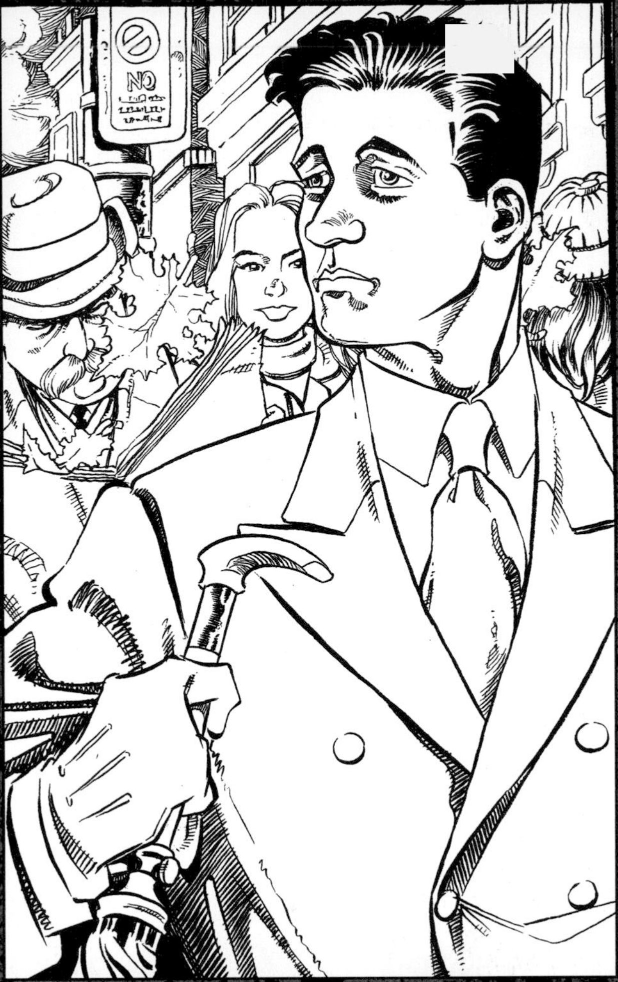
NO

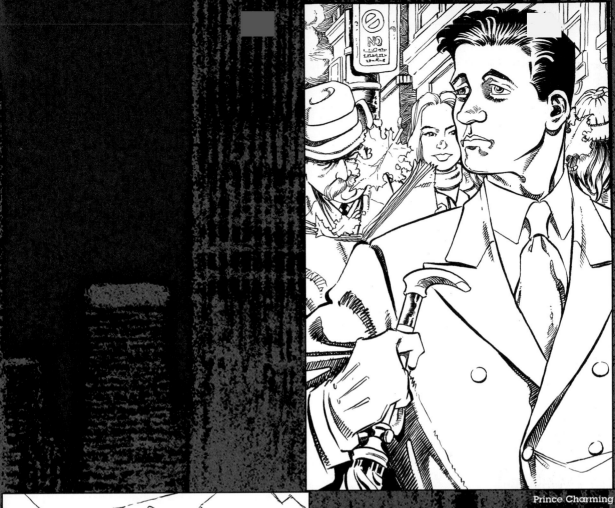

Prince Charming

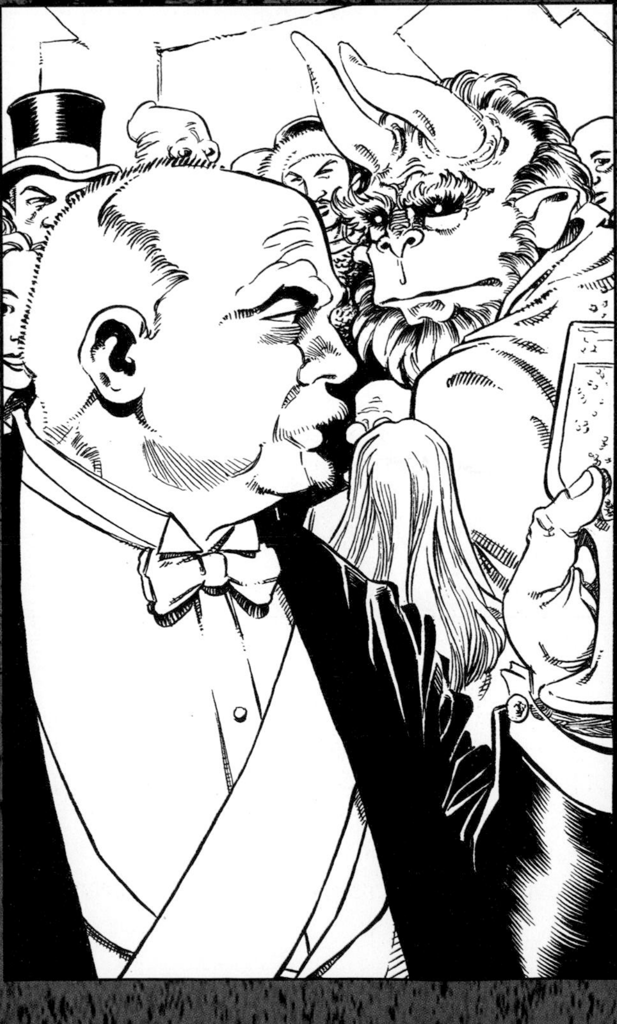

King Cole

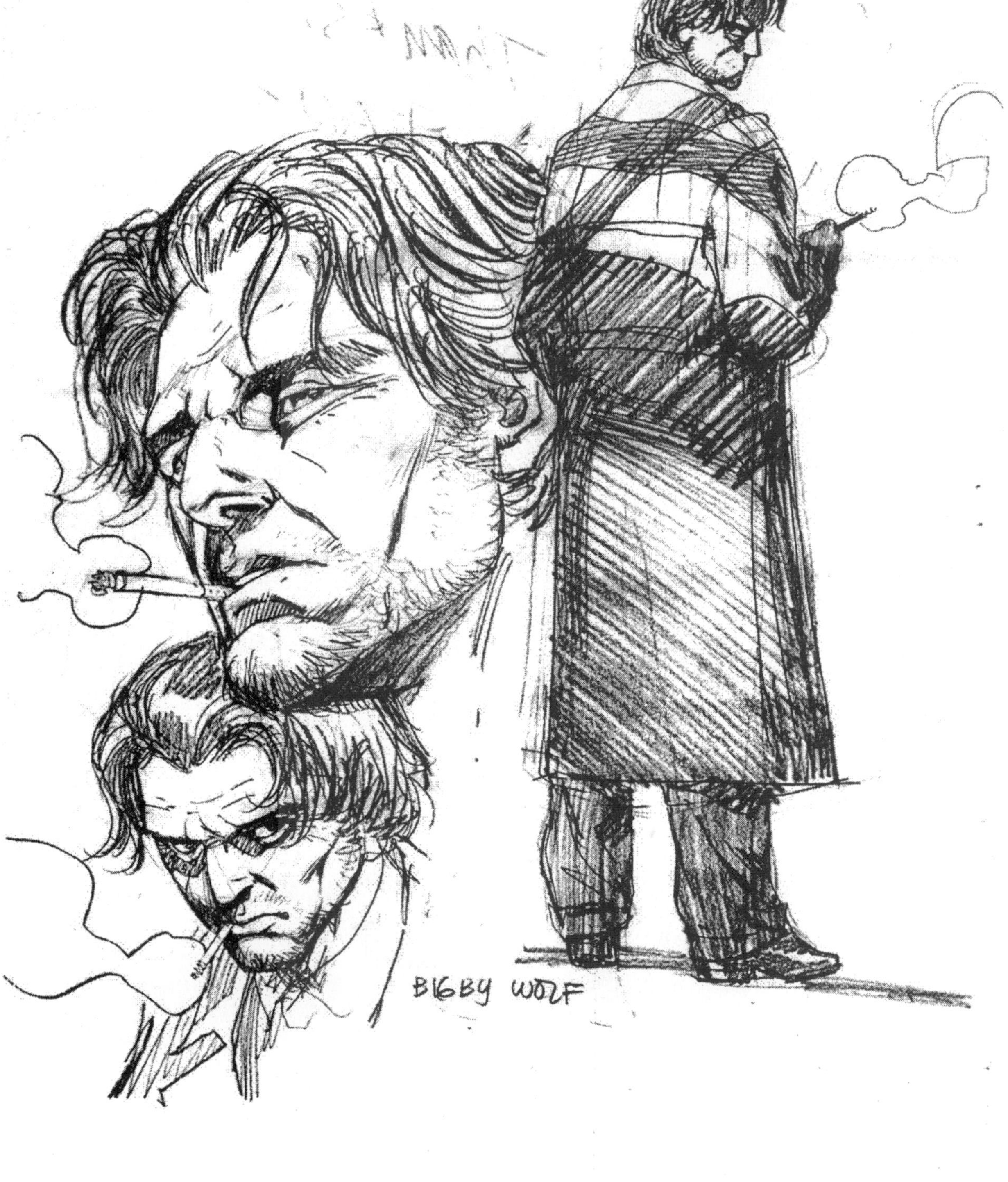
BIGBY WOLF

Lan Medina's preliminary designs for Bigby Wolf and Snow White.

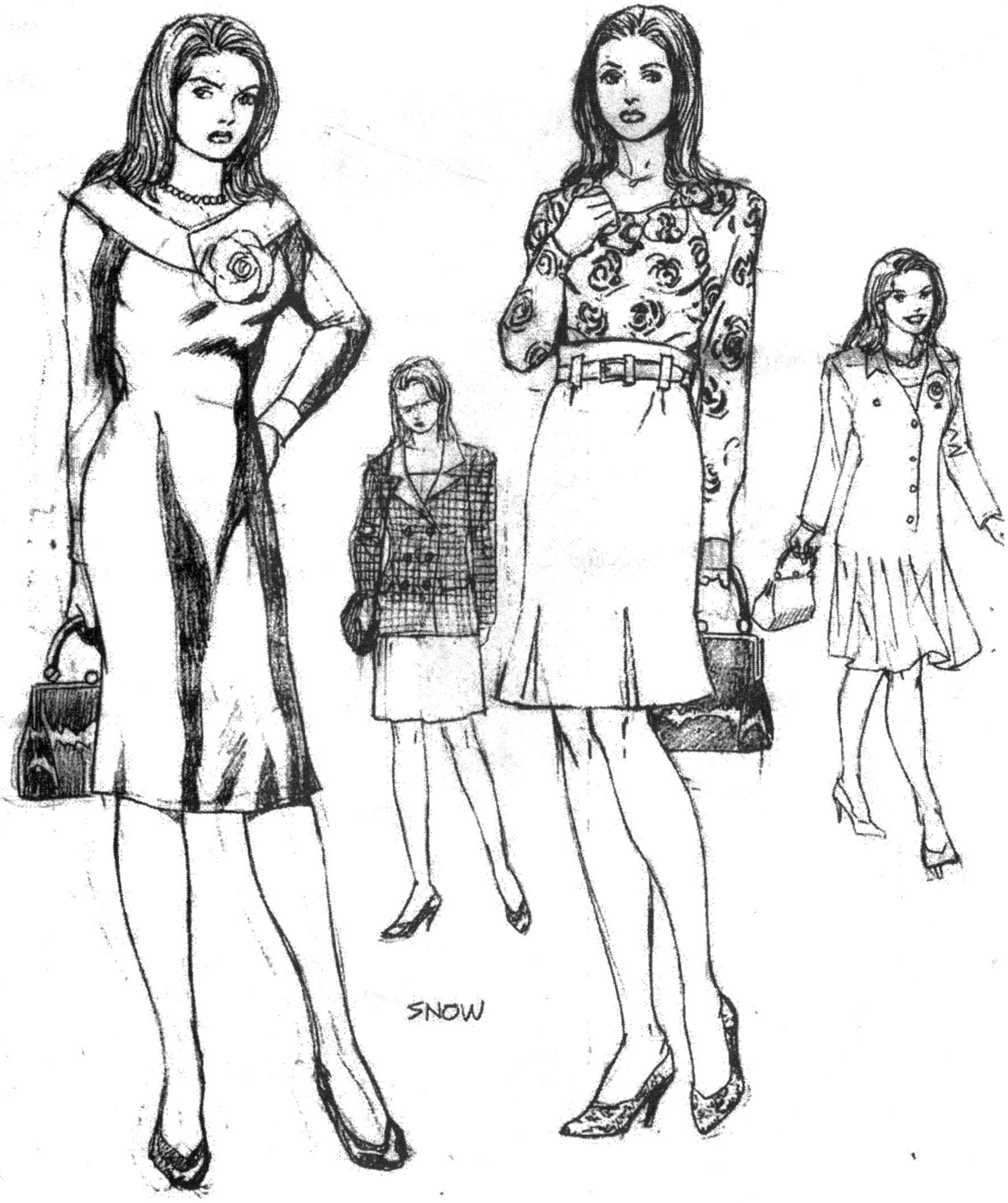
SNOW

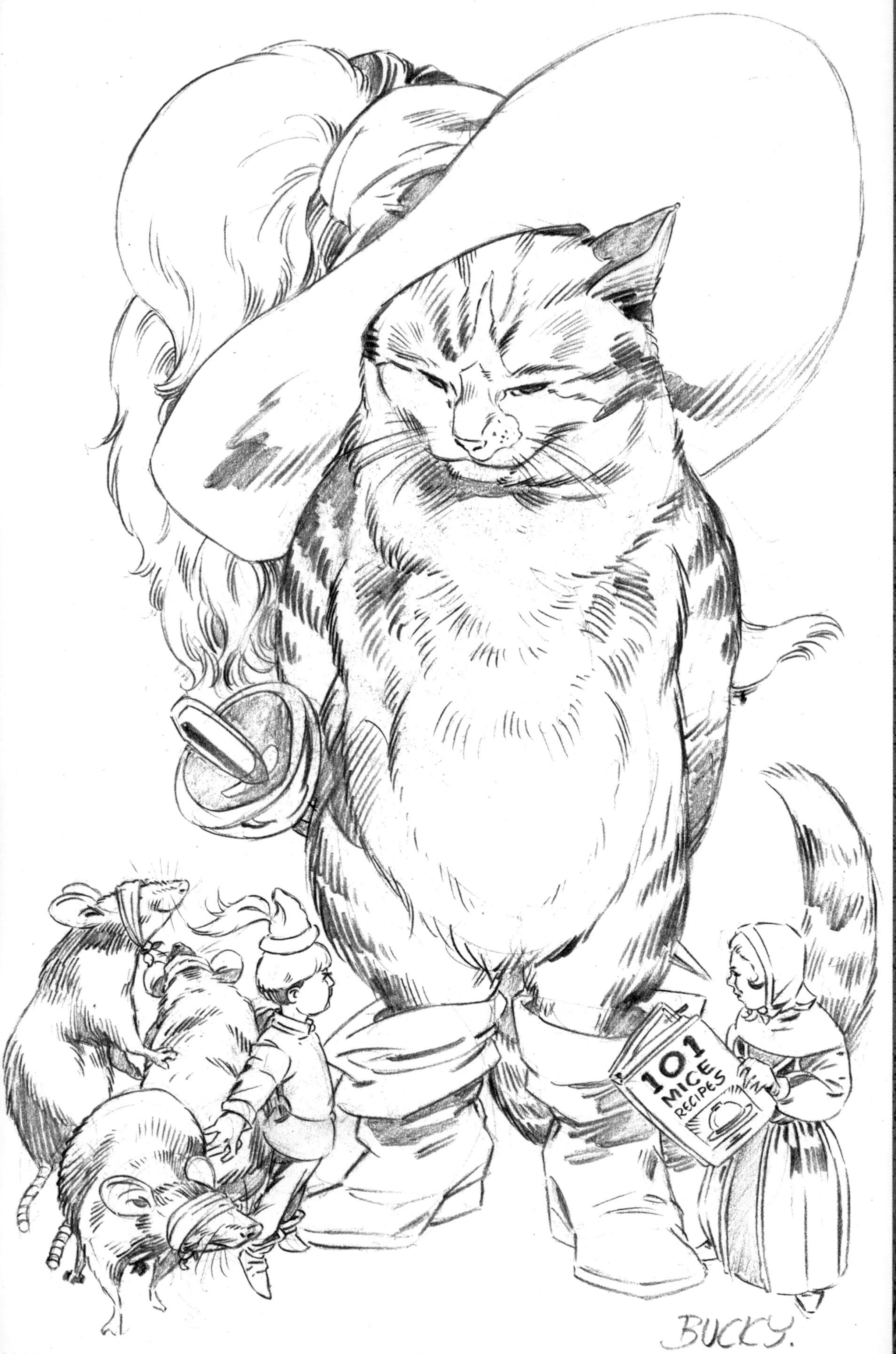
101 MICE RECIPES
BUCKY.

Character sketches for "Animal Farm" by Mark Buckingham.

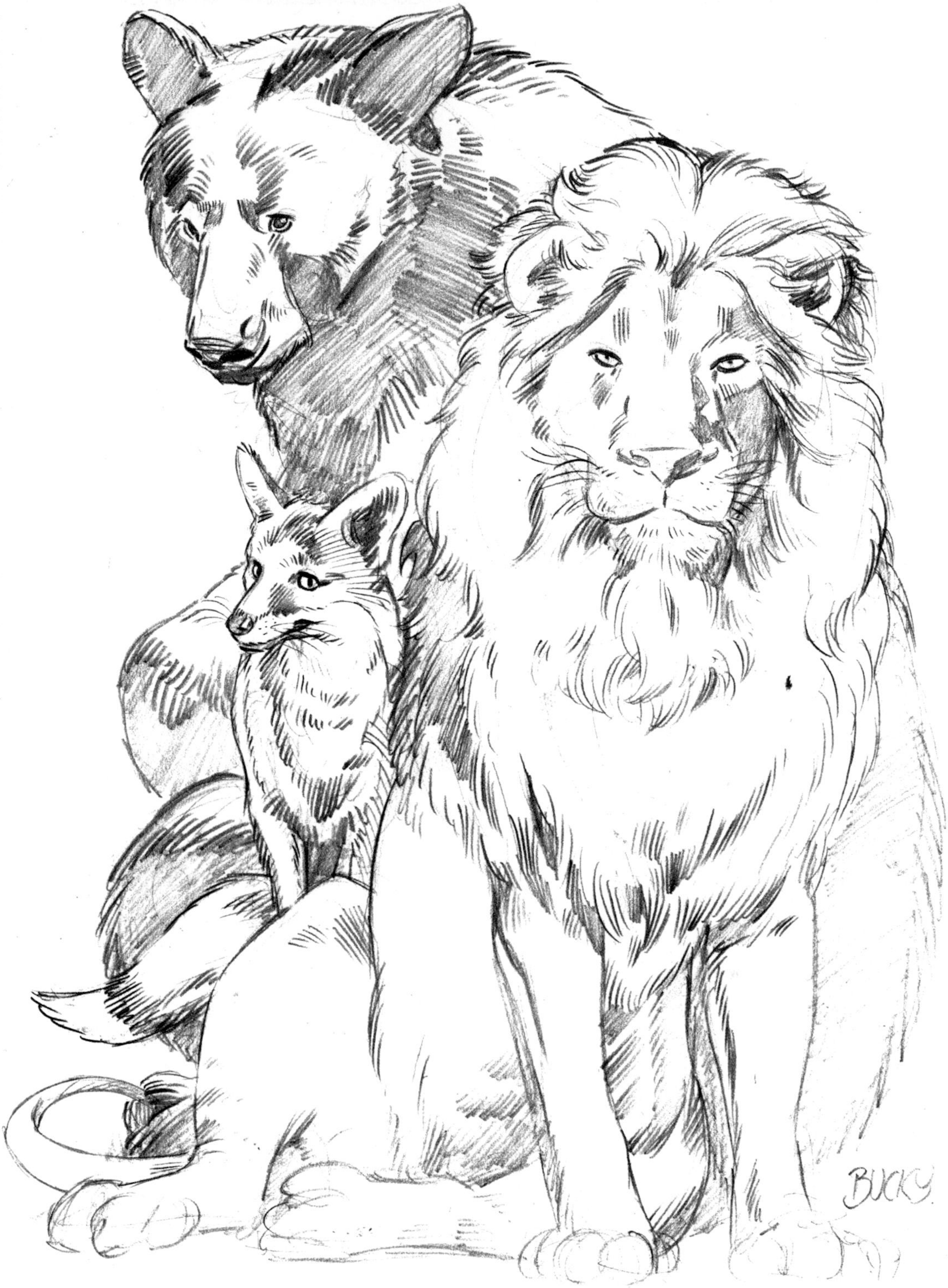
BUCKY

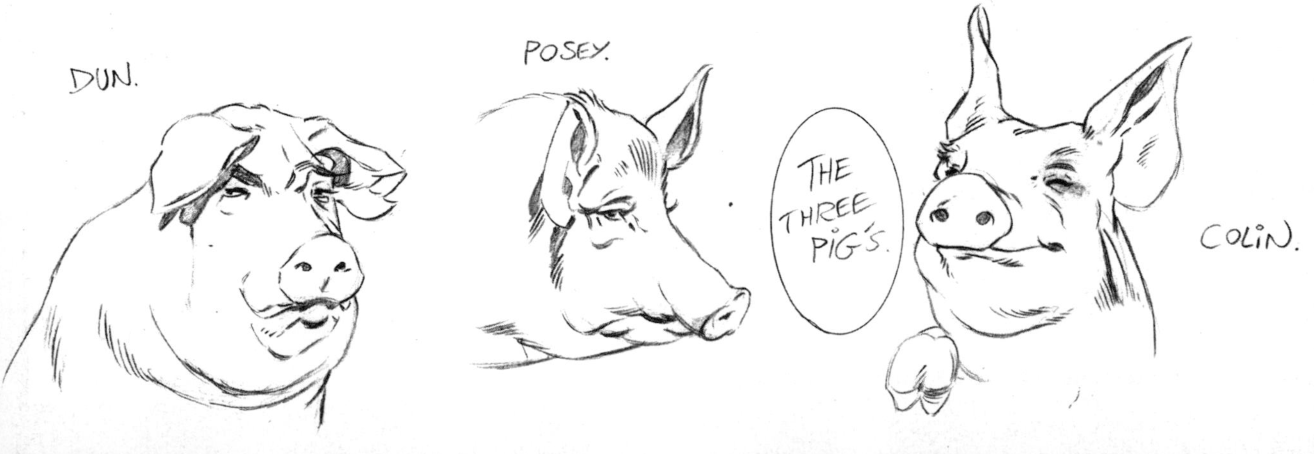
DUN.
POSEY.
THE THREE PIG'S.
COLIN.

Early conceptual sketches by Mark Buckingham
for a Rose Red statue.

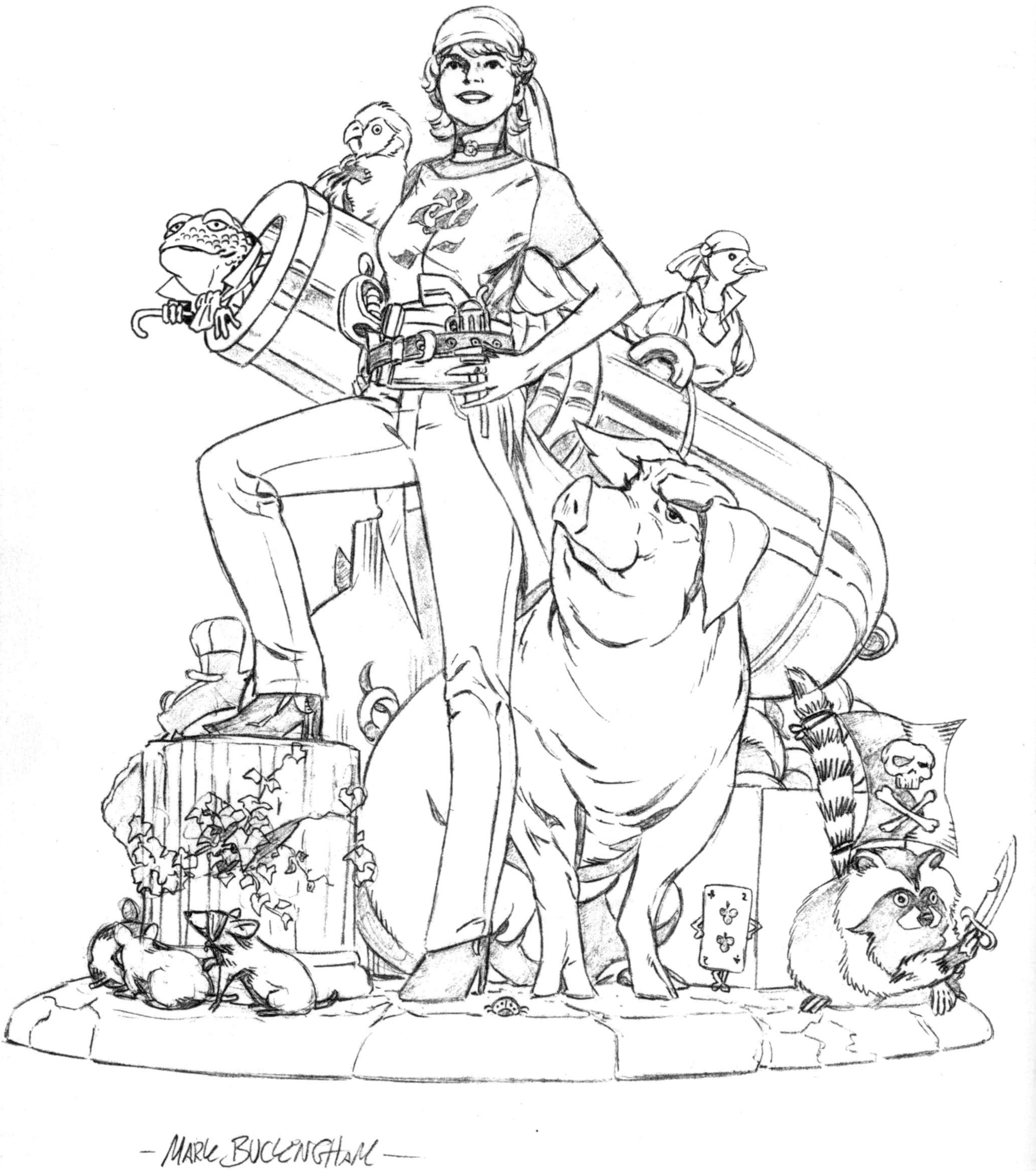
MARK BUCKINGHAM

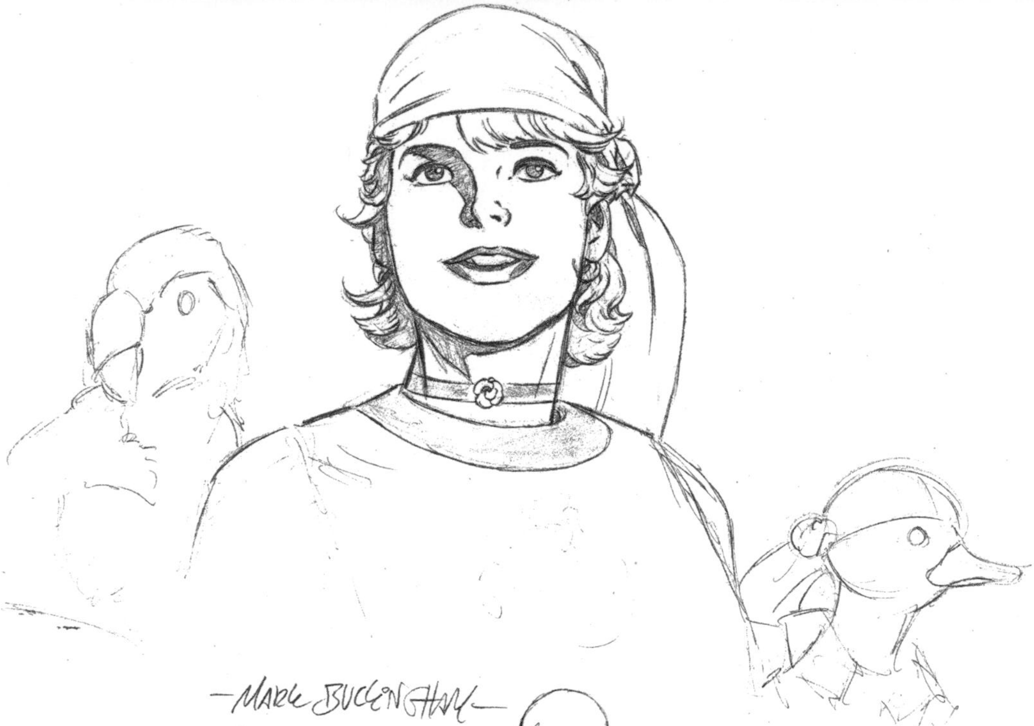
—MARK BUCKINGHAM—

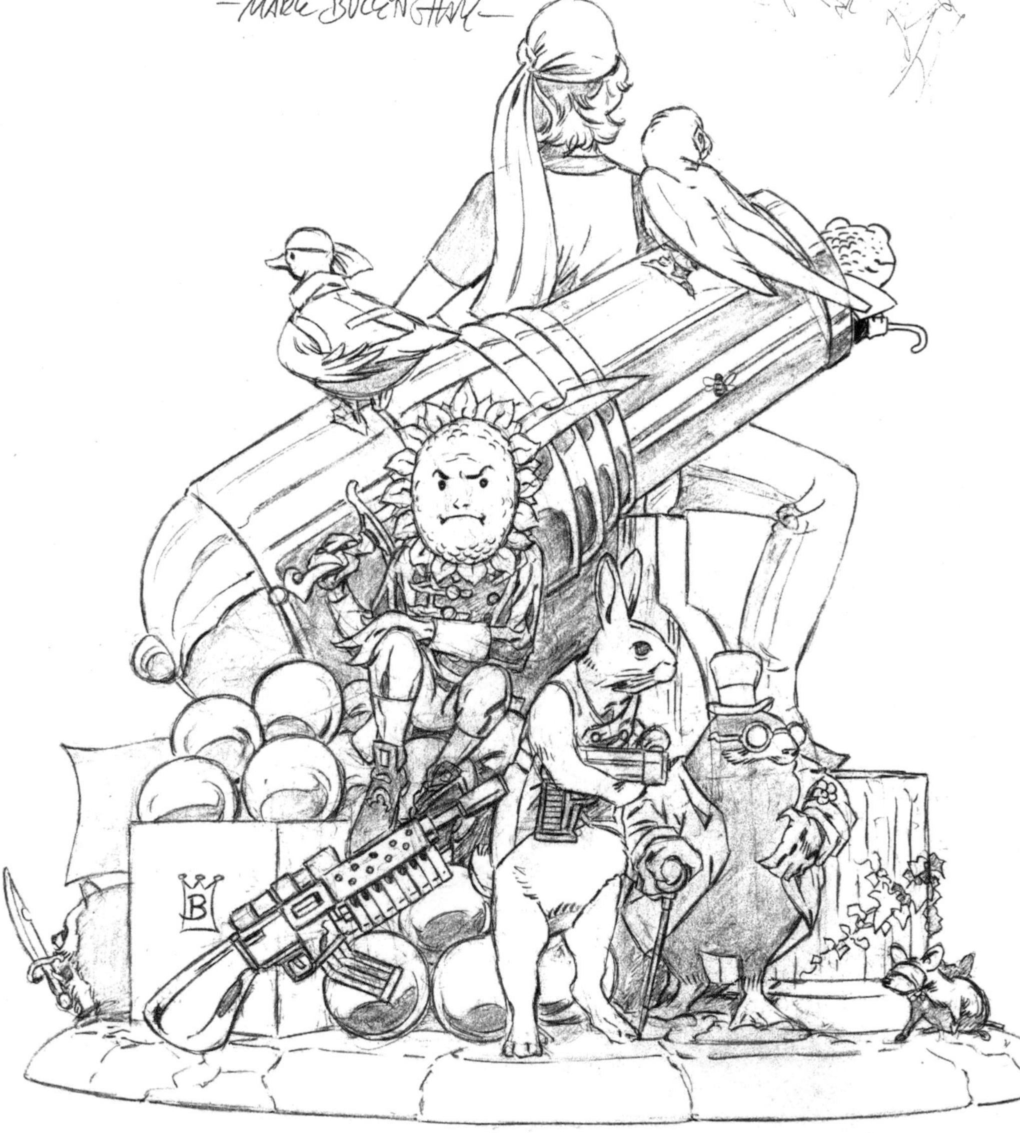
—MARK BUCKINGHAM—

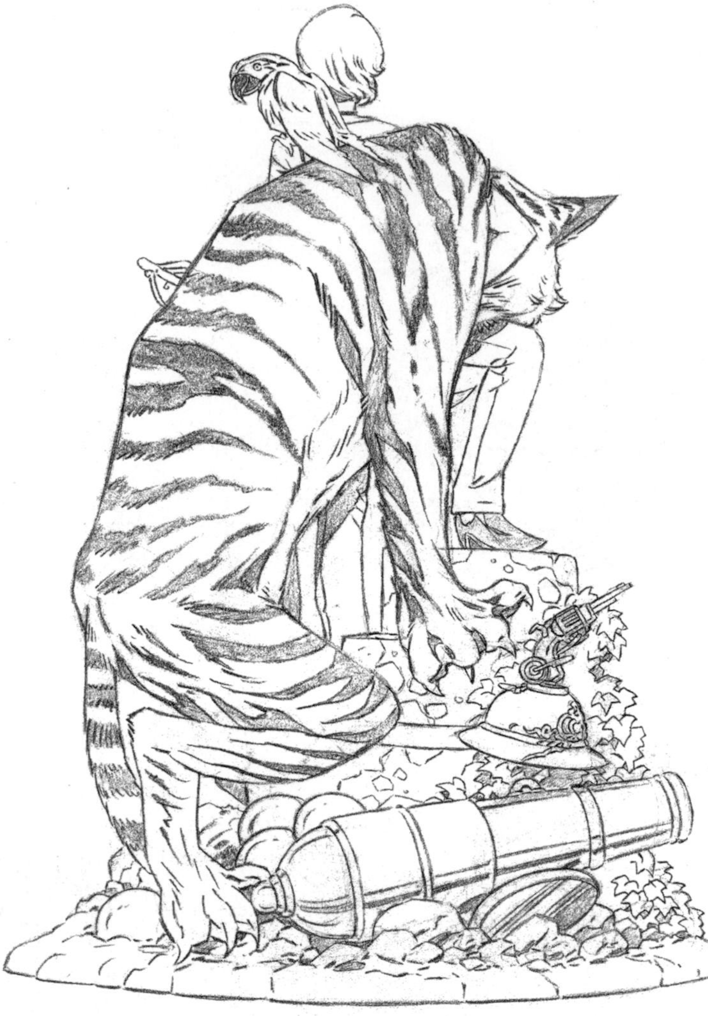

—MARK BUCKINGHAM

#1 INSPIRED BY #8 COVER.

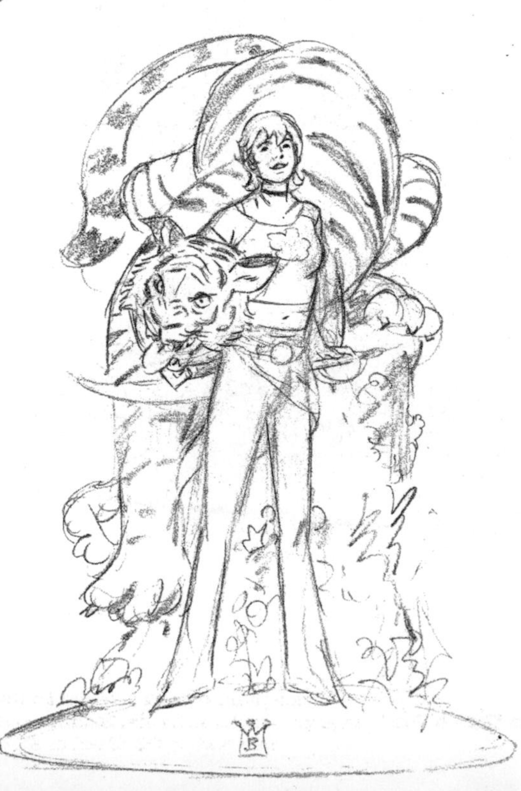

#2 INSPIRED BY ANIMAL FARM TPB COVER.

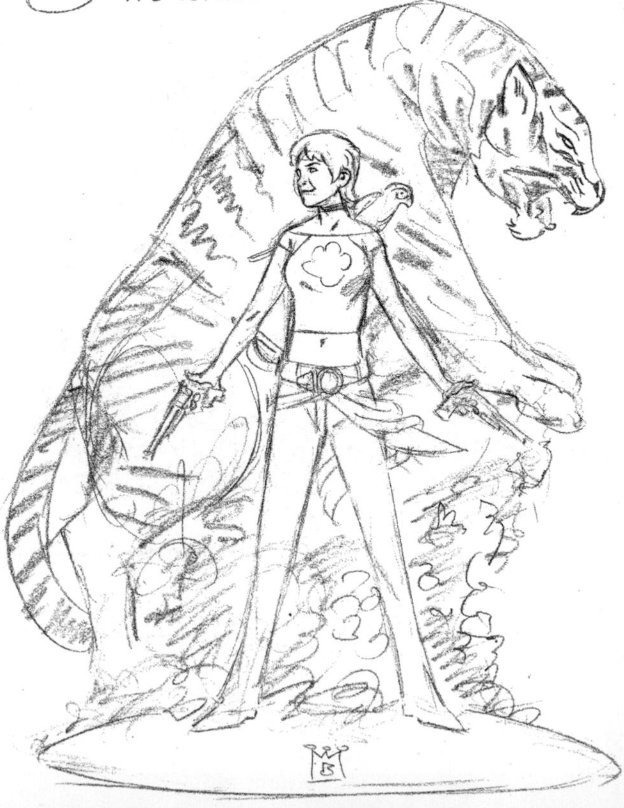

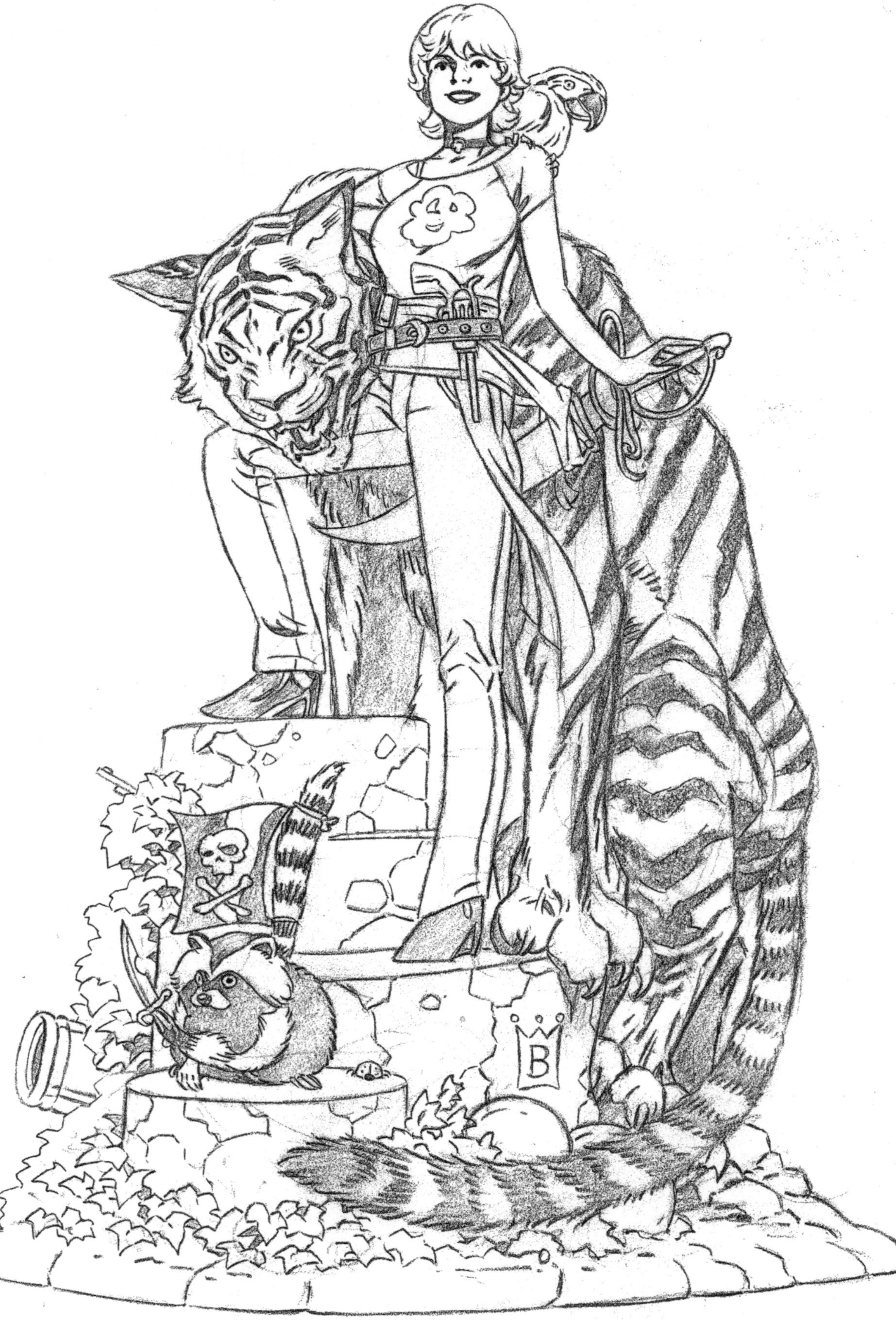

Buckingham's finished design for the
Shere Khan & Red Rose statue, sculpted by Jim Maddox and
released by DC Direct in 2007.

Bill Willingham has been writing, and sometimes drawing, comics for more than twenty years. During that time he's had work published by nearly every publisher in the business and he's created many critically acclaimed comic book series, including *The Elementals*, *Coventry*, PROPOSITION PLAYER and FABLES. His other credits are vast and impressive but far too many to mention here. Currently, he lives in his own personal corner of the American Midwest and can be visited at clockworkstorybook.net.

The first Filipino artist to win an Eisner Award, **Lan Medina** has applied his intricate style to a wide variety of comic book titles. After gaining prominence illustrating Vic J. Poblete's "Devil Car" feature in the 1980s Filipino horror magazine *Holiday*, Medina went on to win acclaim in north America with Image Comics' *Aria* and the Vertigo series AMERICAN CENTURY and FABLES. His other notable works include Marvel's *The Punisher*, *Foolkiller* and *Storm*, for which he earned a Glyph Comics Fan Award.

Born in 1966 in the English seaside town of Clevedon, **Mark Buckingham** has worked in comics professionally since 1988. In addition to illustrating all of Neil Gaiman's run on the post-Alan Moore *Miracleman* in the early 1990s, Buckingham contributed inks to THE SANDMAN and its related miniseries DEATH: THE HIGH COST OF LIVING and DEATH: THE TIME OF YOUR LIFE as well as working on various other titles for Vertigo, DC and Marvel through the end of the decade. Since 2002 he has been the regular penciller for Bill Willingham's FABLES, which has gone on to become one of the most popular and critically acclaimed Vertigo titles of the new millennium. These days he can be found with his wife Irma in the Asturias region of northern Spain.

A thirty-year veteran of the industry, **Steve Leialoha** has worked for nearly every major comics publisher in the course of his distinguished career. Titles featuring his artwork include DC's BATMAN, SUPERMAN and JUSTICE LEAGUE INTERNATIONAL, Vertigo's THE DREAMING, THE SANDMAN PRESENTS: PETREFAX and THE SANDMAN PRESENTS: THE DEAD BOY DETECTIVES, Marvel's *The Uncanny X-Men*, *Spider-Woman* and *Dr. Strange*, Epic's *Coyote*, Harris's *Vampirella* and many of Paradox Press's BIG BOOK volumes. Since 2002, Leialoha has inked Bill Willingham's hit Vertigo series FABLES, for which he and penciller Mark Buckingham won the 2007 Eisner Award for Best Penciller/Inker Team.

Born in Macon, Georgia, **Craig Hamilton** has loved drawing since he was six years old. After completing a year at the Atlanta College of Art, Hamilton began freelancing for DC Comics, where his work on the 1986 AQUAMAN miniseries won him universal fan acclaim. Although he has also built a successful career in commercial illustration over the years, his passion for comics endures — as evidenced by his impressive list of credits, including DC's GREEN LANTERN, LEGION OF SUPER-HEROES and STARMAN, as well as Vertigo's FLINCH and LUCIFER. Still residing in Macon, Hamilton describes himself as "an artist more than anything else" and an "adult fan of LEGO."

James Jean was born in Taiwan in 1979. Raised in New Jersey, he graduated from New York City's School of Visual Arts in 2001. Along with his award-winning cover art for DC Comics, Jean has produced illustrations for *Time Magazine*, *The New York Times*, *Wired*, *Rolling Stone*, *Spin*, *Playboy*, ESPN, Atlantic Records, Target, Nike, and Prada, among many others. He currently lives and works in Santa Monica.

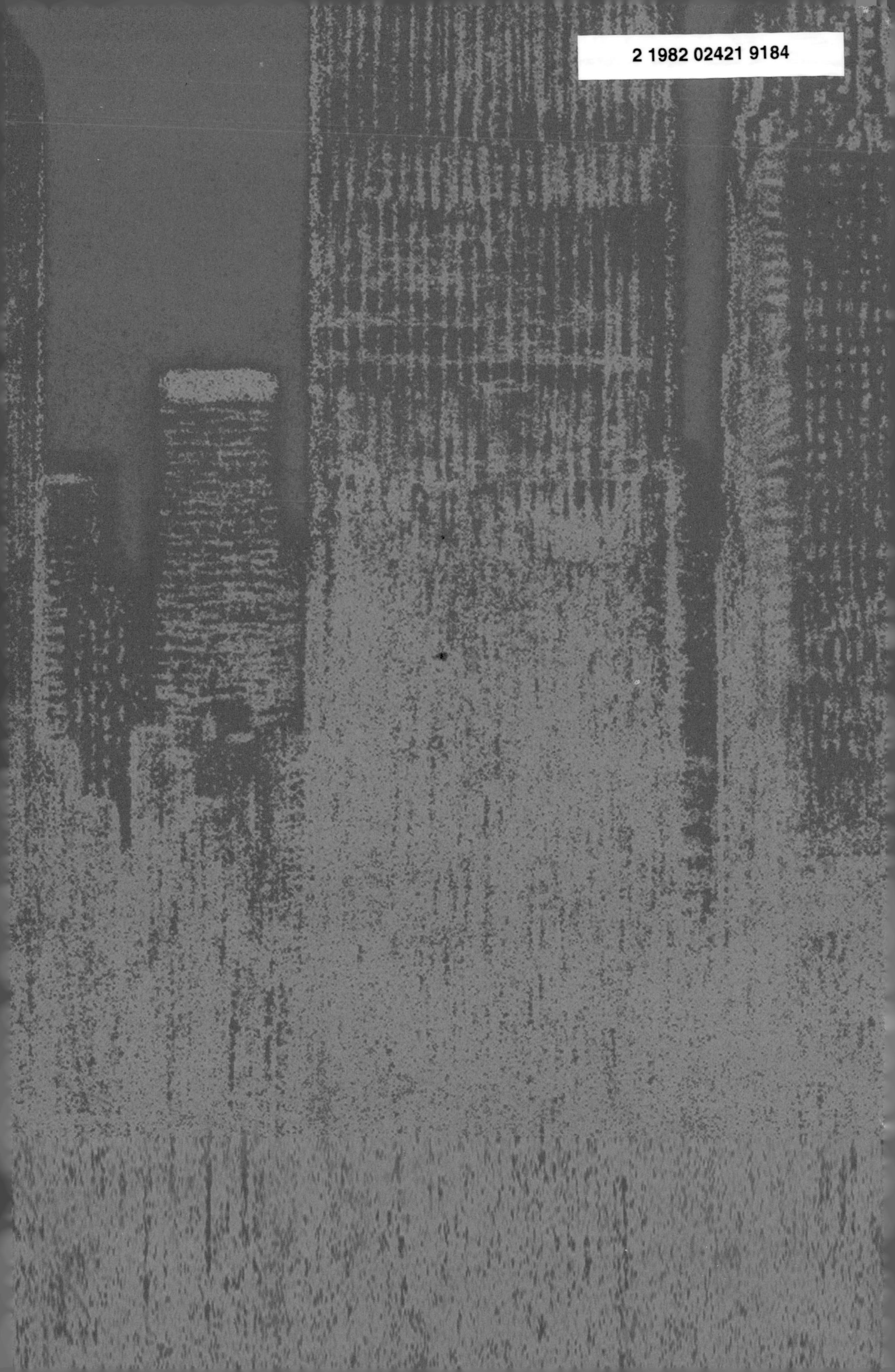